The Hardball Times

Presents...

The 2004 Baseball Annual

The Hardball Times Staff:

Alex Belth
Craig Burley
Joe Dimino
Robert Dudek
Aaron Gleeman
Brian Gunn
Ben Jacobs
Vinay Kumar
Larry Mahnken
Matthew Namee
Lee Sinins
Bryan Smith
Dave Studenmund
Steve Treder

With Special Guest Appearances by:
Bill James
Woody Studenmund

Edited by Dave Studenmund and Greg Tamer

Contents

Introduction

Welcome to *The Hardball Times 2004 Baseball Annual*. In March, just before the start of the 2004 season, a dozen guys with a passion for baseball got together to create The Hardball Times (www.hardballtimes.com), a website where we could write about the game we love. THT covered the 2004 season from the first pitch to the final out, starting with in-depth previews of all 30 teams in the spring and ending with some of the best postseason analysis around in the fall, with hundreds of great articles in between.

In doing so, we built a sizeable audience, got some national recognition, and also expanded to include more writers. Now that we've made the website a reality (or at least a *virtual* reality), we'd like to expand once more, this time with a book. For most of us, baseball books such as Bill James' *Baseball Abstracts* helped make us the baseball fans we are today. So you might call this a return to our roots.

While most of our focus during the season was on the website, we decided that we didn't want our book to simply include republished articles – we wanted it to stand on its own, too. So we wrote a dozen new articles for the book, developed over 150 pages of new stats and graphs, and also added in some of our best work from the 2004 season.

The Hardball Times 2004 Baseball Annual is essentially a review of the 2004 season, which was one of the best and most memorable in recent history. Records were set, greatness was established, youth was served, dramas were played out daily, and the Boston Red Sox rewrote history, coming out on top for the first time since 1918.

In this book you'll find three basic sections:

New Material

- A look at how history will view the 2004 season.
- Reviews of how 2004 played out in each of baseball's six divisions.
- A recap of one of the most exciting Octobers in recent memory.
- An in-depth look at the year in the minor leagues.
- The 2004 fantasy baseball review.
- The season in college and Japanese baseball.
- A groundbreaking new fielding study of outfield flies.

Best Of

- Our very best work from throughout the 2004 season, in two sections:

- **Meanwhile, On the Internet,** including analysis and commentary on the events and trends of the 2004 season as they happened, such as Greg Maddux's 300th career win, Ichiro Suzuki's assault on the all-time hits record, the blockbuster midseason trades, and much more.
- **Contemplating the Baseball Cosmos,** including perspectives on baseball's fascinating past, as well as how the players, teams and performances from 2004 fit into the sport's long history.

Stats and Graphs

- In-depth team stats.
- Team-by-team individual numbers.
- League leaderboards.
- Graphs of the divisional races.
- Special stats you won't find anywhere else, such as Net Win Shares Values, Fielding Win Shares per 1,000 innings, and detailed plate appearance outcomes for every single pitcher and hitter in baseball.

We hope that *The Hardball Times 2004 Baseball Annual* is a book you'll want to keep on your shelf, as both a reference guide and an interesting look back at a great baseball season.

Over the last year, we've received a lot of help and encouragement along the way. We'd like to thank Rob Neyer, Bill James, Eric Neel, and the many baseball bloggers and writers who referenced and used our site. We'd also like to thank Baseball Info Solutions (www.baseballinfosolutions.com) for their daily statistical updates to our site throughout the year, as well as the stats you'll find in this book. Finally, thanks to Kasia Wandowska (www.artkasia.com) for the graphical art that made our site and the cover of this book look so good.

And most of all we'd like to thank you for supporting our website, buying this book, and making this whole thing worthwhile. Our coverage will continue throughout the offseason and right into the start of the 2005 baseball season, which is just a few long months away. And next November, look for *The Hardball Times 2005 Baseball Annual*.

Happy Baseball,

Aaron Gleeman
Editor-in-Chief, The Hardball Times

Fifty Years Ago: The 2004 Season

By Steve Treder

Caught up in the moment, dazzled by the rush of immediacy, sometimes it's difficult to truly comprehend or appreciate events as they happen. Clear understanding often requires the passage of time. Things that seemed momentous quickly fade in importance, and things that were scarcely noticed take on ever-greater meaning. Historical perspective has a way of distilling matters into their deeper essence, allowing us to discern the significant from the mundane in ways that weren't apparent at first glance.

The just-completed 2004 baseball season still swirls in immediate consciousness, not yet consigned to memory, not yet assuming the shape it will with the benefit of hindsight. How will 2004 be remembered decades from now? Will it be forever prominent, the way certain seasons are for us today – 1920, 1947, 1961, 1998 – the mere mention of the year itself immediately conjuring timeless images of players, teams, and achievements? Or will it recede into obscurity, just another year in the endless procession, its personalities and events given over to the province of trivia?

Climb aboard The Baseball Time Machine. We're setting the dial to the year 2054. We're going to find out what baseball historians will be saying about 2004 ...

In this, the fiftieth anniversary edition of *The Hardball Times Baseball Annual*, let's look back at the baseball season of half a century ago, when The Hardball Times was a modest little startup website (remember that quaint term: "website"?). The year THT was launched was a season featuring several dramatic moments and accomplishments, only some of which are well remembered today.

First, let's establish a bit of historical context for the 2004 season. Those not old enough to remember the early 21st century should understand that it was a simpler, less fast-moving time than we inhabit today. The vast majority of Americans still got around in private gasoline-powered vehicles (the emblem of the era was the lumbering "SUV"), still sat in front of large non-portable "computers" (there's another lexiconical blast from the past for you!) both at home and in the workplace, and still passively "watched" television programming that was entirely one-way, non-interactive. In many ways, 2004 was a time little changed from the 20th century.

Much of the world of baseball in 2004 reflected this. Such antiquities as Fenway Park, Wrigley Field, and Yankee Stadium were still in use. The old National and American League arrangement was still in place (with just 30 total major league teams!), and the oddity of a different rule structure for each of the two leagues (the Designated

Hitter was used by the AL only), an awkward holdover dating all the way back to the 1970s, still applied. Umpires still made all their calls without technological assistance, and players were still scandalized by rumors of steroid use – genetic and nanotechnological manipulation concerns were yet to be encountered. It was a simpler and more innocent time.

The baseball season of 2004 was, in a sense, correspondingly placid. The management-labor strife that had plagued the sport in preceding years (and would again in years to follow) was on the back burner. The notorious syndicate-status of the Montreal Expos franchise moved toward resolution, as the decision was finally made in the summer of 2004 that the Expos would transfer to Washington D.C. The management scandals that would eventually culminate in the clamorous downfall of Commissioner-for-Life Bud Selig, and the rescinding of MLB's anti-trust exemption, had not yet come to light. Fans in 2004 were largely able to focus on the game on the field.

Fans were rewarded with a season of particular drama and interest. By far the most memorable element was the playoff and World Series triumph achieved by the Boston Red Sox; indeed, if the 2004 season is noted for anything by most fans of today, it is for that alone. In the years since 2004, the Red Sox have won six more league pennants (four of them under the old American League structure that abided in '04), and four more World Series titles, but most longtime Sox fans would agree that none of them have matched 2004 for sheer excitement and passionate joy. The 86-year drought between ultimate victories that the Red Sox overcame in 2004 wasn't the longest in major league baseball, even at the time – the Chicago Cubs' stretch of frustration was 96 years long at the time, and would of course eventually reach 117 seasons – but it was certainly the most prominent such "curse" in the national imagination.

Prior to the Red Sox' 2004 redemption, perhaps the only scenario that approached it in baseball history was that enjoyed by the Brooklyn Dodgers nearly 50 years earlier, in 1955. Entering that season, not only had the Dodgers never achieved a World Series victory in their 65-year existence, but they had gone down to defeat at the hands of their cross-town rivals, the New York Yankees, with daunting regularity in recent years: 1941, 1947, 1949, 1952, and 1953. The Dodgers' seventh-game vanquishing of the Bronx Bombers in 1955 was a moment of near-spiritual catharsis for the team and their fans, finally overcoming what had come to seem an insurmountable

3

obstacle, defeating the opponent that had come to seem ordained by some cosmic force to perpetually prevail.

So it was with the '04 Red Sox, who, like the Dodgers, had suffered for decades from an inability to overcome the Yankees. Boston's perennial frustration had taken on a mystical mantle, in the media if not in the actual perspective of many fans, with "The Curse of the Bambino" imagery dominating coverage of the rivalry. Not only had the Red Sox not won the World Series since Babe Ruth was clad in scarlet hose, but the arch-rival Yankees had done so no fewer than 26 times in the intervening period. And to make matters worse, it was the Yankees themselves thwarting strong Red Sox challenges several times in the years leading up to 2004. Most acutely in the memory of everyone in 2004, it had been the Yankees defeating the Red Sox in dramatic late-inning come-from-behind fashion in the seventh game of the 2003 American League Championship Series.

Thus a Red Sox' ALCS defeat of their nemesis in 2004 would have been seen as a significant historical turning point no matter how it occurred. It did then occur, of course, in staggeringly improbable fashion, the highlights of which are still often recited: not only did the Sox overcome a three-games-to-none deficit in the best-of-seven series, which had never occurred before in the entire history of major league baseball (and has only occurred one time since), but they also did so after having suffered a trouncing of epic record-smashing proportion on their home turf in the third game, and they also did so by navigating arduous come-from-behind extra-inning marathon wins in both game four and game five, and they also did so by having their injured ace pitcher Curt Schilling, emergency-stitched together and literally bleeding through his bandages, gallantly hurl seven brilliant innings in Yankee Stadium in game six to bring the series back to even. Such grand operatic spectacle served to elevate the triumph to a status far beyond mere lofty heights: the Red Sox-Yankees games of October 12-20, 2004, are seared forever into the innermost core of baseball legend.

The World Series that followed was therefore, almost by necessity, something of an anti-climax, despite the historical import of the Red Sox holding with their grasp the opportunity to exorcise the venerable Curse. No matter how momentous the prospect of a Red Sox World Series victory, it seemed that the actual games themselves couldn't hope to measure up to those of the preceding week in terms of tension and drama. In fact they didn't; the Red Sox handily dispatched the NL champ St. Louis Cardinals in four straight games, none of which were particularly memorable contests. Indeed, while all Red Sox fans today (and most fans generally) can easily identify 2004 as the year in which the Sox finally vanquished the Yankees and The Curse, not everyone knows the World

Series victory was a sweep, and few even can name the Cardinals as the opponent.

The 2004 Red Sox won eight consecutive postseason games, a feat that had never been achieved in a single postseason, and has been achieved only once since. That St. Louis would be the victim of the final four was an outcome predicted by no one at the time, but in the years following 2004 it became apparent that the '04 Cards were a good team, but not as good as they appeared at the time. They had romped through most of the season, going 105-57 and dominating the National League's stat boards, but their squeaker seven-game verdict over the Houston Astros in the NLCS might have served as a portent that the Cardinals weren't without vulnerabilities. That particular St. Louis squad never had another year that approached 2004's performance, and from this distant vantage point it's clear that their pitching staff was a no-name bunch that overachieved. The immortal Albert Pujols (just 24 at the time, with his magnificent peak not yet reached, and the great bulk of his 812 career home runs yet to be struck) was the key to the offense; he was joined that one season by nearly equal contributions from Scott Rolen and Jim Edmonds, a happenstance that would never occur again, and in fact commenced its disappearance in that year's World Series.

The St. Louis Cardinals are just one of many elements of the 2004 season that were celebrated at the time, but rarely remembered today. Fans that year witnessed the last truly great season from Barry Bonds, the best player of the late 20th century. The prodigious slugger turned 40 in July of 2004, but still managed to hit 45 homers (surpassing the 700 mark for his career), and lead the National League in batting and slugging. Bonds was so profoundly feared that he set three records in 2004 that stand to this day: 232 overall bases on balls, 120 intentional walks, and a .609 on-base percentage.

Bonds, of course, would go on in 2006 to break Hank Aaron's career record for home runs, before retiring with 765. But throughout 2004, Bonds was hounded by a murky steroid-distribution scandal, the particulars of which are little remembered today, but were disquieting headline news at the time. No legal charges would ever be filed against Bonds, nor would he ever suffer sanctions from MLB, but he became one in a long line of players to have his reputation tainted by steroid suspicion. The early 2000s, of course, marked the beginning of the era of performance enhancement controversies in baseball, an issue which has churned in various forms ever since.

The first of the five slugging greats who would go on to eclipse Bonds' 765-homer mark was, of course, Alex Rodriguez. 2004 was his first season in New York, arriving from the Texas Rangers in a controversial offseason deal in which the Yankees assumed much of A-Rod's enormous (for the era) contract. The trade prompted the sort of protests that were frequently sounded during much of Yankee owner George Steinbrenner's tenure, namely that the Bronx Bombers were leveraging an unfair market advantage to gobble up the best available talent and buy the championship. However valid the complaint may have been in principle, in practice things didn't work out that way in 2004, as Rodriguez, ill-advisedly shifted from shortstop to third base by the Yankees, had a very-good-but-not-great season (his least impressive showing since 1999, in fact) and proved unable to compensate for the team's pitching insufficiencies.

No one could have known it at the time, of course, but the 2004 ALCS appearance (with its humiliating loss to the Red Sox) would be the last hurrah for that great Yankee ball club of the late 1990s and early 2000s. A-Rod would go on to perform brilliantly, but the team around him would increasingly succumb to age-and-injury problems over the next few seasons. Rodriguez would be the only remaining member from the 2004 Yankees' roster when the ball club re-emerged as a powerhouse contender in 2008.

No era in history showcased four all-time great pitchers of such luminescence as the late 20th-early- 21st centuries, with Roger Clemens, Greg Maddux, Randy Johnson and Pedro Martinez all glittering. 2004 was the final season in which the four grand aces enjoyed simultaneous success. The fragile Martinez (often referred to at the time as simply "Pedro"), 32 years old in 2004, revealed diminishing effectiveness but was still a strong 16-9 for the champion Red Sox. The 38-year-old Maddux returned as a free agent to his original team, the Cubs, and won his 300th game along the way to a 16-11 performance. The 40-year-old Johnson (who truly did go by the nickname "The Big Unit"), laboring for a dreadful Arizona Diamondbacks club that lost a franchise-record 111 games, led the major leagues in strikeouts and had a 171 ERA+. Perhaps most remarkable of all was Clemens, who turned 42 in August, being coaxed out of retirement the previous winter to pitch for his hometown Houston Astros, and proceeding to turn in a scintillating 18-4 contribution that propelled the team to a Wild Card playoff berth.

Aside from Bonds, two players broke single-season records in 2004. One was Cincinnati's Adam Dunn, who struck out 195 times, a record that has of course been surpassed several times since. The other was the Seattle Mariners' Ichiro Suzuki (called simply "Ichiro!" by the fans of the day), who topped the 84-year-old mark for base hits in a season by slapping 262. Like those set by Bonds in 2004, Suzuki's record still stands fifty years later. As records go, this one wasn't the most captivating, but Suzuki did command a fair amount of attention over the 2004 season's closing weeks as he implacably closed in on the standard. Casual fans today may not have heard much of Suzuki, but perhaps as a function of his then-unusual status as a Japanese import, he was a star of significant magnitude in his time, even winning the American League MVP in 2001.

All in all, the 2004 season was highly colorful and exciting. While little of it is noted today beyond the legendary Red Sox' story, it was a thoroughly entertaining year in general. This is reflected in the fact that attendance per game in 2004 was 30,075: the highest mark since the strike-shortened season of 1994, and the third-highest in history at the time. If old-timers today warmly recall 2004 as a season of particular fun amid a simpler time, they can be forgiven. There's much to justify such a characterization.

American League East Review

By Ben Jacobs

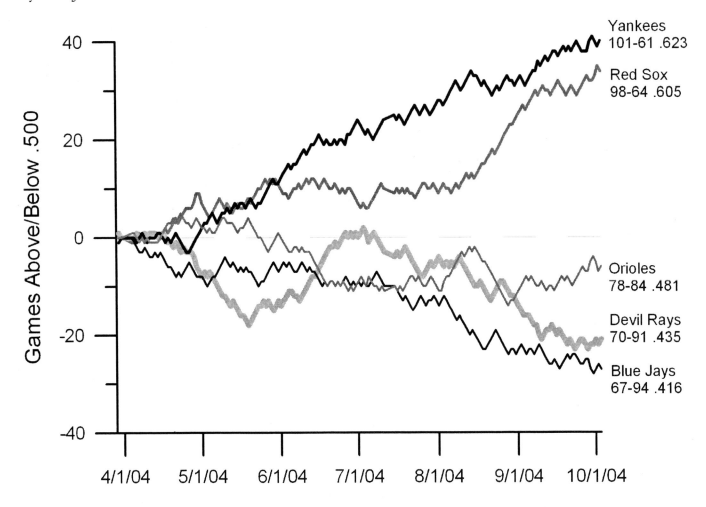

Ever since attaining its current form for the 1998 season, the final standings for the AL East have always been the same: New York Yankees, Boston Red Sox, Toronto Blue Jays, Baltimore Orioles, Tampa Bay Devil Rays.

This year, things were a little more unpredictable, and for a time it appeared each of the five teams might finish in a different spot in the standings. It didn't happen, but there was a change. The top two teams remained the same but Toronto fell into the basement and Baltimore and Tampa Bay each moved up a spot.

It all started on a different continent this year, when the Yankees and Devil Rays traveled to Japan to play a couple of games a week before anybody else. The standings were turned upside down right away as the Yankees lost their first game of the season to the lowly Devil Rays. They rebounded and won the next game

before getting a week off, but continued to play up-and-down baseball early on.

In fact, the top four teams in the AL East all had four losses when the Yankees visited Boston for the first of six heated series between the rivals. The Red Sox took the first game 6-2 by getting to Javier Vazquez in his first game of the rivalry. They took the second game 5-2, welcoming Curt Schilling to their side of the rivalry. The Yankees got a game back the next day 7-3, but Boston overcame a 4-1 deficit for a 5-4 win on Monday, April 19 to take three of four from the Yankees and drop New York to 8-8.

Although they had drawn first blood against the Yankees, the Red Sox had not yet drawn first place in the standings at 7-5. The Orioles had gotten off to a 7-4 start against Boston and Tampa Bay to hold that spot very early. The Orioles, Red Sox and Yankees each won two of their next three to keep the standings the same when the Red Sox traveled to Yankee Stadium the following weekend.

The Red Sox routed the Yankees 11-2 to win the first game of that series. After blowing a 2-0 lead in the second game, the Red Sox hung on to win 3-2 in 12 innings and clinch their second series win against the Yankees of the young season. Pedro Martinez pitched a seven-inning gem on Sunday, April 25 and Manny Ramirez's two-run shot off Vazquez was enough for a 2-0 Boston win and a three-game sweep that shocked the Yankees.

Suddenly, the Red Sox, who finished April with three straight wins to go to 15-6, had a four-game lead over the Yankees and had won six of the first seven games against New York. Baltimore was able to finish April in second place, a game ahead of the Yankees, while the Devil Rays and Blue Jays fell off the pace right away at 7-14 and 7-15, respectively.

The good feelings didn't last long for Boston, however. The Red Sox lost their first five games in May, allowing the Yankees to completely erase their deficit in the standings in the matter of a week. The two teams stayed close throughout May, swapping first place eight times and finishing the month tied atop the standings at 31-20 for Boston and 30-19 for New York. While the Yankees rode a hot offense to an 18-8 May against some tough competition from the AL West, the Red Sox struggled to a 16-14 May against lesser foes.

The Yankees saw Alex Rodriguez (.333/.427/.627 in May) and Hideki Matsui (.351/.453/.629) rebound from poor Aprils with outstanding months. They also got their only meaningful contribution from Jason Giambi (.310/.385/.638 in 15 games) in May and an incredibly hot month from Ruben Sierra (.356/.400/.678 in 17 games). The Red Sox didn't hit poorly in May, but they struggled in the rotation. Curt Schilling put up a 2.74 ERA in the month, but the rest of the rotation had a 5.62 ERA.

While the two titans in the East were battling for first place, Baltimore slid back toward .500, finishing the month five games back of first at 24-23. And Toronto and Tampa Bay continued to keep each other company at the bottom of the standings. Toronto used a decent May to move three games ahead of the Devil Rays and finish 22-29.

Unfortunately, that's about as good as things would get for the Blue Jays. Carlos Delgado, who struggled at the plate the first two months of the season, missed all of June with an injury. Vernon Wells joined Delgado on the disabled list midway through June and didn't return until after the All-Star Break. And Roy Halladay missed two starts in early June before missing two months after the All-Star break.

After going 15-14 in May, Toronto had four consecutive losing months, bottoming out with a 9-20 August. After a five-game losing streak in early August

dropped the Blue Jays to 47-64, manager Carlos Tosca lost his job and was replaced by John Gibbons. Toronto fought to stay out of last place through the All-Star break before finally dropping into the cellar for good on July 15.

The other team trying to avoid the cellar changed during June, however. Toronto was 3 ½ games ahead of Tampa Bay after both teams won on June 9, but the Devil Rays would not lose again until June 23. By then they were in third place, 3 ½ games ahead of both the Blue Jays and Orioles.

Thanks to that 12-game winning streak, Tampa Bay was able to go 20-6 in June. Jose Cruz Jr. carried the offense by hitting .268/.417/.598 in the month and Carl Crawford showed off all his tools by hitting .345 with six doubles, four triples, two homers and 11 steals. The Devil Rays even got production at the plate from Rey Sanchez, who hit .333 with six doubles, two triples and two homers in the month.

The key to the month, however, was pitching. Dewon Brazelton, Victor Zambrano and Mark Hendrickson combined to go 8-0 with a 2.73 ERA in 89 innings. Relievers Danys Baez, Jesus Colome and Jorge Sosa pitched in with a 2.21 ERA in 40 2/3 innings. When their great month ended, the Devil Rays sat above .500 at 38-37 and were 5 ½ games ahead of Toronto and Baltimore.

While Tampa Bay was surging in June, Baltimore was slumping through an 8-19 month. Rafael Palmeiro had an absolutely terrible month (.185/.287/.315) and only Javy Lopez (.330/.368/.523), Jerry Hairston Jr. (.333/.439/.420) and Miguel Tejada (.300/.339/.500) even hit decently in full-time action.

Meanwhile, three-fifths of the rotation fell apart. Erik Bedard and Daniel Cabrera posted a 2.60 ERA between them, but only pitched 65 2/3 innings in 11 starts as Bedard averaged fewer than five innings per start in the month. In the other 16 starts, Rodrigo Lopez, Sidney Ponson, Matt Riley and Eric Dubose put up an ugly 7.21 ERA.

The Orioles played about .500 ball the next two months (14-14 in July and 13-15 in August) before a hot final surge (19-13 to close the season) put them solidly in third place. Tampa Bay went into a freefall after June, going 11-17 in July, 10-18 in August and 11-19 in September and October. That late-summer swoon made things close, but the Devil Rays never did pass the Blue Jays for the bottom spot.

While the bottom three teams in the division rearranged themselves, Boston's only losing month of the year knocked the Red Sox from an early-season lead at the end of April to a tie atop the standings at the end of May to 5 ½ games behind New York by the time the two teams squared off again.

The Red Sox didn't play terribly in June, but they got no life out of the return of Nomar Garciaparra (.235/.274/.382 in the month) to the lineup and they went 11-14. The Red Sox got routed 11-3 in that first game back at Yankee Stadium on June 29 and then blew a 2-0 lead late to lose 4-2 in the second game of the series. Facing a sweep that would cripple their chances of winning the division, the Red Sox gave Garciaparra the day off, watched Derek Jeter hurl himself into the stands after catching a pop up and took a 4-3 lead in the top of the 13th only to watch the Yankees score two runs in the bottom of the inning to sweep Boston to 8 ½ games back.

The Yankees followed their sweep of Boston by getting swept by the Mets, but the Red Sox couldn't take advantage because they lost two out of three to the Braves. At 43-37, the Red Sox were more than twice as many games behind the Yankees (7 ½) as they were games ahead of the Devil Rays (3 ½).

Almost a month later, New York's lead stretched to 9 ½ games when Boston blew an early lead, rallied to tie the game at 7-7 and then let New York score a run in the ninth to win 8-7 on July 23. The next day looked like it would stretch the lead to double digits after a wild game complete with a brawl, but Bill Mueller tagged Mariano Rivera for a two-run homer and an 11-10 win and the Red Sox hung on for a 9-6 win the next day.

Six days later, Boston traded Garciaparra away for Orlando Cabrera and Doug Mientkiewicz and picked up Dave Roberts in a separate deadline deal. Six days after that, the Red Sox caught fire. They took seven of 10 from Tampa Bay and Detroit before losing two of three to the White Sox. They followed that with successive sweeps of Toronto and the White Sox and, after a loss to the Blue Jays, six straight wins over Toronto and Detroit.

When the dust settled, the Red Sox had burned through the easiest part of their schedule with 20 wins and six losses. The Boston offense was unstoppable in August thanks to Ramirez (.290/.365/.634), Jason Varitek (.449/.513/.826), Mueller (.380/.467/.543) and Mark Bellhorn (.325/.426/.575 in 11 games), and the pitching was on cruise control with Martinez and Schilling combining to go 8-2 with a 2.69 ERA in 87 innings.

The Yankees had played pretty well themselves, but Boston still managed to cut the lead all the way down to 4 ½ games. Fortunately for New York, with one day left in August, Boston had nine games coming up against Anaheim, Texas and Oakland.

They won eight of those games. The Yankees went 5-3 in the same nine-day stretch and the lead was a mere two games. Unfortunately for the Red Sox, while those amazing nine games against the AL West locked up the Wild Card, they only made the division race interesting.

The lead was back to 3 ½ when the Red Sox made their way back to Yankee Stadium for the final time during the regular season, and they pretty much had to win at least two games. They got the first one by getting to Rivera again for a 3-2 win, but were never in contention the next two games, losing 14-4 and 11-1.

Boston needed to sweep the Yankees at Fenway Park the next-to-last weekend of the season to have a chance. Once they lost the first game 6-4 thanks to three New York runs in the late innings, it didn't really matter that they rallied to win the next two 12-5 and 11-4. New York was able to clinch the division by sweeping Minnesota out of the Bronx the very next series.

And so the order of the top two stayed the same – Yankees, Red Sox – after a long rollercoaster ride that ended with the teams at the back of the pack getting mixed up – Orioles, Devil Rays, Blue Jays.

American League Central Review

By Aaron Gleeman

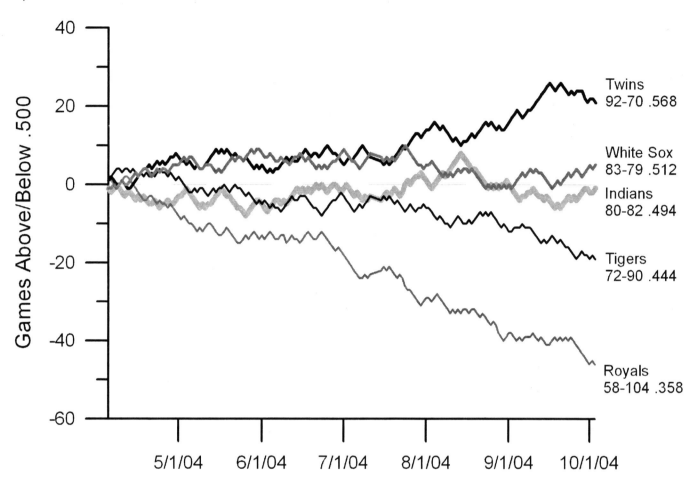

While most schools have, for lack of a better name, a "dumb class," Major League Baseball has the American League Central. Ever since the birth of the division in 1994, the AL Central has struggled to produce even one legitimately good team each year, and has more often than not produced what is essentially a default champion, a team that is rewarded with a trip to the postseason simply because they were the smartest kid in the dumb class.

This year, the Minnesota Twins won the AL Central for the third straight season, going 92-70 to win the division by nine games over the Chicago White Sox. They finished with the fourth-best record in the AL, but even that doesn't tell the whole story, because the three teams in front of them (New York, Boston, Anaheim) and the two teams directly behind them (Oakland, Texas) were forced to play far tougher schedules.

In fact, according to ESPN's "Relative Power Index," which not only takes a team's record into account, but also their strength of schedule, the Twins were the sixth-best team in the league and just the 12th-best team in baseball. While Minnesota won a very impressive-sounding 92 games, they also played the easiest schedule in baseball.

That's not to say what Minnesota has done over the last three years isn't impressive, because clearly the goal of any team is to beat their competition and advance to the playoffs. Three straight years accomplishing that shows what a good job Terry Ryan and the rest of the Twins' management has done, but it also shows just how much of an impact the quality of a team's competition can have.

Is there any doubt, for instance, that the Oakland A's, who won 91 games while playing a significantly more difficult schedule in the AL West and missed the postseason, couldn't have won the AL Central this year? And what about the Texas Rangers, who won 89 games and missed the playoffs? Couldn't they have come up with three more wins if their division had included Kansas City, Detroit, Cleveland and Chicago, rather than Anaheim, Oakland and Seattle?

At the same time, even if you stick the Twins in the AL East and continue to give them credit for the 92 wins they got while playing the AL Central patsies, they would have finished in third place. If you stick them in the AL West and make even a slight adjustment in their win total because of the changes in schedule, they very likely would have finished in *fourth* place.

Actually, you don't even have to stretch your imagination that far. Over the last three years, the Twins have gone 140-88 (.615) against AL Central teams and 105-98 (.517) against AL East and AL West teams. Over the course of a single season, that's the difference between being a 100-win team and an 84-win team, and the difference between going to the playoffs and watching them on TV. And it's not just the Twins; the White Sox, Indians, Tigers and Royals have also stunk outside of the Central. During the Twins' three-year run as President of the Dumb Class, the AL Central has won just 42.7% of its games against non-division opponents.

Of course, *someone* has to win every division in baseball, regardless of the level of competition, and to their credit the Twins fought through a very close race at midseason to pull ahead and beat second-place Chicago for a third straight season, this time by nine games. Interestingly though, it wasn't Chicago that gave the Twins their biggest scare in 2004, it was the Cleveland Indians.

After taking two out of three games in series against the Red Sox and Angels, the Twins were sitting at 61-46 on August 5, comfortably leading the division. They then dropped three out of four at home to the A's before traveling to Seattle, where they lost two out of three to the lowly Mariners. Suddenly they were 63-51, their division lead had shrunk to just three games over the Indians, and they were headed to Jacobs Field for a three-game series.

It was as if the Indians had snuck up on the entire division, completely without warning. First they were that team everyone was waiting for to become contenders a couple of years down the road and then, all of a sudden, there they were in second place and in a position to move to the top of the division with a sweep at home. And for the first two games, it looked like they'd do just that, beating Minnesota 8-2 and 7-1 to cut the deficit to a single game.

On the brink of giving up a division lead that looked nearly impenetrable just a couple of weeks earlier, the Twins turned to a very unlikely source to save their season: 41-year-old lefty Terry Mulholland, whom they acquired from the Mariners earlier in the year for one dollar in cash. Mulholland improbably came up big, giving the Twins eight innings of two-run pitching, and with the game tied at two apiece in the top of the 10th inning, Corey Koskie blasted a two-run homer off of Rick White, and then Joe Nathan came in and slammed the door with a 1-2-3 bottom of the inning.

And that was where the drama ended, although certainly no one knew it at the time. With the Indians two games back and the Twins reeling, the schedule called for Minnesota to go back home, where they'd first host the first-place Yankees, a team that had dominated them like no other for years, and then the Indians would be back, with another chance to make up ground in the division (if there was any ground left to make up by then).

Little did anyone know at the time that Cleveland's loss to the Twins in that pivotal third game would be the first of nine in a row. By the end of the first week in September, the division race was non-existent, as the Indians had dropped 16 out of 20 games to fall to 67-71 on the year. Minnesota coasted home with their third straight title and, amazingly, the six games the Twins and Indians played in the season's final two weeks involved a lot of September callups and very little drama.

While Cleveland was fading down the stretch, the Twins were riding the best pitcher in the AL, Johan Santana, who went 13-0 with an extraordinary 1.21 ERA in 15 second-half starts. Santana, who had offseason surgery to clear out bone chips in his elbow, started the year very poorly and was 2-3 with a 5.61 ERA at the end of May. He then went 18-3 with a 1.58 ERA in the final four months of the season, turning in one of the most dominant pitching performances in baseball history.

In addition to Santana's incredible year, the Twins' pitching staff also got big contributions from two players acquired in offseason trades. Joe Nathan, who came over from the Giants for A.J. Pierzynski, saved 44 games with a 1.62 ERA and was nearly unhittable for long stretches. Carlos Silva, who Minnesota got from the Phillies for Eric Milton, went 14-8 with a 4.21 ERA in 203 innings, essentially matching Milton's production (14-6 with a 4.75 ERA in 201 innings) for about 3% of the price.

In his 10th season with the Twins, Brad Radke had his best year, throwing 219.2 innings with a career-best 3.48 ERA, while walking an astoundingly low 26 batters. Radke only won 11 games because of poor run support, but he was one of the top handful of pitchers in the league, and he and Santana formed the most effective 1-2 punch in baseball.

On the offensive side, Lew Ford, who began the season at Triple-A, came up when Torii Hunter hurt himself early in the year and ended up being the most valuable position player on the team. If not for a loophole in the rules, Ford would have run away with the AL Rookie of the Year award. Justin Morneau once again tore up the minors, but whereas he struggled in his tryout with the Twins in 2003, Morneau was outstanding this season, hitting .271/.340/.536 with 19 homers, 17 doubles and 58 RBI in 74 games. He was so good, in fact, that the Twins not only committed to playing him every day, they traded away Doug Mientkiewicz to clear room at first base.

Of course, the season wasn't all good news for Minnesota. Joe Mauer suffered a major knee injury in his second major-league game, came back briefly, and then had to shut things down for the rest of the season when the same knee acted up again. When he was on the field, Mauer was outstanding, hitting .308/.369/.570 while playing great defense behind the plate, but he played just 35 games and there are now doubts about his long-term health and ability to stay at catcher.

For the third straight year, the Chicago White Sox finished right behind the Twins in the standings as the Vice President of the Dumb Class (which doesn't have nearly as much cache). The White Sox were definitely in a position to challenge for the division title, but in the end injuries did them in. Frank Thomas hit .271/.434/.563 and Magglio Ordonez batted .292/.351/.485, but the two star sluggers combined to play in just 126 games, including only seven after the All-Star break, all by Ordonez.

Aaron Rowand picked up a lot of the slack with an outstanding, breakout year, hitting .310/.361/.544 while playing excellent defense in center field. Though barely anyone noticed, he was quietly one of the top position players in the entire league. Paul Konerko, Juan Uribe and Carlos Lee also had solid years, but Joe Crede, Jose Valentin, Timo Perez and Joe Borchard all got significant playing time and all posted sub-.300 on-base percentages.

Over in Cleveland, the Indians' rebuilding plan was about a year ahead of schedule. Their offensive attack came together in a big way this year, as Victor Martinez (.283/.359/.492) and Travis Hafner (.311/.410/.583) had breakout years and role players like Ronnie Belliard, Matt Lawton, Casey Blake, Coco Crisp and Ben Broussard were very productive.

Cleveland's lineup carried them for much of the season, but in the end their pitching was just too thin to stay with the Twins. Jake Westbrook and C.C. Sabathia combined to go 25-19 with a 3.72 ERA in 402.2 innings, but the rest of the Indians' pitching staff went just 55-63 with a 5.89 ERA. The bullpen was particularly bad, posting a 4.88 ERA, blowing an AL-worst 28 saves, and seemingly naming a new closer every week.

The Detroit Tigers won 29 more games than they did last year and still finished a distant fourth in the division, which tells you just how awful their 2003 season was. Detroit's offseason moves paid off for the most part, as Carlos Guillen was one of the most valuable players in the league before his season-ending injury, and Ivan Rodriguez and Rondell White had solid years.

Things weren't so good on the pitching side of things, as Jason Johnson, another free agent signing, went 8-15 with a 5.13 ERA and the Tigers finished 13th in the league in ERA. One of the only bright spots was Jeremy Bonderman, who made major improvements from his rookie year and had a 3.70 ERA and 85 strikeouts in 90 second-half innings. He looks like a future stud.

After a surprisingly good 2003 season, the Kansas City Royals had an awful 2004, falling back to the cellar while trading away Carlos Beltran at midseason. David DeJesus had a fine second half in place of Beltran, hitting .314/.385/.453, and Zack Greinke was one of the best rookies in baseball, but those were pretty much the only positives in Kansas City.

American League West Review

By Robert Dudek

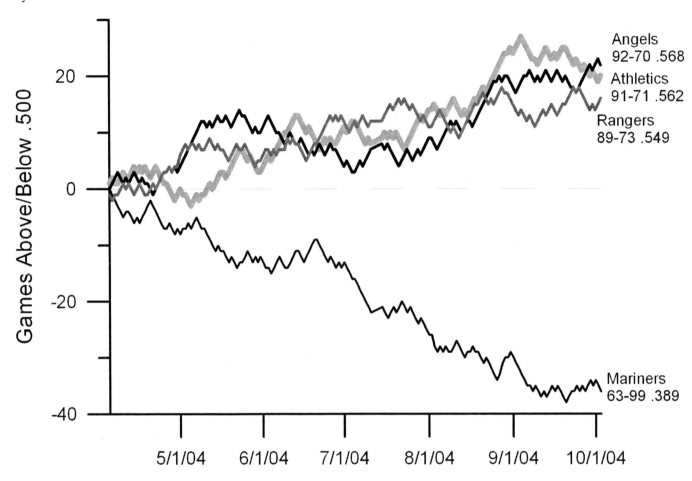

SHOWALTER'S CHARGES SURPRISE; TROUBLES in the PACIFIC NORTHWEST

Before we turn to the exploits of the principal actors in the Major Leagues' most exciting pennant race, let's examine the rapid demise of the Seattle Mariners. Despite playing in a pitcher's paradise, Seattle had scored a copious (though declining) number of runs in recent years. The outfield defense of 2003, with Mike Cameron, Randy Winn and Ichiro Suzuki, was one of the best in baseball. Cameron signed with the Mets, Winn moved to center and Raul Ibanez was signed to play left. The starting rotation seemed solid enough with two young hurlers, Joel Pineiro and Gil Meche, complementing cagey veteran Jamie Moyer as the front three. The bullpen, though weakened by the departures of Arthur Rhodes and Kaz Sasaki, looked solid with fireballer Rafael Soriano, steady Shigetoshi Hasegawa and former Twins closer Everyday Eddie Guardado. Certainly, there were signs of decline, but no one could

have anticipated that Seattle would allow nearly 200 more runs in 2004 than they had the year before.

A club that won over 62% of its games over the last 3 seasons turned into the dregs of the league overnight. An exceptionally poor start prompted management to jettison veterans in favor of a youth movement. John Olerud was released mid-season. Freddy Garcia was traded to the White Sox, bringing top prospect Jeremy Reed the other way. Edgar Martinez announced that he would be hanging up his spikes at the conclusion of the season, and age caught up to the 35-year-old Bret Boone.

One of the few bright spots was the play of the incomparable Ichiro Suzuki. As the season wore on, Ichiro's hitting got better and better. Playing everyday, leading off, walking infrequently and hitting over .370 conspired to create a new single-season record for hits. In game #160, Ichiro bested the 85-year-old mark of 257 hits set by George Sisler, ending up with the remarkable total of 262 hits.

In Arlington, fans were initially more realistic about their chances after Tom Hicks traded away the league's highest paid and most talented player, Alex Rodriguez, for second baseman Alfonso Soriano. The Rangers still had two of the best young hitters in the game – Hank Blalock and Mark Teixeira. Mike Young made the transition to shortstop almost seamlessly, and proved to be an effective and durable leadoff hitter.

The big surprise was the progress in sorting out the pitching, and manager Buck Showalter deserves full marks for that. He sorted through dozens of arms and came up with enough quality to lower opponent scoring by 175 runs, compared to 2003. That vaulted Texas into the thick of the pennant race.

Kenny Rogers and Ryan Drese tallied over 200 strong innings on the front end of the rotation, but it was the bullpen that lifted the Rangers out of mediocrity. Francisco Cordero, the closer since mid-season 2002, became one of the ten best closers in the game. Cordero converted 49 of 54 save opportunities, struck out 79 and walked 32 in 71.2 innings, allowing just 1 home run and posting a 2.13 ERA. He was capably supported by Ron Mahay (67 IP, 2.55 ERA), rookie Frank Francisco (51.1, 3.33) and lefty specialist Brian Shouse (44.1, 2.23).

The Texas bullpen was arguably the most valuable in the league. The Rangers' pen finished a close second behind Anaheim with a 3.51 ERA despite being burdened with the 4th heaviest workload in the AL and plying their trade in one of the best hitter's parks in baseball. Their credentials included a league-best 80% conversion rate of save opportunities and a 34-15 win-loss record.

Change was in the air in the offseason in Oakland, as the A's brain trust continued their gradual shift away from offense to defense. Ace reliever Keith Foulke bolted for big money in Boston and superstar shortstop Miguel Tejada did likewise in Baltimore. Veteran catcher Ramon Martinez was traded to San Diego, with Mark Kotsay, a talented defensive centerfielder, the main player coming to Oakland. AAA graduate Bobby Crosby was installed at short and Beane picked up Damian Miller to fill in the vacancy at catcher. Ted Lilly departed, but was capably replaced by ex-Marlin Mark Redman.

At the All-Star break, Oakland was sitting in third, 2 games behind surprise front runners Texas. No worries – the Athletics put on a couple of their patented hot streaks to edge ahead of their rivals. On the morning of September 5th, Oakland was 4 in front of Anaheim and 6.5 ahead of Texas and their hold on the division title looked firm.

Unfortunately, all was not well in the Baysiders' rotation. After a good start, Tim Hudson strained an oblique muscle, missed all of July and posted an "ordinary" 4.28 ERA in the second half. Mark Mulder suffered through an extended period of ineffectiveness for the first

time since his rookie season. The Cy Young favorite though July, Mulder's 2nd half ERA ballooned to 6.13 and he struck out just 48 batters against 42 walks.

Every year the Athletics make one or more rental trades to boost their playoff chances and 2004 was no exception. Arthur Rhodes's ineffectiveness and injuries left a void in the back of the bullpen, and Octavio Dotel was acquired to bolster it. Though Dotel struck out 72 batters and walked only 18 in 50.2 innings, the 9 gopher balls and 6 blown saves added up to less than was expected of him. In one memorable contest less than two weeks from season's end, the Rangers rallied for 3 runs in the bottom of the ninth off Dotel to win 5-4 and tighten the three-way race.

Following a world championship with a sub-.500 finish usually puts the faithful into a funk. Angels owner Arte Moreno blasted that possibility to dust when he opened up his wallet and brought four impact Latin American players to town. The greatest of these was undoubtedly Vlad Guerrero, one of the greatest natural talents the game has ever produced. The rotation was bolstered with the portly Bartolo Colon and the enigmatic Kelvim Escobar. Outfielder Jose Guillen was thrown into the mix, becoming one of the few leftfielders ever to have a cannon arm and forcing the shift of Garret Anderson to centerfield and Darin Erstad to first base.

THE HOMESTRETCH

With 20 games left to play, all against division rivals, Oakland held a 2-game edge over Anaheim with Texas 5 games back. But the Angels lost gold-glove caliber second baseman Adam Kennedy for the season on September 21st after he injured his knee, and would soon have to deal with another loss of personnel for an altogether different reason.

Jose Guillen threw his glove at the dugout wall after being removed for a pinch runner on the penultimate Saturday of the season. This was not the first incident of questionable behavior involving Guillen, and Mike Scioscia talked to his outfielder and the team behind closed doors. The baseball world was shocked to learn that the Angels had suspended Guillen for the balance of the regular season and eventual playoffs.

The final week would be a showdown of the three contenders. Anaheim took a road trip to Arlington, while Oakland hosted spoil-minded Seattle. The A's held a slim 1-game advantage over the Angels with the Rangers just 2 back. The four games in Texas would knock one of the two teams out of the picture.

In the first game, Bartolo Colon tossed 8 strong innings and the Angels rallied with 4 runs in the final 3 frames to win 5-3. Oakland broke a 5-5 deadlock in the 9th after a leadoff double by Erubiel Durazo and an eventual sacrifice fly which scored pinch-runner Esteban German.

The final Tuesday of the regular season would spell more bad news for Rangers as Chan Ho Park failed to hold down the Angels offense. Kelvim Escobar and the bullpen held the powerful Texas lineup to just 2 runs on the way to an 8-2 victory. Seattle's win over Oakland moved Anaheim into a tie for first, with the Rangers now 3 back with 5 to play.

Game 3 saw the Angels drive a stake into the Rangers. Curtis Pride tied the game in the 9th with a double off Francisco Cordero which plated Vladimir Guerrero. Troy Glaus's 11th inning 2-run home run proved to be enough for the Angels to prevail 8-7. In Oakland, the A's were stymied by rookie Bobby Madritch, who hurled a complete game 3-hitter, while Seattle scored 3 runs in the 8th off tiring starter Rich Harden and reliever Jim Mecir. Seattle prevailed 4-2, knocking the A's into second place with 4 games left to play.

Thursday's contests saw reversals, as Oakland scraped by Seattle and Texas defeated Anaheim. The two

California teams were now tied with only 3 head-to-head contests left to decide the A.L. West championship.

In the opening tilt, Mark Mulder lasted but 2 innings and gave up 4 runs before Ken Macha pulled the plug. Super prospect Joe Blanton restored order, but was knocked out in the 6th inning as the Angels scored 4 more runs to put the game out of reach. Bartolo Colon shut out the A's for 7 innings and the Angels coasted to an easy 10-0 victory.

Needing only one more win to take the pennant, Anaheim entrusted Kelvim Escobar with the task. Things looked promising for the Athletics – Barry Zito pitched effectively and his club had a 2-0 lead through 5 innings. Vlad Guerrero tied it in the 6th with a two-run blast to left-centerfield, but Oakland strung three hits together to take a 4-2 lead. The A's bullpen couldn't hold the lead however: Darin Erstad doubled in two runs to tie the game and Garret Anderson's single plated the go-ahead marker. The Angels' vaunted bullpen did the rest and when Troy Percival retired the side in the 9th, Anaheim had secured their invitation to the Big Dance.

The A.L. West Homestretch Up Close

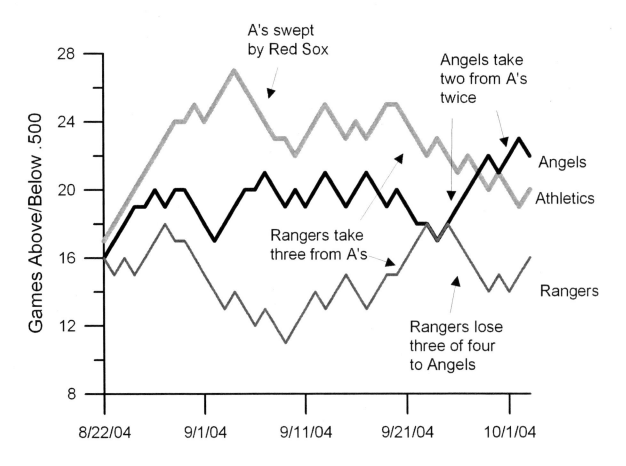

National League East Review

By Vinay Kumar

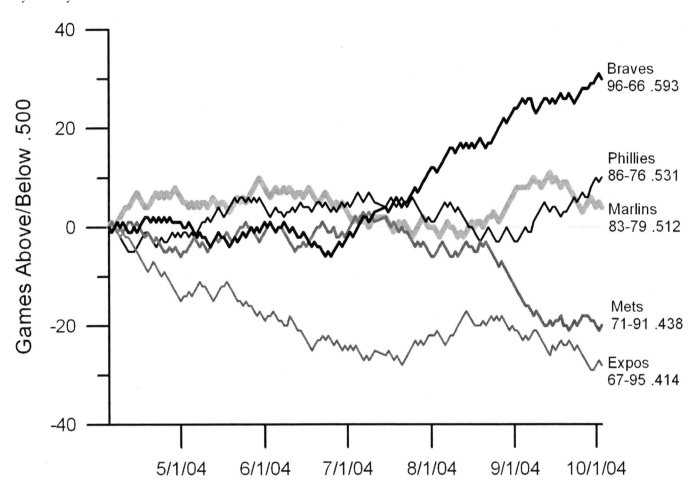

Never underestimate Leo Mazzone. More than anything else, that's what the National League East taught us this year.

After thoroughly dominating the division for a decade (plus a few NL West titles when they still resided there), the Braves' run appeared over this spring. They let Greg Maddux return to Chicago, severing their final tie with the vaunted pitching rotation that symbolized their run (since John Smoltz now closes). They bid adieu to Gary Sheffield and Javy Lopez, the keys to 2003's powerhouse offense. They entered 2004 in the unfamiliar position of underdog.

Oh, people had written the Braves off before. In fact, the 2003 division title was a surprise to many pundits. But in the spring of 2004, it appeared that Braves management cared more about Time Warner's bottom line than about continuing their run. The upstart Florida Marlins had just won their second World Series title (which must've been especially painful to the Atlanta faithful, as the Braves have

won the big trophy just once during their 14-year dynasty), and the Phillies were much-improved and heading into the brand new Citizen's Bank Park. A lineup full of question marks and a pitching staff full of retreads looked utterly overmatched.

The Braves lived down to expectations for much of the spring, entering July languishing below .500 and in fourth place. But inconsistent starts from the Phillies and Marlins kept the Braves within striking distance. And they still had Leo Mazzone.

Under Mazzone, Atlanta has had a near-stranglehold on the league's ERA leadership. Much of the credit had been due to having three future Hall of Fame starters spending their long peaks together. Indeed, without the "big three," the 2003 club relied on a powerful offense to carry the team to the division title; the team's ERA was seventh in the league. But this year Mazzone took an unlikely cast of characters back to their familiar perch, leading the NL with a 3.74 ERA. Jaret Wright, arguably the worst pitcher in the league in 2003, finally had the type of year expected from him for so long in Cleveland (15-8, 3.28 ERA). While none of Russ Ortiz, John Thomson, Paul Byrd and Mike Hampton pitched like All-Stars, they were all above average. A similarly unimpressive bullpen cast, anchored by star John Smoltz, combined for a 3.55 ERA. The key to the staff's success was its consistency: everybody stayed healthy and pitched at least passably; there were no 6.00 ERAs in the #5 rotation slot or middle-inning relief. If there was any debate whether Leo Mazzone belongs in the Hall of Fame, this Braves staff should end it.

The Braves were able to replace Sheffield and Lopez with J.D. Drew (acquired in a trade with St. Louis) and Johnny Estrada (acquired a year earlier in a trade for Kevin Millwood). I'm not sure which is more surprising: Drew's health or Estrada's hitting. Drew has always had MVP-level talent, but his first season in Atlanta was the first in his six-year career that he played enough to even qualify for the batting title. Hitting .305/.436/.539, Drew set career highs in games (145), plate appearances (645) and virtually every offensive category, with a superb all-around season. Estrada defied all expectations by hitting .314/.378/.450. In fact, every front-line Braves player had a solid year with the bat, and Atlanta finished 5th in the NL with 803 runs.

As the divisional chart shows, the Braves looked like a juggernaut for the second half of the season, going 63-27 over the final 90 games and easily pulling away from the pack in the NL East. Meanwhile every other team in the division had a disappointing season.

The Phillies had been looking forward to 2004 for years, as they ushered in a new era of Philadelphia baseball in Citizens' Bank Park. Management had been adding talent (most notably slugger Jim Thome) in advance to put together a championship-level team for 2004. With a lineup core of Thome (.274/.396/.581 and 42 HR) and perennially underrated Bobby Abreu (.301/.428/.544), rebound performances from 3B David Bell (.291/.363/.458) and Pat Burrell (.257/.365/.455), quality seasons from every starter (except for slumping sophomore, Marlon Byrd, who played his way out of the everyday CF job) and some help from the generous home ballpark, the Phillies offense lived up to expectations, scoring 840 runs (just 15 fewer than St. Louis's league-leading total).

The Phillies' downfall, however, was starting pitching. Newcomer Eric Milton couldn't even keep up with the guy he was traded for (4.75 ERA vs. Carlos Silva's 4.21; let's not even mention the $9 million salary difference). Despite his reputation, pedigree and contract, Milton is merely an average pitcher. The rest of the Philly rotation regressed from 2003, as Randy Wolf, Brett Myers, Kevin Millwood and Vicente Padilla all turned in disappointing

years. The high-priced bullpen was decent, but not really worth the money. Billy Wagner was as dominating as expected, but injuries limited him to 48.1 innings over 38 games. Rookie Ryan Madson was the highlight of the pitching staff, emerging from nowhere to post a 2.34 ERA in 77 innings. However, the rest of the Philly pen cashed nearly $9 million in paychecks and provided league-average results. With most of the pen on the wrong side of age 30, things don't look to improve much in 2005. The Phillies will have to hope for a rebound in the rotation, possibly in the form of top prospect Gavin Floyd.

Heading into the season, the defending champion Marlins seemed to be reading from a script written seven years ago, waving goodbye to some key players due to financial reasons (Pudge Rodriguez, Derrek Lee, and Ugueth Urbina). But the team retained enough young talent that they still expected to compete with the vulnerable Braves. Wunderkind Miguel Cabrera continued to develop, hitting .294/.366/.512 with 31 2B and 33 HR at the tender age of 21. Away from the bright lights of New York, Armando Benitez quietly dominated National League hitters, sporting a miniscule 1.29 ERA while saving 47 games. Carl Pavano blossomed into the pitcher the Expos expected him to be when they traded Pedro Martinez for him, going 18-8 with a 3.00 ERA. Dontrelle Willis, Josh Beckett, Brad Penny and AJ Burnett joined Pavano to form a young, effective, but oft-injured rotation.

As July drew to a close, the Marlins were on the outskirts of the playoff race, trailing San Diego by 6 games in the Wild Card hunt. With gaping holes in the bullpen and behind the plate, the Marlins dealt two young players (slugging 1B Hee Seop Choi and talented starter Brad Penny) to Los Angeles for veteran catcher Paul Lo Duca, lights-out setup man Guillermo Mota and overpaid RF Juan Encarnacion. Most of the media frenzy over this deal surrounded the Dodgers, and whether it made sense to trade their "heart and soul" for young players while the team was in a tight division battle of its own. Lost was the impact on the Marlins, as Lo Duca and Mota immediately filled holes. Unfortunately, neither was nearly as effective for Florida (Lo Duca experienced his usual second-half fade and hit .258/.314/.376 as a Marlin, while Mota's ERA ballooned from 2.14 to 4.81), and the Marlins faded to an 83-79 finish.

The Mets are an organization without any clear vision or direction. They provided a fascinating story for outsiders in 2004 (though fans probably considered it excruciating). For years, they had uttered nonsensical excuses like, "You can't rebuild in New York," while occupying themselves as much with the cross-town Yankees as with their own state of affairs. But after an embarrassing 69-92 season in 2003, the Mets came to grips with reality and conceded that it would take an overhaul to really compete again. They didn't trade any of their top young talent over the offseason and signed outfielder Mike Cameron to a reasonable contract. They added dynamic shortstop Kazuo Matsui from Japan, who optimistically projected to be a Barry Larkin type of player. It was looking like 2004 would be a return to respectability for the Mets, hopefully followed by years of contention for a team anchored by homegrown talents like Jose Reyes, David Wright, and Scott Kazmir.

Things started going wrong almost from day one. Reyes couldn't stay healthy. Matsui was decent but unspectacular with the bat, and a complete disappointment with the glove. Mike Piazza got hurt again; the Mets responded by experimenting with him at 1B, where he was so atrocious that the whole ordeal took his hitting down with his defense. The Mets persevered, however, and stayed above .500 through the All-Star break.

In retrospect, that mid-season flirtation with the Wild Card race might've been the worst thing that could've happened to the Mets. They scrapped their slow-growth plan and traded for pitchers Victor Zambrano and Kris Benson. To acquire Benson, the Mets parted with prospects Justin Huber and Matt Peterson (along with infielder Ty Wigginton); an excessive price to pay for a pitcher on the verge of free agency. More egregious was the trade for Zambrano, in which the Mets surrendered twenty-year-old Scott Kazmir, arguably the top pitching prospect in the minors at the time.

Pitching coach Rick Peterson defended the trade, saying that Kazmir was a few years away from big-league success. Apparently, time flies faster in Florida, as Kazmir threw five shutout innings against the Seattle Mariners just three weeks later. OK, so the 2004 Mariners aren't really a major-league caliber team; Kazmir shut down the potent Red Sox lineup for six innings just a month later.

As more and more criticism for the trade crossed the airwaves and newsstands, many Mets employees publicly denied their culpability. Everybody from owner Fred Wilpon to Chief Operating Office Jeff Wilpon, from GM Dan Duquette to pitching coach Rick Peterson to rotation anchor Al Leiter raced to defend themselves. While all of them were eager to defend the organization and themselves publicly, they unwittingly admitted that they all had some input on the deal. So it's no wonder that the Mets have no unified direction or plan; they have too many people involved in each decision. The Mets solved their too-many-cooks-in-the-kitchen problem by hiring yet another cook, head of baseball operations Omar Minaya. They didn't fire Duquette; they just installed Minaya above him. While Minaya is reputedly a sharp talent evaluator, he openly eschews modern statistical research and completely bungled the Bartolo Colon trades (among others) during his tenure as GM in Montreal.

Amid the furor over the trades and management structure of the Mets, many have already forgotten that

two of the most exciting young players in baseball will start at Shea next season. While Jose Reyes' recurring hamstring problems take some of the shine off his luster, he is still an electrifying player with an impressive resume at age 21. 3B David Wright tore through AA and AAA on his way to a magnificent major-league debut (.293/.332/.525 in 69 games). With 52 doubles and 32 HR across the majors and minors last year at just age 21, Wright projects to be an awesome hitter for the Mets. And with the Mets' revenue stream, they are poised to add even more marquee talent this offseason. With all that has gone wrong the last few months in Flushing, it's been easy to ignore that things are still looking up.

The few remaining fans of the Montreal Expos must surely be the most loyal fans in all of sports, having to put up with the abuse they've taken from MLB, their former owners and jokesters across America the last few years. The sham continued for another year, as MLB continued to perpetrate the biggest conflict of interest imaginable. MLB's rules specifically forbid an owner to hold shares in multiple teams, but apparently they've chosen to waive that rule if they *all* do it.

After the club tried the experiment of playing some games in San Juan, Puerto Rico in 2003, the players decided that they didn't like it (gee, who wouldn't like being on the road for an extra three weeks per season?) and couldn't put up with it for another year. The owners bullied them into accepting the plan again in 2004, however, by threatening to cut the budgets even further if they would not change their votes. It amazes me that this story didn't receive more coverage. Maybe the public is just so used to these types of shenanigans from MLB that this isn't considered news. I wish great public humiliation on Bud Selig and everybody involved in this disgusting episode.

Lost amid all of this controversy were fine seasons from Brad Wilkerson (.255/.374/.498) and Juan Rivera (.307/.364/.465) as well as Livan Hernandez's re-emergence as a stud starter (3.60 ERA over a league-leading 255 innings). Orlando Cabrera and Jose Vidro have quietly been a very strong middle-infield duo over the years, and both were rewarded this season: Cabrera with a trade to Boston and a World Series ring, and Vidro with a $30 million, 4-year extension.

MLB is moving forward with plans to relocate the team to Washington in 2005. Given the pending RICO suit, I hesitate to call this a done deal. Given everything that the players and fans have gone through for the last few years, it would be for the best if the franchise can get a fresh start in Washington in 2005. I just hope that the 36 years in Montreal aren't forgotten, and that the city's reputation isn't tarnished permanently in baseball circles due to the greed of MLB and former owner Claude Brochu.

National League Central Review

By Joe Dimino

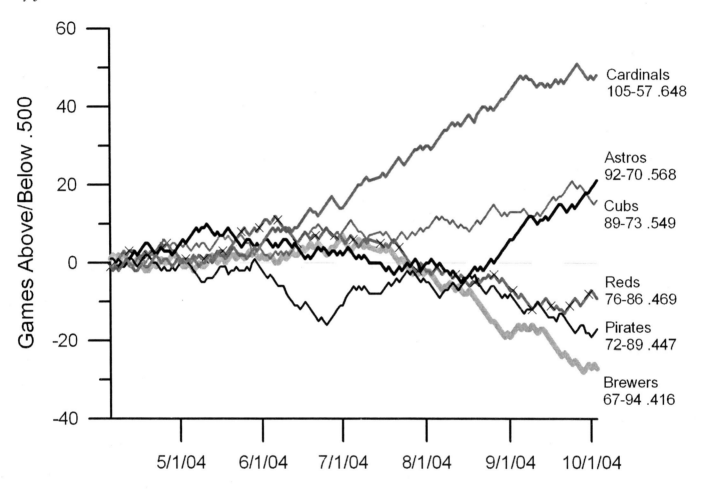

The NL Central was quite a pleasant surprise in 2004. Picked by many to be the second worst division in the game, the entire division was over .500 (even the Brewers!) as late as May 29 – when the Pirates sat in last place with a 23-22 record.

Even within the division there were surprises, early in the season at least – most thought there was going to be a two-team race between the teams with the best rotations in the Senior Circuit, the Cubs and Astros. A few felt the Cardinals would contend as well, but most forecasters had St. Louis slated for third. The Reds, picked no better than fourth and under .500 by most – led the division as late as June 10.

In late May, the Redbirds were right where most figured they'd be with a 23-22 record. The offense was expected to be strong, but there were major question marks for a pitching staff that didn't have a true ace.

Things gelled May 27. That day, the Cardinals started a 9-1 run that saw them take 4 of 5 from the Astros during the stretch. After alternating wins and losses for a week, they reeled off 11 more wins in 13 games. After a minor speed bump in the form of being swept by the Pirates, Tony LaRussa's club turned around and won 20 of 25 to close out July at 66-37, basically ending the race.

As expected, the pitching didn't appear to be anything special on the surface, as no starter was dominant. Yet St. Louis finished with the 2nd best ERA in the NL. None of the starters were awful, and the bullpen was amazing, as five pitchers had an ERA lower than 3.00 while pitching at least 45 innings.

But the real story in St. Louis was the offense, which led the NL with 855 runs despite playing in a pitcher's park and giving over 400 PA to Mike Matheny (and his 67 OPS+). Albert Pujols was his usual self (175 OPS+), while Scott Rolen (160) and Jim Edmonds (173) had career years. Larry Walker came over from Colorado to join the party in August and posted a 146 OPS+ in 150 AB.

It all came together in the form of a truly magical season for the Cardinals – 105 wins, and their first NL pennant in 17 seasons.

The Astros season finished right where many forecasted, 92 wins and a Wild Card berth. However, the path to that end was the most unlikely of any postseason team.

After losing 6 of 7 to the less-than-stellar Expos and Mets August 7-14, the Astros' season appeared over. They were 56-60 at that point. Andy Pettitte and Wade Miller were lost for the season. Manager Jimy Williams had been replaced at the All-Star break by Phil Garner, though it hadn't seemed to matter.

But something clicked August 15. The Astros scored 3 runs in the top of the 9th to pull out a 5-4 win in the finale with Montreal. From that point on, the Astros were the best team in baseball, going 36-10 the rest of the way; they clinched the Wild Card on the final day of the regular season.

Despite the postseason heroics of Beltran, Lance Berkman was the key cog in this offense. Berkman hit .316 with 127 walks, good for the 3rd best OBP in the NL and the #5 OPS+ (161) in the Senior Circuit. Beltran posted a 136 OPS+ after coming over from Kansas City (he played 90 games for Houston) and was the perfect complement at the top of the order.

The great run over the last 46 games masked the continued decline of Jeff Bagwell. While still a middle-of-the-pack NL offensive first baseman (117 OPS+), 2004 was the 5th consecutive season in a decline period that has seen his OPS+ go 169, 152, 141, 137, 127, 117. Bagwell failed to hit 30 HR and SLG .500 for the first time since 1995.

As for the pitching, Brad Lidge emerged as the top closer in baseball, posting a 1.90 ERA. He struck out 157 and walked 30 in 95 innings. Lidge brings back memories of Goose Gossage – whose NL record (151) he broke for relief strikeouts in a season.

Roger Clemens started the All-Star Game for the NL, finished 18-4 and posted his best ERA+ (145) since 1998. Roy Oswalt was the only 20-game winner in the NL and posted a 3.49 ERA over 237 IP (3rd in the league).

With the addition of Greg Maddux, Derrek Lee, and LaTroy Hawkins, almost everyone thought the Cubs would be much improved in 2004. Back in March, they were the consensus favorites to represent the National League in the World Series.

As Kenny Mayne says, they don't play games on paper; they play them inside television sets. The Cubs did 'improve', winning one more game during the regular season in 2004 than in their magical 2003 campaign that came so close - but yet so far away.

The Cubs were in control of the Wild Card race most of the way - unfortunately, they ran into an awful spell of luck the last nine days of the season. They lost 5 one-run games and 7 of 8 total from September 25 through October 2 – including 5 of 6 to the Mets (71-91) and Reds (76-86). So despite having the 3rd best Pythagorean record in the NL (94-68), the Cubs watched the 2004 postseason from the luxury of their living rooms.

The main reasons for the stagnation in Chicago (it really wasn't a step backwards) were the injuries to Mark Prior, Kerry Wood and Alex Gonzalez.

Prior posted just a 113 ERA+ (175 in 2003), throwing only 119 IP after missing the first two months with an Achilles injury. He was awful in July and August (5.56 ERA) before pitching great down the stretch, though it was too little too late. Wood was off to a great start (2.82 ERA after 7 starts) when he went down in May. He was limited to just 22 starts on the season and his ERA was 4.14 after his return. Finally, Gonzalez played just 37 games with a 50 OPS+. He and his counterparts at SS did an incredible impression of Doug Flynn, before a 4-team deal brought Nomar Garciaparra to the Cubs – again, too little too late.

There were positives. Carlos Zambrano took the next step and became one of the best pitchers in the National League - at the age of just 23. He allowed just 14 home runs and fanned 188 in 210 IP. It added up to a 16-8 record and a 2.75 ERA. Free-agent-to-be Matt Clement also pitched pretty well, despite his 9-13 record, recording a career high 123 ERA+, striking out 190 in 181 innings.

But Corey Patterson and Sammy Sosa took serious steps backwards. Sosa is 35 and showed it, as this was his worst year since 1997. Sosa tailed off to .253 with 'just' 35 home runs while missing 36 games.

Patterson appeared to have finally gotten things together in 2003, before tearing his ACL that July. 2004 was a regression though it didn't appear to be related to the injury (he had 32 SB). Patterson lost 32 points off his batting average and 59 off his slugging. Despite playing for a manager that doesn't like walks, because, 'they clog up the basepaths', Patterson was more patient at the plate (his walks and strikeouts were up) but his overall results were off. He's still just 25 and he is young enough to experience these ups and downs while developing his game – the batting average drop-off could have just been random chance, and the increase in walks is encouraging.

Chili Davis had a similar 'setback year' in 1983, though he was a year younger. His batting average dropped 28 points and his slugging 58, while his BB and K rates went up. In 1984, he broke out, hitting .315 with 21 home runs (which meant something back then, as it was good enough for 8th in the NL) and a 148 OPS+. Cubs fans are hoping Patterson will follow a similar path.

For the Cincinnati Reds, this was yet another season of the rapidly evaporating Ken Griffey Jr. era that never materialized. This was somewhat due to injuries, but mostly the result of the worst pitching staff in the Major Leagues – one that allowed more home runs than any team, while striking out fewer batters than all but two National League teams. They gave up 907 runs, more than anyone but the Rockies (and 52 more than the Cardinals scored, for perspective).

The team had the best record in the NL in early June (making the finish all the more frustrating). Adam Dunn came through with a breakout season (152 OPS+). Sure, he broke the late Bobby Bonds' strikeout record, but much more importantly he finished 2nd in the NL with 46 home runs while drawing 108 walks. Those strikeouts may be a negative, but you can't hit into a double play when you are striking out, and Dunn only hit into 8 all season.

Sean Casey had a career year as well, with a 142 OPS+, but Austin Kearns falling off a cliff offset that. Two years ago Kearns looked on track for first-tier stardom. He posted a 130 OPS+ in two-thirds of a season as a rookie after tearing up the minors. The OPS+ dipped to 113 while Kearns missed half the season in 2003; but hopes were high for a full recovery this season.

It wasn't to be. On June 1, Kearns had only played 28 games, was hitting .195 and headed for thumb surgery. After his return in August he played reasonably well (.254/.317/.469) for someone coming off surgery, but it was a second lost year in his development.

For the 4th consecutive season Griffey spent significant time on the DL. He's now played just 206 games over the past 3 seasons. It's time to move Griffey to first base. Considering that he can still handle centerfield, once he gets some reps at first, he'll likely be a star defensively – and his bat is likely to stay in the lineup if he isn't running and diving all over the place.

Even perennial doormats like the Pirates and Brewers showed signs of life early in the season. The Pirates were 23-22 after knocking off the Cubs for the third consecutive game on May 29. As mentioned earlier, they were in last place, but it was an encouraging start for a team that hasn't finished better than 79-83 since the elder Bush was in the White House.

Then, it all fell apart. The Bucs were blown out 12-1 in the final game of the Cub series and Hurricane Cardinal came to town and swept 4 straight – combined score 25-9.

Those were the first five games of a stretch that saw the Pirates lose 21 of 24. Of course, they followed that up with a 10-game winning streak (including a sweep of the Cardinals) – and by July 25 they were within 2 games of .500 again! From there, the Bucs lost 9 of 11. In the end, they would finish roughly where expected at 72-89 and in 5th place, but it was a wild ride.

Individually, the most encouraging thing for Pirate fans had to be the breakout season of Jack Wilson. After 3 years of making Pirate fans wax nostalgic for the days of Kevin Polcovich, Lou Collier and Mike Benjamin, Wilson posted 23 Win Shares, hitting .308 with a .459 SLG and was in a pack among the best shortstops in the National League. He only walked 26 times, but his newfound power (41 2B, 12 3B, 11 HR) put him among the top offensive shortstops in the NL anyway.

After missing the first month of the season with an injury, Jason Bay was a Rookie of the Year candidate, posting 17 WS and a 135 OPS+. The offense in Pittsburgh had some of the cogs needed for success. The foundation of Bay and Craig Wilson (122 OPS+) was solid. Jason Kendall turned 30 in June, but he's still a good hitter for a catcher (110 OPS+), though he basically has no power (32 2B and 3 HR).

With the help of Bay, Oliver Perez made the Brian Giles trade look like a coup for beleaguered GM Dave Littlefield. Perez, who turned 23 in August, was 12-10 with a 2.98 ERA. He fanned 239 batters in just 196 IP and is arguably the best young pitcher in the National League (Jake Peavy being the other choice).

Sean Burnett gave Pirate fans hope as well. He came up for good June 19, and had a 2.18 ERA after his 7th start on July 20. But he was hit hard in 5 of his next 6 starts and was shut down in late August with a torn ligament in his elbow. His 2005 campaign is likely over before it begins, leaving Pittsburgh fans disappointed yet again.

One might look at Milwaukee's 67-95 record and think that it was the same old, same old in Brew Town. It wasn't – the team actually showed progress in 2004; for the first time in memory they appear to be moving forward.

The Brewers were similar to the Pirates in that they got off to a solid start and had a few players post breakout seasons. Coming into 2004, Ben Sheets was a solid pitcher with a low-to-mid 4's ERA over the past few seasons. He'd consistently pitch 200+ innings with an ERA around the league average – your typical innings eater, but nothing special – very similar to Ben McDonald, another promising young Louisiana righthander who struggled at age 23 and 24.

2004 saw Sheets become a star, a pitcher that would have been considered for the Cy Young Award if he wasn't doomed to a 12-14 record pitching in Milwaukee. Sheets posted a 2.70 ERA and fanned 264 batters in 237 IP, walking just 32! It all came together for Sheets, as it did for McDonald in his age-25 season. Coincidentally, McDonald also had a tough-luck year, going 13-14 despite a 130 ERA+ in 1993.

The biggest holes in the Brewer lineup were players like Scott Podsednik and the catchers, Gary Bennett and Chad Moeller. Podsednik did his best impression of Omar

Moreno. He stole 70 bases and was caught just 13 times, which is outstanding. But his .313 OBP and 79 OPS+ were just awful for a major-league outfielder – and exactly Moreno's career OPS+ to boot. Bennett and Moeller hit .224/.297/.329 and .208/.265./303 – consuming 536 AB.

The National League's best top-to-bottom division appropriately sent both representatives to the NLCS. Every team in the division except the Cardinals has a strong case that they could be better in 2005 than in 2004, so this promises to be a division to be reckoned with for the foreseeable future.

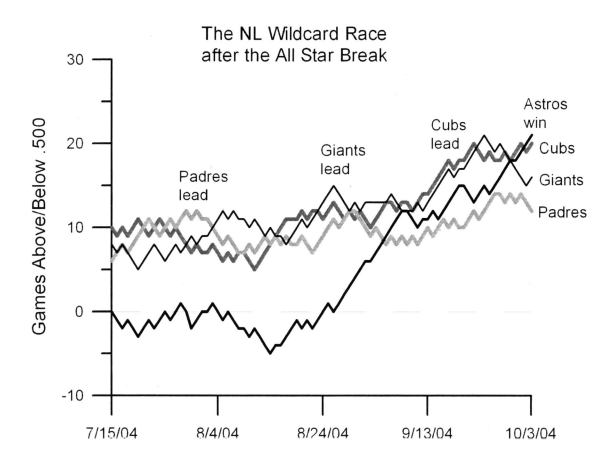

National League West Review

By Steve Treder

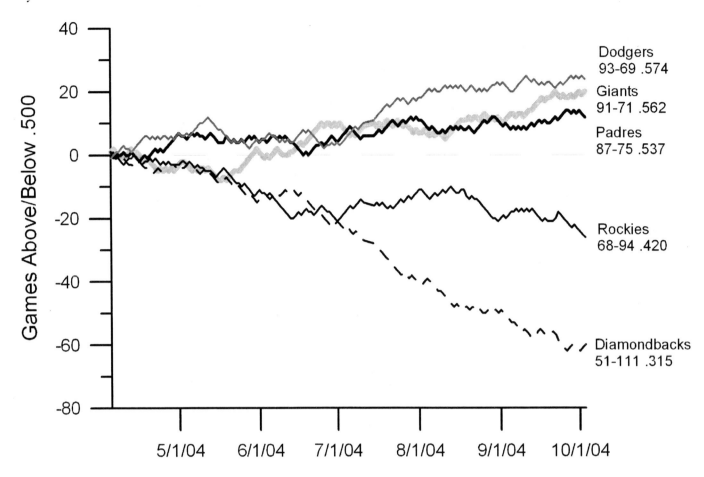

The 2004 National League West was a surprising, exciting, and fun division. Wait -- actually, the 2004 NL West was a surprising, exciting, and fun division except for the Arizona Diamondbacks, who were surprising, but neither exciting nor fun. And -- well, to be honest, the Colorado Rockies were neither exciting nor fun, and that was, alas, no surprise at all.

Okay, then, let's try this: the Los Angeles Dodgers, San Francisco Giants, and San Diego Padres presented surprising, exciting, and fun baseball in 2004. The Rockies and Diamondbacks -- well, we'll get to them.

Let's start with the division-winning 2004 Dodgers, one of the more interesting ball clubs in the franchise's storied history. In startling contrast to the 2003 pitching-and-defense-and-absolutely-nothing-else edition, the '04 Dodgers blasted 203 homers and scored 761 runs (spiking from 124 and 574 in '03), flashing a rambunctious offense that routinely ticked stunning late-inning comebacks off the to-do list.

The Dodger most responsible for this transformation was, emphatically, third baseman Adrian Beltre. A promising underachiever for several years, Beltre suddenly played like an all-time great at age 25, hitting .334/.388/.629, with 48 home runs. Beltre's fielding was brilliant as well, and altogether his performance piled up 37 Win Shares, fourth best in the NL.

Los Angeles won nine of their first twelve in 2004, and played well nearly all year, suffering only one real slump (a 2-12 slide in late May). From July through October, they only once lost as many as three games in a row (that micro-skid being, perhaps ominously, a sweep at the hands of the Cardinals in early September).

Dodgers' rookie GM Paul DePodesta stunned the baseball world (or at least the mainstream baseball media) when he pulled off a blockbuster deadline deal with the Florida Marlins, surrendering popular catcher Paul Lo Duca and top-notch setup man Guillermo Mota in a package that netted starter Brad Penny and young first baseman Hee Seop Choi. The trade worked out poorly for the Dodgers, but not for the reason nearly all the pundits expected. What happened was that Penny immediately got hurt and was essentially useless, and Choi didn't hit and was quickly buried on the Dodger bench; what had been widely predicted was that the team would be emotionally devastated by the midseason departure of the fiery Lo Duca. Instead Jim Tracy's team showed, if anything, more spunk than ever down the stretch, and the Dodgers came up with a young stud reliever in Yhency Brazoban to replace Mota in support of peerless closer Eric Gagne, and a young stud bat in Jayson Werth (and an old stud bat in Steve Finley) to pick up the offensive slack.

The Dodgers needed every bit of spunk and studliness they could muster, because they were pursued to the wire by the depleted, but still surprisingly formidable Giants. In a payroll-cutting mode, San Francisco surrendered several key assets from its 2003 division-champion ball club to free agency, and did little more than rifle through the bargain bin to find replacements. Giants' fans' worst fears seemed doomed to validation when the team stumbled out of the gate and was gasping along at 15-23 in mid-May.

But suddenly and unexpectedly, the Giants got red hot, exploding for a 27-9 surge, capped by a four-game sweep of the Dodgers at SBC Park in late June that catapulted San Francisco into first place. They were soon overtaken, but never fell out of the race again, either for the division or the Wild Card, and it took a seven-run ninth inning bullpen implosion at Chavez Ravine on October 2nd to finally put the Giants away.

That bullpen meltdown was a fitting *coup de grace* for the 2004 Giants, as relief pitching was the team's chronic weakness. Matt Herges, the first-half closer, was simply horrible, prompting Felipe Alou to shift starter Dustin Hermanson into the role. While Hermanson did reasonably well, overall the Giants' bullpen was quite bad (4.53 ERA, 13th in the NL). Ace starter Jason Schmidt (18-7, 3.20, with a San Francisco record 251 strikeouts) was the team's only consistently good pitcher.

Without question, the Giants were as successful as they were due to yet another other-worldly performance by Barry Bonds (.362/.609/.812, 53 major-league-leading Win Shares, and a mind-boggling all-time record 232 walks). Bonds was walked so astoundingly often because opponents had little fear of the rest of the team's hitters, but while it's true that the Giants lacked another imposing bat, their ultra-veteran lineup scored 850 runs (second in the league, and the most by a Giant team since 2000) because it had Bonds and (once they dumped Neifi Perez) no holes. The worst OPS of any Giants' regular was .729, and they got an especially good contribution from J.T. Snow (.327/.429/.529, including an astonishing .387/.496/.646 after the All-Star break).

San Diego was the third California team to have a surprisingly good year. Inaugurating their waterfront ballpark, the Padres brought in some newcomers (Brian Giles, David Wells, Ramon Hernandez) to complement their familiar core (Phil Nevin, Trevor Hoffman, Ryan Klesko) and their bevy of impressive young talent (Jake Peavy, Kahlil Greene, Sean Burroughs). By and large, everyone contributed nicely, and no Padre was better than veteran second baseman Mark Loretta, who turned in a career year at age 32 (.335/.391/.495, with 47 doubles, good for 33 Win Shares). A 64-98 dud in 2003, the Padres were never a serious threat to win the division in '04, but they played well all season long, and were in the race until the season's final few days.

PETCO Park played as one of the toughest home run parks in the majors (much to Klesko's particular frustration; he hit just 9 homers, 3 at home, though he was good otherwise, with a .399 OBP). The brand of ball the Padres displayed was in keeping with their little-bit-of-this, little-bit-of-that roster: they didn't overpower anyone, and had no superstars, but they were solid in every phase of the game, presenting their best showing by far since their pennant-winning season of 1998.

This concludes the good news in the 2004 NL West. Outside the California state lines, things didn't go well at all: for one team, in a dull, familiar way, and for the other in a stunning what-was-*that*-all-about fashion.

Let's get the boring story out of the way first. Is there any drearier franchise in baseball than the Colorado Rockies? Here are their records from 1998 through 2003: 77-85, 72-90, 82-80, 73-89, 73-89, 74-88. The only change with the Rockies in 2004 was that they were a little worse than usual, slogging in at 68-94.

Every season it seems the Rockies make a go of it with the same tired formula: they bring in a crew of over-the-hill mediocrities, they get fooled (by gaudy thin-air batting stats) into thinking these journeymen are rejuvenated, and then they scratch their heads, wondering why all those crooked numbers in the RBI column don't yield a winning team. This year's cast, reading from the dog-eared script, included Vinny Castilla (reprising his old role), Jeromy Burnitz, Royce Clayton, and Charles Johnson. The Rockies are MLB's version of *The Love Boat*; all that's missing is the guest turn from John Forsythe. Standout first baseman Todd Helton is an Olivier amid this dreck.

In 2004 the Rockies did add one twist: manager Clint Hurdle determined that one of his mediocre young pitchers, Shawn Chacon (a hunky guest star love interest for Lauren Tewes, perhaps?), just *had* to be the one-and-only closer, and Hurdle kept him there through thick and thin. The problem was that there turned out to be no thick, just thin. Chacon was incredibly bad, and it wasn't just a mile-high stat illusion: his overall 1-9, 7.11 record included a 6.19 ERA in 32 innings on the road, with 24 walks and 5 home runs allowed.

The Rockies' ineffectual 2004 was encapsulated perfectly in the season's final week, in which the schedule put them in the role of potential spoiler, facing the Dodgers for four games, and the Wild Card-chasing Houston Astros for three. Not only did the Rockies lose six of the seven (much to the chagrin of the Giants), in Los Angeles they did so in flamboyant fashion: they blew late-inning leads in three of the four games, the most egregious being the September 28th affair, in which Chacon, holding a 4-0 lead with one out in the ninth inning, walked Alex Cora, Robin Ventura, Jose Hernandez, and Cesar Izturis in succession, setting the Dodgers up for a 5-run walk-off rally.

Perhaps no team in baseball was more surprising in 2004 than the Arizona Diamondbacks, but their surprises were all of the unpleasant variety. Picked by some intrepid prognosticators to win the NL West (one particular such prognosticator, whose initials might stand for Stupid Try, and whose last name rhymes with "cheddar," shall remain anonymous), the Snakes instead not only finished last, they did it with a grand flourish, going 51-111, including an appalling 25-74 mark from mid-June onward. (Note from Stupid Try: nobody prognosticated *that*, did they? *Did they?!?*)

Just about everything that could go wrong did go wrong for Arizona. Injuries hit them very hard, limiting marquee slugger Luis Gonzalez to 105 games, blockbuster acquisition Richie Sexson to just 23, and closer Matt Mantei to 12. Two key young players who appeared to be on the verge of stardom – pitcher Brandon Webb and shortstop Alex Cintron -- regressed instead. The Diamondbacks were bad in all respects, and it's hard to say exactly which was the worst mess: their pitching, which employed twelve different starters and nineteen different relievers on the way to compiling a 4.98 team ERA; their fielding, which trailed only the Rockies in the NL with a .684 Defensive Efficiency Ratio; or their hitting, which despite playing its home games in a good hitters' park, was last in runs, home runs, OBP, and OPS.

Only one star shone in Arizona, and even that glow was dimmed by the gloomy atmosphere. The amazing 40-year-old Randy Johnson came back from an injury-plagued 2003 to pitch nearly as well as he ever has, finishing second in the league in ERA (to the Padres' Peavy) with a 2.60 mark, second in innings pitched with 246, and leading the majors with 290 strikeouts. Johnson led all NL pitchers in Win Shares with 25. But dismal support from his teammates held him to a 16-14 won-lost record: the D-backs scored two or fewer runs in 17 of his 35 outings.

Arizona couldn't even cash in on The Big Unit's value by dealing him. Ardent trade-deadline entreaties from the Dodgers, Red Sox, Yankees, and Angels all failed to satisfy either Johnson's no-trade-clause-waiver demands, or the Diamondbacks' trade requirements, and the great southpaw remained clad in purple-and-turquoise through to the bitter end of 2004.

THT Excerpt: The Dodgers clinch the title *(from October 3, 2004)*:

On October 2nd, the Dodgers came back from a 3-0 ninth-inning deficit against the Giants to win the NL West. Giant reliever Dustin Hermanson simply could not find the plate, walking in a run before being relieved. The inning was capped by a grand slam home run by Steve Finley, and the Dodgers won the crazy game 7-3.

Some perspective: Between 1979 and 1990 there were almost 3,000 games in which the home team trailed by exactly three runs in the bottom of the ninth, and they managed to come back and win only 99 of them. That's less than a 4% Win Expectancy.

Here's a chart of how the Dodgers' play-by-play Win Expectancy rose from 4% to 100% in the fateful ninth:

Play	WE	Diff	Impact
Beginning of Inning	0.038		
Green singled	0.096	0.058	
Ventura walked	0.193	0.097	
Cora struck out	0.110	-0.083	
Hernandez walked	0.214	0.104	
Choi walked, run scores	0.343	0.129	
Error by Ransom, run scores	0.544	0.201	Second most important play
Werth singled, run scores	0.835	0.291	THE key play
Finley home run	1.000	0.165	

It was Jayson Werth's single to right that really made the difference. Cody Ransom had just been inserted at shortstop in the ninth as a defensive substitute, but his error was the second-most crippling play of the inning for the Giants. This was a case of the Giants beating themselves. Marquis Grissom had two big hits and Brett Tomko pitched an excellent game. But Dustin Hermanson's wildness, coupled with the Ransom error, did them in.

The Playoffs and World Series

By Larry Mahnken

Every year, eight teams qualify for the postseason, and one team is crowned World Champions. They may not be the best team that year, or even in the series that they win, but it doesn't matter. The goal in Major League Baseball is not to have the best team, but to win the World Series. Everything else is window dressing.

For 86 years, the Boston Red Sox had not reached that goal. Every season ended in failure, sometimes in excruciating fashion. Four times they had come within one win of the championship, one time they had even come within one strike, but for 86 years that final win was beyond their grasp. It wasn't just the failure, but how close they had so often come to success, and how often their failure had come at the hands of the team that nearly everyone despises, the New York Yankees.

2004 was the 100th anniversary of Jack Chesbro's Wild Pitch, which cost the Yankees a shot at their first pennant at the hands of the Red Sox. Until 2004, that moment was perhaps the salient triumph by Boston in 100 years of rivalry. In 2004, that moment, and all the moments before it, was eclipsed by the greatest comeback in the history of baseball, and a long dreamed-of triumph. The Impossible Dream came true, albeit 37 years later.

But before that happened, there were eight teams…

National League Division Series

Houston Astros over Atlanta Braves (3-2)

Three times since 1997, the Astros had faced off against the Braves in the NLDS, and only once had they so much as won a game from the Braves. But these weren't the old Braves, and these weren't the old Astros. This time, everyone expected it to be Houston that dominated.

The Astros took early command of the series, winning the first game 9-3, and taking a 2-0 lead into the seventh in Game Two. But Atlanta fought back to tie the game in the eighth, and Rafael Furcal's homer in the bottom of the 11th sent the series to Houston tied at one.

The Astros took control once again, winning Game Three 8-5, and in Game Four they were poised to close the series out with a 5-2 lead in the sixth behind Roger Clemens. But Clemens was lifted to start the inning, and Chad Qualls was only able to retire one batter before Adam LaRoche hit a three-run homer to tie the game. J.D. Drew drove in the game-winner in the ninth to force a Game Five in Atlanta.

For the first six innings the game remained close, but the Astros broke it open with five runs in the seventh,

cruising to an easy 12-3 win. After 42 seasons, the Astros had finally won a postseason series.

St. Louis Cardinals over Los Angeles Dodgers (3-1)

Neither the Dodgers or Cardinals were expected to make the playoffs in 2004, but both had exceeded expectations and won their respective divisions. Being overmatched in nearly every facet of the game, few gave the Dodgers much of a chance in the NLDS, and this time, expectations were met.

The Dodgers simply didn't have enough to shut down the devastating Cardinals lineup, and they lost two 8-3 games in St. Louis. In LA, Jose Lima gave Dodger fans a faint glimmer of hope by shutting the Cardinals out 4-0, but that hope faded when Odalis Perez and Wilson Alvarez were tagged for five runs in the first four innings in Game Four, and St. Louis cruised to a 6-2 victory. In a welcome show of sportsmanship and class, the Dodgers came out on the field after the final out and congratulated their opponents, giving a rather anticlimactic series a truly memorable moment. As the Dodgers headed home for the winter, the Cardinals headed to their fourth NLCS in nine seasons, trying to win their first pennant since 1987.

American League Division Series

New York Yankees over Minnesota Twins (3-1)

The Twins were hyped entering October as the team that nobody wanted to face, with the best pitcher in the American League, Johan Santana, starting two of five games. The Twins exploited their advantage right away. Santana wasn't at his best in Game One, but the Yankees ran themselves out of rallies and hit into five double plays in a 2-0 defeat. The Twins rallied from a 5-3 deficit in the eighth inning of Game Two, and took a 6-5 lead in the top of the twelfth on Torii Hunter's home run. But the Yankees scored two runs off of a weary Joe Nathan in the bottom of the inning, and the two teams went off to Minnesota tied at 1.

Behind Kevin Brown, the Yankees pounded their way to an easy 8-4 victory in Game Three, pushing the Twins to the brink. Minnesota surged to a 5-1 lead in the eighth inning of Game Four, but the Yankees staged a dramatic rally, capped by Ruben Sierra's game-tying three-run home run, and went on to win it and advance to the ALCS for the seventh time in nine years.

Boston Red Sox over Anaheim Angels (3-0)

In the final days of the season, Jose Guillen earned the ire of Angels management with a hostile reaction to being lifted for a pinch runner. The Angels suspended Guillen for the remainder of the season, sending a powerful message about team discipline, but dealing a powerful blow to the Angels' lineup.

Ultimately, it mattered for very little, as Jose Guillen isn't a very good pitcher. The Red Sox cruised behind Curt Schilling in Game One, winning by a score of 9-3. Game Two was closer, but Anaheim wasn't able to hold a sixth-inning lead with Bartolo Colon. Boston pushed across a go-ahead run against Francisco Rodriguez in the seventh, and in the top of the ninth exploded for four more against Brendan Donnelly.

For most of Game Three, it looked like the Sox would have an easy sweep, taking a 6-1 lead into the seventh. But a bases-loaded walk to Darin Erstad was followed by a grand slam by Vladimir Guerrero, and the game was tied. Anaheim held Boston there until the tenth, when with two outs and a runner on first, Mike Scioscia inexplicably lifted Rodriguez for, of all people, Jarrod Washburn. David Ortiz swatted the first pitch over the Green Monster, and the Red Sox completed only the second postseason sweep in their history. Their reward was a matchup with the Yankees for the third time in six years.

National League Championship Series

St. Louis Cardinals over Houston Astros (4-3)

Perhaps it was the fascination with yet another Yankees-Red Sox matchup, an East Coast bias, or merely an underestimation of one or both of the teams playing, but the NLCS got short shrift from the public. The Astros weren't given much of a chance by many observers, with too much emphasis being placed on their reliance on Roger Clemens and Roy Oswalt. While the praise of the St. Louis lineup was well deserved, the Astros had a formidable one of their own. The new-look "Killer B's" may not have matched up evenly with St. Louis' multiple MVP candidates, but they were capable of putting lots of runs on the board, and in a short series, a difference of .3 runs a game isn't a significant one.

The series started off with a bang, with five home runs and a 10-7 Cardinals triumph, thanks to a six-run outburst against the underbelly of the Astros' bullpen in the sixth. The next night Garner repeated his mistakes from Game One, sending Dan Miceli into a tied game in the eighth instead of a fully rested Brad Lidge, and back-to-back homers won the game for St. Louis, 6-4. With Houston headed home down 0-2, the Cardinals appeared on the verge of putting the pennant away.

But Roger Clemens was able to hold the Cardinals to two runs in seven innings, and a three-run first inning provided the runs the Astros would need to get back in the series, winning 5-2. On Sunday night they tied the series at two with a late-inning comeback, winning it 6-5 on Carlos Beltran's record-tying 8th postseason home run in the seventh. Then came the great game of the series, as Brandon Backe and Woody Williams combined in one of the great pitching duels in postseason history, giving up a total of two singles in 15 innings, with Backe taking a no-hitter two outs into the sixth. The game featured a spectacular diving catch by Beltran in the seventh, and was capped in the ninth by Jeff Kent's walkoff three-run homer. Headed back to St. Louis, the Astros were only one win away from their first-ever pennant.

Rather than trying to slam the door shut with Roger Clemens on short rest, the Astros turned to journeyman Pete Munro, who couldn't get out of the third inning, leaving the game trailing 4-2. Houston clawed back to tie it in the ninth, but in the bottom of the twelfth, Jim Edmonds tagged Dan Miceli with his second loss of the series, driving the ball deep over the wall in right for a two-run homer, sending the series to a seventh game.

In a matchup of Jeff Suppan and Roger Clemens, the Astros seemed to have the clear edge, and after 5½ innings they held a 2-1 lead and were within ten outs of the pennant. But a two-out RBI double by Albert Pujols was followed by a two-run homer by Scott Rolen, and Houston's run came to an end. Jose Vizcaino grounded out to Tony Womack, and the Cardinals were in their first World Series since 1987.

American League Championship Series

Boston Red Sox over New York Yankees (4-3)

This was the series almost everyone wanted, and it more than lived up to the hype. It was hard not to give the Red Sox the edge in this series, with Curt Schilling and Pedro Martinez scheduled to start four, maybe five games. But 86 years of history weighed heavily on the minds of many, and some chose to project victory for the Yankees if only because they couldn't conceive of Boston triumphing. What ended up happening was something that almost nobody could have foreseen.

In Game One, Curt Schilling was battered for six runs in three innings, while Mike Mussina took a perfect game into the seventh. It was 8-0 before Mussina allowed a base runner, but then the floodwaters broke through, and the Red Sox got the tying run to third in the eighth. But the Yankees were able to tack on two in the bottom of the inning, and held on for the 10-7 victory.

Game Two was just as good, as Jon Lieber completely shut down the Boston lineup, and Pedro Martinez held the Yankees to a single run until John Olerud clubbed his 106th pitch over the right field wall. The Yankees won 3-1, and headed to Boston up 2-0.

In Game Three, Kevin Brown could only get through two innings while giving up four runs, and the Red Sox appeared to be on their way. But their pitching let them down completely, and by night's end, the Yankees had humiliated the Red Sox 19-8, putting them in a hole no team had ever recovered from, three games to none.

The Yankees would come within three outs of sweeping the Sox, with a 4-3 lead in the ninth inning of the fourth game and Mariano Rivera on the mound. But Kevin Millar walked, pinch runner Dave Roberts stole second, and Bill Mueller singled him home to tie the game. David Ortiz won it with a two-run homer in the 12th, and the Red Sox were still alive.

In Game Five, the Yankees got to Pedro once again, scoring three in the sixth to take a 4-2 lead. But Joe Torre had wasted Tom Gordon by pitching him in the blowout and two innings the night before, and in the eighth Gordon was unable to retire a single batter. Torre brought Rivera in with the tying run on third and nobody out, and with a fly ball to center the game was even. It continued another six excruciating innings before the Red Sox won it, once again on a base hit by David Ortiz.

With their bullpen shot, the Red Sox needed a miracle start to stay alive, and a miracle is what they got. In the ALDS, Curt Schilling had torn the sheath surrounding a tendon located across the back of his ankle, resulting in his poor Game One start. Before Game Six, he had surgery to secure the tendon with sutures, allowing him to pitch. He gave the Red Sox seven innings, allowing only four hits and one run, and Mark Bellhorn's home run provided the margin to force a Game Seven.

After three straight nail biters, the decisive game was never in doubt, as the Red Sox destroyed Kevin Brown and Javier Vazquez. Boston won 10-3, becoming the first team to ever win after trailing 0-3, and they did it to their archrivals. After winning perhaps the greatest postseason series in history, the World Series seemed almost anticlimactic – and it ended up being just that.

World Series
Boston Red Sox over St. Louis Cardinals (4-0)

To win their first title since 1918, the Red Sox would have to beat the team that had stopped them the first two times they tried to win the World Series after the Ruth sale, as well as the team with the best record in baseball. Everyone expected a great World Series. Everyone was wrong.

In Game One, the Red Sox slugged their way to a 7-2 lead before the Cardinals fought back to tie it in the sixth. Boston took the lead again in the seventh, but two Manny Ramirez errors allowed the Cardinals to tie the game in the top of the eighth. It was the last thing that would go right for St. Louis in the series.

In the bottom of the eighth, Mark Bellhorn clubbed a two-run homer that proved to be the game winner. The next night, the Cardinals didn't bunt against Curt Schilling to try and re-injure his ankle, and they couldn't hit him, either. They went down fairly meekly 6-2, and two nights later they were humbled by Pedro Martinez, 4-1.

Their long-awaited goal within their grasp, the Red Sox finished their journey in short order. Against Derek Lowe, the mighty Cardinals' lineup managed only three singles and a double, and not a single run. The last out was a comebacker to Keith Foulke, who flipped the ball to Doug Mientkiewicz.

And that was it. The earth did not crack open, fire did not rain from the sky, no god came down to pass judgment on mankind, dogs and cats did not live together. After 86 years, it was just a baseball game. A baseball game that made millions of people throughout this country, old and young, happier than they have perhaps ever been in their lives. That is what baseball gives us, a joy that is rare in life. Perhaps the wait was too long, but for those who saw it, even those who had not rooted for it, it was difficult to not be touched by it. There are no curses; baseball is just a game. And for the first time in 86 years, the Boston Red Sox are the champions of it.

2004 Minor League Review

by Bryan Smith

While minor league baseball may not be your fancy, its effects are drastically felt at the Major League level. Take for example, Joe Mauer. Before 2004, Mauer was the unquestioned top prospect in baseball after tearing through level after level. Minnesota had enough confidence in their 21-year-old, former #1 overall pick to trade A.J. Pierzynski, an established All-Star with back-to-back .300 seasons. In return, they landed setup man Joe Nathan and two prospects.

Nine months later, we have a season's worth of data to evaluate Terry Ryan's moves. Nathan was one of the game's best closers, tying Eric Gagne with 14 Win Shares (WS), only one behind Mariano Rivera for the top spot. He had 7 Win Shares Above Average (WSAA), while Pierzynski struggled at times, and finished with 2 WSAA. Joe Mauer spent much of the season on the DL, but he did manage 6 WS (3 WSAA) in very limited time. Most importantly, the Twins made the playoffs for the third consecutive year, despite having very different role players.

One of those role players was Justin Morneau. The 23-year-old slugger spent much of the first half in AAA, where he posted an astounding line of .306/.377/.615 in 72 games. On July 17, Minnesota called up their prized prospect, who played everyday for the next two weeks. On the morning of July 31, Morneau had accumulated 85 major-league at-bats, and was hitting .271/.311/.506. This convinced Terry Ryan that Morneau was ready and that the team would be unaffected by Doug Mientkiewicz's absence.

And the rest is history. Mientkiewicz was part of a four-team trade that sent Nomar Garciaparra to a hero's welcome in Cubdom and put Theo Epstein under fire in Boston. But while trades seldom work out for everyone involved, the Twins, Cubs and Red Sox all improved after the trade. Had Justin Morneau played poorly in Rochester, the Cubs may well have played Neifi Perez all September, and Boston's clubhouse could have become a boxing ring.

The moral of the story is that minor leaguers make a difference, and keeping an eye beneath the surface can be a predictive tool. This season saw great years from prospects, many of whom will likely change the course of Major League organizations.

It was a deadline deal that brought together the New York Mets and Tampa Bay Devil Rays franchises, creating farm systems with very similar talent at the top. After the New York Mets inexplicably traded top prospect Scott Kazmir for Victor Zambrano, both teams' top three prospects were a left-side infielder, a 2003 first-round

outfielder, and a pitcher with some great numbers. Overall, these six players provided some of the best stories of the minor league season.

Prior to the season, the only prospect recognized with near-Mauer talent was shortstop B.J. Upton, the second overall choice from the 2002 draft. In just his age-18 season, Upton reached AA in 2003, looking good in more than 100 plate appearances. This season the league provided little trouble for the teenager, who hit .327/.407/.471, before moving to the Durham Bulls. Still, Upton faced few challenges, hitting .311/.411/.519 before being called up to the Devil Rays. With his defense struggling, Upton's arrival in the Majors precipitated a position battle at shortstop with Piniella-favorite Julio Lugo, which culminated in Upton spending time at the hot corner.

As a prep player, Upton's thirdbase teammate was David Wright, a first-round choice by the Mets in the 2001 draft. Considered a solid prospect before the season, Wright exploded in 2004, evoking comparisons to All-Star Scott Rolen. Far and away the Eastern League's best player, Wright hit .363/.467/.619 in 60 games. The International League provided a few more obstacles, but Wright's line of .298/.388/.579 was enough to convince Jim Duquette to trade Ty Wigginton and call up his stud prospect.

But Wright wasn't the only Met prospect influencing trades, as many believe the progress of Yusmeiro Petit led to the aforementioned Kazmir trade. Few noticed when Petit had an 85/10 K/BB across two short-season levels in 2003. But Petit made headlines this season, striking out 200 in 139.1 innings from low-A to AA.

Ask Chuck Lamar and the Devil Rays though, and they'll take Kazmir. Taken thirteen spots after Upton in the 2002 draft due to salary demands, the Texan southpaw entered the season with a 2.33 ERA in 127.1 professional innings. His success continued this year, when a 2.49 ERA in 101 innings led to a call-up to Tampa Bay and a five-inning scoreless Major League debut. Still creating relief vs. starting debates among scouts, there is little question that Kazmir will contend for the 2005 Rookie of the Year voting.

If Kazmir does win the award next year, the Devil Rays will be favored to go back-to-back, as many expect Delmon Young to win the award in 2006. After much June consideration, the Devil Rays chose the Californian outfielder first overall in the 2003 draft. He did little to make Tampa brass regret the decision, clubbing 25 home runs in 513 South Atlantic League at-bats. And perhaps the season's most impressive achievement was his collection of the league's "Most Outstanding Major League Prospect" award.

New York has an outfield prospect that would have given Young some competition, if not for a promotion to the Florida State League. Another byproduct of being able to draft 'expensive' players, the Mets chose Lastings Milledge twelfth when other teams were afraid of his bonus. New York ponied up, and after 26 unimpressive at-bats last year, began Milledge in low-A after a preseason injury healed. He took little time to get used to professional baseball, posting an OPS (.978) more than fifty points better than Young's in about half the at-bats.

Young's main competition for the prospect award was not Milledge, but a third base prospect that grew up less than 100 miles from Delmon. Chosen tenth overall with promises of huge raw power, Ian Stewart took little time to make the Colorado Rockies thank their lucky stars. Outhitting Young in almost every category, Stewart hit 30 home runs, and had an OPS (.992) better than Young and Milledge. Throw in nineteen stolen bases, and one can understand why scouts are torn between Young and Stewart.

Stewart's magnificent season was a bit overshadowed though, because the Rockies had the player that Baseball America would tab "Minor League Player of the Year". Few noticed when Jeff Francis sensationally closed out an otherwise-mediocre 2003 season, foreshadowing what was to come. This year, the Canadian southpaw had a 13-1 record in the Texas League, posting an ERA of 1.98 with a K/BB ratio of 147/22 in 113.2 innings. A 2.85 in 41 Pacific Coast League innings necessitated a call-up, and his minor-league 6.28 H/9 show that the Rockies might have developed a solution to Coors.

No one changed an organization's plans as a teenager like Doc Gooden, who started his career 58-19 before leading the Mets to the World Series in 1986. Arms like his come once in a generation, and people are already touting his second coming. Felix Hernandez raised eyebrows when, at the tender age of seventeen, he struck out 91 men in his first 69 professional innings. A year later, consider our eyebrows near our hairlines. Hernandez went 9-3, 2.74 ERA in the California League this year, striking out 114 and walking 26 in 92 innings. And for me, his best performance was at the Futures Game, where the whole world saw a mid-90s fastball and a Gooden-esque breaking ball.

Hernandez was one of the few bright spots in a disappointing season for the Mariner organization, who finished with the third-worst record in the Majors. Realizing they were out of the race early, Bill Bavasi decided to trade Freddy Garcia to the Chicago White Sox. In exchange, the Mariners received several players,

including the prospect I labeled 2003's top player: Jeremy Reed. While Reed didn't have a disappointing year, he was passed by fellow 2002 draftees Nick Swisher (.269/.406/.537 in PCL) and Curtis Granderson (.303/.407/.515 in AA).

The one outfielder that came out running and sprinted past everyone was Jason Kubel, a worthy participant in the Player of the Year chase. After a mediocre season in the Florida State League in 2003, Kubel flew through AA and AAA before ending his season on the Twins' postseason roster. Kubel had far more extra-base hits (68) than strikeouts (59), and stole 16 bases to boot. Throw those numbers in with a .352 batting average for the year, and you have a player Terry Ryan refused to trade at the deadline.

Joining Kubel on the AA–to–Major-League-playoffs train was Dallas McPherson, who closed his season starting at the hot corner for the Angels. Showing immense power in the minor leagues, Dallas hit forty home runs and ninety extra-base hits overall. Despite not being a magician at third, McPherson is part of the reason Anaheim is not expected to re-sign Troy Glaus. This is because Bill Stonemann has a plan, one that involves McPherson and Casey Kotchman on the corners.

Most of the hitters mentioned today have been corner players, but I would be remiss to not mention some exemplary seasons by players up the middle. Ian Kinsler went from being a 17th round pick to a hitter that torched the Midwest League with a .440 average in 224 at-bats. Even after being moved up to the Texas League, Kinsler's .866 OPS means Michael Young could be on the move again. Fellow shortstop Joel Guzman is causing a stir in the Dodger front office, as they can't decide what to do with their 6' 6" shortstop. Anytime you have a player of this caliber, it is one damn good problem to have.

Guzman excelled during the second half of his season in the Southern League, which proved to be a difficult task for a lot of players. Rickie Weeks and Prince Fielder of the Brewers both could not top a .275 average, despite entering the season as two of the game's better prospects. Josh Barfield had an OPS of just .730 in the SL, but his 90 RBI still give the Padres hope he might be their replacement for Mark Loretta. Finally, after a Spring Training in which he stole all the headlines, James Loney slugged just .327 in more than 100 games, making Paul DePodesta's acquisition of Hee Seop Choi look phenomenal.

If 1998 was the year of the home run in the Majors, this season was the same in the minor leagues. Five league MVPs made runs at their respective league's home run record, with the short-season Appalachian League MVP Mitch Einertson breaking his with 24 in 227 at-bats. Not bad for being three months removed from graduation. The Cubs had two sluggers almost break records, Brian

Dopirak in the Midwest League (39) and Brandon Sing in the Florida State League (32).

Jim Thome signed with the Phillies to add a home run threat to an already potent lineup, but in effect he has blocked one of the minors' best sluggers: Ryan Howard. In 485 at-bats across the Eastern and International Leagues, Howard hit an astounding 46 home runs, good for a .637 cumulative slugging percentage. The Pirates' Brad Eldred picked up where Howard left off in the Eastern League, hitting 17 home runs in 39 games. This came after being promoted from the Carolina League, where the MVP had hit 21 homers and hit .310 in 91 games.

While it was power hitting that dominated a lot of leagues, power pitching was existent as well. There is no better example than Jose Capellan of the Braves, who after starting the season in high-A, finished pitching with Atlanta in his fourth different league. Reminiscent of Bartolo Colon with thick thighs and high-90s gas, Capellan struck out 156 batters and allowed just one homer while in the minors. While some scouts envision the Dominican righthander as John Smoltz's successor, Capellan should be in line for some starts next season.

Beating out Jose for the strikeout crown was Brandon McCarthy of the Chicago White Sox, who struck out 202 batters in 172 innings pitched. Touted with possessing great control, McCarthy walked just 30 men and won 17 games. Tall and lanky, McCarthy reminded fans of Black Jack McDowell, the Sox ace during the 1990s. Control was also the key trait for the minor league ERA leader, Zach Duke of the Pittsburgh Pirates. The former 20th round pick kept his ERA at just 1.47 for the season, with 148.1 innings split across the Carolina and Eastern Leagues.

If we are recognizing the statistical leaders of the minors, we should also give props to the organization that had the best year. While they were busy winning their umpteenth straight division title in the Majors, the Atlanta Braves also did some great things in prospect development. We already talked about Jose Capellan's great year, and he was joined by southpaw Dan Meyer in a September call-up. The club has great depth in the pitching staff, and one of the best 1-2 hitting prospect combos in Andy Marte and Jeff Francoeur. The two were teammates in AA at season's end, and both promise to be major factors with the Braves very soon.

Because of that, John Scheurholz is very close to making a big decision. Chipper Jones seems capable of playing three positions: left field, third base, and first. The Braves top three young hitters? Marte, Francoeur and Adam LaRoche. There simply isn't room for all four, and the Braves will soon face the same type of decision Terry Ryan made a year ago. Can Scheurholz turn his strengths into sixteen Win Shares? If so, you'll know why.

College Baseball in 2004

By Craig Burley

The Titans of Cal State Fullerton won their fourth national championship in Omaha, Nebraska on June 27, beating Texas 3-2 on a seventh-inning RBI single by catcher Kurt Suzuki to sweep the best-of-three final of the College World Series. Senior righthander Jason Windsor pitched a complete game for Fullerton in the final game -- his second complete game of the CWS -- and he was named the Most Outstanding Player.

The Titans were full measure for their victory, but it would have come as a surprise to observers earlier in the year. Fullerton began their year just 15-16, but playing a tough schedule early on helped mold them into a juggernaut that finished the year on a 32-6 run and vaulted both Suzuki and Windsor to All-American status.

In the Hardball Times College Baseball ranking system, unveiled here for the first time, the Titans' early struggles

meant that they could climb no higher than 13th overall, despite their run to the national championship. Fullerton's vanquished opponent in the finals, the Texas Longhorns, finished at the top of our rankings by a narrow margin after compiling a 58-15 record against one of the nation's toughest schedules. THT's rankings are based on a "true winning percentage" calculated based on a team's record, its opponents' records, and its opponents' opponents' records. The rankings (by winning percentage) are then adjusted for "confidence," since a team that plays a longer schedule is more likely to do well via true talent rather than luck. The following table lists our Top 40 teams for 2004. Interestingly, only four of THT's top twelve teams made the final eight of the College World Series in Omaha, although these included our top three - Texas, Miami, and South Carolina.

Rank	Team	W	L	Div 1 Win %	SOS	True Win%	THT Rating
1	Texas	58	15	.795	.662	.884	.789
2	Miami (FL)	50	13	.794	.674	.888	.786
3	South Carolina	53	17	.757	.669	.863	.761
4	East Carolina	51	13	.797	.570	.839	.738
5	Stanford	46	14	.767	.609	.837	.727
6	Notre Dame	51	12	.800	.543	.826	.723
7	Louisiana State	46	19	.708	.658	.824	.711
8	Rice	46	14	.767	.574	.816	.707
9	Oral Roberts	50	11	.810	.488	.802	.699
10	Arizona State	41	18	.695	.655	.812	.692
11	Vanderbilt	45	19	.703	.634	.804	.689
12	Virginia	44	15	.746	.579	.801	.688
13	Cal State Fullerton	47	22	.681	.650	.799	.686
14	Georgia	45	23	.662	.671	.800	.685
15	Florida	43	22	.662	.672	.801	.683
16	Florida State	45	23	.662	.659	.791	.677
17	Georgia Tech	44	21	.677	.644	.791	.675
18	Arkansas	45	24	.652	.662	.786	.671
19	Wichita State	49	16	.750	.536	.776	.668
20	Florida Atlantic	47	17	.734	.555	.775	.664
21	Mississippi	39	21	.650	.654	.779	.656
22	Central Florida	47	18	.723	.551	.762	.651
23	Texas A&M	42	22	.656	.629	.764	.645
24	Southern Mississippi	45	19	.703	.567	.756	.642
25	Long Beach State	40	21	.656	.626	.761	.640
26	College of Charleston	47	16	.746	.500	.746	.636

Rank	Team	W	L	Div 1 Win %	SOS	True Win%	THT Rating
27	Clemson	39	26	.600	.662	.746	.625
28	Lamar	41	16	.719	.530	.743	.624
29	North Carolina	43	21	.672	.581	.740	.623
30	Washington	39	20	.655	.607	.746	.621
31	Birmingham-Southern	47	18	.714	.523	.732	.619
32	Texas Tech	40	21	.638	.612	.735	.609
33	Tennessee	38	24	.623	.623	.732	.608
34	Oklahoma	38	24	.613	.622	.723	.599
35	North Carolina State	36	24	.600	.632	.721	.594
36	Oklahoma State	38	24	.613	.616	.717	.594
37	Arizona	36	27	.571	.651	.712	.588
38	Nebraska	36	23	.610	.615	.714	.587
39	Tulane	41	21	.661	.551	.705	.585
40	Mississippi State	35	24	.593	.626	.709	.581

Team Stats - Win % is against Division I teams only. SOS is strength of schedule, expressed as the "true winning percentage" of the team's opponents. "True Win %" is the team's own true winning percentage. "THT Rating" is the 97% confidence lower bound of the team's winning percentage. It is 97% likely that the team would do this well or better against a perfectly average schedule.

In addition to these outstanding team performances, there were many outstanding individual performances as well. Long Beach State righthander Jered Weaver blew away his NCAA opponents in record-breaking fashion, drew plaudits from far and wide for his performances, but could only finish #2 in the Hardball Times pitcher rankings for Division I players. Weaver, who was subsequently selected in the first round of the 2004 MLB Entry Draft by the Anaheim Angels, went 15-1 with a 1.62 ERA (a great feat in the world of aluminum bats) and struck out 213 in 144 innings. Weaver led the NCAA in wins, strikeouts, and opponents' batting average and was one of only three NCAA players with a strikeout-to-walk ratio of better than 10:1 (the others being Shawn Phillips of Delaware State and Kevin Slowey of Winthrop). Weaver was also the winner of the 2004 Golden Spikes Award as the top player in the NCAA.

But Weaver simply can't lay claim to the top performance among NCAA pitchers in 2004. That honor belongs to Jason Windsor, who despite a more pedestrian strikeout rate, managed to be nearly one hundred runs better than an average NCAA pitcher for 2004, in 162 innings (leading the college ranks), against some of the top competition on offer. Windsor could only manage a 13-4 record and a 1.72 ERA, but a tougher park for pitchers than Weaver's meant that the Fullerton senior came out substantially on top. When linear weights runs are taken into account instead of simple runs allowed (adjusting for bullpen support and other factors) Windsor's performance was better than 100 runs above average. Third place in the rankings went to Florida's righthanded ace Justin Hoyman. J.P. Howell of Texas, who finished fourth, was the top lefthander.

Rank	Player	Team	W	L	ERA	IP	AdjRA+	AdjRSAA
1	Jason Windsor	Cal State Fullerton	13	4	1.72	162.2	363	102
2	Jered Weaver	Long Beach State	15	1	1.62	144.0	338	86
3	Justin Hoyman	Florida	11	2	2.71	139.2	214	69
4	J. P Howell	Texas	15	2	2.13	135.1	245	65
5	Sam Lecure	Texas	9	3	2.34	123.0	223	62
6	Connor Falkenbach	Florida	10	7	3.34	126.2	219	61
7	Casey Janssen	UCLA	10	4	3.16	116.2	206	57
8	Matt Campbell	South Carolina	10	6	3.05	124.0	191	57
9	Ricky Romero	Cal State Fullerton	14	4	3.37	155.0	194	56

College Baseball in 2004

Rank	Player	Team	W	L	ERA	IP	AdjRA+	AdjRSAA
10	Mike Pelfrey	Wichita State	11	2	2.18	115.1	240	56
11	Cesar Ramos	Long Beach State	12	4	2.29	133.2	237	54
12	Vern Sterry	North Carolina State	9	2	2.20	114.1	246	53
13	Michael Rogers	North Carolina State	9	4	3.08	117.0	208	53
14	Jeremy Sowers	Vanderbilt	10	6	3.08	122.2	203	52
15	Cesar Carrillo	Miami, Florida	12	0	2.69	113.2	229	52
16	Wade Townsend	Rice	12	0	1.80	120.1	296	52
17	Wade Leblanc	Alabama	8	4	2.08	112.2	237	50
18	David Purcey	Oklahoma	9	5	3.11	118.2	192	49
19	Jonathan Ellis	The Citadel	12	3	2.18	136.1	219	49
20	Matt Fox	Central Florida	14	2	1.85	111.2	241	49
21	Mark Roberts	Oklahoma	9	5	3.41	121.1	182	48
22	Glen Perkins	Minnesota	9	3	2.83	111.1	193	46
23	Greg Bunn	East Carolina	10	1	2.70	106.2	227	45
24	Stacen Gant	George Mason	10	1	2.72	119.0	210	45
25	Spencer Grogan	Oklahoma State	12	3	2.95	131.0	216	44
26	Rhett James	Florida State	10	3	3.36	109.2	179	44
27	Will Startup	Georgia	7	2	2.22	81.0	235	43
28	Ryan Mullins	Vanderbilt	9	3	2.58	111.2	215	43
29	Zach Jackson	Texas A&M	10	7	3.58	120.2	164	43
30	Philip Humber	Rice	13	4	2.27	115.0	241	41
31	Eddie Cannon	Florida State	9	7	3.87	111.2	148	41
32	Jason Meyer	Texas A&M	8	2	2.89	106.0	226	41
33	Thomas Diamond	New Orleans	6	4	2.38	113.2	207	41
34	Garrett Broshuis	Missouri	11	0	2.61	114.0	199	40
35	Micah Owings	Georgia Tech	9	3	3.89	113.1	175	40
36	Kyle Bono	Central Florida	8	2	1.94	97.1	204	39
37	Shawn Phillips	Delaware State	10	2	2.02	115.2	191	39
38	Charley Boyce	Arkansas	10	3	3.20	115.1	195	39
39	Joe Koshansky	Virginia	8	3	2.98	102.2	188	38
40	Brett Smith	UC Irvine	8	5	2.54	113.1	192	38
41	Jarrett Grube	Memphis	9	4	2.82	102.0	197	37
42	Zach Kroenke	Nebraska	7	5	3.03	104.0	207	37
43	Andrew Dobies	Virginia	6	3	3.41	108.1	185	37
44	Donnie Smith	Old Dominion	6	2	2.29	86.1	249	37
45	Koley Kolberg	Arizona	9	7	4.70	149.1	142	36
46	Dennis Bigley	Oral Roberts	13	1	2.91	117.2	191	35
47	J. D. Cockroft	Miami, Florida	9	5	3.55	104.0	185	35
48	Andrew Kown	Georgia Tech	10	1	3.46	112.0	210	35
49	Huston Street	Texas	6	1	1.58	57.0	332	35
50	Tom Robbins	Texas State	8	6	3.34	113.1	177	35

Pitcher Stats - W/L/ERA/IP are all unadjusted. AdjRA+ is the ratio of the player's runs allowed to the NCAA's average pitcher, with 100 as average. AdjRSAA is the pitcher's runs saved above an average NCAA pitcher. Both measures are adjusted for parks played in and competition faced.

Unlike Weaver, who had been expected to dominate, the hitters at the top of the Hardball Times hitter rankings for Division I players were both complete and stunning surprises. East Carolina's senior centerfielder/DH Ryan Jones, a 5-7 dynamo coming off a subpar 2003 when he hit just .264 with little power, came out of nowhere to become the NCAA's top hitter in 2004, hitting exactly .400 with terrific power (49 extra-base hits including 19 home runs). Jones more than doubled his slugging percentage and led the Pirates to a #4 finish in The Hardball Times team rankings. His 53.9 runs produced above the average player allowed him to rank #1 overall, just ahead of the aforementioned Kurt Suzuki, whose .413 average and excellent (and unprecedented) power against a tough schedule enabled him to rank #2 - a superb achievement for a top-line defensive catcher. Like Jones, the performance of Stanford's fine second baseman Jed Lowrie came out of the blue. Lowrie was the third-most productive hitter in the NCAA despite being only a sophomore playing his first full season. Each was named Player of the Year in their respective conference (Jones in Conference USA, Suzuki in the Big West, and Lowrie in the Pac-10).

Rank	Player	Team	AVG	OBP	SLG	PA	AdjOWP	AdjRAA
1	Ryan Jones	East Carolina	.400	.511	.823	273	.884	53.9
2	Kurt Suzuki	Cal State Fullerton	.413	.511	.702	326	.870	53.1
3	Jed Lowrie	Stanford	.399	.505	.734	293	.874	51.0
4	Chip Cannon	The Citadel	.358	.514	.681	313	.852	49.8
5	Alex Gordon	Nebraska	.365	.493	.754	272	.863	45.2
6	Eddy Martinez-Esteve	Florida State	.385	.457	.707	315	.840	44.9
7	Matt Vanderbosch	Oral Roberts	.383	.500	.533	300	.825	43.0
8	Mike Costanzo	Coastal Carolina	.359	.479	.740	284	.842	42.5
9	Chris Rahl	William and Mary	.389	.462	.764	264	.828	41.8
10	Jeff Fiorentino	Florida Atlantic	.348	.478	.670	297	.823	40.6
11	Stephen Drew	Florida State	.344	.458	.692	278	.844	40.0
12	Brad Corley	Mississippi State	.380	.442	.678	274	.830	39.4
13	Steve Pearce	South Carolina	.346	.430	.650	312	.812	39.3
14	Richie Robnett	Fresno State	.384	.469	.699	272	.820	38.2
15	Matt Macri	Notre Dame	.367	.465	.667	287	.810	37.9
16	Brian Bixler	Eastern Michigan	.453	.519	.650	284	.813	37.8
17	Warner Jones	Vanderbilt	.414	.445	.660	293	.813	37.6
18	Landon Powell	South Carolina	.330	.427	.611	321	.803	37.5
19	J.C. Holt	Louisiana State	.393	.463	.552	318	.807	37.0
20	Curtis Thigpen	Texas	.378	.465	.568	340	.791	36.8
21	Ryan Norwood	East Carolina	.382	.438	.695	282	.802	36.7
22	Brad McCann	Clemson	.379	.468	.648	299	.816	36.0
23	Mike Ferris	Miami, Ohio	.361	.513	.755	275	.805	35.3
24	Danny Putnam	Stanford	.378	.454	.643	285	.804	35.1
25	Drew Moffitt	Wichita State	.289	.457	.701	282	.790	34.3
26	Jim Burt	Miami, Florida	.371	.460	.678	293	.808	34.0
27	Logan Sorensen	Wichita State	.377	.461	.607	295	.783	34.0
28	Chris Westervelt	Stetson	.385	.484	.634	254	.809	34.0
29	Dan Batz	Rhode Island	.406	.507	.738	229	.824	33.8
30	P.J. Hiser	Pittsburgh	.354	.430	.758	235	.810	33.7
31	Brendan Winn	South Carolina	.305	.403	.618	307	.788	33.7
32	Nick Blasi	Wichita State	.366	.460	.585	314	.773	33.6
33	Josh Brady	Texas Tech	.362	.436	.688	303	.783	33.6
34	Chad Huffman	Texas Christian	.383	.477	.577	298	.792	33.4

College Baseball in 2004

Rank	Player	Team	AVG	OBP	SLG	PA	AdjOWP	AdjRAA
35	Josh Morris	Georgia	.319	.433	.597	300	.795	33.1
36	Dustin Pedroia	Arizona State	.393	.502	.611	302	.800	32.6
37	Nick Shimer	George Mason	.330	.466	.679	268	.794	32.1
38	Patrick Perry	Northern Colorado	.478	.550	.844	222	.821	32.0
39	Eric Nielsen	Nevada-Las Vegas	.402	.508	.701	311	.770	31.9
40	Clay Timpner	Central Florida	.371	.422	.564	288	.768	31.6
41	Jon Zeringue	Louisiana State	.384	.439	.616	294	.783	31.0
42	Jason Vargas	Long Beach State	.354	.469	.531	255	.812	30.9
43	Mark Jurich	Louisville	.353	.432	.702	273	.773	30.8
44	Caleb Moore	East Tennessee State	.455	.509	.752	226	.814	30.7
45	Jeff Frazier	Rutgers	.382	.457	.657	243	.802	30.7
46	Mike Hughes	Illinois-Chicago	.364	.463	.668	258	.770	30.7
47	Cody Ehlers	Missouri	.364	.460	.693	288	.771	30.6
48	Rob Hosgood	Central Connecticut State	.376	.481	.579	271	.767	30.2
49	Graig Badger	Rutgers	.364	.502	.485	256	.800	29.9
50	Steve Sherman	North Carolina-Asheville	.360	.464	.650	250	.785	29.3

Hitter Stats - AVG/OBP/SLG/PA are all unadjusted. AdjOWP is the player's adjusted offensive winning percentage, measured against the NCAA as a whole. AdjRAA is the player's adjusted runs produced (using a custom linear weights method) above the NCAA's average hitter. Both measures are adjusted for parks played in and competition faced.

THT's hitter and pitcher rankings are based on a custom linear weights measurement of offense and defense, and are fully adjusted for the level of competition that each player faces throughout the year, as well as the level of offense in his league and ballpark. They are therefore a comprehensive measure of the 2004 performance of all NCAA Division I players.

And so in the final analysis, the two players left to carry the day for the national champions in the clinching game were two of the outstanding performers in the NCAA this year. To choose between them would be nearly impossible. Battery mates Jason Windsor and Kurt Suzuki are therefore **The Hardball Times 2004 College Players of the Year**, and receive our heartiest congratulations. The Oakland Athletics proved their commitment to drafting top college performers, as they selected both Windsor (third round) and Suzuki (first round) in the 2004 MLB Entry Draft.

There was sad news after the Horizon League season had been completed, as the University of Detroit Mercy announced that it was dropping baseball due to financial pressures (at a school that fields teams in nine women's and seven men's sports). There is no easy answer for the increasing costs of fielding baseball programs; what makes baseball more of a cost-cutting target for schools out of the spotlight is the expense generated by a long schedule and the specialized fields and equipment that baseball requires. About one school a year currently leaves Division I in baseball.

Also following the completion of the season, the NCAA began reviewing the possibility of holding the College World Series in July instead of June, pushing the beginning of the regular season back to March 1, in an attempt to lengthen the season and have more games when the weather is warm in the north. The obvious drawback to such a plan is that it puts more games outside the academic year, but a look at the Hardball Times team rankings -- with only one school (Notre Dame) in the Top 25 located above the Mason-Dixon line -- shows why northern schools are pushing for a more level playing field in the NCAA schedule.

Some of the biggest news of the year was generated by the biggest crowds of the year, as two NCAA games were watched by crowds larger than any other in NCAA history. San Diego State christened the Padres' new ballpark, PETCO Park, in March with a crowd of 40,106 fans who watched the Aztecs down the Houston Cougars 4-0 behind a shutout by Scott Shoemaker. Then in May, Turner Field in Atlanta drew 28,836 fans for an all-Peach State matchup between the University of Georgia and Georgia Tech, with the Yellow Jackets prevailing 12-5. Both games showed how college baseball continues to seep back into the nation's consciousness after decades on the margins. All in all, despite the obstacles that baseball faces at many NCAA schools, the continued popularity of college players amongst Major League franchises at the annual amateur draft ensures that the college game will continue to provide a stage for many of the most talented prospects in the U.S.

Baseball also continued to march forward at the small-college level. The NCAA Division II championship was won by Delta State from Mississippi, and George Fox University of Oregon won the Division III crown. Dixie State College of Utah won the Junior College World Series and Cumberland University of Tennessee won the NAIA World Series.

Japanese Baseball in 2004

By Craig Burley

The most important season in the modern history of Nippon Professional Baseball (NPB), Japan's professional baseball league, ended on October 25 when the Seibu Lions beat the Chunichi Dragons 7-2 in Game 7 of the Japan Series to claim the title. Takashi Ishii won his second game of the series with six shutout innings; he didn't give up an earned run in either game he pitched. A five-run third -- all the runs scored with two outs -- was keyed by a ten-pitch at-bat by leadoff hitter Tomoaki Sato that resulted in a single and the game's first run. The inning was later capped by a two-run homer by Seibu slugger Alex Cabrera, and the Lions cruised the rest of the way to complete a comeback after having been down 3-2 in the series, winning both Game 6 and Game 7 in the unfriendly confines of the Nagoya Dome, the Dragons' home.

It was not on-field events, though, that made the 2004 season historically significant. The story of pro *yakyu* in 2004 was all about events off the field, as the previously docile NPB Players' Association went on strike for the very first time in its history. On September 18 and 19, stadiums stayed dark around Japan as the players walked out to protest the planned merger of the Orix Blue Wave and the Kintetsu Buffaloes and certain issues related to it. The strike, which generated enormous controversy in Japan, was entirely successful, as the goal of forcing NPB to allow an expansion team to begin play for the 2005 season was successful.

A relatively quiet season had been unfolding, with many of Japan's top stars now playing in the U.S., until the Blue Wave and Buffaloes dropped a bombshell on Japan on June 13 by announcing that the Pacific League rivals would merge. Kintetsu Corp., a railway operator and the parent corporation of the Buffaloes, was no longer willing to endure the losses that the ball club was recording and Orix Corp. (a leasing business and the parent of the Blue Wave) were happy to take over. According to media reports at the time, the aim of NPB was to encourage the formation of a 10-team single league, instead of the current setup of 12 teams split into two leagues (without interleague play). This plan had been formulated nearly a decade ago by powerful Yomiuri Giants president Tsuneo Watanabe, but had failed to find willing contraction victims until the Buffaloes -- the only current NPB team never to have won a Japan Series -- stepped forward. The Buffaloes had attempted to sell the team's naming rights to another party, in an attempt to stave off some losses, but the NPB Commissioner (with the all-powerful Watanabe reportedly pulling strings behind the scenes as he often does) ruled against them.

Speculation heightened that the Buffaloes were attempting to pave the way for contracting NPB to 10 teams, after Kintetsu refused to consider an offer to buy the team from Livedoor, an Internet service provider who had been attempting to join the tightly restricted club of NPB for a few years. Kintetsu's president even refused to meet with Livedoor to entertain a bid for the team. However, the other Central League clubs, jealous of their home dates with the Giants, began to agitate against creating a single 10-team league. The Giants are by far the best draw in Japan, and easily more than half of Japanese baseball fans are Giants fans. This means that the Central League outdraws the Pacific League by 30% or more; hence the desire of the CL owners to freeze the PL out of dates with the Giants. This growing bloc of opposition to contraction emboldened the Players' Association, and when it seemed likely that instead of adding an expansion team in 2005, the NPB would wait until at least 2006, the players decided to force the owners' hand to preserve jobs.

It has now been decided that an expansion team will be added to the Pacific League for the 2005 season, and the owners have now agreed to interleague play (six games against each team from the other league). E-commerce firm Rakuten Inc., as well as Livedoor, are bidding for the new franchise, which would be based in Sendai, which does not currently have an NPB team.

The final shock to NPB before the Japan Series came on October 13 as Yoshiaki Tsutsumi, the owner of the Seibu Lions, announced that he was going to step down as Lions president following the Japan Series. Tsutsumi, one of the most powerful men in Japan and formerly the richest man in the world, stepped down from all his posts within the Seibu organization after some irregularities in financial reporting within the Seibu group of companies. At the time, Seibu had just prevailed in the Pacific League playoffs and was heading to the Japan Series for the 15th time.

On the field, it was a season for pleasant surprises as Chunichi won the Central League title despite having been substantial underdogs to begin the year. As in nearly every year, the Giants were heavily favored but could not find the consistency necessary to make a strong challenge for the CL crown, and the Dragons - under new manager Hiromitsu Ochiai, a legendary two-time Triple Crown winner and iconoclast - struggled early but in June built a lead that they would not relinquish. In the Pacific League, the Fukuoka Daiei Hawks cruised to the regular-season title, and Seibu finished comfortably in second. The third and final playoff spot was fiercely contested between the Nippon Ham Fighters and the Chiba Lotte Marines (under new manager Bobby Valentine), with the Fighters winning the right to match up with Seibu by just half a game. In the Central League, the Giants had been heavy favorites to land another title after adding slugger Tuffy Rhodes from the Buffaloes, as well as third baseman Hiromi Kokubo, who had been let go by the Hawks for nothing in the offseason (enraging the fans in Fukuoka). But the Giants could finish no better than third; and the CL, unlike the PL, doesn't have league playoffs.

In those PL playoffs, the Lions first beat the Fighters 2-1 thanks to some grand slam heroics from Alex Cabrera in the deciding game, then beat the Hawks 3-2, with the deciding game a 10-inning, 4-3 thriller (in which Japan Series hero Ishii provided some foreshadowing by recording the save).

The Pacific League's outstanding individual performance was turned in by first baseman Nobuhiko Matsunaka of the Hawks, who won the Triple Crown. Matsunaka hit .358 with 44 homers and 120 RBI in the 133-game season, and won Japan's first Triple Crown since 1986, though not outright as Fernando Seguignol of the Fighters tied Matsunaka's 44-homer performance. Matsunaka also led the PL in runs scored (118), slugging percentage (.715) and OBP (.464). Another outstanding performance was turned in by Hawks catcher Kenji Jojima (2003 MVP and also the anchor of the bronze-medal winning team at the 2004 Olympics), who batted .338 and slugged .655. Matsunaka was named the league's MVP and won over 90% of the first-place votes.

Pacific League pitchers were led by Hisashi Iwakuma of the Buffaloes, who redeemed an otherwise grim season in Osaka by going 15-2 with a 2.92 ERA.

In the Central League, the MVP award was won by righthander Kenshin Kawakami of the champion Dragons. Kawakami finished just fourth in the CL in ERA with a 3.32 figure, but went 17-7 (his 17 wins led NPB) and finished second in the circuit in strikeouts behind the Hanshin Tigers' lefthanded palmball master Kei Igawa, who threw a no-hitter against the Hiroshima Carp on October 4. Central League hitters were paced by Greg LaRocca of the fifth-place Carp, who led the CL in both OBP and slugging, posting figures of .328/.425/.677. LaRocca lost the batting title to teammate Shigenobu Shima, who batted .337 after having played only two games in all of 2003. New Giants acquisition Tuffy Rhodes led the circuit in home runs, tying with Tyrone Woods of the BayStars at 45. The secret to the Dragons' success was not their bats, as they hit fewer home runs than any other NPB team. Instead, their pitching led the way, with Domingo Guzman and Masahiro Yamamoto joining Kawakami as the league's finest rotation.

With Kazuo Matsui, Akinori Otsuka, and Shingo Takatsu having left Japan for MLB in the preceding offseason, to add to the defections of previous years, it was expected that 2004 would bring fewer fireworks to NPB fields than years past. What nobody bargained for was the fireworks coming from off the field. NPB has not yet achieved a stable economic system, but it can be hoped that 2005 will be a less "interesting" year than 2004.

Note: As this book went to press, it was announced that the Pacific League expansion franchise had been awarded to Rakuten Inc. The Tohoku Rakuten Golden Eagles, who will be more commonly called the Rakuten Eagles, will be based in the city of Sendai, and have named American Marty Kuehnert their first General Manager.

Japanese Baseball in 2004

Final Standings

Central League	Record	Pct	GB
Chunichi Dragons	79-56-3	.585	--
Yakult Swallows	72-64-2	.529	7.5
Tokyo Yomiuri Giants	71-64-3	.526	8.0
Hanshin Tigers	66-70-2	.485	13.5
Hiroshima Toyo Carp	60-77-1	.438	20.0
Yokohama BayStars	59-76-3	.437	20.0

Pacific League	Record	Pct	GB
Fukuoka Daiei Hawks	77-52-4	.597	--
Seibu Lions	74-58-1	.561	4.5
Hokkaido Nippon Ham Fighters	66-65-2	.504	12.0
Chiba Lotte Marines	65-65-3	.500	12.5
Osaka Kintetsu Buffaloes	61-70-2	.466	17.0
Orix Blue Wave	49-82-2	.374	29.0

Notes: "Record" is expressed as wins-losses-ties. In NPB, games are a maximum of 12 innings, so games can end in ties.

Japanese League Leaders

Central League Leaders	Player	Team	Total	Pacific League Leaders	Player	Team	Total
AVG	Shigenobu Shiba	Carp	.338	AVG	Nobuhiko Matsunaka	Hawks	.358
OBP	Greg LaRocca	Carp	.425	OBP	Nobuhiko Matsunaka	Hawks	.464
SLG	Greg LaRocca	Carp	.677	SLG	Nobuhiko Matsunaka	Hawks	.715
OPS	Greg LaRocca	Carp	1.102	OPS	Nobuhiko Matsunaka	Hawks	1.179
H	Shigenobu Shiba	Carp	189	H (tied)	Nobuhiko Matsunaka	Hawks	171
					Munenori Kawasaki	Hawks	171
2B	Takayuki Shimizu	Giants	39	2B	Kazuya Fukuura	Marines	42
3B	Kosuke Fukudome	Dragons	7	3B	Munenori Kawasaki	Hawks	8
HR (tied)	Tyrone Woods	BayStars	45	HR (tied)	Nobuhiko Matsunaka	Hawks	44
	Tuffy Rhodes	Giants	45		Fernando Seguignol	Fighters	44
BB	Tomoaki Kanemoto	Tigers	79	BB	Benny Agbayani	Marines	86
R	Toshihisa Nishi	Giants	106	R	Nobuhiko Matsunaka	Hawks	118
RBI	Tomoaki Kanemoto	Tigers	113	RBI	Nobuhiko Matsunaka	Hawks	120
SB	Norihiro Akahoshi	Tigers	64	SB	Munenori Kawasaki	Hawks	42
W	Kenshin Kawakami	Dragons	17	W	Hisashi Iwakuma	Buffaloes	15
IP	Kei Igawa	Tigers	200.1	IP	Nagisa Arakaki	Hawks	192.1
ERA	Koji Uehara	Giants	2.6	ERA	Daisuke Matsuzaka	Lions	2.9
K	Kei Igawa	Tigers	228	K	Nagisa Arakaki	Hawks	177
SV	Ryota Igarashi	Swallows	37	SV (tied)	Yukiya Yokoyama	Fighters	28
					Koji Mise	Hawks	28

2004 Fantasy Review

by Ben Jacobs

With fantasy baseball continuing to grow in popularity, what-year-in-review book would be complete without a look back at the fantasy baseball season? We've decided to come up with two teams – the fantasy All-Stars and All-Busts.

All choices are based on 5x5 scoring and players are listed at the position they were eligible for that gives them the most value.

All-Stars

C Ivan Rodriguez, Tigers: There were no great catchers this year, but Rodriguez led all catchers in batting average (.334) and was the only catcher among the top five at his position in all five categories with 19 homers, seven steals, 72 runs and 86 RBI.

C Javy Lopez, Orioles: Lopez's 23 home runs were 20 fewer than last year, which is why he dropped from being one of the top 35 fantasy players to out of the top 100. Still, he hit .316 with 83 runs and 86 RBI, which is good enough for a catcher.

1B Todd Helton, Rockies: Helton was not up to his usual fantasy standards, but Coors Field still helped him enough. He missed 100 RBI (96) for the first time since 1998, but he hit .347 with 32 home runs and 115 runs scored. Blame the first two spots in Colorado's lineup for Helton only being the best fantasy first baseman by a small margin.

1B David Ortiz, Red Sox: Ortiz came off what most people thought was a career year and hit much better. He raised his average from .288 to .301, hit 10 more home runs (41), drove in 38 more runs (139) and scored 15 more runs (94). He also finally showed he can play a full season with 150 games and 582 at-bats.

2B Michael Young, Rangers: He played shortstop all season, but he qualified at second base and was better than anybody who actually played there. He also was coming off what looked like a career year and improved almost across the board. He hit .313 with 22 homers, 12 steals, 114 runs and 99 RBI, going up in every category except steals (13 last year).

2B Jeff Kent, Astros: Kent's just a steady performer offensively and he bounced back nicely from a slight down year in which he missed 32 games. He's obviously not going to put up MVP numbers anymore at age 36, but a .289 average, 27 homers, seven steals, 96 runs and 107 RBI from second base is very solid.

3B Adrian Beltre, Dodgers: This was just a remarkable performance. In 2002 and 2003 combined, missing only seven games, he hit 44 homers, scored 120 runs and drove in 155. This year, he hit 48 homers, scored 104 runs and drove in 121. He also hit .334 after hitting .249 the previous two years.

3B Scott Rolen, Cardinals: Because Rolen was already a star, nobody really talked about how much better he was at the plate this year than normal. He hit above .300 for the first time in his career (.314) and he set career highs in homers (34) and RBI (124). He also scored more than 100 runs (109) for just the second time in his career.

SS Alex Rodriguez, Yankees: Rodriguez had his fewest homers (36) and RBI (106) since 1997 and his lowest average (.286) and fewest runs scored (112) since 1999. He was still able to outperform all the shortstops because he stole more bases (28) than he had since 1998.

SS Miguel Tejada, Orioles: Tejada essentially reproduced his 2002 MVP season, just with 19 more RBI. He hit .308 in 2002 and .311 this year. He hit 34 homers both seasons. He scored 108 runs in 2002 and 107 this year. He stole seven bases in 2002 and four this year. The difference is that he drove in 131 runs in 2002 and an amazing 150 this year.

OF Vladimir Guerrero, Angels: This wasn't Guerrero's best fantasy season (that would be two years ago when he hit .336 with 39 homers and 40 steals), but it was close. He had the average (.336) and the home runs (39), but the steals were down to 15. He almost made up for it by combining for 250 runs (124) and RBI (126).

OF Albert Pujols, Cardinals: The only complaint you can have about the Pujols fantasy era is that he's gone from qualifying at third base, first base and the outfield; to first base and the outfield; to just first base next year. Still, when a player hits .331 with 46 homers, five steals, 133 runs and 123 RBI and nobody's even remotely surprised, you know he's amazing.

OF Bobby Abreu, Phillies: Abreu has been tremendous the last five years, but this was his best season yet. His average was there (.301), he hit 30 homers for the second time in his career and stole 40 bases for the first time. He tied his career high with 118 runs and drove in at least 100 (105) for the third time.

OF Carlos Beltran, Royals/Astros: Well, he didn't quite make it to 40-40, but you can't complain about 38 homers and 42 steals. You also have to like 121 runs and 104 RBI. He did only hit .267, but when he's bringing so much to the table in the other four categories, that's something you can deal with pretty easily.

OF Barry Bonds, Giants: You would think that a player with a .362 average, 45 home runs and 129 runs scored would easily be the best fantasy outfielder, but he's not. Because everybody's afraid of him, he was only able to drive in 101 runs. And because he only had 373 at-bats, his batting average just didn't impact your team as much as you would like.

SP Johan Santana, Twins: Santana's performance as a part-time starter the last two years gave an indication that he would be great, but that he was this great this quickly was something of a surprise. It was especially surprising considering that he had two wins and a 5.61 ERA after two months. To finish with 20 wins, a 2.61 ERA, 0.92 WHIP and 265 strikeouts after that start is remarkable.

SP Randy Johnson, Diamondbacks: Hopefully, you didn't shy away from Johnson due to his age and last year's injuries, because he was as good as ever this year. From 1999 to 2002, he averaged a 2.48 ERA, 1.04 WHIP and 354 strikeouts in 258 innings. This year, he had a 2.60 ERA, 0.90 WHIP and 290 strikeouts in 245 innings. The only negative is that he won just 16 games this year.

SP Ben Sheets, Brewers: In his first three seasons, Sheets had career bests of a 4.15 ERA, 1.25 WHIP and 7.06 strikeouts per nine innings. This year, he somehow finished in the top five in the majors in all three categories with a 2.70 ERA, 0.98 WHIP and 10.03 K/9IP rate (264 strikeouts). Only his 12 wins prevented him from being in the same class as Santana and Johnson.

SP Jason Schmidt, Giants: Schmidt wasn't as great as last year, but he was able to make three more starts, which kept his fantasy value from taking a big hit. His ERA rose from 2.34 to 3.20 and his WHIP went up from 0.95 to 1.08, but he picked up one extra win (18) and 43 extra strikeouts (251).

SP Curt Schilling, Red Sox: Schilling was everything the Red Sox and his fantasy owners expected him to be. He pitched 226.2 innings, won 21 games and posted a 3.26 ERA and 1.06 WHIP. His strikeouts dipped a little more than you might have expected just by adjusting for the league change, be he still had 203 of them.

SP Roger Clemens, Astros: I think I'll retire. No, on second thought, I think I'll try to win another Cy Young award. In a matter of months, Clemens went from being out of baseball to being one of the best fantasy options available with 18 wins, a 2.98 ERA, 1.16 WHIP and 218 strikeouts.

SP Roy Oswalt, Astros: This season was eerily similar to the only other season in which Oswalt was able to stay healthy. In 2002, Oswalt's line read 19 wins, 233 innings, 215 hits, 78 earned runs, 17 home runs, 62 walks, 208 strikeouts and a 3.01 ERA. This year, only three

numbers were appreciably different: 233 hits, 92 earned runs and a 3.49 ERA.

RP Eric Gagne, Dodgers: Gagne wasn't quite as dominant as last year, but his season was almost a carbon copy of 2002. The only difference is that he saved seven fewer games (45) and won three more (seven). The strikeouts (114) were the same and the ERA (2.19) and WHIP (0.91) were very close.

RP Brad Lidge, Astros: Had he been the closer all year, Lidge easily would have been the best fantasy reliever in baseball this season. Instead, he only saved 29 games. Combine that with six wins, a 1.90 ERA, 0.92 WHIP and 157 strikeouts and he was a close second to Gagne.

RP Mariano Rivera, Yankees: The only thing that prevents Rivera from being the best fantasy closer is that he doesn't get as many strikeouts as guys like Gagne and Lidge. He only had 66 this year, but he made up for it with 53 saves, a 1.94 ERA and 1.08 WHIP while setting a career high in appearances (74).

All-Busts

C Mike Piazza, Mets: Seeing time at first base was supposed to help Piazza bounce back from an injury-plagued season. It didn't. Looking only at seasons in which he played at least 100 games, Piazza set career lows in every fantasy category this season by hitting .266 with 20 homers, 47 runs and 54 RBI.

C Matthew LeCroy, Twins: After hitting .287 with 17 homers and 64 RBI in 107 games last year, LeCroy seemed poised for an increase in playing time and production. If he played 140 games, 25 homers and 90-100 RBI didn't seem unreasonable. Instead, he played 88 games and hit .269 with nine homers, 25 runs and 39 RBI.

1B Jason Giambi, Yankees: With several nagging injuries and all sorts of steroid suspicions, Giambi was certainly a risk. But he was coming off a 41-homer, 107-RBI season, so he appeared to be a risk worth taking. Nobody could have predicted what happened, with Giambi missing 82 games and hitting just .208 with 12 homers and 40 RBI in the games he did play.

1B Richie Sexson, Diamondbacks: Sexson had a very clean injury history coming into this season and two of his last three seasons (2001 and 2003) were identically spectacular. But when a player you're counting on for 45-50 homers plays just 23 games before his season's over, he's a bust.

2B Bret Boone, Mariners: If Boone had hit .252 with 24 homers, 10 steals and 83 RBI three years ago, people would have been praising him for having one of his best seasons. But he waited until this year to put up those numbers, and the amazing numbers he produced last year and in 2001 make this year's line disappointing.

2B Alfonso Soriano, Rangers: You might think it's unfair to call a second baseman who hits .280 with 28 home runs, 18 steals, 77 runs and 91 RBI a bust, and you'd normally be right. But not when that second baseman has hit .295 and averaged 38.5 homers, 38 steals, 121 runs and 96.5 RBI the last two seasons.

3B Troy Glaus, Angels: After missing 71 games last year, Glaus owners were hoping that he'd stay healthy and at least put up the numbers he did two years ago. Instead, he missed even more time than he did last year. He played just 58 games and hit .251 with 18 homers, 47 runs and 42 RBI.

3B Morgan Ensberg, Astros: Ensberg hit 25 homers in 127 games last year and was another player who appeared to be ready to flourish in a full-time role. Instead he barely played more games this year (131), and he only hit .275 with 10 home runs and 66 RBI.

SS Nomar Garciaparra, Red Sox/Cubs: Missing exactly half the season certainly didn't help Garciaparra, but even when he played, he only hit .308 with nine homers, four steals, 52 runs and 41 RBI. He averaged 13.5 homers, 6.2 steals, 57.4 runs and 58.4 RBI per 81 games the last two years.

SS Edgar Renteria, Cardinals: Normally, a shortstop who hits .287 with 10 homers, 17 steals, 84 runs and 72 RBI would be more than acceptable. However, Renteria stole twice as many bases, hit 43 points higher and drove in 28 more runs last year. While not bad, this year was disappointing.

OF Magglio Ordonez, White Sox: Ordonez had his worst fantasy season since 1998 last year, and he still hit .317 with 29 homers, nine steals, 95 runs and 99 RBI. So, most people were expecting another great year. Instead, injuries limited him to 52 games and he hit .292 with nine homers and 37 RBI.

OF Preston Wilson, Rockies: Coors Field turned Wilson into a fantasy monster last season, and the expectation was that it would do so again. Unfortunately, injuries got in the way and Wilson hit just .248 with six homers and 29 RBI in 58 games. He fell 30 homers and 112 RBI short of his marks from last year.

OF Vernon Wells, Blue Jays: After a breakout season last year, Wells missed 28 games and his production suffered tremendously. His average (.272) was 45 points lower, he hit 10 fewer homers (23), scored 36 fewer runs (82) and drove in 50 fewer runs (67). The only positive is that he stole five more bases (nine).

OF Brian Giles, Padres: After four years as an elite but underrated hitter, Giles missed some time with injuries last year and was traded mid-season. He was able to play a full season again this year, but he put up the worst numbers in any of his five years with at least 140 games, hitting .284 with 23 homers, 10 steals, 97 runs and 94 RBI.

OF Garret Anderson, Angels: Anderson had played at least 150 games in eight straight seasons entering this year. So, most people were shocked when injuries forced him to miss 50 games. Even when he could play, he wasn't quite the same player he had been the last couple of years as he hit .301 with just 14 homers and 75 RBI.

SP Mark Prior, Cubs: Prior was the hands-down top choice among pitchers until a preseason injury clouded his value. That injury stretched well into the season, and he ended up starting just 21 games. Even in those games, he wasn't great as he won just six of them with a 4.02 ERA, 1.35 WHIP and 139 strikeouts.

SP Roy Halladay, Blue Jays: Halladay threw 266 innings on his way to the Cy Young award last year. This year, he could only manage half that many innings as he may have felt the effects of throwing 505.1 innings in two years. He also managed just eight wins, a 4.20 ERA, 1.35 WHIP and 99 strikeouts.

SP Mike Mussina, Yankees: In his previous nine seasons, Mussina threw 200 innings nine times, won 17 games six times, posted an ERA below 3.80 six times and struck out 170 batters eight times. This year, he missed all those marks with 12 wins, a 4.59 ERA, 1.32 WHIP and 132 strikeouts in 164 2/3 innings.

SP Javier Vazquez, Yankees: Moving from Montreal to New York, Vazquez was supposed to maintain his effectiveness and increase his wins. Instead, he maintained his win total and decreased his effectiveness. His 14 wins are right in line with what he did for the Expos, but his 4.91 ERA, 1.29 WHIP and 150 strikeouts in 198 innings are not even close.

SP Kerry Wood, Cubs: Wood was off to a tremendous start when an injury interrupted his season in May. When he returned, he wasn't nearly as effective and he finished with only eight wins, a 3.72 ERA, 1.27 WHIP and 144 strikeouts in 140 1/3 innings. It's disappointing whether you compare it to last year's ERA of 3.20 or his first month's 2.52 ERA.

SP Josh Beckett, Marlins: Beckett's value went through the roof due to last year's playoff performance, but he had never even pitched enough to qualify for an ERA title and he didn't this year either. He set a career high with 156 2/3 innings, but he won just nine games with a 3.79 ERA, 1.22 WHIP and 152 strikeouts.

SP Matt Morris, Cardinals: Morris' production declined for the second year in a row last season, but he was still good enough to help your team and there was a chance he'd return to his former greatness. He didn't. He won 15 games, but those wins came with a 4.72 ERA, 1.29 WHIP and just 131 strikeouts in 202 innings.

SP Mark Mulder, Athletics: Mulder looked like a lock for the other list when he was 13-2 with a 3.21 ERA just after the All-Star break. Then his season fell apart. He won 17 games, but his ERA (4.43) and WHIP (1.36) were a far cry from last year's 3.13 and 1.18.

SP Barry Zito, Athletics: Zito's declining strikeout rate the last two years warned of danger, but he actually increased his strikeouts (163) and still had the worst season of his career. He only won 11 games and he needed a decent final two months to lower his ERA to 4.48 and his WHIP to 1.39.

RP Billy Wagner, Phillies: Wagner had slowly but surely recovered from his 2000 injury to the point where he had a 1.78 ERA, 44 saves and 105 strikeouts in 86 innings last year. Finally all the way back, he went and got hurt again this year. He had a 2.42 ERA and 0.77 WHIP, but only 21 saves in 48.1 innings.

Hang Time on the Baseball Field

By Robert Dudek

Current methods of defensive analysis rely heavily on categorisation of balls put in play into field zones. The playing field is divided up and the result is noted every time a ball is hit into a given zone. But there are other important factors which increase or decrease the difficulty of turning a batted ball into an out.

Groundballs are complicated things. It's not self-evident that hard hit grounders are more difficult to turn into outs than weakly-hit grounders. Well placed weakly-hit groundballs can be very difficult to turn into outs, while crisply hit grounders right at a fielder are comparatively easy. Balls hit to the right of a fielder are more difficult than those hit to a fielder's left. This is because an infielder fielding a ball to his right has his momentum going away from first base. The exception is a ball hit to a second baseman's right when there is a force play at second base.

Fly balls are much simpler beasts. The fielder only has to worry about catching the ball before it lands (throwing to bases is a separate issue). Visibility and wind conditions are not significant factors most of the time. The main factors affecting the difficulty of turning a fly ball into an out are (a) the distance the ball is hit from a fielder's starting position (i.e. the zone) and (b) how long the ball is in the air – its hang time. It's unfortunate that so much attention has been paid to zones and so very little to hang time.

It stands to reason that the longer a ball is in the air, the easier it is to catch. But how important is hang time? The study I've undertaken is a small step towards understanding the role this factor might play in evaluating pitching and defense.

The Study

I chose eight pitchers for the study, a pair from each of four American League teams (in order to minimize the distorting effect of parks and quality of fielders). One of each pair was a pitcher with a high groundout to airout ratio (go/ao); the other possessed a low go/ao ratio. Each time a ball was hit in the air for at least 1.5 seconds, the hang time, general defensive zone and result (hit/out/error) were recorded. Hang time was clocked from the moment of impact until the ball was touched by a fielder, hit a wall or landed on the ground. Balls that went through the infield below the infielder's eye level were considered line-drives through the infield and were excluded from the study. Ground ball outs, line drive outs at an infielder, infield hits, and balls grounded through the infield were also excluded.

The Condensed Games feature of the mlb.com 2004 Archives was indispensable for this project; where unavailable, the full game archives were used. Games that were not available in condensed or full format were regretfully but necessarily excluded from the study. I wish I could have included pairs of pitchers from every major league team, but recording hang time for each fly ball is a laborious activity. I hope to look at more data in the coming year.

Here is a list of the pitchers in the study and the games *excluded* from the study:

- Erik Bedard – all games available
- Roy Halladay, versus Detroit (April 15), Arizona (June 12)
- Tim Hudson, versus Toronto (June 5), Minnesota (August 7), Seattle (September 18)
- Ted Lilly, versus Arizona (June 13), Anaheim (July 10), Baltimore (September 29)
- Derek Lowe – all games available
- Pedro Martinez – versus San Francisco (June 19)
- Sidney Ponson – all games available
- Barry Zito, versus Kansas City (May 16, May 22)

Once all the work collecting and digitizing the data was complete, I aggregated the data to get a feel for the relationship between hang time and the chance an outfielder would catch the ball (out percentage). To this end, I removed fly balls caught by infielders.

Hang Time	Number	Outs	Out%	Change
1.5-2.0	122	1	0.8	---
2.0-2.5	154	7	4.5	3.3
2.5-3.0	173	49	28.3	23.8
3.0-3.5	168	69	41.1	12.8
3.5-4.0	186	104	55.9	14.8
4.0-4.5	187	126	67.4	11.5
4.5-5.0	181	145	80.1	12.7
5.0-5.5	178	154	86.5	6.4
5.5-6.0	146	140	95.9	9.4
6.0-6.5	110	107	97.3	1.4
6.5-plus	28	27	96.4	-0.8

Note: Change is the gain/loss of each time period over the preceding time period

The key hang times range from 2.5 to 5.0 seconds. In this range, how far a ball is hit from where the outfielder starts is quite important.

If a ball is in the air less than two seconds, it is very likely to be land in front of the outfielder, so unless he is playing very shallow he does not have a realistic opportunity to make the catch. When a ball is in the air for 5 or more seconds, the fielder will very likely catch it unless he has to run a long distance.

Could hang time be as significant a factor as ball location in determining the chances a ball will be caught?

I decided on a simple 12 outfield zone scheme. The five principal zones were left, center, right, left-center and right-center. They each had a deep zone as a complement; any ball hit to the warning track, wall or off the wall was considered to be in one of the deep zones. The other two zones were those encompassing the area near the two foul lines.

Basic zones	Number	Outs	Out%
Centerfield	378	246	65.1
Rightfield	287	177	61.7
Leftfield	262	159	60.7
Leftcenterfield	132	73	55.3
Rightcenterfield	124	77	62.1

Other zones	Number	Outs	Out%
Deep Center	69	46	66.7
Deep Left	83	43	51.8
Deep Right	74	38	51.4
Deep Leftcenter	61	19	31.1
Deep Rightcenter	32	7	21.9
Leftfield Foul Line	68	24	35.3
Rightfield Foul Line	63	27	42.9

As you can see, the variance of out conversion rates from zone to zone isn't especially large. **Hang time is a more important factor in determining whether the ball is caught than the (broadly defined) zone into which the ball is hit.**

Groundball and Flyball Pitchers – A Breed Apart?

Sinkers, sliders, sharp curves and splitters are the tools of the trade for the groundball specialist. The most extreme groundball pitcher among American League starters is Derek Lowe of the Boston Red Sox – everything he throws has late downward movement. Roy Halladay throws a sharp curve and slider that he tries to locate down in the zone. Tim Hudson throws a heavy sinker that cuts away from lefthander hitters; he also throws a tight splitter.

Fly ball pitchers like to pitch up in the strike-zone, resorting to fastballs and changeups when doing so. Pedro Martinez relies on changeups and moving fastballs up in the zone and complements them with an assortment of breaking pitches. Ted Lilly has an excellent change up and cuts his fastball into right-handed hitters. Barry Zito is famous for a great 12-to-6 curveball which he relies on for strikeouts and weak grounders, but the fastballs and changeups he throws induce many fly balls.

The differences between these two pitcher types show up in the stats, if you know where to look. Here are seasonal stats for the pitchers in the study:

Pitcher	IP	G/F	BB/9	K/9	HR/9	BABIP	ERA
Lowe	182.2	3.36	3.50	5.17	0.74	.327	5.42
Hudson	188.2	2.19	2.10	4.91	0.38	.297	3.53
Halladay	133.0	2.06	2.64	6.43	0.88	.308	4.20
Ponson	215.2	1.82	2.88	4.80	0.96	.327	5.30
Martinez	217.0	0.85	2.53	9.41	1.08	.291	3.90
Zito	213.0	0.78	3.42	6.89	1.18	.291	4.48
Bedard	137.1	0.74	4.65	7.93	0.85	.323	4.59
Lilly	197.1	0.74	4.06	7.66	1.19	.261	4.06
Groundball	180.0	2.36	2.78	5.33	0.74	.315	4.61
Flyball	191.1	0.78	3.67	7.97	1.08	.292	4.26

The last two lines are the un-weighted averages for the two groups of pitchers. The ground-out-to-air-out ratio is taken directly from mlb.com – double plays count as two outs.

Some differences are already apparent. The fly ball pitcher group is in line with the classic power pitcher profile – high walks, high strikeouts and somewhat prone to the gopher ball. Groundball pitchers keep the ball in the park, but tend to give up hits in play more frequently.

A few years ago, Mike Emeigh of Baseball Think Factory had an idea that got me thinking. He theorized that groundball pitchers like Tim Hudson try to get groundballs, so when they give up a fly ball it's very likely a result of a mistake pitch. We would expect that mistake pitches are hit harder and that the out rate on fly balls hit off a pitcher like Hudson should therefore be lower than from a pitcher who tries to produce fly balls.

Does this hold up? What can hang time tell us about groundball and fly ball pitchers? In order to study only those fly balls that stayed in play, I filtered out homeruns (except for one inside-the-park homerun hit off Pedro Martinez by David Newhan).

Pitcher	Flyballs	Out%	Avg HangTime	Popups	%	Easy Flies	%
Derek Lowe	198	49%	3.86	19	10%	38	19%
Tim Hudson	191	59%	4.02	28	15%	35	18%
Roy Halladay	133	61%	3.96	19	14%	20	15%
Sidney Ponson	314	61%	4.18	38	12%	77	25%
Pedro Martinez	301	67%	4.48	50	17%	86	29%
Barry Zito	333	69%	4.38	72	22%	83	25%
Erik Bedard	232	68%	4.22	47	20%	47	20%
Ted Lilly	285	73%	4.57	75	26%	76	27%
Groundball	209	58%	4.01	26	12%	43	20%
Flyball	288	69%	4.41	61	21%	73	25%

Notes: a popup is either a bunt caught in the air or a ball caught by an infielder with a hang time of at least 2.5 seconds; an easy fly is defined as a non-pop up with a hang time of at least 5 seconds.

Hang Time on the Baseball Field

A sample size of just eight pitchers isn't enough to draw firm conclusions; nevertheless a number of interesting findings present themselves:

1)   When a fly ball is hit off a fly ball pitcher it hangs in the air longer.

2)   A much greater percentage of fly balls off fly ball pitchers are infield pop ups.

3)   Fly balls off fly ball pitchers are easier to convert into outs.

These propositions are interrelated. Pop ups are the easiest of fly balls: almost 99% of the pop ups in this study resulted in outs. The longer that fly balls hang in the air, the more likely they will find a glove. More pop ups plus higher fly balls lead inevitably to a higher out conversion rate (and a lower hit rate on balls in play).

Let's now turn to the matter of all the other balls in play - the groundballs, bunts and liners through the infield. At what rate do these batted balls become hits? The following summarizes data from the games that were available for study (errors are considered non-hits).

Pitcher	Flyballs	Hit%	Other BIP	Hit%	Overall Hit%
Derek Lowe	198	50%	442	25%	33%
Tim Hudson	191	40%	357	24%	30%
Roy Halladay	133	38%	237	27%	31%
Sidney Ponson	314	40%	425	28%	33%
Pedro Martinez	301	33%	257	25%	29%
Barry Zito	333	31%	273	28%	29%
Erik Bedard	232	32%	189	32%	32%
Ted Lilly	285	27%	217	25%	26%
Groundball	209	42%	365	26%	32%
Flyball	288	31%	234	28%	29%

At the risk of generalising, groundball pitchers have an advantage when a non-fly ball is hit into play, but it is slight. Fly ball pitchers, inducing many more pop ups and easy flies have a massive edge in converting fly balls into outs. Overall, the edge shrinks but is maintained by the fly ball pitchers. The equaliser is a fly ball pitcher's tendency to give up more homeruns than a groundball pitcher.

Mike Emeigh's theory seems to be hold water: groundball pitchers are much better off when allowing groundballs. The same relationship doesn't seem to hold for the four fly ball pitchers in the study, however.

A Thought in Lieu of a Conclusion

As I write this, Derek Lowe is about to file for free agency after two sterling performances in the playoffs for the Boston Red Sox. He may yet re-sign with the Red Sox; it would be a shame if he didn't. The combination of an extreme groundball pitcher and the smallest left field territory in the major leagues might have set the stage for an interesting experiment.

Excluding pop ups, how many balls were caught in leftfield at Fenway Park when Derek Lowe was pitching in 2004? The answer is seven – in 19 starts. To be sure there were other balls caught in left-center (6 to be precise), but imagine if we had Johnny Damon shaded towards the left-center gap to catch those, with Trot Nixon in the right-center gap?

Our nominal leftfielder, let's call him Kevin Millar, becomes an extra infielder. Suppose we station him near first base. The first baseman could play where the second sacker normally does but shading to the hole. The second baseman would play either to the right or left of second base depending on the batter, getting to all those balls bouncing and floating up the middle. The shortstop could play extra deep, helping Damon out on shallow flies and snaring the liners that normally go through the hole or over the leaping shortstop's glove. The third baseman would play off the line, to cut off the dribblers headed for the shortstop.

Anywhere from 10 to 20 would-be hits could be turned into outs with the cost of a half dozen extra hits to the outfield. It's an idea … maybe someday someone will try it.

Meanwhile, on the Internet...

Meet Me in New Orleans

By Alex Belth

Will Carroll, who writes the "Under the Knife" injury column for Baseball Prospectus, was one of the first Internet writers I developed a relationship with. I started "Bronx Banter", a Yankee-based baseball blog, in the fall of 2002, and sometime the following spring, Carroll e-mailed me about a piece I wrote concerning Robbie Alomar and homosexuality in sports. Carroll and I are roughly the same age, and we became chummy in no time. Before long, Will told me the best thing I could do for myself all year would be to attend the baseball winter meetings in New Orleans. The previous year, Carroll, on a lark, showed up at the meetings in Nashville and promptly made contacts with the likes of Jayson Stark and Peter Gammons.

Carroll had the good fortune to write about a topic that wasn't covered anywhere in the mainstream or alternative media. He offered analysis and education about baseball injuries and carved himself out a nice niche. Big shots like Peter Gammons picked up on his newsletter, which eventually became a website and later a regular column for Baseball Prospectus. My site didn't provide anything remotely as specialized, but that didn't stop my sense of grandiosity from imagining being whisked away by Gammons and some of his pals to talk shop over lunch.

As the 2003 season unfolded, Will kept on me about attending the meetings. In addition to covering the Yankees, I started conducting lengthy interviews for my site, mostly with sportswriters. Going to the meetings started to make more sense. I could meet some of the guys I had interviewed over the phone and get a chance to hang out with Will and some of his pals from Baseball Prospectus. I convinced fellow blogger, Jay Jaffe, whose Futility Infielder is one of the longest-running independent baseball websites on the Net, to share a room with me. After all, what did we have to lose? It would be a good chance to meet some sportswriters and get a glimpse at what their world is all about.

Jay and I arrived in New Orleans on a cool and rainy Friday night. Our hotel was roughly a ten-minute walk from the Marriott, where the action was taking place. Earlier in the week I had e-mailed Tom Verducci from Sports Illustrated, whom I had previously interviewed, about meeting him at some point during the weekend. I wondered where we could connect. He replied that I'd find him in the lobby of the Marriott. Jay and I checked into our room and quickly made an appearance.

In short order, we found Will and the Baseball Prospectus gang. Carroll is a sturdy, round, animated guy. He wore glasses and a dress shirt. He was flanked by Joe Sheehan, also round, and wearing a navy blue suit. On first glance, the two could pass as distant relatives. But their demeanors were completely different. Will was forthcoming and engaging while Joe was guarded, suspicious. Along with them were BP interns Chaim Bloom, Ryan Wilkins and Nate Silver, all about ten years younger than Joe and Will. Carroll excitedly looked around the room and pointed people out to the group as if he were a tour guide. Jay and I introduced ourselves and got to know the guys some, then got ourselves a drink. It wasn't long before I grew impatient standing around in our little cipher. I hate standing in one place too long, so I drifted off on my own and took the place in.

Smack dab in the middle of the hotel lobby was a squared-off bar area, raised up off the floor by a couple of feet, carpeted and outfitted with tables. Everything seemed to be tinged in gold. The room was populated with up to several hundred men—agents, scouts, front office assistants, kids looking for jobs, and of course, the members of the media. Essentially, the scene looked like a cocktail party on steroids. Groups of men clustered together and chatted like a bunch of clandestine yentas. It's the kind of set-up where you see a guy pull another guy aside and say, "Step into my office."

It was not an inviting atmosphere. The mood wasn't exactly dour, just forced, and tense underneath the chuckles and backslapping. After all, the winter meetings aren't a social gathering, it's a business affair. The teams are in the business of signing players and making trades, the agents are in the business of selling their clients, and the media's business is to be up in everybody's business. As a result, everyone is checking everybody else out. When Jay and I first walked in, we got the once over too. A few guys shot me suspicious, dark looks, as if to say, "Now who the hell is this?" Others looked at me more openly, with curiosity, as if to say, "Who the hell is that? Do I need to know him?"

The attention didn't last long, but it was constant. Once someone determined I was nobody that interested them, another guy was staring at me. Repeat cycle. And this wasn't just me, of course. This is what the entire room was doing to everyone. It is an odd sensation, watching a room full of guys checking each other out, eyes darting from face to face. The overall effect has all the charm (not to mention awkwardness) of a seventh-grade dance, except there aren't any girls.

Which isn't to say there weren't objects of desire. It's just the "girls" in this case, were other, more famous men. There wasn't anything inherently sexual about it, but essentially, the Marriott was a room filled with men hanging around in clusters scoping out other guys. A regular meat market of a different color. Oh, look, there is Peter Gammons, the homecoming queen. And there is Dusty Baker, and Felipe Alou, the dashing old-timers. Do I dare go up and talk to them, or do I just sit here with my back-against-the-wall and gawk at them? Ohmygod, I'm so nervous. Is my make-up right? Do I have my business card handy? What if he blows me off?

Some of the men were clearly built to thrive in the schmoozy atmosphere, while others looked hopelessly stiff, concerned and ill at ease. Some just stood around looking nervous and alert, as if they were limo drivers at the airport waiting to pick someone up. There was a range of faces and personality types, but as a whole, it all added up to way too much testosterone in one confined place. There were some women present, but few with anything to do with the meetings. The vibe wasn't anti-female; they just didn't have anything to do with the business at hand. They were flocks of high school cheerleaders, in town for a big high school football weekend. They pranced along the lobby floor, self-consciously, in short skirts, their backs-arched, presenting perky breasts for anyone who cared to notice.

Sharing the lobby with baseball's best and brightest were scores of families from the Midwest, hurrying about the place with bags of McDonald's or KFC. Add the hotel staff to the mix—cleaning women, doormen, bellhops, bartenders—and you had a room full of people who were all seemingly unaware of each other's existence, all happily self-contained and self-absorbed.

There were plenty of hard, old baseball faces, former ballplayers who were now scouts, guys from the front office, veteran sportswriters. Many of them had red necks and pink faces, suggesting they hadn't seen much snow recently. As a contrast, there were also many boyish-looking men, walking around as if they were five-year-olds at a fair who lost their mother. In general, the men were dressed casually. Some preferred sneakers and short-sleeve shirts, while others wore suits and loafers. The older guys donned sweaters. There were a few bonafide Oscar Madison slobs in untucked, rumpled shirts, but not nearly as many as I had imagined there would be. I suspect that the agents were the guys in the loafers, reeking of cologne (hello Drakar Noir). There were uniformly good-looking, classically handsome jocular types. Many of the writers were pale zhlubs with bad hair. Virtually everybody had a drink in their hand. (Jack McKeon, fresh off the Marlins World Series championship, loitered outside of the hotel entrance working on his cigar much of the time, shaking more hands than a Presidential candidate.)

There was a conference room upstairs, but most of the print media walked laps around the bar in the lobby, looking for their next lead, for new information. The Red Sox and the Rangers were close to making a deal involving Alex Rodriguez. This was the hottest story of the weekend, though of course, nothing transpired. The beat reporters were especially active as they had stories to file for the following day. Agents and their assistants were on their cell phones arranging meetings. The teams all set up shop upstairs in suites, creating, in effect, their own individual war rooms. Ostensibly, they poured over data, schemed, and plotted-out their plan of attack. For the most part, the general managers remained in seclusion, preferring to send out assistants to comb the lobby to see what was shaking down. (The Yankees took this to the extreme, as Boss Steinbrenner didn't allow any Yankee representatives to attend the meetings, no doubt a punitive measure after the Bronx Bombers failed to win the World Serious.) Even when nothing was officially happening, the buzz was steady. I overheard a guy say, "Well, if this team makes this move and this guy signs with that team, then we are going to make this move and sign this player."

After spending a few hours in at the hotel on Friday night, the mystique that these proceedings held in my imagination before we arrived quickly wore off. It was a humanizing experience. Yes, this was the heart of baseball business, and look, these guys are human just like the rest of us. So many of us invest so much time and energy in this game, and the powers that be aren't so removed and magical. They seemed so, well, regular. Hey, there is Scott Boras talking to a reporter; oh, there is Jeff Brantley and Jayson Stark. Stark is taller than I would have imagined. Bruce Bochy is a house. Here comes J.P. Riccardi—a slick and dashing figure—and whoa, there is Lee Mazzilli. How about Tony Perez and Omar Minaya?

These men were regular in the sense that they didn't glow, or have a spotlight following them around the room (although the more recognizable figures like Baker and the ESPN television guys were steadily approached by casual fans who happened to spot them.) Still, it was a surreal situation to be in as an outsider. I worked in and around the movie business for over a decade, so being around famous people was nothing new for me. But even though I've been in close proximity to some of the hotshot actors, and have had conversations and even relationships with others, I've never been in a single room that was a who's-who of celebrities quite like this.

Will introduced me to Jayson Stark briefly on Saturday morning. Later on, I walked up to Gammons and introduced myself. Shockingly, I wasn't invited to lunch. I received a quick handshake and an acknowledgement that he had visited my blog. That would have to suffice. I was momentarily deflated but had more success striking up a conversation with Verducci, a tall, athletic man, with youthful good looks that will probably never desert him. Verducci was a cool customer, friendly, but aloof. He was able to engage in conversation while seemingly surveying the room for something or somebody else. We spoke for a good twenty minutes, and then I introduced myself to Jack Curry of the New York Times. Curry isn't as lanky as Verducci; he's stockier and has blond hair, but he's equally as handsome. The two were the golden boys of the sportswriters I saw. They were well dressed without being formal, and both courteous and extremely professional.

Late in the afternoon, I spotted Howard Bryant of The Boston Herald. After I introduced myself, he said something to the effect of, "Oh yeah, I've been by your site. You were pretty tough on my book." Gulp. Indeed I had been. The worst of it was I didn't exactly remember what I had written. A chill ran through my body, but I didn't rattle. After nervously fumbling over my words for a minute, we ended up having an interesting conversation about his book's subject—racism in the Boston sports world. Bryant was sharp and bright, and he didn't rip me for being critical of his work. I was glad that I had approached him. It was my first taste of what it's like to be confronted by someone whose work I had criticized. It could not have gone better.

Pleased with the face-to-face contacts I had made, I felt like there wasn't much else to be gained from the experience. It is awkward checking out somebody that you would like to meet, and then waiting for them to break away from their present conversation, only to jump into their face, shake their hands, introduce yourself and stick a business card in their palm. It felt like that Looney Tunes cartoon where Bugs Bunny goes to the dog races and falls in love with the mechanical rabbit. After whooshing by him once, Bugs spits out his spiel to her as fast as his gums can flap before she zips away again. It was rewarding to get the opportunity to meet professional sportswriters and baseball men. But it was also taxing and socially painful at the same time. There was no glamour or glitz, not that I had expected anything short of being wined and dined by Peter Gammons. So in short, I was ready to go home.

I spent Saturday evening with a friend of mine from high school who settled in New Orleans after she graduated from Tulane University. It was a real treat getting to see a part of the city other than the French quarter. I made a short appearance on Bourbon Street later on where the BP guys were whooping it up, but since neither drinking or walking around in claustrophobic crowds are my scene, I kept it short and sweet. The following day, Jay and I woke up to learn that the Iraqi President, Saddam Hussein had been captured by American troops. But if the news barely penetrated the insulated world of the baseball winter meetings -- at least as I experienced them -- it did provide a framework to encapsulate the day in our memories for a long time. Everything seemed heightened, lifted.

After a thoroughly mediocre brunch in the French Quarter, we arrived back at the Marriott and found the Baseball Prospectus guys. Initially, they busted my chops for making like a ghost on Saturday. Honestly, I don't think they knew what to make of me. Jay had spent most of his time with them, and here I was, wandering off on my own the whole time. But I simply wanted to get the chance to meet as many people as I could; it was nothing personal against Prospectus.

Jay and I joined Ryan and Chaim around a table in the center area of the hotel lobby. Sheehan and Will buzzed in and out as they worked the room. Nate Silver eventually joined us, as did Tim Marchman of The New York Sun and Jeff Silver, a former front office analyst for the Reds (Tim, Jeff and Joe are all New York natives). These guys felt like my peers. After spending the first day at the meetings scrambling to meet newspaper men, engaging in brief, distracted conversation, I spent the better part of Sunday afternoon in fine company and had a terrific time.

We sat around and talked baseball all day. We didn't care much about what was going on around us. We talked quickly, but not over each other. We listened too, and I learned a lot. Sure, the trade rumors kept us going, but we didn't regulate our conversation to what was happening in baseball at that very moment. If I really felt lifted that afternoon, it was because of the quality of the conversation. The common bond shared by the guys I was talking to was that they were all stunningly bright and shamelessly enthusiastic about the game, its history, and its future. You could even say that they'll be part of its future. I would not be surprised to see Chaim or Nate--not to mention Joe and Will---working inside the game in the near future. We were the outsiders, representing an alternative, sabermetric way of looking at the game. Though BP is an established entity, while guys like Jay and I were amateur writers, to the rest of the room, we were the same. Perhaps we looked conspicuous, but I was enjoying myself too much to notice or care.

At one point on Monday morning, when most of the weekend's wheeling and dealing was complete, Jack Curry approached a group of us and asked me chidingly, "So what the hell are you guys doing here anyway?" He was more curious than anything else. "Ah, I just wanted to see what you guys do and what this is all about." Truthfully, unless you are getting paid to be there, it isn't all too exciting. But my hunch is that there will be more baseball bloggers and Internet writers with each passing year. Maybe that will get boring quickly too. But if you ever check it out for yourself, there is a good chance that you can connect with some decent people and infuse your soul talking baseball. And that is worth the trip.

Ebullient on Opening Day

By Craig Burley

Opening Day (the real one, not the quasi-exhibition series between the New York Ricohs and the Tampa Bay Ricohs, or the made-for-TV hootenanny from Baltimore, or the first game for the stragglers in Florida, Arizona, Atlanta, and Seattle) is just now behind us. A marvelous day.

Now signs of spring were not exactly plentiful this weekend in the frozen wastes of the Great White North; when I left for work yesterday morning it was -7 degrees (19 for those of you to the south) and there had been rumors of snow all through the weekend. Still, the day dawned bright, blue and crystalline, and as I caught the glare of the sun off the Credit River as the train wended its way to Toronto, I saw signs of spring all over.

Globe and Mail sports reporter extraordinaire Stephen Brunt in line at the train station, buying his ticket, no doubt heading for the game. Two fans in head-to-toe Blue Jays regalia - the brand new jerseys and hats, already adorned with dozens of pins. Two young boys with their parents sitting just across from me (for what child takes an intercity train on a Monday school day, if not for the ballgame?). Sure enough, as I remove my headphones to catch their conversation, I find out they are headed to the museum and then to SkyDome.

For me, the start of the season means it is spring, atmospheric evidence be damned, and as long as Lake Ontario doesn't have ice on it (nope, I am looking at it now - blue, white capped and marvelous) then spring is here and it's time for my winter mood to evaporate like a Rangers lead.

Opening Day is the day for the fans. The one day that is about us, not about anything else, not about making money or chasing a batting title or preserving a lead in the pennant race or saving the manager's job. Opening Day is the day we earn with five months of shoveling snow, fantasy drafts, and interminable college football games. Five months of nothing to watch at night, five months of no morning box scores, five months of drudgery slogging through the forecasting magazines. If you didn't enjoy it, even from afar, you have cheated yourself out of your just reward.

In fact, my ebullience on Opening Day is so profound that nothing can touch it... not a dreary day in the office with the ballpark beckoning in full sight of my window (my view onto SkyDome is my office's greatest blessing and greatest curse), not an agonizing, never-ending afternoon following the pitch-by-pitch on Sportsline as the Tigers pound Roy Halladay and the Blue Jays 7-0, not even

a train ride home squeezed next to Canada's fattest man and opposite the world's least convincing transvestite. Lest you think I am joking, I assure you she was the spitting image of George Foster - possibly with a touch of Jeffrey Leonard around the chin and mouth. As for the rotund fellow, I am north of 200 myself but if this guy wasn't well over twice my weight I'll eat his lunch. I don't mind, but I didn't exactly have a lot of elbow room.

Basically, I was in the zone. I hope you were too, as it's 364 days until the next Opening Day and if you don't enjoy it you put in a long winter for nothing.

And nobody will have enjoyed yesterday as much as Tigers fans. A 7-0 pasting of a pretty good team? Shutting out a fine offense? Three home runs off the Cy Young winner? Leading the AL Central? Yeah, after last season, that's a heckuva good day.

Well, Cubs fans, who finally got to erase the Alex Gonzalez/Steve Bartman/Mark Prior/Joe Borowski fiasco from their "last game" stack, might be happier. They beat the Reds 7-4, the pen was incredible (four innings, one hit, no walks, five strikeouts) and their new catcher got himself two hits.

Giants' fans had a good day; not only did they win the game, but Barry Bonds edged to within one home run of Willie Mays, setting up a date with history tomorrow. Bonds had an incredible day -- 3-3 with three RBI, two runs scored, a walk, two doubles and the aforementioned home run -- all off Roy Oswalt, currently the NL's best active pitcher.

I am not going to get into Barry's legal situation here -- no one's in the mood for a rant against governments using criminal investigations and prosecutions for political purposes. His baseball situation is, especially today, a lot more interesting and newsworthy. Is it possible that his troubles, focusing his anger and frustration in his performance, could make him more devastating than before? We know from experience that Bonds has great powers of concentration and focus. There is no telling what he may do if the world makes him mad. Yesterday was the 30th anniversary of Hank Aaron passing the Babe's home run mark, and one wonders whether Aaron's own mark might hold up against Barry Bonds on a mission to prove himself.

Padres fans in particular have a lot to feel happy about, as their up-and-coming team pasted the despised Dodgers 8-2, stranding 15 Dodger runners, turning three double plays and watching a healthy Phil Nevin pound a grand slam off Hideo Nomo, who's due for an off year now that

Ebullient on Opening Day

he's on my fantasy team's roster (of course, the same handicap didn't seem to hurt Jason Johnson).

Royals' fans, after a wonderful, improbable six-run comeback in the bottom of the ninth, are probably still celebrating. Luckily, they get until Wednesday at 1:10 to sleep it off - that weird Tuesday off day comes in handy when there's partying to do.

Indians and Twins fans may have had the best day of all -- extra baseball. The Twins finally prevailed 7-4 (on a three-run blast by Shannon Stewart -- watch for the MVP talk to start again soon), but Ben Broussard had a terrific day at first base for Cleveland, going 4-for-4 and starting a 3-6-3 double play to boot. Unfortunately, he limped off the field in the 11th and was replaced by Lou Merloni. No word as this article went to press on whether he was seriously hurt.

Opening day is the real New Year's Day (surely it's not a coincidence that New Year's used to fall at around this time), the first heartbeat that sets a rhythm that will beat for months and months, keeping time for everything else that happens in our lives. Baseball, if you let it, can be the foundation stone from which you can build everything else that's worth having. At least until October -- but it's the fact that the season eventually ends that makes Opening Day possible once more.

Even for those of us who might not have normally enjoyed these games, Opening Day just can't compare to other games on other days. White Sox fans may have choked in agony as their bullpen blew another lead against their division rivals (yes, Cliff Politte's arm looks to be, essentially, cooked) but how can you get down when there are 161 more ballgames to look forward to? Blue Jays fans are so keyed up that despite seeing their team get pounded 7-0 by the worst team in baseball, one Jays fan likened the game to the launching of a ship by smashing a champagne bottle into it.

Opening Day is the key that unlocks the door into summer. I hope you seize it, and keep it well.

Happy Baseball!

This article originally appeared on The Hardball Times on April 6, 2004 at http://www.hardballtimes.com/main/article/ebullient_on_opening_day/

The Victor Zambrano Award

By Matthew Namee

With his first two games scheduled to be against Mike Mussina and the Yankees, I don't think anyone expected Victor Zambrano to sport a 2-0 record on April 8. Yet, the man has turned the trick, thanks in no small part to what appears to be a multi-hemispherical collapse by Mussina.

That 2-0 record is a bit deceiving, of course. In 11 innings thus far, the 28-year-old Zambrano has walked eight batters, hit another, and thrown one wild pitch. This is par for the course with Victor, who achieved a remarkable (if dubious) feat of wildness last season. You see, Victor Zambrano won the rare Triple Crown of Wild in 2003, leading his league in Walks (106), Hit Batsmen (20), and Wild Pitches (15).

Intuitively, I'd expect this to happen reasonably often. Guys wild enough to lead the league in one category are probably wild enough to lead the league in all three, right? So much for intuition -- only two other players in the history of baseball have led their league in all three of those categories in the same season, and both of those guys did it before World War II was over.

The first (and until Zambrano, the only) AL pitcher to lead his league in walks, hit batsmen, and wild pitches was Cleveland's George Uhle, in 1926. That year, Uhle walked 118 batters, hit eight more (tied with the Browns' Win Ballou), and tossed 13 wild pitches.

If you're a baseball history buff, you might recognize "George Uhle, 1926." See, while Uhle (known as "The Bull") was pretty wild in '26, he was also the best pitcher in the Junior Circuit. His 318 innings led the league, as did his remarkable 27-11 record. His 2.83 ERA was second only to Lefty Grove, but Uhle pitched 60 more innings than Lefty. If the Cy Young award had been around back then, George Uhle would have been a unanimous pick.

Uhle is one of the men credited with inventing the slider, but that didn't happen until late in his career. At this point, he was mainly a fastball-curve pitcher. In 1930, umpire George Moriarty said of Uhle, "When right, [Uhle] is a masterful pitcher. No predecessor or contemporary ever knew more about the science and technique of box work than this veteran."

That sort of testimony calls to mind cerebral pitchers like Curt Schilling or Greg Maddux; I wouldn't expect a pitcher like that to come close to a triple crown like this one. And while Uhle did hit a lot of batters in his career, his career walk rate was very good.

As one might expect, those 318 innings in 1926 took a toll on the Bull, and he was never quite the same afterwards.

The other pitcher in this strange little club is Hal Gregg, a tall righthander with the Brooklyn Dodgers. With most of the best players at war in 1944, the 22-year-old Gregg was pressed into the Dodger rotation. He led the team with 198 innings, but they were pretty awful -- his 5.46 ERA was 35% worse than the league average. Gregg allowed 137 walks, hit nine batters, and threw 10 wild pitches -- all league-leading figures. The Dodgers, an outstanding team before and after the War, lost 91 games to finish in 7th place.

Despite such an awful season, Gregg was back in the Dodger rotation in '45. This time, he was pretty good, too: 18-13 with a 3.47 ERA in 254 innings. He led the league in walks again that year with 120, but his walk rate dropped from 6.5/9 IP to 4.5/9 IP.

A sore arm (probably caused by overwork as a young pitcher) pretty much killed Gregg's career; he won just 13 more games. Gregg still had one more big contribution left for the Dodgers, though.

In December 1947, Branch Rickey sent Gregg, young starter Vic Lombardi, and aging star/racist Dixie Walker to the Pirates. None of the three did much for Pittsburgh, but in return, the Dodgers got Preacher Roe and Billy Cox. Roe went on to have six fine years for Brooklyn, while Cox became the regular third baseman for the Boys of Summer. A third player, Gene Mauch, went to the Dodgers in the trade, but his mark was made as a manager, not as a player.

As for Victor Zambrano, he wasn't all that bad in 2003, wildness notwithstanding. Zambrano went 12-10 with a 4.21 ERA in 188 innings -- not 27 wins like Uhle, but also not a 65 ERA+ like Gregg.

I'm going out on a not-so-far limb here and predicting that Zambrano will match his feat in 2004 -- he's the D-Rays' ace, and he'll probably top 200 innings this year. And if his first two games are any indication, the wildness hasn't gone anywhere.

Zambrano was traded from the Devil Rays to the Mets on July 31st. At the time, he was leading the majors in hit batsmen (16) and walks (96) but was 22nd in wild pitches (5). Shortly after being traded to the Mets, he was placed on the DL, losing his chance for another Triple Crown of Wild. This article originally appeared April 8, 2004 on The Hardball Times website at http://www.hardballtimes.com/main/article/the_victor_zambrano_award/

Visiting the New Ballparks

By Woody Studenmund

Since one of my hobbies is visiting every Major League baseball stadium, this is a great time of the year. I first completed my "collection" in 1975 or so, and I've kept up to date ever since. I just returned from games at PETCO Park in San Diego and Citizens Bank Park in Philadelphia, and I thought you might be interested in my evaluations of the new stadiums.

PETCO is a true gem. Set in the Gaslamp district just two blocks from San Diego Bay, PETCO is so close to the surrounding downtown hotels, restaurants, and bars that it even has a bridge from the second deck to the lobby of the Omni Hotel next door. The stadium itself is small (low 40,000s in capacity) but unique.

The outside is sheathed in a glowing tan rock facade that is quite different from anything I've seen. In addition, the structure of the upper decks at PETCO isn't continuous -- it's almost like three different stadiums broken up by fairly tall (and wide) light towers behind first and third. The stands actually come to a halt for these towers, and it's impossible for a fan to walk from one section to another. I've never seen anything like it.

Finally, and most endearingly, the stadium was built around a century-old brick structure, Western Metal Supply. It's a great idea. You can walk from new to old without a hitch, a portion of the old building is in fair territory, and each floor of the factory has been converted to a luxury suite, complete with an overhanging deck. My guess is that the Western Metal Supply building will become PETCO's signature feature, and deservedly so.

The field itself is free from gimmicks except for a fun "porch" in right field that juts out just left of the foul pole and then scoots abruptly back not long after. You can expect a ton of triples (off the odd angles) and some extra homers to dead right, but, except for that, the stadium looks to be a pitchers' park. Not only are the power alleys fairly deep, but the sea air seems to hold the ball up.

The amenities, including the food, in the stadium are good but not great, but all the other basics are fantastic. The sight lines are superb (though some seats aren't angled quite right), and the two upper decks are very close to the field and very steep. As a result, everyone in the ballpark (including those in the upper decks) feels close to the game. Given that, and given that the grass is real and the scoreboards are numerous, the overall feel is quite similar to Coors or the Jake. It's a blast!

Nothing is perfect, so it won't surprise you that PETCO has a couple of weaknesses, at least one of which really can't be fixed. What you notice first is a shortage of

bathrooms. I've been to many parks where I've seen lines outside of women's rooms, and I've even been to a couple where I've seen lines outside of men's rooms around the 7th inning, so I'm not expecting perfection here. However, PETCO is so short of bathrooms (and the bathrooms have so few fixtures) that there seemed to be long lines outside every men's room during every inning.

A second weakness is that it may well be too much of a pitchers' park. Time and time again, the deep power alleys combined with the moist, heavy sea air to convert extra base hits into flyouts. Whether this will change when the weather heats up is questionable, since the bay is so close.

The final and most important drawback to the park is that it doesn't take advantage of its location. If you're sitting in the stadium, you really have no idea that you're right next to a beautiful bay. When you walk to your car, you see craggy Point Loma, the soaring Coronado bridge, the huge aircraft carriers at the naval airbase, and hundreds of sailboats, but in the stadium, you might as well be landlocked. I understand that pointing the stadium at the bay might have caused some sun problems for someone, but it's still a shame to have had a chance to rival PacBell (uh, SBC) and to have dropped the ball.

Even given these drawbacks, however, PETCO is a smashing success. It's bound to provide a wonderful venue for the Padres long after the excitement of a new stadium is gone.

Eight days after I attended opening day in PETCO, I was at the first night game ever in Philadelphia's Citizens Bank Park, and I was immediately struck by a number of parallels between the two stadiums. They're quite similar in seating capacity, they avoid glitzy gimmicks, and they've got a cozy, "high quality" look to them. After that, however, some interesting differences grab your attention.

Citizens Bank Park is just yards away from a demolished Vet, but it's light years away in terms of quality. The outside of the new stadium is all brick, the insides are painted a Fenway green, and the seats are all deep blue. The seats are comfortable and well-angled, and there's a metal "Phillies" logo at the end of each row of seats. The result is a rich, textured, five-tiered "old time stadium" that grows on you without getting "old." It's clearly a fan's ballpark!

Sitting behind home plate, five magnificent attractions are all in view simultaneously. In left is perhaps the best scoreboard in baseball, rising high into the night with a huge script "Phillies" logo on top. Even better, the "diamond vision" portion of the scoreboard is the clearest

I've ever seen -- imagine a digital image four times the size of the Dodger Stadium scoreboard and you'll be about right. At times, I was tempted to watch the game on the scoreboard rather than directly … that's how unbelievable it was!

Off in center are the bullpens, situated side by side at different levels, so that they appear to be stacked on top of one another if viewed from home plate. In right center, the stands approach the field in a series of sharp angles (one on each of three levels) that narrow to a point, one seat wide, from which the occupant is literally surrounded by baseball … the field in front and the bullpen behind.

Behind all this is a food court, aptly named for Richie Ashburn, that outdoes them all (with the possible exception of Atlanta) with wonderful BBQ from "Bull Luzinski" (see Boog Powell), foot-long hot dogs, Philly cheesesteaks, and various entertainments. Finally, off in right field, there's a huge neon "Liberty Bell" that swings and "bongs" whenever a Phillie hits a homer. All in all, it's one spectacular outfield.

I suppose it's picky to point out that the stadium was opened before it was complete, so that the scoreboard wasn't fully ready and the floors had a distinctly unfinished and scruffy look to them. And it's obviously unfair to quote that architectural reviewer who derided the park for looking as if it were in a suburban mall. Considering that Citizens Bank Park is in a huge parking lot in South Philly, a suburban mall might actually be a good thing!

These quibbles aside, I do have two criticisms of the ballpark. First, the field level has too many seats and the slope of the aisles is too shallow; this results in some difficult sight lines and frequent "Siddown ya jerk" calls from behind. In addition, the extra seats mean that all the upper decks are too far from the field.

Second, as spunky as the outfield is, the regular stands and the field itself are almost completely lacking in individuality. I understand that we go to a stadium to watch the game, and I hate those gimmicks in Enron/MinuteMaid, but at least one quirk would have made things a bit more fun, no?

All that said, what the fans in Philadelphia have is one of the best new ballparks built to date. My guess is that fans will love this park as they loved Shibe … a great and personal place to watch the Phils.

Which new stadium, you ask, do I like better? Well, I like the two almost equally, but if I had to pick one (which I obviously do), I'd rank Citizens Bank a hair ahead of PETCO. Both, however, are superb ballparks. In comparison to the rest of the new Major League stadiums, they fit nicely between the true brilliance that thrives in San Francisco and Pittsburgh and the acceptable new parks that have been built in Milwaukee and Detroit.

My current rankings (with apologies to your favorite) are:

1. SBC (San Francisco)
2. Safeco (Seattle)
3. Wrigley (Chicago Cubs)
4. Camden Yards (Baltimore)
5. Fenway (Boston)
6. PNC (Pittsburgh)
7. Jacobs (Cleveland)
8. Coors (Colorado)
9. Dodger Stadium (LA)
10. Yankee Stadium (NY)
11. Citizens Bank (Philadelphia)
12. PETCO (San Diego)
13. The Great American Ballpark (Cincinnati)
14. Kaufman (Kansas City)
15. Skydome (Toronto)
16. Turner (Atlanta)
17. Minute Maid (Houston)
18. The BOB (Arizona)
19. Comerica (Detroit)
20. Angels Stadium (Anaheim)
21. Miller (Milwaukee)
22. The Ballpark (Texas)
23. Busch (St. Louis)
24. Comiskey (Chicago Sox)
25. Network (Oakland)
26. Metrodome (Minnesota)
27. Shea (NY Mets)
28. Pro Player (Florida)
29. Olympic (Montreal)
30. Tropicana (Tampa Bay)

That should do it for this year. I note with joy that only six unimproved old ballparks remain in the majors and that the Expos should be playing in a new stadium by next year.

PETCO Park's Park Factor was 0.84 last year, the lowest run-scoring park in the majors. This article originally appeared April 22, 2004 on The Hardball Times website at http://www.hardballtimes.com/main/article/visiting-the-new-ballparks/

Woody Studenmund is an econometrician at Occidental College in Los Angeles, but his main claims to fame (in order of importance) are that he is Studes' brother, was born in Cooperstown, and started the first play-by-mail APBA league (still going strong) in 1961.

Old Man Franco

By Aaron Gleeman

HAMPTON, Va., May 29 -- The Peninsula Pilots completed a six-game sweep of the Alexandria Dukes last night with a 5-0 triumph.

Paul Kiess, who entered the game batting .144, slammed a two-run homer in the third to start the Pilots on a four-run inning. Julio Franco's single and Will Culmer's double, both to left field, drove in the final two runs of the uprising.

-- *The Washington Post, May 30, 1980: "Pilots Blank Dukes For 6-Game Sweep"*

A 21-year-old Julio Franco, then a promising shortstop prospect, hit .321 for Peninsula that year. He went on to hit .301 at Reading in 1981 and an even .300 at Oklahoma City in 1982, before making his Major League debut with the Philadelphia Phillies that season. Following the 1982 season, in which he hit .276/.323/.310 in 16 games with the Phillies, Philadelphia traded Franco to the Cleveland Indians.

Here's a story on the trade from the December 10, 1982 edition of The New York Times:

HONOLULU, Dec. 9 -- After three days of mostly frustrating talks, trading activity picked up today at the winter meetings. The Cleveland Indians sent Von Hayes, an outfielder with a promising future, to the Philadelphia Phillies for five players, including Manny Trillo, an established second baseman who is 31 years old.

Besides Trillo, one of the best second basemen in the National League, the Indians received George Vukovich, an outfielder who hit .272 in 123 games last season; Julio Franco, a 21-year-old minor leaguer whom the Indians expect to be their starting shortstop, and two other minor leaguers, Jay Baller, a 6-foot-6-inch pitcher, and Jerry Willard, a catcher.

A little less than a month after the trade was a made, a boy named Aaron Jay Gleeman was born in a St. Paul, Minnesota hospital. Yes, that's how old Julio Franco is.

Franco did indeed become Cleveland's starting shortstop and he had a nice rookie season in 1983, batting .273/.306/.388 when .273/.306/.388 wasn't bad for a shortstop. He drove in 80 runs, stole 32 bases, and scored 68 times.

Here's part of an article from the November 23, 1983 edition of The New York Times:

Ron Kittle, the left-fielder who helped lead the Chicago White Sox to a division championship, today was named the American League Rookie of the Year.

In voting by the Baseball Writers Association of America, Kittle out-polled Julio Franco, the Indians' shortstop, and Mike Boddicker, the Orioles' pitcher. Kittle collected 15 of the 28 first-place votes while Franco received 8 and Boddicker 5.

Ron Kittle's final season was 1991 and Mike Boddicker was finished after 1993. Thirteen years after Kittle was done and 11 years after Boddicker hung em up, Julio Franco is currently batting .286/.412/.393 as a platoon first baseman for the Atlanta Braves. Yes, that's how long Julio Franco has been playing.

Take a look at some of the differences in baseball between Franco's first season, 1982, and Franco's 19th season, 2003:

	1982	2003
Runs/Game	4.09	4.61
League ERA	3.60	4.28
Steals/Team	149	81
Homers/Team	108	169
League OPS	.692	.744
Strikeouts/Team	858	1062

Homers and stolen bases basically flip-flopped, and offense went up about 13% in the process. Not coincidentally, the average team struck out nearly 25% more often last year than in 1982.

Dontrelle Willis was born about two weeks after Julio Franco made his Major League debut. Jose Reyes, Edwin Jackson, Joe Mauer and Miguel Cabrera had not even been conceived when Franco played his first major-league game.

Since Franco finished third in the voting in 1983, there have been 40 Rookie of the Year winners. 15 of them are retired. Of those 15, one is the manager of an American League team, one is a television announcer for ESPN, and one very briefly held the all-time single-season home run record.

A total of 82 people have been inducted into baseball's Hall of Fame since Julio Franco played his first big-league game. The two players the baseball writers voted into the Hall the year Franco debuted were Hank Aaron and Frank Robinson.

Old Man Franco

Players who were still playing during Franco's first season in the majors include Willie Stargell, Johnny Bench, Carl Yastrzemski, Fergie Jenkins, Gaylord Perry, Bill Lee, Luis Tiant, Joe Rudi and Mark Belanger.

The New York Yankees have a television channel called the YES Network. They use multiple color commentators, but their main guys are Ken Singleton, Jim Kaat and Bobby Murcer. All three were still playing when Franco began his Major League career.

Some of Franco's teammates on the Phillies in 1982 include Pete Rose, Mike Schmidt, Steve Carlton, Sparky Lyle and Tug McGraw. Also on that team was Gary Matthews, whose son Gary Jr. has played over 500 games in the majors and was recently let go by Franco's Braves. Mike Krukow, who is currently an announcer for the San Francisco Giants, went 13-11 with a 3.12 ERA for the Phillies in 1982 and was their starting pitcher in Franco's first game.

Dave LaRoche, a left-handed relief pitcher who played 14 years in the majors, retired following the 1983 season -- Franco's rookie year. LaRoche had a son named Adam while he was doing his second stint with the Angels. Adam LaRoche is now 25 years old and he is currently Julio Franco's platoon partner at first base for the Braves.

Okay, so I think we've established that Julio Franco is really old and has been playing for a really long time. He finally fessed up to his true age a little while back, which means he turned 45 years old last August. He'll turn 46 on his next birthday, but for baseball purposes, this is his "age-45" season.

We're not even a full month into the 2004 season, so it's obviously tough to predict what Franco's final numbers will look like. Thus far, he's hit .286/.412/.393 in 14 games. Assuming he can keep up a reasonably similar pace (Franco hit .294/.372/.452 last year and .290/.365/.413 over the past three years), is there a chance he could have the greatest season in baseball history for a 45-year-old hitter?

Well, the competition for that honor is extremely limited. In fact, in the history of baseball, only two 45-year-olds have had more than 100 plate appearances in a season.

Way back in 1897, Cap Anson had 497 plate appearances with the Chicago Cubs. And then, 90 years later, Pete Rose had 272 plate appearances with the Cincinnati Reds. And that's it, those are the only two 45-year-olds who had any sort of significant playing time.

Here's what Franco has to compete with for the title of Best 45-Year-Old Hitter Ever:

	G	AB	PA	AVG	OBP	SLG	OPS+	RC
Anson	114	424	497	.285	.379	.361	92	57
Rose	72	237	272	.219	.316	.270	61	19

I think it's safe to assume that Julio Franco will be better this season than Pete Rose was as a 45-year-old. Of course, assuming anything for a 45-year-old hitter is never all that safe. Still, Rose simply wasn't very good at all. After just 14 games and 34 plate appearances, Franco already has 4.4 Runs Created, 23% of Rose's total, and Franco will destroy Rose's performance in all of the "rate" stats like batting average, on-base percentage, slugging percentage and OPS+.

Beating Cap Anson is going to be significantly more difficult. For one thing, Anson played nearly everyday in 1897, playing in 86% of his team's games while accumulating nearly 500 plate appearances. While Franco may play in a similar percentage of Atlanta's games thanks to pinch-hitting, it is extremely unlikely that he'll even come close to 500 plate appearances.

For one thing, Franco hasn't had that many plate appearances in a season since 1997. For another, he had just 223 plate appearances for Atlanta last year and is on pace for just 290 this season. And finally, assuming LaRoche starts to heat up a little offensively (he's only hitting .212/.255/.346 thus far), Franco could see the starts he is getting right now dry up quickly.

So, it's not looking like Franco will be able to top Cap Anson when it comes to the counting stats like plate appearances or Runs Created. Still, there's a decent shot he could beat Anson's batting average, on-base percentage, slugging percentage and/or OPS+.

I bet that would be a pretty big honor for Julio Franco too, because I heard he was a big Cap Anson fan back in the late 1800s.

Franco finished the year with 361 plate appearances, 53 Runs Created and a .309/.378/.441 batting line with a 112 OPS+, according to baseball-reference.com. This article originally appeared on The Hardball Times on April 28, 2004 at http://www.hardballtimes.com/main/article/old-man-franco/

Adam Dunn: A True (Outcomes) Hero

By Aaron Gleeman

I've been wanting to write about Adam Dunn for a long time. To me, he is one of the most intriguing players in baseball, and guys like me have been expecting big things from him for quite a while now.

Back in 2001, Dunn had one of the best seasons you'll ever see a 21-year-old have. Between Double-A, Triple-A and the Majors, Dunn put up these totals:

G	AB	AVG	OBP	SLG	2B	HR	RUN	RBI	BB	SB
160	594	.305	.405	.633	40	51	128	127	100	10

What's not to like there? .305 batting average, 40 doubles, 51 homers, 100 walks, 10 stolen bases. That's just a beautiful stat line. The only downside is that Dunn struck out 156 times, but we'll get to that in a minute.

66 of those 160 games came with the Reds, with whom Dunn batted .262/.371/.578 with 19 homers, 18 doubles and 38 walks. As you can imagine, Dunn was in the majors to stay at that point.

Dunn started the 2002 season with the Reds and he was crushing the ball early. He hit .288/.433/.506 in April, .323/.480/.594 in May, .303/.417/.506 in June and .253/.452/.590 in July. He was at .300/.452/.544 with 17 homers, 14 doubles and 78 walks at the All-Star break, and it looked like we had a 22-year-old superstar on our hands.

Then the second-half of the season started, and Dunn suddenly couldn't buy a hit. He was still walking and he was still hitting for some power, but Dunn collected just 48 hits in 252 second-half at-bats, leading to a post All-Star break performance of .190/.339/.353.

Here's an interesting little tidbit from Dunn's second-half struggles: he drove in 54 runs in 283 first-half at-bats, but then knocked in a total of just 17 runs in 252 at-bats in the second-half. 17 runs in 252 at-bats from a guy who stayed healthy and batted almost entirely in the middle of the lineup is pretty damn amazing, regardless of how badly he hit.

A .190 batting average in the second-half will do some serious damage to season totals, and Dunn ended 2002 hitting a solid but somewhat disappointing .249/.400/.454 with 26 homers, 28 doubles and 128 walks.

Last season, Dunn once again got off to a hot start, hitting .253/.382/.627 with nine homers in April. Also like 2002, Dunn struggled in the second-half, hitting .255 with a .383 slugging percentage, while getting only 94 at-bats due to injuries. Whereas his hot hitting in 2002 lasted for several months, 2003's hot start was only April, so Dunn's final numbers looked very unappealing: .215/.354/.465.

Now, don't get me wrong, there are quite a few corner outfielders who would take a .353 on-base percentage or a .465 slugging percentage, but the first two full seasons of Adam Dunn's career didn't exactly look like many expected them to.

Fast forward now to this season. Adam Dunn is once again off to a very good start. In fact, aside from the freak of nature playing left field in San Francisco, Dunn has been the best hitter in the National League this year.

His 2004 totals:

G	AB	AVG	OBP	SLG	2B	HR	RUN	RBI	BB	SB
26	76	.303	.518	.697	3	9	21	19	33	2

That's a 55 HR/120 RBI/130 R/200 BB pace. I see that and all of those high expectations I had for Dunn start popping up again and I start thinking about what kind of incredible power and walk numbers he can put up in his career. Of course, then I remember that he came out of the gates strong in 2002 and 2003 too, and that didn't exactly lead to MVP-caliber seasons.

The other day I talked about Jim Thome, who got off to very slow starts from 2000-2003, but still managed to have incredible overall numbers when each season ended. Adam Dunn, so far at least, seems to be the opposite of that. He has done extremely well from the outset in each of his four seasons in the majors.

From his great MLB debut in 2001, to his outstanding first-half in 2002, and his .627 April slugging percentage last year. And then, of course, what he's done so far this season. Yet, for all of those good months and all of those good beginnings, Dunn is a career .244 hitter with a .489 slugging percentage.

Despite Dunn's up-and-down seasons, the one skill he has consistently shown, even through the struggles, is very

Adam Dunn: A True (Outomes) Hero

good plate discipline. Take a look at his walk rates in his various "halves":

	BB/PA
'01 2nd	0.133
'02 1st	0.215
'02 2nd	0.162
'03 1st	0.160
'03 2nd	0.158
'04 1st	0.300

Dunn is walking like a madman this year, but aside from that his walk rates look pretty similar. Another way of looking at that is to prorate those per-plate-appearance numbers over the course of a full season (~650 plate appearances):

	BB/650
'01 2nd	87
'02 1st	140
'02 2nd	105
'03 1st	104
'03 2nd	103
'04 1st	195

Unless he plans on becoming Barry Bonds full-time this year, he won't keep up his current walk rate. Still, if he keeps slugging in the .600s, he'll cruise past 100 walks.

While there is some fluctuation in those walk rates, compare that to his power by halves (using Isolated Power, which is SLG minus AVG):

	ISO
'01 2nd	.316
'02 1st	.244
'02 2nd	.163
'03 1st	.289
'03 2nd	.128
'04 1st	.394

Whereas his second-half walk rates have been fairly similar to his first-half rates, his Isolated Power is all over the place and has plummeted in his two full-season second halves.

The first question that comes to mind when I think of a guy like Dunn -- lots of walks, lots of homers, lots of strikeouts, struggling for huge parts of seasons -- is whether or not his propensity for whiffing is becoming more of an issue during his struggles. Well, let's take a look...

	SO/AB
'01 2nd	.303
'02 1st	.325
'02 2nd	.310
'03 1st	.348
'03 2nd	.277
'04 1st	.381

Dunn's strikeout rate is actually pretty consistent too. I certainly don't see much of a correlation between his struggles and his strikeouts.

Finally, let's take a look at Dunn, not by halves but by whole seasons:

	BB/PA	SO/AB	ISO
2001	.133	.303	.316
2002	.189	.318	.205
2003	.158	.330	.250
2004	.300	.381	.394

Aside from this season (which should probably just be ignored because of sample-size issues and such), there hasn't been that much difference, season-to-season, in Dunn's ability to walk or make contact. That's just the type of player he is; whether he's slumping or killing the ball, he's going to be walking and he's going to be striking out.

The real issue with Dunn, in my opinion, is always going to be his ability to hit singles. That may sound like a weird thing for a player like Dunn, but his singles-hitting is going to determine what his batting average will look like. And, with his relatively consistent rates for walks, strikeouts and power, that will essentially determine what kind of overall season he'll have.

Just by looking at his walks and power in his career, which have been very stable, you can see how different Dunn's overall production becomes when the batting average changes. If he hits .280, he's one of the best offensive players in the league (.280/.425/.550 or so). If he hits .250, he's an All-Star (.250/.390/.500). If he hits .220, he'll be hearing about all of his strikeouts (.220/.365/.470).

Dunn is the epitome of a "Three True Outcomes" player, meaning strikeouts, walks and home runs. In other words, the stuff fielders have no impact on. For a young player (Dunn is 24 this season) to be such an extreme 3TO hitter is pretty rare throughout baseball history.

Take a look at how Dunn ranks among all players in baseball history with at least 900 plate appearances through age-23 in regard to the Three True Outcomes...

Adam Dunn: A True (Outomes) Hero

Walks Per Plate Appearance

Frank Thomas	.194
Ted Williams	.189
Charlie Keller	.170
ADAM DUNN	.168
Eddie Mathews	.153
Eddie Yost	.150
Joe Morgan	.147
Rickey Henderson	.146
Harlond Clift	.146
Mickey Mantle	.145

The top 10 walkers includes Dunn, four Hall of Famers, one future first-ballot Hall of Famer, and another guy who I think should be a first-ballot Hall of Famer but (sadly) probably won't be. And then you've got Eddie Yost, who is one of the great walkers in baseball history, and two other guys who had good but not great careers.

Strikeouts Per At-Bat

Pete Incaviglia	.337
Larry Hisle	.329
ADAM DUNN	.319
Dean Palmer	.319
Reggie Jackson	.294
Bobby Bonds	.292
Willie Crawford	.280
Troy Glaus	.279
Sammy Sosa	.277
Rick Monday	.276

As you might expect, the strikeout leaders are a much less star-studded group. Reggie Jackson is the lone Hall of Famer, though Sammy Sosa will very likely join him there one day. Aside from those two, this is basically a list of good-to-very good players.

Home Runs Per At-Bat

Eddie Mathews	.073
Bob Horner	.067
Juan Gonzalez	.067
Harmon Killebrew	.066
Albert Pujols	.064
Reggie Jackson	.063
ADAM DUNN	.062
Darryl Strawberry	.061
Manny Ramirez	.060
Ted Williams	.060

The home run top 10 is pretty interesting. You've got four Hall of Famers and two of today's top sluggers. Then you've also got Juan Gonzalez who, while being very overrated, has been a very good hitter for a long time. Darryl Strawberry was perhaps headed towards a Hall of Fame career before everything went downhill. And, finally, Bob Horner, who started his career extremely fast and extremely well, and then was out of baseball at age 30.

By ranking 4th, 3rd and 7th, Adam Dunn is the only player to appear in the top 10 of all the Three True Outcomes rankings through the age of 23. Because of that, I think it's safe to say that no player in baseball history has gotten off to a better start on his Three True Outcomes career than Adam Dunn.

Adam Dunn set the major league record for most strikeouts in a season, with 195 strikouts in 681 plate appearances. He also batted .266/.388/.569 with a .303 ISO, walked 108 times and hit 46 home runs. This article originally appeared on The Hardball Times on May 5, 2004 at http://www.hardballtimes.com/main/article/adam-dunn-three-true-outcomes/

Making the Leap

By Aaron Gleeman

While watching the NBA playoffs over the past few weeks (that Miami/New Orleans first-round series lasted just slightly longer than the Tampa Bay Devil Rays' playoff chances), I've been thinking about a topic that my favorite sports columnist, Bill Simmons, often discusses: "The Leap."

Simmons is more of a basketball and football guy, unless it has to do with the Red Sox, but we'll forgive him for not being as obsessed with baseball as he should be. While Simmons often talks about this concept in regard to his two favorite sports, The Leap is something that works beautifully in other areas too. It can work in music or movies or even, as Simmons once discussed, dating. And, of course, baseball.

The Leap is, as you might guess, something a player makes. That is, an already good player enters a new level of excellence. Usually it is a younger player who, whether physically or emotionally or simply through experience and hard work, steps his game up a notch or two and enters a whole different realm of dominance.

About Len Bias, a tragic figure in Simmons' beloved New England sports history, he writes:

I almost broke an ankle hurling myself onto the Bias Bandwagon. There was one play when Bias drained a 15-footer, then came flying back in to steal the inbounds pass and dunk the ball behind his head, fluidly, all in one motion. I can't even really describe it. When somebody makes The Leap right before your eyes in sports ... well, you remember. You always remember.

In a column entitled "Beware the heartbreakers", on former Patriots wide receiver Terry Glenn, another somewhat tragic figure in New England sports history, Simmons writes:

With Glenn, maybe fate played a bigger factor than anything. Every time he seemed to be making The Leap, something held him back. The loss of Parcells. An untimely leg injury in '97. A deteriorating offensive line that couldn't protect Bledsoe. Constant double-teaming from opponents. Off-field distractions. There was always an excuse.

And finally, regarding Michael Jordan, a guy I think we are all familiar with, Simmons writes:

His fifth season, normally the season when a star player makes The Leap and starts scratching the limits of his talents.

Jordan carried a mediocre Bulls team during the '88-'89 season and carried a mediocre Bulls team to the Eastern Conference Finals (during a time when the league was extremely competitive, no less).

As a pure scorer, this was the year when he peaked -- his athletic ability was unparalleled; the referees were awarding him "Larry/Magic"-level respect; he would never be faster or more explosive; and he did whatever he wanted offensively. You needed three people to guard him. Period.

I've been thinking about The Leap as it applies to the 2004 baseball season. Which player is a prime candidate and who is showing signs of making The Leap right now?

Well, as I said earlier, Leapers tend to be young players, though not too young. They need some time to establish themselves first as simply good players, before turning into great ones. As Simmons said, somewhere around the fifth season is usually a good time. And in baseball, the general idea is that hitters peak right around the age of 27.

With that in mind, I bring you the guy I think is making The Leap this season...

Carlos Beltran/CF/Kansas City Royals/Age: 27

There are, I would think, two kinds of Leaps. One is a player going from being a good, solid everyday player to an All-Star. The other, more impressive Leap, is going from being a star to a superstar. This is when an All-Star turns into an annual MVP candidate, an elite player.

I think we can all agree that Carlos Beltran has been a star for a few years now. Though he hasn't been an All-Star yet (can you believe that?), he has been one of the better centerfielders in the American League for the past three seasons. He had his only top 10 MVP finish last year, when he placed ninth, between Vernon Wells and Bret Boone.

This is the year I think Beltran goes beyond that level. This is the year I think he becomes one of the best players in baseball. Perhaps not coincidentally, this is also his "contract year."

Beltran is really an amazing talent. Whether you want to talk about him as a "five-tool player" or a "seven-skill player," he's got it all. He does just about everything there is to do on a baseball field well, and he's a phenomenal athlete.

Perhaps his most overlooked skill -- and maybe his best skill -- is baserunning. Look at Beltran's yearly stolen base numbers and try not to drool all over your book.

YEAR	SB	CS	PCT
1998	3	0	100%
1999	27	8	77%
2000	13	0	100%
2001	31	1	97%
2002	35	7	83%
2003	41	4	91%
2004	7	0	100%

That's really quite amazing. His worst season as a base stealer was in 1999, when he was a very respectable 27-for-35. Take that year out and Beltran is 130-for-142 during the rest of his career, which works out to an incredible 91.5% success rate.

The funny thing is, if Beltran weren't so good at hitting doubles, triples and homers (the stuff that keeps him from standing on first base), he could probably be one of the great base stealers in baseball history. I'm referring to total stolen bases, of course, because Beltran already is one of the greats in baseball history when it comes to his success rate.

Caught stealing totals are a little sketchy (and often non-existent) in early baseball history, but take a look at how Beltran's stolen base percentage stacks up over the last 60 years (among players with 150+ stolen bases).

	SB	CS	PCT
CARLOS BELTRAN	157	20	89%
Tim Raines	808	146	85%
Eric Davis	349	66	84%
Tony Womack	318	63	83%
Willie Wilson	668	134	83%
Barry Larkin	378	77	83%
Davey Lopes	557	114	83%
Stan Javier	246	51	83%
Doug Glanville	161	36	82%
Julio Cruz	343	78	81%

Not bad, huh? For those of you wondering, the king of stolen bases, Rickey Henderson, is at 80.8% for his career (1,406 SB, 335 CS). The worst success rate? None other than Charlie Hustle, at 57.1% (198 SB, 149 CS).

While Beltran's base stealing has always been amazing, his ability to get on base hasn't always been that great. From 1998-2000, Beltran had an on-base percentage of just .327. As is the case with any player, much of his OBP was tied to the amount of walks he drew.

During his rookie season, Beltran drew a total of just 46 walks in 723 plate appearances, and two of those were

intentional. However, take a look at how his non-intentional walk rate has improved over the years.

YEAR	BB/PA
1998	.048
1999	.061
2000	.080
2001	.074
2002	.097
2003	.113
2004	.132

Aside from an extremely slight step back in 2001, Beltran's walk rate has been on a constant rise since he debuted in 1998. Even setting aside his numbers so far this season, he has essentially doubled his walk rate, going from .061 BB/PA in his rookie season to .113 BB/PA last year. Over the course of 700 plate appearances, that is the difference between 42 walks and 79 walks, or about 53 points of OBP. He's on pace for over 100 walks this year.

Along with the hike in walks, Beltran's strikeout rate is another sign that he might be stepping things up a notch:

YEAR	SO/PA
1998	.190
1999	.170
2000	.167
2001	.176
2002	.187
2003	.134
2004	.116

After whiffing in 17-19% of his plate appearances from 1998-2002, Beltran struck out in just 13.4% of his plate appearances last season. And he's whiffing even less so far in 2004, with just 14 strikeouts in 121 plate appearances (11.6%).

And, of course, as you might expect from a guy whose walk rate is rising and whose strikeout rate is falling, Beltran's strikeout/walk ratio has seen some pretty huge improvements:

YEAR	SO/BB
1998	4.00
1999	2.80
2000	2.09
2001	2.40
2002	1.93
2003	1.19
2004	0.88

You can see some fairly steady improvements from 1998 to 2002, then the big jump last year, and another big jump this season.

From 1998-2002, Beltran struck out 459 times versus just 207 walks, a ratio of 2.22 SO/BB. Then last year, his strikeout and walk totals were close to even, with 81 strikeouts and 68 non-intentional walks. Right now, Beltran is on pace for more walks than strikeouts for the first time in his career. He's on track for 99 non-intentional walks and 87 strikeouts this season, which is simply a great ratio.

I'm a big believer in improvements in plate discipline and strike zone control leading to positive developments in other areas. Like what? Ah, good question...

Isolated Power is a stat that takes a player's slugging percentage and subtracts his batting average, to show strictly what type of power a hitter has. Take a look at Beltran's ISO numbers over the years:

YEAR	ISO
1998	.190
1999	.161
2000	.118
2001	.207
2002	.228
2003	.215
2004	.354

It is my general feeling that someone is officially "hitting for power" when their ISO reaches .200 or better. Beltran has been at that level now for three seasons, and he's hitting for huge power so far in 2004.

In particular, look at his home run rates:

YEAR	HR/AB
1998	.000
1999	.033
2000	.019
2001	.039
2002	.046
2003	.050
2004	.081

Once again, a nice, mostly steady climb. It's unlikely that Beltran will continue to hit .081 homers per at-bat this season (that would put him on pace for about 50), but I definitely wouldn't put 35-40 long balls past him.

Perhaps the most telling stat in regard to Beltran's all-around improvement over the years is his Secondary Average. Essentially, Secondary Average is a stat that looks at everything a player does offensively, beyond batting average. In other words, it takes into account power and walks and even stolen bases, all of the "secondary" skills. Beltran's improvements here are undeniable:

YEAR	SecA
1998	.293
1999	.259
2000	.247
2001	.340
2002	.383
2003	.424
2004	.616

That's what happens when you have a guy who is getting better in just about every area of his offensive game. Beltran has gone from a great talent who was a good player, to a guy who hits for average, draws walks, controls the strike zone, hits for power and is exceptional at stealing bases. He also switch-hits and plays outstanding defense in center field. In other words, he has turned himself into the total package.

Since I mentioned the fact that Beltran switch-hits, I might as well point out his career totals from each side of the plate:

	AVG	OBP	SLG	OPS	GPA
as LHB	.288	.352	.481	.833	.279
as RHB	.289	.356	.495	.850	.284

As with just about everything else, Carlos Beltran is great at switch-hitting too.

One final thing to note about Beltran is that he has played his home games in Kauffman Stadium, a good ballpark for hitters. During his career, Beltran has definitely performed better at home. In 379 career games at Kauffman, he has an .863 OPS. In 373 games away from Kauffman, he has an .812 OPS. That's a difference of about 6%. His GPA gap is similar, with a 7% home advantage.

However, in general most players do better at home than on the road. Over the last five seasons, American League batters as a whole had a home OPS that was about 4% better than their road OPS. In that sense, Beltran and Kauffman aren't like, for example, Todd Helton playing his home games in Coors Field. During his career, spent entirely with the Rockies, Helton's OPS at home has been about 28% better than it is on the road and his home GPA has been about 26% better.

Okay, so let's see...

Base Running? Check.
Defense? Check.
Hitting For Average? Check.
Hitting For Power? Check.
Plate Discipline? Check.

Strike Zone Control? Check.

Ready To Make The Leap? Check.

As Bill Simmons might say, I wish I could buy stock in things like "Carlos Beltran will be the best centerfielder in baseball for the rest of this decade." This is what The Leap looks like.

Combining his time with Kansas City and Houston, Beltran batted .267/.367/.548 in 2004, with an ISO of .281. He hit 38 home runs and stole 42 bases while being caught stealing three times. He walked 92 times and struck out 101 times. In the postseason, he batted .435/.536/1.022 with eight home runs in 46 at bats. This article originally appeared on The Hardball Times on May 7, 2004 at http://www.hardballtimes.com/main/article/making-the-leap/

No Such Thing as a Free Pass

By Larry Mahnken

Lately, there's been a lot of discussion about Barry Bonds and the intentional walk. Bonds had walked 54 times through Sunday; 29 times intentionally, 37 times on four pitches. While Bonds' .628 on-base percentage is undoubtedly a good thing for the Giants, it's a fair question whether or not the almost universal practice of pitching around the game's best hitter is good for the game itself.

Many have dismissed the idea of changing the rules regarding intentional walks by saying that you shouldn't change the rules for one player, especially one who will retire in a couple of seasons. But the issue is not whether Bonds should be pitched to; it's a question of whether or not pitching to certain batters as a matter of course is a detriment to the popularity of Major League Baseball.

Fans, particularly casual fans, want to see Bonds hit home runs, or at least try to. While putting Bonds on base improves the Giants' chances of winning, it's also incredibly boring, and people aren't willing to put down their money to watch someone walk. There will be no fireworks or on-field ceremony when Bonds sets the career walks record, impressive though it is. Fans would rather see Bonds strikeout than walk, because it at least carries with it the possibility of a home run.

Even more, it doesn't really matter if this rule is put in place when Bonds is still playing or not. All Bonds has done is highlight a stupid exploit of the rules, one that

should be removed. This wouldn't be a new thing, but it is something that hasn't been done in a long time, because people have since viewed the game as "perfect."

The original Cartwright Rules stated: "Three balls being struck at and missed and the last one caught is a hand out; if not caught, is considered fair, the striker bound to run." A batter could take all the pitches he wanted until he got one he wanted to hit. A pitcher could throw the ball wide of the batter all afternoon if he wanted. It's not hard to see how this would slow down the game.

In 1858, the rules were changed so that the umpire could call a strike when the batter refused to swing at a "good ball," what exactly a "good ball" was being left up to the judgment of the umpire. This did nothing to prevent the pitcher from throwing wide, though, and in 1863, the "ball" was invented, and batters awarded first base when, in the judgment of the umpire, and after a warning, the pitcher had thrown three unfair balls before the batter had struck out.

The rule changes were made because the exploit was obviously being widely abused. But the abuse was the symptom, not the disease. Other exploits, like the stolen base, were kept in the game because they added something to it. Wide pitches and overly selective batters did not, and neither does the intentional walk. It doesn't matter if it's only being overdone on Barry Bonds, it's a bad exploit, and it should be removed.

No Such Thing as a Free Pass

If the intentional walk was banned, pitchers could get around it by throwing pitches wide of the plate, or in the dirt, accomplishing the same result. In a recent online chat, Rob Neyer suggested that all four-pitch walks be considered "intentional" in certain situations, but that creates problems of its own. Sometimes a pitcher will walk a batter on four pitches because he has no control, not because he's trying to pitch around him.

I would recommend making this something of a judgment call for the umpire, just as balls and strikes originally were, but more in the mode of the modern strike zone. My proposal:

1) A pitch striking the ground in front of home plate, passing home plate over the batter's shoulders, behind the batter, or in or wide of the batter's box opposite the batter, shall be considered an "intentional ball" by the umpire, unless a previous pitch shall have been a strike or foul, or two unintentional balls have been pitched. An umpire shall audibly call such a pitch an "intentional ball."

2) If a pitcher walks a batter on four pitches, three of which are called "intentional balls," the umpire shall declare the at-bat an "intentional walk."

3) If a batter walks and the fourth ball is thrown in such a manner as to obviously be intentionally wide of the plate, the umpire shall declare the at-bat an "intentional walk," regardless of the pitches that preceded it.

This rule would prevent teams from "pitching around" Bonds. Teams could still not try to get him out -- but they'd have to give him two pitches that he might be able to hit. There would be pitchers who'd try to pitch to Bonds but be so wild that they can't throw a ball that would be considered "unintentional," but in those situations, the penalty of an intentional walk is probably the least of your worries.

But what should be the penalty for the intentional walk? More importantly, should that penalty always be applied? The intentional walk has its utility, there are situations where it's a good idea to use it, and it shouldn't necessarily be eliminated because it's being exploited.

So I recommend limiting its use, not totally banning it. Rather than limit it to one per batter, or forbid it in certain situations (which will undoubtedly lead to much confusion and several mistakes by umpires), limit it to, say, two or three times a game per team, perhaps with teams allowed to issue an additional intentional walk for every three extra innings. You could use it on Bonds, but eventually you'd have to pitch to him. And by limiting them in such a fashion, it would encourage teams to not intentionally walk a batter until they really needed to.

As for the penalty, I would recommend that the batter be awarded second base, with all base runners advancing at least one base. A runner on third would always score, and walking a batter with the bases loaded would score two runs.

It's a not a rule change that's likely to impact the game very much, but it would put the bat back in Bonds' hands. Bonds will still walk 150 times a year, but pitchers will be put in situations where they have to throw pitches that, if they miss, could end up in McCovey Cove.

It'll hurt the Giants' offense, and Bonds probably won't hit that many more home runs than he does now. But at least he'll have a chance, which is better than what the fans are getting now.

Bonds set new major league records for most walks (232) and intentional walks (120) in 2004. The Intentional Base on Ball rules did not change. This article originally appeared on The Hardball Times on May 19, 2004 at http://www.hardballtimes.com/main/article/no-such-thing-as-a-free-pass/

Fiction Is Dead

by Larry Mahnken

Now it is done. Now the story ends. And there is no way to tell it. The art of fiction is dead. Reality has strangled invention. Only the utterly impossible, the inexpressibly fantastic, can ever be plausible again.

--- Red Smith, October 4, 1951

New York 5, Boston 4 (13)

If I hadn't seen it, I wouldn't have believed it -- and I'm still not sure I do. This was the type of game that makes you believe in miracles and curses, mystique and aura, and destiny. It had heroes and it had goats, unlikely comebacks and lost opportunities, highlight-reel plays and errors. It was the kind of game that makes you a baseball fan until the day you die.

And it began with a mismatch.

With Kevin Brown on the disabled list -- and now diagnosed with a parasite just like the ailing Jason Giambi -- rookie Brad Halsey was matched up against the great Pedro Martinez. Halsey had pitched a fantastic game against the Dodgers two weeks ago, but was terrible last Saturday against the Mets. Against one of the best hitting teams in baseball, with one of the best pitchers in the game on the mound, the Yankees' chances seemed bleak.

But the Yankees caught a break before a pitch was even thrown, as Nomar Garciaparra was given a day off to rest his Achilles' Heel, which had cost him a third of the season already.

And then Halsey pitched fantastically well, giving up only two hits and two walks through the first five innings, while striking out four. Pedro only gave up two hits through the first five, too -- but both of those went over the wall, and entering the sixth, the Yankees led 3-0, and an improbable sweep was in their grasp.

But now the Yankees started to make mistakes on defense, mirroring the bumbling of the Red Sox in the previous two games. After Mark Bellhorn struck out swinging, David Ortiz hit a fly ball down the left-field line. Hideki Matsui, playing Ortiz to pull, made the long run ... and missed the catch. Not an error, but a defensive miscue nonetheless, and the ball bounced into the stands for an automatic double.

Three pitches later, Manny Ramirez hit a ball off the front of the black center field bleachers to bring the Red Sox within one. That ended the night for Halsey, who walked off the mound to a standing ovation, and with Paul Quantrill coming in, and Tom Gordon and Mariano Rivera

looming, a reasonable expectation of collecting his second major league win.

But in the seventh, the Yankees' gloves cost them another run. Kenny Lofton was unable to hold on to a deep fly ball by Dave McCarty -- a ball that was in his grasp, but popped out and fell to the ground. Again, it was not called an error, but the damage was the same. "Euclis, The Greek God of Walks" singled McCarty to third, who scored to tie the game on a Pokey Reese double play.

And tied it would remain, though not for lack of trying. The Yankees put two on with two out in the bottom of the seventh, but Kenny Lofton flew out to left to end the threat. They loaded the bases with one out in the bottom of the ninth, but Ruben Sierra swung at two straight pitches over his shoulders, and Lofton again ended the threat, grounding out to second.

Again the Yankees got the winning run to third in the 10th, but Bernie Williams lined out to Youkilis, and now it was the Red Sox's turn to waste an opportunity -- in an unbelievably dramatic way.

Mariano Rivera had struck out the side in the ninth Wednesday, and struck out two of the three batters he faced in the 10th. But David Ortiz worked the count full and slapped a single into left field. Manny Ramirez then singled to center field, and as David Ortiz raced to third base, Bubba Crosby threw the ball past Alex Rodriguez, and Ramirez moved to second. Jason Varitek was intentionally walked, and the Red Sox now had the bases loaded with *nobody out.*

As unlikely as it was, they failed to score a single run. Kevin Millar ripped a 1-0 pitch down the third base line, but Alex Rodriguez dove and grabbed it, touched third base, and threw around pinch-runner Gabe Kapler *from his knees* to get the out at home. Posada fired back to third, and Rodriguez tagged Manny Ramirez.

For an instant, it appeared the Yankees had gotten out of the inning on a triple play, and Rodriguez protested the umpire's call that it was only two -- before realizing that by touching third base he had already retired Ramirez. Everyone had a good laugh, and Rivera got McCarty to fly out to left to get the actual third out.

The Yankees failed to take advantage of any of that momentum, though, and went quietly in the bottom of the 11th.

Again the Red Sox threatened with Tanyon Sturtze relieving Rivera in the 12th. Youkilis did what's made him famous, and led off with a walk. Pokey Reese sacrificed pinch-runner Cesar Crespo to second, and Johnny Damon singled to left to, once again, put the go-ahead run on third with less than two outs.

But Mark Bellhorn popped the first pitch to second, and pinch-hitter Trot Nixon popped a 1-2 pitch down the third base line. Derek Jeter raced out to make an excellent catch (in case you hadn't noticed, he's actually playing good defense this season), and his momentum carried him into the stands ... face-first into a chair.

Jeter came up dazed, bruised and bloodied, and was escorted to the locker room. With Jeter due to bat second in the bottom of the inning, and Enrique Wilson, their only other infielder, already out of the game, the Yankees were faced with the undesirable possibility of having to play someone out of position if they couldn't score a run.

Miguel Cairo delivered exactly what the Yankees needed, smashing a ball off the left-center field wall, reaching third when the ball bounced over Johnny Damon's head. With the winning run 90 feet away with no outs, the Red Sox brought Kevin Millar in from the outfield to play the infield, and the Yankees turned to the ailing Jason Giambi to hit for Jeter. But Old Wormy couldn't make contact, and struck out swinging. Sheffield was plunked, A-Rod intentionally walked, and the Yankees had the bases loaded, one out, and rookie Bubba Crosby at the plate.

Crosby worked the count full, but couldn't get the ball out of the infield, grounding hard to short. Pokey Reese forced Cairo out at home, and Varitek may well have made the double play at first had Cairo not come in with a takeout slide, clipping Varitek's leg and throwing him off-balance. It was all for naught, though, as Bernie Williams struck out to end the threat.

Now the Yankees had to make a tough choice -- who would they bring in to play the infield? Torre chose Gary Sheffield to play third, a position he had not played since 1993 -- and not all that well even then. To fill in Sheffield's spot, Bernie Williams vacated the DH slot to play center, and the Yankees were now playing by NL rules with only eight hitters, only John Flaherty on the bench, short reliever Bret Prinz and the starters in the bullpen, and perhaps the worst defense ever fielded by a great team.

But before all those disadvantages could hurt them, Manny Ramirez did, clubbing another homer over the left-field fence, and the Red Sox finally had the lead. After Varitek struck out, Sheffield made a nice pick on a hard

grounder by Millar, but overthrew Tony Clark for an error. Dave McCarty walked to move Millar to second, but with Garciaparra on the bench, Cesar Crespo was left in to bat ... and hit the first pitch to second for an inning-ending double-play.

It didn't seem like that would matter, of course. The Yankees had made 24 outs without scoring, and with Posada, Clark and Sierra batting from their weaker sides in the bottom of the inning, to be followed by Cairo and Sturtze, a rally seemed unlikely.

But apparently the Heart of Gold was in port, because last night the improbable came true again and again. Posada and Clark were retired, but Ruben Sierra was able to keep the game alive with a single into center. Curtis Leskanic, who had worked out of the 12th inning jam of his own making so brilliantly, now got ahead of Miguel Cairo quickly 0-2. But Varitek was unable to sell strike three, and Cairo fouled off the 1-2 pitch.

The next pitch was belt-high, over the outside part of the plate. Cairo went with it, and drove it hard into right-center. Millar couldn't cut it off, it rolled to the wall, and Sierra scored without a throw, and improbably, the game was tied. But it wasn't over yet.

John Flaherty, a 36-year-old backup catcher with a .669 career OPS, pinch-hit for Sturtze, and as Bret Prinz hurriedly warmed up, Flaherty worked the count to 3-1. And again, Leskanic threw it belt-high, over the middle of the plate. Manny Ramirez, turned, ran, and then slowed and watched it hit the warning track 30 feet from him, bounce into the stands, and end the game.

If it wasn't Yankees/Red Sox, if it wasn't such a crucial game for the Red Sox, it still would have been the best game of the year. That it *was* these two teams, that so much did ride on it for Boston, makes it one of the great games in Yankees history. It wasn't Bucky Dent, it wasn't Aaron Boone, but it was almost as exhilirating, almost as heartbreaking, and every bit as memorable.

There are people in this world who do not like baseball, there are people who find it boring. But last night's game showed, once again, why baseball is the greatest game ever invented; it will always find a new way to surprise you. Even a poorly played game like last night's contest can be a classic. If that's boring, then nothing in this world is interesting.

This article originally appeared on The Hardball Times on July 2, 2004 at http://www.hardballtimes.com/main/article/fiction-is-dead

Analyzing the Deadline Deals

By Aaron Gleeman

Wow. A lot happened since last we spoke. Rather than try to come up with some clever introduction, let's just get right to the trades ...

TO CHICAGO:	TO BOSTON:	TO MONTREAL:	TO MINNESOTA:
Nomar Garciaparra	Orlando Cabrera	Alex Gonzalez	Justin Jones
Matt Murton	Doug Mientkiewicz	Brendan Harris	
		Francis Beltran	

I don't think this was a good trade for the Boston Red Sox. Actually, I take that back ... If Boston was absolutely sure that either Nomar Garciaparra is more injured than generally thought and/or Garciaparra was simply not going to re-sign with them this offseason, then the trade is at least understandable. Still not a good one, but understandable.

The one thing the Red Sox have done here is upgrade their defense significantly, which is an area of weakness and a major issue this year. Doug Mientkiewicz is the best defensive first baseman that I have ever seen and Orlando Cabrera is, by nearly every metric you can look at, one of the top defensive shortstops in baseball.

So, if Boston GM Theo Epstein set out to make the defense better, he's certainly done that. They now have Mientkiewicz at first base and Cabrera at shortstop, along with Johnny Damon in center field and Pokey Reese as an option at second base. Their corner outfield defense will still be weak when Dave Roberts (whom they acquired in a separate deal) isn't playing, but they are now very strong up the middle defensively, which is always the biggest key.

Still, I don't think this was a good trade for Boston. Garciaparra, with all his injuries and faults as a player, is simply one of the best shortstops in baseball. He may never again approach the offensive levels he reached in 1999 and 2000 (when he hit a combined .365/.426/.601), but he has settled nicely into the .300/.350/.500 range over the last few seasons. Last season, Garciaparra hit .301/.345/.524 and ranked third among all major-league shortstops in Win Shares, behind only Alex Rodriguez and Miguel Tejada. In 2002, he hit .310/.352/.528 and also ranked third among shortstops in Win Shares, behind Rodriguez and Edgar Renteria.

There are differing schools of thought on Garciaparra's defense, but regardless of what you think of him in the field, he's clearly one of the top 3-5 all-around shortstops in baseball. In trading him, the Red Sox got two solid players, good defenders who have done well offensively in

the past, but neither are in Garciaparra's league as overall players.

Cabrera came close last season, hitting .297/.347/.460 to rank sixth among major-league shortstops in Win Shares, about 20% behind Garciaparra. And 2003 was far and away Cabrera's best season offensively, whereas Garciaparra has played at that level (and above) for years. Cabrera has been awful offensively this season, hitting just .246/.298/.336 in 103 games with the Expos.

Mientkiewicz is similar, in that he had a very nice season in 2003, hitting .300/.393/.450, but has been far worse this season, hitting just .246/.340/.363 in 78 games with the Twins. Mientkiewicz had the same problem a few years ago, when he hit .306/.387/.464 in 2001 and followed it up by hitting a measly .261/.365/.392 in 2002.

If Cabrera and Mientkiewicz play up to their full potential and more or less duplicate their 2003 performances, this trade is a decent one for Boston. They've swapped a top-five shortstop for a top-10 shortstop and a top-10 first baseman. On the other hand, if, as is more likely, Cabrera and Mientkiewicz play somewhere in between their 2003 and 2004 levels offensively, they've swapped Garciaparra for an average shortstop and an average first baseman. That is not a swap I'd like to make, and that's giving both Cabrera and Mientkiewicz the benefit of the doubt that they'll improve upon their current numbers.

However, there are clearly issues beyond simply on-field performance when it comes to Garciaparra, and it's difficult to say how much the off-field stuff motivated this move. Still, in the end, I think the Red Sox have traded away one of their best players and, at best, have made themselves just slightly worse. I am a big believer in paying (or even overpaying) for top-of-the-line talent and Garciaparra, with all his faults, is a top-of-the-line talent.

From the Cubs' point of view, this is an excellent deal, assuming Garciaparra is healthy, of course. They gave up their starting shortstop, Alex Gonzalez, and prospects

Brendan Harris, Francis Beltran and Justin Jones, while receiving Garciaparra and Matt Murton, Boston's first-round pick last year.

Jones is a good prospect and I like Harris quite a bit too, but Gonzalez and Beltran are guys they won't miss much now or in the future. If you simplify things and say that Murton and Harris essentially cancel each other out as far as value is concerned, then the Cubs just traded Gonzalez, Jones and Beltran for Garciaparra. While that's not an extraordinary trade if Garciaparra is only around for the remainder of this season, I think the considerable upgrade from Gonzalez to Garciaparra makes it a good trade.

And trust me, the upgrade is considerable ...

2004	AVG	OBP	SLG	OPS	GPA
Garciaparra	.321	.367	.500	.867	.290
Gonzalez	.217	.241	.364	.605	.199

2001-2003	AVG	OBP	SLG	OPS	GPA
Garciaparra	.305	.349	.523	.872	.288
Gonzalez	.243	.303	.406	.709	.238

Garciaparra has been about 45% better than Gonzalez offensively this season and was about 21% better from 2001-2003. That's huge; it would be like if the Giants replaced J.T. Snow at first base with Albert Pujols.

In the end, this trade makes the Cubs a better team for 2004. If Mientkiewicz and Cabrera play like they did last season, it doesn't necessarily make the Red Sox any worse, it simply makes them different. If Mientkiewicz and Cabrera don't improve upon what they've done so far in 2004, Boston has gotten worse, although they have helped fill the void created by Trot Nixon's injury by being able to shift Kevin Millar from first base to right field now that Mientkiewicz is onboard. Plus, they probably won't have to hear as many people complain about their defense, which is an added bonus.

TO NEW YORK:	TO TAMPA BAY:
Victor Zambrano	Scott Kazmir
Bartolome Fortunato	Joselo Diaz

This is just an awful, awful trade for the New York Mets.

Victor Zambrano is a back-of-the-rotation starting pitcher. He has fairly good stuff, but absolutely no clue where the ball is going once it leaves his hand. This year, Zambrano has a 4.47 ERA as a starter, with a 108-to-95 strikeout-to-walk ratio. Last year, Zambrano had a 4.23 ERA as a starter, with a 128-to-102 strikeout-to-walk ratio.

In 2002, he had a 4.27 ERA as a starter, with a 42-to-33 strikeout-to-walk ratio. See the pattern here? Mediocre ERAs and horrendous strikeout-to-walk ratios. And Zambrano's not even young; he turns 29 years old in August.

So the Mets just traded for a soon-to-be 29-year-old pitcher with severe control issues who has never had an ERA below 4.00 as a starter in the major leagues. And what did they give up for him? Here's where this deal gets crazy ... They gave up one of the best -- and perhaps the best -- pitching prospect in all of baseball, Scott Kazmir. And that's not all, they also gave up Joselo Diaz, who is an intriguing low-minors prospect with some potential.

With David Wright being called up to the big leagues a little while back, Kazmir was the crown jewel of New York's farm system. A first-round pick in 2002, Kazmir dominated the competition during his first two pro seasons, throwing 127 innings with a 2.34 ERA and 179 strikeouts in the low minors. After posting a 3.42 ERA in 50 innings at Single-A this season, he moved up to Double-A, where he had a 1.73 ERA in 26 innings before the trade.

Here's what Kazmir's done in three years as a pro ...

IP	ERA	SO	BB	H
203	2.53	259	82	149

How you look at those numbers from a 20-year-old power lefty who was a former first-round pick, has incredible raw talent, and has already reached (and pitched well at) Double-A, and decide to trade him away for a 28-year-old pitcher with a 4.47 career ERA is beyond me. It honestly boggles my mind, particularly because the Devil Rays aren't exactly known for ripping other teams off in trades.

I ranked Kazmir as the #8 prospect in baseball coming into this season and certainly, with the way he's pitched thus far and the fact that several of the guys ahead of him are now in the majors, he's a top-five prospect right now. You can argue that you like this prospect or that prospect more than Kazmir, and I probably wouldn't put up a fight, but he's certainly an elite prospect, the type of guy you build your pitching staff around. And not the type of guy you trade for someone like Victor Zambrano.

Honestly, if you'd have told me the Devil Rays traded Zambrano to the New York Mets for just Joselo Diaz, I would have thought that made sense. A mediocre, 28-year-old starting pitcher for a mediocre-but-intriguing 24-year-old prospect? Yeah, that seems about right. The idea that Scott Kazmir was just sent from the Mets to the Devil Rays in a trade that revolved around Victor Zambrano is enough to make you wonder whether or not you're following the same game as some of the people in charge of actually making these decisions.

Kudos to the Devil Rays, who just shocked the hell out of me by not only making a smart trade, but actually robbing another team blind. Tampa Bay already has an impressive collection of young talent throughout their organization, and Kazmir gives them another piece to add to the puzzle. They're in the wrong division to make waves, but the Devil Rays are going to be very interesting to watch in a couple years.

As for the Mets, they aren't the first team to trade away the future for the present, but they might be one of the only teams to trade away the future for a present that isn't even good. I mean really, Victor Zambrano? Rick Peterson better be a miracle worker. This trade has John Smoltz-for-Doyle Alexander potential, except Zambrano is no Doyle Alexander and the Mets aren't going to make the playoffs.

TO METS:	TO PIRATES:	TO KC:
Kris Benson	Ty Wigginton	Justin Huber
Jeff Keppinger	Matt Peterson	
	Jose Bautista	

Just to show that I'm not biased against the Mets, let me say that I think this deal was merely a bad one for them, as opposed to the horrendous deal they made with the Devil Rays.

Kris Benson is a better pitcher than Victor Zambrano, but his hype went off the charts over the past couple weeks, as his name was mentioned in a seemingly endless number of trade rumors. I've seen fans of my favorite team, the Minnesota Twins, gradually increase their rating of Benson with each passing day and swirling rumor. First he was a guy who would be nice to add to the rotation, someone to complement the team's #1 and #2 starters. Then, before I could figure out what was happening, he was a potential season-maker, a guy who would make a huge difference down the stretch and into the playoffs, a guy teams that wanted help in their rotation had to acquire.

And the whole time, I kept looking at Kris Benson's numbers and wondering if people were talking about the same guy. Yeah, he pitched pretty well over his last 10 starts before the trade, going 4-4 with a 3.01 ERA in 71.2 innings, but his ERA for the year was a thoroughly mediocre 4.22. He also had a 4.97 ERA last year and a 4.70 ERA in 2002.

Benson's best season in the majors came way back in 2000, and even that wasn't such a great year -- he went 10-12 with a 3.85 ERA in 217.2 innings. And not only have three and a half years passed since that season, Benson has had Tommy John surgery and missed an entire year (2001) since. He's a 29-year-old pitcher with a 4.26 career ERA whose best season, 2000, wasn't all that great to begin

with. Not to mention the fact that he then had major arm surgery and was out of action the next year.

Now, the funny thing is that I think Benson, despite all the stuff I just said about him, is a better pitcher than Zambrano. Yet, it was Zambrano who fetched one of baseball's elite prospects, while all the Pirates got for Benson is a decent everyday third baseman and two mid-level prospects.

Ty Wigginton is the guy the Mets have apparently been centering most of their trade offers around this season, which was smart on their part. Not only did they have a better, younger player at his position in David Wright, Wigginton simply isn't that good. He's versatile defensively, but he's not a good defender. He has a little power, but he's not a power hitter. He's not old, but he's not young. Wigginton is just a 26-year-old third baseman who is hitting .285/.334/.487 this year, after hitting .255/.318/.396 for the Mets last season. There are worse guys to acquire to be your starting third baseman, but Wigginton is definitely not the type of player you want to build around.

Even when Wigginton is playing very well for him, which I think is the case this season, he's only a league-average hitter. Wigginton's .285/.334/.487 performance so far translates to a .272 GPA. The average major-league third baseman has hit .270/.336/.446 this season, which translates to a .263 GPA. Even if you factor in that Shea Stadium is a pitcher's ballpark, Wigginton has only been slightly above-average offensively. Add in his defense, and the fact that he hit far worse than average last season, and I think I'd peg him as exactly an "average" everyday third baseman.

In addition to Wigginton, the Pirates also got Matt Peterson, who is a very solid 22-year-old pitching prospect. Peterson had a 3.34 ERA in 371.2 career minor-league innings coming into this season and had a 3.27 ERA in 104.2 innings at Double-A before the trade. He's big, he throws hard and he gets a fair amount of strikeouts, although his strikeout-to-walk ratio is not outstanding. I'd say he's a B-minus/C-plus pitching prospect who is fairly close to being major-league ready.

The second prospect the Pirates got came by way of the Kansas City Royals. Pittsburgh apparently coveted Jose Bautista, so the Mets sent Justin Huber to Kansas City for him, and then flipped him to the Pirates. The weird thing about all of this is that Bautista was actually in the Pirates' organization this time last year. They took him in the 20th round of the 2000 draft and he played three seasons in the Pittsburgh organization before the Orioles grabbed him in the Rule 5 draft this offseason.

The Orioles decided they didn't want to hold onto him all year (Rule 5 picks have to remain in the big leagues or be offered back to their original teams), so they put him on waivers, where he was claimed by the Tampa Bay Devil

Rays. A few weeks later, the Devil Rays dealt him to the Royals for "cash considerations." Yes, you read that right. A month ago, the Royals acquired Bautista for essentially nothing, and they just traded him to the Mets for Huber, one of the best catching prospects in baseball.

As much as I have to applaud the Devil Rays for making a rare great move and for ripping off the Mets by getting Kazmir for Zambrano, I have to give at least that much credit to the Royals for basically getting their hands on one of the top prospects in baseball for nothing. I have a feeling New York GM Jim Duquette called up Kansas City GM Allard Baird in a panic, saying he needed to find another prospect to include in the deal with Pittsburgh and the Pirates wanted Bautista back. I imagine the conversation went something like this ...

Duquette: I need Jose Bautista. Would you deal him?

Baird: Sure, I'd consider giving him up.

Duquette: Great. That's great! Okay, so do we have anyone in our system who you like?

Baird: Hmm, I don't know if I can think of anyone off the top of my head. I know we obviously like Kazmir and Huber ...

Duquette: Well, we're dealing Kazmir for Victor Zambrano, but I'd give you Huber.

Baird: Wait, what?

Duquette: Would you do Huber for Bautista?

Baird: Justin Huber, the catcher?

Duquette: Yeah.

Baird: [Holding his hand over the phone as he looks around the room to see if perhaps he is on Punk'd] Yeah, I could do that.

Duquette: Great, done deal. Nice doing business with you Allard. Thanks for helping me out on such short notice.

Baird: Okay ... no problem ... I guess. By the way, did you just say you traded Scott Kazmir for Victor Zambrano?

As I see it, the Royals are the only real winners in this trade. They gave up a mid-level prospect who they had just acquired for cash for one of the best catching prospects in baseball.

The Mets acquired a decent #3 or #4 starter who is a free agent this offseason for an average, 26-year-old third baseman who didn't really have a place to play, plus a mid-level pitching prospect and an upper-level catching prospect. Losing Wigginton is no loss, although he certainly had value, but giving up two good prospects for a dozen starts from Kris Benson seems rather foolish.

Of course, the Mets could sign Benson to a long-term deal, but they could have done that this offseason anyway. The only other way this deal gets better from the Mets' perspective is if they offer Benson arbitration, he declines and signs with another team, and then the Mets pick up a

couple of draft picks as compensation. Even still, Wigginton, Peterson and Huber for two months of Kris Benson and two draft picks isn't my idea of a good deadline deal.

As for the Pirates ... I can't say that this is really a bad deal, but it seems like a very unimpressive package of players to end up with after all the enticing rumors about what they had been offered and were asking for Benson. They'd have been much better off simply taking Huber, Wigginton and Peterson from the Mets, which would have made trading Jason Kendall at some point much easier.

TO LOS ANGELES:	TO FLORIDA:
Brad Penny	Paul Lo Duca
Hee Seop Choi	Guillermo Mota
Bill Murphy	Juan Encarnacion

When I first saw this trade, courtesy of a Lee Sinins e-mail, my immediate reaction was that it was a very good trade for the Dodgers. Then I started to go around the Internet, looking for reaction to the trade from others, and I was shocked to find that almost every "expert" and every fan of the Dodgers thought the Marlins robbed L.A.

While everyone spoke of Paul Lo Duca like he's Johnny Bench and Guillermo Mota like he's Goose Gossage, I didn't hear one person say or write something positive about Hee Seop Choi. In fact, most of the analysis of the trade that I saw barely even mentioned Choi. It was like he was the invisible man.

I saw former Cincinnati GM and current ESPN baseball expert Jim Bowden say that Choi couldn't hit breaking balls, and then I watched as Peter Gammons repeated the exact same thing with great authority whenever he spoke of the trade over the next few days. ESPN.com's Buster Olney wrote that "Choi hits homers and draws walks, but he had 78 whiffs in 281 at-bats this year, and he was hitting .238 with runners in scoring position; part of the reason the Marlins needed to make this trade was because rallies tended to die with Choi." Olney later wrote: "Choi has had the type of long swing that can get exploited by good pitchers."

After reading that, I thought maybe I had mistakenly thought of Choi as a good, young hitter all this time. So I looked up his numbers: .270/.388/.495 with 15 homers, 16 doubles, 52 walks, 40 RBI and 48 runs scored in 95 games with the Marlins. He was leading Florida in on-base percentage and walks, and was third in slugging percentage, OPS and homers. And while it's true that Choi was "hitting .238 with runners in scoring position," what Olney conveniently left out was that Choi had a .407 on-base percentage and a .547 slugging percentage in those situations, both great numbers.

Analyzing the Deadline Deals

While everyone was busy picking on (or not even talking about) the 25-year-old hitter with the .388 on-base percentage and .495 slugging percentage, I didn't see many people mentioning Juan Encarnacion's inability to hit any pitching or Lo Duca's .273/.335/.377 performance last year or the fact that he hit just .252/.306/.374 after the All-Star break during the past three years. All I heard about was how Lo Duca was the "leader" and the "heart and soul" of the Dodgers, how Encarnacion was "a good bat," and how Choi was either non-existent or worse.

Well, let me respectfully disagree: Hee Seop Choi is a damn good player. He's 25 years old, he has power and plate discipline, and he's been one of the better offensive first basemen in the National League this year. Just a few months ago, the Marlins valued him enough to trade Derrek Lee to the Cubs for him. Now, just a few months later, after Choi has actually been a very good hitter for Florida, he's just some guy who feasts on bad pitching, can't hit with runners on base, and flails away at breaking balls.

Paul Lo Duca is a good player, a solid defensive catcher who hits for nice batting averages and can play nearly every day. As for his leadership, heart, soul, and ability to create chemistry, I'll quote long-time baseball writer Ross Newhan, in yesterday's Los Angeles Times: "Chemistry, of course, is a mysterious thing, but it is worth remembering that Dodger chemistry wasn't worth much in the second half of last season when Lo Duca slumped badly, a management concern that was compounded by his falloff this June and July."

Chemistry, along with winning, is always a "chicken or egg" issue, as in which came first, the winning or the chemistry? This trade makes the Dodgers a better team and whether you want to call that the chicken or the egg, the chemistry will follow. You see, it has to, because as most mainstream baseball writers and TV personalities will tell you, time after time after time, all good teams have good chemistry. And the Dodgers are a good team.

They strengthened their starting rotation with Brad Penny, added to their offense (and their future) with Choi, and later used Bill Murphy, the third player acquired from the Marlins, in the trade for Steve Finley. The Dodgers' new catching duo of David Ross (a career .224/.310/.466 hitter) and Brent Mayne is unlikely to be as productive offensively as Lo Duca, but the addition of Choi and the fact that he allows Shawn Green to move back to right field, replacing Encarnacion, will likely make up for those offensive losses and then some.

Guillermo Mota, who was also sent to Florida in the deal, is a very good, very valuable player, one of the best relievers in baseball, both this year and last year. But the Dodgers clearly felt that their bullpen, with a combined ERA of 2.98, was an area of strength, so they dealt from it in order to improve an area of weakness, their rotation. Unless you believe that chemistry can come and go with one player and is more important to a team's record than hitting and pitching, this trade was good one for the Los Angeles Dodgers.

This article originally appeared on The Hardball Times on August 2, 2004 at http://www.hardballtimes.com/main/article/analyzing-the-deadline-deals/

Weren't These Guys Supposed to Finish Third?

By Brian Gunn

If baseball were played by preseason pundits, the Cardinals would have lost the National League Central by about eight games. Almost no one picked them to top the division -- no one at Baseball Prospectus; no one at ESPN.com; no one at All-Baseball.com; not even one lonely soul at The Hardball Times. Heck, I didn't even pick St. Louis to win the division, and I bleed Cardinal red (then again, most people bleed red whether they like the Cards or not).

Now, of course, the Cards don't have the division wrapped up -- there's plenty of time for them to go all '64 Phillies or '95 Angels on us. But they're setting a pretty nice pace. They're 30 games over .500. They're on track for 104 wins. They're nine games up on the Cubs. They're second in the league in runs scored and fourth in fewest runs allowed. They haven't lost a road series all year. And they just completed a stretch of games where they went a staggering 43-14.

To paraphrase David Byrne: "You may ask yourself -- how did we get here?"

In one sense everyone knows how the Cardinals got where they are. Scott Rolen, Albert Pujols, and Jim Edmonds are terrorizing NL pitchers, the Cards' rotation has been surprisingly solid, and their bullpen is stepping up large. But is there anything about the team's success that we could have predicted back in April? Is there anything all the prognosticators missed, anything that might teach us how to build a better ball club?

Here are a few possible lessons ...

Lesson 1: A Lot of Pitching is Actually Defense

Before the season started, the Cards' rotation looked much like Swiss cheese. Matt Morris was coming off a troubled 2003, Woody Williams was awful down the stretch last season, Jeff Suppan seemed little more than an innings sponge, and Jason Marquis and Chris Carpenter had just finished the year with a grand total of zero major-league wins.

But GM Walt Jocketty was very shrewd about the pitchers he kept and the new ones he acquired. He knew he didn't have enough resources to land a first-class power pitcher, so instead he stockpiled guys who had a history of keeping the ball down, in the park, and in the strike zone.

The theory was this: the Cardinals wouldn't strike out many guys, but they'd take advantage of the team's vaunted defense and turn a lot of batted balls into outs. And when the staff did surrender a home run or two, hopefully there wouldn't be enough guys on base to do serious damage.

So far the plan has worked beautifully. The Cardinals are near the bottom of the league in strikeouts -- only 6.12 per nine innings. But they've issued fewer walks than any team in the NL and they've more or less kept the ball in the park (the only hiccup: Morris, who leads the NL in gopher balls). Meanwhile, the defense has kept up its end of the bargain by turning more double plays than anyone else and gobbling up more batted balls than any team but the Dodgers.

The poster child for this approach is Carpenter. He actually leads the team in strikeouts, but his fastball isn't much to write home about. He succeeds because he gets a ton of groundballs (he's got a 1.9 ground/fly ratio against a league average of 1.29), keeps runners off the bases (only two walks per nine innings), and lets his fielders work for him (the team Defensive Efficiency Ratio when he pitches is .721 vs. the league average of .698). In turn, he's extraordinarily efficient on the mound, which allows him to pitch deeper into games without putting excessive wear and tear on his mending shoulder.

It's doubtful that Carpenter -- or really, any of the Cardinals' pitchers -- would be as successful with a different defense behind him. Does this make them worse pitchers? Maybe in some abstract sense, yes, but that's precisely the point. In the context in which they perform, Cardinals pitchers are highly effective. This is a textbook example of assembling a team holistically rather than discretely, whereby each player's strength is maximized by the players around him.

Lesson 2: Don't Underestimate Superstars

One of the tenets of Moneyball is that you shouldn't overpay for replaceable parts. But there's a flipside to that advice: you should pay, and sometimes pay dearly, for irreplaceable parts. And one of the hardest things to replace is a superstar.

The Cardinals have three no-doubt-about-it superstars on their roster: Pujols, Rolen, and Edmonds. Put together they'll make $35 million this year, more than the Brewers' entire payroll. But they're worth it -- so good, in fact, that they make up for a lot of mediocrities in the Cardinals' lineup. Here's where the Cardinals rank in terms of team OPS at various positions:

Catcher	12th
Second Base	10th
Shortstop	3rd
Left Field	14th
Right Field	13th

Weren't These Guys Supposed to Finish Third?

With all those holes in the lineup, how are the Cardinals second in the league in runs?

First Base	1st
Third Base	1st
Center Field	1st

Those are some Cardinals' OPS rankings that you probably know already: Pujols, Rolen, and Edmonds. Here's what they've each done so far this year, projected out to a full season:

	G	AB	AVG	OBP	SLG	2B	HR	RUN	RBI
Pujols	154	596	.323	.412	.636	44	47	141	119
Rolen	157	578	.333	.410	.611	37	38	115	147
Edmonds	156	527	.301	.411	.649	47	44	112	119

That's just astonishing, like having three MVPs, one after another, in the heart of your order. On top of that, each of these guys is among the top glovemen at his position. Pujols is 5th in fielding Win Shares at first (a former third baseman, he's very handy with the leather), Edmonds is 2nd in center (those SportsCenter "web gems" aren't just hype), and Rolen, of course, is the best third baseman in the league.

In the old, pre-sabermetrics days, sportswriters used to wax rhapsodically (almost hilariously so) over great players. It was as if you could just add Babe Ruth, Lou Gehrig, two cups of water, and -- presto -- you've got the '27 Yankees! Nowadays us wise folks recognize that a great team is more than just the sum of its great players. But I sometimes wonder if the revisionist movement among statheads hasn't gone too far. After all, you can't build greatness out of effective role players and spare parts; and in one respect the old-timers had it right: nothing is as useful, reliable, or predictable as a great player. And the Cardinals have more of them than any team in baseball.

Lesson 3: Stay Healthy

Okay, this isn't really a lesson anyone needed to learn, but team health really has been a key to this Cardinals team. Before the season began, the Cardinals looked as banged-up and holey as that dude from the board game "Operation." There were question marks about Williams' shoulder, Tony Womack's elbow, Carpenter's labrum, Ray Lankford's back, Marquis' elbow, Morris' shoulder, Jason Isringhausen's labrum, Pujols' elbow, Edgar Renteria's back, Rolen's shoulder (and neck), Edmonds' shoulder (and hamstrings), and Reggie Sanders' entire body.

According to most baseball folks, the Cards -- who have a number of key players on the wrong side of 34 (Williams, Womack, Edmonds, Lankford, and Sanders) -- should have buckled as the season wore on. So far it hasn't happened. The Cardinals have actually gotten stronger as the season has progressed, going 12-11 in April, 15-12 in May, 19-9 in June, and 20-5 in July. And they've done it all without suffering any catastrophic injuries.

I should note, however, that the Cardinals have not been entirely injury free. Renteria has a weak back, which in my opinion has limited his power. Morris seems to be playing with a bum shoulder, which puts a serious crimp in his fastball. Mike Lincoln, who had the lowest OPS allowed of anyone on the Cards' staff, is out for the year with a severe elbow strain. And Lankford, Williams, Mike Matheny, and Rolen -- who's been playing with excruciating pain in his knee -- have all battled various injuries. Nevertheless, Cardinals' starting pitchers have missed only one start all year, and most of the team's key players have answered the call day in and day out. That's crucial for an organization like St. Louis, which has been poor at acquiring and developing secondary talent.

So how have the Cardinals managed to stay so healthy? I asked Baseball Prospectus' Will Carroll this question, and while he noted the good work done by the Cards' medical staff with regard to Carpenter, Cal Eldred, and Kiko Calero, he also said their team health picture is largely the residue of dumb luck.

Fair enough. But I should point out that the same commentators who overplayed the Cards' injury risks in the preseason probably underplayed the shakiness of the Cards' chief competitors. The Astros, for example, are an old team, plain and simple, and it's no surprise that some of their best players have spent time on the shelf this year. Same goes for the Cubs -- they've got an old lineup and a fledgling pitching staff: a recipe for the DL if there ever was one. So yes, the Cards have been lucky when it comes to health, but relatively speaking that's not as unexpected as it seems. Which segues nicely into our last point ...

Lesson 4: Under Certain Circumstances, You May Expect to Get Lucky

No doubt about it, the 2004 Cards have been lucky. Not supremely lucky, mind you -- they're only one game over their Pythagorean win total, and they haven't been all that fortunate in relation to their performance elements (for instance, their record in one-run games is worse than their record in all other games). But the Cards have been getting a lot of breaks.

Weren't These Guys Supposed to Finish Third?

Some of them are scheduling breaks. The Cardinals played their last game against the Chicago Cubs on July 20, which means they played most of their games against their top rival with several Cubs on the DL (and without that Nomar Garciaparra kid I've been hearing so much about). The Cards also had a three-game set with the Royals right after they traded Carlos Beltran. They faced Seattle right after they unloaded Freddy Garcia. It's been that kind of season. Take the other night: the Cards fall behind 3-0 to the Giants; Jerome Williams is cruising on the mound. In the fourth inning, Williams strains his triceps -- he's out of the game. Enter the Giants' bullpen; dissolve to Cardinals victory.

So yes, they're lucky. But it's not as random as you might think. There's a certain phenomenon at work here, and it even has a name: the "Plexiglas Principle." Coined by Bill James, the theory says that any team that improves dramatically one season is likely to decline the next season. Conversely, any team that declines dramatically one season is likely to improve the next season. The thinking is that statistical glitches and quirks tend to smooth out over hundreds and hundreds of games.

The Cubs were classic "over-achievers" in 2003, finishing 21 games better than they had the year before. And sure enough, the improvement wasn't as rock solid as it might appear at first blush. Example: the Cubs were 27-17 last year in one-run games. The Cards, on the other hand, were a putrid 14-25. This year those numbers have reversed themselves. The Cubs have been on the bad end of some bad luck, going 13-20 in games decided by one run, while the Cards are 17-11 in such contests.

Some of you might be saying, So what? Luck is luck, you can't do anything but wait for it. But that's not entirely true. GMs constantly make rash moves by over-estimating or under-estimating their team's chances, so it's important to understand just how much of a team's success is "real" and how much is mere luck. Looking back on it, it appears that the Cards' mediocre 85-win season in 2003 was an anomaly, a downward blip between two immensely strong Cardinal ball clubs in 2002 and 2004. In fact, the nucleus of these teams is the same, suggesting that they're scarcely different ball clubs at all.

Fortunately, Walt Jocketty seemed to recognize all of this in the offseason. He didn't panic, he didn't shed precious commodities (even after several outfits, including the St. Louis Post-Dispatch and, I'm embarrassed to admit, my own weblog, urged him to unload Edmonds). Instead he made a series of small, pinpointed air strikes. He beefed up the bullpen simply by shedding deadweights like Esteban Yan and Jeff Fassero, and replaced them with Ray King and Julian Tavarez. He installed serviceable major leaguers like Sanders in right field and (it's time for us to fess up) Womack at second base.

Mind you, these weren't big deals, and no one is claiming the Cards' success is primarily due to Womack and Tavarez. But the Cardinals, whose constituent parts were better than their record would indicate last year, were only one or two decent players away from a kind of tipping point in 2004. Jocketty went out, got those players, and his team, much to the relief of Redbird fans everywhere, tipped.

This article originally appeared on The Hardball Times on August 6, 2004 at
http://www.hardballtimes.com/main/article/werent-these-guys-supposed-to-finish-third/

Enigmatic Disappointment to Superstar in 465 At-Bats

By Aaron Gleeman

Whenever a player has what I would call a unique career path, one of my favorite things to do is reconstruct his career, year by year, to create what looks like a more normal pattern of development. For instance, I've done this in the past with Troy Glaus, who burst onto the scene in his second full season, at the age of 23, hitting .284/.404/.604 with 47 homers, 37 doubles and 112 walks, and then essentially performed at a lower level each season thereafter (prior to this year, which has been very good but ruined by injuries).

While watching Adrian Beltre smack his 40th home run of the season Tuesday night against the Expos, I decided I'd do a little remodeling with Beltre's career to see if I could come up with something that resembled the notion of a career path we're all familiar with (improvement through the early 20s, peak around 26-29).

Beltre is a very maddening player to get a handle on because he debuted when he was just 19 years old and actually had his two best seasons (prior to this year) in his first two full seasons, at the ages of 20 and 21. Coming into this season, he was a 25-year-old who had hit just .254/.300/.421 in the previous three years, never getting his on-base percentage above .310 and never slugging above .426.

But if you do a little creative mixing and matching, you can actually make Beltre's career resemble a "normal" one:

AGE	AVG	OBP	SLG	OPS	GPA
19	.215	.278	.369	.647	.217
20	.240	.290	.424	.714	.236
21	.257	.303	.426	.729	.242
22	.265	.310	.411	.721	.242
23	.275	.352	.428	.780	.265
24	.290	.360	.475	.835	.281
25	.334	.380	.646	1.026	.333

Doesn't look so crazy now, does it?

You've got a 19-year-old who struggled during his first taste of the majors and then slowly improved at 20, 21 and 22, with his batting average rising each season. Then, at 23, he made his first big jump, boosting his OPS and Gross Production Average (GPA) by nearly 10% each over his age-22 season.

Age 24 brought another significant improvement, as his batting average once again rose, career highs in on-base percentage and slugging percentage were reached, and his OPS topped .800 for the first time. And then you get the big breakout at age 25, not hugely out of line with the age we usually associate with someone's "peak."

All in all, you've got a guy who came into the league as a 19-year-old and saw his batting average, on-base percentage and GPA rise every year, culminating in this tremendous breakout season we're currently seeing at the age of 25. The only problem, of course, is that the order I've put those seasons in actually goes like this: 1998, 2003, 2002, 2001, 1999, 2000, 2004. Or, if you prefer ages, it goes: 19, 24, 23, 22, 20, 21, 25. Basically, it looks like Beltre picked his seasons out of a hat or lined 'em all up, blindfolded himself and threw seven darts.

This type of career path, while weird, isn't totally unheard of, but Beltre actually has a couple interesting things that make his situation fairly unique. For one, his appendix burst while he was in the Dominican Republic prior to the 2001 season and the emergency appendectomy was botched. When he came back to America, he had all sorts of problems, ranging from not being able to eat and losing tons of weight to an issue with not healing properly. He eventually had to have another surgery to fix the wound, and missed the first month of the season.

So, if you look at Beltre with that in mind, you see a guy who had a very nice season as a 20-year-old in 1999 and then improved significantly upon that in 2000, hitting .290/.360/.475 as a 21-year-old in Dodger Stadium, which is tremendously impressive. With the knowledge of the appendix problems, the fact that he regressed in 2001 suddenly doesn't seem so strange. Of course, why he played just as poorly (and perhaps worse) in both 2002 and 2003 is another issue.

Regarding his breakout this year, one thing to remember is that this is Beltre's "contract year." In other words, he's a free agent this offseason and this season, more than any before it, is going to have an impact on the type of long-term contract he can expect to get. Now, I don't completely buy into the theory about most players doing better the year before they become free agents, but it's certainly worth noting in this case. At the very least, Beltre is guilty of impeccable timing.

For someone to have predicted Beltre's amazing breakout this year, I think they likely would have had to base it on believing some combination of these four things:

1) He was headed for stardom before being derailed by the appendix problem.

2) He is an incredible talent with amazing skills and athleticism that went beyond any of his actual, on-field performance.

3) He's 25 years old and it takes a while for a player who got started so young to truly reach his full potential.

4) He wasn't sufficiently motivated to play at his highest level until free agency was right around the corner.

Other than those things (or slight variations of them), I'm not sure there's anything that points to Beltre doing what he's doing right now, this season.

For instance, after averaging 18 homers and 49 total extra-base hits a season in his first five years and never having more than 23 homers or 55 extra-base hits, Beltre now has 40 homers and 64 extra-base hits in 120 games this season, putting him on pace for 50 homers and 80 extra-base hits.

Yet, if you examine his Isolated Power (slugging percentage minus batting average) numbers, there is nothing that sticks out in any meaningful way.

YEAR	ISO
1998	.154
1999	.152
2000	.184
2001	.145
2002	.169
2003	.184

This year his Isolated Power is .312, 70% higher than his previous career high.

If you think trying to figure Beltre's career out is difficult, trying putting yourself in the Dodgers' position. They've now had Beltre in the organization for a decade, including seven years at the major league level, and they've invested millions of dollars, thousands of at-bats and countless hours of coaching in him. They stuck by him through his various struggles and now he's having his best season, and perhaps one of the best seasons ever for a third baseman, all at the age of 25.

And in about two months, he'll be free to choose another team to play for.

Beltre finished the year batting .334/.388/.629 with a .295 ISO, 48 home runs and 80 extra-base hits. This article originally appeared on the Hardball Times website on August 26, 2004 at http://www.hardballtimes.com/main/article/enigmatic-disappointment-to-superstar-in-465-at-bats/

Ichiro's Edge

By Bill James

In the September 8, 2004, edition of SABR-L, Dan Heisman posed a question which seemed to me to be worthy of a few hours' research. As I cannot really improve on his phrasing of the issue, I have asked for and received permission from him to quote his letter:

Subject: The effect of stat frequency on the 162 game "asterisk"

The more frequently a statistic occurs, the larger the effect of a longer season. For example, the chances of breaking the record for most plate appearances is clearly more enhanced with 162 games compared to 154 when compared to the chances of breaking the record for Most Perfect games pitched in a season.

Many of the SABR-L members are statisticians. Is it possible for them to speculate how much easier it is for Ichiro to break Sisler's 154 game hit record in 162 games than it was for Maris to break Ruth's record? I would guess the answer is easier, but not dramatically so, but I am curious if anyone can give a quantitative answer to this question.

Dan Heisman
Baseball's Active Leaders

On a certain level, the question that Dan poses is obviously un-answerable. The impact of the longer schedule on the probability of a player breaking the home run record is different if the player needs to hit 62 homers than it is if he needs to hit 61. It is very significantly different if he needs to hit 65. The impact is different if the player's "true level of ability" -- his sustainable production level -- is 40 homers per 600 at-bats than if it is 45 homers per 600 at-bats. The impact of the longer schedule is different on every player that you could come up with -- thus, there is no general answer to the question.

Nonetheless, while we cannot make a perfectly objective answer to the question which covers a wide range of players, we can perhaps offer a reasonable answer to the question, based on reasonable assumptions. Suppose that there is a hitter who, in a typical season, given his real level of ability, can be expected to play 150 games (out of 154), bat 570 times, and hit 42 home runs. We will call this player "Roger Marix". What is the chance that that player, given a 154-game schedule, will hit 60 or more home runs? What is the chance that that player, given a 162-game schedule, will hit 60 or more? What is the difference between the two?

I wrote a very simple computer program to run that problem. In this program, it was first randomly determined whether or not Marix would play in this game, assuming that he should play in 150 of every 154 games.

Second, if Marix did play in this game, the computer randomly assigned him a number of at-bats for the game:

- 2 at-bats in 5% of the games
- 3 at-bats in 33% of the games
- 4 at-bats in 41% of the games
- 5 at-bats in 19% of the games
- 6 at-bats in 2% of the games

That works out to 3.80 at-bats per game, which is 570 at-bats per 150 games.

For each at-bat, the computer then randomly determined whether or not Marix would hit a home run, on the assumption that he should hit 42 home runs per 570 at-bats.

We will note in passing that there are many elements of the Roger Maris argument that this simulation does not deal with. This simulation does not deal with the fact that the expansion of the schedule may have weakened the level of competition. The simulation does not deal with the fact that one of the two new teams added to the league played in a band box. The simulation does not deal with the fact that Roger Maris' hair fell out and HBO made a movie about it. Roger Marix is a much simpler creature than Roger Maris. We're just dealing with one element of the problem, which is the impact of having 162 games on the schedule, as opposed to having 154.

I ran Marix through 200,000 simulated seasons of 154 games each. In those 200,000 seasons, Marix hit 60 or more home runs 806 times, or once every 248 years.

I then changed just one tiny element of the program, changing the season from 154 games to 162, and repeated the experiment. Marix hit 60 or more home runs 2,229 times, or once every 90 years. The eight extra games increased the number of times Marix hit 60 or more home runs by 177%.

I then created a comparable "clone" for Ichiro -- Ichirox -- using the same program, but just very slightly different parameters. Like Marix, Ichirox played in 150 of every 154 games, on average -- some seasons 154, some seasons 140, but 150 on average. Ichirox had more at-bats per game:

- 2 at-bats in 2% of the games

- 3 at-bats in 20% of the games
- 4 at-bats in 41.5% of the games
- 5 at-bats in 27.5% of the games
- 6 at-bats in 8% of the games
- 7 at-bats in 1% of the games

That works out to 4.225 at-bats per game, which is 634 at-bats per 150 games, or 651 at-bats per 154 games, or 684 at-bats per 162 games. Ichirox hits .350 overall -- .400 once in a great while, .299 some seasons, but .350 overall.

In this study, Ichirox collected 257 or more hits in a 154-game schedule 845 times in 200,000 seasons -- essentially the same as the frequency with which Marix hit 60 or more homers. This was the operating assumption -- I actually had to re-run the study several times and jiggle the numbers to make it come out in that area, so that we would have a basis to compare the effect of the longer schedule on Ichirox vs. Marix. Ichirox had 257 or more hits 845 times, which is once every 237 years.

I then changed one number in the program, changing the season from 154 games to 162, and re-ran the study.

Given the eight extra games, Ichirox tied or broke Sisler's record 8,462 times in 200,000 seasons, or once every 24 years. Whereas the longer schedule increased Marix' chance of breaking or tying Ruth's record by 177%, it increased Ichirox' chance of breaking or tying Sisler's record by 901%.

For me to try to tell you how surprised I am by this answer would be a waste of my time and yours, but ... I certainly did not expect this. Heisman speculated that it would be "easier, but not dramatically so." I would have agreed. In fact, the impact is (about) five times greater on Ichiro than it was on Maris.

The irony is that whereas the extra eight games on the schedule created a mega-furor when Maris broke Ruth's record, the same factor is being almost totally ignored as Ichiro gets set to cruise past Sisler, even though this edge was a hamster for Maris, and is a gorilla for Ichiro. The reason for the muted reaction, of course, is that, when Maris had his moment broiling in the sun, the 162-game schedule was new, and thus controversial. But most of you reading this weren't even born then, and the 162-game schedule has long since ceased to be a curiosity. On the one hand, the 162-game schedule has been around so long, and so many players have already "had" Ichiro's advantage, that this no longer seems to be any big deal, while on the other hand, Barry Bonds in the last few years has so thoroughly trashed the record book that we're all sort of numb to it. Nobody cares about that stuff anymore.

One other note. I also kept track of the frequency with which Ichirox would hit .400, just because this seemed like an obvious thing to want to know. In 200,000 seasons, Ichirox hit .400 or better 809 times -- essentially the same as the frequency with which Marix or Ichirox would break their respective "counting" records in a 154-game schedule. But, of course, as the longer schedule makes it easier to collect 257 hits, it makes it harder to maintain a .400 average. On the 154-game schedule, Ichirox hit .400 or better 954 times, or about 18% more often.

Maybe that is next year's story; maybe next year Ichiro will miss 40 games with an injury, and hit .410 in the other 122. A friend of mine claims that it is obviously impossible for a modern hitter to hit .400, because, if it could be done, Barry Bonds . would have done it by now.

Bill James, Chairman Emeritus
Swift Boat Veterans for Kevin Youkilis

Ichiro broke Sisler's record in the 160th game of the season, and finished with 262 hits. This article originally appeared on the Hardball Times website on September 13, 2004 at http://www.hardballtimes.com/main/article/ichiros-edge/.

Bill James is the author of many superb baseball books, including the Historical Baseball Abstracts. He is currently employed by the Boston Red Sox.

Timing is Everything

By Ben Jacobs

I was watching the Yankees-Royals game on TV Wednesday afternoon when they gave the scouting report for Darrell May and mentioned that he had 17 losses this season. I was shocked, not because I thought May was a better pitcher than that, but because I hadn't heard anything this year about anybody approaching 20 losses.

I hopped on the ol' Internet, checked the league leaders and saw that May was leading the majors in losses thanks to a five-start losing streak. He only gave up three runs in 6.1 innings against the Yankees, but that was enough for his sixth consecutive loss and 18th of the season.

With 17 games left on the schedule for Kansas City, May should get three more starts. He only needs to lose two of them to reach 20 losses. But even if he loses his next one, Brian Kingman won't be flying to Chicago or Kansas City to jinx May's attempt at No. 20.

The reason, of course, is that Mike Maroth lost 21 games last year, becoming the first pitcher to lose at least 20 games in a season since Kingman did it in 1980. And now nobody cares if a pitcher loses 20 games. At least not for that specific reason.

This is a good thing, because there's nothing inherently wrong with losing 20 games. You generally need to pitch badly to do so, but the number itself doesn't transform your season from bad to disastrous. There's no appreciable difference between losing 20 games and losing 19 games, which at least one pitcher did in seven of the full seasons between Kingman and Maroth.

But people see a nice round number and they notice that it hasn't been reached in a long time and they decide that it must be a really bad thing to do. So several pitchers over the last few years had their spot in the rotation toyed with to provide fewer opportunities to lose that 20th game and several more pitchers had to answer stupid questions about pitching in the shadow of 20 losses and Jayson Stark wrote several columns featuring Kingman.

Maroth didn't have his spot in the rotation toyed with, but he did have to answer plenty of stupid questions and Stark did write plenty of columns featuring Kingman. May probably won't have to answer any of those questions and Stark certainly won't be writing any columns featuring Kingman, and hopefully May won't have his spot in the rotation toyed with.

May's not having a good season, but he hasn't been terrible. He's 9-18 with a 5.48 ERA and 1.55 WHIP and he's averaging 5.74 K/9IP and 2.74 BB/9IP. The only acceptable reason to remove him from the rotation is to give a young pitcher a chance to show what he's got.

However, three of the other members of Kansas City's rotation have pitched worse than May, so one of them should get the boot if there's a youngster in the Royals organization who simply must have a major-league start this year.

I will be very happy if May gets all three of the starts he's entitled to the rest of this season, whether he wins them all or loses them all. He gives Kansas City a better chance to win than anybody they could use in his place, and it's just stupid to hurt your team's chances of winning (even when the season's a total loss) to prevent a player from reaching a stat that isn't all that bad.

Take a look at May's line (listed first) compared with another AL pitcher this season:

G	IP	H	ER	BB	SO	ERA
28	174	217	106	53	111	5.48
28	171.1	205	105	61	105	5.52

Esteban Loaiza has a winning record (9-7), while May has a chance to lose 20 games. But is there much of a difference between what they've done this year? Loaiza has already lost his spot in the rotation because the Yankees have (at least) five pitchers who are better than him.

If the Royals have five pitchers who are better than May, then they should replace him. But they don't, so they shouldn't, whether he might lose 20 games or not. And I don't think they will replace him, thanks to Maroth.

For a similar reason, I'm hoping Adam Dunn strikes out 19 more times this season. The record for strikeouts in a season, of course, is held by Bobby Bonds with 189 in 1970.

Since 2000, there have been six instances in which a player struck out more than 180 times, but did not reach Bonds' mark. In some of those instances, the player in question got some days off near the end of the season specifically to reduce his chances of breaking the record.

As stupid as it is to pull a pitcher from the rotation because he's about to lose 20 games, this is worse. You pretty much have to be having a bad season (these days, anyway) to have a shot at losing 20 games. You can set the single-season record for strikeouts and still be having a good season.

Jose Hernandez was having a good season when he struck out 188 times in 2002. He "missed" eight of the Brewers last 11 games that season, and Milwaukee lost six of those eight games. Would the Brewers have won any of them with Hernandez in the lineup? Nobody knows, but they certainly would have had a better chance, and their fans should have been irate that he wasn't.

Preston Wilson was having a fine season when he struck out 187 times in 2000. In two of Florida's last five games, he only entered the game as a pinch-hitter. His final strikeout came in the final game in the season, and one can only surmise that if he had reached 187 -- or 188 -- sooner, he might have seen more time on the bench.

Dunn has 171 strikeouts, which puts him on pace for 191 on the season. He also has 42 home runs, a .398 on-base percentage and a .581 slugging percentage. Along with Sean Casey, he's been far and away one of Cincinnati's two best players this season. If he gets

benched at all down the stretch because he's approaching a record that seems pretty bad, his manager should be fired, plain and simple.

A manager's job is to win ballgames. You do that by using the best players available to you, no matter what numbers he's getting close to. Dunn is the best player the Reds have available to play his position, and it shouldn't make a difference whether he strikes out 175 times or 200 times this season.

It looks like Maroth's milestone last year may have rid managers of the need to sit pitchers who are approaching 20 losses. Hopefully, Dunn can do the same thing for the need to sit hitters who are approaching Bonds' record for strikeouts in a season.

Darrell May finished the year with nine wins and nineteen losses. He skipped his final turn in the rotation. Adam Dunn broke the strikeout record with 195 strikeouts. This article originally appeared on The Hardball Times on September 16, 2004 at http://www.hardballtimes.com/main/article/timing-is-everything/

Cy Santana

By Aaron Gleeman

If there was any doubt about who the best pitcher in the world is, hopefully Johan Santana erased most of it yesterday afternoon. With the Twins on the verge of clinching their third straight American League Central championship, Santana tossed eight shutout innings against the Orioles, striking out 14 Baltimore hitters without issuing a walk.

Santana threw 78 of his 103 pitches for strikes on his way to increasing his scoreless innings streak to 30. He has now won 12 straight decisions, including wins in 11 straight starts, and has not lost since July 11, when he gave up two runs to the Tigers and the Twins' offense came up empty. Yesterday's dominant outing was his 20th consecutive Quality Start.

Santana improved to 19-6 on the season, raised his league-leading strikeout total to 254, and lowered his major league-leading ERA to 2.65. He is 12-0 with a 1.16 ERA (yes, 1.16) since the All-Star break, a span of 13 starts in which he has 118 strikeouts, 18 walks, and just 51 hits allowed. And since the beginning of June, Santana is 17-3 with a 1.50 ERA in 21 starts, with 200 strikeouts in 156 innings pitched.

Just in case all of that didn't convince you and you need some more evidence, here's how Santana compares to the guy some people mistakenly think is a legitimate Cy Young candidate, Curt Schilling ...

	IP	ERA	RA/9	SO	BB	OAVG	QS
Santana	217.0	2.65	2.82	254	49	.194	24
Schilling	211.2	3.40	3.49	183	30	.249	20

It's not that Schilling has been bad, because he's actually been fantastic this year. It's just that no one comes close to Santana. Santana has thrown more innings than Schilling, and has been 22.1% better preventing earned runs and 19.2% better preventing runs, period. Santana has 38.8% more strikeouts, has held opponents to a batting average that is 55 points and 22.1% better than what batters have hit off of Schilling, and has more Quality Starts.

Here are some more numbers for you to chew on ...

	OBP	SLG	OPS	GPA	RSAA	WS	WSAA
Santana	.248	.317	.565	.191	48	25	13
Schilling	.277	.406	.683	.226	36	19	7

Santana has been 10.5% better than Schilling at keeping runners off base, his slugging percentage allowed is 21.9% better, and his total offense allowed is either 17.3% better or 15.5% better than Schilling's, depending on if you'd rather use OPS allowed or Gross Production Average (GPA) allowed.

Moving on to some of the more advanced metrics, you can see that Santana has a 33.3% advantage in Runs Saved Above Average (RSAA), a 31.5% lead in Win Shares (WS), and is blowing Schilling away in Win Shares Above Average (WSAA), 13 to seven. And the amazing thing is that, because all of those advanced metrics aren't updated as frequently as regular stats, those totals are from before Santana's 14-strikeout masterpiece against the Orioles.

A pitcher's job is quite simple: throw as many innings as you can and give up as few runs as you can, and Santana has been better than Schilling at both those things in 2004.

In fact, the only significant thing Schilling has done better than Santana this year is receive better run support, which has led to Schilling winning 20 games and Santana winning 19.

Quite simply, Schilling pitches for a team with a great offense and Santana pitches for a team with a lineup that has struggled for much of the season, so Schilling has a slightly higher total in the one number most baseball fans (and far too many mainstream media members) look to first for pitchers. Unfortunately, what they don't look at is that wins and losses for pitchers come not only from what they do on the mound, but from the support their offense provides them, which is something AL pitchers have absolutely no control over.

Schilling has received the most run support in the American League, with the Red Sox scoring 7.57 runs per nine innings while he's on the mound. Meanwhile, Santana has gotten just 5.51 runs of support per nine innings from the Twins, 27.2% fewer runs to work with than Schilling has received. You give Schilling's run support to Santana and Santana's run support to Schilling, and not only isn't this even a contest, Santana is probably being hyped as a legitimate MVP candidate (which he is anyway, but that's another issue).

If Schilling does end up taking Santana's Cy Young award this year, it will be just about all you need to know about the mainstream media's obsession with pitchers' wins. By any objective measure that does not rely on the amount of support a pitcher has gotten from his offense -- something the pitcher has absolutely no control over, particularly in the American League -- Santana has been significantly better than Schilling.

In fact, this could be one of those times when the side someone takes in a debate is a way to determine what kind of person they are, and whether or not your world view is at all compatible. Ask someone the age-old question of "Bull Durham or Field of Dreams?" and you can get a pretty good feel for whether or not the two of you can get along. The same thing goes for the equally-important "Britney or Christina?" quandary, and, of course, the always-dangerous, "Who are you voting for?"

"Santana or Schilling?" has the potential to be one of those questions. I know for me, I hope to find out which voters cast their ballot for Schilling, so that I can avoid reading their work for the rest of my life. Because in my mind, anyone who sees what Santana and Schilling have done this year and comes away thinking anything other than that Santana has been the better pitcher is completely undeserving of an audience, and probably should have a scarlet "W" permanently placed on their press-pass.

And if for some reason you need even more evidence that I'm right, consider that John Kruk and Jeff Brantley are in complete agreement that Schilling deserves the award.

This article originally appeared on The Hardball Times on September 20, 2004 at http://www.hardballtimes.com/main/article/cy-santana/

Contemplating the Baseball Cosmos

Stop and Smell the Roses

By Larry Mahnken

Whether or not you think Barry Bonds is the greatest player who ever lived is wholly subjective. I, for one, am still partial to Babe Ruth, because he did it in an era when home runs were rare, was more valuable over the course of his career than Bonds (or anyone else for that matter), was an elite pitcher at the beginning of his career, and, of course, was a Yankee.

But you can counter with the facts that black players were barred from the game, that home runs were rare in that era largely because no other players were trying to hit them like Ruth was, that he was a good pitcher, but a poor defensive player (while Bonds was excellent in his prime), and that the Yankees suck. All fair points, but I'll still go with Ruth. As I said, it's wholly subjective.

Whether or not he's the best player in the game today is not. People say that Alex Rodriguez (in spite of his dreadful start) is the best all-around player in baseball, because Barry doesn't run anymore, isn't a Gold-Glove fielder anymore, and plays a far less valuable position than A-Rod does.

No matter -- Bonds' value at the plate is so incredible that Rodriguez would have to win the Gold Glove at both third base and shortstop this year to match it. Nobody even comes close to Barry, and unless he gets hurt, another MVP is a foregone conclusion -- or it should be, but we know how the writers like to complicate things.

What Bonds has been doing so far this season makes one wonder not whether he'll break Hank Aaron's record, but whether he'll do it this season. Seriously, of course he'll slow down, but a slump for Barry is what most players would consider a hot streak.

Aaron Gleeman previously talked about Barry hitting .400, and he may well. Despite what many analysts have said before, Barry Bonds is exactly the type of player who has the best chance to hit .400 -- he walks a lot (minimizing the number of at-bats), hits a lot of home runs (hits with no chance of becoming outs), and doesn't strike out much (minimizing the number of outs without a chance for a hit). More likely than Bonds hitting .400 is another run at the single-season home run record, which, if he approaches it, would make the breaking of Hank Aaron's record next season a virtual lock.

What Bonds has done the past few seasons is simply awe-inspiring, and 50 years ago sportswriters would have been falling all over each other to come up with new metaphors to describe him. But these days, the media seems more interested in tearing down heroes than building them up, and Bonds' media-unfriendly attitude doesn't do much to dissuade them.

Is Barry Bonds on steroids? There are plenty of reasons to be suspicious: he's freakishly huge, and gained much of that weight in a relatively short time. He's experienced an astounding late-career surge, and his past three seasons may have been the three single greatest offensive seasons in history. He's associated with a supplements lab that's been indicted for distributing performance enhancing drugs to athletes, and his personal trainer has been indicted as well. Reports have come out that federal agents were told he received steroids.

Bonds may well have used steroids, but it's unlikely that he's taking any known steroids right now, with baseball having begun mandatory testing this season. Perhaps he's using HGH, for which there is no test, but that's something we'll never know, unless proof -- not accusations -- surface that he received and used it. Unless the test samples that were seized this month include samples from Bonds, and they come back positive, we'll probably never know if Barry Bonds used performance enhancers.

But we know for certain that we'll *never* know that he *didn't* use steroids. If the standard becomes guilty until proven innocent, then all ballplayers are forever guilty. What good does that do us?

By all means, federal investigations should continue, and agents should seek out all relevant information, including evidence that Bonds and others have used steroids. Investigative journalists should follow leads and inform the public when something important arises. But until there's something more than hearsay and speculation, shut up.

By focusing on what Bonds *may* have done, we're failing to appreciate what he is in fact doing right now, and how great a player he is. Forget how big he is for a moment, and watch his swing. If you were to build a robot that swung a baseball bat perfectly, that's what it would look like. Performance-enhancing drugs can make a ballplayer swing a bat faster, see a ball better and react to it quicker -- but no drug can make you swing a bat like that. It's a thing of absolute beauty, especially in profile. Being able to rewind and watch it again is reason enough to get a digital video recorder, being able to see it almost every night is reason enough to buy the Extra Innings package.

Someday, after Bonds is long retired, all the talk of steroids might be forgotten, as it's unlikely to turn up anything on Bonds. Many people will see old footage of

Bonds, think back to these years, and realize that while they could have enjoyed the show, they were too busy trying to prove that it wasn't real. Don't be one of those people. If it turns out to be an illusion, then maybe you'll feel dirty for having suspended disbelief. But if, as is more likely, we never really find out, then you'll regret not having watched.

And after all, it's just a game, you shouldn't feel dirty about enjoying it anyway.

This article originally appeared on The Hardball Times on April 23, 2004 at http://www.hardballtimes.com/main/article/stop-and-smell-the-roses/

A Tale of Two Leagues

By Steve Treder

The American League began operation in 1900, but in a status that wasn't considered "Major League." Beginning in 1901 it was recognized as a "major" league, of equal status to the National League.

What's been in effect ever since (with the brief exception of 1914-15, when the Federal League operated) is a two-major-league system in baseball. What may have also prevailed ever since is a sense that the two leagues, American and National, have represented essentially equal and similar brands. This may not be a valid perception.

In fact, the two leagues, while generally presenting equivalent styles and qualities of play over the decades, have often differed quite a bit. Let's compare and contrast the AL and NL in their century of companionship.

1901-1919: A Great Start for the Junior Circuit

In their first two decades of co-existence, the two leagues presented similar products in terms of style. Scoring levels between the leagues were consistently within 10% of each other, with neither league sustaining a period of scoring superiority.

There was no significant difference between the leagues in batting average. The National League consistently featured more home runs (probably mostly due to the effect of Baker Bowl in Philadelphia), but in that era home runs were such an overall rarity that the NL's advantage didn't yield a difference in scoring, especially since the AL, increasingly through the 1910s, tended to have higher walk rates. Stolen base rates were at all-time highs in both leagues, and while there were generally slightly more in the AL, the differences weren't dramatic -- generally only a few percentage points of distinction between the leagues.

But while the leagues were rather indistinguishable in style of play, they weren't equal at the turnstile: almost from the start, the upstart American League was better-attended than the Senior Circuit. NL attendance per game exceeded that of the AL in 1901 and 1903, but then never again for the entire period.

The attendance advantage of the AL wasn't always dramatic -- generally within 10-15% of the NL (with one anomaly in the Federal League's initial season of 1914, when National League attendance took a sharp dip). But in the last three years of the period (1917-19) the AL's attendance superiority assumed a more significant posture, with successive seasons of 22%, 24%, and 27% dominance over the NL.

Why this was so is an interesting question. Both leagues shared the major city markets (New York, Chicago, Philadelphia, Boston, St. Louis); indeed the NL had two franchises in New York City. A systemic market-based explanation for the AL's attendance advantage doesn't suggest itself. More likely the primary reason for the AL's greater popularity is simply a function of the quality of the product: the American League probably presented a generally superior level of play in those decades.

Think of the very greatest players, the first-tier Hall of Fame-quality talent of that era: Honus Wagner, Christy Mathewson, and Grover Cleveland Alexander were in the NL. But the AL featured Cy Young, Nap Lajoie, Ty Cobb, Walter Johnson, Tris Speaker, Eddie Collins, and Joe Jackson. Counting superstars is a less-than-scientific method of comparing league quality, but it does seem to be the case that the very best players in (white) baseball in the 1901-1919 era tended to be in the AL. Couple this with the junior loop's near-total superiority in attendance, and it's a fair inference that fans preferred the American League product because it was generally just better.

Oh, yeah. There was one other young star who emerged in the American League toward the end of the period ... a southpaw pitcher. The kid could hit a little, too. Already a superstar in 1915-19, he would take the sport by storm in 1920, coming to New York and leading a transformation into a new mode of play.

1920-30: Balance in the Jazz Age

The cork-centered "live" ball had been introduced to the major leagues long before 1920 -- in 1911, to be exact. Hitting and scoring in both leagues took a dramatic jump in 1911-12. But pitchers soon learned to counteract the livelier new ball by perfecting, ever more ardently, methods to deface and defile it: spitballs, tobacco balls, coffee balls, mudballs; baseballs scratched and torn and stained and altered to such a degree that they became easier to curve and more difficult to see and hit. Scoring levels in both leagues declined after 1912, and for the rest of the decade they were nearly as low as they had been before 1911.

In 1920, both leagues adopted a new rule: pitchers were no longer allowed to deface the ball (under a grandfather clause, a few career spitballers were allowed to continue to ply their trade). As a means of enforcing the rule, a fresh, new, clean white baseball would be inserted into the game whenever the current ball became stained or scratched.

The rule change was made primarily in the interest of keeping the ball sanitary -- getting rid of those brown slimy horrors -- but the impact on scoring was unanticipated and enormous. With a fresh, new, clean, white, live cork-centered baseball in play at all times, batters suddenly entered the promised land.

Babe Ruth led the way, of course. But tremendous as his impact was, he was not the only hitter who enjoyed huge and immediate success in the new conditions. Hitting and scoring soared in 1920, 1921, and 1922, at a rate of increase never seen before or since.

The effect was pretty even across both leagues: once stabilized in the new circumstances, neither league outscored the other by as much as 10% in any season between 1922 and 1930. The leagues presented remarkably equal batting averages, strikeout rates, and stolen base rates across the decade. The differences between the leagues that had been apparent earlier -- the NL featuring more home runs, the AL featuring more bases on balls -- continued, though not as dramatically as before, and indeed by the end of the 1920s the walk rate difference had disappeared.

Even in terms of attendance, the 1920-30 period is one of great balance between the two leagues. Babe Ruth

notwithstanding, the AL superiority in attendance disappeared in the '20s. By 1926, the leagues were almost exactly even in attendance, and from 1927 through 1930 the NL was better attended -- essentially for the first time in the 20th century -- by rates of 5% to 15%.

Why the shift in the attendance trend? Performing the superstar count for the era reveals a roughly equivalent strength in "name brands": along with the aging stars Johnson, Cobb, and Speaker, there was Ruth, George Sisler, Harry Heilmann, Lou Gehrig, Al Simmons, and the emerging Lefty Grove in the American League. But the NL countered with the aging star Alexander, plus Rogers Hornsby, Frankie Frisch, Dazzy Vance, Paul Waner, Hack Wilson, Pie Traynor, and the emerging Mel Ott. Perhaps the talent advantage that the AL had enjoyed was no longer there by the late 1920s.

1931-42: Keep Your Eye On the Ball

The 1920s had featured higher and higher scoring, and the 1930 season was the highest, with record-setting levels in both leagues. Suddenly in 1931, things changed -- but only in the National League.

In the American League, scoring continued along its merry way throughout the 1930s, consistently exceeding 1920s levels. In 1936 the AL posted the highest-scoring season in its history. Often, today, the 1930s are referred to as an extremely high-scoring era, and this is true -- for the American League.

But the 1930s National League was quite a different story. Run scoring in the NL in 1931 dropped by 1.2 runs per team per game, the largest single-season decline in major league history, taking the NL back down to a scoring level it hadn't seen since 1920. In every year from 1931 through 1942, the American League outscored the National. Never was the difference in scoring less than 8%, and it was as much as 26%. Among the 15 greatest scoring difference seasons between the leagues in history, eight occurred between 1931 and 1942:

YEAR	DIFF	RANK
1933	26%	1st
1938	22%	3rd
1936	20%	4th
1939	17%	6th
1937	16%	8th
1931	15%	11th
1932	14%	13th
1940	13%	14th

What explains this? How could the leagues suddenly go from being consistently equivalent as scoring environments through 1930, to dramatically and persistently different scoring environments from 1931 through 1942? The NL didn't suddenly adopt new, pitcher-friendly ballparks in 1931. Neither league adopted any significant playing rule changes in 1931. Great hitters didn't suddenly get traded from the NL to the AL in exchange for great pitchers.

I think there's only one possible explanation: the baseball. Each league in those days authorized and used its own private-label baseball; there was no such thing as a single standard "major league" ball. Given the evidence, I don't think there's any possible conclusion to draw but this: whether intentionally or not, the National League used a distinctly less lively baseball than the American League from 1931 through 1942.

Neither league, as far as I know, ever clearly acknowledged this, although I've read many oblique references and rumors regarding it over the years. The closest thing my (admittedly not very thorough) research has been able to find is this "Editorial Comment" by John B. Foster which opens the 1934 *Spalding Official Base Ball Guide* (in 1933 NL scoring had dropped to its lowest level since 1919, and the difference in scoring between the leagues was the greatest in history):

> *...under the platform of separate balls for the two big leagues, made in such a manner as to create heavier batting for one as opposed to the other, there was no question about the batting. It was then attributed to the slightly different method employed in the manufacture of the ball, which was sensible enough, since the National League openly avowed that its ball was slightly slower than that used by the American League, and consequently its batters could not be expected to do quite as much execution with it.*
>
> *The difference between the ball used by the National League and that which was in use in the American League was in the manner of sewing and in the cover, which was slightly heavier in the National League...*
>
> *Now all this has been abolished and done away with. The ball that will be used in the American League will be of the same construction as that employed by the National League, and the players of one organization will not have the slightest advantage over those of the other.*

What the evidence suggests really happened, I think, is that the NL agreed to liven up its extraordinarily "dead" 1933 ball, but that the leagues didn't truly adopt standardized baseball specs until World War II forced them to -- which we'll get into shortly.

But this is something very important to keep in mind when assessing players of the 1931-42 era. We may tend to see the best hitters of that time as being in the AL (Gehrig, Foxx, Greenberg, etc.), with the NL's best hitters (Ott,

Klein, Medwick, etc.) as not quite measuring up. Maybe the best hitters were American Leaguers, but a careful assessment of the scoring environment needs to be applied in order to be certain.

Looking at attendance in the 1931-42 period reveals something interesting as well: even though the AL featured a distinctly more action-packed brand of play, the AL was not a more popular product. Attendance between the leagues was remarkably equivalent: in the 12 seasons, the AL had higher attendance six times, and the NL also six. It seems fair to conclude that even though fans obviously comprehended the two leagues as presenting different styles, neither style was generally more popular than the other. Nor, as revealed by their attending habits, did fans perceive either league as presenting a higher quality of play.

The 1931-42 period stands, therefore, as one of the most interesting in history: the two leagues were providing extraordinarily different styles of product, each of which was equally valued by customers.

1943-1955: Sowing the Seeds of Change

In 1943 National League scoring matched American League scoring for the first time since 1930. This happened not because the NL increased its slugging, but because the AL finally dropped down to the NL's lower-scoring mode. The explanation, again, may clearly be found in the baseball itself.

World War II raw material restrictions were fully in effect by 1943, and both leagues were forced to adopt a baseball constructed with inferior components. Derisively nicknamed the "balata ball," despite various construction methods, the wartime ball was distinctly non-lively; home runs and scoring plunged in both leagues to levels not seen since before 1920. Whether they preferred it or not, neither league could maintain exclusive control over the specs of its ball for the duration of the war.

Beginning in 1946, however, such restrictions were removed. While it took a year or two for scoring to rebound all the way to pre-war levels, it's clear that the "balata ball" was discarded: home runs increased in 1946 and began a long upward climb. But what's striking is the degree to which, as scoring increased in the late 1940s, it did so in both leagues.

The clear distinction between the AL and NL that had prevailed in 1931-42 didn't reassert itself: in the 10 seasons from 1946 through 1955, the AL outscored the NL five times, the NL outscored the AL four times, and in one year they were exactly equal. In no season in that period did either league outscore the other by more than 10%.

The only conclusion one can draw from this is that, after World War II, at least, John B. Foster's 1934 pronouncement was finally true: "The ball that will be used in the American League will be of the same construction as that employed by the National League."

Beneath similarities in overall scoring levels, however, there were some remarkable differences between the leagues in 1946-55. The NL resumed the superiority in home run rates that it had held until the 1930s. The AL consistently featured more walks, though not as many more as had prevailed in the '30s. The NL generally had a few more stolen bases, though its stolen base advantage was not as great as that which the AL had shown in most of the seasons in the '30s and early '40s.

But the most striking difference between the leagues in 1946-55 was, of course, the degree to which the leagues racially integrated. It wasn't just that Jackie Robinson was in the NL a few months before Larry Doby was in the AL; through the entire period, players of color began to be deployed much more readily by NL teams than by AL teams. While in 1955, only two AL teams (the Tigers and Red Sox) remained all-white, as opposed to one in the NL (the Phillies), the different levels of integration go much deeper than that.

Players of color used in significant roles in the AL in 1955 were Larry Doby, Elston Howard, Connie Johnson, Hector Lopez, Minnie Minoso, Carlos Paula, Dave Pope, Vic Power, Harry Simpson, and Al Smith: 10 players, several of them stars, one who would be elected to the Hall of Fame.

In the NL in 1955 were Hank Aaron, Sandy Amoros, Gene Baker, Ernie Banks, Bill Bruton, Roy Campanella, Roberto Clemente, George Crowe, Lino Donoso, Jim Gilliam, Ruben Gomez, Chuck Harmon, Monte Irvin, Sam Jones, Brooks Lawrence, Willie Mays, Roman Mejias, Don Newcombe, Jackie Robinson, Hank Thompson, and Bob Thurman: 21 players, many of them stars, seven who would become Hall of Famers.

The very different rate of introduction of black talent into the two leagues would continue in the years following 1955, and would inevitably lead to different levels of quality of play between the two leagues: it was entirely impossible for the AL to offset, in deployment of greater white talent (which it didn't do anyway), the huge talent advantage it ceded to the NL in black talent.

While the AL tended to have better attendance than the NL in the 1946-55 period (leading the NL in seven of the 10 seasons), the growing advantage in quality of players that the NL was accumulating would soon change that. The period following 1955 would see the greatest attendance disparities between the leagues in history, a situation which would bring the AL to a state of crisis by the early 1970s.

1956-1972: Reaping Different Harvests

By 1960, the AL was making use of 17 black players, and the NL featured 38. Over the next decade, the American League finally began to seriously integrate, but was still unable to catch up: in 1965 the tally was 42 players of color in the AL, 57 in the NL; in 1970 it was AL 63, NL 82.

Moreover, the distinction was much more than a matter of quantity. After Larry Doby and Satchel Paige were signed by the Indians in 1947-48, no AL organization developed a player of color who would go on to the Hall of Fame until Rod Carew (Twins) and Reggie Jackson (A's), both of whom entered the league in 1967.

By that year, NL teams had already brought 18 black Hall of Famers to the majors, including several who are widely considered to be among the greatest players of all time: Roy Campanella, Willie Mays, Hank Aaron, Roberto Clemente, Frank Robinson, Bob Gibson, and Joe Morgan.

In both quantity and quality, such a staggering inequity in new talent infusion couldn't help but have a significant impact on the overall caliber of play. From the mid-to-late 1950s through at least the early 1970s, there's little question that the National League was presenting generally better players and better teams than the American League.

The NL gained other important advantages in this period. In most of the biggest, fastest-growing, affluent new markets, NL teams were the first arrivals, gaining high ground in Southern California, the San Francisco Bay Area, Houston, and Atlanta. The AL, meanwhile, claimed only Baltimore, Kansas City, and Minneapolis-St. Paul before making an abortive move into Seattle in 1969. In 1970 the AL took the Milwaukee market that the NL had already exploited and abandoned, and moved into Dallas-Fort Worth in 1972.

Brand-new ballparks were unveiled in the NL in San Francisco (1960), Los Angeles (1962), New York (1964), Houston (1965), Atlanta (1966), St. Louis (1966), San Diego (1969), Pittsburgh (1970), Cincinnati (1970), and Philadelphia (1971). The only new facilities introduced by the AL in the period were in Minneapolis-St. Paul (1961), Washington (1962), Anaheim (1966) and Oakland (1968).

As if better players, better markets, and newer facilities weren't enough, the NL featured more competitive pennant races throughout the era too. The AL had already been dominated by the Yankees for much of the time since the 1920s, and this monotony continued: in the nine seasons from 1956 through 1964, the Yankees won the AL pennant every year but one, and rarely in close fashion.

In the meantime six different teams were claiming at least one NL championship, and there were several multi-team races in the NL (1956, 1959, 1962, and 1964) that were extraordinarily competitive and compelling. It wasn't until 1965 that AL races became comparable to the NL's in terms of unpredictability.

All this added up to enormously different box office stories. In 1956, the NL began a 33-year streak of attendance superiority over the AL. From the mid-1960s through the mid-1970s, the NL's attendance dominance was the most extreme in history. Among the 10 greatest attendance difference seasons in history, eight occurred between 1958 and 1974:

YEAR	DIFF	RANK
1965	53%	2nd
1966	47%	3rd
1971	45%	4th
1958	40%	5th
1970	38%	6th
1972	36%	7th
1964	31%	9th
1974	30%	10th

By the early '70s, the AL's circumstances were becoming dire. Better players in better markets had attracted more fans for NL teams, which provided them greater revenues with which to sign and develop still better players. It was a cycle without a happy resolution in sight for the American League. In the *New Yorker* in June 1972, Roger Angell put it this way:

Among the ... hovering anxieties is the deepening disparity in quality and attendance between the two major leagues. Last year's record total attendance did not conceal the fact that the National League outdrew the American by nearly five and a half million customers... The gap is widening this year... The difference between the leagues in quality and attractiveness of play is harder to prove, but it can be suggested: so far this spring, National League batters have hit over one hundred more home runs than their American League counterparts.

Indeed, the 1972 season would present not only an attendance disparity of historic proportions, but also one in hitting. The NL outscored the AL by 13% in 1972; only twice in history (1903 and 1945) was the AL outscored more distinctly. Run production in the American League had been sputtering for years; the 1969 rule changes adopted by both leagues (shrinking the strike zone and lowering the mound) had been temporarily effective at revitalizing offense in the AL, but in 1972 AL scoring plunged again. Only in 1908, 1909, and 1968 did the American League produce runs less regularly than in 1972.

Faced with a chronically less popular product than the National League, and a major deficit in hitting and scoring, following the 1972 season the American League was ready to take bold action; one might even call it an act of desperation. The AL voted to conduct an "experiment" with the Designated Hitter rule in 1973. Jerome Holtzman in the *Sporting News Baseball Guide* aptly described it: "The most significant rule change in modern baseball history."

1973-1992: Road to Redemption

The DH had an immediate impact on scoring. American League run production in 1973 jumped by 23%, an even bigger bounce than had occurred in 1920. As an offensive tonic, the DH was an obvious success, and its "experimental" status was quickly dropped. Thanks primarily to the DH, the AL would be a higher-scoring league than the NL in every season but one from 1973 through 2003 -- though it's important to note that, despite the DH, the AL's scoring superiority over the NL since 1973 hasn't matched the disparity seen in 1931-42.

The DH's impact on the American League's popularity was perhaps less dramatic, though unquestionably positive: AL attendance in 1973 was up 12%. However, the AL's per-game attendance in '73 remained less than it had been in 1967 or 1968, and far below the peak rates it had achieved way back in the late 1940s. Moreover, it was still 24% less than the NL's 1973 attendance.

It would take a long time for AL attendance to creep back into a realm of competitiveness. It dropped back to 30% below the NL in 1974, and 25% in 1975. But after that, the march back toward attendance parity was steady, if slow. From 1975 to 1980 American League per-game attendance was within 10% and 15% of the National's every year, and from 1981 through 1988, though never quite matching the NL, the disparity was never as great as 10%.

It took more than the Designated Hitter rule to achieve this gradual comeback. The AL expanded in 1977, capturing a large new market in Toronto that would host one of MLB's best franchises of the 1980s. The AL's flagship, the Yankees, rebounded in the mid-70s to become a near-perennial contender -- but not resuming the numbingly dull league dominance of the '50s and early '60s.

Overall the American League in the 1980s featured competitive balance of a robustness rarely seen in history: in 10 seasons, five of the seven AL West teams, and six of the seven AL East teams, were Division Champs. Eight different AL teams won the pennant in the 1980s.

Most significantly, however, was the fact that in this period the American League overcame the NL's superiority in quality of play. One key indicator of this was the gradual elimination of the disparity in deployment of players of color. In 1970 the NL had used 82 black players in significant roles, compared to just 63 in the AL. By 1975 the difference was nearly gone: 88 players of color in the NL, 81 in the AL.

In 1980 the NL regained its edge, with 96 black players in its 12-team league (or 8 players per team), compared to 83 on the AL's 14 teams (a little under 6 per team). But by 1985 the disparity had finally vanished: 101 players of color in the American League (7.2 per team), 85 in the National (7.1 per team).

The NL's overwhelming advantage in elite-quality superstars disappeared. There are 20 players in the Hall of Fame who had their peak seasons in the 1973-1992 period: two (Nolan Ryan and Dave Winfield) spent nearly equal peak time in both leagues, seven (Joe Morgan, Steve Carlton, Phil Niekro, Don Sutton, Mike Schmidt, Gary Carter, and Ozzie Smith) were National Leaguers. Eleven of the era's Hall of Famers were American Leaguers: Rod Carew, Reggie Jackson, Jim Palmer, Catfish Hunter, Rollie Fingers, Carlton Fisk, George Brett, Robin Yount, Dennis Eckersley, Eddie Murray, and Kirby Puckett. (There are five other stars from the era who will almost certainly be elected to the HOF, and the AL has the edge here too: Rickey Henderson, Cal Ripken, and Wade Boggs over Tim Raines and Tony Gwynn.)

There's every reason to believe that by sometime around 1980 or 1985, the American League had worked its way back to a quality of play that was every bit the equal of the National. In 1989, for the first time since 1955, the AL exceeded the NL in per-game attendance, and would do so every season though 1992. It marked the climax of a twenty-year journey of redemption for the American League.

Thus, the 1980s may be seen as a return to the pattern of 1931-42: the two leagues presented a stable "separate but equal" offering, with the AL the high-scoring brand, the NL the little-ball brand, but each of equal quality, and each of equal popularity.

1993-2003: Just What Is a League, Anyway?

The National League expanded prior to the 1993 season, adding Colorado and Florida. In the fall 1992 expansion draft to stock the new rosters, something unprecedented occurred: despite the fact that these were two new National League teams, all existing MLB franchises -- both AL and NL -- were subject to the draft. In all previous expansions, the drafts were strictly intra-league.

This was a harbinger. The management structure of MLB would truly amalgamate the leagues in this period, with the positions of League President eventually being dispensed with altogether. Among the dizzying array of innovations and transformations punctuating the era are

two that strike at the very heart of the meaning of a "league": inter-league play was introduced in 1997, and an existing franchise (the Milwaukee Brewers) was transferred from the AL to the NL in 1998. The American and National Leagues, rivals for so long, in recent years have come to intermingle and resemble one another more than ever. Perhaps this is emblematic of the era, a time of ironies and contradictions.

Since the early 1990s, the whirl of new ballpark construction (among the ironies is that nearly all of the new parks affect an ardently "retro" style) has transformed the look and feel of both leagues: Chicago, Baltimore, Cleveland, Arlington, Seattle, and Detroit in the AL, and Denver, Atlanta, Phoenix, Houston, San Francisco, Milwaukee, Pittsburgh, and Cincinnati in the NL. (Plus, beginning in 2004, Philadelphia and San Diego.)

The ubiquitous new facilities have eliminated any distinctive ballpark style for either league: in the '70s and '80s, the NL was full of sleek modern arenas (a/k/a sterile Astroturfed ashtrays), the AL full of quaint historic charmers (shabby crumbling anachronisms?). In 1993-2003, increasingly, extravagant luxury boxes in theme-park "unique" pleasure palaces have become emblematic of both leagues.

A characteristic the new parks tend to have (along with 8-buck microbrews) is a cozy hitter-friendliness. This factor, along with ever-stronger batters (whether steroid-enhanced or not), and a persistent tendency of umpires to refuse to call the high strike (despite what have appeared to be sincere and diligent efforts on the part of MLB to correct them, most recently with Questec), combined to ignite an offensive explosion in the mid-1990s.

The soaring levels of run production -- at their peaks, 25% above 1992 in the AL (achieved in 1996), and 29% above 1992 in the NL (achieved in 2000) -- have occurred at remarkably similar rates in both leagues. In the 11 seasons from 1993 through 2003, the AL has outscored the NL every season, by a rate of between 3% and 15%, and at an average rate of 8%. This differs almost not at all from the pattern of the previous 11 years (1982-92), when the AL outscored the NL between 2% and 12% every season, at an average rate of 9%. The scoring binge of 1993-2003 has been a league-neutral phenomenon.

Robust scoring in spiffy new ballparks has proven to be an attractive package; one of the most striking features of 1993-2003 has been booming attendance (setting the stage for one of the era's contradictions: strident ownership complaints of financial distress, even the need to contract franchises, amid an environment of unprecedented customer demand). Among the 10 greatest total-MLB attendance-per-game seasons of all time, nine occurred between 1993 and 2003:

A Tale of Two Leagues

YEAR	ATT/G	RANK
1994	31,256	1st
1993	30,964	2nd
2001	29,881	3rd
2000	29,378	4th
1998	29,030	5th
1999	28,888	6th
2002	28,007	7th
1997	27,877	8th
2003	27,831	9th

The salient theme of 1993-2003 is that if it weren't for the DH -- a major caveat, to be sure -- there would be no significant points of difference between the American and National Leagues. They present products of similar style and quality in similar venues, and are similarly popular.

Among the ironies to consider in this regard is that of the Designated Hitter rule: invoked in desperation to address a run production problem that no longer exists, and an attendance crisis that no longer exists, it remains in place 30 years later as a dramatic rule difference dividing the sport (neither the NFL, NBA, or NHL feature anything remotely analogous).

Both leagues have enjoyed the attendance-fest. But the NL has resumed the status of generally better-attended league that it held for so long before 1989: only once since 1992 has the AL led the NL in per-game attendance. The margins of NL superiority have been in the 2% to 11% range, not approaching the stark differences that prevailed in the 1960s and 1970s.

As the American and National Leagues enter their second century of co-existence, they're more tightly integrated than ever before, and yet as sharply segregated in the rulebook as they've ever been. How this odd circumstance will be resolved -- or if it will -- is one of the most intriguing questions to ponder as the leagues move more deeply into the 21st century.

The league statistics used for this article were taken from the baseball-reference.com league pages: http://www.baseball-reference.com/leagues/AL.shtml and http://www.baseball-reference.com/leagues/NL.shtml

An excellent source of information on players of color in the major leagues in the 1947-59 period is Moffi and Kronstadt's Crossing the Line: Black Major Leaguers, 1947-1959.

Any researcher looking into the quantitative magnitude of the racial integration of baseball is forced to perform a preposterous exercise: to categorize every ballplayer as either "white" or "black". This is biologically absurd, yet it's precisely what MLB did, not only pre-1947, but for a long time after; as late as the early 1960s, some guidebooks categorized players by race.

In the counts of players of color in the 1960s, 1970s, and 1980s which I've performed here, I was forced to make a judgement as to whether certain Latin American players with neither very dark nor very light skin -- Jose Cruz Sr., for example -- would have been considered "colored" in baseball's segregated era. To make this judgement, I have brought to bear my knowledge of each player in question, and my many years of research into the subject, but I fully recognize that this is an inherently imprecise task.

Another researcher might come up with slightly different counts than I have. Nonetheless, for purposes of this article, the potential for error must be seen as applying equally to the AL and NL, and thus the differential proportions of players of color in the two leagues remains undeniable, even if the exact numbers are problematic

This article originally appeared on The Hardball Times on April 13 and 20, 2004 at http://www.hardballtimes.com/main/article/a_tale_of_two_leagues_part_one/ and http://www.hardballtimes.com/main/article/a-tale-of-two-leagues-part-two-1956-2003/

Smart Growth and Major League Baseball: A Virtual History

By Steve Treder

In 1952, there were 16 major league teams, covering the following markets:

- 3 teams in New York City
- 2 teams in Chicago
- 2 teams in Boston
- 2 teams in Philadelphia
- 2 teams in St. Louis
- 1 team in each of Washington, Pittsburgh, Cincinnati, Cleveland, and Detroit

Things had been that way (except for the brief intrusion of the Federal League in 1914-15) for half a century.

Here's the lineup a half-century later:

- 2 teams in New York City
- 2 teams in Chicago
- 2 teams in the Los Angeles area
- 2 teams in the San Francisco Bay Area

1 team in each of Miami, Tampa-St. Petersburg, Atlanta, Baltimore, Boston, Montreal, Toronto, Philadelphia, Pittsburgh, Cincinnati, Cleveland, Detroit, Milwaukee, Minneapolis-St. Paul, St. Louis, Kansas City, Dallas-Ft. Worth, Houston, Denver, Phoenix, San Diego, and Seattle

Clearly things have changed quite a bit. It's quite fair to say that it was inevitable that things would change quite a bit since 1952. But there's no reason to believe it was inevitable that things would turn out exactly as they did, and especially, that it was inevitable that every franchise movement and expansion entry since 1952 would occur as it did. Just because things happened doesn't mean things had to be that way.

As we all know, the way things have occurred, while succeeding in bringing Major League Baseball to many very deserving and grateful markets, also delivered huge frustration and bitterness to many communities, including Brooklyn, Washington DC, Milwaukee, Kansas City, Seattle, and of course, Montreal. Moreover, nearly every current major league city has gone through the agitation of being threatened with abandonment, and all that ensues from that.

There were many different scenarios under which Major League Baseball might have grown and captured all its new markets over the past 50 years. I suggest that without the application of franchise relocation, in any but

the most dire circumstances, the past half-century of MLB would have been an entirely more acceptable and enjoyable enterprise for everyone involved (except for the few greedy soulless millionaires who actually profited, hugely, from what actually transpired -- and, most assuredly, none of us should care a whit about their selfish concerns).

I'd like to present a scenario which, while admittedly is best-case and in many ways fanciful, offers an alternative in which:

- All existing MLB markets (and then some) are served
- There was only one franchise relocation

Let's give this virtual history a whirl ...

In the early 1950s, the Boston Braves franchise was suggested as one that would no longer be viable, and should be moved. However, reasonable voices prevailed, offering the obvious truths that the Boston market was a huge and affluent baseball town, then and looking forward, and could and should support two properly managed major league franchises.

But by the 1953 season, it had become evident that St. Louis was a market that couldn't sustain two major league franchises. Following that season, it was agreed by all other major league teams that the extraordinary measure of a franchise relocation should be enacted. Kansas City was the logical and reasonable site for the relocation: a growing market, within the same general geography as St. Louis, thus retaining as much of the existing fan base as possible, and therefore retaining that part of the viable market for the American League. Thus the first geographic franchise shift since 1903 took place prior to the 1954 season: the St. Louis Browns became the Kansas City Blues.

There was some suggestion in the early 1950s that the Philadelphia Athletics franchise should be moved, but the greater wisdom was understood that Philadelphia, like Boston, was a large and great baseball market that should be catered to, not retreated from. All further suggestions that either Philadelphia team might be moved were greeted with deserving dismissal; the proper thing to do if a franchise was struggling would be to focus on improving its management.

By the late 1950s, all Major League Baseball owners had agreed that it was time for the beginning of expansion of the venerable 16-team structure, as well as extension to the West Coast. Everyone understood that, as this process unfolded, decreasing any presence in strong traditional markets (such as New York) would be idiotic; the focus would always be on growth, not retreat or abandonment.

So, effective for the 1958 season, two new franchises were added to each league. Both leagues adopted a new 162-game schedule, under which each team played each of its rivals 18 times (9 home and 9 away), 9 x 18 = 162.

The new major league roster looked like this (*new expansion teams in italics*):

American League, 1958-64:

Boston Red Sox
Chicago White Sox
Cleveland Indians
Detroit Tigers
Kansas City Blues
Los Angeles Angels
New York Yankees
Philadelphia Athletics
San Francisco Seals
Washington Senators

National League, 1958-64:

Baltimore Orioles
Boston Braves
Brooklyn Dodgers
Chicago Cubs
Cincinnati Reds
Milwaukee Brewers
New York Giants
Philadelphia Phillies
Pittsburgh Pirates
St. Louis Cardinals

This new arrangement proved to be a great success. Indeed the installation of the vibrant new West Coast franchises in the American League appeared to give new life and competitiveness to the circuit that had appeared to be becoming rather languid under chronic domination by the New York Yankees.

As the 1960s unfolded, it was agreed by everyone that further expansion into new and viable markets was

appropriate, including further development of the booming Los Angeles market. Effective 1965, each league split into two divisions, adding a best-of-7 League Championship Series to the postseason. The new alignment was as follows, with each team playing each division rival 18 times, and each other-division rival 12 times (18 x 5 = 90) + (12 x 6 = 72) = 162:

American League, 1965-71:

East Division	West Division
Boston Red Sox	*Atlanta Peaches*
Cleveland Indians	Chicago White Sox
Detroit Tigers	Kansas City Blues
New York Yankees	Los Angeles Angels
Philadelphia Athletics	*Minnesota Twins*
Washington Senators	San Francisco Seals

National League, 1965-71:

East Division	West Division
Baltimore Orioles	Chicago Cubs
Boston Braves	Cincinnati Reds
Brooklyn Dodgers	*Houston Astros*
New York Giants	*Los Angeles Stars*
Philadelphia Phillies	Milwaukee Brewers
Pittsburgh Pirates	St. Louis Cardinals

After seven seasons in this arrangement, it was agreed that the sport was ready for another expansion. Two

additional West Coast franchises were added, and MLB incorporated a Canadian market for the first time as well.

The AL's Atlanta franchise was moved into the league's East Division, making more time zone sense. To accommodate the 7-team divisions, a 166-game schedule was adopted (16 x 6 = 96) + (10 x 7 = 70) = 166.

There was some discussion that the slightly longer schedule would taint the legitimacy of statistical records. However, the prevailing understanding was that a few games worth of difference in the schedule was a small price to pay to preserve the more important principle of each team in a division playing its rivals the same number of games, as well as preserving an even number of games home and away against each competitor.

Many ballparks in the 1960s and 1970s introduced artificial turf into the game. Initially it was an exciting novelty, but after the first few years, it began to be obvious that the phony turf, on balance, negatively impacted the quality and character of play. Therefore in 1975 it was

agreed that artificial turf would be phased out of the game as quickly as reasonably possible. The domed stadium in Houston was agreed to be replaced with a retractable-roof ballpark within 15 years, and no new non-retractable domes would be allowed. Baseball on real grass was recognized to be the way the game ought to be played.

There was also discussion during this period that perhaps a Designated Hitter rule might be invoked. But the logic prevailed that undermining the fundamental 9-player structure of the game, as well as diminishing the tactical challenges faced by managers, would not be a worthwhile tradeoff to gain additional offense. Adjusting ballpark conditions, and perhaps modifying the strike zone, were understood to be much more appropriate approaches to infusing more run-scoring into the game as desired.

American League, 1972-79:

East Division	West Division
Atlanta Peaches	Chicago White Sox
Boston Red Sox	*Dallas Spurs*
Cleveland Indians	Kansas City Blues
Detroit Tigers	Los Angeles Angels
New York Yankees	Minnesota Twins
Philadelphia Athletics	San Francisco Seals
Washington Senators	*San Diego Padres*

National League, 1972-79:

East Division	West Division
Baltimore Orioles	Chicago Cubs
Boston Braves	Cincinnati Reds
Brooklyn Dodgers	Houston Astros
Montreal Nordiques	Los Angeles Stars
New York Giants	Milwaukee Brewers
Philadelphia Phillies	*Oakland Oaks*
Pittsburgh Pirates	St. Louis Cardinals

After another eight years, it was time to grow again. The American League was ready to go north of the border, and a third MLB entry was added in each of the enormous Chicago and Los Angeles-area markets. It was understood that the sport's largest markets could and should support multiple franchises, and inhibiting any one or two franchises from gaining too much access to the financial power of the largest markets was understood to be a way to avoid any potential competitive balance issues before they developed.

There was discussion during this period (as there always has been) that baseball was expanding too fast or

too far, that the availability of talent couldn't keep up with the number of MLB teams, and so the quality of play (particularly it was often said, for some reason, pitching) was being "watered down."

However, it was more generally understood that both the US population, as well as the extra-U.S. populations (especially Latin America) from which professional baseball recruits talent, had been and would likely continue to grow at rates very ample to provide outstanding athletes to MLB. Indeed, as the amount of money in the game continued to increase, and as training, conditioning, and sports medicine capabilities continued to progress, most observers recognized that the quality of play in MLB was continually improving.

With each league featuring 8-team divisions, the schedule returned to its previous 162-game length: (14 x 7 = 98) + (8 x 8 = 64) = 162.

American League, 1980-91:

East Division	West Division
Atlanta Peaches	*Chicago Lakers*
Boston Red Sox	Chicago White Sox
Cleveland Indians	Dallas Spurs
Detroit Tigers	Kansas City Blues
New York Yankees	Los Angeles Angels
Philadelphia Athletics	Minnesota Twins
Toronto Blue Jays	San Francisco Seals
Washington Senators	San Diego Padres

National League, 1980-91:

East Division	West Division
Baltimore Orioles	*Anaheim Oranges*
Boston Braves	Chicago Cubs
Brooklyn Dodgers	Houston Astros
Cincinnati Reds	Los Angeles Stars
Montreal Nordiques	Milwaukee Brewers
New York Giants	Oakland Oaks
Philadelphia Phillies	St. Louis Cardinals
Pittsburgh Pirates	*Seattle Mariners*

By 1992, MLB was ready to add a fourth franchise to its most lucrative market, the New York City area, as well as three fast-growing Southern and Western cities. Moving to 9-team divisions led to the adoption of a 160-game regular-season schedule: (12 x 8 = 96) + (8 x 8 = 64) = 160.

There was discussion at this point that perhaps the leagues should be split into three divisions, but the consensus decided that the necessity of incorporating a Wild Card team, and a third tier of postseason play, would lessen the urgency of division pennant races, as well as watering down the prestige and excitement of the hugely successful League Championship Series and, of course, World Series. Some even raised the possibility that Interleague Play might be incorporated, but that silly idea was roundly dismissed as a gimmick that this marvelous sport most definitely didn't need.

American League, 1992-present:

East Division	West Division
Atlanta Peaches	Chicago Lakers
Boston Red Sox	Chicago White Sox
Cleveland Indians	*Colorado Rockies*
Detroit Tigers	Dallas Spurs
Newark Bears	Kansas City Blues
New York Yankees	Los Angeles Angels
Philadelphia Athletics	Minnesota Twins
Toronto Blue Jays	San Francisco Seals
Washington Senators	San Diego Padres

Smart Growth and Major League Baseball: A Virtual History

National League, 1992-present:

East Division	West Division
Baltimore Orioles	Anaheim Oranges
Boston Braves	*Arizona Diamondbacks*
Brooklyn Dodgers	Chicago Cubs
Cincinnati Reds	Houston Astros
Miami Marlins	Los Angeles Stars
Montreal Nordiques	Milwaukee Brewers
New York Giants	Oakland Oaks
Philadelphia Phillies	St. Louis Cardinals
Pittsburgh Pirates	Seattle Mariners

Current plans call for another round of expansion to occur probably within the next five years. Tampa Bay and Portland are expected to join the American League, while Raleigh-Durham and Sacramento will likely enter the National. 10-team divisions will probably invoke a 168-game schedule: $(12 \times 9 = 108) + (6 \times 10 = 60) = 168$.

Thus, by 2010, MLB will feature the following market coverage:

- 4 teams in the New York City area (2 in each league)
- 3 teams in Chicago (2 in the AL, 1 in the NL)
- 3 teams in the Los Angeles area (2 in the NL, 1 in the AL)
- 2 teams in Boston (1 in each league)
- 2 teams in Philadelphia (1 in each league)
- 2 teams in the San Francisco Bay Area (1 in each league)
- 2 teams in the Baltimore-Washington area (1 in each league)
- 1 team in each of Miami, Tampa-St. Petersburg, Atlanta, Raleigh-Durham, Montreal, Toronto, Pittsburgh, Cincinnati, Cleveland, Detroit, Milwaukee, Minneapolis-St. Paul, St. Louis, Kansas City, Dallas-Ft. Worth, Houston, Denver, Phoenix, San Diego, Sacramento, Portland, and Seattle

There are no plans to invoke any such nonsense as the DH, the Wild Card, or Interleague Play. The game has been free of artificial turf for years, and will always remain so.

The careful, steady growth plan that MLB has followed over the past 50 years, adding new markets, adding additional teams to its most robust existing markets, not abandoning any market, has been credited as one of the explanations for the sport's burgeoning financial vitality and loyal, ever-growing fan base. There is every reason to expect that baseball will continue to follow a path of prudent yet confident development as the 21st century unfolds.

Okay, it's a fantasy, all right? And it's my fantasy, so I can have it go any way I want.

But I sincerely believe that baseball certainly could have and should have managed its growth and expansion into emerging new markets in the second half of the 20th century far more intelligently and decently than it did. Relocation of a franchise should have been a last resort, to be avoided if at all possible, yet instead between 1953 and 1972, MLB allowed 10 teams to move, and over the years has threatened to move countless more. I believe it's very fair to say that of all the teams that did move, only the St. Louis Browns were a franchise that was truly not viable in the long term.

I love baseball as it is. But the way it is isn't the only way it could have possibly turned out to be. I would love Major League Baseball even more if it had followed a more enlightened growth path.

This article originally appeared on The Hardball Times on June 23, 2004 at http://www.hardballtimes.com/main/article/smart-growth-and-mlb-a-virtual-history/

The Butterfly Effect

By Matthew Namee

Have you seen the movie *The Butterfly Effect*? It came out earlier this year, and in the movie, the Ashton Kutcher character goes back in time and changes one specific thing. That change has far-reaching implications, altering his entire reality.

Kutcher then goes back numerous other times, but we're going to just take one trip back. Back to the second half of the 1992 baseball season. A 26-year-old rookie, Eric Young, has just taken over the Dodgers' second-base job. The Dodgers are in the midst of a nightmarish 99-loss season, but the farm system is stocked with talent. Young, who has just batted .337 at Albuquerque (a .277 Major League Equivalent, or MLE) looks like the second baseman of the future.

Here is our one little change. In real life, Young hit .258/.300/.258 in his 49 games that year, and was drafted by the Rockies in the expansion draft that fall. Let's do one little, tiny thing: let's add four hits to Young's 1992 total. Four hits is nothing; it's less than one every dozen games. But four hits is the difference between Young's .258 average and .280, which was essentially his MLE.

So Young hits .280, and his trial is not considered a failure. He is protected by the Dodgers in the expansion draft and remains the second baseman of the future. The Rockies draft Jody Reed (who they actually drafted and then traded to LA), and Reed becomes the original Colorado 2B.

Meanwhile, Eric Young does a passable job in his rookie season and hangs onto the second-base job. With no hole at second, the Dodgers don't trade Pedro Martinez to Montreal for Delino DeShields. Still, the Expos need to trade DeShields, who is in his arbitration years and beginning to get expensive.

The Yankees are an obvious trading partner, with the uninspiring Pat Kelly at second base, and they send young pitchers Bob Wickman (coming off a 14-4 season) and Sterling Hitchcock to the Expos in exchange for DeShields. DeShields is the Yankee 2B from 1994-96, batting in the .290s every year and helping the club to the World Series in '96.

In reality, the Yankees had some decent one-year guys at second base, but nobody really reliable during the 1994-97 period. Hitchcock was actually traded to the Mariners in December 1995, in a deal that brought Tino Martinez and Jeff Nelson to the Bronx. Wickman went to Milwaukee in 1996, where he emerged as a solid reliever. And in real life, DeShields was a bust in his 3 years in Los Angeles, batting

.241/.326/.327. Of course, the Yankees did win the World Series in '96.

After the season, a number of the team's best players leave as free agents -- DeShields, John Wetteland, Jimmy Key. DeShields signs with the Cardinals, and after a season of stopgaps at second base, the Yankees trade for Minnesota's Chuck Knoblauch.

Well, that's pretty much what actually happened. DeShields did sign with St. Louis after the '96 season, though he was hardly a star at that point. Wetteland and Key also left New York. And after a season of stopgaps at second base in 1997, the Yanks acquired Chuck Knoblauch from the Twins.

Back to the Dodgers. Pedro Martinez stays in the bullpen in 1994, and with Pedro there, the Dodgers see no need to rush prospect Darren Dreifort. In 1995, Martinez moves into the rotation, joining his brother Ramon and Japanese sensation Hideo Nomo. Dreifort is called up to the big leagues that September, and pitches well down the stretch as the Dodgers win the division but fall to the Reds in the playoffs.

In the real 1994, Pedro went 11-5 with a 3.42 ERA as a starter for Montreal. The Dodgers did rush Darren Dreifort, and he ended up having Tommy John surgery (twice, actually). In '95, Pedro had another decent season with the Expos, going 14-10 with a 3.51 ERA. And the Dodgers did win the division but lost to Cincy in the playoffs.

1996 is a great season for the Dodgers. Eric Young hits .300, Mike Piazza has a monster year, and Pedro wins 18 games. The Dodgers have one of the best rotations in recent memory, with the Martinez brothers, Nomo, and young pitchers Ismael Valdez and Pedro Astacio. Chan Ho Park makes some starts late in the year, and Darren Dreifort emerges as a dominant middle reliever.

Real life: 1996 was a decent season for the Dodgers. Eric Young hit .324 (for the Rockies), Mike Piazza did have a monster year (.336/.422/.563, 36 HR), and Pedro won 14 games (for Montreal). The Dodgers had a solid rotation, with Ramon Martinez, Nomo, and young pitchers Ismael Valdez and Pedro Astacio (also Tom Candiotti). Chan Ho Park made some starts late in the year, but Darren Dreifort was no great shakes in 19 games (24 SO in 23.2 IP, but a 4.94 ERA).

The Dodgers win 97 games and go on to face the Yankees in the World Series. They lose, but after the season Piazza is signed to a 6-year, $65 million deal that makes him the highest-paid player in the game. At the press conference, owner Peter O'Malley addresses rumors that he wants to sell the club. "They're nonsense," he says. "We just won the pennant. The Dodger-Yankee rivalry is back. Revenues couldn't be better. This isn't the time to sell a ball club; it's the time to enjoy it."

The Dodgers won 90 games and the Wild Card, but were swept by Atlanta in the Division Series. Piazza wanted a contract extension, but didn't get one. As for the rumors that O'Malley wanted to sell the team... well, read on.

The next year, Pedro Martinez goes 21-5 with a 1.75 ERA. Todd Worrell struggles in the closer role, and Dreifort takes over the job. Los Angeles rides Pedro through the playoffs, and the Dodgers sweep the Indians in the World Series that October. The next month, Piazza is awarded the NL MVP.

The real 1997 season saw Pedro make "the Leap" into superstardom with the Expos, going 17-8 with a 1.90 ERA. Todd Worrell struggled all year as the Dodger closer (5.28 ERA), and Dreifort had his only really good year (2.86 ERA and 63 SO in 63 IP), but had just 4 saves. The Dodgers won 88 games and missed the playoffs, and the Marlins beat the Indians in 7 games in the World Series. The next month, Larry Walker was awarded the NL MVP.

In January '97, Peter O'Malley announced plans to sell the Dodgers. By May he was negotiating with media mogul Ruppert Murdoch, and the deal is done on March 19, 1998.

Two weeks after winning the World Series, the Dodgers ink Pedro to a 5-year, $60 million contract extension that keeps him in Los Angeles through 2003. Dan Duquette and the Red Sox, looking to acquire a big-name starting pitcher, send Carl Pavano and Tony Armas Jr. to the Marlins for ace Kevin Brown, whom they promptly sign to a 4-year extension.

In November, Dan Duquette and the Red Sox traded Pavano and Armas to the Expos for Pedro. The champion Marlins traded Kevin Brown to San Diego in December, for Derrek Lee and a couple other guys.

After a failed attempt at the championship, Marlins owner H. Wayne Huizenga claims that the club lost $50 million in 1997, and he proceeds to dismantle the team. Moises Alou is the first to go, and Kevin Brown and Al Leiter (to San Diego for Derrek Lee) are gone before the new year. Then in May 1998, the Marlins trade Gary Sheffield, Bobby Bonilla, and Jim Eisenreich to the Red Sox for Troy O'Leary, Trot Nixon, and Brian Rose.

After winning the championship, Huizenga claimed that the Marlins lost $34 million in '97, and he proceeded to dismantle the team. Alou went to Houston, Brown went to San Diego, and Leiter went to the Mets (for A.J. Burnett, among others). Then in May '98, the Marlins traded Sheffield, Bonilla, Eisenreich, Charles Johnson, and Manuel Barrios to the Dodgers for Piazza and Todd Zeile. Piazza was traded to the Mets 8 days later, for Preston Wilson, Ed Yarnall, and Geoff Goetz, and then Zeile was dumped on the Rangers.

The Padres win 91 games and the Wild Card, and after setting the home run record, Mark McGwire beats out Sammy Sosa for the NL MVP award. Darren Dreifort is outstanding in his first full season as a closer, with 44 saves and a 2.50 ERA. The Dodgers finish the year 94-68, but lose to the Astros in the NLDS. San Diego upsets the Braves and then Houston, and meets the 114-win Yankees in the World Series, where the Pads lose in four straight.

With Kevin Brown leading the way, the Padres won 98 games and the NL West title, and despite setting the home run record, McGwire lost out to Sosa in the MVP voting (thanks in large part to Sosa's Cubs winning the Wild Card). The Dodgers finished the year 83-79, a distant third place, and with no reliable closer, they traded prospects Paul Konerko and Dennys Reyes to the Reds for Jeff Shaw over the All-Star break. Thinking it would help him avoid injury (it didn't), the Dodgers moved Darren Dreifort to the starting rotation, where he had a mediocre year (8-12, 4.00 ERA). San Diego beat Houston and then the Braves to cop the NL pennant, and were swept by the Yankees in the World Series.

In need of a center fielder, the Dodgers send first base prospect Paul Konerko to the White Sox for Mike Cameron that winter. Cameron goes on to have a breakthrough season, batting .245/.345/.450 with 18 homers and 45 steals.

In September '98, the Dodgers' Fox ownership named Kevin Malone the new GM. Malone proceeded to make a series of questionable moves, including signing Kevin Brown to a huge long-term contract and bringing in the aging Devon White. And after the 1998 season, the Reds sent Konerko to the White Sox for Mike Cameron, who batted .256/.357/.469 with 21 homers and 38 steals for Cincinnati.

Obviously, the face of baseball has changed. In real life, the Reds packaged Cameron in a trade to Seattle that sent Ken Griffey Jr. to Cincy before the 2000 season. With no Cameron, the Reds' position wouldn't be nearly as strong, and a team like the Yankees would be in a great position to acquire Junior. So, let's say the Yankees send a comparable package... Alfonso Soriano, Ted Lilly, and Ricky Ledee.

But that leaves the M's without a center fielder. In real life, Houston traded CF Carl Everett to Boston for infielder Adam Everett that offseason, but with Gary Sheffield in the lineup, the Sox wouldn't really need Carl Everett's bat. Instead, the Mariners could acquire Everett as a one-season rental, sending shortstop Carlos Guillen back to Houston (where he began his career).

We could keep going on like this for hours (and pages), but you get the point -- a few hits can mean more than anyone realizes at the time. Eric Young's disappointing cup of coffee in 1992 set off a chain of events that nobody could have foreseen.

This article originally appeared on The Hardball Times on July 1, 2004 at http://www.hardballtimes.com/main/article/the-butterfly-effect/

So, Billy, What Does Work in the Playoffs?

By Vinay Kumar

"My s*** doesn't work in the playoffs."
-- Billy Beane, Oakland Athletics GM, in Michael Lewis'
Moneyball

Those words are some of the most famous uttered by a general manager in the last decade. Many have repeated Beane's words or paraphrases thereof, often to mean different things. Statheads see Beane recognizing that anything can happen in a short series (in fact, the foul-mouthed Beane continued, "My job is to get us to the playoffs. Everything after that is f****** luck."). Critics of sabermetrics interpret Beane's statement as an admission that sabermetrics don't apply to the postseason (which is a misunderstanding itself, since "sabermetrics" is defined as "the objective study of baseball," and not any specific principles).

Many people have theorized what kind of teams win in the playoffs. Since teams skip their fifth and sometimes fourth starters in the playoffs (giving more starts and innings to the top starters), it makes sense that front-line starting pitching is more important than depth. While many people have long understood that idea, the 2001 Diamondbacks drove the point home.

With the Athletics' well-chronicled four-year streak of losing in the first round, many pundits have talked about the importance of "small ball" and manufacturing runs. Many of these theories make sense -- in theory. But I don't know whether any data supports them; most of the time, people point to single instances to support their ideas, like the 2002 Angels or 2003 Marlins.

I'll ignore the holy wars and agendas while trying to answer the obvious follow-up question: what has worked in the playoffs? What are the traits of teams that have been successful in the playoffs?

Major League Baseball moved to an expanded playoff system in 1995 (well, they planned to move to the system

in 1994, but the strike caused the cancellation of the 1994 playoffs). Offensive levels jumped in 1993 and rose again for the next few years; the brand of baseball we've watched for the last decade differs noticeably from that of the previous few decades (in particular, there have been more long balls and strikeouts, and relief pitching roles have become increasingly specialized).

There has been much more talk during this past decade about baseball's finances and supposed competitive imbalance. Combine all these factors, and it makes sense to look at the playoffs since 1995 only, as the results from 1993 and earlier aren't necessarily relevant to today's postseason.

So which traits do translate into postseason success? I looked at all 63 postseason series that have been played since 1995 and looked at which team fared better in various statistical categories over the regular season, compared with which team won the series. For instance, the team with more regular season home runs has won 32 of the series, while losing 31 times -- a virtual dead heat.

While it may be tempting to infer that home run hitting is not important to playoff success, that isn't a fair reading of the data. Sixty-three series represents a lot of baseball, but still constitutes a small sample statistically. Furthermore, there are times when the "underdog" in the category isn't exactly a pipsqueak; the Yankees hit 230 HR last year, but counted as one of the low-HR upsets when they knocked off the 238-HR Red Sox. So I don't think any meaningful conclusions can be drawn from such a comparison; I think this exercise is useful just to add some actual data to the discussion and to see which arguments don't even have a leg to stand on.

So on to the data; here is the won-lost record (in terms of series won and lost, not games) of the teams which fared better in each measure:

Statistical Category	Series Won-Lost	Type of Statistic
Won-lost record	28-33	Overall
Run ratio (RS/RA)	34-29	Overall
Runs scored	27-36	Batting
Batting average	34-29	Batting
On-base percentage	34-29	Batting
Slugging percentage	31-32	Batting
Doubles	26-37	Batting

So, Billy, What Does Work in the Playoffs?

Statistical Category	Series Won-Lost	Type of Statistic
Triples	29-31	Batting
Home runs	32-31	Batting
Batters walks	31-31	Batting
Batters strikeouts (fewer)	37-26	Batting
Stolen bases	35-28	Base-stealing
Stolen base attempts (more)	36-27	Base-stealing
Net stolen bases (SB-2*CS)	27-35	Base-stealing
Stolen base percentage	27-36	Base-stealing
Caught stealing (fewer)	26-36	Base-stealing
Runs allowed	35-28	Pitching
ERA	34-29	Pitching
Pitchers strikeouts	38-25	Pitching
Pitchers walks (fewer)	32-30	Pitching
Hits allowed (fewer)	41-22	Pitching
Home runs allowed	37-26	Pitching
Complete games	31-28	Pitching
Pitchers shutouts	38-19	Pitching
Saves	31-28	Pitching
Saves by team leader	29-31	Pitching
Bullpen ERA *	34-29	Pitching
Errors committed (fewer)	38-24	Fielding
Defensive efficiency *	32-31	Fielding
Fielding double plays	29-31	Fielding

The wins and losses don't always add up to 63 because of cases where both teams tied; for instance, the 2000 Mets and Cardinals each walked 675 times, so their NLCS matchup is ignored for that category. For stats such as batters' strikeouts where it's ambiguous whether a higher or lower total is more desirable, the "fewer" or "more" indicates which one is considered the leader.

Well, this is quite interesting, as some of the results are very counter-intuitive; who would've guessed that the higher-scoring team would go only 27-36 in the playoffs? And the biggest head-scratcher is the 28-33 record for the team with the better regular-season record (feel free to use those tidbits in bar bets; just cut me in on a percentage).

I already identified a couple of reasons why these records are unreliable, and in some cases downright misleading. One thing I noticed is that in many cases, the two teams are pretty evenly matched in a particular category (like the aforementioned Yankees and Red Sox). Cases like that show up in the won-loss records above, though they don't really tell us anything (especially because the numbers are affected by a myriad of factors, like home parks, schedule vagaries, etc.).

So let's throw them out; for instance, instead of looking at all cases where one team steals more bases than the other, even if it's only by a couple of bags, let's look only at cases where one team steals 30 more than the other. This will leave us looking at just the series where the teams had a meaningful difference in skills.

I didn't pick the number 30 out of thin air; I went through each category and found the gap that would weed out roughly half of the series. After doing that, here is the same table, with one new column (the minimum spread between teams for the series to be included here), and now sorted by playoff success. The pitching/fielding statistics are shaded grey:

So, Billy, What Does Work in the Playoffs?

Statistical Category	Minimum Gap	Series Won-Lost
Hits allowed (fewer)	70	24-9
Errors committed (fewer)	12	24-10
Batters strikeouts (fewer)	65	22-10
Pitchers shutouts	2	22-11
Runs allowed	55	22-12
Home runs allowed	20	20-11
Stolen bases	30	21-12
Complete games	3	22-14
ERA	0.4	20-13
Defensive efficiency *	0.01	19-13
Pitchers strikeouts	90	18-13
Stolen base attempts (more)	35	18-13
Won-lost record	5	18-14
Saves by Team Leader	9	18-15
Run ratio (RS/RA)	0.1	16-15
Triples	5	17-16
Batters walks	60	16-16
On-base percentage	0.012	15-16
Bullpen ERA *	0.3	16-18
Pitchers walks (fewer)	50	15-17
Batting average	0.01	15-18
Saves	5	15-18
Fielding double plays	12	15-18
Net stolen bases (SB-2*CS)	20	15-20
Slugging percentage	0.025	12-18
Doubles	18	13-20
Stolen base percentage	0.05	14-22
Runs scored	65	12-19
Home runs	32	13-21
Caught stealing (fewer)	10	12-21

Now some of the quirks are eliminated; the team with the better regular-season record goes 18-14, about what we'd expect. But the most striking thing about this list is that it supports the old adages: you win in the postseason with pitching, fielding, and speed. Eleven of the 12 most important categories (by this crude measure) demonstrate skill on the mound, in the field and on the bases. Obviously some of those categories are inter-related (a gopherball is not just a HR allowed, but also a hit allowed, at least one run allowed and it ruins a shutout), but their dominance on this list is remarkable.

Only after these categories do we get to the measures of overall team success (won-lost record and run ratio) and then all the batting categories. Batting prowess (and power specifically) look completely irrelevant, as the teams that score more runs and hit for more power (whether measured by home runs, doubles, or slugging percentage) have done quite poorly in the postseason.

Interestingly, the only batting category that shows as a strong indicator of postseason success is batters' strikeouts -- the one category that sabermetricians have long called meaningless. I initially didn't consider this alarming, because HR and K are highly negative-correlated; the players who knock a lot of balls over the fences also whiff more than their share of the time. So strikeouts and home runs would have to balance, I thought; once you know

So, Billy, What Does Work in the Playoffs?

how poorly homers show up on the list, it's not additionally surprising that contact hitting shows up so high.

But then I looked at the data, and while strikeouts and home runs are strongly related for individuals, that's not the case for teams; the team with more home runs than its opponent struck out more often only 33/63 times (another way to put this: the correlation between home runs and strikeouts among playoff teams is only .091 -- virtually nothing). So maybe the statheads have been missing something.

The other stats at the bottom are times caught stealing and stolen base percentage (which are obviously related). Teams that run themselves into outs during the regular season are winning in the postseason; so it looks like maybe speed and daring are more important than judicious decision-making.

Interestingly, a strong bullpen (as measured by bullpen ERA) and a dominant relief ace (represented by a big gap in saves by the team leader) don't show up as important.

One thing we know is that the top closers pitch far more innings in the postseason than they do in the regular season, and thus have a greater impact.

All of this runs counter to most "stathead" thinking. The usual thought process is that a run earned is just as valuable as a run saved, to close approximation. Well, maybe that approximation breaks down in the postseason. More importantly, it does appear that the stronger pitching in the playoffs neutralizes some offenses, and differences in pitching, fielding and speed show up more.

Now that we know what recent series winners have excelled at, it's tempting to turn those into recommendations, or to grade actual teams against those criteria (note that Beane's most recent incarnation of the Athletics placed among the league's elite in many of the most telling categories). However, it's important to remember that correlation does not imply causation; recent winners have had certain traits in common, but it doesn't mean they won because of those traits.

Most of the statistics used here come from The Baseball Archive's fabulous Lahman database. A few were culled from the equally-fabulous Baseball-Reference.com.

I appreciate the help from other members of The Hardball Times staff in choosing what categories to examine and how to present the data. Special thanks to Craig Burley and Studes.

Bullpen ERA: I didn't have access to starting/relieving splits for this entire period. Instead, I approximated bullpen ERA by using the composite ERA of all pitchers who made at least 2/3 of their appearances that season in relief. This means that each team's bullpen ERA misses a few relief appearances and catches a handful of starts, but shouldn't impact the outcomes.

Defensive efficiency rating measures how effective a defensive unit turns balls in play into outs; basically it's (non-strikeou) outs divided by balls in play. I didn't have access to ball-in-play data, so I approximated DER as (IP*3-K)/(IP*3+H-HR-K-DP). Since I used the same approximation for every team, and we're only interested in the relative differences between teams, it's unlikely that this approximation affected the results at all. It's impossible to completely separate the impacts of pitchers from fielders; DER is an attempt to isolate the fielders' impact, while K, BB and HR allowed measure fielding-independent outcomes.

This article originally appeared on The Hardball Times on May 12, 2004 at http://www.hardballtimes.com/main/article/so-billy-what-does-work-in-the-playoffs/

Perfection Never Lasts Forever

By Robert Dudek

It's finally over - Eric Gagne doesn't make the century mark. His consecutive saves streak ended at 84 when Arizona strung three hits together to plate 2 runs and tie the game 5-5 in the 9th. Gagne's streak is 30 games longer than the previous record, set by Tom Gordon 5 years ago. No doubt it is a wonderful accomplishment, but baseball history is filled with other interesting streaks of pitching perfection.

The ultimate goal of pitching is to prevent runs, and so the consecutive scoreless innings streak has been of great significance for a long time. The record is held by Orel Hershiser at 59 consecutive scoreless innings, achieved in 1988 during the greatest season of his illustrious career. 1988 was a pitcher's year and Dodgers Stadium was one of the toughest parks in baseball to score a run in.

The former record holder was also a Dodger -- Don Drysdale. He tossed 58.1 consecutive scoreless innings during the height of the second deadball era (1968). Before Drysdale, the record was held by one of the greatest pitchers of all-time: Walter Johnson (56 innings). There was much fanfare attached to Hershiser's accomplishment -- it was hailed by Sam McManus of the L.A. Times as comparable to Joe Dimaggio's 56-game hit streak in difficulty and significance.

The record for consecutive punch outs also has a high profile. Tom Seaver had a string of 10 punch outs (5 of them called third strikes) on April 22, 1970 against the San Diego Padres. There may be a longer streak spread over two or more games, but I've found no mention of one. Seaver mowed down the last ten hapless Padres he faced before running out of innings. His next start was against the Dodgers -- Maury Wills grounded out to end Seaver's strikeout streak.

Another rare feat is striking out the side on 9 pitches - an ultra-perfect inning, so to speak. It turns out that this has been done only 37 times, including once this season by Ben Sheets. Three pitchers have accomplished the feat twice (and they may be familiar names to some of you): Lefty Grove (1928), Sandy Koufax (1962, 1964) and Nolan Ryan (1968, 1972). Needless to say, no one has done it in two consecutive innings.

The most talked about feat of perfect pitching is the perfect game. A perfect game is defined for official purposes as at least nine innings in length, in which the pitcher earns a complete game and retires all opposing batters without any reaching base. Since 1900, there have been only 15 official major-league perfect games (and two in the 19th century).

Most of you know that Randy Johnson tossed the most recent perfecto on May 18, 2004, the first in the major leagues since David Cone's in 1999. In his previous start (May 12th versus the Mets), Johnson gave up a single to Joe McEwing to leadoff the 6th and then retired the next six batters before leaving the game. In the start after the perfect game, Johnson retired the first 6 batters before allowing a leadoff double in the third to Florida's Abraham Nunez. But how many baseball fans were aware that if Johnson had been able to get through a 1-2-3 third inning, he would have broken the record for consecutive batters retired? Johnson's perfect streak ended at 39 batters, two shy of the longest streak on the books.

Listed in the table are most of the perfect game pitchers from Catfish Hunter's 1968 gem to the present and the number of batters they retired consecutively over multiple games. Of necessity, those occurring from 1993 to 1998 are not included due to the unavailability of play-by-play logs from an online source.

Date of Perfect Game	Pitcher	Next Game	Broken up by	Consecutive Retired	By K
'68 May 8th	C.Hunter	May 14th	R.Carew	**29**	11
'81 May 15th	L.Barker	May 20th	B.Bochte	**31**	13
'84 Sept 30th	M.Witt	April 9('85)	K.Puckett	**28**	10
'88 Sept 16th	T.Browning	Sept 21st	W.Clark	**40**	12
'91 July 28th	D.Martinez	August 2nd	W.Chamberlain	**31**	5
'99 July 18th	D.Cone	July 23rd	K.Lofton	**30**	11
'03 May 18th	R.Johnson	May 23rd	A.Nunez	**39**	14

Perfection Never Lasts Forever

Around the same time Hershiser was making headlines, Tom Browning wrote his name into history with his perfect game. Browning is not the kind of pitcher we expect to have a long streak of batters retired; nevertheless his streak of 40 is the second longest in history (we think). The pitcher who holds the record was not dissimilar to Tom Browning, except that he was not lefthanded. Righthander Jim Barr established the high water mark, retiring 41 consecutive batters in 1972.

Jim Barr and Tom Browning - Mirror Images?

Browning	Innings	K/9	BB/9	H/9
1987	183.0	5.75	3.00	9.89
1988	250.2	4.45	2.30	7.36
1989	249.2	4.25	2.31	8.69
Barr	Innings	K/9	BB/9	H/9
1972	179.0	4.32	2.06	8.35
1973	231.1	3.42	1.91	9.34
1974	239.2	3.15	1.76	8.37

Jim Barr established the record in his second major league season, not long after his conversion to starting pitching. To do it, he mowed down some of the best batsmen of the early '70s - Lou Brock, Willie Stargell, Roberto Clemente, Joe Torre and Ted Simmons among them. He retired the last 21 Pirates he faced on August 23, 1972 and then the first 20 Cardinals on August 29th before Bernie Carbo doubled with two outs in the 7th. Barr completed the game and earned a 3-hit shutout. What is amazing is that he struck out only 3 batters during the 41-batter streak, which means his fielders converted all 38 balls in play into outs during that stretch.

I didn't know about Barr's streak until a month ago, when it was the answer to a trivia question during one of the games I was watching on Extra Innings. In the course of researching perfect pitching streaks, I stumbled upon a very interesting article by Baseball Prospectus' Keith Woolner, which may have been the source material for the trivia question. Woolner found that between 1972 and 2003, there have been 68 streaks of 27 or more batters retired consecutively by a particular pitcher, including the seven official perfect games during that time. That's about two a year on average. The fact that Eric Gagne didn't retire as many as 27 straight batters in his dominating 2003 season illustrates how difficult it will be to break Barr's record.

How unlikely is it for a pitcher to retire 41 consecutive batters? Let's build a probability chart and find out. The first column will represent the chances of a particular pitcher getting a particular hitter out; the second will represent the chance of stringing together 41 successful outcomes (outs) at a given out probability:

Out Probability	Odds of 41 Straight
0.62	1 in 325.04 million
0.65	1 in 46.83 million
0.68	1 in 7.36 million
0.71	1 in 1.25 million
0.74	1 in 230 thousand
0.77	1 in 45 thousand
0.80	1 in 9.4 thousand

A streak like this can only start after a plate appearance in which a batter reaches base. I don't have a precise count, but I estimate it to be about 63,380 in the majors in 2003. That's about how many chances there were to start a consecutive batters retired streak.

Thus, if every pitcher were average in his ability to retire batters, and that average were around 68% (it was about 66.2% in 2003), the chances of a 41-batter streak occurring in a given year would be about 1 in 116 (7.36 million divided by 63,380). In reality, the odds are probably a tiny bit better than that because of the way pitching talent is distributed, and because consecutive batting events are not completely independent.

The one common feature of all streaks of perfect pitching is that they end. When you see a pitcher throw up a bunch of zeroes or strikeout a string of hitters, you'll know exactly how far away they are from the records held by Jim Barr, Orel Hershiser and Tom Seaver.

This article originally appeared on The Hardball Times on July 8, 2004 at http://www.hardballtimes.com/main/article/perfection-never-lasts-forever/

Re-Examining 300

by Aaron Gleeman

The next game Greg Maddux wins -- possibly tomorrow against the Brewers -- will be his 299th in the major leagues. Now, there are two ways to look at that piece of information. One is that Maddux is just two wins away from joining some very exclusive company in the 300-win club. The other is that Maddux, despite starting at age 20, having essentially an injury-free career and being one of the greatest pitchers in baseball history, is still two wins from 300.

Maddux, and Roger Clemens just slightly before him, show what I think is probably the upper limit for a pitcher in the current, five-man-rotation era. Maddux is in his 19th season, he's had 15 or more wins in every season except

his first two, he's thrown 200+ innings in 15 of his last 16 years, and he has a .637 career winning percentage. And yet, if he continues to pitch at this level until he's 40 (which is no given, certainly), he'll end up with maybe 330 wins.

It wasn't always this way, but the 300-win club has become the toughest to join. At the moment, 25 players have reached 3,000 hits, 20 players have reached 500 home runs, and 21 (soon to be 22) players have reached 300 wins.

However, take a look at how many members each club had at the beginning of each decade ...

CLUB	1960	1970	1980	1990	2000	NOW
3000 Hits	7	7	14	15	22	25
300 Wins	12	14	14	19	20	21
500 Home Runs	3	8	12	14	16	20

In other words, since 1960, 18 players have reached 3,000 hits, 17 players have reached 500 home runs, and just nine players have reached 300 wins. For those of you who don't want to look quite that far back in history, consider that, since 1990, 10 hitters have reached 3,000 hits and six hitters have reached 500 home runs, but just Nolan Ryan and Clemens (and soon to be Maddux) have reached 300 wins.

After Maddux gets #300 this year, I don't see anyone getting there for quite a while. The closest active pitchers after Maddux are Tom Glavine (258), Randy Johnson (240), Mike Mussina (208), David Wells (206) and Kevin Brown (204). I would give Wells and Brown absolutely zero shot at getting to 300 and, while I think Glavine, Johnson and Mussina all have some sort of a chance, I wouldn't bet on any of them getting there. Johnson is 40, Glavine is 38 and Mussina, though "only" 35, has a 5.20 ERA this season and would need to average 18 wins a year through age 40 to get #300.

So who does that leave? Well, the active pitcher under 35 years old who has the most wins is Pedro Martinez, who is 32 years old and has 176 wins. Assuming Pedro gets another 6-7 wins this year, he would then need to average 17-18 wins per year through age 39 to reach 300. I'm generally for not putting anything past Pedro Martinez, but even that might be a little much for him, considering his current ERA and always-tender right arm.

All of which is a very long way of saying that I think the "standard" of 300 wins for greatness (or an automatic

ticket to the Hall of Fame) for a pitcher probably needs to be re-examined. If hitters are joining both the 500-homer and 3,000-hit clubs at double the rate pitchers are joining the 300-win club, and pitchers in this era are starting far fewer games than pitchers were when the 300-win club was being filled up, doesn't it only make sense to lower the threshold for greatness?

In other words, if we're going to use "magic numbers" for career milestones, we should at least recognize when the numbers start getting easier or harder to reach. In the case of the number 300, it is no longer effective in identifying great pitchers -- it is good at identifying *extraordinary* pitchers. I'm thinking 250 wins might be the new number. At 250 wins, you've got Glavine in, Johnson joining early next year, Mussina still needing three more good years, and guys like Wells and Brown on the outside, looking in. All of which sounds just about right to me.

Now, I'm not going to say that no one is going to join the 300-win club after Maddux, because that sort of thinking is just silly. Clearly, if Maddux and Clemens have gotten there, in (more or less) this current era of offense and rotation size, then it can and most likely will be done again. It's just going to take an extremely special pitcher to do so, someone along the lines of Clemens or Maddux, which is to say one of the greatest handful of pitchers in baseball history.

Meanwhile, guys will be joining the 500-homer club and, to a lesser extent, the 3,000-hit club at much more frequent paces. Hell, just in the past several years, Barry

Bonds, Mark McGwire, Sammy Sosa, Rafael Palmeiro, and Ken Griffey Jr. have hit their 500th career home runs, and Fred McGriff is just seven long balls short. In another few years, it's very likely that Frank Thomas (436), Jeff Bagwell (432), Jim Thome (412), and maybe even guys like Juan Gonzalez (434) and Gary Sheffield (399), will hit their 500th homers. And then right on their tails you've got Alex Rodriguez (369) and Manny Ramirez (374), who both seem like pretty safe bets to make it right now.

But if, as I just discussed, the group of active wins leaders like Glavine, Johnson and Mussina doesn't look likely to provide a bunch of 300-game winners, who might the next 300-game winners be? Well, honestly, I think it's probably more likely that, aside from Maddux and Clemens, no one pitching in the major leagues right now will ever win 300 games than it is that even one more pitcher will. That might sound severe, but that's how tough it is to win 300 in your career when, at most, you're starting 35 games per season.

To see just how many things have to go right for a pitcher to win 300 games in this current era, take a look at where Clemens and Maddux stood in wins through each age ...

	20	21	22	23	24	25	26	27	28	29
Clemens	0	9	16	40	60	78	95	116	134	152
Maddux	2	8	26	45	60	75	95	115	131	150

So -- and I suppose this makes sense -- Clemens and Maddux were both basically half way there at the end of their 20s. I think it's also interesting to notice just how close they were to each other through each age. They were both at 60 wins through 24, 95 wins through 26, etc.

Also, if you look at the year-by-year path of **Tom Seaver**, the only other 300-game winner to do so in similar circumstances (that is, not getting 40+ starts in a season several times), it also looks very similar ...

	20	21	22	23	24	25	26	27	28	29
Clemens	0	9	16	40	60	78	95	116	134	152
Maddux	2	8	26	45	60	75	95	115	131	150
Seaver	0	0	16	32	57	75	95	116	135	146

Again, it looks to me like you'd better start racking up wins very early, get to around 75 wins by age 25, and be half way to 300 by the time you finish up your age-29 season. With that in mind, there's one obvious question: Is there anyone out there right now who looks like they can do that?

Let's take a look. Below you'll find the year-by-year win totals of every significant or noteworthy starting pitcher (as far as I could determine) currently between the ages of 20 and 29, along with the average of Clemens, Seaver and Maddux through each age. Years marked with an asterisk are the current, in-progress season, so the win total isn't finished.

	20	21	22	23	24	25	26	27	28	29
Roger/Greg/Tom	0	6	19	39	59	76	95	116	133	149
Edwin Jackson	4*									
Zack Greinke	2*									
Jeremy Bonderman	6	12*								
Dontrelle Willis	0	14	21*							
Jerome Williams	0	7	16*							
Oliver Perez	4	8	14*							
Rich Harden	0	5	9*							
C.C. Sabathia	17	30	43	49*						
Carlos Zambrano	1	5	18	27*						
Mark Prior	0	6	24	26*						
Jake Peavy	0	6	18	25*						
Jon Garland	4	10	22	34	41*					
Josh Beckett	0	2	8	17	21*					
Mark Buehrle	0	4	20	39	53	63*				

Re-Examining 300

	20	21	22	23	24	25	26	27	28	29
Roger/Greg/Tom	**0**	**6**	**19**	**39**	**59**	**76**	**95**	**116**	**133**	**149**
Joel Pineiro	0	1	7	21	37	42*				
Ben Sheets	0	0	11	22	33	42*				
Johan Santana	0	2	3	11	23	31*				
Mark Mulder	0	0	9	30	49	64	77*			
Barry Zito	0	0	7	24	47	61	66*			
Roy Oswalt	0	0	0	14	33	43	52*			
Brad Penny	0	0	8	18	26	40	48*			
Javier Vazquez	0	5	14	25	41	51	64	75*		
Roy Halladay	0	1	9	13	18	37	59	66*		
Kerry Wood	0	13	13	21	33	45	59	64*		
Sidney Ponson	0	8	20	29	34	41	58	63*		
Randy Wolf	0	0	6	17	27	38	54	58*		
Jeff Weaver	0	0	9	20	33	44	51	58*		
Wade Miller	0	0	0	6	22	37	51	58*		
Kip Wells	0	0	4	10	20	32	42	46*		
Tim Hudson	0	0	0	11	31	49	64	80	87*	
Freddy Garcia	0	0	0	17	26	44	60	72	80*	
Eric Milton	0	0	8	15	28	43	56	57	68*	
Kelvim Escobar	0	3	10	24	34	40	45	58	63*	
Kevin Millwood	0	0	5	22	40	50	57	75	89	97*
Livan Hernandez	0	0	9	19	27	44	57	69	84	90*
Matt Morris	0	0	12	19	19	22	44	61	72	82*
Matt Clement	0	0	0	3	12	25	34	46	60	67*
Jarrod Washburn	0	0	0	6	10	17	28	46	56	66*

Okay, that's one gigantic table, but what does it say? Well, I listed the year-by-year win totals of 38 different active pitchers, from guys currently in their age-20 season to guys currently in their age-29 season. The big question is obviously which of them are at or ahead of the paces of Clemens, Maddux and Seaver at the same age?

Setting aside guys like Edwin Jackson, Zack Greinke and Jeremy Bonderman, all of whom simply started pitching at a younger age than the 300-win threesome, four of the remaining 35 pitchers are at least close to the paces of Clemens, Maddux and Seaver, and all four are either in their age-22 or age-23 seasons.

Dontrelle Willis has 21 wins already, which puts him ahead of the pace of the 300-win threesome, who had an average of 19 wins at the end of their age-22 season. Jerome Williams and Oliver Perez, also 22-year-olds, are not to 19 wins yet, but they should be there or very close by season's end.

C.C. Sabathia is the guy who is the furthest ahead of the pace. Sabathia is in his age-23 season and has 49 wins. The average of the 300-win threesome through age-23 was 39, so Sabathia has a chance to get even further ahead of the pace before the end of the year. If Sabathia can win five more games between now and the end of this season, he would then need just six wins next year (his age-24 season) to stay on the pace.

Above and beyond everything else, what the above table shows is that, the younger you are, the better chance you have of being at or better than the Clemens/Maddux/Seaver pace. All of which says to me just how tough it is for someone to maintain that pace as they get to 26, 27, 28 years old. I mean, Sabathia is ahead of the pace, and has a very good shot at being ahead of the pace after next year too, but do you think he has a good chance of getting to 149 wins through his age-29 season?

Assuming he wins five more games this year, he would then need to win an average of 16 games per season from age 24 to age 29. Sabathia has won at least 16 games in a season just one time, his rookie year, when he won 17 games as a 20-year-old. He won 13 games in both his second and third seasons and is on pace for just 10 wins this season.

Of course, what makes getting 300 wins so incredibly tough is not necessarily staying on pace through your 20s. I mean, let's say Sabathia benefits from a Cleveland lineup that appears to be getting very good, and he wins those 16 games per year from 24-29. Then he's sitting at 149 wins after his age-29 season. And guess what? He's half-way there!

Here's what Clemens, Maddux and Seaver did after turning 30 ...

	30	31	32	33	34	35	36	37	38	39	40	41
Clemens	11	20	30	40	61	81	95	108	128	141	158	169*
Seaver	22	36	57	73	89	99	113	118	127	142	158	165
Maddux	15	34	52	71	90	107	123	139	148*			

If the part about getting to 150 wins by the end of your 20s doesn't kill your chances, the part about getting 150 wins after you turn 30 almost certainly will. So who will the next 300-game winner be, after Maddux gets there this season? My guess is that the guy is probably playing Little League ball right now, and there's a chance he hasn't even been born yet.

Greg Maddux finished the year with 305 lifetime victories. C.C. Sabathia finished with 54. This article originally appeared on The Hardball Times on July 26, 2004 at http://www.hardballtimes.com/main/article/re-examining-300/

Fearsome Foursomes

By Aaron Gleeman

Last week, Brian Gunn of Redbird Nation penned a guest column for THT about the first-place St. Louis Cardinals. In it, he discussed how one of the main reasons for St. Louis' surprising dominance this year has been the outstanding play of their three superstars -- Albert Pujols, Jim Edmonds and Scott Rolen.

Brian described it as "like having three MVPs, one after another, in the heart of your order" and gawked over their amazing offensive numbers, which now look like this ...

	AVG	OBP	SLG	OPS	GPA	2B	HR	RUN	RBI
Edmonds	.302	.417	.654	1.071	.351	31	31	76	80
Rolen	.332	.411	.611	1.022	.338	27	26	81	98
Pujols	.317	.402	.620	1.022	.336	30	32	95	81

Less than 24 hours after Brian's piece appeared here, the Cardinals went out and made a big trade, acquiring Larry Walker from the Colorado Rockies for minor leaguers Luis Martinez, Chris Narveson and Jason Burch.

If you thought the heart of the Cardinals' batting order had some ridiculous numbers last week, take a look at what they've got now ...

	AVG	OBP	SLG
2) Larry Walker, RF	.316	.467	.607
3) Albert Pujols, 1B	.317	.402	.620
4) Scott Rolen, 3B	.332	.411	.611
5) Jim Edmonds, CF	.302	.417	.654

The crazy offensive numbers those four have put up so far this year get only slightly less crazy if you look at what they did from 2001-2003 ...

	AVG	OBP	SLG
2) Larry Walker, RF	.325	.431	.583
3) Albert Pujols, 1B	.334	.412	.613
4) Scott Rolen, 3B	.280	.372	.510
5) Jim Edmonds, CF	.297	.406	.580

Of course, Walker did much of that damage while playing in Colorado, which means his numbers are definitely Coors-inflated. However, even if you completely toss out the work he's done in Colorado over the years, Walker is still a very good offensive player. For this year, he's hitting a Bonds-like .298/.515/.723 away from Coors Field, but in only 70 plate appearances. From 2001-2003, Walker hit .279/.392/.494 away from Coors (as opposed to an incredible .370/.469/.668 at Coors).

If you consider that most players, even those who play in normal environments, tend to do better at home, plus the fact that some studies have shown that Rockies' hitters have a sort of "hangover" effect that hurts their road numbers, I think it's probably safe to say Walker's non-Coors level of performance over the past 3+ seasons is about .300/.400/.500 or so.

Here's how Walker's OPS+ (which adjusts for home ballparks) compares to his new teammates over the past three years ...

	2001	2002	2003	Avg
Albert Pujols	158	155	189	167
Jim Edmonds	150	163	161	158
Larry Walker	160	146	124	143
Scott Rolen	126	132	139	132
TOTALS	149	149	153	150

That is some serious hitting. Basically, that foursome has averaged a 150 OPS+ between them over the past three years, and that number will likely be even higher this season. To put that into some context, only 37 players in baseball history with at least 3,000 plate appearances have a career OPS+ of 150 or higher.

However, I think what truly makes the Cardinals' foursome unique is not only that they are all great offensively, but that they are also all very good defensively. As Brian Gunn wrote while talking about Pujols, Edmonds and Rolen:

On top of [the offense], each of these guys is among the top glovemen at his position. Pujols is fifth in fielding Win Shares at first (a former third baseman, he's very handy with the leather), Edmonds is second in center (those SportsCenter "web gems" aren't just hype), and Rolen, of course, is the best third baseman in the league.

Now they've added Walker, who is certainly no slouch defensively; he is a seven-time Gold Glove winner and is considered by many to be among the greatest defensive rightfielders in baseball history. Along with Walker's seven Gold Gloves, Edmonds has six of his own and Rolen has five. The Gold Glove count leaves Pujols as the odd man out, but this is his first season as an everyday first baseman.

Just how good, offensively and defensively, are Rolen, Pujols, Edmonds and Walker? Well, thanks to the wonder of Win Shares, we can actually examine that question in a meaningful way.

First, let's look at what the St. Louis foursome has been worth according to Win Shares over the past three years ...

	2001	2002	2003	Tot
Albert Pujols	29	32	41	102
Scott Rolen	29	28	25	82
Jim Edmonds	30	29	22	81
Larry Walker	25	26	18	69
TOTALS	113	115	106	334

From 2001-2003, the foursome was worth an average of 28 Win Shares apiece per season, which is phenomenal. How good is that? Well, Bill James wrote in *The New Bill James Historical Baseball Abstract* that, "A 30-Win Share season is, in general, an MVP candidate-type season."

This year, Walker's Win Share total is low because he's missed even more time than he usually does with injuries, but Rolen, Pujols and Edmonds are each having fantastic seasons. Right now, Rolen is on pace for an all-time great season of 45 Win Shares, while Pujols (38) and Edmonds (35) are also on pace for MVP-caliber seasons. Walker is on pace for just 10 Win Shares, but that pace should quickly pick up if he remains healthy. And, even if Walker ends up with only 10 on the year, the foursome would be looking at an average of 32 each if the other three stay on their current pace.

Fearsome Foursomes

With the help of THT's Win Shares expert, Studes, I looked at the "established" Win Shares for foursomes throughout baseball history. In other words, taking the three-year averages of players together on one team. So, if you're talking about the 2004 St. Louis Cardinals' foursome, you take their averages from 2001-2003 and that's their established Win Shares level. If you're talking about the 1927 New York Yankees' foursome, you take their averages from 1924-1926. Simple enough, right?

What I basically wanted to find was how good the players were at the point they were together. Rolen, Walker, Edmonds and Pujols are all, more or less, in their primes right now (or at least playing at very high levels), whereas there were many combos that included a washed up former star or a future star just getting started. For instance, Hank Aaron and Robin Yount played together on the 1976 Milwaukee Brewers, but Aaron was a 42-year-old hitting .229/.315/.369 in his final season and Yount was a 20-year-old hitting .252/.292/.301. We could find a couple more good players on that team (Darrell Porter, Gorman Thomas) to a make an impressive-sounding foursome, but that's misleading.

Using the three-year averages for their established level of play, the top foursome in baseball history comes from the 1930 New York Yankees, with Babe Ruth, Lou Gehrig, Earle Combs and Tony Lazzeri. Between them, the four Hall of Famers averaged 133 Win Shares per season from 1927-1929. Similarly, the same group from the 1929 Yankees (with the averages being from 1926-1928) came in second all-time, with an average of 131 Win Shares per season.

This year's Cardinals team (using their levels of play from 2001-2003) comes in 40th all-time, which frankly doesn't sound all that impressive. However, if you narrow the search down to only modern teams, the Cardinals shoot way up the list. In fact, the last foursome to have a higher established Win Shares level than this Cardinals' group came from the Cincinnati Reds during the "Big Red Machine" days of the 1970s. The Reds bettered this year's Cardinals' foursome multiple times behind Joe Morgan, Johnny Bench, Pete Rose and Tony Perez, all of whom are Hall of Famers or would be if they were allowed in.

The highest established Win Shares foursome of the last 50 years comes from the 1975 Cincinnati Reds, whose foursome of Morgan, Bench, Rose and Perez averaged a combined 127 Win Shares per season from 1972-1974. The other Big Red Machine teams weren't too shabby either. The 1976 Reds have the second-best established Win Shares total of any team of the past 50 years and the 1974 Reds come in third during that stretch. The 1973 Reds (117 established Win Shares), 1977 Reds (119) and 1978 Reds (115) also rank among the top dozen foursomes of the past 50 years.

Let's take a closer look at that foursome from 1975 ...

First of all, I guess it should come as no surprise that the team with the best foursome of the past 50 years ended up winning 108 games and the World Series. The '75 Reds won the division by 20 games over the Dodgers, swept the Pirates in the National League Championship Series, and then beat the Red Sox in seven games to capture the World Series.

Here's what their Win Shares totals looked like coming into the 1975 season ...

	1972	1973	1974	Tot
Joe Morgan	39	40	37	116
Johnny Bench	37	26	34	97
Pete Rose	32	34	27	93
Tony Perez	25	32	20	77
TOTALS	133	132	118	383

Compare those numbers to the St. Louis foursome who, from 2001-2003, were worth 113, 115 and 106 Win Shares, for a total of 334 Win Shares. The '75 Cincinnati foursome had an established Win Shares level that was 15% higher than the Cardinals' foursome, which is pretty astounding.

In the three years prior to 1975 (the years counted for their established levels in 1975), here's what the Reds' foursome did ...

	AVG	OBP	SLG	NOTES
Joe Morgan	.291	.416	.474	183 SBs; two Gold Gloves; 4th, 4th, 8th in MVP voting
Johnny Bench	.268	.362	.492	'72 NL MVP; three Gold Gloves; NL RBI champ in '72 & '74
Pete Rose	.310	.389	.414	'73 NL MVP; '73 batting champ
Tony Perez	.287	.358	.494	7th, 6th, 7th in RBI; 7th in '73 MVP voting

At first glance, those numbers don't seem all that extraordinary. After all, none of the four slugged over .500 in the three-year period. However, you have to remember that the levels of offense were a lot lower back then, particularly when it came to power. If you adjust their hitting from 1972-1974 to the offensive environment that

Fearsome Foursomes

Pujols, Rolen and Edmonds were in last season, for instance, the numbers come out looking a lot more impressive ...

	AVG	OBP	SLG
Joe Morgan	.301	.429	.533
Johnny Bench	.276	.373	.554
Pete Rose	.320	.401	.466
Tony Perez	.296	.369	.556

Suddenly Morgan is a Gold Glove second baseman hitting .301/.429/.533 and stealing 60 bases a year, Bench is a Gold Glove catcher hitting .276/.373/.554, Rose is hitting .320 and getting on base 40% of the time, and Perez is slugging .556. The Reds' foursome had at least two players among the top dozen MVP vote-getters each year. They finished 1st (Bench), 4th (Morgan) and 12th (Rose) in 1972, 1st (Rose), 4th (Morgan), 7th (Perez) and 10th (Bench) in 1973, and 4th (Bench) and 8th (Morgan) in 1974.

Also, the one big advantage the Reds' foursome had over the Cardinals' foursome is their health, which makes a difference when we're talking about their total value to a team. From 2001-2003, the Cardinals' foursome missed a combined total of 157 games, or 8.1% of their total games. From 1972-1974, the Reds' foursome missed a combined

total of 76 games, or 4.0% of their total games (1972 was a 154-game season).

I've been very critical of Joe Morgan's work as an announcer and writer for ESPN and ESPN.com, but there is absolutely no denying his greatness as a baseball player. In fact, I believe Joe Morgan is one of the most underrated and under-appreciated players in baseball history. Looking up some of the numbers for this article just hammered that point home with me.

Consider that, in 1975, he hit .327/.466/.508, led the league in on-base percentage, OPS, walks and OPS+, ranked among the top 10 in the league in batting average, slugging percentage, runs scored and stolen bases, won a Gold Glove at second base, and was the MVP of the National League. Adjusted to current levels of offense, Morgan hit approximately .330 with a .470 on-base percentage and a .570 slugging percentage, while stealing 67 bases at an 87% clip.

And then he went ahead and did even better the next year, hitting .320/.444/.576 while leading the league in on-base percentage, slugging percentage, OPS and OPS+, ranking second in runs scored, RBI, walks, extra-base hits and stolen bases, and winning another Gold Glove at second base on his way to back-to-back NL MVPs. Translated to today's levels of offense, that works out to around .325/.455/.660, which is absolutely amazing.

The Cardinals' Big Three combined for 114 Win Shares, the fifth-highest total of any threesome since 1900, and Walker added another 7 in approximately one-third of a season. This article originally appeared on The Hardball Times August 12, 2004 at http://www.hardballtimes.com/main/article/fearsome-foursomes/

The Pitcher is a Pinch Hitter

By Dave Studenmund

Pinch hitters typically bat for the pitcher (at least in the National League), but how often have you seen a pitcher regularly bat as a pinch hitter? Well, if you had been alive 70 to 100 years ago, you would have seen it plenty of times.

In fact, the player most commonly believed to be the first true "professional" pinch hitter was a pitcher. That would be one Dode Criss, who played for the St. Louis Browns from 1908 to 1911. Criss was the first player to pinch hit at least 100 times in his career, compiling 35 hits in 147 at bats for a .239 average. Most notably, he batted .341 as a pinch hitter his rookie year, and led the American League in pinch hits all four of his major league years.

Criss was a righty pitcher, lefty hitter who compiled a lackluster pitching record (3-9 with a 4.38 ERA). In fact, manager Jimmy McAleer gave him some playing time in the outfield and first base, and Criss garnered 30 games on the mound, 26 at first and 11 in the outfield. He wound up with 12 batting Win Shares and only 2 pitching Win Shares, but wasn't a good enough hitter to be a regular. Yet his historic role as the first regular pinch hitter preserves his place in baseball history.

Several other pitchers have also set pinch hitting milestones. Going back in time, the first pinch hitter to record more than one pinch hit in a season was a pitcher -- Baltimore's Kid Gleason in 1894. 1893 was the year that baseball moved the pitching mound back to today's 60' 6", which hurt Gleason's pitching effectiveness. So he morphed into a pinch hitter, and then became a regular infielder for twelve years with the Giants, Tigers and Phillies.

Gleason also has a unique place in baseball history because he was reportedly the first manager to issue an intentional walk to the opposing team's best hitter (don't tell Barry Bonds!). But he'll unfortunately be most remembered for managing the 1919 Black Sox.

After Criss, the next notable Pitcher as Pinch Hitter (or PAPH) was George "The Bull" Uhle, who was a fine pitcher and hitter in the 1920's. Uhle won 200 games and batted .282 (albeit in a hitter's era), and he's the third all-time PAPH with 44 base hits in 169 at bats. Unlike Criss, Uhle was a pitcher first; he compiled 210 pitching Win Shares and 20 batting Win Shares. Really, Uhle was a classic PAPH who never played a position in the field other than pitcher.

But Uhle was paving the way for the 1930's and the three of the finest PAPH's in major league history: Red Ruffing, Wes Ferrell and Red Lucas.

Red Ruffing is a Hall of Famer who won 273 games with a 3.80 ERA, and he was a mainstay of the Yankee rotation throughout the 1930's. Less well known, however, was the fact that Ruffing was a fine hitter, and the second most prolific PAPH in history with 58 hits in 228 at bats for a .255 average. Altogether, Ruffing racked up 290 pitching Win Shares and 30 batting Win Shares.

Wes Ferrell holds two hitting records for pitchers: most home runs in a season (nine) and career (38). As you can imagine, he was also called on to pinch hit frequently, but the role didn't seem to agree with him. Ferrell produced only 31 hits in 139 at bats for a .223 average, compared to an overall batting average of .280. Still, Ferrell compiled 208 pitching Win Shares and 25 batting Win Shares.

But the all-time best PAPH was Red Lucas, the Manny Mota of his day. Lucas was not only the best PAPH ever, he was the best pinch hitter ever, at his time. He set a standard for career pinch hitting, with 114 hits in 437 at bats for a .261 batting average that remained the best career pinch hitting record for more than thirty years.

Like Criss, Lucas threw righty and batted lefty. But unlike Criss, Lucas was a good pitcher who stayed on the mound his entire career. Over 15 years from 1923 to 1938, he compiled a 157-134 record with a 3.72 ERA. But he was most valued for his bat off the bench, as he hit more than 13 pinch hits in a season five years in a row, from 1929 to 1933, and led the league in both pinch at bats and hits three different years. He finished with 172 pitching Win Shares and 23 batting Win Shares.

Sadly, they don't make hitting pitchers like they used to. To illustrate what I mean, here's a graph of the average number of batting Win Shares by pitchers per year, grouped by decade. I'm using batting Win Shares, because they are adjusted for the general hitting level of each league, each year.

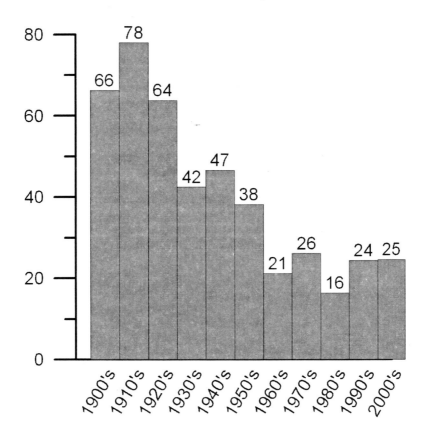

Average Batting Win Shares Per Year
Pitchers Only

Although Win Shares has its faults, it's still a useful stat in this case (I used to say there were no useless stats, until someone invented Productive Outs), because it effectively tracks the top batting pitchers from each year. In other words, this is a graph of the batting productivity of each decade's top batting pitchers. And when it comes to batting pitchers, they just don't make them like they used to.

It's true that today's top hitting pitchers are better than those of the 1980's, but pitchers really haven't been hitting like they used to for half a century. In other words, Brooks Kieschnick is not only a rarity, he's a throwback.

Coming out of the University of Texas in 1993, Kieschnick was a first-round choice of the Chicago Cubs, nine picks behind Alex Rodriquez and a full round ahead of Scott Rolen. Although he was a fine college pitcher, the Cubs most valued him for his potentially powerful bat. Kieschnick developed well at first and Baseball America ranked him the number one Cubs' prospect during his first three professional years.

Unfortunately, Kieschnick never produced on the major league level and the Cubs let him go. It looked like he would remain a AAA lifer until the Cubs' cross-town rivals decided to try him on the mound. For some reason,

even the White Sox eventually let him go, and the Brewers picked him up as a minor league free agent a couple of years ago. Give Kieschnick and manager Ned Yost credit for trying something that hasn't been done since the days of Red Lucas -- putting a PAPH on the roster and making it work.

Last year, Kieschnick compiled a 5.26 ERA in 53 innings, and batted .300 with a .614 slugging average. A righty pitcher and lefty batter, he looked more like Dode Criss than Red Lucas. As a pinch hitter, he was 8 for 21 with two home runs, and he also played a few games as the DH and in left field. Overall, he compiled 1.6 pitching Win Shares and 1.9 batting Win Shares.

It's a different story this year, as Kieschnick has compiled a 3.82 ERA and already has 2.3 pitching Win Shares, along with 1.6 batting Win Shares.

Unfortunately, Kieschnick hasn't actually been hitting that well this year. Last year, Brooks was dynamite, with seven home runs in only 70 at bats and a .969 OPS. He was truly Ferrell-esque. This year is another story, however. Kieschnick has only hit one home run in 50 at bats, and his OPS is a pedestrian .784.

What's more, our THT stats indicate that he's been pretty lucky with the bat this year. He hasn't been putting

The Pitcher is a Pinch Hitter

any loft on the ball -- his Groundball/Flyball ratio is 2.1 -- and his line drive rate is only .056. However, his BABIP (Batting Average on Balls in Play) is an extraordinarily high .400. Typically BABIP is a batter's line drive rate plus .110, or .167 in this case. Kieschnick has seen a lot of ground balls go his way.

Still, pinch hitting is a tough job and he is pinch hitting pretty well; he is batting .263 in the role and he's tied for fifth in the majors in total pinch hits (10 for 38).

Just how valuable is it to have a pitcher who can also pinch hit? In a word, very. If a pitcher can act as an effective pinch hitter, it frees up a roster spot for the manager to include another player; it's like having a 26-man roster. Overall, that could potentially add a win or two over a full season.

There's a statistical way to look at this phenomenon. Here at The Hardball Times, we track a stat called WSAA (Win Shares Above Average). To calculate WSAA, we first compute the average number of Win Shares that a player would be expected to produce in his playing time, depending on whether he is a batter or pitcher. Pitchers are expected to produce less with the bat, so the standard of comparison is different. And because Kieschnick is a pitcher, he overwhelms his batting standard.

Kieschnick has four Win Shares, but he is only expected to have one at this point, given his playing time. Unfortunately, Kieschnick was just placed on the disabled list with shoulder tendinitis, so he may be stuck at three WSAA above average for a while. But that still makes him the fourth most valuable player on the Brewers -- which is the direct result of the unique role he plays.

So here's to Brooks Kieschnick, Pitcher as Pinch Hitter. Let's hope he's not the last of his kind.

Kieschnick returned in September and finished with four Win Shares and 3 WSAA, which was the third-best WSAA total on the team. This article originally appeared on The Hardball Times on August 17, 2004 at http://www.hardballtimes.com/main/article/the-pitcher-is-a-pinch-hitter/

Opposite Directions

By Ben Jacobs

Last year, the Seattle Mariners finished 50 games ahead of the Detroit Tigers in the standings. Seattle went 93-69 while Detroit finished 43-119. Usually, when a team finishes that far ahead of another team in the standings, you'd expect them to finish ahead of the same team again the next year. This season, however, is providing a reminder that it doesn't always work out that way.

Today, Seattle (58-94) is 10 games behind Detroit (68-83). If things stay the way they are, that two-team swing of about 60 games in the standings from one year to the next will be one of the biggest in major league history.

This isn't the first time a team has finished at least 40 games ahead of another team one year and behind that team the next. As far as I can tell, it's happened five other times. Here's a brief look at what went on each time.

2001-02 Mariners and Angels

In 2001, Seattle was the toast of baseball with its 116-46 record while Anaheim had a nondescript, third-place 75-87 campaign. The next year, the Mariners didn't have everything go their way as they had the year before and fell to "only" 93-69. The Angels, meanwhile, caught fire and went 99-63 on their way to winning the World Series.

The Mariners simply had everything fall right in 2001. Several players had career years and Seattle led the majors in both runs scored (927) and runs allowed (627). Even with those run totals, the Mariners won seven more games than the Pythagorean Theorem says they should have. Those kinds of seasons just don't happen twice in a row.

Some players (Olerud, Guillen, Moyer, John Halama) were actually better in 2002 than in 2001, but not enough. Boone had a good season instead of a historic one, Martinez, Ichiro and Cameron all slipped a bit, Cirillo wasn't as good as David Bell had been and Seattle's offense went from a .360 OBP and .445 SLG to a .350 OBP and .419 SLG. That cost the Mariners 113 runs and dropped them to sixth in the AL.

On the pitching side, Garcia was significantly worse, Pineiro pitched more innings but wasn't as ridiculously good and James Baldwin was terrible. The Mariners saw their ERA rise from 3.54 to 4.07 and fell to fifth in the league in runs allowed (699).

This time, the Mariners did exactly what those run totals said they should have, and the result was a loss of 23 games in the standings. The Angels, meanwhile, were going the other direction with almost exactly the same team.

The Anaheim middle infield of Adam Kennedy and David Eckstein improved dramatically, Garret Anderson

had his first legitimately great season, Tim Salmon rebounded nicely from his worst season and Brad Fullmer arrived and hit .289/.357/.503.

All that helped the Angels to improve from .261/.327/.405 and 691 runs scored (12th in the league) to .282/.341/.433 and 851 runs scored (fourth in the league).

The pitching changed almost as dramatically. In 2001, only one Anaheim pitcher who started more than one game posted an ERA below 4.30. In 2002, only two Anaheim pitchers who started more than one game posted an ERA above 4.30.

Ramon Ortiz and Jarrod Washburn both improved their numbers significantly while Kevin Appier and John Lackey both arrived in Anaheim and had solid seasons. The bullpen was excellent thanks to Troy Percival, Ben Weber, Brendan Donnelly and Scot Shields and the team's ERA fell from 4.20 to 3.69. After finishing fourth in the league with 730 runs allowed in 2001, the Angels led the league with 644 runs allowed in 2002.

The Angels actually underperformed by a couple of wins in 2002, but they were still good enough for a 47-game swing between them and the Mariners.

1993-94 Giants and Mets

In 1993, San Francisco and New York had mirror records. The Giants went 103-59 while the Mets went 59-103. Things were much different for both teams the next year. The Mets stood near .500 at 55-58 while the Giants were a game further below even at 55-60 when the strike ended the season.

One year after winning 103 games but still missing the playoffs, everything fell apart for the Giants.

Todd Benzinger (.265/.304/.399) replaced Will Clark (.283/.367/.432) at first base after he signed with Texas, John Patterson (.237/.315/.325) replaced Robby Thompson (.312/.375/.496) at second base after Thompson could only play 35 games, Kirt Manwaring and Royce Clayton both went from bad to awful, and Barry Bonds wasn't quite as great as he had been the previous year.

The result? The 1993 Giants hit .276/.338/.427 and finished second in the league with 808 runs scored. The next year, they hit .249/.313/.402 and were 10th in the league with 504 runs when the season ended.

The pitching wasn't quite as bad, but it didn't help stave off the collapse. Bill Swift was good in 1994, but not as good as in 1993. Salomon Torres and Bryan Hickerson were terrible. The excellent bullpen trio of Rod Beck, Mike

Jackson and Kevin Rogers was reduced to the excellent bullpen duo of Beck and Jackson.

San Francisco's ERA rose from 3.61 to 3.99 and the Giants went from finishing third in the league with 636 runs allowed to finishing fifth in the league with 500 runs allowed. It certainly didn't help matters that the Giants were underperforming their Pythagorean record by three games when their season ended, either.

The Mets actually didn't need to get much better to get much better. In 1993, the Amazin's amazingly underperformed their Pythagorean record by 14 games, and that's pretty tough to do two years in a row. The Mets scored 672 runs (13th in the league) and allowed 744 runs (ninth in the league) and while that's bad, it's not 59-103 bad.

In 1994, Todd Hundley and Jeff Kent were both significantly better, and the Mets improved from 13th in the league in runs to ninth (506). The pitching was pretty much a wash as the ERA went up from 4.05 to 4.13 but the Mets improved from ninth in the league in runs allowed to eighth (526).

Bobby Jones was excellent in 1994 and Bret Saberhagen was even better than he had been in 1993, but Pete Smith had a 5.55 ERA in about 130 innings and nobody but those three reached 10 starts or 70 innings. Dwight Gooden and Eric Hillman combined for a 3.66 ERA in 353.2 innings in 1993 and then combined for a 6.99 ERA in 76 innings in 1994.

So, the Mets improved a bit on offense, but about two-thirds of the improvement in their record came from simply doing what they should have done given their run totals. That, combined with San Francisco's collapse, was good for a 45-game swing between the two teams.

1933-34 Senators and Browns

In 1933, the Senators finished first in the American League at 99-53 while the Browns finished last at 55-96. The next year, the Browns improved slightly to sixth place at 67-85 while the Senators plummeted to seventh at 55-86.

Washington didn't tear its team apart or anything like that; it simply suffered a reversal of fortune. Not only did the Senators outplay their Pythagorean record by six games in 1933, but they were also remarkably healthy.

Of the eight regulars in their starting lineup, only catcher Luke Sewell failed to reach 500 at-bats and he had 474. With Hall-of-Famers Joe Cronin and Heinie Manush leading the way, the Senators finished third in the league with 850 runs scored.

The next year, only Manush, Cronin, Fred Schulte and Buddy Myers were able to reach 500 at-bats and Cronin hit significantly worse than he had the year before. Manush hit even better than he had in 1933, but it wasn't enough to overcome the fact that the Senators needed to rely on their

bench players much more and they fell to sixth in the league with 729 runs scored.

The pitching problems were even worse. In 1933, Earl Whitehill, Alvin Crowder, Lefty Stewart and Monte Weaver combined to post a 3.64 ERA in about 950 innings as none of them had an ERA above 4.00. The next year, the four hurlers combined for a 4.83 ERA in 692 innings as none of them had an ERA below 4.00.

The Senators fell from leading the league with 665 runs allowed to finishing sixth in the league with 806 runs allowed. Placing sixth in both runs scored and runs allowed dropped the Senators six spots from first to seventh.

The Browns aren't nearly as interesting because they only improved by 11.5 games and most of that was because they underperformed their Pythagorean record by seven games in 1933 and outperformed it by three games the next year.

The offense improved from a .320 OBP and .360 SLG to a .333 OBP and .373 SLG, but only scored five more runs (from 669 to 674) and actually fell from seventh in the league to eighth.

The pitching did improve a bit, mainly because not as many guys were truly awful in 1934. In 1933, the Browns had five pitchers throw more than 50 innings and post an ERA above 5.00, and four of those pitchers threw at least 80 innings. In 1934, only one pitcher had an ERA above 5.00 in at least 50 innings and he only threw 61.2 innings.

The staff improved from a 4.82 ERA in 1933 to a 4.49 ERA the next year and went from finishing last with 820 runs allowed to finishing fifth with 800 runs allowed. So, an improvement of 25 runs in run differential led to an improvement of 11.5 games in the record, which led to a 44.5-game swing between the teams.

1917-18 White Sox and Browns

The White Sox went 100-54 in 1917 and won the World Series and went 88-52 in 1919 and I think we all know that story. The year in between? Chicago went 57-67 and finished sixth in the AL. The Browns only won one more game in 1918 than in 1917, but they lost 33 fewer in the war-shortened season, improving from 57-97 to 58-64.

So, how does a team that went to the World Series twice in three years finish 10 games below .500 in the year in between? Well, maybe the team's best hitter was limited to 17 games because of the war and the team's best pitcher for some reason had an average year in between to amazing years.

Joe Jackson hit .301/.375/.429 in 1917, and back then that was good for a 143 OPS+. In 1918, he only got to play 17 games because of World War I. Some other players -- Ray Schalk, Eddie Collins, Buck Weaver -- hit worse in 1918 than in 1917, but the main reason the White Sox went from leading the league with 656 runs scored in 1917 to placing sixth with 457 runs scored in 1918 was the loss of Shoeless Joe.

On the other side of the ball, Eddie Cicotte picked 1918 to have one of the worst seasons of his career. He went 28-12 with a 1.53 ERA (174 ERA+) in 346.2 innings in 1917 and 29-7 with a 1.82 ERA (173 ERA+) in 306.2 innings in 1919. In 1918, he went 12-19 with a 2.77 ERA (99 ERA+) in 266 innings.

With their ace having an average year, even good seasons from some of the other pitchers only meant that the White Sox slipped from second in the league with 464 runs allowed to third in the league with 446 runs allowed. You might notice that they went 57-67 despite outscoring their opponents by 11 runs, and that's another reason it wasn't much of a surprise that they bounced back in 1919.

The main difference for the Browns was that they got to keep their superstar in 1918. George Sisler hit .353/.390/.453 (161 OPS+) in 1917 and then stayed around to hit .341/.400/.440 (157 OPS+) the next year. Another plus was that the Browns didn't have as many terrible hitters in 1918. Among players with at least 200 at-bats, only Joe Gedeon and Fritz Maisel were truly bad offensively. In 1917, Doc Lavan, Burt Shotton, Tod Sloan and Armando Marsans all struggled mightily at the plate.

Overall, St. Louis improved from last in the league with 510 runs to seventh in the league with 426 runs. Not a monumental leap, but better than falling five spots like the White Sox did.

On the pitching staff, Allen Sothoron improved from 14-19 with a 2.83 ERA (92 ERA+) in 276.2 innings to 12-12 with a 1.94 ERA (141 ERA+) in 209 innings, and Urban Shocker had his first great, albeit abbreviated, season with a 1.81 ERA in 94.2 innings.

The Browns went from seventh in the league with 687 runs allowed to fifth in the league with 448 runs allowed. Amazingly, St. Louis hit its Pythagorean record exactly both years. The only reason there was a 45-game swing between these two teams is that the White Sox were hurt more by the war and Cicotte had an off year.

1914-15 Athletics and Naps/Indians

Cleveland didn't actually have very much to do with this swing as there was only a 6.5-game improvement from 1914, when then Naps went 51-102, to 1915, when the Indians went 57-95. The reason for this 62.5-game swing in the standings between these two teams is that Philadelphia crashed from 99-53 in 1914 to 43-109 in 1915. It wasn't a freak occurrence.

After the 1914 season, Connie Mack dismantled the A's. Eddie Collins was sold to the White Sox. Frank Baker didn't play in 1915 and was sold to the Yankees in 1916. Eddie Murphy was sold to the White Sox in July of 1915, Herb Pennock was claimed by the Red Sox in June of 1915 and Bob Shawkey was sold to the Yankees in July of 1915. Chief Bender and Eddie Plank both jumped to the Federal League in 1915.

The people Mack replaced all of those good-to-excellent players with were not up to the task, and the A's went from first in the league in runs scored (749) and third in runs allowed (529) to sixth in runs scored (545) and last in runs allowed (888).

So, Mariners fans, while your team has gone from 40-plus games ahead of a team one year to behind them the next year twice this decade, at least you can take solace in the fact that ownership has yet to intentionally and completely dismantle the ball club.

Seattle finished 63-99 and Detroit finished 72-90 to complete a 59-game swing from 2003. This article originally appeared on The Hardball Times on September 23, 2004 at http://www.hardballtimes.com/main/article/opposite-directions/

Bing and Bob, Starring in "The Road to October"

By Steve Treder

Bob Gibson and Lou Brock were both tremendous players, of course. Their places in the Hall of Fame are well deserved. Gibson was a 20-game winner 5 times, a Cy Young Award winner and an MVP, and of course, that 1.12 ERA in 1968 was a signature accomplishment. Brock had over 3,000 hits, scored over 1,600 runs, and retired with the all-time single-season and career stolen base records.

Still, it must be acknowledged that a significant part of the lore of both -- the saga of exploits that burned the images of **"Bob Gibson"** and **"Lou Brock"** deep into the heart of baseball immortality -- were the duo's heroic deeds in the World Series.

With prominent roles in the scintillating seven-game nail-biters of 1964, 1967, and 1968, both were amazingly brilliant in the national spotlight of The Fall Classic. Gibson's dramatic seventh-game victory in 1964 earned the famous tribute from his manager, Johnny Keane: "I had a commitment to his heart." In 1967, Gibson had three more complete game wins, and then in the opening game of the '68 Series, he delivered one of the very greatest single-game pitching performances in World Series history: shutout, 5 hits, 1 walk, and 17 strikeouts. As if that weren't enough, Gibson hit a World Series home run in both '67 and '68.

Brock hit with slashing, punishing power in all three of those Octobers, while also setting the all-time single-Series record (which still stands) for stolen bases with seven in 1967 - and then matching it in 1968. His 14 career World Series stolen bases tie him with Eddie Collins for the all-time record, a mark that may well stand forever.

Gibson's total Series stat line is as follows:

G	GS	CG	IP	W	L	H	BB	SO	ShO	ERA
9	9	8	81	7	2	55	17	92	2	1.89

And here is Brock's:

G	AB	R	H	2B	3B	HR	RBI	BB	SO	SB	CS	BA	OBP	SLG
21	87	16	34	7	2	4	13	5	10	14	2	.391	.424	.655

Those are two of the most stupendously great performances any player has ever had in World Series competition.

But ...

Fade to Ominous Dream Sequence

... suppose the Cardinals hadn't won any pennants in the 1960s. Suppose therefore that neither Gibson nor Brock ever appeared in the Series. Take that part of their careers away, and certainly neither would have achieved quite the national superstardom they did while active, and likely neither would be quite as well-remembered today. Gibson's reputation might be obscured behind that of Juan Marichal as the "other" pitcher from the 60s (alongside Koufax, of course) -- given that, as we know, it was Marichal's Giants winning the NL pennant in 1964, '67, and '68, giving The Dominican Dandy that national stage upon which to dazzle us. Brock might be known today as little more than a poor man's Rickey Henderson.

The legacies of both Gibson and Brock owe a lot to the fact that their ball club won three pennants in a five-year period. And *that* fact must be understood as one of the greatest feats of team construction in major league history: the 1960s St. Louis Cardinals simply had no business winning any pennants at all, based on the talent produced by their farm system. The 1960s Cardinals were, in fact, almost certainly the greatest trade-built baseball team of all time.

Bing and Bob are Coming Along Here Soon

The St. Louis Cardinals spent the decade of the 1950s in a state of near-perpetual frustration. They had dominated the National League in the 1940s - four pennants and five second-places - and they entered the '50s with an all-time great still in his prime (Stan Musial), plus several other top stars: Enos Slaughter, Red Schoendienst, Marty Marion, and Howie Pollet. There was every expectation that the Cards would continue to be a strong contender, but as the new decade unfolded, year after year the Cardinals fell short. Despite sustained brilliance from Musial, they were never able to put a completely solid team around him, and again and again the Cards were able to do no better than middle-of-the-pack.

By the late '50s, Musial was aging, and it was obvious that no Cardinal team with Stan the Man as its centerpiece was ever again going to be a winner. The team went into a period of rebuilding.

Enter Bing, Stage Left

On November 12, 1957, Cardinals' GM Frank Lane resigned, and was replaced by Bing Devine. (Okay, before we go any further here -- his name really was Vaughan P. "Bing" Devine. "Bing Devine." That was really his name: one that would have seemed outlandish in a Busby Berkeley extravaganza. That was really his name. Anyway, back to our story ...)

Here's the best of what Devine had on hand to work with in 1958-60, in addition to the still-good-but-declining Musial:

- The one star the organization had come up with in the mid-50s: third baseman Ken Boyer, a terrific all-around player.
- One reliable workhorse starting pitcher in Larry Jackson.
- A strong-but-inconsistent relief ace in Lindy McDaniel

Devine did find a couple of pearls in their farm system, to be sure -- Gibson obviously, and Tim McCarver, signed as a much-ballyhooed teenager in 1959 -- but the rest of the home-grown talent they came up with in those years was nothing special: pitchers Ray Sadecki and Ray Washburn, catcher Gene Oliver, and outfielder Charlie James were little more than role players. Bonus baby pitcher Bob Miller was promising, but the Cards ended up losing him in the October 1961 expansion draft.

It wasn't the kind of core that a team can build around; major elements were lacking. But the Cardinals filled in the remaining pieces through a series of amazingly clever acquisitions. Devine made the following deals:

December 5, 1957: Traded pitchers Willard Schmidt, Marty Kutyna, and Ted Wieand to the Cincinnati Reds for outfielders Curt Flood and Joe Taylor.

October 8, 1958: Traded catcher Hobie Landrith, pitcher Billy Muffett, and infielder Benny Valenzuela to the San Francisco Giants for pitchers Marv Grissom and Ernie Broglio.

March 25, 1959: Traded pitchers Sam Jones and Don Choate to the San Francisco Giants for first baseman Bill White and third baseman Ray Jablonski.

May 20, 1960: Signed pitcher Curt Simmons as a free agent.

May 28, 1960: Traded pitcher Wilmer "Vinegar Bend" Mizell and infielder Dick Gray to the Pittsburgh Pirates for second baseman Julian Javier and pitcher Ed Bauta.

Conducted in a period of two and a half years, this series of acquisitions is among the most remarkable of all time. In four separate trades, the Cardinals acquired four young players (Flood, Broglio, White, and Javier) with little or no

major league experience - each of whom would become a star. The talent the Cardinals gave up in exchange was marginal, with the obvious exceptions of Jones (a veteran ace whom Lane had stolen from the Cubs in a 1956 swindle) and Mizell (a solid starter who did well for the Pirates in 1960 before running out of gas). Many teams will go ten or twenty years without pulling off a single trade like this. All in all, the true value exchange for the Cardinals in these four trades was astoundingly advantageous.

And the pickup of Simmons was one of the best scrap-heap snares of all time. The one-time "Whiz Kid" southpaw star had been dragged down with arm trouble, until the Phillies finally just gave up and released him. But immediately upon signing with the Cardinals, Simmons regained his health, and emerged as a crafty control artist, one of the better starting pitchers in the majors from 1960 through 1964.

These moves reinvigorated the Cardinals, and the team was good in 1960 and 1961 as their young talent developed. In '62, they stepped forward in run differential (92-70 Pythagorean record), but didn't win the close games, coming in at 84-78, in 6th place. Gibson, White, Broglio, Flood, and Javier had all emerged as stars, but the team hadn't yet emerged as a contender.

So in the fall of 1962, Devine made two more major trades:

October 17, 1962: Traded pitchers Larry Jackson and Lindy McDaniel and catcher Jimmie Schaffer to the Chicago Cubs for outfielder George Altman, pitcher Don Cardwell, and catcher Moe Thacker.

November 19, 1962: Traded Cardwell and infielder Julio Gotay to the Pittsburgh Pirates for shortstop Dick Groat and pitcher Diomedes Olivo.

Unlike the previous series of deals, these acquisitions weren't about picking up prospects with an eye toward the future. These trades were focused on winning now: Altman was an established heavy-hitting right fielder, and Groat was a standout veteran, the NL MVP in 1960. Devine was clearly rolling the dice; the Cardinals were going for it in 1963.

They almost got there in '63; in Musial's final season the Cards came on with a late-season rush and just fell short, finishing in second place at 93-69, their best performance since 1949. Groat had a great year, completing the quartet of Boyer-Groat-Javier-White that was one of the best all-around infields ever seen, before or since. Gibson and Broglio each won 18 games, giving the Cardinals a pair of aces, and Flood was firmly established as a high-average hitter and a brilliant defensive center fielder. McCarver completed his minor league apprenticeship and settled in as a standout catcher. Altman's lackluster performance was one of the few disappointments on the roster, and he was immediately traded away for a serviceable pitcher in Roger Craig.

The team went into 1964 with high expectations, but as of June 15th, they were languishing at 28-31, in eighth place. So on that trading deadline day, Devine pulled the trigger again on a major deal, surrendering one of his ace starters in a package that yielded a toolsy young outfielder who hadn't yet hit well at the major league level:

June 15, 1964: Traded pitchers Ernie Broglio and Bobby Shantz and outfielder Doug Clemens to the Chicago Cubs for outfielder Lou Brock and pitchers Paul Toth and Jack Spring.

We all know what happened then.

What may not be as well-remembered today is that on August 17, 1964, just two months after pulling off one of the most successful trades of all time, Bing Devine was fired. Owner Gussie Busch was frustrated with his team's 62-55, fifth-place record, and Devine was the fall guy. The team would go 31-14 the rest of the way, and the GM who had navigated the Cardinals' seven-year journey to a championship wouldn't be there to celebrate it.

Now Here's Bob's Big Entrance, Stage Right

Devine's replacement was Bob Howsam, an up-and-coming executive in his first big league GM job. Howsam's road became a rough one from the get-go: the 1965 Cardinals slumped badly, to 80-81, seventh place, as Boyer, Groat, and Simmons all suddenly showed their age.

Howsam demonstrated no hesitation. Few times in history has a former champion been torn apart quite so decisively as this:

October 20, 1965: Traded third baseman Ken Boyer to the New York Mets for pitcher Al Jackson and third baseman Charley Smith.

October 27, 1965: Traded first baseman Bill White, shortstop Dick Groat, and catcher Bob Uecker to the Philadelphia Phillies for outfielder Alex Johnson, pitcher Art Mahaffey, and catcher Pat Corrales.

The Boyer trade worked out well; both Jackson and Smith did well for the Cardinals in 1966. The deal with the Phillies came out dismally, as Johnson, the prize talent in the package, was a spectacular bust. But that trade served the purpose of clearing room for the deployment of new talent;

defensive whiz Dal Maxvill stepped in as the new regular shortstop.

And the space created at first base led to this blockbuster early the next season:

May 8, 1966: Traded pitcher Ray Sadecki to the San Francisco Giants for first baseman Orlando Cepeda.

Thus in the space of less than two years, the Cardinals pulled off two of the greatest steals in trading history.

But the '66 Cardinals were a .500-ish team again, as overall the team didn't hit as well as it could have. That offseason, Howsam made this deal:

December 8, 1966: Traded third baseman Charley Smith to the New York Yankees for outfielder Roger Maris.

This was an interesting move: taking on the injury-diminished former slugging star Maris to play right field, and transplanting incumbent right fielder Mike Shannon -- who had a tremendous arm, but not really a corner outfielder's bat -- to third base to replace Smith. While this parlay was not decisive in itself, Maris was better than Smith (116 OPS+ in 1967 to 84), and his presence along with the shift of Shannon would improve the Cardinals.

For his troubles, Bob Howsam was fired by Busch in January of 1967.

The Cardinals surged to back-to-back runaway pennants in '67 and '68. In both of those seasons, as in 1964, a huge portion of the ball club's core talent had been acquired in deals that were spectacularly one-sided. In the history of baseball, there has never been a championship team so dependent upon clever trade acquisitions as the 1960s Cardinals. But just like Devine before him, Howsam didn't survive as Cardinals' GM to taste the fruits of his labor.

We remember Bob Gibson's and Lou Brock's tremendous World Series deeds, as we should. But let's also acknowledge the amazing work of two different General Managers who made it possible.

(Cue exit music ... Bing Devine and Bob Howsam together, wearing exotic hats and riding an elephant or something ... there's Dorothy Lamour in her sarong ...)

This article originally appeared on The Hardball Times on September 8, 2004 at http://www.hardballtimes.com/main/article/bing-and-bob-starring-in-the-road-to-october/

Statistics

A Statistical What's What

Because we like baseball, we like statistics. Baseball statistics, that is. You can thoroughly enjoy baseball without paying any attention to its statistics, of course. But to really understand the game deeply, you've got to dive in. That's why the Hardball Times site tracked a wealth of baseball stats throughout the year, thanks to our business partners, Baseball Info Solutions (www.baseballinfosolutions.com). We thought we'd include many of them in these pages as well.

Like many baseball fans, we get frustrated by the inappropriate use of common baseball stats, such as RBI and pitcher Wins or Losses, to pick the "best" or "most valuable" player. So we stretch things a bit to uncover the truth behind the numbers. Sometimes, we venture into unknown territory, but we think the journey is part of the fun.

Still, we want you to come on the journey with us, so we've prepared this list of statistical definitions to help you follow along. This is a definition of virtually every stat included in the 2004 Baseball Annual. All of the source statistics listed here are reported by Baseball Info Solutions, though we perform most of the calculations ourselves.

We have lots of statistical lists on our website too, at http://www.hardballtimes.com/main/stats/. We didn't want to just repeat them here, because that's silly and repetitive. For the Annual, we developed a different set of stats for you to enjoy instead. For instance, we didn't include a list of Win Shares, because you can find Win Shares on our site. Instead, we've included new information such as fielding Win Shares per 1,000 innings and Net Win Shares Value.

In addition, we like graphs because we think pictures really do tell a story. So there are almost forty graphs included in these pages. Hopefully, you'll find something new about the 2004 season as you peruse our graphs and stats.

By the way, when you see a writer refer to a batter's performance in this way -- .275/.338/.425 (insert your own numbers) – he's referring to the batter's BA/OBP/SLG. If you're not sure what those are, read on.

A: Assists. The number of times a fielder makes a throw that results in an out.

AB: At Bats

AB/RSP: At Bats with Runners in Scoring Position (second and/or third base).

BA: Batting Average, Hits divided by At Bats.

BA/RSP: Batting Average with Runners in Scoring Position.

BABIP: Batting Average on Balls in Play. The exact formula we use is (H-HR)/(AB-K-HR)

BB: Bases on Balls, otherwise known as walks.

BFP: Batters Faced by Pitcher. The pitching equivalent of Plate Appearances for batters.

CS: Caught Stealing

DER: Defense Efficiency Ratio. The percent of times a batted ball is turned into an out by the teams' fielders, not including home runs. The exact formula we use is (BFP-H-K-BB-HBP-0.6*E)/(BFP-HR-K-BB-HBP)

DP: Double Plays

DPS: Double Plays Started, in which the fielder typically gets only an assist.

DPT: Double Plays Turned, in which the fielder records both an assist and an out.

ERA: Earned Run Average

ERA+: ERA measured against the league average, and adjusted for ballpark factors. An ERA+ over 100 is better than average, less than 100 is below average.

FE: Fielding Errors, as opposed to Throwing Errors (TE)

FIP: Fielding Independent Pitching, a measure of all those things for which a pitcher is specifically responsible. The formula is (HR*13+(BB+HBP)*3-K*2)/IP, plus a league-specific factor (usually around 3.2) to round out the number to an equivalent ERA number. FIP helps you understand how well a pitcher pitched, regardless of how well his fielders fielded. FIP was invented by Tangotiger.

FPct: Fielding Percentage, or the number of fielding chances handled without an error. The formula is (A+PO)/(A+PO+E).

G: Games played.

GIDP (or **GDP**): Grounded Into Double Plays.

GPA: Gross Production Average, a variation of OPS, but more accurate and easier to interpret. The exact formula is (OBP*1.8+SLG)/4, adjusted for ballpark factor. The scale of GPA is similar to BA: .200 is lousy, .265 is around average and .300 is a star.

GS: Games Started, a pitching stat.

HRA: Home Runs Allowed, also a pitching stat.

ISO: Isolated Power, which measures the "true power" of a batter. The formula is SLG-BA.

K: Strikeouts

L: Losses

LD%: Line Drive Percentage. Baseball Info Solutions tracks the trajectory of each batted ball and categorizes it as a groundball, flyball or line drive. LD% is the percent of batted balls that are line drives. Line drives are not necessarily the hardest hit balls, but they do fall for a hit around 75% of the time.

OBP: On Base Percentage, the proportion of plate appearances in which a batter reached base successfully, including hits, walks and hit by pitches.

Op: Save Opportunities

OPS: On Base plus Slugging Percentage, a crude but quick measure of a batter's true contribution to his team's offense. See GPA for a better approach.

OPS+: OPS measured against the league average, and adjusted for ballpark factors. An OPS+ over 100 is better than average, less than 100 is below average.

P/PA: Pitches per Plate Appearance.

PA: Plate Appearances, or AB+BB+HBP+SF+SH.

PO: Putouts, the number of times a fielder recorded an out in the field. First basemen and outfielders get lots of these.

POS: Position played in the field.

Pythagorean Record: A formula for converting a team's Run Differential into a projected Won/Loss record. The formula is $RS^2/(RS^2+RA^2)$. Teams' won/loss records tend to mirror their pythagorean records.

RA: Runs Allowed

RBI: Runs Batted In

RC: Runs Created. Invented by Bill James, RC is a very good measure of the number of runs a batter truly contributed to his team's offense. The basic formula for RC is OBP*TB, but it has evolved into over fourteen different versions. We use the most complicated version, which includes the impact of hitting well with runners in scoring position, and is adjusted for ballpark impact.

RCAA: Runs Created Above Average. A stat invented and tracked by Lee Sinins, the author of the Sabermetric Baseball Encyclopedia. Lee calculates each player's Runs Created, and then compares it to the league average, given that player's number of plate appearances. Lee uses a different version of RC than we do, though the two are very similar.

RF: Range Factor, a measure of the total chances fielded in a player's playing time. The formula we use is 9*(PO+A)/Innings in Field.

RS: Runs Scored

RSAA: Runs Saved Above Average. This stat, which is also tracked and reported by Lee Sinins, is a measure of a pitcher's effectiveness and contribution. The formula is RA/IP minus league-average RA/IP, times total innings pitched.

Run Differential: Runs Scored minus Runs Allowed.

SB: Stolen Bases

SB%: The percent of time a runner stole a base successfully. The formula is SB/SBA.

SBA: Stolen Bases Attempted.

SBA/G: Stolen Base Attempts per 9 innings played.

ShO: Shutouts

SLG: Slugging Percentage. Total Bases divided by At Bats.

SO: Strikeouts

Sv: Saves

Sv%: Saves divided by Save Opportunities

TB: Total Bases, calculated as 1B+2B*2+3B*3+HR*4.

TBA: Total Bases Allowed. A pitching stat.

TE: Throwing Errors, as opposed to Fielding Errors (FE).

UER: Unearned Runs

UERA: Unearned Run Average, or the number of unearned runs allowed for each nine innings pitched.

W: Wins

WP+PB/G: Wild Pitches and Passed Balls per Nine Innings played. A fielding stat for catchers.

WS: Win Shares. Invented by Bill James. Win Shares is a very complicated statistic that takes all the contributions a player makes toward his team's wins and distills them into a single number that represents the number of wins contributed to the team, times three. We have tweaked James' original formula somewhat, and you can read more about our version of Win Shares at http://www.hardballtimes.com/main/article/2004-win-shares-have-arrived/

WSAA: Win Shares Above Average. A stat calculated and tracked by THT, WSAA represents the number of Win Shares a player contributed above the league average, given his playing time.

WSAR: Win Shares Above Replacement, which is similar to WSAA, but based on 75% of league-average Win Shares. This is an estimate of the average value of a "replacement player" – typically a bench or AAA player.

American League Team Stats

Runs Scored and Allowed
(adjusted for ballpark factors)

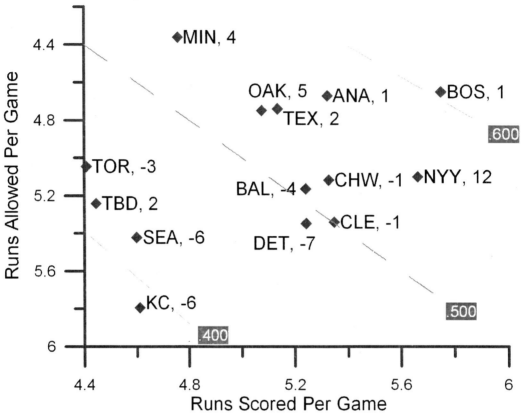

Notes: The dotted lines represent winning percentage based on run differential. The number after each team name represents the difference between the team's actual won/loss record and its run differential.

	Team Record					Scoring Runs			Stopping Runs			
Team	W	L	RS	RA	RS-RA	AB/RSP	BA/RSP	HR	ERA	HRA	K	DER
ANA	92	70	836	734	102	1,496	.278	162	4.28	170	1,164	.689
BAL	78	84	842	830	12	1,495	.276	169	4.70	159	1,090	.687
BOS	98	64	949	768	181	1,554	.295	222	4.18	159	1,132	.694
CHW	83	79	865	831	34	1,276	.292	242	4.91	224	1,013	.694
CLE	80	82	858	857	1	1,519	.269	184	4.81	201	1,115	.685
DET	72	90	827	844	-17	1,401	.273	201	4.93	190	995	.682
KC	58	104	720	905	-185	1,334	.268	150	5.15	208	887	.676
MIN	92	70	780	715	65	1,368	.277	191	4.03	167	1,123	.685
NYY	101	61	897	808	89	1,388	.272	242	4.69	182	1,058	.686
OAK	91	71	793	742	51	1,459	.260	189	4.17	164	1,034	.699
SEA	63	99	698	823	-125	1,431	.263	136	4.76	212	1,036	.700
TBD	70	91	714	842	-128	1,388	.262	145	4.81	192	923	.701
TEX	89	73	860	794	66	1,387	.270	227	4.53	182	979	.687
TOR	67	94	719	823	-104	1,389	.258	145	4.91	181	956	.692
Average	81	81	811	808	3	1,420	.272	186	4.63	185	1,036	.690

Scoring Runs:
OBP and Slugging

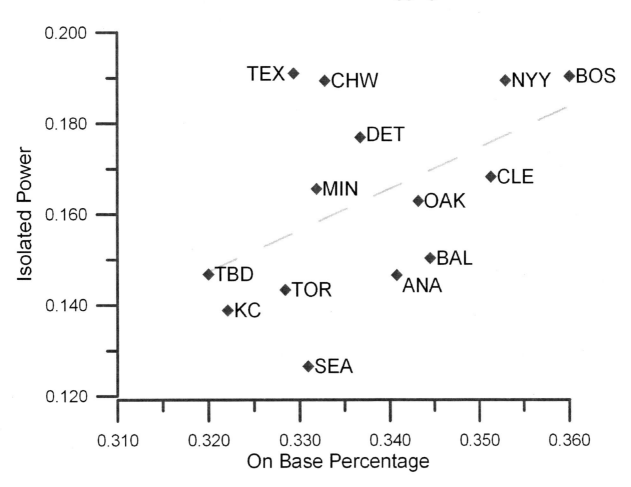

Batting Statistics

Team	RS	PA	H	1B	2B	3B	HR	TB	SO	BB	HBP	SH	SF	BA	OBP	SLG	GPA	ISO
ANA	836	6,296	1,603	1,132	272	37	162	2,435	942	450	73	56	41	.282	.341	.429	.261	.147
BAL	842	6,431	1,614	1,108	319	18	169	2,476	949	528	57	46	62	.281	.345	.432	.263	.150
BOS	949	6,515	1,613	993	373	25	222	2,702	1,189	659	69	12	55	.282	.360	.472	.280	.190
CHW	865	6,197	1,481	936	284	19	242	2,529	1,030	499	63	58	42	.268	.333	.457	.264	.189
CLE	858	6,452	1,565	1,007	345	29	184	2,520	1,009	606	78	47	42	.276	.351	.444	.269	.168
DET	827	6,285	1,531	992	284	54	201	2,526	1,144	518	50	50	43	.272	.337	.449	.264	.177
KC	720	6,153	1,432	992	261	29	150	2,201	1,057	461	76	40	38	.259	.322	.397	.244	.139
MIN	780	6,286	1,494	969	310	24	191	2,425	982	513	64	46	40	.266	.332	.431	.257	.166
NYY	897	6,364	1,483	940	281	20	242	2,530	982	670	80	37	50	.268	.353	.458	.273	.189
OAK	793	6,459	1,545	1,005	336	15	189	2,478	1,061	608	55	25	43	.270	.343	.433	.263	.163
SEA	698	6,362	1,544	1,112	276	20	136	2,268	1,058	492	54	46	48	.270	.331	.396	.248	.127
TBD	714	6,098	1,416	947	278	46	145	2,221	944	469	55	35	56	.258	.320	.405	.245	.147
TEX	860	6,256	1,492	908	323	34	227	2,564	1,099	500	61	23	57	.266	.329	.457	.262	.191
TOR	719	6,178	1,438	969	290	34	145	2,231	1,083	513	71	20	42	.260	.328	.403	.249	.143
Average	**811**	**6,309**	**1,518**	**1,001**	**302**	**29**	**186**	**2,436**	**1,038**	**535**	**65**	**39**	**47**	**.270**	**.340**	**.433**	**.261**	**.163**

Preventing Runs:
Pitching and Fielding (sort of)

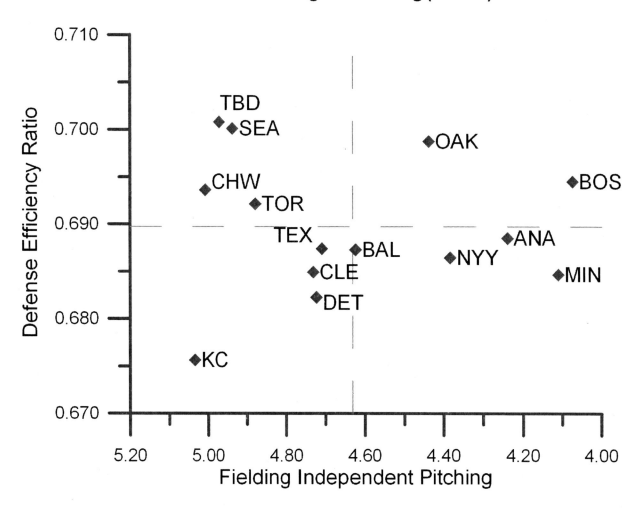

Pitching Statistics

Team	RA	BFP	H	HRA	TBA	K	BB	ShO	Sv	Op	%Save	Holds	ERA	FIP	UERA	DER
ANA	734	6,246	1,476	170	2,330	1,164	502	11	50	67	75%	54	4.28	4.24	0.26	.689
BAL	830	6,459	1,488	159	2,274	1,090	687	10	27	47	57%	54	4.70	4.62	0.43	.687
BOS	768	6,222	1,430	159	2,287	1,132	447	12	36	49	73%	53	4.18	4.07	0.58	.694
CHW	831	6,189	1,505	224	2,501	1,013	527	8	34	46	74%	57	4.91	5.01	0.31	.694
CLE	857	6,450	1,553	201	2,550	1,115	579	8	32	60	53%	55	4.81	4.73	0.45	.685
DET	844	6,296	1,542	190	2,477	995	530	9	35	63	56%	58	4.93	4.72	0.35	.682
KC	905	6,320	1,638	208	2,689	887	518	3	25	47	53%	48	5.15	5.03	0.58	.676
MIN	715	6,269	1,523	167	2,317	1,123	431	9	48	68	71%	48	4.03	4.11	0.33	.685
NYY	808	6,240	1,532	182	2,438	1,058	445	5	59	76	78%	70	4.69	4.38	0.35	.686
OAK	742	6,313	1,466	164	2,293	1,034	544	8	35	63	56%	71	4.17	4.44	0.37	.699
SEA	823	6,389	1,498	212	2,491	1,036	575	7	28	49	57%	42	4.76	4.94	0.31	.700
TBD	842	6,261	1,459	192	2,413	923	580	5	35	45	78%	46	4.81	4.97	0.54	.701
TEX	794	6,345	1,536	182	2,426	979	547	9	52	66	79%	76	4.53	4.71	0.44	.687
TOR	823	6,281	1,505	181	2,397	956	608	11	37	53	70%	47	4.91	4.88	0.30	.692
Average	**808**	**6,306**	**1,511**	**185**	**2,420**	**1,036**	**537**	**8**	**38**	**57**	**67%**	**56**	**4.63**	**4.63**	**0.40**	**.690**

Running and Miscellaneous Batting Stats

Team	SB	CS	SB%	GIDP	P/PA	LD%	BABIP	G/F
ANA	143	46	76%	124	3.66	.190	.315	1.25
BAL	101	41	71%	126	3.80	.192	.313	1.14
BOS	68	30	69%	123	3.93	.183	.323	1.05
CHW	78	51	60%	118	3.76	.177	.291	0.99
CLE	94	55	63%	143	3.82	.183	.308	1.15
DET	86	50	63%	111	3.75	.185	.311	1.11
KC	67	48	58%	130	3.81	.168	.296	1.22
MIN	116	46	72%	130	3.72	.166	.293	1.26
NYY	84	33	72%	157	3.80	.173	.288	1.21
OAK	47	22	68%	141	3.89	.188	.303	1.06
SEA	110	42	72%	132	3.78	.182	.311	1.40
TBD	132	42	76%	98	3.64	.171	.289	1.20
TEX	69	36	66%	91	3.77	.189	.295	0.93
TOR	58	31	65%	137	3.83	.204	.300	1.38
Average	90	41	69%	126	3.78	.182	.303	1.16

Fielding and Miscellaneous Pitching Stats

Team	DER	Fld %	UER	SBA	CS	%CS	PO	Err	TE	FE	DP	GIDP	LD%	G/F	IF/Fly
ANA	.689	.985	42	131	44	34%	11	90	33	54	125	98	.170	1.03	12.6%
BAL	.687	.982	70	121	39	32%	11	110	60	48	163	137	.180	1.25	12.2%
BOS	.694	.981	94	154	31	20%	10	118	54	63	130	106	.183	1.27	14.0%
CHW	.694	.984	49	138	48	35%	23	100	42	54	165	137	.185	1.16	12.4%
CLE	.685	.983	73	157	40	25%	8	106	33	73	152	119	.189	1.19	12.5%
DET	.682	.977	56	112	41	37%	8	144	69	74	160	145	.175	1.25	10.6%
KC	.676	.978	92	119	35	29%	19	131	65	65	170	143	.191	1.04	12.0%
MIN	.685	.984	54	117	44	38%	11	102	52	46	160	132	.179	1.20	13.3%
NYY	.686	.983	56	122	32	26%	7	99	45	51	148	117	.179	1.11	12.5%
OAK	.699	.986	60	123	49	40%	29	91	41	49	172	146	.181	1.34	13.2%
SEA	.700	.983	51	102	38	37%	12	103	51	50	137	115	.185	0.94	14.9%
TBD	.701	.980	85	99	32	32%	17	119	58	59	140	124	.182	1.01	12.8%
TEX	.687	.981	70	110	39	35%	16	117	49	66	152	131	.187	1.21	13.8%
TOR	.692	.985	48	132	41	31%	4	91	48	42	148	120	.187	1.23	13.4%
Average	.690	.982	64	124	40	32%	13	109	50	57	152	126	0.182	1.15	12.9%

Amercian League Leaderboard

Batting Leaders

RCAA		
T1	Guerrero	56
T1	Suzuki	56
3	Mora	54
4	Hafner	51
5	Ramirez	49
6	Ortiz	46
7	Matsui	44
8	Sheffield	40
9	Durazo	38
10	Guillen	36

RUNS		
1	Guerrero	124
2	Damon	123
3	Sheffield	117
4	Young	114
5	Rodriguez	112
T6	Jeter	111
T6	Mora	111
T8	Lawton	109
T8	Matsui	109
10	Ramirez	108

RBI		
1	Tejada	150
2	Ortiz	139
3	Ramirez	130
4	Guerrero	126
5	Sheffield	121
6	Konerko	117
7	Teixeira	112
8	Blalock	110
9	Hafner	109
T10	Martinez	108
T10	Matsui	108

PLATE APPEARANCES		
1	Suzuki	762
2	Young	739
3	Roberts	734
4	Tejada	725
5	Jeter	721
6	Blalock	713
7	Winn	703
8	Damon	702
9	Rodriguez	698
10	Sheffield	684

HITS		
1	Suzuki	262
2	Young	216
3	Guerrero	206
4	Tejada	203
5	Kotsay	190
6	Damon	189
7	Jeter	188
8	Mora	187
9	Crawford	185
10	Lopez	183

SINGLES		
1	Suzuki	225
2	Young	152
3	Kotsay	135
T4	Crawford	129
T4	Eckstein	129
6	Damon	128
T7	Figgins	127
T7	Tejada	127
T7	Vizquel	127
10	Guerrero	126

DOUBLES		
1	Roberts	50
2	Belliard	48
3	Ortiz	47
T4	Jeter	44
T4	Ramirez	44
T6	Hafner	41
T6	Lugo	41
T6	Mora	41
9	Tejada	40
T10	Byrnes	39
T10	Guerrero	39

TRIPLES		
1	Crawford	19
2	Figgins	17
3	Guillen	10
T4	Infante	9
T4	Young	9
6	Cruz	8
T7	Hudson	7
T7	Inge	7
T7	Lofton	7
T7	Newhan	7
T7	Rios	7

HOME RUNS		
1	Ramirez	43
T2	Konerko	41
T2	Ortiz	41
4	Guerrero	39
5	Teixeira	38
T6	Rodriguez	36
T6	Sheffield	36
8	Tejada	34
T9	Blalock	32
T9	Delgado	32

TOTAL BASES		
1	Guerrero	366
2	Ortiz	351
3	Tejada	349
4	Ramirez	348
5	Young	333
6	Suzuki	320
7	Blalock	312
8	Lee	310
9	Mora	309
10	Rodriguez	308

EXTRA BASE HITS		
1	Ortiz	91
2	Ramirez	87
3	Guerrero	80
4	Tejada	76
5	Teixeira	74
6	Blalock	73
7	Hafner	72
T8	Jeter	68
T8	Lee	68
T8	Mora	68

ISOLATED POWER		
1	Ramirez	.305
2	Ortiz	.302
3	Teixeira	.279
4	Hafner	.272
5	Delgado	.266
6	Guerrero	.261
7	Valentin	.258
8	Konerko	.258
9	Sheffield	.244
10	Rowand	.234

STOLEN BASES		
1	Crawford	59
2	Suzuki	36
3	Figgins	34
4	Roberts	29
5	Rodriguez	28
T6	Jeter	23
T6	Lawton	23

CAUGHT STEALING		
1	Crawford	15
T2	Crisp	13
T2	Figgins	13
T2	Sanchez	13
5	Roberts	12
T6	DeJesus	11
T6	Suzuki	11

WALKS		
1	Chavez	95
2	Sheffield	92
T3	Bellhorn	88
T3	Matsui	88
T3	Posada	88
6	Palmeiro	86
7	Williams	85

STRIKEOUTS		
1	Bellhorn	177
2	Blalock	149
3	Pena	146
4	Crosby	141
T5	Blake	139
T5	Valentin	139
7	Boone	135

T8	Hunter	21		T6	Uribe	11		8	Ramirez	82		8	Ortiz	133
T8	Lugo	21		9	Jones	10		9	Rodriguez	80		9	Rodriguez	131
T8	Winn	21		T10	Lawton	9		T10	Cruz	76		10	Dye	128
				T10	Young	9		T10	Damon	76				

BATTING AVERAGE			SLUGGING AVERAGE			ON BASE PERCENTAGE			OPS		
1	Suzuki	.372	1	Ramirez	.613	1	Mora	.419	1	Ramirez	1.009
2	Mora	.340	2	Ortiz	.603	2	Suzuki	.414	2	Hafner	0.993
3	Guerrero	.337	3	Guerrero	.598	3	Hafner	.410	3	Guerrero	0.989
4	Rodriguez	.334	4	Hafner	.583	4	Posada	.400	4	Ortiz	0.983
5	Durazo	.321	5	Mora	.562	5	Chavez	.397	5	Mora	0.981
6	Guillen	.318	6	Teixeira	.560	6	Ramirez	.397	6	Teixeira	0.929
7	Lopez	.316	7	Rowand	.544	7	Durazo	.396	7	Sheffield	0.927
8	Kotsay	.314	8	Guillen	.542	8	Sheffield	.393	8	Guillen	0.921
9	Young	.313	9	Delgado	.535	9	Guerrero	.391	9	Durazo	0.919
10	Hafner	.311	10	Konerko	.535	10	Varitek	.390	10	Matsui	0.912

SACRIFICE HITS			SACRIFICE FLIES			HIT BY PITCHES			OUTS		
1	Vizquel	20	1	Tejada	14	T1	Hafner	17	1	Roberts	499
2	Jeter	16	2	Delgado	11	T1	Millar	17	2	Young	481
3	Roberts	15	3	Palmeiro	9	3	Guillen	15	3	Jeter	477
4	Eckstein	14	T4	Blalock	8	T4	Cairo	14	4	Winn	470
5	Guzman	13	T4	Cruz Jr.	8	T4	Jeter	14	5	Crawford	466
T6	Cairo	12	T4	Guerrero	8	T6	Delgado	13	6	Tejada	465
T6	Sanchez	12	T4	Hatteberg	8	T6	Eckstein	13	7	Blalock	462
T8	Blanco	11	T4	Lugo	8	T6	Ford	13	8	Suzuki	458
T8	Uribe	11	T4	Ortiz	8	T6	Kennedy	13	9	Boone	455
10	Figgins	10	T4	Randa	8	T10	Five tied at	12	10	Soriano	450
			T4	Sheffield	8						

Pitching Leaders

ERA			INNINGS PITCHED			RSAA			FIP		
1	Santana	2.61	1	Buehrle	245.1	1	Santana	54	1	Santana	3.16
2	Schilling	3.26	2	Santana	228.0	2	Schilling	42	2	Schilling	3.34
3	Westbrook	3.38	3	Schilling	226.2	3	Radke	31	3	Hudson	3.64
4	Radke	3.48	4	Mulder	225.2	4	Buehrle	29	4	Radke	3.78
5	Hudson	3.53	5	Radke	219.2	5	Westbrook	28	5	Martinez	3.82
6	Lopez	3.59	T6	Garland	217.0	6	Rodriguez	26	6	Lieber	3.94
7	Buehrle	3.89	T6	Maroth	217.0	T7	Foulke	25	7	Harden	3.95
8	Martinez	3.90	T6	Martinez	217.0	T7	Nathan	25	8	Escobar	3.96
9	Escobar	3.93	T9	Ponson	215.2	T7	Ryan	25	9	Arroyo	4.06
10	Harden	3.99	T9	Westbrook	215.2	T10	Cordero	24	10	Mussina	4.18
						T10	Hudson	24			
						T10	Martinez	24			

STRIKEOUTS			WALKS			STRIKEOUT/WALK RATIO			HIT BY PITCHES		
1	Santana	265	T1	Batista	96	1	Schilling	5.8	1	Arroyo	20
2	Martinez	227	T1	Zambrano	96	2	Lieber	5.7	T2	Martinez	16
3	Schilling	203	T3	Cabrera	89	3	Radke	5.5	T2	Wakefield	16
4	Escobar	191	T3	Lilly	89	4	Santana	4.9	T2	Zambrano	16
5	Garcia	184	5	Contreras	84	5	Martinez	3.7	5	Park	13

T6	Bonderman	168	6	Mulder	83	6	Mussina	3.3	T6	Hudson	12
T6	Lilly	168	T7	Harden	81	7	Buehrle	3.2	T6	Mulder	12
8	Harden	167	T7	Lee	81	8	Arroyo	3.0	T6	Villone	12
9	Buehrle	165	T7	Zito	81	9	Escobar	2.5	T9	Brazelton	11
10	Zito	163	T10	Escobar	76	10	Vazquez	2.5	T9	Drese	11
			T10	Garland	76				T9	Lee	11
			T10	Lohse	76				T9	Moyer	11
									T9	Vazquez	11

HITS/9 INNINGS			STRIKEOUTS/9 INNINGS			WALKS/9 INNINGS			BASERUNNERS/9 INNINGS		
1	Santana	6.2	1	Santana	10.5	1	Lieber	0.9	1	Santana	8.6
2	Lilly	7.8	2	Martinez	9.4	2	Radke	1.1	2	Schilling	9.8
3	Martinez	8.0	3	Escobar	8.3	3	Schilling	1.4	3	Radke	10.7
4	Harden	8.1	4	Bonderman	8.2	4	Silva	1.6	4	Martinez	11.2
5	Schilling	8.2	5	Lee	8.1	5	Buehrle	1.9	5	Westbrook	11.4
6	Bonderman	8.2	6	Schilling	8.1	6	Hudson	2.1	6	Buehrle	11.6
7	Escobar	8.3	7	Harden	7.9	7	Santana	2.1	7	Lopez	11.6
8	Sabathia	8.4	8	Lilly	7.7	8	Mussina	2.2	8	Escobar	11.9
9	Arroyo	8.6	9	Mussina	7.2	9	Hendrickson	2.3	9	Hudson	11.9
10	Lopez	8.7	10	Arroyo	7.2	10	Arroyo	2.4	10	Arroyo	12.0

WINS			LOSSES			WINNING PERCENTAGE			SAVES		
1	Schilling	21	1	May	19	1	Schilling	.778	1	Rivera	53
2	Santana	20	2	Franklin	16	2	Santana	.769	2	Cordero	49
T3	Colon	18	T3	Hendrickson	15	3	Mulder	.680	3	Nathan	44
T3	Rogers	18	T3	Johnson	15	T4	Hudson	.667	4	Percival	33
5	Mulder	17	T3	Ponson	15	T4	Rogers	.667	5	Foulke	32
T6	Buehrle	16	T6	Batista	13	6	Martinez	.640	6	Baez	30
T6	Martinez	16	T6	Bonderman	13	T7	Lee	.636	T7	Dotel	22
T8	Nine pitchers	14	T6	Lackey	13	T7	Lieber	.636	T7	Julio	22
			T6	Lohse	13	T7	Silva	.636	9	Urbina	21
			T6	Maroth	13	10	Buehrle	.615	10	Takatsu	19
			T6	Moyer	13						

GAMES			GAMES STARTED			COMPLETE GAMES			GAMES FINISHED		
1	Quantrill	86	T1	Buehrle	35	T1	Mulder	5	1	Rivera	69
2	Gordon	80	T1	Rogers	35	T1	Ponson	5	T2	Cordero	63
3	Rincon	77	T3	Colon	34	T1	Westbrook	5	T2	Nathan	63
T4	Ryan	76	T3	Lohse	34	4	Buehrle	4	4	Foulke	61
T4	Timlin	76	T3	Radke	34	T5	Hudson	3	5	Baez	59
6	Myers	75	T3	Santana	34	T5	May	3	6	Julio	50
T7	Marte	74	T3	Zito	34	T5	Schilling	3	7	Percival	48
T7	Rivera	74	T8	12 pitchers	33	T8	12 pitchers	2	8	Urbina	46
T7	Romero	74							9	Takatsu	45
T10	Grimsley	73							10	Dotel	41
T10	Nathan	73									

National League Team Stats

Runs Scored and Allowed
(adjusted for ballpark factors)

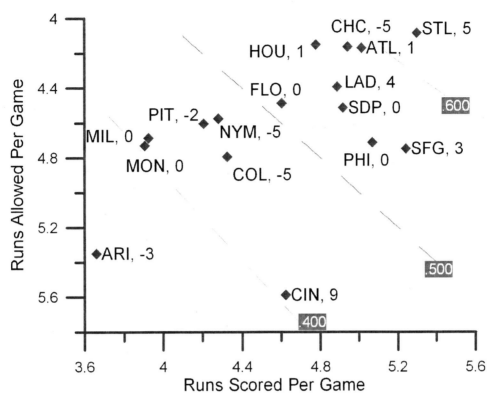

Notes: The dotted lines represent winning percentage based on run differential. The number after each
team name represents the difference between the team's actual won/loss record and its run differential.

Team	Team Record					Scoring Runs			Stopping Runs			
	W	**L**	**RS**	**RA**	**RS-RA**	**AB/RSP**	**BA/RSP**	**HR**	**ERA**	**HRA**	**K**	**DER**
ARI	51	111	615	899	-284	1,271	.257	135	4.98	197	1,153	.684
ATL	96	66	803	668	135	1,477	.263	178	3.74	154	1,025	.690
CHC	89	73	789	665	124	1,321	.266	235	3.82	169	1,346	.698
CIN	76	86	750	907	-157	1,341	.248	194	5.19	236	992	.690
COL	68	94	833	923	-90	1,453	.259	202	5.54	198	947	.678
FLO	83	79	718	700	18	1,409	.255	148	4.10	166	1,116	.700
HOU	92	70	803	698	105	1,412	.274	187	4.05	174	1,282	.686
LAD	93	69	761	684	77	1,341	.256	203	4.01	178	1,066	.711
MIL	67	94	634	757	-123	1,392	.221	135	4.24	164	1,098	.695
MON	67	95	635	769	-134	1,278	.239	151	4.33	191	1,032	.696
NYM	71	91	684	731	-47	1,336	.245	185	4.09	156	977	.698
PHI	86	76	840	781	59	1,439	.257	215	4.46	214	1,070	.703
PIT	72	89	680	744	-64	1,324	.266	142	4.29	149	1,079	.685
STL	105	57	855	659	196	1,437	.270	214	3.75	169	1,041	.711
SDP	87	75	768	705	63	1,494	.258	139	4.03	184	1,079	.695
SFG	91	71	850	770	80	1,457	.271	183	4.29	161	1,020	.696
Average	**81**	**81**	**751**	**754**	**-3**	**1,386**	**.257**	**178**	**4.30**	**179**	**1,083**	**.695**

Scoring Runs:
OBP and Slugging

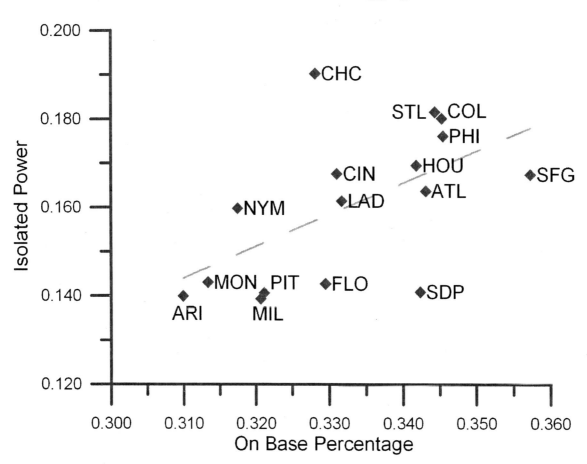

Batting Statistics

Team	RS	PA	H	1B	2B	3B	HR	TB	SO	BB	HBP	SH	SF	BA	OBP	SLG	GPA	ISO
ARI	615	6,114	1,401	933	295	38	135	2,177	1,022	441	35	56	37	.253	.310	.393	.238	.140
ATL	803	6,339	1,503	984	304	37	178	2,415	1,158	587	59	75	48	.270	.343	.434	.263	.164
CHC	789	6,281	1,508	936	308	29	235	2,579	1,080	489	38	78	48	.268	.328	.458	.262	.190
CIN	750	6,278	1,380	871	287	28	194	2,305	1,335	599	81	55	25	.250	.331	.418	.253	.168
COL	833	6,333	1,531	964	331	34	202	2,536	1,181	568	54	97	37	.275	.345	.455	.269	.180
FLO	718	6,160	1,447	992	275	32	148	2,230	968	499	58	77	40	.264	.329	.406	.250	.143
HOU	803	6,269	1,458	941	294	36	187	2,385	999	590	61	98	52	.267	.342	.436	.263	.170
LAD	761	6,244	1,450	991	226	30	203	2,345	1,092	536	62	69	35	.262	.332	.423	.255	.161
MIL	634	6,195	1,358	896	295	32	135	2,122	1,312	540	68	56	40	.248	.321	.387	.241	.139
MON	635	6,138	1,361	907	276	27	151	2,144	925	496	35	100	33	.249	.313	.392	.239	.143
NYM	684	6,209	1,376	882	289	20	185	2,260	1,159	512	61	69	34	.249	.317	.409	.245	.160
PHI	840	6,456	1,505	964	303	23	215	2,499	1,133	645	58	64	46	.267	.345	.443	.266	.176
PIT	680	6,115	1,428	980	267	39	142	2,199	1,066	415	95	79	42	.260	.321	.401	.245	.141
STL	855	6,297	1,544	987	319	24	214	2,553	1,085	548	51	73	70	.278	.344	.460	.270	.182
SDP	768	6,313	1,521	1,046	304	32	139	2,306	910	566	56	52	66	.273	.342	.414	.257	.141
SFG	850	6,466	1,500	970	314	33	183	2,429	874	705	72	92	51	.270	.357	.438	.270	.168
Average	**751**	**6,263**	**1,454**	**953**	**293**	**31**	**178**	**2,343**	**1,081**	**546**	**59**	**74**	**44**	**.263**	**.333**	**.423**	**.256**	**.160**

Preventing Runs:
Pitching and Fielding (sort of)

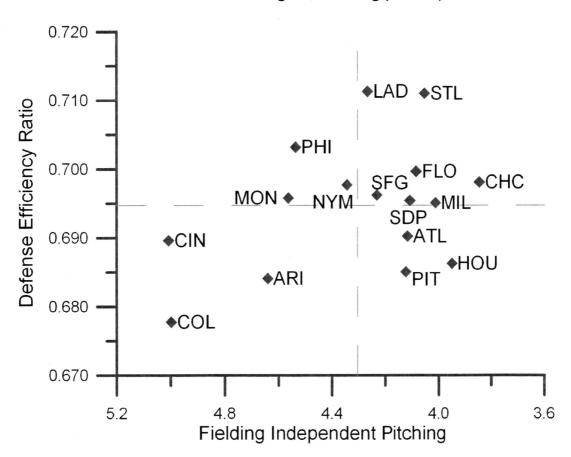

Pitching Statistics

Team	RA	BFP	H	HR	TBA	K	BB	ShO	Sv	Op	%Save	Holds	ERA	FIP	UERA	DER
ARI	899	6,418	1,480	197	2,440	1,153	668	6	33	55	60%	55	4.98	4.64	0.66	.684
ATL	668	6,218	1,475	154	2,221	1,025	523	13	48	68	71%	71	3.74	4.12	0.40	.690
CHC	665	6,262	1,363	169	2,177	1,346	545	6	42	66	64%	68	3.82	3.84	0.27	.698
CIN	907	6,451	1,595	236	2,740	992	572	8	47	77	61%	80	5.19	5.01	0.47	.690
COL	923	6,535	1,634	198	2,650	947	697	2	36	70	51%	67	5.54	5.00	0.25	.678
FLO	700	6,110	1,395	166	2,245	1,116	513	14	53	75	71%	54	4.10	4.08	0.28	.700
HOU	698	6,201	1,416	174	2,291	1,282	525	13	47	70	67%	74	4.05	3.95	0.30	.686
LAD	684	6,155	1,386	178	2,227	1,066	521	6	51	60	85%	57	4.01	4.27	0.23	.711
MIL	757	6,204	1,440	164	2,319	1,098	476	10	42	64	66%	59	4.24	4.01	0.49	.695
MON	769	6,307	1,477	191	2,392	1,032	582	11	31	49	63%	59	4.33	4.56	0.45	.696
NYM	731	6,333	1,452	156	2,256	977	592	6	31	52	60%	70	4.09	4.34	0.45	.698
PHI	781	6,308	1,488	214	2,520	1,070	502	5	43	68	63%	82	4.46	4.54	0.35	.703
PIT	744	6,197	1,451	149	2,261	1,079	576	8	46	69	67%	76	4.29	4.12	0.40	.685
STL	659	6,104	1,378	169	2,208	1,041	440	12	57	73	78%	89	3.75	4.05	0.33	.711
SDP	705	6,135	1,460	184	2,392	1,079	422	8	44	64	69%	76	4.03	4.11	0.37	.695
SFG	770	6,321	1,481	161	2,368	1,020	548	8	46	74	62%	87	4.29	4.23	0.46	.696
Average	**754**	**6,266**	**1,461**	**179**	**2,357**	**1,083**	**544**	**9**	**44**	**66**	**66%**	**70**	**4.30**	**4.30**	**0.39**	**.695**

Running and Miscellaneous Batting Stats

Team	SB	CS	SB%	GDP	P/PA	LD%	BABIP	G/F
ARI	53	32	62%	136	3.68	.187	.289	1.25
ATL	86	32	73%	124	3.73	.187	.313	1.32
CHC	66	28	70%	120	3.64	.200	.295	1.13
CIN	77	25	75%	125	3.84	.188	.297	1.25
COL	44	33	57%	133	3.79	.183	.317	1.25
FLO	96	43	69%	142	3.75	.182	.297	1.24
HOU	89	30	75%	129	3.69	.196	.297	1.13
LAD	102	41	71%	120	3.81	.178	.294	1.24
MIL	138	40	78%	120	3.86	.189	.303	1.28
MON	109	38	74%	117	3.81	.183	.275	1.29
NYM	107	23	82%	129	3.81	.183	.284	1.11
PHI	100	27	79%	122	3.84	.200	.300	1.14
PIT	63	40	61%	117	3.69	.178	.301	1.46
STL	111	47	70%	120	3.78	.197	.313	1.18
SDP	52	25	68%	129	3.72	.195	.305	1.20
SFG	43	23	65%	142	3.60	.180	.293	1.19
Average	**84**	**33**	**72%**	**127**	**3.75**	**.188**	**.298**	**1.23**

Fielding and Miscellaneous Pitching Stats

Team	DER	Fld %	UER	SBA	CS	%CS	PO	Err	TE	FE	DP	GIDP	LD%	G/F	IF/Fly
ARI	.684	.977	105	147	50	34%	12	139	64	74	144	117	.194	1.35	12.1%
ATL	.690	.981	65	120	29	24%	6	116	50	63	172	150	.193	1.42	10.0%
CHC	.698	.986	44	147	39	27%	7	86	38	48	126	104	.191	1.27	13.7%
CIN	.690	.981	75	96	29	30%	1	113	54	57	123	100	.192	1.14	13.3%
COL	.678	.986	40	143	32	22%	24	89	51	37	161	138	.190	1.27	13.5%
FLO	.700	.986	45	156	38	24%	11	86	35	48	154	123	.182	1.17	13.7%
HOU	.686	.983	48	140	39	28%	7	101	43	57	136	119	.195	1.24	12.8%
LAD	.711	.988	37	136	40	29%	10	73	37	34	145	129	.190	1.05	14.7%
MIL	.695	.981	78	118	29	25%	13	117	42	72	132	109	.179	1.17	12.7%
MON	.696	.984	73	99	41	41%	8	99	43	55	171	136	.189	1.24	11.4%
NYM	.698	.978	73	139	39	28%	11	137	57	75	145	124	.188	1.29	13.5%
PHI	.703	.987	57	129	26	20%	1	81	34	43	142	121	.181	1.09	13.7%
PIT	.685	.983	64	110	38	35%	8	103	42	57	189	160	.188	1.26	12.3%
STL	.711	.984	54	82	29	35%	5	98	37	60	154	130	.181	1.45	11.2%
SDP	.695	.982	59	94	25	27%	6	108	44	60	145	126	.190	1.14	11.7%
SFG	.696	.984	75	96	24	25%	11	101	38	62	154	130	.183	1.24	12.5%
Average	**.695**	**.984**	**62**	**122**	**34**	**28%**	**9**	**103**	**44**	**56**	**150**	**126**	**.188**	**1.23**	**12.7%**

National League Leaderboard

Batting Leaders

RCAA			RUNS			RBI			PLATE APPEARANCES		
1	Bonds	152	1	Pujols	133	1	Castilla	131	1	Pierre	748
2	Helton	78	2	Bonds	129	2	Rolen	124	2	Izturis	728
3	Pujols	75	3	Rollins	119	3	Pujols	123	3	Rollins	725
4	Edmonds	73	T4	Abreu	118	4	Beltre	121	4	Abreu	713
T5	Abreu	69	T4	Drew	118	5	Cabrera	112	5	Podsednik	712
T5	Berkman	69	6	Helton	115	6	Edmonds	111	6	Giles	711
7	Drew	66	7	Wilkerson	112	T7	Batista	110	7	Loretta	707
8	Beltre	64	8	Rolen	109	T7	Burnitz	110	8	Finley	706
9	Rolen	57	9	Loretta	108	9	Kent	107	9	Biggio	700
10	Dunn	52	10	Alou	106	T10	Alou	106	10	Wilson	693
						T10	Berkman	106			

HITS			SINGLES			DOUBLES			TRIPLES		
1	Pierre	221	1	Pierre	184	1	Overbay	53	T1	Pierre	12
2	Loretta	208	T2	Izturis	148	2	Pujols	51	T1	Rollins	12
3	Wilson	201	T2	Kendall	148	3	Helton	49	T1	Wilson	12
4	Beltre	200	T4	Castillo	143	T4	Abreu	47	4	Izturis	9
5	Pujols	196	T4	Loretta	143	T4	Biggio	47	T5	Drew	8
6	Izturis	193	6	Womack	140	T4	Loretta	47	T5	Durham	8
T7	Helton	190	7	Wilson	137	T7	Casey	44	T5	Freel	8
T7	Rollins	190	8	Miles	129	T7	Lowell	44	T5	Kent	8
9	Casey	185	9	Burroughs	128	T9	Castilla	43	T9	Beltran	7
10	Kendall	183	10	Redman	122	T9	Rollins	43	T9	Castillo	7

HOME RUNS			TOTAL BASES			EXTRA BASE HITS			ISOLATED POWER		
1	Beltre	48	1	Pujols	389	1	Pujols	99	1	Bonds	.450
T2	Dunn	46	2	Beltre	376	T2	Edmonds	83	2	Edmonds	.341
T2	Pujols	46	3	Helton	339	T2	Helton	83	3	Pujols	.326
4	Bonds	45	4	Alou	335	4	Castilla	81	4	Thome	.307
T5	Edmonds	42	5	Dunn	323	T5	Beltre	80	5	Dunn	.303
T5	Thome	42	6	Edmonds	320	T5	Dunn	80	6	Beltre	.294
7	Alou	39	7	Ramirez	316	T7	Abreu	78	7	Rolen	.284
8	Burnitz	37	T8	Abreu	312	T7	Alou	78	8	Burnitz	.276
T9	Finley	36	T8	Castilla	312	9	Bonds	75	9	Helton	.272
T9	Ramirez	36	10	Cabrera	309	T10	Berkman	73	10	Alou	.265
						T10	Wilkerson	73			

STOLEN BASES			CAUGHT STEALING			WALKS			STRIKEOUTS		
1	Podsednik	70	1	Pierre	24	1	Bonds	232	1	Dunn	195
2	Pierre	45	2	Podsednik	13	T2	Abreu	127	2	Wilson	169
3	Abreu	40	T3	Bradley	11	T2	Berkman	127	3	Patterson	168
4	Freel	37	T3	Renteria	11	T2	Helton	127	T4	Jenkins	152
5	Roberts	33	5	Freel	10	5	Drew	118	T4	Wilkerson	152
T6	Chavez	32	T6	Izturis	9	6	Dunn	108	6	Edmonds	150
T6	Patterson	32	T6	Patterson	9	7	Wilkerson	106	7	Cabrera	148

8	Rollins	30	T6	Rollins	9	8	Thome	104	8	Jones	147
9	Furcal	29	T9	Clark	8	9	Edmonds	101	9	Thome	144
10	Beltran	28	T9	Kendall	8	10	Bagwell	96	10	Cameron	143

	BATTING AVERAGE			SLUGGING AVERAGE			ON BASE PERCENTAGE			OPS	
1	Bonds	.362	1	Bonds	.812	1	Bonds	.609	1	Bonds	1.422
2	Helton	.347	2	Pujols	.657	2	Helton	.469	2	Helton	1.088
3	Loretta	.335	3	Edmonds	.643	3	Berkman	.450	3	Pujols	1.072
4	Beltre	.334	4	Beltre	.629	4	Drew	.436	4	Edmonds	1.061
5	Pujols	.331	5	Helton	.620	5	Abreu	.428	5	Beltre	1.017
6	Pierre	.326	6	Rolen	.598	6	Edmonds	.418	6	Berkman	1.016
7	Casey	.324	7	Thome	.581	7	Pujols	.415	7	Rolen	1.007
8	Kendall	.319	8	Ramirez	.578	8	Rolen	.409	8	Drew	1.006
9	Ramirez	.318	9	Drew	.569	9	Kendall	.399	9	Thome	.977
10	Berkman	.316	10	Dunn	.569	10	Thome	.396	10	Abreu	.971

	SACRIFICE HITS			SACRIFICE FLIES			HIT BY PITCHES			OUTS	
1	Clayton	24	1	Loretta	16	1	Wilson	30	1	Podsednik	504
2	Everett	22	2	Kent	11	2	LaRue	24	2	Izturis	501
T3	Benson	15	T3	Batista	10	3	Kendall	19	3	Pierre	498
T3	Hernandez	15	T3	Renteria	10	4	Cora	18	4	Rollins	484
T3	Pierre	15	T5	Giles	9	T5	Biggio	15	5	Finley	481
T6	Oswalt	13	T5	Pujols	9	T5	Pierzynski	15	6	Batista	480
T6	Schmidt	13	T7	Barrett	8	7	Rolen	13	7	Patterson	478
T6	Tomko	13	T7	Cabrera	8	T8	Freel	12	8	Biggio	469
T9	Chavez	12	T7	Castilla	8	T8	Hill	12	9	Wilson	467
T9	Cintron	12	T7	Edmonds	8	T8	Hillenbrand	12	10	Jenkins	461
T9	Cora	12	T7	Greene	8	T8	Jenkins	12			
T9	Izturis	12				T8	Polanco	12			

Pitching Leaders

	ERA			INNINGS PITCHED			RSAA			FIP	
1	Peavy	2.27	1	Hernandez	255.0	1	Johnson	50	1	Johnson	2.32
2	Johnson	2.60	2	Johnson	245.2	2	Sheets	45	2	Sheets	2.67
3	Sheets	2.70	T3	Oswalt	237.0	3	Zambrano	42	3	Schmidt	2.94
4	Zambrano	2.75	T3	Sheets	237.0	4	Clemens	32	4	Clemens	3.13
5	Clemens	2.98	5	Schmidt	225.0	T5	Peavy	31	5	Peavy	3.16
6	Perez	2.98	6	Pavano	222.1	T5	Schmidt	31	6	Oswalt	3.18
7	Pavano	3.00	7	Weaver	220.0	T7	Kennedy	27	7	Wright	3.30
8	Schmidt	3.20	8	Clemens	214.1	T7	Pavano	27	8	Perez	3.46
9	Leiter	3.21	9	Maddux	212.2	9	Lidge	26	9	Pavano	3.56
10	Perez	3.25	10	Glavine	212.1	10	Perez	25	T10	Zambrano	3.59
									T10	Davis	3.59

	STRIKEOUTS			WALKS			STRIKEOUT/WALK RATIO			HIT BY PITCHES	
1	Johnson	290	1	Webb	119	1	Sheets	8.3	1	Zambrano	20
2	Sheets	264	2	Ortiz	112	2	Johnson	6.6	2	Williams	17
3	Schmidt	251	3	Estes	105	3	Wells	5.1	3	Weaver	14
4	Perez	239	4	Jennings	101	4	Maddux	4.6	4	Kim	13
5	Clemens	218	5	Ishii	98	5	Carpenter	4.0	5	Clement	12
6	Oswalt	206	6	Leiter	97	6	Oswalt	3.3	T6	Estes	11

National League Stats

7	Clement	190	T7	Hernandez	83	7	Peavy	3.3	T6	Leiter	11
8	Zambrano	188	T7	Trachsel	83	8	Schmidt	3.3	T6	Oswalt	11
9	Hernandez	186	T9	Perez	81	9	Perez	3.0	T6	Pavano	11
10	Peavy	173	T9	Zambrano	81	10	Eaton	2.9	T6	Peavy	11
									T6	Webb	11
									T6	Wood	11

HITS/9 INNINGS			STRIKEOUTS/9 INNINGS			WALKS/9 INNINGS			BASERUNNERS/9 INNINGS		
1	Johnson	6.5	1	Perez	11.0	1	Wells	0.9	1	Johnson	8.5
2	Schmidt	6.6	2	Johnson	10.6	2	Sheets	1.2	2	Sheets	9.0
3	Perez	6.7	3	Schmidt	10.0	3	Maddux	1.4	3	Schmidt	9.8
4	Clemens	7.1	4	Sheets	10.0	4	Johnson	1.6	4	Wells	10.4
5	Leiter	7.2	5	Clement	9.5	5	Lima	1.8	5	Perez	10.4
6	Zambrano	7.5	6	Peavy	9.4	6	Carpenter	1.9	6	Carpenter	10.6
7	Sheets	7.6	7	Clemens	9.2	7	Pavano	2.0	7	Clemens	10.7
8	Clement	7.7	8	Zambrano	8.1	8	Perez	2.0	8	Perez	10.8
9	Peavy	7.9	9	Oswalt	7.8	9	Eaton	2.4	9	Maddux	11.0
10	Ishii	8.1	10	Wright	7.7	10	Oswalt	2.4	10	Pavano	11.0

WINS			LOSSES			WINNING PERCENTAGE			SAVES		
1	Oswalt	20	1	Webb	16	1	Clemens	.818	T1	Benitez	47
T2	Clemens	18	T2	Fossum	15	2	Carpenter	.750	T1	Isringhausen	47
T2	Pavano	18	T2	Hernandez	15	3	Lima	.722	3	Gagne	45
T2	Schmidt	18	T4	Eaton	14	4	Schmidt	.720	4	Smoltz	44
T5	Johnson	16	T4	Glavine	14	5	Peavy	.714	5	Mesa	43
T5	Maddux	16	T4	Johnson	14	6	Milton	.700	T6	Graves	41
T5	Suppan	16	T4	Lawrence	14	7	Pavano	.692	T6	Hoffman	41
T5	Zambrano	16	T4	Sheets	14	8	Marquis	.682	8	Kolb	39
T9	8 pitchers	15	T9	Clement	13	T9	Oswalt	.667	9	Chacon	35
			T9	Trachsel	13	T9	Zambrano	.667	T10	Lidge	29
			T9	Vogelsong	13				T10	Looper	29
			T9	Weaver	13						

GAMES			GAMES STARTED			COMPLETE GAMES			GAMES FINISHED		
1	Brower	89	T1	Hernandez	35	1	Hernandez	9	1	Isringhausen	66
2	King	86	T1	Johnson	35	T2	Lidle	5	2	Mesa	65
T3	Cormier	84	T1	Oswalt	35	T2	Sheets	5	3	Smoltz	61
T3	Reitsma	84	T1	Webb	35	T4	Johnson	4	T4	Chacon	60
T3	Torres	84	T5	Davis	34	T4	Schmidt	4	T4	Looper	60
T6	Eyre	83	T5	Estes	34	6	Morris	3	T6	Benitez	59
T6	Stanton	83	T5	Lawrence	34	T7	10 pitchers	2	T6	Gagne	59
8	Ayala	81	T5	Lidle	34				T6	Graves	59
9	Lidge	80	T5	Milton	34				9	Hoffman	51
10	Alfonseca	79	T5	Ortiz	34				10	Hawkins	50
			T5	Sheets	34						
			T5	Weaver	34						

Anaheim Angels

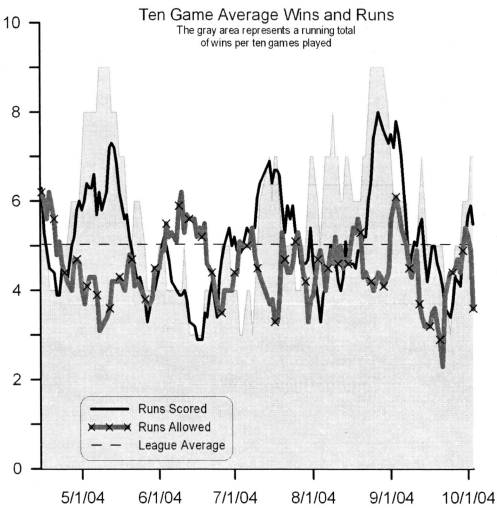

Ten Game Average Wins and Runs
The gray area represents a running total
of wins per ten games played

Legend:
- Runs Scored
- Runs Allowed
- League Average

4/13: Anderson signs
four-year deal for $48M;
4/28: on DL for month

6/2: Vlad has nine
RBIs for club record

8/26: DaVanon
hits for cycle

10/2: 5-4 win over
A's clinches title

8/22: Sweep
Yankees

9/26: Guillen
suspended

5/18: Glaus
on DL, misses
91 games

Team Batting and Pitching/Fielding Stats by Month						
	April	May	June	July	Aug	Sept
Wins	14	17	10	15	19	17
Losses	10	10	17	11	8	14
OBP	.332	.346	.329	.361	.354	.325
SLG	.438	.442	.400	.439	.449	.410
FIP	4.05	4.44	4.19	4.59	4.47	3.29
DER	.667	.717	.702	.750	.666	.700

Batting Stats

Player	RC	Runs	RBI	PA	Outs	H	BB	HR	TB	BA	OBP	SLG	GPA	ISO	SB	CS	GDP
Guerrero V.	128	124	126	680	426	206	52	39	366	.337	.391	.598	.326	.261	15	3	17
Guillen J.	102	88	104	621	414	166	37	27	281	.294	.352	.497	.283	.204	5	4	11
Figgins C.	94	83	60	638	425	171	49	5	242	.296	.350	.419	.262	.123	34	13	6
Erstad D.	78	79	69	543	359	146	37	7	198	.295	.346	.400	.256	.105	16	1	9
Anderson G.	72	57	75	475	313	133	29	14	197	.301	.343	.446	.266	.145	2	1	3
Kennedy A.	61	70	48	533	352	130	41	10	190	.278	.351	.406	.260	.128	15	5	9
Eckstein D.	59	92	35	637	425	156	42	2	188	.276	.339	.332	.235	.057	16	5	10
DaVanon J.	48	41	34	337	211	79	46	7	119	.277	.372	.418	.272	.140	18	3	2
Molina B.	45	36	54	363	262	93	18	10	136	.276	.313	.404	.242	.128	0	1	17
Glaus T.	44	47	42	242	164	52	31	18	119	.251	.355	.575	.304	.324	2	3	6
Quinlan R.	35	23	23	177	107	55	14	5	84	.344	.401	.525	.312	.181	3	1	1
Salmon T.	21	15	23	206	141	47	14	2	60	.253	.306	.323	.218	.070	1	0	2
Molina J.	20	26	25	218	156	53	10	3	76	.261	.296	.374	.227	.113	4	1	5
Kotchman C.	14	7	15	128	92	26	7	0	32	.224	.289	.276	.199	.052	3	0	2
Halter S.	12	10	13	121	95	23	7	4	40	.202	.248	.351	.199	.149	1	1	3
Paul J.	10	11	10	81	54	17	7	2	26	.243	.308	.371	.231	.129	2	1	0
McPherson D	5	5	6	43	31	9	3	3	19	.225	.279	.475	.244	.250	1	0	0
Amezaga A.	5	12	11	105	82	15	3	2	23	.161	.212	.247	.157	.086	3	2	2
Pride C.	4	5	3	42	31	10	0	0	13	.250	.268	.325	.202	.075	1	0	1
Riggs A.	2	2	3	37	31	7	1	0	10	.194	.216	.278	.167	.083	1	0	2
Galarraga A.	1	1	2	11	8	3	0	1	6	.300	.364	.600	.314	.300	0	0	1
Washburn J.	1	0	1	7	3	2	0	0	2	.400	.400	.400	.280	.000	0	0	0
Turnbow D.	0	0	0	1	1	0	0	0	0	.000	.000	.000	.000	.000	0	0	0
Sele A.	0	0	0	1	1	0	0	0	0	.000	.000	.000	.000	.000	0	0	0
Shields S.	0	0	0	1	1	0	0	0	0	.000	.000	.000	.000	.000	0	0	0
Hensley M.	0	0	0	1	1	0	0	0	0	.000	.000	.000	.000	.000	0	0	0
Escobar K.	0	0	0	2	2	0	0	0	0	.000	.000	.000	.000	.000	0	0	0
Lackey J.	0	0	0	2	2	0	0	0	0	.000	.000	.000	.000	.000	0	0	0
Colon B.	0	0	0	3	3	0	0	0	0	.000	.000	.000	.000	.000	0	0	0
Mondesi R.	-1	2	1	37	31	4	2	1	8	.118	.189	.235	.144	.118	0	1	0
Ortiz R.	-1	0	0	3	4	0	0	0	0	.000	.000	.000	.000	.000	0	0	1

Pitching Stats

Player	IP	BFP	G	GS	P/PA	H	K	BB	HR	W	L	Sv	Op	Hld	RA	ERA	FIP	DER
Colon B.	208.3	897	34	34	3.79	215	158	71	38	18	12	0	0	0	5.27	5.01	5.21	.718
Escobar K.	208.3	878	33	33	3.91	192	191	76	21	11	12	0	0	0	3.93	3.93	3.96	.707
Lackey J.	198.3	855	33	32	3.75	215	144	60	22	14	13	0	0	0	4.90	4.67	4.31	.689
Washburn	149.3	640	25	25	3.77	159	86	40	20	11	8	0	0	0	4.88	4.64	4.76	.716
Sele A.	132.0	593	28	24	3.79	163	51	51	16	9	4	0	0	0	5.73	5.05	5.37	.687
Ortiz R.	128.0	543	34	14	3.60	139	82	38	18	5	7	0	0	0	4.50	4.43	4.82	.698
Shields S.	105.3	454	60	0	3.79	97	109	40	6	8	2	4	7	17	3.59	3.33	3.19	.693
Gregg K.	87.7	377	55	0	4.08	86	84	28	6	5	2	1	2	3	4.41	4.21	3.33	.688
Rodriguez	84.0	335	69	0	4.04	51	123	33	2	4	1	12	19	27	2.25	1.82	1.89	.722
Percival T.	49.7	211	52	0	4.10	43	33	19	7	2	3	33	38	0	3.44	2.90	5.12	.758
Donnelly B.	42.0	172	40	0	4.22	34	56	15	5	5	2	0	0	5	3.00	3.00	3.32	.695
Hensley M.	27.7	120	16	0	3.78	32	30	7	5	0	2	0	0	0	4.88	4.88	4.45	.645
Weber B.	22.3	117	18	0	3.85	37	11	15	4	0	2	0	1	2	9.67	8.06	6.65	.621
Turnbow D.	6.3	26	4	0	3.81	2	3	7	0	0	0	0	0	0	0.00	0.00	5.66	.875
Dunn S.	3.0	17	3	0	4.06	7	2	1	0	0	0	0	0	0	9.00	9.00	2.96	.500
Bergman D	2.0	11	1	0	2.64	4	1	1	0	0	0	0	0	0	13.50	13.50	3.79	.556

Fielding Stats

Catchers

Name	Innings	SBA/G	CS%	ERA	WP+PB/G
B Molina	762.0	0.80	25%	4.31	0.543
J Molina	524.3	0.72	45%	4.31	0.326
Paul	168.0	0.91	24%	4.07	0.375

Infielders and Outfielders

Name	POS	Inn	PO	A	TE	FE	FPct	RF	DPS	DPT
D Erstad	1B	1065.0	989	62	1	2	.996	8.88	14	1
C Kotchman	1B	270.3	230	15	0	3	.988	8.16	2	0
R Quinlan	1B	93.0	96	7	0	0	1.000	9.97	0	0
S Halter	1B	9.7	10	1	0	0	1.000	10.24	0	0
A Galarraga	1B	9.0	9	1	0	0	1.000	10.00	0	0
J Molina	1B	6.0	5	1	0	0	1.000	9.00	0	0
A Riggs	1B	1.0	1	1	0	0	1.000	18.00	0	0
A Kennedy	2B	1225.0	256	387	3	9	.982	4.72	35	38
C Figgins	2B	141.0	26	42	1	0	.986	4.34	1	6
A Amezaga	2B	58.3	7	17	0	1	.960	3.70	0	2
S Halter	2B	29.0	4	7	0	0	1.000	3.41	1	1
A Riggs	2B	1.0	0	1	0	0	1.000	9.00	0	0
D Eckstein	SS	1191.0	198	309	3	3	.988	3.83	37	32
A Amezaga	SS	167.0	37	57	0	1	.989	5.07	2	1

Anaheim Angels

Name	POS	Inn	PO	A	TE	FE	FPct	RF	DPS	DPT
C Figgins	SS	80.7	19	24	1	1	.956	4.80	2	3
S Halter	SS	15.0	3	4	0	0	1.000	4.20	0	1
C Figgins	3B	707.3	57	130	6	5	.944	2.38	10	0
R Quinlan	3B	218.0	13	44	0	1	.983	2.35	2	0
S Halter	3B	213.3	26	46	5	5	.878	3.04	2	0
T Glaus	3B	165.0	11	27	2	0	.950	2.07	2	1
D McPherson	3B	93.0	8	20	0	0	1.000	2.71	1	0
A Amezaga	3B	57.7	3	8	0	1	.917	1.72	4	0
J Guillen	LF	1165.0	268	9	2	4	.979	2.14	2	0
J DaVanon	LF	157.3	42	0	0	1	.977	2.40	0	0
C Pride	LF	44.0	15	0	0	0	1.000	3.07	0	0
A Riggs	LF	36.0	11	1	0	0	1.000	3.00	0	0
R Quinlan	LF	16.0	3	0	0	0	1.000	1.69	0	0
T Salmon	LF	14.0	0	0	0	0	.000	0.00	0	0
J Paul	LF	13.0	2	0	0	0	1.000	1.38	0	0
C Figgins	LF	9.0	4	0	0	0	1.000	4.00	0	0
G Anderson	CF	791.7	212	5	1	1	.991	2.47	2	0
C Figgins	CF	336.0	92	0	0	1	.989	2.46	0	0
J DaVanon	CF	247.7	75	1	0	0	1.000	2.76	1	1
R Mondesi	CF	71.0	20	1	0	0	1.000	2.66	0	0
C Pride	CF	8.0	3	0	0	0	1.000	3.38	0	0
V Guerrero	RF	1234.0	308	13	0	9	.973	2.34	3	0
J DaVanon	RF	126.3	26	1	0	0	1.000	1.92	2	0
T Salmon	RF	39.0	15	1	0	0	1.000	3.69	0	0
J Guillen	RF	22.0	4	0	0	0	1.000	1.64	0	0
C Pride	RF	16.0	7	0	0	0	1.000	3.94	0	0
C Figgins	RF	10.0	4	1	0	0	1.000	4.50	0	0
R Quinlan	RF	7.0	1	0	0	0	1.000	1.29	0	0

143

Baltimore Orioles

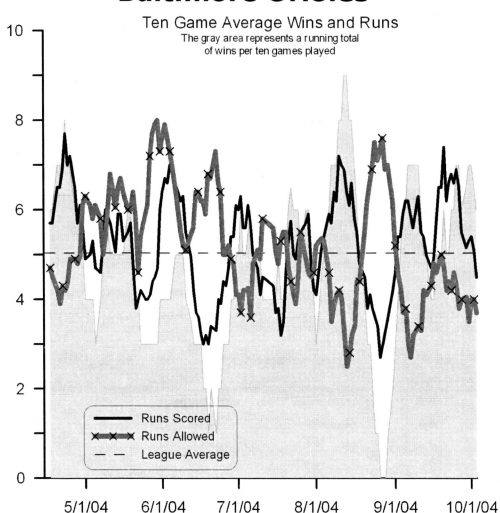

Ten Game Average Wins and Runs
The gray area represents a running total
of wins per ten games played

4/16: Beat Toronto 11-2 to move to 5-4; will stay above .500 until 5/23

5/11: Call up Cabrera, who goes 9-5 with 3.71 ERA in first 19 appearances before slumping

5/20: Lopez becomes starter; goes 11-7 with a 3.95 ERA

6/20: Newhan promoted, bats .433 in first 24 games

7/17: Beat Tampa Bay 3-2 to move out of last place for the final time

8/31: Defeat Tampa Bay 10-6 to move into third place in the AL East to stay.

Team Batting and Pitching/Fielding Stats by Month						
	April	**May**	**June**	**July**	**Aug**	**Sept**
Wins	12	12	9	13	13	19
Losses	10	14	18	14	15	13
OBP	.363	.354	.330	.320	.359	.343
SLG	.416	.451	.401	.428	.437	.452
FIP	4.41	4.95	4.21	4.52	4.90	4.29
DER	.723	.662	.704	.694	.681	.745

Batting Stats

Player	RC	Runs	RBI	PA	Outs	H	BB	HR	TB	BA	OBP	SLG	GPA	ISO	SB	CS	GDP
Tejada M.	126	107	150	725	473	203	48	34	349	.311	.360	.534	.296	.224	4	1	22
Mora M.	116	111	104	636	379	187	66	27	309	.340	.419	.562	.329	.222	11	6	10
Roberts B.	91	107	53	736	481	175	71	4	241	.273	.344	.376	.249	.103	29	12	3
Lopez J.	90	83	86	638	412	183	47	23	291	.316	.370	.503	.292	.187	0	0	16
Palmeiro R.	82	68	88	651	422	142	86	23	240	.258	.359	.436	.271	.178	2	1	13
Newhan D.	69	66	54	412	262	116	27	8	169	.311	.361	.453	.276	.142	11	1	4
Bigbie L.	66	76	68	531	351	134	45	15	204	.280	.342	.427	.260	.146	8	3	4
Surhoff B.	54	49	50	378	246	106	30	8	144	.309	.365	.420	.269	.111	2	0	9
Hairston Jr.	45	43	24	334	209	87	29	2	114	.303	.378	.397	.269	.094	13	8	1
Gibbons J.	38	36	47	380	271	85	29	10	131	.246	.303	.379	.231	.133	1	1	9
Matos L.	28	36	28	359	265	74	19	6	110	.224	.275	.333	.207	.109	12	4	5
Raines Jr T.	9	14	5	101	74	24	4	0	30	.255	.293	.319	.212	.064	7	3	1
Segui D.	9	8	7	65	43	20	5	1	26	.339	.400	.441	.290	.102	0	1	3
Garcia K.	6	9	11	73	53	14	4	3	23	.212	.247	.348	.198	.136	0	0	1
Gil G.	5	1	4	35	23	9	3	0	11	.281	.343	.344	.240	.063	0	0	0
Lopez L.	3	7	8	97	73	16	3	1	24	.182	.211	.273	.163	.091	0	0	1
Mottola C.	3	2	3	16	12	2	2	1	6	.143	.250	.429	.220	.286	0	0	0
McDonald D.	2	3	1	34	27	5	2	0	6	.156	.206	.188	.140	.031	1	0	0
Leon J.	1	4	8	69	60	12	2	2	20	.182	.203	.303	.167	.121	0	0	6
Machado R.	1	5	3	77	64	11	4	1	17	.151	.195	.233	.146	.082	0	0	2
Bautista J.	1	3	0	12	8	3	1	0	3	.273	.333	.273	.218	.000	0	0	0
Huckaby K.	0	1	0	12	10	2	0	0	3	.167	.167	.250	.138	.083	0	0	0
Majewski V.	0	3	1	13	11	2	0	0	3	.154	.154	.231	.127	.077	0	0	0
Parrish J.	0	0	0	1	1	0	0	0	0	.000	.000	.000	.000	.000	0	0	0
DeJean M.	0	0	0	1	1	0	0	0	0	.000	.000	.000	.000	.000	0	0	0
Cust J.	0	0	0	1	1	0	0	0	0	.000	.000	.000	.000	.000	0	0	0
Rodriguez E.	0	0	0	1	1	0	0	0	0	.000	.000	.000	.000	.000	0	0	0
Bedard E.	0	0	0	5	4	0	1	0	0	.000	.200	.000	.090	.000	0	0	0
Riley M.	0	0	0	2	2	0	0	0	0	.000	.000	.000	.000	.000	0	0	0
DuBose E.	0	0	0	2	2	0	0	0	0	.000	.000	.000	.000	.000	0	0	0
Cabrera D.	0	0	0	4	4	0	0	0	0	.000	.000	.000	.000	.000	0	0	0
Ponson S.	-1	0	0	5	5	0	0	0	0	.000	.000	.000	.000	.000	0	0	0
Osik K.	-2	0	0	25	24	2	0	0	2	.080	.080	.080	.056	.000	0	0	1

Pitching Stats

Player	IP	BFP	G	GS	P/PA	H	K	BB	HR	W	L	Sv	Op	Hld	RA	ERA	FIP	DER
Ponson S.	215.7	954	33	33	3.47	265	115	69	23	11	15	0	0	0	5.68	5.30	4.68	.673
Lopez R.	170.7	714	37	23	3.82	164	121	54	21	14	9	0	1	4	3.74	3.59	4.46	.723
Cabrera D	147.7	662	28	27	3.77	145	76	89	14	12	8	1	1	0	5.18	5.00	5.34	.728
Bedard E.	137.3	633	27	26	4.21	149	121	71	13	6	10	0	0	0	5.44	4.59	4.46	.677
Ryan B.	87.0	361	76	0	4.47	64	122	35	4	4	6	3	7	21	2.48	2.28	2.33	.698
Parrish J.	78.0	353	56	1	3.92	68	71	55	4	6	3	1	1	2	4.50	3.46	4.37	.709
DuBose E	74.7	338	14	14	3.77	76	48	44	12	4	6	0	0	0	6.63	6.39	5.98	.723
Julio J.	69.0	306	65	0	3.92	59	70	39	11	2	5	22	26	2	4.57	4.57	5.16	.738
Riley M.	64.0	292	14	13	3.98	60	60	44	11	3	4	0	0	0	6.05	5.63	5.76	.722
Borkowski	56.0	247	17	8	3.98	65	45	15	6	3	4	0	1	1	5.95	5.14	4.04	.669
Bauer R.	53.7	230	23	2	3.92	49	37	20	4	2	1	0	1	0	5.20	4.70	4.22	.727
Groom B.	52.7	236	60	0	3.49	67	32	16	6	4	1	0	2	8	5.13	4.78	4.53	.663
Chen B.	47.7	196	8	7	3.81	39	32	16	7	2	1	0	0	0	3.59	3.02	4.87	.773
Rodriguez	43.3	193	29	0	4.18	36	37	30	5	1	0	0	0	0	4.78	4.78	5.51	.733
DeJean M	39.7	197	37	0	3.64	49	36	28	2	0	5	0	0	1	6.58	6.13	4.70	.624
Grimsley	36.3	167	41	0	3.75	37	21	20	3	2	4	0	6	12	6.19	4.21	5.03	.719
Williams T	31.3	126	29	0	3.62	26	13	9	2	2	0	0	0	3	2.87	2.87	4.63	.753
Ainsworth	30.7	151	7	7	3.65	39	20	20	6	0	1	0	0	0	9.98	9.68	6.98	.670
Cubillan D	10.0	50	7	0	3.96	13	8	7	3	0	0	0	1	0	6.30	5.40	7.69	.688
Rakers A.	4.3	19	3	0	3.58	5	3	1	0	0	0	0	0	0	4.15	4.15	2.60	.667
Maine J.	3.7	19	1	1	3.53	7	1	3	1	0	1	0	0	0	9.82	9.82	8.75	.571
Bautista D	2.0	15	2	0	4.40	6	1	2	1	0	0	0	0	0	36.00	36.00	13.29	.500

Fielding Stats

Catchers

Name	Innings	SBA/G	CS%	ERA	WP+PB/G
Lopez	1092.3	0.73	23%	4.68	0.503
Machado	188.7	0.52	64%	4.58	0.525
Gil	78.0	0.81	43%	3.58	0.462
Osik	59.3	0.61	25%	6.98	0.758
Huckaby	37.0	0.97	25%	4.86	0.486

Infielders and Outfielders

Name	POS	Inn	PO	A	TE	FE	FPct	RF	DPS	DPT
R Palmeiro	1B	1137.0	1090	93	2	5	.993	9.36	11	1
J Gibbons	1B	112.7	112	12	0	1	.992	9.91	1	0
J Leon	1B	95.0	82	9	0	0	1.000	8.62	2	1
B Surhoff	1B	50.0	46	4	0	0	1.000	9.00	0	1
L Lopez	1B	22.0	22	0	1	0	.957	9.00	0	0
D Segui	1B	18.0	17	0	0	0	1.000	8.50	0	0

Baltimore Orioles

Name	POS	Inn	PO	A	TE	FE	FPct	RF	DPS	DPT
D Newhan	1B	11.0	10	1	0	0	1.000	9.00	0	0
K Garcia	1B	9.0	10	1	0	0	1.000	11.00	0	0
B Roberts	2B	1322.0	235	426	3	5	.988	4.50	37	55
J Hairston J	2B	102.0	21	36	1	0	.983	5.03	3	6
L Lopez	2B	31.0	3	9	0	0	1.000	3.48	1	1
M Tejada	SS	1421.0	263	526	10	14	.970	5.00	57	52
L Lopez	SS	32.7	7	10	0	1	.944	4.68	1	2
M Mora	SS	1.0	0	0	0	0	.000	0.00	0	0
M Mora	3B	1210.0	122	258	12	9	.948	2.83	18	1
D Newhan	3B	141.0	11	23	3	2	.872	2.17	2	0
L Lopez	3B	64.0	6	15	2	2	.840	2.95	2	0
J Leon	3B	32.0	1	8	0	1	.900	2.53	1	0
J Bautista	3B	5.0	0	0	0	0	.000	0.00	0	0
J Hairston J	3B	3.0	0	1	0	0	1.000	3.00	0	0
L Bigbie	LF	915.0	215	2	0	2	.991	2.13	0	0
B Surhoff	LF	268.3	69	0	0	0	.986	2.31	0	0
D Newhan	LF	159.0	41	0	0	0	1.000	2.32	1	0
J Hairston J	LF	77.3	17	1	0	1	.947	2.09	1	0
C Mottola	LF	20.7	4	0	0	0	1.000	1.74	0	0
D McDonald	LF	9.0	1	0	0	0	1.000	1.00	0	0
T Raines Jr	LF	6.0	2	0	0	0	1.000	3.00	0	0
L Matos	CF	781.3	219	3	0	1	.996	2.56	1	0
L Bigbie	CF	242.7	74	1	0	0	1.000	2.78	0	1
T Raines Jr	CF	159.3	44	1	0	0	1.000	2.54	0	0
J Hairston J	CF	127.7	35	0	0	0	1.000	2.47	0	0
K Garcia	CF	99.7	24	0	0	0	1.000	2.17	0	0
D McDonald	CF	28.0	6	0	0	0	1.000	1.93	0	0
V Majewski	CF	16.7	8	0	0	0	1.000	4.32	0	0
J Gibbons	RF	555.3	116	6	1	1	.984	1.98	2	0
B Surhoff	RF	302.0	65	3	1	0	.986	2.03	4	0
J Hairston J	RF	210.3	53	2	0	0	1.000	2.35	2	0
D Newhan	RF	190.7	31	3	0	0	1.000	1.60	0	0
T Raines Jr	RF	54.0	15	1	0	0	1.000	2.67	0	0
D McDonald	RF	48.3	14	0	0	0	1.000	2.61	0	0
K Garcia	RF	44.7	9	0	0	0	1.000	1.81	0	0
J Bautista	RF	24.0	4	1	0	0	1.000	1.88	0	0
C Mottola	RF	17.0	3	0	0	0	1.000	1.59	0	0
V Majewski	RF	9.0	3	0	0	0	1.000	3.00	0	0

Boston Red Sox

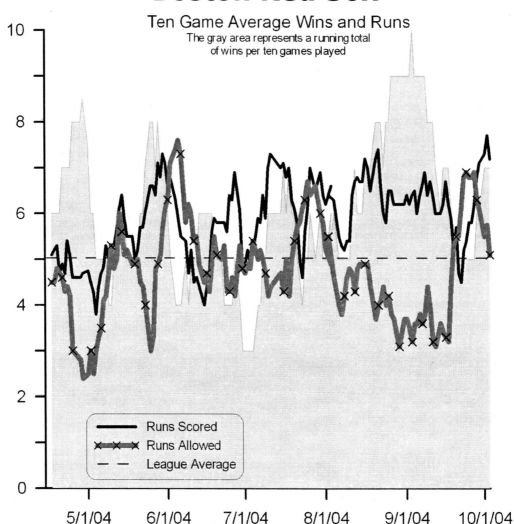

Ten Game Average Wins and Runs
The gray area represents a running total
of wins per ten games played

Legend:
— Runs Scored
×—×—× Runs Allowed
– – League Average

4/25: Boston sweeps 3 games from Yankees for a 4 1/2 game lead

5/11: Option Kim to Pawtucket and give Arroyo spot in the rotation. Arroyo goes 9-8 with a 3.93 ERA

6/9: Nomar returns from DL; Red Sox at 34-23

7/31: Nomar traded to Cubs: Sox get Cabrera and Mientkiewicz; also get Roberts from LA

8/7: Begin stretch of 28 wins in next 34, and 40 of final 55 games.

9/8: Sweep the A's to go 8-1 in nine-game stretch against top three AL West teams, take five-game lead in wild card race.

Team Batting and Pitching/Fielding Stats by Month						
	April	**May**	**June**	**July**	**Aug**	**Sept**
Wins	15	16	11	14	21	21
Losses	8	13	14	11	7	11
OBP	.351	.365	.348	.373	.375	.354
SLG	.418	.469	.473	.527	.496	.467
FIP	3.73	3.78	4.22	4.07	3.74	4.36
DER	.728	.701	.714	.677	.722	.726

Batting Stats

Player	RC	Runs	RBI	PA	Outs	H	BB	HR	TB	BA	OBP	SLG	GPA	ISO	SB	CS	GDP
Ortiz D.	131	94	139	669	419	175	75	41	351	.301	.380	.603	.322	.302	0	0	12
Ramirez M.	127	108	130	663	414	175	82	43	348	.308	.397	.613	.332	.305	2	4	17
Damon J.	115	123	94	702	448	189	76	20	296	.304	.380	.477	.290	.172	19	8	8
Bellhorn M.	96	93	82	620	394	138	88	17	232	.264	.373	.444	.279	.180	6	1	8
Millar K.	90	74	74	588	374	151	57	18	241	.297	.383	.474	.291	.177	1	1	16
Varitek J.	80	67	73	536	340	137	62	18	223	.296	.390	.482	.296	.186	10	3	11
Mueller B.	61	75	57	460	296	113	51	12	178	.283	.365	.446	.276	.163	2	2	8
Youkilis K.	36	38	35	248	156	54	33	7	86	.260	.367	.413	.268	.154	0	1	1
Mirabelli D.	33	27	32	182	120	45	19	9	84	.281	.368	.525	.297	.244	0	0	5
Kapler G.	31	51	33	310	220	79	15	6	113	.272	.311	.390	.237	.117	5	4	5
Cabrera O.	31	33	31	248	166	67	11	6	106	.294	.320	.465	.260	.171	4	1	4
Garciaparra	26	24	21	169	110	50	8	5	78	.321	.367	.500	.290	.179	2	0	4
Nixon T.	23	24	23	167	105	47	15	6	76	.315	.377	.510	.297	.195	0	0	3
Reese P.	20	32	29	268	197	54	17	3	74	.221	.271	.303	.198	.082	6	2	5
McCarty D.	17	24	17	168	117	39	14	4	61	.258	.327	.404	.248	.146	1	0	5
Mientkiewicz	12	13	10	119	88	23	10	1	34	.215	.286	.318	.208	.103	0	1	3
Roberts D.	12	19	14	101	68	22	10	2	38	.256	.330	.442	.259	.186	5	2	2
Daubach B.	11	9	8	86	59	17	10	2	31	.227	.326	.413	.250	.187	0	0	1
Hyzdu A.	3	3	2	11	7	3	1	1	8	.300	.364	.800	.364	.500	0	0	0
Burks E.	2	6	1	37	28	6	3	1	9	.182	.270	.273	.190	.091	2	0	1
Gutierrez R.	1	6	3	42	31	11	2	0	12	.275	.310	.300	.214	.025	1	0	2
Lowe D.	1	0	1	5	3	1	0	0	2	.250	.250	.500	.238	.250	0	0	0
Snyder E.	1	0	0	4	4	1	0	0	1	.250	.250	.250	.175	.000	0	0	1
Dominique A.	0	0	1	11	9	2	0	0	2	.182	.182	.182	.127	.000	0	0	0
Martinez P.	0	0	0	2	2	0	0	0	0	.000	.000	.000	.000	.000	0	0	0
Wakefield T.	0	0	0	2	2	0	0	0	0	.000	.000	.000	.000	.000	0	0	0
Schilling C.	0	0	0	7	6	1	0	0	1	.143	.143	.143	.100	.000	0	0	0
Martinez S.	0	0	0	4	4	0	0	0	0	.000	.000	.000	.000	.000	0	0	0
Arroyo B	-1	0	0	7	6	0	0	0	0	.000	.000	.000	.000	.000	0	0	0
Crespo C.	-1	6	2	79	67	13	0	0	17	.165	.165	.215	.128	.051	2	0	1

Pitching Stats

Player	IP	BFP	G	GS	P/PA	H	K	BB	HR	W	L	Sv	Op	Hld	RA	ERA	FIP	DER
Schilling C	226.7	910	32	32	3.75	206	203	35	23	21	6	0	0	0	3.34	3.26	3.34	.716
Martinez P	217.0	903	33	33	3.86	193	227	61	26	16	9	0	0	0	4.11	3.90	3.82	.709
Wakefield	188.3	831	32	30	3.60	197	116	63	29	12	10	0	0	1	5.78	4.87	5.31	.723
Lowe D.	182.7	839	33	33	3.66	224	105	71	15	14	12	0	0	0	6.80	5.42	4.50	.673
Arroyo B.	178.7	764	32	29	3.68	171	142	47	17	10	9	0	0	0	4.99	4.03	4.06	.714
Foulke K.	83.0	333	72	0	3.80	63	79	15	8	5	3	32	39	0	2.39	2.17	3.39	.756
Timlin M.	76.3	320	76	0	3.58	75	56	19	8	5	4	1	4	20	4.13	4.13	4.12	.711
Embree A.	52.3	217	71	0	3.77	49	37	11	7	2	2	0	1	20	4.82	4.13	4.30	.739
Mendoza	30.7	119	27	0	3.45	25	13	7	3	2	1	0	0	3	3.52	3.52	4.49	.768
Williamson	28.7	120	28	0	3.93	11	28	18	0	0	1	1	2	3	1.88	1.26	3.53	.845
Leskanic	27.7	119	32	0	3.84	24	22	16	3	3	2	2	3	2	3.58	3.58	4.95	.727
Dinardo L.	27.7	130	22	0	3.82	34	21	12	1	0	0	0	0	0	5.53	4.23	3.76	.649
Adams T.	27.0	119	19	0	3.85	35	21	6	6	2	0	0	0	1	6.33	6.00	5.40	.659
Malaska M	20.0	93	19	0	4.10	21	12	12	2	1	1	0	0	1	4.95	4.50	5.34	.712
Kim B.	17.3	77	7	3	3.74	17	6	7	1	2	1	0	0	0	7.79	6.23	4.90	.738
Myers M.	15.0	66	25	0	3.89	16	9	6	2	1	0	0	0	2	4.20	4.20	5.02	.714
Martinez A	10.7	52	11	0	3.81	13	5	6	2	2	1	0	0	0	8.44	8.44	6.75	.711
Astacio P.	8.7	43	5	1	3.58	13	6	5	2	0	0	0	0	0	10.38	10.38	6.63	.633
Brown J.	7.7	41	4	0	3.66	15	6	4	1	0	0	0	0	0	8.22	5.87	4.98	.533
Anderson	6.0	28	5	0	3.64	10	3	3	0	0	0	0	0	0	6.00	6.00	3.79	.545
Alvarez A.	5.0	25	1	1	3.80	8	2	5	2	0	1	0	0	0	9.00	9.00	10.69	.625
McCarty D	3.7	14	3	0	4.57	2	4	1	0	0	0	0	0	0	2.45	2.45	1.92	.778
Seibel P.	3.7	18	2	0	3.67	0	1	5	0	0	0	0	0	0	0.00	0.00	7.65	1.000
Jones B.	3.3	20	3	0	4.30	3	3	8	1	0	1	0	0	0	5.40	5.40	12.59	.750
Nelson J.	2.7	17	3	0	4.65	4	5	3	0	0	0	0	0	0	16.88	16.88	5.16	.429
Castillo F.	1.0	4	2	0	5.25	1	0	1	0	0	0	0	0	0	0.00	0.00	6.29	.667

Fielding Stats

Catchers

Name	Innings	SBA/G	CS%	ERA	WP+PB/G
Varitek	1062.7	0.82	21%	4.18	0.212
Mirabelli	375.7	1.27	13%	4.31	0.815
Martinez	11.0	0.00	0%	0.82	0.818
Dominique	2.0	0.00	0%	4.50	0.000

Infielders and Outfielders

Name	POS	Inn	PO	A	TE	FE	FPct	RF	DPS	DPT
K Millar	1B	512.0	466	57	1	5	.989	9.19	10	0
D McCarty	1B	288.0	287	30	1	2	.991	9.91	4	0
D Mientkiewi	1B	272.0	263	25	0	1	.997	9.53	1	0
D Ortiz	1B	260.3	253	21	0	3	.986	9.47	0	0

Boston Red Sox

Name	POS	Inn	PO	A	TE	FE	FPct	RF	DPS	DPT
B Daubach	1B	100.0	100	10	1	1	.982	9.90	3	0
A Dominique	1B	19.0	25	1	1	0	.963	12.32	0	0
M Bellhorn	2B	1044.0	189	348	3	8	.980	4.63	24	36
P Reese	2B	152.0	49	63	0	1	.991	6.63	7	7
B Mueller	2B	120.0	22	34	2	1	.949	4.20	3	2
R Gutierrez	2B	68.0	15	24	0	0	1.000	5.16	4	3
C Crespo	2B	59.7	12	19	0	0	1.000	4.68	2	1
D Mientkiewi	2B	7.0	2	2	0	0	1.000	5.14	1	0
P Reese	SS	507.7	85	189	2	4	.979	4.86	18	16
O Cabrera	SS	491.0	78	147	3	5	.966	4.12	13	9
N Garciaparr	SS	311.3	52	82	4	2	.957	3.87	5	8
C Crespo	SS	96.3	20	30	1	2	.943	4.67	4	4
R Gutierrez	SS	36.0	7	9	1	0	.941	4.00	2	1
M Bellhorn	SS	9.0	2	3	0	0	1.000	5.00	0	1
B Mueller	3B	827.7	71	162	10	4	.943	2.53	15	1
K Youkilis	3B	506.0	47	106	0	5	.968	2.72	5	0
M Bellhorn	3B	108.7	10	31	1	2	.932	3.40	2	0
E Snyder	3B	9.0	2	3	0	0	1.000	5.00	0	0
M Ramirez	LF	1087.0	198	4	2	5	.967	1.67	0	0
K Millar	LF	116.0	25	0	0	0	1.000	1.94	0	0
G Kapler	LF	64.3	13	0	0	0	1.000	1.82	0	0
D Roberts	LF	50.0	10	0	0	0	1.000	1.80	0	0
D McCarty	LF	47.0	6	1	0	0	1.000	1.34	2	0
B Daubach	LF	44.0	7	1	0	0	1.000	1.64	0	0
A Hyzdu	LF	27.0	6	0	0	0	1.000	2.00	0	0
C Crespo	LF	15.3	2	0	0	0	1.000	1.17	0	0
J Damon	CF	1256.0	349	5	2	3	.986	2.54	4	0
G Kapler	CF	92.0	24	1	1	1	.926	2.45	0	0
D Roberts	CF	74.0	18	0	0	0	1.000	2.19	0	0
C Crespo	CF	29.0	10	0	0	0	1.000	3.10	0	0
G Kapler	RF	590.7	133	5	2	0	.986	2.10	0	0
K Millar	RF	425.7	96	1	1	2	.970	2.05	0	0
T Nixon	RF	306.0	63	1	1	0	.985	1.88	0	0
D Roberts	RF	86.0	25	1	0	1	.963	2.72	2	0
D McCarty	RF	21.0	7	0	0	0	1.000	3.00	0	0
C Crespo	RF	9.0	1	0	0	0	1.000	1.00	0	0
B Daubach	RF	8.0	1	0	0	0	1.000	1.13	0	0
A Hyzdu	RF	5.0	0	0	0	0	.000	0.00	0	0

Chicago White Sox

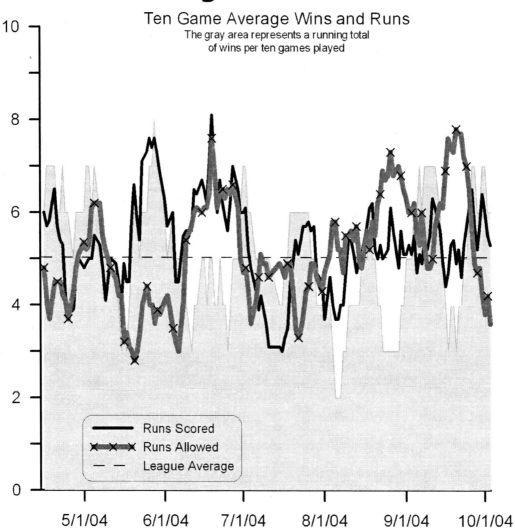

Ten Game Average Wins and Runs
The gray area represents a running total
of wins per ten games played

6/27: Trade Olivo, 7/10: Thomas on
Reed and MinL for DL; out for year
Garcia and Davis

6/16: Lee sets new   7/1: Finish   7/23: Ordonez on
franchise mark with sweep of   DL; out for year
28 game hit streak   Twins

7/29: Swept by
Twins, end of
contention

Team Batting and Pitching/Fielding Stats by Month						
	April	**May**	**June**	**July**	**Aug**	**Sept**
Wins	14	15	13	10	12	19
Losses	9	12	12	16	17	13
OBP	.350	.353	.357	.288	.320	.327
SLG	.476	.461	.503	.389	.457	.453
FIP	5.10	4.17	5.31	4.59	5.35	4.99
DER	.722	.704	.715	.716	.680	.711

Batting Stats

Player	RC	Runs	RBI	PA	Outs	H	BB	HR	TB	BA	OBP	SLG	GPA	ISO	SB	CS	GDP
Lee C.	112	103	99	658	426	180	54	31	310	.305	.366	.525	.296	.220	11	5	10
Konerko P	105	84	117	643	430	156	69	41	301	.277	.359	.535	.295	.258	1	0	23
Rowand A.	92	94	69	534	346	151	30	24	265	.310	.361	.544	.299	.234	17	5	5
Uribe J.	80	82	74	553	381	142	32	23	254	.283	.327	.506	.273	.223	9	11	10
Valentin J.	66	73	70	504	362	97	43	30	213	.216	.287	.473	.248	.258	8	6	3
Crede J.	59	67	69	543	385	117	34	21	205	.239	.299	.418	.239	.180	1	2	10
Thomas F.	59	53	49	311	177	65	64	18	135	.271	.434	.563	.336	.292	0	2	0
Harris W.	50	68	27	472	313	107	51	2	132	.262	.343	.323	.235	.061	19	7	4
Gload R.	41	28	44	260	172	75	20	7	112	.321	.375	.479	.288	.158	0	3	10
Ordonez	38	32	37	222	148	59	16	9	98	.292	.351	.485	.279	.193	0	2	3
Perez T.	38	38	40	321	231	72	15	5	99	.246	.285	.338	.213	.092	3	1	9
Everett C.	23	22	21	169	116	41	8	5	65	.266	.320	.422	.249	.156	1	0	3
Olivo M.	21	21	26	156	108	38	10	7	70	.270	.316	.496	.266	.227	5	4	1
Burke J.	20	22	15	133	82	40	10	0	49	.333	.386	.408	.276	.075	0	0	2
Davis B.	15	21	16	171	126	37	9	6	64	.231	.276	.400	.224	.169	1	1	2
Borchard J	13	25	20	222	170	35	19	9	68	.174	.249	.338	.197	.164	1	0	4
Alomar S	12	15	14	164	115	35	11	2	45	.240	.298	.308	.211	.068	0	0	4
Drnsfeldt	6	5	4	30	20	10	0	0	10	.333	.333	.333	.233	.000	0	0	0
Alomar R.	5	4	8	65	52	11	2	1	15	.180	.203	.246	.153	.066	0	0	2
Valdez W.	2	8	4	46	36	10	2	1	14	.233	.267	.326	.201	.093	1	2	1
Cotts N.	1	0	0	1	0	1	0	0	2	1.000	1.000	2.000	.950	1.000	0	0	0
Scneweis	0	0	0	2	1	1	0	0	2	.500	.500	1.000	.475	.500	0	0	0
Garland J.	0	0	0	5	3	1	0	0	1	.250	.250	.250	.175	.000	0	0	0
Diaz F.	0	0	0	1	1	0	0	0	0	.000	.000	.000	.000	.000	0	0	0
Munoz A.	0	0	0	1	1	0	0	0	0	.000	.000	.000	.000	.000	0	0	0
Buehrle M.	0	0	0	5	3	0	0	0	0	.000	.000	.000	.000	.000	0	0	0
Loaiza E.	-1	0	0	5	6	0	0	0	0	.000	.000	.000	.000	.000	0	0	1

Pitching Stats

Player	IP	BFP	G	GS	P/PA	H	K	BB	HR	W	L	Sv	Op	Hld	RA	ERA	FIP	DER
Buehrle M.	245.3	1016	35	35	3.64	257	165	51	33	16	10	0	0	0	4.37	3.89	4.42	.705
Garland J.	217.0	923	34	33	3.70	223	113	76	34	12	11	0	0	0	5.18	4.89	5.39	.728
Loaiza E.	140.7	604	21	21	3.76	156	83	45	23	9	5	0	0	0	5.18	4.86	5.22	.706
Schoeneweis	112.7	500	20	19	3.83	129	69	49	17	6	9	0	0	0	5.91	5.59	5.41	.691
Garcia F.	103.0	432	16	16	3.88	96	102	32	14	9	4	0	0	0	4.63	4.46	4.16	.706
Contreras J.	74.7	333	13	13	3.89	73	68	42	9	5	4	0	0	0	5.79	5.30	4.81	.698
Marte D.	73.7	303	74	0	4.22	56	68	34	10	6	5	6	12	21	3.42	3.42	4.72	.755
Cotts N.	65.3	281	56	1	4.25	61	58	30	13	4	4	0	2	4	6.20	5.65	5.62	.729
Takatsu S.	62.3	245	59	0	3.98	40	50	21	6	6	4	19	20	4	2.45	2.31	4.05	.795
Adkins J.	62.0	271	50	0	3.65	75	44	20	13	2	3	0	0	5	5.08	4.65	5.61	.679
Politte C.	51.3	225	54	0	4.30	52	48	22	6	0	3	1	1	19	4.56	4.38	4.34	.687
Diaz F.	49.3	226	18	7	3.88	62	33	16	13	2	5	0	0	0	6.93	6.75	6.54	.696
Jackson M.	46.7	210	45	0	3.76	55	26	15	7	2	0	0	0	3	5.21	5.01	5.28	.698
Grilli J.	45.0	203	8	8	3.89	52	26	20	11	2	3	0	0	0	7.60	7.40	6.85	.713
Koch B.	23.3	114	24	0	4.23	24	25	16	3	1	1	8	11	1	5.79	5.40	5.13	.691
Wright D.	17.7	88	4	4	3.99	24	6	11	5	0	4	0	0	0	8.66	8.15	8.50	.703
Munoz A.	14.3	75	11	1	4.01	20	11	12	4	0	1	0	0	0	10.05	10.05	8.11	.660
Rauch J.	8.7	43	2	2	3.35	16	4	4	0	1	1	0	0	0	6.23	6.23	3.75	.543
Bajenaru J.	8.3	44	9	0	3.59	15	8	6	0	0	1	0	0	0	10.80	10.80	3.53	.500
Stewart J.	7.7	41	3	2	4.07	16	5	3	3	0	1	0	0	0	15.26	15.26	8.25	.567
Wunsch K.	2.0	8	3	0	3.63	2	1	1	0	0	0	0	0	0	0.00	0.00	3.79	.667
Darensbourg	1.3	4	2	0	4.50	1	0	1	0	0	0	0	0	0	0.00	0.00	5.54	.667

Fielding Stats

Catchers

Name	Innings	SBA/G	CS%	ERA	WP+PB/G
Davis	397.0	0.93	22%	5.15	0.544
Alomar Jr.	377.0	0.81	21%	4.99	0.310
Olivo	366.3	0.66	26%	4.69	0.393
Burke	292.0	0.55	39%	4.78	0.123

Infielders and Outfielders

Name	POS	Inn	PO	A	TE	FE	FPct	RF	DPS	DPT
P Konerko	1B	1177.0	1149	79	2	3	.995	9.39	11	0
R Gload	1B	218.3	218	12	0	0	1.000	9.48	2	0
F Thomas	1B	32.3	31	3	0	0	1.000	9.46	0	0
J Burke	1B	4.0	4	2	0	0	1.000	13.50	1	0
W Harris	2B	673.7	163	223	1	3	.990	5.16	14	35
J Uribe	2B	616.7	152	200	3	3	.983	5.14	16	29
R Alomar	2B	112.0	24	37	0	1	.984	4.90	5	9

Chicago White Sox

Name	POS	Inn	PO	A	TE	FE	FPct	RF	DPS	DPT
W Valdez	2B	30.0	9	4	0	0	1.000	3.90	1	1
J Valentin	SS	1025.0	187	373	6	13	.966	4.92	50	33
J Uribe	SS	287.3	54	115	1	2	.983	5.29	19	11
W Valdez	SS	80.0	13	23	1	0	.973	4.05	3	1
K Dransfeldt	SS	39.7	4	14	0	1	.947	4.08	1	0
J Crede	3B	1235.0	90	241	5	6	.965	2.41	20	2
J Uribe	3B	180.7	14	41	1	1	.965	2.74	5	0
K Dransfeldt	3B	13.3	2	0	0	0	1.000	1.35	0	0
J Burke	3B	2.7	0	0	0	0	.000	0.00	0	0
C Lee	LF	1277.0	282	11	0	0	1.000	2.06	4	0
R Gload	LF	94.0	20	0	0	1	.952	1.91	0	0
T Perez	LF	51.7	8	1	0	1	.900	1.57	0	0
C Everett	LF	7.0	1	1	0	0	1.000	2.57	0	0
W Harris	LF	2.0	2	0	0	0	1.000	9.00	0	0
A Rowand	CF	1018.0	290	8	2	4	.980	2.63	1	0
W Harris	CF	222.7	55	1	0	1	.982	2.26	0	0
T Perez	CF	179.7	44	2	1	0	.979	2.30	2	0
R Gload	CF	6.3	2	0	0	0	1.000	2.84	0	0
J Borchard	CF	5.0	2	0	0	0	1.000	3.60	0	0
J Borchard	RF	460.7	99	4	1	2	.972	2.01	0	0
T Perez	RF	383.7	82	5	0	0	1.000	2.04	5	0
M Ordonez	RF	364.0	95	0	0	1	.990	2.35	0	0
R Gload	RF	137.3	37	1	0	2	.950	2.49	0	0
A Rowand	RF	76.7	14	2	1	1	.889	1.88	0	0
J Burke	RF	10.0	2	0	0	0	1.000	1.80	0	0

Cleveland Indians

Ten Game Average Wins and Runs
The gray area represents a running total
of wins per ten games played

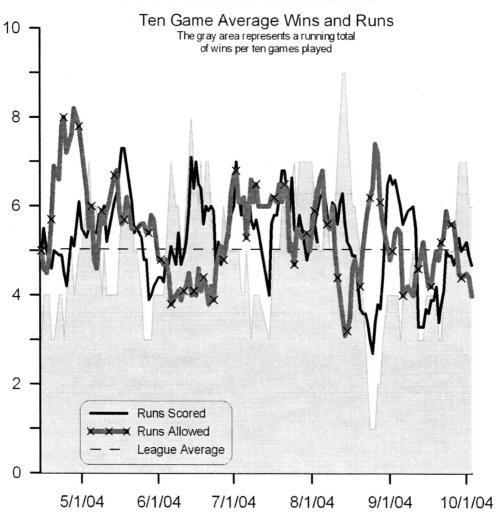

Runs Scored
Runs Allowed
League Average

5/1/04　6/1/04　7/1/04　8/1/04　9/1/04　10/1/04

4/5: Lose to Twins 7-4, after leading 4-0 in the 8th. First of 28 blown team saves

7/25: Sweep Royals and are above .500 for the first time. Including sweep, Tribe wins 17 of next 23.

8/15: Lose to Twins, 3-2 after taking first two games of series and moving within one game of division lead; lose next nine.

8/31: Beat Yankees, 22-0, worst defeat in Yankee history

Team Batting and Pitching/Fielding Stats by Month						
	April	May	June	July	Aug	Sept
Wins	10	12	16	15	14	13
Losses	13	14	12	12	15	16
OBP	.367	.353	.351	.354	.357	.328
SLG	.425	.405	.458	.466	.495	.408
FIP	4.80	4.50	4.82	4.40	4.62	4.75
DER	.695	.684	.708	.680	.710	.716

Batting Stats

Player	RC	Runs	RBI	PA	Outs	H	BB	HR	TB	BA	OBP	SLG	GPA	ISO	SB	CS	GDP
Hafner T.	105	96	109	576	343	150	68	28	281	.311	.410	.583	.330	.272	3	2	9
Martinez V.	91	77	108	591	388	147	60	23	256	.283	.359	.492	.284	.210	0	1	14
Blake C.	89	93	88	668	454	159	68	28	285	.271	.354	.486	.281	.215	5	8	18
Belliard R.	88	78	70	663	449	169	60	12	255	.282	.348	.426	.263	.144	3	2	17
Vizquel O.	84	82	59	651	419	165	57	7	220	.291	.353	.388	.256	.097	19	6	11
Lawton M.	84	109	70	680	457	164	74	20	249	.277	.366	.421	.270	.144	23	9	21
Broussard B.	79	57	82	485	312	115	52	17	204	.275	.370	.488	.288	.213	4	2	7
Crisp C.	73	78	71	538	365	146	36	15	219	.297	.344	.446	.266	.149	20	13	7
Gerut J.	60	72	51	548	375	121	54	11	195	.252	.334	.405	.252	.154	13	6	9
Merloni L.	28	25	28	214	144	55	14	4	81	.289	.343	.426	.261	.137	1	2	7
Sizemore G.	21	15	24	159	104	34	14	4	56	.246	.333	.406	.251	.159	2	0	0
Escobar A.	17	20	12	179	122	32	23	1	47	.211	.318	.309	.220	.099	1	1	1
Phelps J.	10	13	10	80	57	23	4	5	44	.303	.338	.579	.297	.276	0	0	4
Laker T.	9	12	17	128	97	25	7	3	36	.214	.262	.308	.195	.094	0	0	5
McDonald J.	7	17	7	100	75	19	4	2	32	.204	.237	.344	.193	.140	0	0	1
Bard J.	6	5	4	23	11	8	3	1	13	.421	.478	.684	.386	.263	0	0	0
Ludwick R.	4	3	4	54	39	11	2	2	19	.220	.278	.380	.220	.160	0	0	0
Peralta J.	2	2	2	28	20	6	3	0	7	.240	.321	.280	.215	.040	0	1	0
Little M.	1	0	2	23	16	4	0	0	4	.200	.261	.200	.167	.000	0	0	0
Young E.	1	0	0	5	2	2	1	0	2	.500	.600	.500	.395	.000	0	0	0
Davis J.	1	1	1	5	4	1	0	1	4	.200	.200	.800	.290	.600	0	0	0
Phillips B.	0	1	1	24	21	4	2	0	6	.182	.250	.273	.181	.091	0	2	1
Lee C.	0	0	0	3	2	1	0	0	1	.333	.333	.333	.233	.000	0	0	0
Elarton S.	0	1	0	3	2	1	0	0	1	.333	.333	.333	.233	.000	0	0	0
Tadano K.	0	1	0	3	2	1	0	0	1	.333	.333	.333	.233	.000	0	0	0
Martinez S.	0	0	0	2	2	0	0	0	0	.000	.000	.000	.000	.000	0	0	0
Westbrook J.	0	0	0	4	3	0	0	0	0	.000	.000	.000	.000	.000	0	0	0
Sabathia C.	0	0	0	4	3	1	0	0	1	.250	.250	.250	.175	.000	0	0	0
Gonzalez R.	-1	0	0	11	10	1	0	0	1	.091	.091	.091	.064	.000	0	0	0

Pitching Stats

Player	IP	BFP	G	GS	P/PA	H	K	BB	HR	W	L	Sv	Op	Hld	RA	ERA	FIP	DER
Westbrook	215.7	895	33	30	3.51	208	116	61	19	14	9	0	0	0	3.96	3.38	4.28	.728
Sabathia	188.0	787	30	30	3.95	176	139	72	20	11	10	0	0	0	4.31	4.12	4.46	.716
Lee C.	179.0	802	33	33	3.95	188	161	81	30	14	8	0	0	0	5.68	5.43	5.21	.696
Elarton S.	117.3	498	21	21	4.05	107	80	42	25	3	5	0	0	0	4.76	4.53	5.87	.764
Davis J.	114.3	540	26	19	3.66	148	72	51	13	2	7	0	0	1	6.38	5.51	4.95	.663
White R.	78.3	339	59	0	3.70	88	44	29	15	5	5	1	3	2	5.97	5.29	5.84	.707
Riske D.	77.3	337	72	0	4.10	69	78	41	11	7	3	5	12	9	3.72	3.72	4.79	.717
Betancourt	66.7	286	68	0	3.82	71	76	18	7	5	6	4	11	12	4.32	3.92	3.19	.654
Miller M.	55.3	226	57	0	3.68	42	55	23	1	4	1	1	2	7	3.58	3.09	3.11	.709
Durbin C.	51.3	239	17	8	4.11	63	38	24	10	5	6	0	0	0	7.01	6.66	5.98	.675
Tadano K.	50.3	225	14	4	3.64	55	39	18	6	1	1	0	0	0	5.36	4.65	4.54	.692
Howry B.	42.7	178	37	0	4.29	37	39	12	5	4	2	0	2	8	2.95	2.74	3.97	.733
Jimenez J.	36.3	170	31	0	3.65	45	21	14	6	1	7	8	11	1	9.17	8.42	5.77	.688
D'Amico J.	30.7	144	7	7	3.69	45	16	6	6	1	2	0	0	0	8.51	7.63	5.48	.661
Wickman	29.7	129	30	0	3.53	33	26	10	4	0	2	13	14	4	4.25	4.25	4.51	.667
Bartosh C.	19.3	91	34	0	3.91	22	25	11	4	1	0	0	2	3	4.66	4.66	5.10	.647
Denney K.	16.0	86	4	4	3.88	32	13	8	3	1	2	0	0	0	9.56	9.56	5.60	.532
Cressend	15.7	78	11	0	3.82	22	8	10	4	0	1	0	0	2	6.32	6.32	7.50	.679
Robertson	14.0	75	8	0	3.57	22	6	9	5	1	1	0	1	2	14.14	12.21	9.43	.679
Stewart S.	13.7	70	23	0	3.99	23	18	6	2	0	2	0	2	4	9.22	7.24	3.88	.523
Guthrie J.	11.7	49	6	0	3.61	9	7	6	1	0	0	0	0	0	4.63	4.63	5.01	.765
Stanford J.	11.0	50	2	2	3.80	12	5	5	0	0	1	0	0	0	0.82	0.82	4.02	.692
Dawley J.	8.3	37	2	2	3.95	7	8	7	1	0	0	0	0	0	5.40	5.40	5.45	.714
Cruceta F.	7.7	39	2	2	3.72	10	9	4	1	0	1	0	0	0	10.57	9.39	4.60	.625
Cabrera F.	5.3	20	4	0	4.10	3	6	1	0	0	0	0	0	0	5.06	3.38	1.60	.769
Lee D.	4.3	27	4	0	4.00	8	4	4	0	0	0	0	0	0	14.54	10.38	4.21	.579
Pote L.	3.0	13	2	0	4.54	3	5	1	0	0	0	0	0	0	9.00	9.00	0.96	.571
Robbins J.	1.7	8	2	0	3.88	3	0	0	1	0	0	0	0	0	5.40	5.40	11.09	.714
Anderson	1.0	8	1	0	5.00	1	1	4	1	0	0	0	0	0	45.00	45.00	26.29	1.000
Laker T.	1.0	4	1	0	4.00	1	0	1	0	0	0	0	0	0	0.00	0.00	6.29	.667

Fielding Stats

Catchers

Name	Innings	SBA/G	CS%	ERA	WP+PB/G
Martinez	1108.0	0.93	23%	4.99	0.357
Laker	298.7	0.87	24%	4.31	0.271
Bard	53.0	1.02	33%	3.91	0.679
Martinez	7.0	3.86	33%	6.43	1.286

Cleveland Indians

Infielders and Outfielders

Name	POS	Inn	PO	A	TE	FE	FPct	RF	DPS	DPT
B Broussard	1B	1019.0	989	77	0	6	.994	9.42	14	0
L Merloni	1B	297.7	282	14	0	1	.997	8.95	2	0
T Hafner	1B	81.7	81	9	0	0	1.000	9.92	0	0
J Phelps	1B	56.0	43	2	0	1	.978	7.23	0	0
C Blake	1B	12.0	12	0	0	0	1.000	9.00	0	0
R Belliard	2B	1320.0	278	426	1	13	.981	4.80	32	54
B Phillips	2B	56.7	17	19	0	1	.973	5.72	0	4
J McDonald	2B	48.3	10	23	0	0	1.000	6.14	3	2
L Merloni	2B	41.0	12	17	1	0	.967	6.37	1	3
O Vizquel	SS	1245.0	200	395	2	9	.982	4.30	49	36
J McDonald	SS	166.7	25	65	3	2	.947	4.86	5	10
J Peralta	SS	55.0	7	17	0	3	.889	3.93	2	0
C Blake	3B	1352.0	121	275	6	20	.938	2.64	27	0
L Merloni	3B	80.3	1	20	0	1	.955	2.35	1	0
J McDonald	3B	24.3	1	12	0	0	1.000	4.81	0	0
J Peralta	3B	9.7	1	2	0	0	1.000	2.79	0	0
M Lawton	LF	1070.0	231	7	2	1	.988	2.00	4	0
C Crisp	LF	293.3	81	2	0	0	1.000	2.55	2	0
A Escobar	LF	66.0	20	0	0	0	1.000	2.73	0	0
L Merloni	LF	19.0	2	1	0	1	.750	1.42	0	0
J Gerut	LF	11.0	0	0	0	0	.000	0.00	0	0
M Little	LF	6.0	2	1	0	0	1.000	4.50	0	0
R Gonzalez	LF	1.0	0	0	0	0	.000	0.00	0	0
C Crisp	CF	807.3	205	3	0	4	.981	2.32	0	0
G Sizemore	CF	348.3	105	0	0	1	.991	2.71	0	0
A Escobar	CF	188.3	53	3	0	0	1.000	2.68	2	0
J Gerut	CF	100.0	25	0	0	0	1.000	2.25	0	0
M Little	CF	22.7	5	0	0	0	1.000	1.99	0	0
J Gerut	RF	1009.0	242	7	1	3	.984	2.22	2	0
M Lawton	RF	167.7	35	2	0	1	.974	1.99	2	0
A Escobar	RF	129.0	29	6	0	1	.972	2.44	2	0
R Ludwick	RF	119.7	32	0	1	0	.970	2.41	0	0
M Little	RF	24.0	5	0	0	0	1.000	1.88	0	0
R Gonzalez	RF	17.0	7	0	0	0	1.000	3.71	0	0

Detroit Tigers

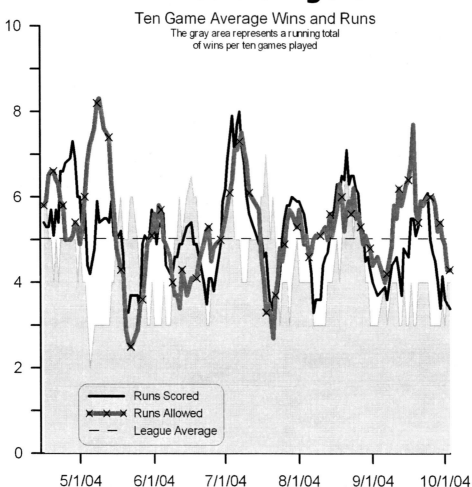

Ten Game Average Wins and Runs
The gray area represents a running total
of wins per ten games played

Legend:
— Runs Scored
×—×—× Runs Allowed
– – League Average

*4/5: Tigers beat Blue
Jays on Opening Day,
start year 4-0; last
year's start was 3-25*

*7/16: Beat Yankees
8-0; 43rd win of the
year, matching last
year's total*

*8/23: Bonderman hurls
complete game, 14 K
shutout vs. White Sox;
ends up with a 3.70 ERA
and 85 strikeouts in 90
second-half innings.*

*10/2: Beat Devil Rays
5-1, giving 72 wins;
improvement of 29
games over 2003*

*5/8: Lose wild game,
16-15 to Rangers
in 10 innings. Lead
14-4 top of 5th, give up
10 runs bottom of 5th.*

Team Batting and Pitching/Fielding Stats by Month						
	April	**May**	**June**	**July**	**Aug**	**Sept**
Wins	13	10	14	13	11	11
Losses	11	17	12	14	17	19
OBP	.349	.360	.341	.324	.337	.312
SLG	.416	.459	.463	.464	.455	.435
FIP	4.84	4.65	4.50	4.76	4.51	4.60
DER	.689	.697	.734	.723	.675	.694

Batting Stats

Player	RC	Runs	RBI	PA	Outs	H	BB	HR	TB	BA	OBP	SLG	GPA	ISO	SB	CS	GDP
Guillen C.	105	97	97	583	369	166	52	20	283	.318	.379	.542	.306	.224	12	5	8
Rodriguez I.	102	72	86	575	370	176	41	19	269	.334	.383	.510	.300	.176	7	4	15
Pena C.	78	89	82	562	376	116	70	27	227	.241	.338	.472	.270	.231	7	1	10
Higginson B.	74	63	64	531	349	110	70	12	174	.246	.353	.388	.256	.143	5	2	9
Infante O.	72	69	55	556	381	133	40	16	226	.264	.317	.449	.255	.185	13	7	4
White R.	71	76	67	498	342	121	39	19	203	.270	.337	.453	.265	.183	1	2	13
Monroe C.	69	65	72	481	328	131	29	18	218	.293	.337	.488	.273	.195	3	4	8
Inge B.	64	43	64	458	299	117	32	13	185	.287	.340	.453	.266	.167	5	4	4
Young D.	60	72	60	432	290	106	33	18	187	.272	.336	.481	.271	.208	0	1	6
Munson E.	51	36	49	357	254	68	29	19	143	.212	.289	.445	.242	.234	1	1	0
Sanchez A.	40	41	26	352	242	107	7	2	128	.322	.335	.386	.247	.063	19	13	4
Thames M.	32	24	33	184	127	42	16	10	84	.255	.326	.509	.274	.255	0	1	3
Logan N.	15	12	10	152	99	37	13	0	46	.278	.340	.346	.240	.068	8	2	1
Smith J.	14	20	19	169	120	37	8	5	67	.239	.280	.432	.234	.194	1	2	0
Vina F.	10	21	7	131	96	26	9	0	31	.226	.308	.270	.206	.043	2	1	6
Shelton C.	4	6	3	56	39	9	9	1	13	.196	.321	.283	.215	.087	0	0	2
Granderson	2	2	0	28	20	6	3	0	9	.240	.321	.360	.235	.120	0	0	1
DiFelice M.	1	3	2	25	22	3	3	0	5	.136	.240	.227	.165	.091	0	0	3
Norton G.	1	9	2	99	74	15	12	2	22	.174	.276	.256	.188	.081	0	0	3
Raburn R.	1	4	1	31	25	4	2	0	5	.138	.194	.172	.130	.034	1	0	0
Knotts G.	0	2	0	5	2	1	1	0	1	.333	.500	.333	.308	.000	0	0	0
German F.	0	0	0	1	1	0	0	0	0	.000	.000	.000	.000	.000	0	0	0
Johnson J.	0	0	0	4	3	0	0	0	0	.000	.000	.000	.000	.000	0	0	0
Robertson N.	0	0	0	3	3	0	0	0	0	.000	.000	.000	.000	.000	0	0	0
Maroth M.	0	0	1	5	4	0	0	0	0	.000	.000	.000	.000	.000	0	0	0
Bonderman J.	-1	0	0	7	7	0	0	0	0	.000	.000	.000	.000	.000	0	0	0

Pitching Stats

Player	IP	BFP	G	GS	P/PA	H	K	BB	HR	W	L	Sv	Op	Hld	RA	ERA	FIP	DER
Maroth M.	217.0	928	33	33	3.60	244	108	59	25	11	13	0	0	0	4.60	4.31	4.71	.700
Johnson J.	196.7	859	33	33	3.67	222	125	60	22	8	15	0	0	0	5.54	5.13	4.47	.691
Robertson N.	196.7	852	34	32	3.61	210	155	66	30	12	10	1	1	0	5.31	4.90	4.77	.698
Bonderman J	184.0	793	33	32	3.67	168	168	73	24	11	13	0	0	0	4.94	4.89	4.51	.722
Knotts G.	135.3	599	36	19	3.64	142	81	58	20	7	6	2	2	2	5.59	5.25	5.39	.720
Yan E.	87.0	379	69	0	3.65	92	69	32	8	3	6	7	17	11	4.45	3.83	4.14	.684
Levine A.	70.7	310	65	0	3.54	83	32	24	10	3	4	0	1	16	4.71	4.58	5.29	.700
Walker J.	64.7	277	70	0	3.52	69	53	12	8	3	4	1	7	18	3.90	3.20	3.86	.700
Urbina U.	54.0	234	54	0	4.02	38	56	32	7	4	6	21	24	0	4.67	4.50	4.85	.772
Ledezma W.	53.3	225	15	8	3.73	55	29	18	3	4	3	0	1	0	4.73	4.39	4.06	.699
Patterson D.	41.7	179	37	0	3.49	44	24	16	7	0	4	2	4	3	5.18	4.75	5.84	.709
Colyer S.	32.0	146	41	0	4.05	33	31	24	8	1	0	0	0	4	6.75	6.47	6.95	.695
Dingman C.	29.3	142	24	0	3.82	33	16	22	3	2	2	0	2	0	6.75	6.75	6.19	.691
Cornejo N.	25.7	125	5	5	3.65	42	12	11	4	1	3	0	0	0	8.77	8.42	5.79	.608
Novoa R.	21.0	94	16	0	3.60	25	15	6	4	1	1	0	1	3	6.43	5.57	5.48	.687
Ennis J.	16.0	75	12	0	3.68	20	13	5	3	0	0	1	2	0	9.00	8.44	5.04	.685
German F.	14.7	73	16	0	3.93	17	8	11	4	1	0	0	1	1	9.20	7.36	8.00	.740
Urdaneta L.	0.0	6	1	0	4.33	5	0	1	0	0	0	0	0	0	0.00	0.00	3.29	.000

Fielding Stats

Catchers

Name	Innings	SBA/G	CS%	ERA	WP+PB/G
Rodriguez	1051.0	0.48	29%	4.86	0.454
Inge	312.7	1.38	38%	5.09	0.576
DiFelice	59.0	0.31	50%	4.88	0.763
Shelton	16.0	0.00	0%	6.19	1.688
Munson	1.0	0.00	0%	0.00	0.000

Infielders and Outfielders

Name	POS	Inn	PO	A	TE	FE	FPct	RF	DPS	DPT
C Pena	1B	1159.0	1137	74	0	6	.995	9.40	8	2
D Young	1B	211.3	203	17	0	0	1.000	9.37	1	0
G Norton	1B	43.0	36	2	0	0	1.000	7.95	0	0
C Shelton	1B	26.0	22	4	0	0	1.000	9.00	0	0
O Infante	2B	868.7	203	276	5	7	.976	4.96	29	44
J Smith	2B	258.0	66	89	0	2	.987	5.41	8	14
F Vina	2B	248.3	73	86	2	3	.970	5.76	7	16
R Raburn	2B	64.7	9	22	0	1	.969	4.31	2	3
C Guillen	SS	1151.0	220	415	11	6	.974	4.97	42	45
O Infante	SS	188.7	28	67	3	1	.960	4.53	7	5

Detroit Tigers

Name	POS	Inn	PO	A	TE	FE	FPct	RF	DPS	DPT
J Smith	SS	100.0	16	35	0	1	.981	4.59	3	2
E Munson	3B	740.7	52	175	9	7	.934	2.76	18	0
B Inge	3B	524.7	42	131	4	8	.935	2.97	12	0
G Norton	3B	117.7	7	19	1	0	.963	1.99	0	0
O Infante	3B	29.3	2	8	0	0	1.000	3.07	2	0
J Smith	3B	20.7	5	5	2	0	.833	4.35	2	0
D Young	3B	6.7	1	1	0	0	1.000	2.70	0	0
R White	LF	614.7	127	2	1	2	.977	1.89	0	0
C Monroe	LF	446.0	102	1	3	4	.928	2.08	0	0
M Thames	LF	298.7	78	3	0	0	1.000	2.44	2	0
B Inge	LF	49.0	7	2	0	1	.900	1.65	0	0
D Young	LF	16.0	2	0	0	0	1.000	1.13	0	0
G Norton	LF	15.3	2	0	0	0	1.000	1.17	0	0
A Sanchez	CF	661.0	176	2	1	8	.952	2.42	2	0
N Logan	CF	359.7	117	3	0	2	.984	3.00	2	0
C Monroe	CF	189.0	49	1	0	0	1.000	2.38	0	0
B Inge	CF	136.0	35	2	0	0	1.000	2.45	2	0
C Granderson	CF	61.0	16	1	0	0	1.000	2.51	0	0
O Infante	CF	32.0	10	0	0	0	1.000	2.81	0	0
A Torres	CF	1.0	0	0	0	0	.000	0.00	0	0
B Higginson	RF	979.3	222	13	0	6	.975	2.16	2	0
C Monroe	RF	386.0	110	3	1	2	.974	2.63	2	0
M Thames	RF	68.3	16	0	0	0	1.000	2.11	0	0
B Inge	RF	5.0	1	1	0	0	1.000	3.60	0	0
C Shelton	RF	1.0	1	0	0	0	1.000	9.00	0	0

Kansas City Royals

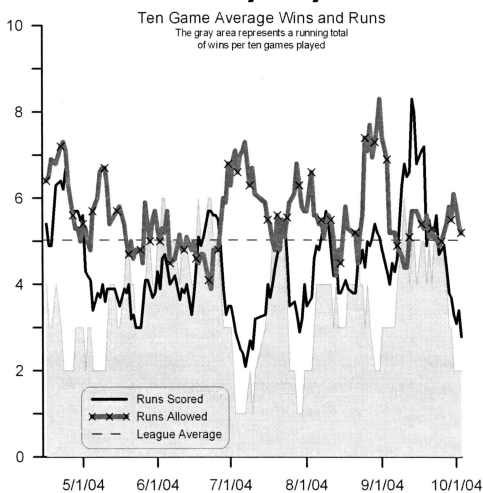

Ten Game Average Wins and Runs
The gray area represents a running total
of wins per ten games played

Runs Scored
Runs Allowed
League Average

4/5: Beat ChiSox 9-7 by
scoring 6 runs in bottom
of 9th, featuring HR's by
Lopez and Beltran

6/8: Greinke records
first major-league victory
with seven shutout innings
against Expos; has 3.97
ERA and 100 K's and
26 walks for season

6/25: Beltran traded
to Astros in 3-way
deal that nets them
three prospects;
Royals go 2-13
in their next 15
games

8/13: Beat A's 10-3;
first team in history
to have two rookies
(Buck and Nunez)
hit grand slams in
same game

9/9: Beat
Detroit 26-5

Team Batting and Pitching/Fielding Stats by Month						
	April	May	June	July	Aug	Sept
Wins	7	11	11	7	10	12
Losses	15	16	16	19	19	19
OBP	.345	.307	.315	.306	.335	.325
SLG	.450	.380	.379	.369	.424	.390
FIP	4.86	5.34	4.55	4.87	5.33	4.74
DER	.687	.692	.698	.688	.699	.690

Batting Stats

Player	RC	Runs	RBI	PA	Outs	H	BB	HR	TB	BA	OBP	SLG	GPA	ISO	SB	CS	GDP
Sweeney M.	77	56	79	452	301	118	33	22	207	.287	.347	.504	.282	.217	3	2	6
Stairs M.	68	48	66	496	333	117	49	18	198	.267	.345	.451	.268	.185	1	0	11
Randa J.	68	65	56	539	357	139	40	8	198	.287	.343	.408	.257	.122	0	1	10
Berroa A.	61	72	43	554	396	134	23	8	197	.262	.308	.385	.235	.123	14	8	10
Beltran C.	60	51	51	309	199	74	37	15	142	.278	.367	.534	.299	.256	14	3	4
Harvey K.	59	47	55	494	338	131	28	13	192	.287	.338	.421	.257	.134	1	1	12
DeJesus D.	53	58	39	413	276	104	33	7	146	.287	.360	.402	.263	.116	8	11	6
Relaford D.	37	45	34	430	309	84	34	6	116	.221	.296	.305	.209	.084	5	4	9
Graffanino T	35	37	26	314	211	73	27	3	93	.263	.332	.335	.233	.072	10	2	4
Buck J.	28	36	30	258	186	56	15	12	101	.235	.280	.424	.232	.189	1	1	3
Nunez A.	27	31	29	247	176	50	25	5	74	.226	.304	.335	.220	.109	0	1	4
Pickering C.	26	21	26	142	98	30	18	7	61	.246	.338	.500	.277	.254	0	0	6
Brown D.	21	19	24	209	149	49	11	4	68	.251	.293	.349	.219	.097	2	2	1
Santiago B.	20	15	23	189	137	48	8	6	76	.274	.312	.434	.249	.160	1	2	8
Gonzalez J.	18	17	17	138	96	35	9	5	56	.276	.326	.441	.257	.165	0	1	3
Gotay R.	16	17	16	166	116	41	9	1	57	.270	.315	.375	.236	.105	0	1	4
Blanco A.	11	9	5	67	43	19	5	0	25	.317	.379	.417	.275	.100	1	2	0
Castillo A.	10	12	11	105	68	24	14	1	33	.270	.365	.371	.257	.101	0	2	1
Stinnett K.	9	10	7	69	41	18	5	3	27	.305	.379	.458	.285	.153	0	0	0
Guiel A.	8	15	13	157	117	21	17	5	40	.156	.263	.296	.192	.141	1	1	2
Mateo R.	6	9	7	98	78	18	3	0	28	.194	.235	.301	.181	.108	1	1	2
Gomez A.	3	1	4	31	22	8	2	0	9	.276	.323	.310	.223	.034	0	0	1
Gettis B.	3	7	1	49	33	7	8	0	10	.179	.327	.256	.211	.077	0	1	0
Murphy D.	2	1	3	27	23	5	0	0	8	.185	.185	.296	.157	.111	1	0	1
Berger B.	1	5	2	36	30	7	0	0	9	.200	.200	.257	.154	.057	1	1	1
Guerrero W.	1	7	1	32	26	7	0	0	9	.219	.219	.281	.169	.063	1	0	1
Brown A.	1	0	0	11	8	3	0	0	3	.273	.273	.273	.191	.000	0	0	0
Jackson D.	1	1	2	16	13	2	1	0	4	.133	.188	.267	.151	.133	0	0	0
Lopez M.	1	4	4	44	37	4	4	1	7	.105	.209	.184	.140	.079	0	0	3
Bautista J.	0	1	1	26	20	5	1	0	6	.200	.231	.240	.164	.040	0	0	0
Phillips P.	0	2	0	6	4	1	0	0	1	.200	.333	.200	.200	.000	0	0	0
George C.	0	0	0	3	2	0	1	0	0	.000	.333	.000	.150	.000	0	0	0
Anderson B.	0	0	0	2	1	0	0	0	0	.000	.000	.000	.000	.000	0	0	0
Gobble J.	0	0	0	2	2	0	0	0	0	.000	.000	.000	.000	.000	0	0	0
Wood M.	0	0	0	2	2	0	0	0	0	.000	.000	.000	.000	.000	0	0	0
Greinke Z.	0	0	0	2	2	0	0	0	0	.000	.000	.000	.000	.000	0	0	0
Thompson R.	0	1	0	1	2	0	0	0	0	.000	.000	.000	.000	.000	1	0	1
May D.	0	0	0	4	4	0	0	0	0	.000	.000	.000	.000	.000	0	0	0
Reyes D.	-1	0	0	6	6	0	0	0	0	.000	.000	.000	.000	.000	0	0	0
Tonis M.	-1	0	0	7	7	0	1	0	0	.000	.143	.000	.064	.000	0	0	1

Pitching Stats

Player	IP	BFP	G	GS	P/PA	H	K	BB	HR	W	L	Sv	Op	Hld	RA	ERA	FIP	DER
May D.	186.0	831	31	31	3.61	234	120	55	38	9	19	0	0	0	6.29	5.61	5.58	.682
Anderson	166.0	746	35	26	3.72	217	70	53	33	6	12	0	0	2	6.67	5.64	6.01	.688
Gobble J.	148.0	638	25	24	3.58	157	49	43	24	9	8	0	0	0	5.72	5.35	5.67	.744
Greinke Z.	145.0	599	24	24	3.82	143	100	26	26	8	11	0	0	0	3.97	3.97	4.95	.733
Reyes D.	108.0	482	40	12	3.77	114	91	50	12	4	8	0	1	5	5.33	4.75	4.55	.686
Wood M.	100.0	432	17	17	3.63	112	54	28	16	3	8	0	0	0	6.03	5.94	5.31	.707
Affeldt J.	76.3	344	38	8	3.77	91	49	32	6	3	4	13	17	0	5.78	4.95	4.41	.665
Camp S.	66.7	287	42	0	3.34	74	51	16	10	2	2	2	3	5	5.00	3.92	4.66	.688
Sullivan S.	60.3	273	49	0	3.68	73	45	24	8	3	4	0	1	6	5.07	4.77	5.07	.656
Cerda J.	45.7	206	53	0	4.22	41	33	30	1	1	4	2	3	12	4.14	3.15	4.30	.712
Field N.	44.3	191	43	0	3.66	40	30	19	5	2	3	3	5	2	5.08	4.26	4.83	.741
George C.	42.3	207	10	7	3.65	60	15	25	1	1	2	0	0	0	8.29	7.23	4.66	.645
Carrasco D	35.3	163	30	0	3.70	41	22	15	5	2	2	0	3	4	5.60	4.84	5.41	.695
Serrano J.	32.7	141	10	5	3.87	35	25	12	5	1	2	0	0	0	4.68	4.68	4.94	.694
Bautista D.	27.7	127	5	5	3.78	38	18	11	2	0	4	0	0	0	6.51	6.51	4.34	.617
Grimsley J.	26.7	118	32	0	3.76	24	18	15	1	3	3	0	3	5	3.71	3.38	4.23	.723
Huisman J.	25.0	116	14	0	3.53	36	13	8	3	0	0	1	1	1	7.20	6.84	4.89	.637
Seanez R.	23.0	100	16	0	3.65	21	21	11	0	0	1	0	1	1	3.91	3.91	2.90	.691
Kinney M.	16.3	84	11	0	4.02	27	21	7	3	0	1	0	0	0	7.71	7.16	4.76	.529
Leskanic C	15.7	85	19	0	3.96	23	15	14	5	0	3	2	5	4	9.19	8.04	8.21	.647
MacDougal	11.3	61	13	0	4.03	16	14	9	2	1	1	1	3	0	6.35	5.56	5.76	.600
Bukvich R.	7.3	30	9	0	3.90	4	7	7	0	0	0	1	1	1	3.68	3.68	4.25	.750
Appier K.	4.0	22	2	2	3.91	7	2	3	0	0	1	0	0	0	18.00	13.50	4.54	.588
Villacis E.	3.3	20	1	1	3.30	6	0	4	1	0	1	0	0	0	13.50	13.50	10.79	.667
Vasquez J.	3.3	17	2	0	3.65	4	4	1	1	0	0	0	0	0	10.80	8.10	6.59	.700

Fielding Stats

Catchers

Name	Innings	SBA/G	CS%	ERA	WP+PB/G
Buck	575.0	0.58	19%	5.31	0.517
Santiago	416.0	0.74	18%	4.65	0.519
Castillo	242.3	0.71	26%	5.09	0.297
Stinnett	155.0	0.75	15%	5.57	0.523
Tonis	17.0	0.53	0%	8.47	1.588
Phillips	15.0	0.00	0%	7.20	0.000

Infielders and Outfielders

Name	POS	Inn	PO	A	TE	FE	FPct	RF	DPS	DPT
K Harvey	1B	630.0	610	51	1	3	.994	9.44	4	0
M Sweeney	1B	471.0	463	34	0	4	.992	9.50	6	0
M Stairs	1B	229.0	206	11	2	1	.986	8.53	1	0

Kansas City Royals

Name	POS	Inn	PO	A	TE	FE	FPct	RF	DPS	DPT
C Pickering	1B	61.0	60	3	0	0	1.000	9.30	1	0
J Randa	1B	24.0	20	2	0	0	1.000	8.25	0	0
W Guerrero	1B	3.0	3	0	0	0	1.000	9.00	0	0
M Lopez	1B	2.3	0	0	0	0	.000	0.00	0	0
T Graffanino	2B	630.3	185	219	2	3	.988	5.77	21	43
R Gotay	2B	368.3	78	97	2	1	.983	4.28	13	16
D Relaford	2B	278.3	69	93	1	2	.982	5.24	12	11
D Murphy	2B	61.0	12	17	0	0	1.000	4.28	4	5
W Guerrero	2B	49.3	8	16	1	0	.960	4.38	0	2
M Lopez	2B	32.0	10	6	1	0	.941	4.50	1	1
D Jackson	2B	1.0	0	0	0	0	.000	0.00	0	0
A Berroa	SS	1143.0	207	388	14	14	.955	4.69	60	40
A Blanco	SS	162.0	30	64	2	2	.959	5.22	11	6
D Relaford	SS	89.3	14	28	0	0	1.000	4.23	3	3
M Lopez	SS	19.0	2	2	0	0	1.000	1.89	1	0
W Guerrero	SS	5.0	1	2	0	0	1.000	5.40	0	0
D Jackson	SS	2.0	0	0	0	0	.000	0.00	0	0
J Randa	3B	1021.0	85	241	5	6	.967	2.87	22	0
D Relaford	3B	315.7	24	77	5	3	.927	2.88	5	0
J Bautista	3B	58.0	5	17	0	1	.957	3.41	2	0
M Lopez	3B	21.0	2	7	0	1	.900	3.86	0	1
W Guerrero	3B	4.0	0	0	0	0	.000	0.00	0	0
D Brown	LF	433.0	93	4	0	3	.970	2.02	0	0
A Guiel	LF	307.3	82	3	2	1	.966	2.49	0	0
D Relaford	LF	152.0	39	2	0	1	.976	2.43	0	0
M Stairs	LF	113.7	23	2	1	0	.962	1.98	4	0
R Mateo	LF	89.0	21	3	0	0	1.000	2.43	2	0
B Gettis	LF	88.0	25	1	2	0	.929	2.66	1	0
B Berger	LF	86.0	25	1	0	0	1.000	2.72	1	0
A Gomez	LF	45.0	11	0	0	1	.917	2.20	0	0
D DeJesus	LF	32.0	9	0	0	0	1.000	2.53	0	0
K Harvey	LF	30.0	4	0	0	0	1.000	1.20	0	0
A Brown	LF	27.0	9	0	0	0	1.000	3.00	0	0
M Lopez	LF	10.0	0	0	0	0	.000	0.00	0	0
W Guerrero	LF	6.0	2	0	0	0	1.000	3.00	0	0
R Thompson	LF	1.0	0	0	0	0	.000	0.00	0	0
D Jackson	LF	0.3	0	0	0	0	.000	0.00	0	0
D DeJesus	CF	732.3	231	3	0	4	.983	2.88	0	0
C Beltran	CF	597.0	197	5	2	1	.985	3.05	2	0
R Mateo	CF	41.0	12	0	0	0	1.000	2.63	0	0
A Nunez	CF	28.0	6	2	0	0	1.000	2.57	0	0
D Relaford	CF	14.0	2	0	0	0	1.000	1.29	0	0
W Guerrero	CF	4.0	0	0	0	0	.000	0.00	0	0
A Gomez	CF	3.0	1	0	0	0	1.000	3.00	0	0
D Jackson	CF	1.0	1	0	0	0	1.000	9.00	0	0

Kansas City Royals

Name	POS	Inn	PO	A	TE	FE	FPct	RF	DPS	DPT
A Nunez	RF	459.3	129	1	0	1	.992	2.55	0	0
M Stairs	RF	450.3	108	3	0	1	.991	2.22	0	0
J Gonzalez	RF	237.0	52	3	1	2	.948	2.09	2	0
R Mateo	RF	82.0	19	1	0	0	1.000	2.20	0	0
D Relaford	RF	55.7	10	0	0	0	1.000	1.62	0	0
B Gettis	RF	48.0	13	1	1	0	.933	2.63	0	0
D DeJesus	RF	32.0	6	0	0	0	1.000	1.69	0	0
A Gomez	RF	26.0	9	0	0	0	1.000	3.12	0	0
M Lopez	RF	13.0	6	0	0	1	.857	4.15	0	0
D Jackson	RF	8.0	1	0	0	0	1.000	1.13	0	0
R Thompson	RF	4.0	2	0	0	0	1.000	4.50	0	0
A Brown	RF	2.0	0	0	0	0	.000	0.00	0	0
B Berger	RF	1.0	0	0	0	0	.000	0.00	0	0
A Guiel	RF	1.0	0	0	0	0	.000	0.00	0	0
J Bautista	RF	1.0	0	0	0	0	.000	0.00	0	0

Minnesota Twins

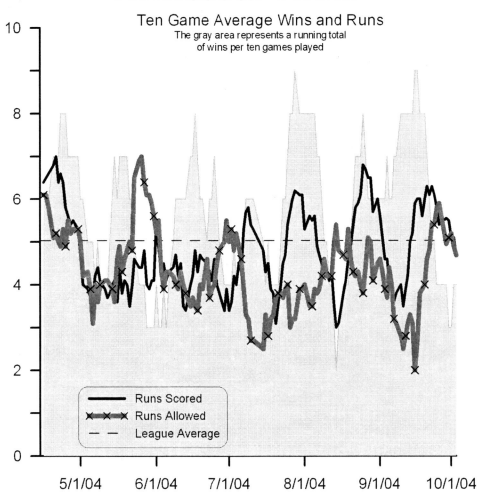

Ten Game Average Wins and Runs
The gray area represents a running total
of wins per ten games played

Legend:
— Runs Scored
—X—X—X— Runs Allowed
– – League Average

4/5: Beat Indians in 11 innings, 7-4, in comback win, behind Stewart HR

6/9: Santana K's 10 Mets and allows one run. Has 5.51 ERA before game, goes 18-2 with 1.35 ERA for rest of year

7/26: Beat White Sox 6-2 as Hunter plows over catcher Burke on a close play at home; go on to sweep all three games

9/19: Santana starts September with 33 consecutive scoreless innings.

8/15: Beat Indians on Koskie's 10th inning HR, take AL Central lead for good

Team Batting and Pitching/Fielding Stats by Month						
	April	**May**	**June**	**July**	**Aug**	**Sept**
Wins	15	13	13	17	15	19
Losses	8	15	13	9	13	12
OBP	.364	.320	.298	.336	.333	.341
SLG	.456	.404	.392	.438	.469	.431
FIP	4.21	4.35	4.12	3.87	3.77	3.87
DER	.668	.690	.708	.733	.688	.706

Batting Stats

Player	RC	Runs	RBI	PA	Outs	H	BB	HR	TB	BA	OBP	SLG	GPA	ISO	SB	CS	GDP
Ford L.	102	89	72	658	415	170	67	15	254	.299	.381	.446	.283	.148	20	2	14
Jones J.	75	69	80	608	436	141	40	24	237	.254	.315	.427	.249	.173	13	10	12
Hunter T.	74	79	81	569	405	141	40	23	247	.271	.330	.475	.267	.204	21	7	19
Koskie C.	70	68	71	488	325	106	49	25	209	.251	.342	.495	.278	.244	9	3	6
Stewart S.	68	46	47	430	269	115	47	11	169	.304	.380	.447	.283	.143	6	3	3
Guzman C.	66	84	46	624	438	158	30	8	221	.274	.309	.384	.235	.109	10	5	15
Cuddyer M.	52	49	45	382	262	89	37	12	149	.263	.339	.440	.263	.177	5	5	7
Morneau J.	50	39	58	312	208	76	28	19	150	.271	.340	.536	.287	.264	0	0	4
Rivas L.	36	44	34	358	259	86	13	10	145	.256	.283	.432	.235	.176	15	1	8
Mientkiewicz	34	34	25	328	225	70	38	5	103	.246	.340	.363	.244	.116	2	2	9
LeCroy M.	33	25	39	287	199	71	16	9	112	.269	.321	.424	.250	.155	0	0	6
Blanco H.	27	36	37	353	261	65	21	10	116	.206	.260	.368	.209	.162	0	3	8
Offerman J.	24	22	22	202	130	44	29	2	68	.256	.363	.395	.262	.140	1	1	1
Mauer J.	22	18	17	122	74	33	11	6	61	.308	.369	.570	.309	.262	1	0	0
Punto N.	15	17	12	103	68	23	12	2	29	.253	.340	.319	.233	.066	6	0	0
Kubel J.	13	10	7	67	43	18	6	2	26	.300	.358	.433	.270	.133	1	1	0
Ojeda A.	11	16	7	72	40	20	10	2	27	.339	.429	.458	.307	.119	1	1	0
Borders P.	6	3	5	44	30	12	0	0	16	.286	.302	.381	.231	.095	2	0	0
Restovich M.	6	9	6	51	35	12	4	2	21	.255	.314	.447	.253	.191	0	0	0
Tiffee T.	6	7	8	48	34	12	3	2	22	.273	.333	.500	.275	.227	0	0	2
Ryan M.	4	9	7	75	57	17	4	0	21	.239	.280	.296	.200	.056	1	1	2
Bowen R.	2	1	2	32	25	3	4	1	6	.111	.226	.222	.157	.111	0	0	1
Santana J.	2	0	2	8	5	3	0	0	3	.375	.375	.375	.263	.000	0	0	0
Prieto A.	2	4	4	36	26	8	3	1	12	.250	.306	.375	.231	.125	0	1	1
Bartlett J.	1	2	1	14	11	1	1	0	1	.083	.154	.083	.090	.000	2	0	0
Nathan J.	0	0	0	1	1	0	0	0	0	.000	.000	.000	.000	.000	0	0	0
Rincon J.	0	0	0	1	1	0	0	0	0	.000	.000	.000	.000	.000	0	0	0
Guerrier M.	0	0	0	1	1	0	0	0	0	.000	.000	.000	.000	.000	0	0	0
Radke B.	0	0	0	3	2	0	0	0	0	.000	.000	.000	.000	.000	0	0	0
Mulholland T	0	0	0	2	2	0	0	0	0	.000	.000	.000	.000	.000	0	0	0
Lohse K.	0	0	0	4	3	0	0	0	0	.000	.000	.000	.000	.000	0	0	0
Silva C.	0	0	0	3	3	0	0	0	0	.000	.000	.000	.000	.000	0	0	0

Pitching Stats

Player	IP	BFP	G	GS	P/PA	H	K	BB	HR	W	L	Sv	Op	Hld	RA	ERA	FIP	DER
Santana J.	228.0	880	34	34	3.89	156	265	54	24	20	6	0	0	0	2.76	2.61	3.16	.750
Radke B.	219.7	901	34	34	3.71	229	143	26	23	11	8	0	0	0	3.77	3.48	3.79	.707
Silva C.	203.0	869	33	33	3.33	255	76	35	23	14	8	0	0	0	4.43	4.21	4.61	.682
Lohse K.	194.0	883	35	34	3.77	240	111	76	28	9	13	0	0	0	5.94	5.34	5.31	.679
Mulholland	123.3	549	39	15	3.42	163	60	33	17	5	9	0	0	2	5.55	5.18	5.04	.664
Rincon J.	82.0	327	77	0	4.30	52	106	32	5	11	6	2	6	16	2.96	2.63	2.74	.742
Romero J.	74.3	319	74	0	4.01	61	69	38	4	7	4	1	8	16	3.87	3.51	3.87	.719
Nathan J.	72.3	284	73	0	4.31	48	89	23	3	1	2	44	47	0	1.74	1.62	2.41	.731
Roa J.	70.0	318	48	0	3.54	84	47	24	9	2	3	0	1	2	4.89	4.50	4.86	.678
Greisinger	51.0	233	12	9	3.67	68	36	15	12	2	5	0	0	0	7.06	6.18	5.94	.667
Fultz A.	50.0	216	55	0	3.90	50	37	23	5	3	3	1	4	5	5.04	5.04	4.55	.700
Balfour G.	39.3	172	36	0	4.30	35	42	21	4	4	1	0	1	4	4.35	4.35	4.23	.699
Crain J.	27.0	109	22	0	4.08	17	14	12	2	3	0	0	1	2	2.00	2.00	4.66	.813
Guerrier M	19.0	84	9	2	3.95	22	11	6	5	0	1	0	0	0	6.16	5.68	6.66	.721
Pulido C.	11.3	56	6	0	3.52	16	9	4	2	0	0	0	0	1	10.32	8.74	5.32	.650
Durbin J.	7.3	38	4	1	3.92	12	6	6	0	0	1	0	0	0	7.36	7.36	4.11	.538
Thomas B.	2.7	16	3	0	3.25	7	0	1	0	0	0	0	0	0	16.88	16.88	4.42	.533
Beimel J.	1.7	15	3	0	3.13	8	2	2	1	0	0	0	0	0	43.20	43.20	12.29	.300

Fielding Stats

Catchers

Name	Innings	SBA/G	CS%	ERA	WP+PB/G
Blanco	872.3	0.58	45%	4.25	0.371
Mauer	257.0	0.56	31%	3.40	0.175
LeCroy	144.3	1.00	6%	3.55	0.249
Borders	120.7	1.12	33%	4.55	0.298
Bowen	81.7	0.77	14%	3.97	0.220

Infielders and Outfielders

Name	POS	Inn	PO	A	TE	FE	FPct	RF	DPS	DPT
D Mientkiewi	1B	668.7	662	35	0	4	.994	9.38	7	0
J Morneau	1B	538.3	523	41	0	2	.995	9.43	5	0
M LeCroy	1B	181.7	173	2	1	0	.994	8.67	1	0
J Offerman	1B	51.0	52	6	0	1	.983	10.24	3	0
M Cuddyer	1B	35.0	34	2	0	0	1.000	9.26	0	0
T Tiffee	1B	1.3	2	0	0	0	1.000	13.50	0	0
L Rivas	2B	860.3	176	317	1	2	.994	5.16	31	40
M Cuddyer	2B	327.3	54	114	1	2	.982	4.62	6	9
N Punto	2B	111.3	20	34	0	1	.982	4.37	5	5
A Ojeda	2B	110.0	19	43	1	1	.969	5.07	5	4

Minnesota Twins

Name	POS	Inn	PO	A	TE	FE	FPct	RF	DPS	DPT
A Prieto	2B	55.0	10	20	0	0	1.000	4.91	2	4
J Offerman	2B	11.0	3	3	2	0	.750	4.91	0	1
J Bartlett	2B	1.0	0	1	0	0	1.000	9.00	0	0
C Guzman	SS	1304.0	234	438	5	7	.982	4.64	51	50
N Punto	SS	88.0	16	33	0	0	1.000	5.01	5	2
A Ojeda	SS	43.3	8	14	0	0	1.000	4.57	2	2
J Bartlett	SS	22.0	5	11	1	1	.889	6.55	1	2
A Prieto	SS	18.0	4	4	0	0	1.000	4.00	1	1
C Koskie	3B	1004.0	79	207	5	6	.963	2.56	16	0
M Cuddyer	3B	338.0	33	51	2	4	.923	2.24	10	0
T Tiffee	3B	94.0	11	17	1	0	.966	2.68	0	0
A Ojeda	3B	20.0	1	6	0	0	1.000	3.15	1	0
A Prieto	3B	16.0	1	3	0	0	1.000	2.25	0	0
N Punto	3B	4.0	0	0	0	0	.000	0.00	0	0
L Ford	LF	680.7	149	5	1	0	.994	2.04	0	0
S Stewart	LF	639.3	103	2	0	2	.972	1.48	0	0
M Restovich	LF	55.0	13	0	0	0	1.000	2.13	0	0
M Ryan	LF	48.0	8	0	0	0	1.000	1.50	0	0
M Cuddyer	LF	35.0	3	0	0	0	1.000	0.77	0	0
J Kubel	LF	18.0	3	1	0	0	1.000	2.00	2	0
T Hunter	CF	1100.0	311	5	1	3	.988	2.59	0	0
L Ford	CF	341.0	101	1	2	1	.971	2.69	0	0
N Punto	CF	13.0	2	1	0	0	1.000	2.08	0	0
M Ryan	CF	13.0	3	0	0	0	1.000	2.08	0	0
J Jones	CF	9.0	4	0	0	0	1.000	4.00	0	0
J Jones	RF	1237.0	314	5	0	2	.994	2.32	2	0
L Ford	RF	85.0	18	1	0	0	1.000	2.01	0	0
M Cuddyer	RF	49.0	13	0	0	0	1.000	2.39	0	0
J Kubel	RF	44.0	11	0	0	0	1.000	2.25	0	0
M Restovich	RF	41.0	7	0	0	0	1.000	1.54	0	0
M Ryan	RF	20.0	7	0	0	1	.875	3.15	0	0

New York Yankees

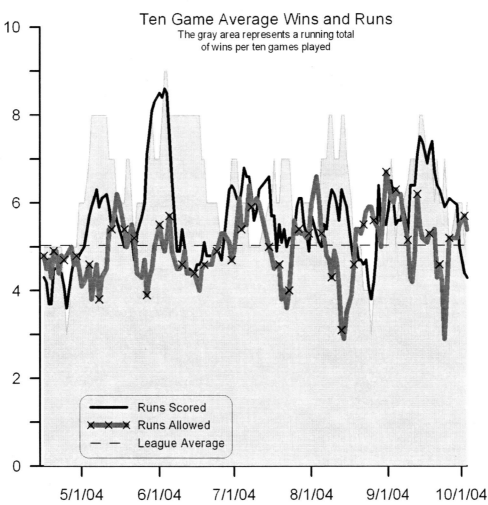

Ten Game Average Wins and Runs
The gray area represents a running total
of wins per ten games played

Runs Scored
Runs Allowed
League Average

5/20: After a terrible season start, Jeter goes 2-for-5 with a homer. He'll hit .329 with 22 homers in his final 116 games.

7/1: Win a classic 5-4 in 13 innings to sweep Red Sox and take an 8 1/2-game lead in the AL East.

7/23: Giambi goes 0-for-3 and is 0-for-last-21. Won't play again until 9/14

9/3: Brown punches wall and breaks left hand

7/11: Hernandez wins 2004 debut. He won't lose until 9/22, and will finish 8-2 with a 3.30 ERA.

7/16: Vazquez allows 8 runs in 4 1/3 innings. He'll go 4-5 with a 6.92 ERA after the break

Team Batting and Pitching/Fielding Stats by Month						
	April	**May**	**June**	**July**	**Aug**	**Sept**
Wins	13	18	19	15	16	20
Losses	11	8	7	12	12	11
OBP	.344	.371	.344	.340	.360	.355
SLG	.402	.505	.444	.455	.482	.448
FIP	4.41	4.45	4.04	4.36	4.72	3.87
DER	.714	.707	.711	.682	.696	.690

Batting Stats

Player	RC	Runs	RBI	PA	Outs	H	BB	HR	TB	BA	OBP	SLG	GPA	ISO	SB	CS	GDP
Sheffield G.	124	117	121	684	428	166	92	36	306	.290	.393	.534	.310	.244	5	6	15
Matsui H.	117	109	108	680	420	174	88	31	305	.298	.390	.522	.306	.224	3	0	10
Rodriguez A.	113	112	106	698	450	172	80	36	308	.286	.375	.512	.297	.226	28	4	17
Jeter D.	101	111	78	721	478	188	46	23	303	.292	.352	.471	.276	.179	23	4	19
Williams B.	82	105	70	651	437	147	85	22	244	.262	.360	.435	.271	.173	1	5	18
Posada J.	79	72	81	547	353	122	88	21	216	.272	.400	.481	.300	.209	1	3	23
Cairo M.	50	48	42	408	264	105	18	6	150	.292	.346	.417	.260	.125	11	3	6
Sierra R.	47	40	65	338	237	75	25	17	140	.244	.296	.456	.247	.212	1	0	5
Giambi J.	42	33	40	322	215	55	47	12	100	.208	.342	.379	.248	.170	0	1	5
Clark T.	38	37	49	283	203	56	26	16	116	.221	.297	.458	.248	.237	0	0	6
Lofton K.	35	51	18	313	207	76	31	3	109	.275	.346	.395	.255	.120	7	3	4
Olerud J.	26	16	26	188	123	46	21	4	65	.280	.367	.396	.264	.116	0	0	5
Wilson E.	24	19	31	262	196	51	15	6	78	.213	.254	.325	.195	.113	1	2	5
Flaherty J.	14	11	16	135	101	32	5	6	59	.252	.286	.465	.245	.213	0	2	4
Crosby B.	7	8	7	58	45	8	2	2	16	.151	.196	.302	.164	.151	2	0	0
Phillips A.	1	1	2	8	7	2	0	1	5	.250	.250	.625	.269	.375	0	0	1
Navarro D.	1	2	1	7	5	3	0	0	3	.429	.429	.429	.300	.000	0	0	1
Halsey B.	0	0	0	2	1	1	0	0	1	.500	.500	.500	.350	.000	0	0	0
Lieber J.	0	0	0	3	3	1	0	0	1	.333	.333	.333	.233	.000	0	0	1
Vazquez J.	0	1	0	5	4	1	0	0	2	.250	.250	.500	.238	.250	0	0	1
Gordon T.	0	0	0	1	1	0	0	0	0	.000	.000	.000	.000	.000	0	0	0
Mussina M.	0	0	0	1	1	0	0	0	0	.000	.000	.000	.000	.000	0	0	0
Sturtze T.	0	0	0	3	3	0	0	0	0	.000	.000	.000	.000	.000	0	0	0
Quantrill P.	0	0	0	1	2	0	0	0	0	.000	.000	.000	.000	.000	0	0	1
Escalona F.	-1	1	0	9	8	0	0	0	0	.000	.111	.000	.050	.000	0	0	0
Bush H.	-1	2	0	8	8	0	0	0	0	.000	.125	.000	.056	.000	1	0	1
Lee T.	-1	1	2	20	19	2	1	0	3	.105	.150	.158	.107	.053	0	0	2
Contreras J.	-1	0	0	8	8	0	0	0	0	.000	.000	.000	.000	.000	0	0	0

Pitching Stats

Player	IP	BFP	G	GS	P/PA	H	K	BB	HR	W	L	Sv	Op	Hld	RA	ERA	FIP	DER
Vazquez J.	198.0	849	32	32	3.78	195	150	60	33	14	10	0	0	0	5.18	4.91	5.02	.728
Lieber J.	176.7	749	27	27	3.40	216	102	18	20	14	8	0	0	0	4.84	4.33	3.95	.677
Mussina M.	164.7	697	27	27	3.73	178	132	40	22	12	9	0	0	0	4.97	4.59	4.19	.689
Brown K.	132.0	551	22	22	3.71	132	83	35	14	10	6	0	0	0	4.43	4.09	4.28	.716
Contreras J	95.7	425	18	18	4.00	93	82	42	22	8	5	0	0	0	6.21	5.64	6.07	.740
Quantrill P.	95.3	424	86	0	3.53	124	37	20	5	7	3	1	5	22	5.10	4.72	3.95	.668
Gordon T.	89.7	342	80	0	3.87	56	96	23	5	9	4	4	10	36	2.31	2.21	2.68	.765
Hernandez	84.7	359	15	15	3.99	73	84	36	9	8	2	0	0	0	3.30	3.30	4.14	.716
Rivera M.	78.7	316	74	0	3.62	65	66	20	3	4	2	53	57	0	1.94	1.94	3.06	.721
Sturtze T.	77.3	337	28	3	3.89	75	56	33	9	6	2	1	1	1	5.70	5.47	4.87	.717
Loaiza E.	42.3	214	10	6	3.90	61	34	26	9	1	2	0	0	0	9.14	8.50	6.43	.636
Heredia F.	38.7	182	47	0	3.71	44	25	20	5	1	1	0	1	5	6.52	6.28	5.39	.700
Halsey B.	32.0	153	8	7	3.96	41	25	14	4	1	3	0	0	0	7.31	6.47	4.85	.657
Prinz B.	28.3	124	26	0	3.77	28	22	14	5	1	0	0	0	1	5.40	5.08	5.62	.720
Proctor S.	25.0	118	26	0	3.99	29	21	14	5	2	1	0	0	2	6.48	5.40	5.89	.692
White G.	20.7	104	24	0	3.40	33	8	7	2	0	1	0	2	3	8.27	8.27	5.08	.635
Osborne D.	17.7	79	9	2	3.82	25	10	5	3	2	0	0	0	0	8.15	7.13	5.56	.627
Nitkowski	13.0	65	19	0	3.58	18	10	6	1	1	1	0	0	0	7.62	7.62	5.06	.614
Padilla J.	11.3	50	6	0	3.44	16	5	4	1	0	0	0	0	0	3.97	3.97	4.62	.625
DePaula J.	9.0	38	3	1	3.61	9	2	4	2	0	1	0	0	0	6.00	5.00	7.07	.767
Karsay S.	6.7	27	7	0	3.81	5	4	2	2	0	0	0	0	0	4.05	2.70	6.89	.842
Graman A.	5.0	31	3	2	3.90	14	4	2	1	0	0	0	0	0	19.80	19.80	5.49	.458
Marsonek	1.3	6	1	0	3.83	2	0	0	0	0	0	0	0	0	0.00	0.00	3.29	.667

Fielding Stats

Catchers

Name	Innings	SBA/G	CS%	ERA	WP+PB/G
Posada	1102.3	0.73	26%	4.65	0.482
Flaherty	328.3	0.77	18%	4.93	0.302
Navarro	13.0	0.00	0%	1.38	0.000

Infielders and Outfielders

Name	POS	Inn	PO	A	TE	FE	FPct	RF	DPS	DPT
T Clark	1B	623.7	601	49	2	1	.994	9.38	10	0
J Olerud	1B	400.0	368	25	0	1	.997	8.84	2	1
J Giambi	1B	375.0	370	14	1	3	.990	9.22	2	0
T Lee	1B	42.0	44	4	0	0	1.000	10.29	0	0
M Cairo	1B	3.0	2	0	0	0	1.000	6.00	0	0
M Cairo	2B	856.0	195	274	1	4	.987	4.93	26	33
E Wilson	2B	564.7	124	179	4	3	.977	4.83	10	12

New York Yankees

Name	POS	Inn	PO	A	TE	FE	FPct	RF	DPS	DPT
H Bush	2B	23.0	7	4	0	0	1.000	4.30	1	1
D Jeter	SS	1341.0	273	392	6	7	.981	4.46	43	44
E Wilson	SS	59.0	10	25	1	0	.972	5.34	0	5
F Escalona	SS	22.0	3	7	0	0	1.000	4.09	1	0
M Cairo	SS	19.0	0	5	0	0	1.000	2.37	1	0
A Rodriguez	SS	2.0	1	1	0	0	1.000	9.00	0	1
A Rodriguez	3B	1364.0	101	261	4	9	.965	2.39	21	1
M Cairo	3B	54.3	4	13	2	0	.895	2.82	0	0
A Phillips	3B	22.0	2	5	0	0	1.000	2.86	0	0
G Sheffield	3B	2.0	0	0	1	0	.000	0.00	0	0
F Escalona	3B	1.0	0	0	0	0	.000	0.00	0	0
H Matsui	LF	1388.0	303	8	1	6	.978	2.02	4	0
B Crosby	LF	33.3	3	0	0	0	1.000	0.81	0	0
R Sierra	LF	22.3	4	0	0	0	1.000	1.61	0	0
B Williams	CF	830.3	214	2	0	1	.995	2.34	2	0
K Lofton	CF	539.3	162	3	0	1	.994	2.75	6	0
B Crosby	CF	59.0	19	0	1	0	.950	2.90	0	0
H Matsui	CF	15.0	4	0	0	0	1.000	2.40	0	0
G Sheffield	RF	1178.0	270	11	1	4	.983	2.15	4	0
R Sierra	RF	159.0	37	1	0	1	.974	2.15	0	0
B Crosby	RF	54.0	14	0	0	0	1.000	2.33	0	0
K Lofton	RF	52.0	18	1	0	1	.950	3.29	2	0

Oakland Athletics

Ten Game Average Wins and Runs

The gray area represents a running total
of wins per ten games played

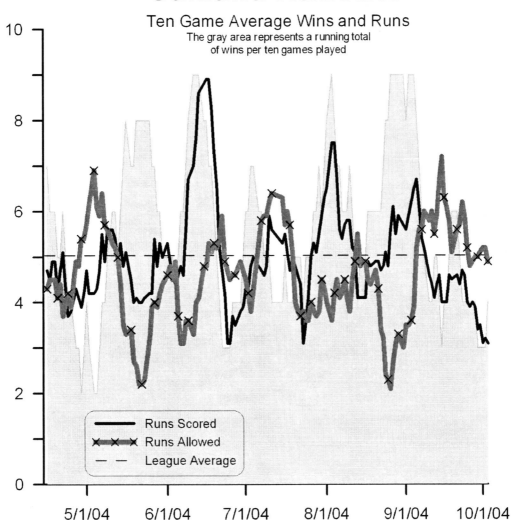

6/2: Chavez on
DL over a month

7/10: Mulder is 12-2 with
3.21 ERA; goes 5-6 and
6.13 ERA after

9/5: Lead by four
games; bat .184
with RISP rest of year

6/10: Score 40 runs in
three games vs. Reds;
most in Oakland history

8/19: Durazo homers
three times in 5-4 win

6/24: Pick up
Dotel from Astros

6/26: Hudson placed
on DL for over a month

Team Batting and Pitching/Fielding Stats by Month						
	April	**May**	**June**	**July**	**Aug**	**Sept**
Wins	12	15	17	14	20	13
Losses	12	11	10	12	8	18
OBP	.331	.339	.351	.359	.343	.336
SLG	.408	.433	.464	.455	.443	.394
FIP	4.22	4.07	4.04	5.12	4.13	4.54
DER	.702	.702	.697	.730	.740	.696

Batting Stats

Player	RC	Runs	RBI	PA	Outs	H	BB	HR	TB	BA	OBP	SLG	GPA	ISO	SB	CS	GDP
Durazo E.	109	80	88	578	356	164	56	22	267	.321	.396	.523	.309	.202	3	2	7
Kotsay M.	100	78	63	673	426	190	55	15	278	.314	.370	.459	.281	.145	8	5	5
Byrnes E.	96	91	73	632	418	161	46	20	266	.283	.347	.467	.273	.185	17	1	9
Hatteberg S.	95	87	82	638	404	156	72	15	231	.284	.367	.420	.270	.136	0	0	10
Chavez E.	91	87	77	577	368	131	95	29	238	.276	.397	.501	.304	.225	6	3	21
Dye J.	76	87	80	590	406	141	49	23	247	.265	.329	.464	.264	.199	4	2	13
Crosby B.	68	70	64	623	434	130	58	22	232	.239	.319	.426	.250	.187	7	3	16
Miller D.	58	39	58	442	307	108	39	9	160	.272	.339	.403	.253	.131	0	1	17
Scutaro M.	52	50	43	477	339	124	16	7	179	.273	.297	.393	.232	.121	0	0	8
Kielty B.	32	29	31	278	192	51	35	7	88	.214	.321	.370	.237	.155	1	0	5
McLemore M.	31	29	21	295	193	62	41	2	82	.248	.355	.328	.242	.080	0	2	3
Melhuse A.	23	23	31	231	164	55	16	11	99	.257	.309	.463	.255	.206	0	1	4
German E.	8	9	7	65	46	15	4	0	18	.250	.297	.300	.209	.050	0	1	0
Swisher N.	8	11	8	71	47	15	8	2	25	.250	.352	.417	.263	.167	0	0	2
Karros E.	8	8	11	111	84	20	7	2	32	.194	.243	.311	.187	.117	1	0	1
McMillon B.	7	10	11	102	77	17	8	3	30	.185	.255	.326	.196	.141	0	1	1
Mulder M.	0	2	0	6	4	0	1	0	0	.000	.333	.000	.150	.000	0	0	0
Rose M.	0	1	0	2	2	0	0	0	0	.000	.000	.000	.000	.000	0	0	0
Hudson T.	0	0	0	3	3	0	0	0	0	.000	.000	.000	.000	.000	0	0	0
Zito B.	0	0	0	4	4	0	0	0	0	.000	.000	.000	.000	.000	0	0	0
Castro R.	-1	2	3	16	14	2	1	0	3	.133	.188	.200	.134	.067	0	0	1
Redman M.	-1	0	0	5	5	0	0	0	0	.000	.000	.000	.000	.000	0	0	0
Harden R.	-1	0	0	5	5	0	0	0	0	.000	.000	.000	.000	.000	0	0	0
Menechino F.	-1	0	1	35	32	3	1	0	3	.091	.143	.091	.087	.000	0	0	2

Pitching Stats

Player	IP	BFP	G	GS	P/PA	H	K	BB	HR	W	L	Sv	Op	Hld	RA	ERA	FIP	DER
Mulder M.	225.7	952	33	33	3.46	223	140	83	25	17	8	0	0	0	4.75	4.43	4.75	.714
Zito B.	213.0	926	34	34	3.98	216	163	81	28	11	11	0	0	0	4.90	4.48	4.74	.709
Redman M.	191.0	832	32	32	3.75	218	102	68	28	11	12	0	0	0	5.18	4.71	5.29	.697
Harden R.	189.7	803	31	31	3.93	171	167	81	16	11	7	0	0	0	4.27	3.99	3.96	.711
Hudson T.	188.7	793	27	27	3.48	194	103	44	8	12	6	0	0	0	3.91	3.53	3.64	.703
Duchscherer	96.3	398	53	0	3.75	85	59	32	13	7	6	0	2	6	3.46	3.27	4.97	.751
Bradford C.	59.0	251	68	0	3.61	51	34	24	5	5	7	1	4	14	4.88	4.42	4.72	.749
Hammond C	53.7	223	41	0	3.69	56	34	13	4	4	1	1	3	3	3.52	2.68	3.89	.692
Dotel O.	50.7	210	45	0	4.08	41	72	18	9	6	2	22	28	0	4.09	4.09	4.00	.704
Mecir J.	47.7	212	65	0	3.95	45	49	19	5	0	5	2	7	21	3.97	3.59	4.05	.704
Rincon R.	44.0	201	67	0	4.07	45	40	22	3	1	1	0	4	18	4.50	3.68	3.93	.689
Rhodes A.	38.7	182	37	0	4.08	46	34	21	9	3	3	9	14	3	5.35	5.12	6.19	.686
Lehr J.	32.7	145	27	0	3.61	35	16	14	3	1	1	0	1	5	5.23	5.23	4.98	.709
Saarloos K.	24.3	112	6	5	3.72	27	10	12	4	2	1	0	0	0	4.81	4.44	6.33	.726
Blanton J.	8.0	30	3	0	4.27	6	6	2	1	0	0	0	0	0	5.63	5.63	4.17	.762
Garcia J.	5.7	32	4	0	4.34	5	5	9	3	0	0	0	0	0	12.71	12.71	13.70	.857
Harville C.	2.7	11	3	0	2.73	2	0	1	0	0	0	0	0	1	3.38	3.38	4.42	.800

Fielding Stats

Catchers

Name	Innings	SBA/G	CS%	ERA	WP+PB/G
Miller	963.7	0.60	28%	4.24	0.290
Melhuse	504.7	0.62	23%	4.05	0.375
Rose	3.0	3.00	0%	3.00	3.000

Infielders and Outfielders

Name	POS	Inn	PO	A	TE	FE	FPct	RF	DPS	DPT
S Hatteberg	1B	1280.0	1281	85	1	8	.993	9.60	10	1
E Karros	1B	147.3	165	16	1	1	.989	11.06	1	0
E Durazo	1B	19.0	14	1	1	1	.882	7.11	0	0
N Swisher	1B	18.0	19	0	0	0	1.000	9.50	0	0
B McMillon	1B	5.0	4	1	0	0	1.000	9.00	0	0
A Melhuse	1B	2.0	2	1	0	0	1.000	13.50	0	0
M Scutaro	2B	968.7	231	310	0	3	.994	5.03	30	46
M McLemore	2B	373.3	113	123	1	5	.975	5.69	8	29
F Menechino	2B	85.0	16	29	0	1	.978	4.76	0	1
E German	2B	44.3	9	21	0	0	1.000	6.09	3	3
B Crosby	SS	1356.0	242	503	9	10	.975	4.94	65	38
M Scutaro	SS	113.3	25	42	2	0	.971	5.32	9	1
R Castro	SS	2.0	0	2	0	0	1.000	9.00	0	0

Oakland Athletics

Name	POS	Inn	PO	A	TE	FE	FPct	RF	DPS	DPT
E Chavez	3B	1129.0	113	276	7	5	.968	3.10	28	2
M McLemore	3B	202.0	17	46	1	0	.984	2.81	2	0
E German	3B	102.7	8	21	2	0	.935	2.54	2	0
R Castro	3B	30.0	1	4	0	0	1.000	1.50	0	0
A Melhuse	3B	6.7	1	2	1	0	.750	4.05	1	0
M Scutaro	3B	1.0	0	0	0	0	.000	0.00	0	0
E Byrnes	LF	871.3	172	7	0	2	.989	1.85	4	0
B Kielty	LF	366.7	71	1	0	1	.986	1.77	0	0
B McMillon	LF	126.0	23	0	0	0	1.000	1.64	0	0
N Swisher	LF	98.0	19	0	0	1	.950	1.74	0	0
M McLemore	LF	5.0	0	0	0	0	.000	0.00	0	0
E Chavez	LF	4.3	2	0	0	0	1.000	4.15	0	0
M Kotsay	CF	1255.0	347	11	4	2	.984	2.57	7	0
E Byrnes	CF	215.3	62	3	1	0	.985	2.72	0	0
N Swisher	CF	1.0	0	0	0	0	.000	0.00	0	0
J Dye	RF	1178.0	257	3	1	1	.992	1.99	3	0
E Byrnes	RF	154.0	30	1	0	0	1.000	1.81	0	0
B Kielty	RF	109.3	26	0	0	0	1.000	2.14	0	0
N Swisher	RF	28.0	5	0	0	2	.714	1.61	0	0
B McMillon	RF	2.0	0	0	0	0	.000	0.00	0	0

Seattle Mariners

Ten Game Average Wins and Runs
The gray area represents a running total
of wins per ten games played

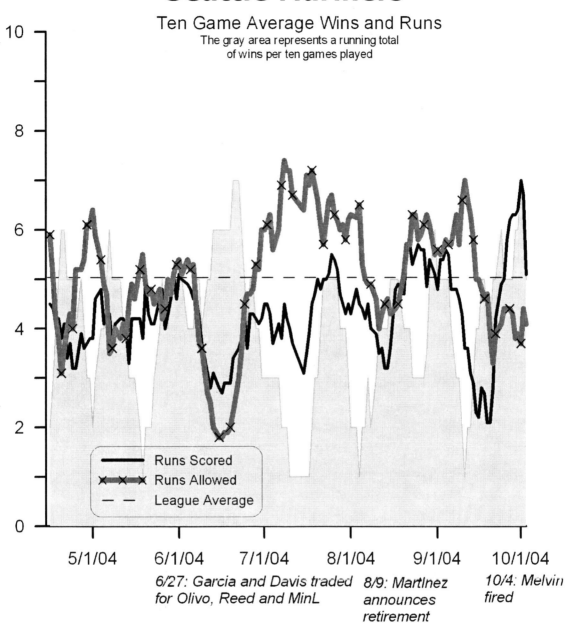

Legend:
— Runs Scored
✕—✕—✕ Runs Allowed
– – League Average

6/27: Garcia and Davis traded
for Olivo, Reed and MinL

8/9: Martinez
announces
retirement

10/4: Melvin
fired

7/23: Olerud released,
signs with Yankees

10/1: Suzuki breaks
single-season hit
record

Team Batting and Pitching/Fielding Stats by Month						
	April	**May**	**June**	**July**	**Aug**	**Sept**
Wins	8	11	13	7	12	12
Losses	16	16	13	19	16	19
OBP	.321	.330	.327	.334	.344	.328
SLG	.373	.388	.376	.418	.440	.380
FIP	4.85	4.40	4.14	6.22	4.83	4.75
DER	.689	.723	.717	.705	.712	.732

Batting Stats

Player	RC	Runs	RBI	PA	Outs	H	BB	HR	TB	BA	OBP	SLG	GPA	ISO	SB	CS	GDP
Suzuki I.	138	101	60	762	459	262	49	8	320	.372	.414	.455	.300	.082	36	11	6
Winn R.	104	84	81	703	469	179	53	14	267	.286	.346	.427	.262	.141	21	7	15
Boone B.	78	74	83	658	465	149	56	24	251	.251	.317	.423	.249	.172	10	5	16
Ibanez R.	77	67	62	524	347	146	36	16	227	.304	.353	.472	.277	.168	1	2	10
Martinez E.	69	45	63	549	372	128	58	12	187	.263	.342	.385	.250	.121	1	0	14
Cabrera J.	51	38	47	391	276	97	16	6	138	.270	.312	.384	.236	.114	10	3	11
Spiezio S.	35	38	41	415	296	79	36	10	127	.215	.288	.346	.216	.131	4	1	7
Olerud J.	34	29	22	312	203	64	40	5	94	.245	.354	.360	.249	.115	0	0	6
Wilson D.	31	23	33	359	247	80	26	2	99	.251	.305	.310	.215	.060	0	1	7
Aurilia R.	28	27	28	292	208	63	22	4	88	.241	.304	.337	.221	.096	1	0	10
Jacobsen B.	26	17	28	176	119	44	14	9	80	.275	.335	.500	.276	.225	0	0	3
Lopez J.	24	28	22	218	161	48	8	5	76	.232	.263	.367	.210	.135	0	1	1
Bloomquist W	21	27	18	201	146	46	10	2	62	.245	.283	.330	.210	.085	13	2	2
Hansen D.	16	14	12	97	59	22	18	2	33	.282	.412	.423	.291	.141	0	0	3
Leone J.	16	15	13	115	80	22	9	6	45	.216	.298	.441	.245	.225	1	0	0
Olivo M.	15	25	14	173	132	32	10	6	62	.200	.260	.388	.214	.188	2	2	2
Reed J.	12	11	5	66	38	23	7	0	27	.397	.470	.466	.328	.069	3	1	2
Bocachica H.	10	9	6	107	73	22	12	3	36	.244	.337	.400	.251	.156	5	4	1
Dobbs G.	5	4	9	56	41	12	1	1	16	.226	.250	.302	.188	.075	0	0	0
Borders P.	2	6	5	55	45	10	1	1	15	.189	.204	.283	.162	.094	1	1	1
Moyer J.	1	0	2	2	1	1	0	0	1	.500	.500	.500	.350	.000	0	0	0
Lopez M.	1	1	0	6	3	1	1	0	1	.250	.500	.250	.288	.000	0	0	0
Santiago R.	1	8	2	45	33	7	3	0	8	.179	.256	.205	.166	.026	0	0	1
Pineiro J.	0	0	0	5	4	1	0	0	2	.200	.200	.400	.190	.200	0	0	0
Franklin R.	0	0	0	5	3	0	1	0	0	.000	.250	.000	.113	.000	0	0	0
Nageotte C.	0	0	0	2	2	0	0	0	0	.000	.000	.000	.000	.000	0	0	0
Rivera R.	0	0	0	3	3	0	0	0	0	.000	.000	.000	.000	.000	0	0	0
Garcia F.	0	0	0	4	4	0	0	0	0	.000	.000	.000	.000	.000	0	0	0
Guardado E.	0	0	0	1	2	0	0	0	0	.000	.000	.000	.000	.000	0	0	1
McCracken Q	-1	6	0	23	19	3	2	0	3	.150	.227	.150	.140	.000	1	1	1
Davis B.	-2	1	2	37	32	3	3	0	3	.091	.162	.091	.096	.000	0	0	2

Pitching Stats

Player	IP	BFP	G	GS	P/PA	H	K	BB	HR	W	L	Sv	Op	Hld	RA	ERA	FIP	DER
Moyer J.	202.0	888	34	33	3.84	217	125	63	44	7	13	0	0	0	5.66	5.21	5.98	.732
Franklin R	200.3	870	32	32	3.69	224	104	61	33	4	16	0	0	0	5.21	4.90	5.46	.711
Pineiro J.	140.7	596	21	21	3.77	144	111	43	21	6	11	0	0	0	4.93	4.67	4.66	.705
Meche G.	127.7	565	23	23	4.09	139	99	47	21	7	7	0	0	0	5.15	5.01	5.10	.700
Villone R.	117.0	523	56	10	3.96	102	86	64	12	8	6	0	1	7	4.92	4.08	5.10	.742
Garcia F.	107.0	446	15	15	3.61	96	82	32	8	4	7	0	0	0	3.28	3.20	3.68	.727
Madritsch	88.0	359	15	11	3.80	74	60	33	3	6	3	0	0	0	3.38	3.27	3.63	.726
Hasegawa	68.0	300	68	0	3.72	67	46	31	5	4	6	0	5	12	5.56	5.16	4.35	.713
Putz J.	63.0	275	54	0	3.78	66	47	24	10	0	3	9	13	3	5.00	4.71	5.24	.704
Mateo J.	57.7	248	45	0	3.58	56	43	16	11	1	2	1	4	6	4.68	4.68	5.37	.740
Guardado	45.3	176	41	0	3.90	31	45	14	8	2	2	18	25	0	2.78	2.78	4.59	.787
Nageotte	36.7	185	12	5	3.71	48	24	27	3	1	6	0	0	0	7.61	7.36	5.58	.646
Thornton	32.7	148	19	1	4.09	30	30	25	2	1	2	0	0	0	4.13	4.13	4.55	.692
Baek C.	31.0	139	7	5	3.94	35	20	11	5	2	4	0	0	0	6.68	5.52	5.36	.703
Atchison S	30.7	133	25	0	4.29	29	36	14	4	2	3	0	0	2	3.52	3.52	4.01	.684
Myers M.	27.7	126	50	0	3.99	29	23	17	3	4	1	0	0	8	4.88	4.88	5.10	.679
Blackley T	26.0	134	6	6	4.15	35	16	22	9	1	3	0	0	0	10.73	10.04	9.21	.698
Sherrill G.	23.7	104	21	0	3.99	24	16	9	3	2	1	0	0	3	4.56	3.80	4.86	.720
Jarvis K.	13.0	63	8	0	3.78	20	7	5	4	1	0	0	0	0	8.31	8.31	7.37	.660
Kida M.	9.7	47	7	0	3.96	15	5	5	1	0	0	0	0	0	8.38	8.38	5.46	.600
Williams R	4.7	22	6	0	4.18	3	4	6	0	0	0	0	0	1	5.79	5.79	5.43	.750
Taylor A.	3.7	19	5	0	4.00	5	4	3	2	0	0	0	0	0	9.82	9.82	10.66	.700
Soriano R.	3.3	23	6	0	4.13	9	3	3	0	0	3	0	1	0	16.20	13.50	4.19	.471

Fielding Stats

Catchers

Name	Innings	SBA/G	CS%	ERA	WP+PB/G
Wilson	827.3	0.66	28%	4.83	0.207
Olivo	394.0	0.37	25%	4.39	0.640
Borders	138.0	0.85	54%	5.02	0.130
Davis	97.0	0.37	50%	5.47	0.557
Rivera	3.0	0.00	0%	0.00	0.000

Infielders and Outfielders

Name	POS	Inn	PO	A	TE	FE	FPct	RF	DPS	DPT
J Olerud	1B	645.3	547	52	0	1	.998	8.35	6	1
S Spiezio	1B	279.0	252	24	1	2	.986	8.90	1	0
B Jacobsen	1B	175.0	168	12	0	3	.984	9.26	0	0
J Cabrera	1B	148.7	149	7	0	0	1.000	9.44	3	0
W Bloomquist	1B	99.0	69	8	0	2	.975	7.00	1	1

Seattle Mariners

Name	POS	Inn	PO	A	TE	FE	FPct	RF	DPS	DPT
R Ibanez	1B	78.3	57	2	0	1	.983	6.78	0	0
D Hansen	1B	34.0	22	4	0	0	1.000	6.88	0	0
B Boone	2B	1308.0	280	349	5	9	.978	4.33	47	43
J Cabrera	2B	140.7	38	40	0	1	.987	4.99	5	7
M Lopez	2B	9.0	1	4	0	0	1.000	5.00	0	0
W Bloomquist	2B	1.0	0	0	0	0	.000	0.00	0	0
R Aurilia	SS	634.0	114	185	1	2	.990	4.24	16	23
J Lopez	SS	490.0	91	125	6	4	.956	3.97	9	14
W Bloomquist	SS	139.3	26	36	2	1	.954	4.00	3	8
R Santiago	SS	105.0	22	31	3	0	.946	4.54	2	6
J Cabrera	SS	83.0	11	13	1	0	.960	2.60	2	1
J Leone	SS	8.0	3	1	1	0	.800	4.50	0	0
S Spiezio	3B	587.7	56	131	3	3	.964	2.86	14	1
J Cabrera	3B	277.7	33	63	2	1	.970	3.11	6	0
J Leone	3B	242.0	25	48	5	3	.901	2.71	3	0
W Bloomquist	3B	221.3	24	36	3	2	.923	2.44	6	0
G Dobbs	3B	108.7	5	21	1	1	.929	2.15	3	0
D Hansen	3B	21.0	6	5	0	0	1.000	4.71	0	0
J Lopez	3B	1.0	0	0	0	0	.000	0.00	0	0
R Ibanez	LF	949.3	227	10	1	3	.983	2.25	6	0
R Winn	LF	288.0	74	0	0	0	1.000	2.31	0	0
J Cabrera	LF	158.0	42	1	1	0	.977	2.45	0	0
W Bloomquist	LF	29.0	7	0	0	0	1.000	2.17	0	0
Q McCracken	LF	24.0	3	0	0	0	1.000	1.13	0	0
H Bocachica	LF	7.0	0	0	0	0	.000	0.00	0	0
J Reed	LF	4.0	1	0	0	0	1.000	2.25	0	0
R Winn	CF	1070.0	342	5	1	3	.989	2.92	2	0
H Bocachica	CF	217.7	63	0	0	0	1.000	2.60	0	0
J Reed	CF	123.3	50	0	0	1	.980	3.65	0	0
Q McCracken	CF	34.0	8	1	0	0	1.000	2.38	0	0
W Bloomquist	CF	8.0	7	0	0	0	1.000	7.88	0	0
J Cabrera	CF	6.0	4	1	0	0	1.000	7.50	2	0
I Suzuki	RF	1405.0	372	12	1	2	.992	2.46	4	0
H Bocachica	RF	34.0	5	0	0	0	1.000	1.32	0	0
R Ibanez	RF	18.0	2	0	0	0	1.000	1.00	0	0
J Cabrera	RF	2.0	0	0	0	0	.000	0.00	0	0

Tampa Bay Devil Rays

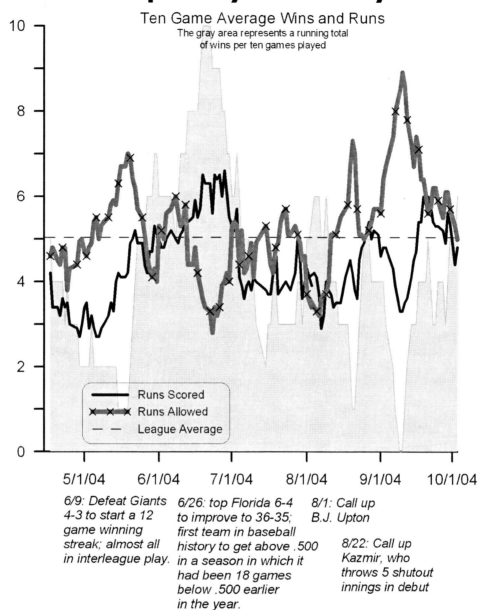

Ten Game Average Wins and Runs
The gray area represents a running total of wins per ten games played

Legend:
— Runs Scored
✕✕✕ Runs Allowed
— — League Average

X-axis: 5/1/04, 6/1/04, 7/1/04, 8/1/04, 9/1/04, 10/1/04

6/9: Defeat Giants 4-3 to start a 12 game winning streak; almost all in interleague play.

6/26: top Florida 6-4 to improve to 36-35; first team in baseball history to get above .500 in a season in which it had been 18 games below .500 earlier in the year.

8/1: Call up B.J. Upton

8/22: Call up Kazmir, who throws 5 shutout innings in debut

7/30: Trade Zambrano and minL for Kazmir and minL.

Team Batting and Pitching/Fielding Stats by Month						
	April	May	June	July	Aug	Sept
Wins	7	11	20	11	10	11
Losses	15	17	6	16	18	19
OBP	.312	.306	.355	.319	.313	.315
SLG	.367	.403	.432	.405	.400	.415
FIP	5.12	5.82	4.30	4.70	4.79	4.64
DER	.733	.739	.709	.729	.719	.679

Batting Stats

Player	RC	Runs	RBI	PA	Outs	H	BB	HR	TB	BA	OBP	SLG	GPA	ISO	SB	CS	GDP
Huff A.	100	92	104	667	430	178	56	29	296	.297	.360	.493	.285	.197	5	1	7
Crawford C.	99	104	55	672	458	185	35	11	282	.296	.331	.450	.261	.155	59	15	2
Lugo J.	89	83	75	655	433	160	54	7	230	.275	.338	.396	.251	.120	21	5	7
Cruz J.	82	76	78	636	424	132	76	21	236	.242	.333	.433	.258	.191	11	6	5
Martinez T.	80	63	76	538	347	120	66	23	211	.262	.362	.461	.278	.199	3	1	8
Baldelli R.	73	79	74	565	389	145	30	16	226	.280	.326	.436	.256	.156	17	4	12
Hall T.	44	35	60	441	319	103	24	8	148	.255	.300	.366	.227	.111	0	2	16
Blum G.	30	38	35	369	273	73	24	8	118	.215	.266	.348	.207	.133	2	3	4
Sanchez R.	28	23	26	307	222	70	12	2	96	.246	.281	.337	.210	.091	0	1	6
Cantu J.	23	25	17	185	126	52	9	2	80	.301	.341	.462	.269	.162	0	0	5
Upton B.	22	19	12	177	120	41	15	4	65	.258	.324	.409	.248	.151	4	1	1
Fick R.	21	12	26	238	173	43	20	6	70	.201	.273	.327	.205	.126	0	0	2
Cummings M.	12	10	7	61	39	15	5	2	25	.278	.361	.463	.278	.185	1	0	0
McGriff F.	8	7	7	81	60	13	9	2	22	.181	.272	.306	.199	.125	0	0	1
Fordyce B.	8	14	9	163	122	31	9	2	43	.205	.259	.285	.188	.079	0	0	2
Perez E.	6	2	7	42	31	8	4	1	13	.211	.286	.342	.214	.132	0	0	1
Rolls D.	5	12	9	132	103	19	10	0	24	.162	.231	.205	.155	.043	2	1	4
Gathright J.	4	11	1	57	41	13	2	0	13	.250	.316	.250	.205	.000	6	1	1
Diaz M.	2	3	3	24	17	4	1	1	10	.190	.292	.476	.250	.286	0	0	0
Gipson C.	2	1	0	5	2	2	0	0	2	.500	.500	.500	.350	.000	1	0	0
Zambrano V.	1	1	1	5	4	1	0	0	2	.200	.200	.400	.190	.200	0	0	0
Romano J.	0	0	1	8	7	1	0	0	1	.125	.125	.125	.088	.000	0	0	0
Hendrickson	0	0	0	6	4	1	1	0	1	.200	.333	.200	.200	.000	0	0	0
Bell R.	0	1	0	5	4	1	0	0	2	.200	.200	.400	.190	.200	0	0	0
Simon R.	0	2	0	21	15	2	3	0	2	.118	.286	.118	.158	.000	0	0	0
Gomes J.	0	0	1	15	13	1	1	0	1	.071	.133	.071	.078	.000	0	0	0
Gaudin C.	0	0	0	2	1	0	0	0	0	.000	.000	.000	.000	.000	0	0	0
Colome J.	0	0	0	2	1	0	0	0	0	.000	.000	.000	.000	.000	0	0	0
Brazelton D.	0	0	0	1	1	0	0	0	0	.000	.000	.000	.000	.000	0	0	0
Bautista J.	0	1	1	15	11	2	3	0	2	.167	.333	.167	.192	.000	0	1	0
Halama J.	-1	0	0	3	4	0	0	0	0	.000	.000	.000	.000	.000	0	0	1

Pitching Stats

Player	IP	BFP	G	GS	P/PA	H	K	BB	HR	W	L	Sv	Op	Hld	RA	ERA	FIP	DER
Hendrickson	183.3	803	32	30	3.58	211	87	46	21	10	15	0	0	0	5.55	4.81	4.70	.704
Zambrano V	128.0	588	23	22	4.09	107	109	96	13	9	7	0	0	1	4.78	4.43	5.53	.734
Bell R.	123.0	529	24	19	3.56	121	57	41	16	8	8	0	0	0	5.20	4.46	5.18	.744
Brazelton D.	120.7	535	22	21	3.80	121	64	53	12	6	8	0	0	0	5.30	4.77	5.11	.724
Halama J.	118.7	513	34	14	3.46	134	59	27	17	7	6	0	0	0	5.16	4.70	5.10	.708
Sosa J.	99.3	447	43	8	3.92	100	94	54	17	4	7	1	1	6	6.07	5.53	5.29	.705
Carter L.	80.3	336	56	0	3.77	77	36	23	12	3	3	0	1	7	3.59	3.47	5.23	.754
Harper T.	78.7	331	52	0	3.85	69	59	23	8	6	2	0	1	9	4.23	3.89	4.26	.739

Tampa Bay Devil Rays

Player	IP	BFP	G	GS	P/PA	H	K	BB	HR	W	L	Sv	Op	Hld	RA	ERA	FIP	DER
Waechter D.	70.3	309	14	14	3.86	68	36	33	20	5	7	0	0	0	6.91	6.01	7.54	.778
Baez D.	68.0	295	62	0	3.99	60	52	29	6	4	4	30	33	1	4.10	3.57	4.50	.731
Gonzalez J.	50.3	235	11	8	3.74	72	22	20	9	0	5	0	0	0	7.51	6.97	6.11	.652
Miller T.	49.0	208	60	0	3.60	48	43	15	3	1	1	1	3	9	3.86	3.12	3.43	.688
Abbott P.	47.0	222	10	9	3.82	49	25	27	8	2	5	0	0	0	7.47	6.70	6.36	.742
Gaudin C.	42.7	201	26	4	3.67	59	30	16	4	1	2	0	1	5	5.70	4.85	4.51	.626
Colome J.	41.3	169	33	0	4.08	28	40	18	4	2	2	3	4	8	3.48	3.27	3.99	.774
Kazmir S.	33.3	151	8	7	4.30	33	41	21	4	2	3	0	0	0	5.94	5.67	4.46	.651
Seay B.	22.7	95	21	0	3.96	21	17	5	2	0	0	0	0	0	2.38	2.38	3.87	.725
Nunez F.	10.7	54	8	0	4.11	11	14	7	1	0	3	0	1	0	6.75	5.91	4.70	.655
Standridge	10.0	48	3	1	3.63	14	7	4	5	0	0	0	0	0	9.00	9.00	9.59	.719
Webb J.	9.0	45	4	0	4.44	12	9	7	2	0	0	0	0	0	7.00	7.00	6.85	.615
Moss D.	8.0	43	5	2	3.72	13	6	5	2	0	1	0	0	0	16.88	16.88	7.29	.621
Ritchie T.	8.0	42	4	2	3.93	12	4	6	4	0	2	0	0	0	10.13	9.00	11.42	.704
Gonzalez D.	7.3	32	4	0	3.19	9	7	2	1	0	0	0	0	0	6.14	6.14	3.97	.636
Fortunato B.	7.3	30	3	0	3.70	10	5	2	1	0	0	0	0	0	3.68	3.68	4.52	.591

Fielding Stats

Catchers

Name	Innings	SBA/G	CS%	ERA	WP+PB/G
Hall	1011.3	0.54	28%	4.72	0.418
Fordyce	400.7	0.63	18%	5.12	0.359
Fick	5.0	0.00	0%	1.80	0.000

Infielders and Outfielders

Name	POS	Inn	PO	A	TE	FE	FPct	RF	DPS	DPT
T Martinez	1B	959.7	875	64	2	1	.997	8.81	9	1
A Huff	1B	274.3	268	22	0	1	.997	9.51	5	0
R Fick	1B	75.3	79	2	0	2	.976	9.68	0	0
F McGriff	1B	52.0	53	3	0	0	1.000	9.69	0	0
E Perez	1B	43.7	43	2	0	0	1.000	9.27	0	0
G Blum	1B	10.0	13	0	0	0	1.000	11.70	0	0
R Simon	1B	1.0	0	0	0	0	.000	0.00	0	0
D Rolls	1B	1.0	0	0	0	0	.000	0.00	0	0
R Sanchez	2B	696.0	157	234	3	2	.987	5.06	24	30
G Blum	2B	364.7	76	104	1	0	.994	4.44	7	15
J Cantu	2B	274.0	48	84	2	3	.964	4.34	9	10
J Lugo	2B	69.0	16	16	0	1	.970	4.17	0	2
D Rolls	2B	7.3	2	2	0	0	1.000	4.91	0	0
J Romano	2B	6.0	1	0	0	1	.500	1.50	0	0
J Lugo	SS	1238.0	237	423	16	9	.964	4.80	47	42
B Upton	SS	140.0	23	41	3	4	.901	4.11	6	2

Tampa Bay Devil Rays

Name	POS	Inn	PO	A	TE	FE	FPct	RF	DPS	DPT
R Sanchez	SS	26.0	5	15	0	0	1.000	6.92	0	1
J Cantu	SS	7.0	2	2	0	0	1.000	5.14	0	0
C Gipson	SS	5.0	0	2	0	0	1.000	3.60	1	0
G Blum	SS	1.0	1	0	0	0	1.000	9.00	0	0
A Huff	3B	705.0	69	129	6	6	.943	2.53	13	0
G Blum	3B	382.0	35	77	0	7	.933	2.64	9	0
D Rolls	3B	127.7	16	25	2	0	.953	2.89	4	0
B Upton	3B	103.0	10	12	0	2	.917	1.92	0	0
J Cantu	3B	94.3	9	26	3	0	.921	3.34	0	1
J Bautista	3B	4.0	0	2	0	0	1.000	4.50	0	0
E Perez	3B	1.0	0	0	0	0	.000	0.00	0	0
C Crawford	LF	1010.0	274	5	1	0	.996	2.49	2	0
R Fick	LF	87.7	20	0	0	1	.952	2.05	0	0
D Rolls	LF	76.7	14	0	0	0	1.000	1.64	0	0
A Huff	LF	71.0	17	0	0	0	1.000	2.15	0	0
G Blum	LF	59.3	12	1	0	1	.929	1.97	2	0
J Bautista	LF	25.0	4	0	0	0	1.000	1.44	0	0
J Gathright	LF	22.0	3	0	0	0	1.000	1.23	0	0
M Diaz	LF	20.0	8	0	0	0	1.000	3.60	0	0
M Cummings	LF	17.0	3	0	0	0	1.000	1.59	0	0
E Perez	LF	12.0	2	0	0	0	1.000	1.50	0	0
J Romano	LF	9.0	2	1	0	0	1.000	3.00	0	0
B Upton	LF	7.0	0	0	0	0	.000	0.00	0	0
C Gipson	LF	0.3	0	0	0	0	.000	0.00	0	0
R Baldelli	CF	1047.0	341	11	1	7	.978	3.03	3	0
C Crawford	CF	225.0	76	0	1	0	.987	3.04	0	0
J Gathright	CF	96.0	27	0	0	0	1.000	2.53	0	0
D Rolls	CF	35.0	13	0	0	0	1.000	3.34	0	0
J Cruz	CF	9.0	3	0	0	0	1.000	3.00	0	0
C Gipson	CF	5.0	3	0	0	0	1.000	5.40	0	0
J Cruz	RF	1301.0	312	10	2	8	.970	2.23	1	0
R Fick	RF	55.0	20	0	0	0	1.000	3.27	0	0
D Rolls	RF	31.0	8	1	0	0	1.000	2.61	0	0
M Diaz	RF	9.0	3	0	0	0	1.000	3.00	0	0
E Perez	RF	8.0	3	0	0	0	1.000	3.38	0	0
J Gathright	RF	8.0	0	0	0	0	.000	0.00	0	0
J Bautista	RF	3.3	0	0	0	0	.000	0.00	0	0
A Huff	RF	1.0	0	0	0	0	.000	0.00	0	0

Texas Rangers

Ten Game Average Wins and Runs
The gray area represents a running total of wins per ten games played

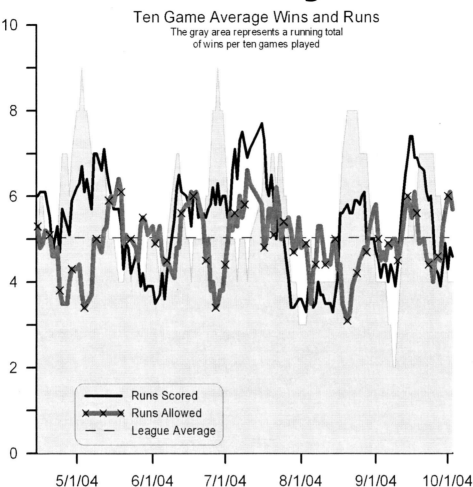

4/25: Move into first place; first time since June 2000

5/2: Sweep Red Sox as Cordero saves all three games

7/19: Teixeira homers in fifth straight game, tying a team record

7/23: Rogers ties MLB lead with 13th win; lead AL West by 4 1/2 games

8/17: Teixeira becomes second Ranger to hit for the cycle

9/14: Francisco throws chair at fan, breaking her nose

9/23: Dellucci hits two-out, two-run double in bottom of ninth for a 5-4 win to complete sweep of Oakland; Rangers within two games of AL West lead.

9/29: Eliminated by Angels

Team Batting and Pitching/Fielding Stats by Month						
	April	**May**	**June**	**July**	**Aug**	**Sept**
Wins	15	13	16	13	16	16
Losses	9	13	10	13	12	16
OBP	.361	.323	.334	.318	.325	.318
SLG	.499	.438	.474	.454	.445	.429
FIP	4.31	4.85	4.47	5.24	4.81	4.33
DER	.692	.704	.730	.679	.718	.688

Batting Stats

Player	RC	Runs	RBI	PA	Outs	H	BB	HR	TB	BA	OBP	SLG	GPA	ISO	SB	CS	GDP
Young M.	117	114	99	739	488	216	44	22	333	.313	.353	.483	.280	.170	12	3	11
Teixeira M.	116	101	112	625	399	153	68	38	305	.281	.370	.560	.306	.279	4	1	6
Blalock H.	115	107	110	713	467	172	75	32	312	.276	.355	.500	.285	.224	2	2	13
Soriano A.	87	77	91	658	450	170	33	28	294	.280	.324	.484	.267	.204	18	5	7
Mench K.	70	69	71	481	322	122	33	26	236	.279	.335	.539	.285	.260	0	0	6
Dellucci D.	54	59	61	387	259	80	47	17	146	.242	.342	.441	.264	.199	9	4	4
Young E.	51	55	27	402	263	99	43	1	131	.288	.377	.381	.265	.093	14	9	9
Matthews Jr.	46	37	36	317	205	77	33	11	129	.275	.350	.461	.273	.186	5	1	1
Barajas R.	43	50	58	389	273	89	13	15	162	.249	.276	.453	.237	.204	0	1	3
Nix L.	43	58	46	400	286	92	23	14	162	.248	.293	.437	.241	.189	1	1	6
Fullmer B.	29	41	33	290	207	60	27	11	114	.233	.310	.442	.250	.209	1	2	7
Jordan B.	14	27	23	233	174	47	16	5	77	.222	.275	.363	.214	.142	2	2	7
Perry H.	13	13	17	153	107	30	14	5	49	.224	.307	.366	.230	.142	0	0	3
Laird G.	10	20	16	168	120	33	12	1	42	.224	.287	.286	.200	.061	0	1	5
Gonzalez A.	6	7	7	44	32	10	2	1	16	.238	.273	.381	.218	.143	0	0	0
Conti J.	4	6	4	60	47	10	5	0	13	.182	.250	.236	.172	.055	0	2	0
Alexander M.	3	3	3	22	16	5	1	0	7	.238	.273	.333	.206	.095	0	0	0
Allen C.	2	4	6	63	46	14	2	0	20	.241	.262	.345	.204	.103	0	1	1
Ardoin D.	1	1	1	11	7	1	3	0	1	.125	.364	.125	.195	.000	0	0	0
Nivar R.	1	3	4	21	15	4	0	0	4	.222	.211	.222	.150	.000	1	1	0
Drese R.	1	1	0	4	2	2	0	0	3	.500	.500	.750	.413	.250	0	0	0
Fox A.	0	2	0	13	11	1	1	0	1	.083	.154	.083	.090	.000	0	0	0
Huckaby K.	0	3	0	43	34	5	5	0	7	.132	.233	.184	.151	.053	0	0	1
Mahay R.	0	0	0	1	1	0	0	0	0	.000	.000	.000	.000	.000	0	0	0
Bierbrodt N.	0	0	0	3	2	0	0	0	0	.000	.000	.000	.000	.000	0	0	0
Rodriguez R.	0	0	0	2	2	0	0	0	0	.000	.000	.000	.000	.000	0	0	0
Wasdin J.	0	0	0	3	3	0	0	0	0	.000	.000	.000	.000	.000	0	0	0
Benoit J.	-1	1	0	6	6	0	0	0	0	.000	.000	.000	.000	.000	0	0	0
Rogers K.	-1	1	0	5	6	0	0	0	0	.000	.000	.000	.000	.000	0	0	1

Pitching Stats

Player	IP	BFP	G	GS	P/PA	H	K	BB	HR	W	L	Sv	Op	Hld	RA	ERA	FIP	DER
Rogers K.	211.7	935	35	35	3.75	248	126	66	24	18	9	0	0	0	4.97	4.76	4.63	.685
Drese R.	207.7	897	34	33	3.46	233	98	58	16	14	10	0	0	0	4.51	4.20	4.34	.696
Dickey R.	104.3	480	25	15	3.77	136	57	33	17	6	7	1	1	0	6.64	5.61	5.38	.678
Benoit J.	103.0	456	28	15	3.99	113	95	31	19	3	5	0	0	0	5.85	5.68	4.97	.690
Park C.	95.7	428	16	16	3.57	105	63	33	22	4	7	0	0	0	5.93	5.46	6.40	.721
Almanzar	72.7	298	67	0	3.44	66	44	19	8	7	3	0	2	20	3.96	3.72	4.46	.740
Cordero F.	71.7	304	67	0	4.24	60	79	32	1	3	4	49	54	0	2.39	2.13	2.64	.691
Mahay R.	67.0	290	60	0	3.83	60	54	29	5	3	0	0	2	14	3.09	2.55	4.03	.725
Wasdin J.	65.0	301	15	10	3.70	83	36	23	18	2	4	0	0	0	7.20	6.78	6.98	.706
Brocail D.	52.3	232	43	0	3.88	54	43	20	2	4	1	1	1	4	4.99	4.13	3.57	.679
Francisco	51.3	216	45	0	4.27	36	60	28	4	5	1	0	3	10	3.33	3.33	3.77	.736
Shouse B.	44.3	184	53	0	3.77	36	34	18	3	2	0	0	0	12	2.44	2.23	3.92	.742
Young C.	36.3	158	7	7	4.23	36	27	10	7	3	2	0	0	0	5.20	4.71	5.29	.741
Ramirez E.	35.7	148	34	0	3.66	34	21	7	5	5	3	0	2	3	4.79	4.29	4.77	.741
Rodriguez	26.7	119	5	4	3.50	28	15	12	1	3	1	0	0	0	3.38	2.03	4.00	.703
Powell J.	24.0	103	23	0	3.84	24	17	11	3	1	1	0	0	4	4.13	3.38	4.87	.708
Nelson J.	23.7	103	29	0	4.21	17	22	19	3	1	2	1	1	9	6.08	5.32	5.48	.763
Dominguez	23.0	98	4	4	3.52	25	14	5	2	1	2	0	0	0	4.30	3.91	4.11	.693
Regilio N.	19.3	91	6	4	4.20	20	12	15	3	0	4	0	0	0	7.45	6.05	6.70	.712
Erickson S.	19.0	94	4	4	3.95	23	6	16	2	1	3	0	0	0	6.16	6.16	6.55	.700
Bierbrodt N	17.0	81	4	4	3.84	14	10	19	4	1	1	0	0	0	5.82	5.82	8.87	.783
Bacsik M.	15.7	63	3	3	3.62	16	6	1	2	1	1	0	0	0	4.60	4.60	4.75	.731
Lewis C.	15.3	71	3	3	4.14	13	11	13	1	1	1	0	0	0	4.11	4.11	5.44	.733
Callaway	11.3	58	4	3	4.31	18	9	7	2	0	1	0	0	0	7.94	7.94	6.11	.590
Garcia R.	6.7	35	4	0	4.00	9	5	5	1	0	0	0	0	0	6.75	5.40	5.99	.667
Loe K.	6.7	29	2	1	3.14	6	3	6	0	0	0	0	0	0	6.75	5.40	5.54	.684
Tejera M.	5.3	29	6	0	4.03	9	7	3	1	0	0	0	0	0	10.13	10.13	5.35	.529
Snare R.	3.3	17	1	0	3.71	5	0	2	3	0	0	0	0	0	13.50	10.80	16.79	.833
Narron S.	2.7	17	1	1	3.59	5	1	4	3	0	0	0	0	0	13.50	13.50	21.66	.778
Hughes T.	1.3	10	2	0	3.80	4	4	2	0	0	0	0	0	0	13.50	13.50	1.79	.000

Fielding Stats

Catchers

Name	Innings	SBA/G	CS%	ERA	WP+PB/G
Barajas	908.7	0.57	28%	4.50	0.238
Laird	397.0	0.66	41%	4.40	0.385
Huckaby	109.0	0.91	27%	5.70	0.578
Ardoin	25.0	1.44	0%	3.60	0.720

Texas Rangers

Infielders and Outfielders

Name	POS	Inn	PO	A	TE	FE	FPct	RF	DPS	DPT
M Teixeira	1B	1223.0	1210	98	3	6	.992	9.63	9	2
H Perry	1B	107.0	104	3	0	0	1.000	9.00	0	0
A Gonzalez	1B	89.0	93	6	0	1	.990	10.01	0	0
B Fullmer	1B	17.7	15	0	0	0	1.000	7.64	0	0
R Barajas	1B	3.0	3	1	0	0	1.000	12.00	0	0
A Soriano	2B	1248.0	308	418	2	21	.969	5.24	37	66
E Young	2B	149.7	39	51	2	4	.938	5.41	4	7
M Alexander	2B	22.0	2	9	1	0	.917	4.50	0	0
A Fox	2B	20.0	3	9	0	0	1.000	5.40	0	2
M Young	SS	1386.0	225	422	10	9	.971	4.20	49	46
M Alexander	SS	27.0	6	11	1	0	.944	5.67	0	1
E Young	SS	26.0	2	4	0	1	.857	2.08	0	1
H Blalock	3B	1377.0	103	279	7	9	.957	2.50	32	0
H Perry	3B	33.0	7	6	1	1	.867	3.55	0	0
M Alexander	3B	21.0	2	2	1	0	.800	1.71	0	0
E Young	3B	6.0	0	1	0	0	1.000	1.50	0	0
A Fox	3B	2.0	0	0	0	0	.000	0.00	0	0
D Dellucci	LF	648.7	152	0	0	2	.987	2.11	0	0
K Mench	LF	362.7	73	1	0	1	.987	1.84	2	0
E Young	LF	326.3	58	3	1	1	.968	168	0	0
C Allen	LF	86.0	13	0	0	0	1.000	1.36	0	0
G Matthews J	LF	11.0	7	1	0	0	1.000	6.55	0	0
B Jordan	LF	3.0	0	0	0	0	.000	0.00	0	0
J Conti	LF	1.0	0	0	0	0	.000	0.00	0	0
A Fox	LF	1.0	1	0	0	0	1.000	9.00	0	0
L Nix	CF	875.7	222	4	0	1	.996	2.32	2	0
G Matthews J	CF	221.7	69	3	0	0	1.000	2.92	0	0
J Conti	CF	131.7	45	0	0	0	1.000	3.08	0	0
E Young	CF	78.0	19	1	0	0	1.000	2.31	0	0
R Nivar	CF	50.0	12	1	0	0	1.000	2.34	0	0
D Dellucci	CF	45.7	14	0	0	0	1.000	2.76	0	0
K Mench	CF	37.0	13	0	0	0	1.000	3.16	0	0
K Mench	RF	500.7	127	5	0	0	1.000	2.37	2	0
G Matthews J	RF	476.3	119	4	1	1	.984	2.32	1	0
B Jordan	RF	358.7	94	1	0	1	.990	2.38	0	0
D Dellucci	RF	43.3	11	0	0	0	1.000	2.28	0	0
M Teixeira	RF	36.7	8	0	0	0	1.000	1.96	0	0
L Nix	RF	13.0	3	0	0	0	1.000	2.08	0	0
C Allen	RF	9.0	1	0	0	0	1.000	1.00	0	0
A Fox	RF	2.0	1	0	0	0	1.000	4.50	0	0

Toronto Blue Jays

Ten Game Average Wins and Runs
The gray area represents a running total of wins per ten games played

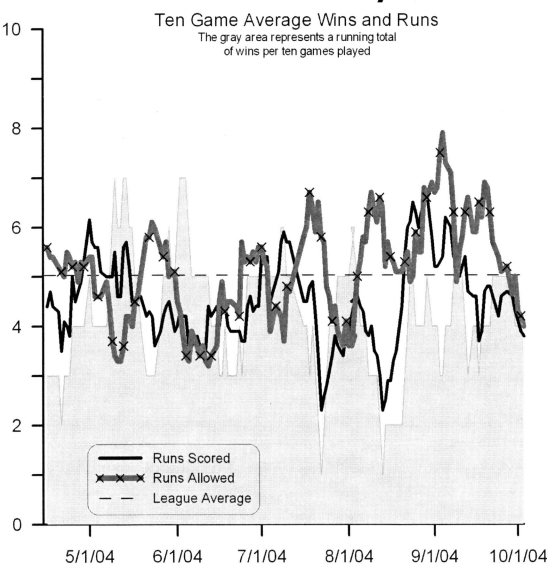

5/27: Bring
up Alexis Rios

5/29: Delgado out; to
miss over a month

6/16: Wells on DL
for a month

7/20: Halladay on DL
for two months

8/8: Fire Tosca; name
Gibbons Manager

Team Batting and Pitching/Fielding Stats by Month						
	April	May	June	July	Aug	Sept
Wins	8	15	12	10	9	13
Losses	16	13	15	14	20	16
OBP	.333	.344	.333	.314	.323	.322
SLG	.404	.399	.397	.406	.402	.412
FIP	4.72	4.17	4.62	4.52	5.62	5.04
DER	.700	.702	.717	.711	.674	.723

Batting Stats

Player	RC	Runs	RBI	PA	Outs	H	BB	HR	TB	BA	OBP	SLG	GPA	ISO	SB	CS	GDP
Delgado C.	89	74	99	551	346	123	69	32	245	.269	.372	.535	.301	.266	0	1	10
Wells V.	73	82	67	590	408	146	51	23	253	.272	.337	.472	.270	.200	9	2	16
Hudson O.	71	73	58	551	372	132	51	12	214	.270	.341	.438	.263	.168	7	3	12
Johnson R.	64	68	61	582	409	145	28	10	204	.270	.320	.380	.239	.110	6	3	14
Hinske E.	60	66	69	634	451	140	54	15	214	.246	.312	.375	.234	.130	12	8	13
Zaun G.	49	46	36	392	256	91	47	6	133	.269	.367	.393	.264	.124	0	2	7
Rios A.	48	55	28	460	319	122	31	1	163	.286	.338	.383	.248	.096	15	3	12
Gomez C.	45	41	37	377	251	96	28	3	118	.282	.337	.346	.238	.065	3	2	4
Menechino F.	43	40	25	276	169	71	36	9	119	.301	.400	.504	.306	.203	0	2	2
Phelps J.	40	38	51	321	233	70	18	12	123	.237	.296	.417	.237	.180	0	0	8
Catalanotto	34	27	26	274	182	73	17	1	97	.293	.344	.390	.252	.096	1	0	6
Woodward C.	24	21	24	232	168	50	14	1	74	.235	.283	.347	.214	.113	1	2	3
Berg D.	15	13	23	162	120	39	4	3	52	.253	.278	.338	.209	.084	0	1	4
Gross G.	14	18	16	149	105	27	19	3	40	.209	.311	.310	.217	.101	2	2	1
Cash K.	11	18	21	197	149	35	10	4	56	.193	.249	.309	.189	.116	0	0	3
Clark H.	11	17	12	133	92	25	13	3	40	.217	.292	.348	.218	.130	0	0	2
Adams R.	11	10	10	78	53	22	5	4	38	.306	.359	.528	.293	.222	1	0	3
Crozier E.	4	5	4	39	28	5	6	2	13	.152	.282	.394	.225	.242	0	0	0
Quiroz G.	4	2	6	57	42	11	2	0	13	.212	.263	.250	.181	.038	1	0	1
Pond S.	2	4	6	56	43	8	5	1	13	.163	.250	.265	.179	.102	0	0	2
Myers G.	1	0	1	20	15	4	2	0	6	.222	.300	.333	.218	.111	0	0	1
Estalella B.	1	1	0	17	11	3	3	0	3	.231	.412	.231	.243	.000	0	0	1
Speier J.	0	0	0	1	1	0	0	0	0	.000	.000	.000	.000	.000	0	0	0
File B.	0	0	0	1	1	0	0	0	0	.000	.000	.000	.000	.000	0	0	0
Bush D.	0	0	0	2	2	0	0	0	0	.000	.000	.000	.000	.000	0	0	0
Lilly T.	0	0	0	4	3	0	0	0	0	.000	.000	.000	.000	.000	0	0	0
Towers J.	0	0	0	3	2	0	0	0	0	.000	.000	.000	.000	.000	0	0	1
Hentgen P.	0	0	0	1	2	0	0	0	0	.000	.000	.000	.000	.000	0	0	1
Batista M.	-1	0	0	5	5	0	0	0	0	.000	.000	.000	.000	.000	0	0	0
Halladay R.	-1	0	0	6	6	0	0	0	0	.000	.000	.000	.000	.000	0	0	0
Hermansen C.	-1	0	0	7	7	0	0	0	0	.000	.000	.000	.000	.000	0	0	0

Pitching Stats

Player	IP	BFP	G	GS	P/PA	H	K	BB	HR	W	L	Sv	Op	Hld	RA	ERA	FIP	DER
Batista M.	198.7	867	38	31	3.76	206	104	96	22	10	13	5	5	0	5.16	4.76	5.18	.713
Lilly T.	197.3	845	32	32	3.91	171	168	89	26	12	10	0	0	0	4.20	4.06	4.75	.739
Halladay R	133.0	561	21	21	3.65	140	95	39	13	8	8	0	0	0	4.47	4.20	4.04	.692
Towers J.	116.3	518	21	21	3.20	148	51	26	16	9	9	0	0	0	5.42	5.11	5.11	.683
Bush D.	97.7	412	16	16	3.58	95	64	25	11	5	4	0	0	0	4.33	3.69	4.40	.725
Miller J.	81.7	375	19	15	3.82	101	47	42	14	3	4	0	0	0	6.39	6.06	6.10	.674
Hentgen P	80.3	373	18	16	3.71	90	33	42	16	2	9	0	0	0	7.51	6.95	6.78	.734
Speier J.	69.0	294	62	0	3.86	61	52	25	8	3	8	7	11	7	4.17	3.78	4.60	.740
Frasor J.	68.3	299	63	0	3.99	64	54	36	4	4	6	17	19	8	4.08	4.08	4.14	.704
Chulk V.	56.0	248	47	0	3.89	59	44	27	6	1	3	2	5	13	4.82	4.66	4.61	.688
Ligtenberg	55.0	263	57	0	3.71	73	49	25	6	1	6	3	5	4	6.55	6.38	4.40	.630
Adams T.	43.0	197	42	0	3.79	49	35	22	4	4	4	3	6	2	4.19	3.98	4.48	.667
Douglass	38.7	179	14	3	4.07	37	36	28	6	0	2	0	0	0	6.28	6.28	5.77	.710
File B.	33.7	154	24	0	3.34	45	15	12	4	1	0	0	0	2	5.08	4.81	5.19	.661
Frederick	28.7	133	22	0	3.72	32	22	16	4	0	2	0	1	3	6.59	6.59	5.35	.689
Nakamura	25.7	114	19	0	3.84	27	24	7	7	0	3	0	0	2	8.06	7.36	6.02	.730
Kershner J	22.3	103	24	2	3.91	30	15	8	3	0	1	0	0	2	6.45	6.04	4.77	.649
Lopez A.	21.0	95	18	0	3.42	21	13	13	5	1	1	0	0	3	6.43	6.00	7.29	.742
Glynn R.	20.0	89	6	2	3.85	19	14	8	4	1	0	0	0	0	4.50	4.50	6.14	.750
Chacin G.	14.0	52	2	2	3.90	8	6	3	0	1	1	0	0	0	2.57	2.57	3.29	.810
de los Santos	11.7	56	17	0	3.61	11	10	10	0	0	0	0	1	0	6.17	6.17	4.15	.694
League B.	4.7	18	3	0	3.50	3	2	1	0	1	0	0	0	1	0.00	0.00	3.08	.800
Peterson	2.7	18	3	0	3.56	7	2	3	1	0	0	0	0	0	16.88	16.88	10.04	.500
Maurer D.	1.3	15	3	0	3.60	6	1	5	1	0	0	0	0	0	54.00	54.00	22.79	.375
Menechino	0.3	3	1	0	3.00	2	0	0	0	0	0	0	0	0	0.00	0.00	3.29	.333

Fielding Stats

Catchers

Name	Innings	SBA/G	CS%	ERA	WP+PB/G
Zaun	789.0	0.92	26%	4.79	0.354
Cash	460.3	0.65	42%	5.08	0.528
Quiroz	114.7	0.55	29%	5.34	0.785
Myers	32.0	1.13	25%	3.38	0.281
Estalella	25.0	1.44	0%	6.48	0.720

Infielders and Outfielders

Name	POS	Inn	PO	A	TE	FE	FPct	RF	DPS	DPT
C Delgado	1B	1038.0	1046	86	0	4	.996	9.82	6	0
C Gomez	1B	115.0	104	12	0	2	.983	9.08	2	0

Toronto Blue Jays

Name	POS	Inn	PO	A	TE	FE	FPct	RF	DPS	DPT
J Phelps	1B	99.7	101	2	1	1	.981	9.30	0	0
H Clark	1B	93.0	106	6	0	0	1.000	10.84	5	0
D Berg	1B	40.0	43	3	0	2	.958	10.35	1	0
E Crozier	1B	34.7	34	1	1	0	.972	9.09	0	0
O Hudson	2B	1124.0	277	449	2	10	.984	5.81	34	57
F Menechino	2B	237.3	53	72	0	0	1.000	4.74	2	11
D Berg	2B	28.0	5	9	0	0	1.000	4.50	0	1
C Gomez	2B	23.0	6	2	0	0	1.000	3.13	0	0
H Clark	2B	8.0	0	0	0	0	.000	0.00	0	0
C Gomez	SS	638.0	109	205	8	2	.969	4.43	24	18
C Woodward	SS	514.7	86	172	2	3	.981	4.51	27	13
R Adams	SS	159.3	27	48	4	1	.938	4.24	9	2
F Menechino	SS	109.0	26	26	0	1	.981	4.29	5	3
E Hinske	3B	1310.0	105	240	3	5	.977	2.37	18	2
F Menechino	3B	59.0	4	14	0	0	1.000	2.75	1	0
C Gomez	3B	31.3	2	8	0	0	1.000	2.87	1	0
D Berg	3B	19.0	0	3	1	1	.600	1.42	0	0
H Clark	3B	1.0	0	0	0	0	.000	0.00	0	0
R Johnson	LF	461.3	97	5	1	1	.981	1.99	2	0
F Catalanott	LF	309.7	66	1	1	1	.971	1.95	1	0
G Gross	LF	289.7	73	5	0	0	1.000	2.42	1	0
D Berg	LF	226.7	36	1	0	1	.974	1.47	0	0
H Clark	LF	64.7	16	2	0	0	1.000	2.51	0	0
S Pond	LF	52.0	10	0	0	0	1.000	1.73	0	0
C Hermansen	LF	17.0	4	0	0	0	1.000	2.12	0	0
V Wells	CF	1135.0	326	5	1	0	.997	2.62	0	0
R Johnson	CF	265.0	82	1	0	0	1.000	2.82	0	0
A Rios	CF	21.0	1	0	0	0	1.000	0.43	0	0
A Rios	RF	943.7	216	11	1	1	.991	2.16	7	0
R Johnson	RF	382.7	88	2	1	0	.989	2.12	0	0
H Clark	RF	66.7	17	0	0	1	.944	2.30	0	0
S Pond	RF	25.0	8	0	0	0	1.000	2.88	0	0
D Berg	RF	3.0	1	0	0	0	1.000	3.00	0	0

Arizona Diamondbacks

Ten Game Average Wins and Runs

The gray area represents a running total
of wins per ten games played

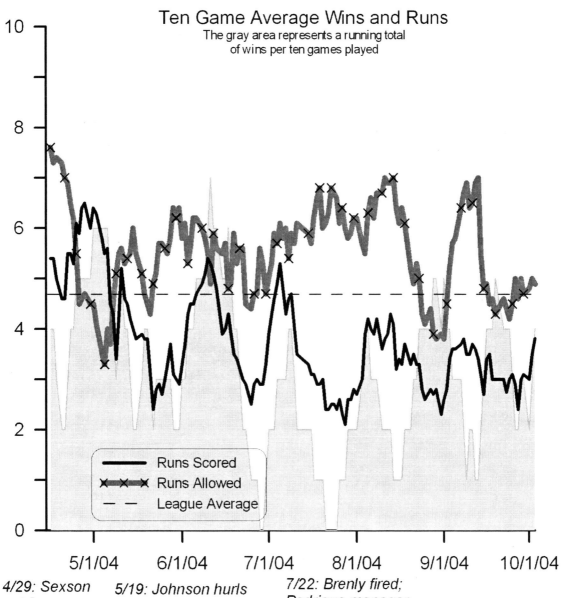

4/29: Sexson out for year

5/19: Johnson hurls perfect game

7/22: Brenly fired; Pedrique manager

5/9: Mantei out for year

6/30: 4,000 K's for Johnson

8/3: Gonzalez on DL for year

Team Batting and Pitching/Fielding Stats by Month						
	April	**May**	**June**	**July**	**Aug**	**Sept**
Wins	10	9	10	4	8	10
Losses	13	20	17	23	18	20
OBP	.338	.299	.322	.305	.305	.297
SLG	.462	.385	.419	.375	.358	.370
FIP	4.55	4.73	4.73	5.13	4.96	4.55
DER	.703	.721	.691	.702	.706	.697

Batting Stats

Player	RC	Runs	RBI	PA	Outs	H	BB	HR	TB	BA	OBP	SLG	GPA	ISO	SB	CS	GDP
Hillenbrand	87	68	80	604	402	174	24	15	261	.310	.348	.464	.273	.155	2	0	14
Bautista D.	71	64	65	582	403	154	35	11	216	.286	.332	.401	.250	.115	6	2	16
Gonzalez L.	66	69	48	451	291	98	68	17	187	.259	.373	.493	.291	.235	2	2	8
Tracy C.	66	44	53	532	356	137	45	8	196	.285	.343	.407	.256	.123	2	3	9
Cintron A.	61	56	49	613	429	148	31	4	205	.262	.301	.363	.226	.101	3	3	10
Finley S.	55	61	48	456	306	111	40	23	198	.275	.338	.490	.275	.215	8	4	9
Hairston S.	34	39	29	364	262	84	21	13	150	.248	.293	.442	.242	.195	3	3	4
Terrero L.	27	21	14	255	179	56	20	4	82	.245	.319	.358	.233	.114	10	2	4
McCracken Q.	20	20	13	172	117	45	13	2	64	.288	.341	.410	.256	.122	2	4	2
Kata M.	20	17	13	178	124	40	13	2	59	.247	.301	.364	.227	.117	4	1	1
Sexson R.	19	20	23	104	71	21	14	9	52	.233	.337	.578	.296	.344	0	0	2
Alomar R.	19	14	16	125	80	34	12	3	52	.309	.382	.473	.290	.164	0	2	2
Hammock R.	16	22	18	210	160	47	13	4	79	.241	.287	.405	.230	.164	3	3	9
Snyder C.	12	9	15	110	74	23	13	5	44	.240	.327	.458	.262	.219	0	0	1
Devore D.	11	5	13	114	85	24	7	3	40	.224	.272	.374	.216	.150	1	1	1
Baerga C.	10	6	11	94	72	20	6	2	28	.235	.309	.329	.221	.094	0	0	7
Mayne B.	9	9	10	111	75	24	13	0	32	.255	.343	.340	.239	.085	1	0	5
Olson T.	8	8	5	114	83	18	16	2	31	.186	.301	.320	.215	.134	1	0	4
Brito J.	8	17	12	184	141	35	9	3	51	.205	.246	.298	.185	.094	1	0	5
Green A.	7	13	4	119	90	22	5	1	29	.202	.241	.266	.175	.064	1	1	2
Hill K.	5	3	6	38	27	9	2	1	13	.250	.289	.361	.221	.111	1	0	0
Zinter A.	4	2	6	40	27	7	5	1	12	.206	.300	.353	.223	.147	0	0	0
Randolph S.	4	4	3	12	7	5	0	0	8	.417	.417	.667	.354	.250	0	0	0
Gil J.	4	3	8	88	73	15	0	0	19	.174	.182	.221	.137	.047	2	0	2
Estalella B.	2	2	4	14	12	2	0	2	8	.143	.143	.571	.207	.429	0	0	0
Kroeger J.	1	5	2	55	48	9	1	0	12	.167	.182	.222	.137	.056	0	1	2
Cormier L.	1	1	1	10	6	2	1	0	3	.250	.333	.375	.244	.125	0	0	0
Dessens E.	1	0	0	25	16	3	3	0	5	.167	.286	.278	.198	.111	0	0	1
Johnson R.	1	1	6	87	71	10	4	0	13	.125	.167	.163	.116	.038	0	0	1
Colbrunn G.	1	1	1	28	24	3	1	0	3	.111	.143	.111	.092	.000	0	0	0
Sparks S.	0	0	1	32	27	4	0	0	4	.129	.129	.129	.090	.000	0	0	0
Durbin C.	0	0	0	1	1	0	0	0	0	.000	.000	.000	.000	.000	0	0	0
Service S.	0	0	0	1	1	0	0	0	0	.000	.000	.000	.000	.000	0	0	0
Aquino G.	0	0	0	1	1	0	0	0	0	.000	.000	.000	.000	.000	0	0	0
Choate R.	0	0	0	1	1	0	0	0	0	.000	.000	.000	.000	.000	0	0	0
Villafuerte	0	0	0	1	1	0	0	0	0	.000	.000	.000	.000	.000	0	0	0
Sadler D.	0	1	0	24	20	3	1	0	5	.130	.167	.217	.129	.087	0	0	0
Gonzalez E.	0	0	0	15	11	2	0	0	2	.154	.214	.154	.135	.000	0	0	0
Gosling M.	0	0	0	8	6	0	1	0	0	.000	.143	.000	.064	.000	0	0	0
Good A.	0	0	1	6	5	0	0	0	0	.000	.000	.000	.000	.000	0	0	0
Webb B.	-1	3	4	71	58	6	3	0	6	.094	.134	.094	.084	.000	0	0	0
Daigle C.	-1	2	0	18	16	2	0	0	4	.118	.118	.235	.112	.118	0	0	1
Fossum C.	-2	3	0	46	39	4	1	0	4	.095	.116	.095	.076	.000	0	0	1

Arizona Diamondbacks

Pitching Stats

Player	IP	BFP	G	GS	P/PA	H	K	BB	HR	W	L	Sv	Op	Hld	RA	ERA	FIP	DER
Johnson	245.7	964	35	35	3.77	177	290	44	18	16	14	0	0	0	3.22	2.60	2.33	.736
Webb B.	208.0	933	35	35	3.69	194	164	119	17	7	16	0	0	0	4.80	3.59	4.44	.715
Fossum C	142.0	652	27	27	3.69	171	117	63	31	4	15	0	0	0	7.04	6.65	5.81	.675
Sparks S.	120.7	545	29	18	3.56	139	57	45	18	3	7	· 0	0	0	6.64	6.04	5.31	.712
Koplove	86.7	371	76	0	3.58	86	55	37	7	4	4	2	8	18	4.36	4.05	4.31	.704
Dessens	85.3	386	38	9	3.76	107	55	23	11	1	6	2	4	4	5.70	4.75	4.31	.676
Randolph	81.7	393	45	6	4.16	73	62	76	11	2	5	0	0	2	6.17	5.51	6.14	.745
Choate R.	50.7	232	74	0	3.91	52	49	28	1	2	4	0	2	10	4.62	4.62	3.35	.658
Daigle C.	49.0	230	10	10	3.53	63	17	27	9	2	3	0	0	0	7.53	7.16	6.55	.691
Gonzalez	46.3	228	10	10	3.57	72	31	18	15	0	9	0	0	0	9.52	9.32	7.44	.642
Cormier L	45.3	218	17	5	3.69	62	24	25	13	1	4	0	0	2	8.34	8.14	7.53	.682
Good A.	40.7	177	17	2	3.67	43	26	13	8	1	2	0	0	0	5.53	5.31	5.54	.724
Aquino G.	35.3	147	34	0	3.82	24	26	17	4	0	2	16	19	1	3.82	3.06	4.69	.796
Bruney B.	31.3	135	30	0	4.57	20	34	27	2	3	4	0	1	2	4.60	4.31	4.42	.746
Valverde	29.7	131	29	0	4.02	23	38	17	7	1	2	8	10	5	5.16	4.25	5.40	.765
Gosling M	25.3	112	6	4	3.70	26	14	13	5	1	1	0	0	0	4.62	4.62	6.31	.731
Service S.	20.3	97	21	0	4.28	24	17	10	5	1	1	0	2	1	7.52	7.08	6.37	.698
Villafuerte	20.0	96	20	0	3.72	25	13	14	2	0	3	0	0	0	4.05	4.05	5.33	.652
Fetters M.	18.7	94	23	0	3.60	23	14	14	2	0	1	1	1	1	10.61	8.68	5.38	.667
Villarreal	18.0	84	17	0	3.57	25	17	7	3	0	2	0	0	2	7.00	7.00	4.69	.607
Nance S.	12.3	69	19	0	3.99	19	9	12	2	1	1	0	1	3	8.03	5.84	7.37	.605
Mantei M.	10.7	55	12	0	3.91	17	13	6	5	0	3	4	7	0	12.66	11.81	8.42	.613
Durbin C.	9.3	52	7	0	3.71	9	10	11	1	1	1	0	0	1	9.64	8.68	6.18	.724
Reynolds	2.0	14	1	1	3.57	6	0	2	0	0	1	0	0	0	27.00	4.50	6.08	.500
Fassero J	1.0	3	1	0	4.67	0	1	0	0	0	0	0	0	0	0.00	0.00	1.08	1.000

Fielding Stats

Catchers

Name	Innings	SBA/G	CS%	ERA	WP+PB/G
Brito	461.7	0.92	26%	4.54	0.507
Hammock	376.7	0.88	27%	3.94	0.430
Snyder	247.3	0.69	32%	4.33	0.473
Mayne	236.7	0.87	39%	6.73	0.723
Hill	83.0	1.19	27%	8.02	1.084
Estalella	30.7	0.00	0%	7.92	0.880

Infielders and Outfielders

Name	POS	Inn	PO	A	TE	FE	FPct	RF	DPS	DPT
S Hillenbran	1B	1113.0	1126	73	4	9	.989	9.70	17	1
R Sexson	1B	204.3	197	26	0	1	.996	9.82	2	1
A Zinter	1B	39.0	42	2	0	1	.978	10.15	0	0

Arizona Diamondbacks

Name	POS	Inn	PO	A	TE	FE	FPct	RF	DPS	DPT
C Baerga	1B	35.7	32	3	0	0	1.000	8.83	0	0
C Tracy	1B	33.0	29	3	1	0	.970	8.73	0	0
G Colbrunn	1B	9.0	7	1	0	0	1.000	8.00	0	0
B Mayne	1B	1.7	2	0	0	0	1.000	10.80	0	0
S Hairston	2B	704.0	173	207	1	10	.972	4.86	17	28
M Kata	2B	320.7	75	111	1	1	.989	5.22	8	16
R Alomar	2B	203.3	48	53	0	3	.971	4.47	5	5
A Cintron	2B	147.0	31	45	1	1	.974	4.65	2	4
A Green	2B	55.0	16	15	1	0	.969	5.07	0	4
D Sadler	2B	6.0	2	1	0	0	1.000	4.50	1	0
A Cintron	SS	1099.0	141	382	4	11	.972	4.28	31	27
J Gil	SS	212.3	35	72	3	2	.955	4.54	8	8
T Olson	SS	97.3	18	29	3	1	.922	4.35	2	6
D Sadler	SS	18.0	3	3	0	0	1.000	3.00	0	1
M Kata	SS	9.3	3	5	0	0	1.000	7.71	0	2
C Tracy	3B	1062.0	104	258	16	9	.935	3.07	25	1
S Hillenbran	3B	133.0	6	29	3	0	.921	2.37	3	0
A Green	3B	117.0	12	32	1	3	.917	3.38	1	0
T Olson	3B	98.3	17	35	1	1	.963	4.76	1	0
M Kata	3B	17.3	4	4	0	0	1.000	4.15	0	0
D Sadler	3B	5.0	1	0	0	0	1.000	1.80	0	0
R Hammock	3B	2.0	1	0	0	0	1.000	4.50	0	0
A Cintron	3B	1.0	1	0	0	0	1.000	9.00	0	0
L Gonzalez	LF	900.3	162	2	1	5	.965	1.64	0	0
Q McCracken	LF	223.7	28	1	0	0	1.000	1.17	0	0
D Devore	LF	107.7	27	2	0	0	1.000	2.42	2	0
R Hammock	LF	79.0	20	1	0	1	.955	2.39	0	0
J Kroeger	LF	57.0	17	0	0	0	1.000	2.68	0	0
A Green	LF	45.3	10	1	0	0	1.000	2.18	0	0
D Sadler	LF	9.0	1	0	0	0	1.000	1.00	0	0
T Olson	LF	8.0	3	0	0	0	1.000	3.38	0	0
S Hairston	LF	4.0	0	0	0	0	.000	0.00	0	0
L Terrero	LF	1.0	0	0	0	0	.000	0.00	0	0
C Tracy	LF	1.0	2	0	0	0	1.000	18.00	0	0
S Finley	CF	896.3	214	5	1	1	.991	2.20	6	0
L Terrero	CF	488.7	111	5	3	3	.951	2.14	5	0
D Bautista	CF	14.0	6	0	0	0	1.000	3.86	0	0
J Kroeger	CF	14.0	7	0	0	0	1.000	4.50	0	0
T Olson	CF	10.7	4	0	0	0	1.000	3.38	0	0
D Sadler	CF	7.0	1	0	0	0	1.000	1.29	0	0
Q McCracken	CF	4.3	3	0	0	0	1.000	6.23	0	0
D Devore	CF	1.0	1	0	0	0	1.000	9.00	0	0
D Bautista	RF	1178.0	265	8	2	2	.986	2.09	2	0
D Devore	RF	100.7	25	0	0	0	1.000	2.24	0	0
Q McCracken	RF	69.0	14	1	0	1	.938	1.96	0	0

Arizona Diamondbacks

Name	POS	Inn	PO	A	TE	FE	FPct	RF	DPS	DPT
J Kroeger	RF	46.3	9	0	0	0	1.000	1.75	0	0
L Terrero	RF	34.0	6	0	0	2	.750	1.59	0	0
T Olson	RF	3.0	0	0	0	0	.000	0.00	0	0
S Hairston	RF	2.7	0	0	0	0	.000	0.00	0	0
D Sadler	RF	1.7	0	0	0	0	.000	0.00	0	0

Atlanta Braves

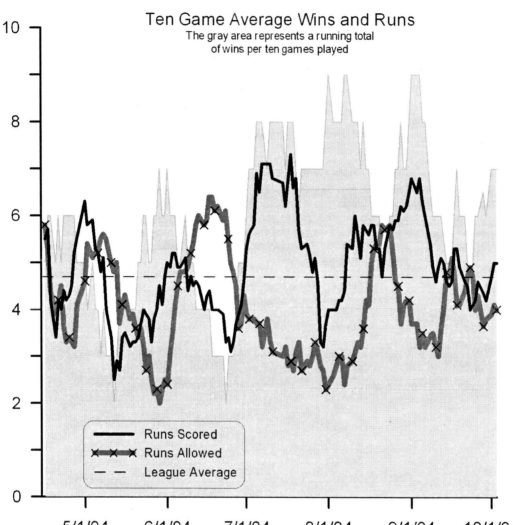

Ten Game Average Wins and Runs
The gray area represents a running total
of wins per ten games played

Runs Scored
Runs Allowed
League Average

5/1/04   6/1/04   7/1/04   8/1/04   9/1/04   10/1/04

5/18: Giles
on DL; misses
two months

6/27: Beat Orioles 8-7
after trailing 7-0; go
46-16 in next 62 games

9/24: Beat Marlins 8-7,
Win division

9/29: Cox wins
2,000th game

7/19: Beat Phillies 4-2
to take first place

7/28: Drew's 28 game
hitting streak stopped

Team Batting and Pitching/Fielding Stats by Month						
	April	May	June	July	Aug	Sept
Wins	12	14	12	19	20	19
Losses	11	14	15	6	8	12
OBP	.345	.297	.339	.358	.378	.340
SLG	.424	.407	.421	.454	.475	.420
FIP	4.56	3.98	4.33	3.50	4.90	4.22
DER	.694	.716	.671	.727	.725	.702

Batting Stats

Player	RC	Runs	RBI	PA	Outs	H	BB	HR	TB	BA	OBP	SLG	GPA	ISO	SB	CS	GDP
Drew J.	126	118	93	645	370	158	118	31	295	.305	.436	.569	.339	.264	12	3	7
Jones C.	87	69	96	567	367	117	84	30	229	.248	.362	.485	.284	.237	2	0	12
Furcal R.	85	103	59	632	419	157	58	14	233	.279	.344	.414	.258	.135	29	6	7
Estrada J.	80	56	76	517	334	145	39	9	208	.314	.378	.450	.283	.136	0	0	17
Jones A.	80	85	91	646	450	149	71	29	278	.261	.345	.488	.277	.226	6	6	23
Giles M.	69	61	48	434	271	118	36	8	168	.311	.378	.443	.281	.132	17	4	6
Franco J.	59	37	57	361	230	99	36	6	141	.309	.378	.441	.280	.131	4	2	7
Marrero E.	52	37	40	280	175	80	23	10	130	.320	.374	.520	.298	.200	4	1	4
La Roche A.	47	45	45	356	241	90	27	13	158	.278	.333	.488	.272	.210	0	0	7
Thomas C.	38	35	31	267	172	68	21	7	105	.288	.368	.445	.277	.157	3	1	3
Green N.	36	40	26	290	194	72	12	3	102	.273	.312	.386	.237	.114	1	2	0
DeRosa M.	25	33	31	345	242	74	23	3	99	.239	.293	.320	.212	.081	1	3	4
Wise D.	21	24	17	175	127	37	9	6	72	.228	.272	.444	.233	.216	6	1	1
Perez E.	13	14	13	188	136	39	11	3	60	.229	.286	.353	.217	.124	0	0	5
Garcia J.	10	14	10	118	90	29	1	1	38	.252	.265	.330	.202	.078	1	2	2
Byrd P.	4	2	4	43	24	6	5	0	6	.200	.314	.200	.191	.000	0	0	0
Hampton M.	3	7	7	71	54	11	3	2	20	.172	.209	.313	.172	.141	0	0	1
Hollins D.	2	3	5	23	14	8	0	0	10	.364	.364	.455	.277	.091	0	0	0
Hessman M.	1	8	5	71	60	9	1	2	18	.130	.155	.261	.135	.130	0	0	0
Cruz J.	0	1	0	6	4	1	1	0	2	.200	.333	.400	.250	.200	0	0	0
Drew T.	0	1	0	3	2	0	1	0	0	.000	.333	.000	.150	.000	0	0	0
Almanza A.	0	0	0	1	0	0	0	0	0	.000	.000	.000	.000!	.000	0	0	0
Thomson J.	0	3	4	76	55	13	0	0	14	.197	.197	.212	.142	.015	0	0	2
McConnell S.	0	0	0	1	1	0	0	0	0	.000	.000	.000	.000	.000	0	0	0
Alfonseca A.	0	0	0	1	1	0	0	0	0	.000	.000	.000	.000	.000	0	0	0
Betemit W.	0	2	3	52	40	8	4	0	8	.170	.231	.170	.146	.000	0	1	0
Capellan J.	0	0	0	2	2	0	0	0	0	.000	.000	.000	.000	.000	0	0	0
Smoltz J.	0	0	0	2	2	0	0	0	0	.000	.000	.000	.000	.000	0	0	0
Smith T.	0	0	0	8	7	1	0	0	1	.125	.125	.125	.088	.000	0	0	0
Ramirez H.	-1	0	1	22	19	2	0	0	2	.095	.095	.095	.067	.000	0	0	0
Ortiz R.	-2	1	1	71	54	6	1	0	8	.102	.131	.136	.093	.034	0	0	1
Wright J.	-2	4	4	65	51	6	2	1	10	.105	.136	.175	.105	.070	0	0	0

Pitching Stats

Player	IP	BFP	G	GS	P/PA	H	K	BB	HR	W	L	Sv	Op	Hld	RA	ERA	FIP	DER
Ortiz R.	204.7	896	34	34	3.87	197	143	112	23	15	9	0	0	0	4.31	4.13	4.83	.717
Thomson J.	198.3	834	33	33	3.52	210	133	52	20	14	8	0	0	0	4.22	3.72	3.92	.695
Wright J.	186.3	781	32	32	3.82	168	159	70	11	15	8	0	0	0	3.82	3.28	3.31	.708
Hampton M.	172.3	760	29	29	3.59	198	87	65	15	13	9	0	0	0	4.49	4.28	4.35	.691
Byrd P.	114.3	482	19	19	3.46	123	79	19	18	8	7	0	0	0	4.49	3.94	4.29	.712
Smoltz J.	81.7	323	73	0	3.54	75	85	13	8	0	1	44	49	0	2.76	2.76	2.75	.691
Reitsma C.	79.7	344	84	0	3.53	89	60	20	9	6	4	2	9	31	4.29	4.07	3.91	.683
Alfonseca A.	73.7	313	79	0	3.60	71	45	28	5	6	4	0	1	13	2.93	2.57	3.88	.719
Cruz J.	72.0	300	50	0	4.01	59	70	30	7	6	2	0	0	2	3.00	2.75	3.73	.728
Ramirez H.	60.3	259	10	9	3.58	51	31	30	7	2	4	0	0	0	3.58	2.39	5.05	.770
Gryboski K.	50.7	217	69	0	3.78	54	24	23	2	3	2	2	4	16	3.91	2.84	4.00	.690
Smith T.	40.7	180	16	4	3.70	48	26	12	12	2	3	0	0	1	6.20	6.20	6.59	.721
Nitkowski C	20.0	95	22	0	3.91	22	16	10	3	1	0	0	0	0	4.95	4.50	5.23	.703
Colon R.	19.0	82	18	0	3.66	18	15	8	0	2	1	0	1	1	4.26	3.32	2.76	.695
Martin T.	17.0	72	29	0	3.79	17	12	5	4	0	1	0	3	7	3.71	3.71	5.61	.745
Drew T.	16.0	73	11	0	3.40	21	7	5	2	0	0	0	0	0	6.19	4.50	4.95	.672
Cunnane W	12.3	59	9	0	3.76	18	11	4	3	1	1	0	1	0	7.30	7.30	5.67	.625
Almanza A.	11.7	54	13	0	4.37	9	13	7	3	1	1	0	0	0	6.17	6.17	6.25	.800
McConnell	9.3	44	10	0	3.68	11	4	4	0	1	0	0	0	0	3.86	3.86	3.83	.686
Capellan J.	8.0	42	3	2	4.21	14	4	5	2	0	1	0	0	0	11.25	11.25	7.20	.613
Meyer D.	2.0	8	2	0	3.50	2	1	1	0	0	0	0	0	0	0.00	0.00	3.58	.667

Fielding Stats

Catchers

Name	Innings	SBA/G	CS%	ERA	WP+PB/G
Estrada	1042.0	0.73	18%	3.77	0.337
Perez	408.0	0.71	34%	3.71	0.154

Infielders and Outfielders

Name	POS	Inn	PO	A	TE	FE	FPct	RF	DPS	DPT
A La Roche	1B	720.0	738	40	2	3	.994	9.73	3	2
J Franco	1B	631.3	628	48	0	1	.997	9.64	14	1
M Hessman	1B	90.3	96	4	1	3	.962	9.96	1	0
E Perez	1B	8.3	10	0	0	0	1.000	10.80	0	0
M Giles	2B	789.0	186	289	5	6	.975	5.42	23	46
N Green	2B	572.0	137	203	3	5	.977	5.35	22	23
J Garcia	2B	53.0	16	19	2	0	.946	5.94	3	2
M DeRosa	2B	34.0	3	11	0	0	1.000	3.71	4	0
R Furcal	2B	2.0	0	0	0	0	.000	0.00	0	0
R Furcal	SS	1134.0	191	412	13	11	.962	4.79	49	50

Atlanta Braves

Name	POS	Inn	PO	A	TE	FE	FPct	RF	DPS	DPT
J Garcia	SS	191.0	31	71	1	3	.962	4.81	5	10
W Betemit	SS	74.7	12	30	0	3	.933	5.06	3	2
M DeRosa	SS	50.3	10	18	1	1	.933	5.01	3	4
C Jones	3B	802.0	58	177	2	4	.975	2.64	12	0
M DeRosa	3B	556.0	27	125	4	6	.938	2.46	8	1
W Betemit	3B	39.0	2	6	0	0	1.000	1.85	2	0
M Hessman	3B	29.0	2	14	1	1	.889	4.97	1	0
J Garcia	3B	12.0	0	3	0	1	.750	2.25	0	0
N Green	3B	12.0	0	2	0	0	1.000	1.50	0	0
C Thomas	LF	560.7	132	6	0	1	.993	2.22	3	0
E Marrero	LF	375.0	80	4	1	0	.988	2.02	2	0
C Jones	LF	238.0	35	2	0	0	1.000	1.40	2	0
D Wise	LF	207.3	40	2	0	0	1.000	1.82	0	0
D Hollins	LF	37.0	7	1	0	0	1.000	1.95	0	0
M Hessman	LF	17.0	4	0	0	0	1.000	2.12	0	0
M DeRosa	LF	15.0	0	0	0	0	.000	0.00	0	0
A Jones	CF	1347.0	389	10	0	3	.993	2.67	5	0
J Drew	CF	49.0	19	1	0	0	1.000	3.67	0	0
D Wise	CF	44.0	11	0	0	0	1.000	2.25	0	0
E Marrero	CF	9.0	0	0	0	0	.000	0.00	0	0
C Thomas	CF	1.0	1	0	0	0	1.000	9.00	0	0
J Drew	RF	1193.0	277	10	0	3	.990	2.17	0	0
E Marrero	RF	171.0	41	2	0	0	1.000	2.26	0	0
D Wise	RF	66.0	10	0	0	0	1.000	1.36	0	0
C Thomas	RF	11.0	4	1	0	0	1.000	4.09	0	0
D Hollins	RF	8.0	1	0	0	0	1.000	1.13	0	0
N Green	RF	1.0	0	0	0	0	.000	0.00	0	0

Chicago Cubs

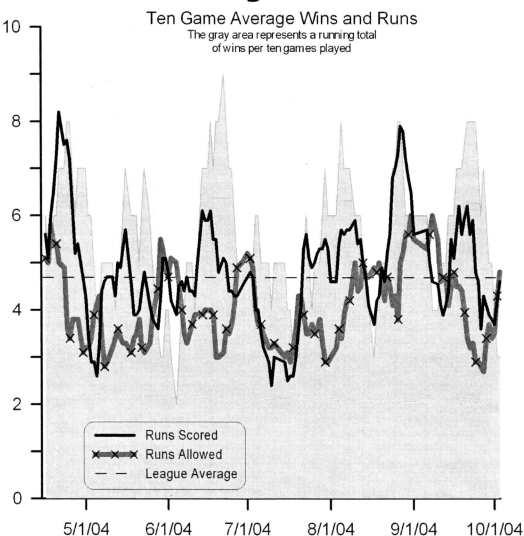

Ten Game Average Wins and Runs
The gray area represents a running total
of wins per ten games played

*4/18: Sosa becomes
all-time club HR
leader w/514 HR's*

*5/20: Wood on
DL; out over a
month*

6/4: Prior returns

*7/31: Trade
for Nomar*

*8/7: Maddux
wins 300*

*9/30: Prior K's
16 and walks
one; Cubs lose
2-1*

*10/3: Lose
7 of last 9*

Team Batting and Pitching/Fielding Stats by Month						
	April	**May**	**June**	**July**	**Aug**	**Sept**
Wins	14	13	16	13	16	17
Losses	9	15	11	13	12	13
OBP	.336	.327	.327	.306	.332	.338
SLG	.497	.421	.450	.455	.490	.444
FIP	4.27	4.03	3.87	4.28	4.36	3.24
DER	.719	.722	.709	.733	.679	.710

Batting Stats

Player	RC	Runs	RBI	PA	Outs	H	BB	HR	TB	BA	OBP	SLG	GPA	ISO	SB	CS	GDP
Alou M.	124	106	106	675	433	176	68	39	335	.293	.361	.557	.302	.265	3	0	8
Lee D.	109	90	98	688	455	168	68	32	305	.278	.356	.504	.286	.226	12	5	13
Ramirez A.	108	99	103	606	398	174	49	36	316	.318	.373	.578	.312	.260	0	2	23
Patterson C.	94	91	72	687	479	168	45	24	285	.266	.320	.452	.257	.185	32	9	7
Sosa S.	74	69	80	539	366	121	56	35	247	.253	.332	.517	.279	.264	0	0	9
Barrett M.	72	55	65	506	342	131	33	16	223	.287	.337	.489	.274	.202	1	4	13
Walker T.	64	60	50	424	275	102	43	15	174	.274	.352	.468	.275	.194	0	3	2
Grudzielanek	37	32	23	278	185	79	15	6	111	.307	.347	.432	.264	.125	1	1	6
Martinez R.	31	22	30	298	199	64	26	3	90	.246	.313	.346	.227	.100	1	0	3
Garciaparra	29	28	20	185	123	49	16	4	75	.297	.364	.455	.277	.158	2	1	6
Hollandswort	28	28	22	167	104	47	17	8	81	.318	.392	.547	.313	.230	1	1	2
Macias J.	23	23	22	204	145	52	5	3	73	.268	.292	.376	.226	.108	4	1	2
Perez N.	14	12	6	67	40	23	3	2	34	.371	.400	.548	.317	.177	1	0	1
Bako P.	11	13	10	157	114	28	15	1	39	.203	.288	.283	.200	.080	1	0	4
Gonzalez A.	9	15	8	135	105	28	4	3	47	.217	.241	.364	.199	.147	1	1	3
Goodwin T.	6	11	3	114	85	21	8	0	29	.200	.254	.276	.184	.076	5	0	1
Ordonez R.	4	2	5	67	52	10	2	1	16	.164	.190	.262	.151	.098	0	0	1
Dubois J.	4	2	5	25	18	5	1	1	10	.217	.240	.435	.217	.217	0	0	0
Grieve B.	3	2	6	19	12	4	0	1	9	.250	.316	.563	.283	.313	0	0	0
Zambrano C.	2	8	5	82	55	16	3	1	20	.229	.257	.286	.187	.057	0	0	1
Harris B.	2	0	1	10	7	2	1	0	3	.222	.300	.333	.218	.111	0	0	0
Murray C.	1	2	1	6	4	1	1	0	1	.200	.333	.200	.200	.000	0	0	0
Clement M.	1	2	2	61	47	8	1	0	9	.145	.158	.164	.112	.018	0	0	0
Jackson D.	1	1	1	18	14	1	3	1	4	.067	.222	.267	.167	.200	0	0	0
Wood K.	0	2	3	53	39	6	2	1	10	.133	.167	.222	.131	.089	0	0	0
Farnsworth K	0	0	0	1	1	0	0	0	0	.000	.000	.000	.000	.000	0	0	0
Anderson J.	0	0	0	1	1	0	0	0	0	.000	.000	.000	.000	.000	0	0	0
Beltran F.	0	0	0	1	1	0	0	0	0	.000	.000	.000	.000	.000	0	0	0
Leicester J.	0	0	0	1	1	0	0	0	0	.000	.000	.000	.000	.000	0	0	0
Remlinger M.	0	0	0	1	1	0	0	0	0	.000	.000	.000	.000	.000	0	0	0
Dempster R.	0	0	0	1	1	0	0	0	0	.000	.000	.000	.000	.000	0	0	0
Wuertz M.	0	0	0	1	1	0	0	0	0	.000	.000	.000	.000	.000	0	0	0
Mercker K.	0	0	0	2	2	0	0	0	0	.000	.000	.000	.000	.000	0	0	0
DiFelice M.	0	0	0	3	3	0	0	0	0	.000	.000	.000	.000	.000	0	0	0
Mitre S.	0	0	0	19	14	1	1	0	2	.067	.125	.133	.090	.067	0	0	0
Prior M.	0	5	0	44	31	5	2	0	5	.139	.184	.139	.118	.000	0	0	0
Kelton D.	0	1	0	10	9	1	0	0	2	.100	.100	.200	.095	.100	0	0	0
Rusch G.	-1	3	3	46	33	6	0	2	13	.154	.154	.333	.153	.179	0	0	0
Maddux G.	-1	5	5	79	59	11	1	0	11	.159	.171	.159	.117	.000	1	0	1

Pitching Stats

Player	IP	BFP	G	GS	P/PA	H	K	BB	HR	W	L	Sv	Op	Hld	RA	ERA	FIP	DER
Maddux G.	212.7	872	33	33	3.35	218	151	33	35	16	11	0	0	0	4.36	4.02	4.39	.716
Zambrano	209.7	886	31	31	3.91	174	188	81	14	16	8	0	0	0	3.13	2.75	3.60	.726
Clement M.	181.0	775	30	30	3.86	155	190	77	23	9	13	0	0	0	3.93	3.68	4.10	.721
Wood K.	140.3	595	22	22	3.73	127	144	51	16	8	9	0	0	0	3.98	3.72	3.83	.702
Rusch G.	129.7	545	32	16	4.01	127	90	33	10	6	2	2	2	3	3.75	3.47	3.55	.713
Prior M.	118.7	510	21	21	4.04	112	139	48	14	6	4	0	0	0	4.02	4.02	3.56	.680
Hawkins L.	82.0	333	77	0	3.58	72	69	14	10	5	4	25	34	4	2.96	2.63	3.56	.739
Farnsworth	66.7	298	72	0	4.13	67	78	33	10	4	5	0	4	18	5.27	4.73	4.26	.674
Mercker K.	53.0	223	71	0	4.16	39	51	27	4	3	1	0	3	16	2.55	2.55	3.83	.746
Mitre S.	51.7	244	12	9	3.41	71	37	20	6	2	4	0	0	0	6.62	6.62	4.55	.633
Leicester J.	41.7	175	32	0	4.09	40	35	15	7	5	1	0	2	5	4.32	3.89	4.66	.720
Remlinger	36.7	156	48	0	4.07	33	35	16	3	1	2	2	6	13	3.93	3.44	3.62	.703
Beltran F.	35.0	153	34	0	3.71	27	40	22	8	2	2	0	0	5	4.89	4.63	5.65	.771
Wuertz M.	29.0	124	31	0	4.18	22	30	17	4	1	0	1	1	1	4.34	4.34	4.56	.753
Wellemeyer	24.3	119	20	0	4.33	27	30	20	1	2	1	0	0	0	5.92	5.92	3.61	.618
Borowski J.	21.3	106	22	0	3.66	27	17	15	3	2	4	9	11	0	8.02	8.02	5 42	.662
Dempster	20.7	93	23	0	4.06	16	18	13	1	1	1	2	2	3	3.92	3.92	4.14	.746
Anderson J	9.7	42	7	0	3.38	9	3	3	0	0	0	1	1	0	4.66	4.66	4.01	.735
Pratt A.	1.7	13	4	0	3.62	0	1	7	0	0	1	0	0	0	21.60	21.60	16.28	1.000

Fielding Stats

Catchers

Name	Innings	SBA/G	CS%	ERA	WP+PB/G
Barrett	1081.3	0.75	20%	3.89	0.408
Bako	377.7	1.22	29%	3.55	0.238
DiFelice	6.3	0.00	0%	9.95	0.000

Infielders and Outfielders

Name	POS	Inn	PO	A	TE	FE	FPct	RF	DPS	DPT
D Lee	1B	1432.0	1258	127	0	6	.996	8.70	16	0
T Hollandswo	1B	21.0	16	4	0	1	.952	8.57	0	0
T Walker	1B	11.0	7	1	0	0	1.000	6.55	0	0
J Dubois	1B	1.3	2	0	0	0	1.000	13.50	0	0
T Walker	2B	749.3	150	213	4	3	.981	4.36	16	13
M Grudzielan	2B	568.0	136	186	1	4	.985	5.10	9	22
J Macias	2B	85.0	15	24	0	0	1.000	4.13	1	2
D Jackson	2B	33.3	8	14	0	1	.957	5.94	2	3
R Martinez	2B	18.7	3	6	0	0	1.000	4.34	0	0
N Perez	2B	11.0	4	4	0	0	1.000	6.55	0	2
R Martinez	SS	529.7	80	174	2	4	.977	4.32	20	15

Chicago Cubs

Name	POS	Inn	PO	A	TE	FE	FPct	RF	DPS	DPT
N Garciaparr	SS	364.7	69	94	2	1	.982	4.02	8	9
A Gonzalez	SS	297.3	64	82	3	2	.967	4.42	9	10
R Ordonez	SS	153.3	31	39	0	3	.959	4.11	2	7
N Perez	SS	120.3	20	41	1	1	.968	4.56	4	6
A Ramirez	3B	1245.0	92	221	7	3	.969	2.26	14	0
R Martinez	3B	112.7	12	21	2	1	.917	2.64	3	0
J Macias	3B	85.3	10	12	1	0	.957	2.32	1	0
B Harris	3B	22.0	4	4	1	0	.889	3.27	0	0
M Alou	LF	1338.0	240	7	1	7	.969	1.66	4	0
T Goodwin	LF	44.7	12	0	0	0	1.000	2.42	0	0
J Macias	LF	37.3	5	0	0	0	1.000	1.21	0	0
T Hollandswo	LF	29.0	5	0	0	0	1.000	1.55	0	0
D Kelton	LF	9.0	2	0	0	0	1.000	2.00	0	0
T Walker	LF	2.0	1	0	0	0	1.000	4.50	0	0
C Murray	LF	2.0	2	0	0	0	1.000	9.00	0	0
J Dubois	LF	2.0	0	0	0	0	.000	0.00	0	0
B Grieve	LF	1.0	1	0	0	0	1.000	9.00	0	0
C Patterson	CF	1367.0	324	8	0	1	.997	2.19	10	0
T Goodwin	CF	59.7	14	0	0	0	1.000	2.11	0	0
J Macias	CF	30.0	4	0	0	0	1.000	1.20	0	0
C Murray	CF	8.0	5	0	0	0	1.000	5.63	0	0
S Sosa	RF	1097.0	238	5	0	4	.984	1.99	3	0
T Hollandswo	RF	232.3	54	2	0	0	1.000	2.17	0	0
J Macias	RF	72.3	21	2	0	0	1.000	2.86	0	0
T Goodwin	RF	25.7	4	0	0	0	1.000	1.40	0	0
J Dubois	RF	20.0	5	0	0	0	1.000	2.25	0	0
B Grieve	RF	12.7	2	0	0	0	1.000	1.42	0	0
D Kelton	RF	2.7	0	0	0	0	.000	0.00	0	0
C Murray	RF	2.0	0	0	0	0	.000	0.00	0	0

Cincinnati Reds

Ten Game Average Wins and Runs
The gray area represents a running total
of wins per ten games played

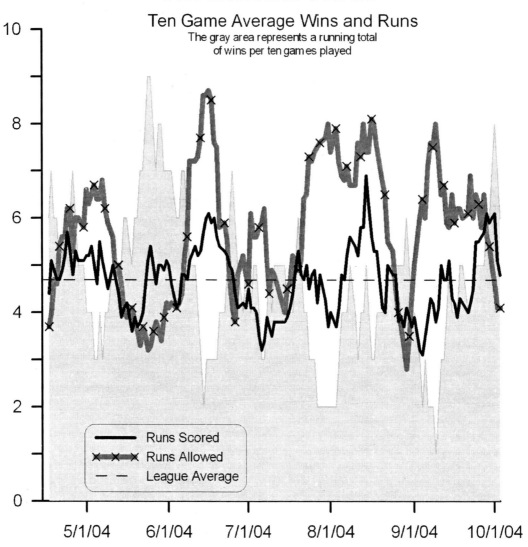

Runs Scored
Runs Allowed
League Average

6/1: Kearns' last game
before thumb surgery;
returns 8/24

6/2: Graves records
26th save. Team only
gets 21 more

6/10: At 34-25, Reds
have best record in
NL; go 42-61 after
(3rd-worst in NL)

7/11: Griffey on DL;
plays just three
more games

7/24: Larkin's final games as
regular SS for the Reds

9/30: Dunn breaks
record with190th K;
finishes with 195

Team Batting and Pitching/Fielding Stats by Month						
	April	**May**	**June**	**July**	**Aug**	**Sept**
Wins	12	19	11	9	11	14
Losses	11	10	15	17	16	17
OBP	.351	.337	.330	.320	.327	.323
SLG	.408	.423	.430	.400	.442	.404
FIP	4.89	4.39	5.22	5.17	5.53	5.61
DER	.682	.731	.693	.693	.709	.710

Batting Stats

Player	RC	Runs	RBI	PA	Outs	H	BB	HR	TB	BA	OBP	SLG	GPA	ISO	SB	CS	GDP
Dunn A.	115	105	102	681	426	151	108	46	323	.266	.388	.569	.317	.303	6	1	8
Casey S.	109	101	99	633	400	185	46	24	305	.324	.381	.534	.305	.210	2	0	14
Jimenez D.	89	76	67	652	433	152	82	12	222	.270	.364	.394	.262	.124	13	7	15
Freel R.	75	74	28	592	382	140	67	3	186	.277	.375	.368	.261	.091	37	10	7
Griffey Jr.	60	49	60	348	231	76	44	20	154	.253	.351	.513	.286	.260	1	0	7
Pena W.	58	45	66	364	257	87	22	26	177	.259	.316	.527	.274	.268	5	2	6
LaRue J.	56	46	55	445	299	98	26	14	168	.251	.334	.431	.258	.179	0	2	5
Larkin B.	47	55	44	386	258	100	34	8	145	.289	.352	.419	.263	.130	2	0	12
Lopez F.	35	35	31	295	202	64	25	7	107	.242	.314	.405	.243	.163	1	1	1
Castro J.	28	36	26	316	235	73	14	5	113	.244	.277	.378	.219	.134	1	0	9
Kearns A.	28	28	32	246	176	50	28	9	91	.230	.321	.419	.249	.189	2	1	8
Valentin J.	21	18	20	222	159	47	17	6	77	.233	.293	.381	.227	.149	0	0	4
Cruz J.	21	22	28	167	119	33	16	3	50	.224	.317	.340	.228	.116	0	0	5
Larson B.	12	13	14	135	95	25	14	3	40	.212	.304	.339	.221	.127	1	0	2
Hummel T.	8	10	7	125	87	24	8	1	31	.218	.281	.282	.197	.064	1	0	1
Machado A.	8	6	4	66	42	15	10	0	22	.268	.379	.393	.269	.125	3	1	0
Bragg D.	7	11	9	103	78	18	8	4	35	.191	.255	.372	.208	.181	1	0	2
Vander Wal J	3	2	4	55	45	6	4	2	14	.118	.182	.275	.150	.157	0	0	0
Romano J.	2	3	3	29	22	4	2	1	7	.154	.214	.269	.164	.115	0	0	0
Clark J.	2	4	2	34	26	4	1	0	5	.133	.212	.167	.137	.033	1	0	0
Van Poppel	1	1	1	23	14	3	1	0	3	.176	.222	.176	.144	.000	0	0	0
Lidle C.	1	2	2	51	36	6	5	0	8	.143	.234	.190	.153	.048	0	0	0
Hancock J.	1	1	1	19	13	2	3	0	2	.133	.278	.133	.158	.000	0	0	0
Hudson L.	1	1	2	18	14	2	1	0	2	.125	.167	.125	.106	.000	0	0	0
Olmedo R.	0	0	0	2	1	0	1	0	0	.000	.500	.000	.225	.000	0	0	0
Valentine J.	0	0	0	1	1	0	0	0	0	.000	.000	.000	.000	.000	0	0	0
Riedling J.	0	0	0	3	3	0	0	0	0	.000	.000	.000	.000	.000	0	0	0
Sanchez J.	0	0	0	5	4	0	0	0	0	.000	.000	.000	.000	.000	0	0	0
Bong J.	0	0	0	4	4	0	0	0	0	.000	.000	.000	.000	.000	0	0	0
Haynes J.	0	0	0	4	4	0	0	0	0	.000	.000	.000	.000	.000	0	0	0
Claussen B.	-1	1	0	22	17	2	1	0	2	.105	.150	.105	.094	.000	0	0	0
Wilson P.	-1	2	2	70	54	6	2	0	8	.100	.143	.133	.098	.033	0	0	0
Miller C.	-2	2	3	49	41	1	6	0	1	.026	.204	.026	.098	.000	0	0	3
Acevedo J.	-3	0	1	52	42	2	3	0	2	.047	.106	.047	.060	.000	0	0	1
Harang A.	-5	1	0	61	54	4	0	0	5	.070	.070	.088	.054	.018	0	0	1

Pitching Stats

Player	IP	BFP	G	GS	P/PA	H	K	BB	HR	W	L	Sv	Op	Hld	RA	ERA	FIP	DER
Wilson P.	183.7	798	29	29	3.60	192	117	63	26	11	6	0	0	0	4.56	4.36	4.80	.716
Harang A.	161.0	711	28	28	3.84	177	125	53	26	10	9	0	0	0	5.03	4.86	4.70	.699
Acevedo J.	157.7	704	39	27	3.59	188	117	45	30	5	12	0	0	2	6.16	5.94	5.02	.688
Lidle C.	149.0	656	24	24	3.45	170	93	44	24	7	10	0	0	0	5.74	5.32	4.91	.702
Van Poppel	115.3	502	48	11	3.78	136	72	32	22	4	6	0	1	2	6.24	6.09	5.22	.694
Riedling J.	77.7	365	70	0	3.59	90	46	40	10	5	3	0	7	14	6.26	5.10	5.27	.698
Graves D.	68.3	290	68	0	3.33	77	40	13	12	1	6	41	50	0	5.14	3.95	4.85	.709
Claussen B	66.0	313	14	14	4.02	80	45	35	9	2	8	0	0	0	6.82	6.14	5.17	.680
Norton P.	65.7	296	69	0	3.61	71	48	38	5	2	5	0	2	9	5.62	5.07	4.43	.675
Jones T.	57.0	235	51	0	3.97	49	37	25	4	8	2	1	6	22	3.95	3.79	4.06	.732
Hancock J.	54.7	251	12	9	3.66	60	31	25	14	5	1	0	0	0	5.60	4.45	6.70	.744
Wagner R.	51.7	242	49	0	3.72	59	37	27	7	3	2	0	3	8	5.40	4.70	5.09	.692
Hudson L.	48.3	204	9	9	4.09	36	38	25	3	4	2	0	0	0	2.98	2.42	3.99	.757
White G.	39.0	161	40	0	3.73	39	33	5	12	1	2	1	3	9	6.23	6.23	5.77	.757
Matthews	30.0	137	35	0	3.82	31	15	16	7	2	1	0	0	5	6.60	6.30	6.91	.753
Valentine J	29.3	136	24	1	3.93	23	29	25	4	2	3	4	4	5	5.52	5.22	5.63	.750
Reith B.	26.0	128	22	0	3.94	30	24	19	5	2	2	0	1	4	7.27	7.27	6.27	.675
Bong J.	15.3	75	3	3	3.85	17	11	10	3	1	1	0	0	0	7.63	4.70	6.14	.725
Haynes J.	15.0	79	5	4	3.71	26	8	7	3	0	3	0	0	0	10.20	9.60	6.41	.610
Sanchez J.	14.3	68	3	3	3.97	18	8	9	4	0	2	0	0	0	7.53	7.53	7.47	.702
Padilla J.	14.3	74	12	0	3.38	23	12	8	6	1	0	0	0	0	10.67	10.67	8.73	.638
Myette A.	4.3	26	5	0	4.46	3	6	8	0	0	0	0	0	0	8.31	8.31	7.23	.700

Fielding Stats

Catchers

Name	Innings	SBA/G	CS%	ERA	WP+PB/G
LaRue	930.0	0.52	30%	4.95	0.542
Valentin	409.7	0.86	31%	5.51	0.571
Miller	104.0	0.26	33%	6.32	0.692

Infielders and Outfielders

Name	POS	Inn	PO	A	TE	FE	FPct	RF	DPS	DPT
S Casey	1B	1245.0	1234	56	3	4	.994	9.33	11	1
A Dunn	1B	58.7	76	4	0	0	1.000	12.27	0	0
T Hummel	1B	50.7	43	8	0	0	1.000	9.06	2	0
J Valentin	1B	37.0	37	1	0	0	1.000	9.24	0	0
J Castro	1B	28.0	27	2	0	0	1.000	9.32	0	0
J Cruz	1B	16.0	10	1	0	0	1.000	6.19	1	0
J Vander Wal	1B	7.7	8	0	0	0	1.000	9.39	0	0
D Jimenez	2B	1263.0	298	388	3	4	.990	4.89	24	45

Cincinnati Reds

Name	POS	Inn	PO	A	TE	FE	FPct	RF	DPS	DPT
R Freel	2B	92.3	25	23	0	0	1.000	4.68	0	3
J Castro	2B	67.3	15	28	1	0	.977	5.75	3	3
J Clark	2B	13.0	4	3	0	0	1.000	4.85	0	1
F Lopez	2B	5.0	1	1	0	1	.667	3.60	0	1
T Hummel	2B	3.0	1	0	0	0	1.000	3.00	0	0
B Larkin	SS	684.3	105	216	2	2	.988	4.22	19	12
F Lopez	SS	391.0	65	137	6	3	.957	4.65	13	13
J Castro	SS	190.3	32	72	0	2	.981	4.92	8	8
A Machado	SS	149.0	23	36	4	0	.937	3.56	2	4
D Jimenez	SS	19.0	7	7	0	0	1.000	6.63	1	0
R Olmedo	SS	9.0	4	4	0	0	1.000	8.00	1	0
T Hummel	SS	1.0	0	0	0	0	.000	0.00	0	0
R Freel	3B	392.3	42	107	7	5	.925	3.42	12	2
J Castro	3B	378.7	38	75	4	1	.958	2.69	6	0
B Larson	3B	272.3	24	50	3	2	.937	2.45	5	1
F Lopez	3B	207.7	24	50	3	2	.937	3.21	2	0
T Hummel	3B	192.7	17	47	1	3	.941	2.99	6	0
A Dunn	LF	1327.0	250	10	1	7	.970	1.76	2	0
R Freel	LF	85.3	29	1	0	0	1.000	3.16	0	0
J Cruz	LF	12.7	1	0	0	0	1.000	0.71	0	0
D Bragg	LF	9.3	1	0	0	0	1.000	0.96	0	0
J Clark	LF	9.0	1	0	0	0	1.000	1.00	0	0
K Griffey Jr	CF	656.3	173	4	0	1	.994	2.43	2	0
W Pena	CF	378.3	143	4	0	3	.980	3.50	1	0
R Freel	CF	271.3	76	4	0	1	.988	2.65	1	0
D Bragg	CF	108.7	43	0	0	1	.977	3.56	0	0
J Romano	CF	26.7	8	0	0	0	1.000	2.70	0	0
A Kearns	CF	1.3	0	0	0	0	.000	0.00	0	0
J Clark	CF	1.0	0	0	0	0	.000	0.00	0	0
A Kearns	RF	508.3	118	1	2	1	.975	2.11	0	0
W Pena	RF	339.7	69	1	0	3	.946	1.85	0	0
R Freel	RF	265.0	79	3	1	1	.976	2.78	3	0
J Cruz	RF	160.3	35	1	0	0	1.000	2.02	0	0
D Bragg	RF	71.0	17	2	0	0	1.000	2.41	0	0
J Vander Wal	RF	43.0	12	1	0	0	1.000	2.72	0	0
J Clark	RF	32.0	9	1	0	0	1.000	2.81	0	0
J Romano	RF	18.3	1	1	0	0	1.000	0.98	0	0
K Griffey Jr	RF	4.0	0	0	0	0	.000	0.00	0	0
J LaRue	RF	2.0	1	0	0	0	1.000	4.50	0	0

Colorado Rockies

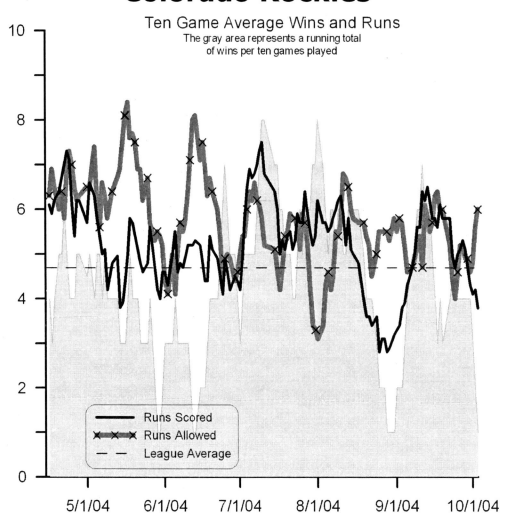

Ten Game Average Wins and Runs
The gray area represents a running total
of wins per ten games played

- —— Runs Scored
- ×—×—× Runs Allowed
- – – League Average

5/1/04   6/1/04   7/1/04   8/1/04   9/1/04   10/1/04

4/13: Wilson on DL with knee surgery; will miss over two months

5/5: Kennedy goes 4-0, will finish 9-7 with 3.66 ERA

5/31: Miles brought back up; hits .395 in June

6/21: Walker comes off DL; plays for first time; 1.104 OPS with Rockies

8/6: After refusing trade to Rangers, Walker is sent to Cardinals for MinL and 2 PTBNL

8/25: Francis brought up to majors

Team Batting and Pitching/Fielding Stats by Month						
	April	**May**	**June**	**July**	**Aug**	**Sept**
Wins	10	10	8	18	9	13
Losses	13	18	18	8	18	18
OBP	.361	.332	.331	.370	.331	.348
SLG	.503	.437	.410	.509	.443	.436
FIP	5.65	4.85	5.44	5.10	5.30	4.64
DER	.715	.672	.680	.703	.681	.689

Batting Stats

Player	RC	Runs	RBI	PA	Outs	H	BB	HR	TB	BA	OBP	SLG	GPA	ISO	SB	CS	GDP
Helton T.	121	115	96	683	369	190	127	32	339	.347	.469	.620	.366	.272	3	0	12
Burnitz J.	84	94	110	607	401	153	58	37	302	.283	.356	.558	.300	.275	5	6	7
Castilla V.	77	93	131	648	445	158	51	35	312	.271	.332	.535	.283	.264	0	0	20
Clayton R.	62	95	54	652	431	160	48	8	228	.279	.338	.397	.251	.118	10	5	12
Miles A.	56	75	47	566	388	153	29	6	192	.293	.329	.368	.240	.075	12	7	12
Holliday M.	52	65	57	439	297	116	31	14	195	.290	.349	.488	.279	.198	3	3	10
Johnson C.	40	42	47	362	239	72	49	13	131	.236	.350	.430	.265	.193	2	1	5
Gonzalez L.	38	42	40	351	238	94	15	12	151	.292	.330	.469	.266	.177	1	5	5
Sweeney M.	30	25	40	215	132	47	32	9	90	.266	.377	.508	.297	.243	1	0	2
Greene T.	24	23	35	209	149	55	13	10	99	.282	.325	.508	.273	.226	0	0	9
Walker L.	22	22	20	138	75	35	25	6	68	.324	.464	.630	.366	.306	2	0	2
Wilson P.	17	24	29	222	161	50	17	6	79	.248	.315	.391	.240	.144	2	1	8
Closser J.	12	5	10	124	80	36	6	1	45	.319	.364	.398	.263	.080	0	0	3
Barmes C.	10	14	10	77	54	20	3	2	31	.282	.320	.437	.253	.155	0	1	2
Piedra J.	9	15	10	98	66	27	5	3	44	.297	.340	.484	.274	.187	0	1	1
Pellow K.	9	15	10	133	94	29	8	2	42	.240	.308	.347	.225	.107	1	0	2
Hawpe B.	9	12	9	118	84	26	11	3	42	.248	.322	.400	.245	.152	1	1	4
Atkins G.	7	3	8	33	18	10	4	1	15	.357	.424	.536	.325	.179	0	0	0
Freeman C.	6	15	11	105	79	17	14	1	27	.189	.298	.300	.209	.111	1	1	5
Jennings J.	5	3	6	78	55	17	2	1	24	.239	.260	.338	.202	.099	0	0	1
Estes S.	4	13	2	80	55	17	1	0	22	.236	.247	.306	.187	.069	0	0	0
Hocking D.	4	7	4	106	79	19	7	0	21	.202	.257	.223	.172	.021	0	1	3
Fassero J.	2	3	1	24	17	4	1	0	4	.190	.227	.190	.150	.000	0	0	0
Kennedy J.	2	2	4	54	42	6	2	0	9	.125	.160	.188	.119	.063	0	0	0
Tracy A.	1	1	1	17	13	3	1	0	4	.188	.235	.250	.168	.063	0	0	0
Elarton S.	0	1	0	14	7	2	1	0	2	.222	.300	.222	.191	.000	0	0	0
Dohmann S.	0	0	0	3	1	0	0	0	0	.000	.500	.000	.225	.000	0	0	0
Reed S.	0	0	0	2	1	1	0	0	1	.500	.500	.500	.350	.000	0	0	0
Young J.	0	0	1	5	2	0	0	0	0	.000	.000	.000	.000	.000	0	0	0
Simpson A.	0	0	0	1	1	0	0	0	0	.000	.000	.000	.000	.000	0	0	0
Gissell C.	0	0	0	1	1	0	0	0	0	.000	.000	.000	.000	.000	0	0	0
Driskill T.	0	0	0	1	1	0	0	0	0	.000	.000	.000	.000	.000	0	0	0
Lopez J.	0	0	0	3	2	0	0	0	0	.000	.000	.000	.000	.000	0	0	0
Reyes R.	0	5	1	66	52	9	5	0	11	.148	.212	.180	.141	.033	0	0	0
Harikkala T.	0	0	0	4	3	0	0	0	0	.000	.000	.000	.000	.000	0	0	0
Bernero A.	0	1	0	6	5	0	0	0	0	.000	.000	.000	.000	.000	0	0	0
Stark D.	0	0	0	9	8	0	1	0	0	.000	.111	.000	.050	.000	0	0	0
Wendell T.	0	0	0	2	3	0	0	0	0	.000	.000	.000	.000	.000	0	0	1
Francis J.	-1	1	0	14	10	0	0	0	0	.000	.000	.000	.000	.000	0	0	0
Wright J.	-1	1	0	27	18	1	0	0	2	.053	.053	.105	.050	.053	0	0	0
Cook A.	-1	1	1	37	31	4	1	0	4	.118	.143	.118	.094	.000	0	0	1

Pitching Stats

Player	IP	BFP	G	GS	P/PA	H	K	BB	HR	W	L	Sv	Op	Hld	RA	ERA	FIP	DER
Estes S.	202.0	904	34	34	3.73	223	117	105	30	15	8	0	0	0	5.93	5.84	5.57	.699
Jennings	201.0	925	33	33	3.61	241	133	101	27	11	11	0	0	0	5.60	5.51	5.11	.674
Kennedy	162.3	705	27	27	3.56	163	117	67	17	9	7	0	0	0	3.77	3.66	4.38	.706
Fassero J	111.0	505	40	12	3.48	136	59	44	9	3	8	0	0	2	5.92	5.51	4.37	.674
Cook A.	96.7	433	16	16	3.41	112	40	39	7	6	4	0	0	0	4.38	4.28	4.62	.691
Wright J.	78.7	361	14	14	3.81	82	41	45	8	2	3	0	0	0	4.46	4.12	5.30	.716
Reed S.	66.0	285	65	0	3.60	72	38	17	7	3	8	0	4	15	3.95	3.68	4.39	.699
Chacon S.	63.3	316	66	0	3.99	71	52	52	12	1	9	35	44	0	7.39	7.11	6.60	.697
Harikkala	62.7	262	55	0	4.03	55	30	23	10	6	6	0	7	15	4.88	4.74	5.34	.773
Dohmann	46.0	198	41	0	3.83	41	49	19	8	0	3	0	4	4	4.30	4.11	4.45	.730
Fuentes	44.7	201	47	0	4.00	46	48	19	5	2	4	0	1	13	6.04	5.64	3.93	.672
Elarton S.	41.3	199	8	8	3.85	57	23	20	8	0	6	0	0	0	9.80	9.80	5.93	.669
Lopez J.	40.7	187	64	0	3.65	45	20	26	1	1	2	0	1	12	7.52	7.52	4.55	.679
Simpson	39.0	183	32	0	4.01	44	46	20	4	2	1	0	1	1	6.00	5.08	3.90	.633
Francis J.	36.7	164	7	7	3.95	42	32	13	8	3	2	0	0	0	5.40	5.15	5.31	.691
Bernero	32.3	147	16	2	3.59	36	21	17	7	1	1	0	1	1	5.57	5.57	6.17	.716
Stark D.	26.0	150	6	6	3.54	53	10	18	9	0	5	0	0	0	14.88	11.42	8.88	.611
Nunez V.	25.7	114	22	0	3.93	26	22	14	6	3	3	0	3	3	7.71	7.01	6.15	.718
Wendell	16.7	80	12	0	4.16	21	11	12	4	0	0	0	1	0	7.02	7.02	7.40	.667
Tsao C.	9.3	37	10	0	3.65	7	11	1	2	0	0	1	2	1	3.86	3.86	3.83	.783
Gissell C.	8.7	48	5	1	3.98	20	11	3	4	0	1	0	0	0	14.54	14.54	7.58	.467
Driskill T.	8.3	39	5	0	3.95	13	6	3	0	0	0	0	1	0	6.48	6.48	2.72	.567
Young J.	8.3	45	2	2	3.84	15	7	5	3	0	1	0	0	0	12.96	12.96	7.88	.600
Kroon M.	6.0	32	6	0	4.31	7	3	10	1	0	0	0	0	0	6.00	6.00	9.24	.667
Jarvis K.	2.0	15	2	0	4.87	6	0	4	1	0	0	0	0	0	27.00	27.00	15.58	.500

Fielding Stats

Catchers

Name	Innings	SBA/G	CS%	ERA	WP+PB/G
Johnson	746.3	0.90	16%	5.68	0.374
Greene	421.0	0.66	6%	5.75	0.599
Closser	259.0	0.83	21%	4.90	0.764
Pellow	9.0	0.00	0%	2.00	0.000

Infielders and Outfielders

Name	POS	Inn	PO	A	TE	FE	FPct	RF	DPS	DPT
T Helton	1B	1320.0	1355	142	3	1	.997	10.21	18	2
M Sweeney	1B	71.7	68	5	0	0	1.000	9.17	0	0
K Pellow	1B	26.0	26	3	0	1	.967	10.04	0	0
G Atkins	1B	17.0	22	1	0	0	1.000	12.18	0	0
A Miles	2B	1029.0	275	353	6	4	.984	5.49	33	40

Colorado Rockies

Name	POS	Inn	PO	A	TE	FE	FPct	RF	DPS	DPT
L Gonzalez	2B	293.0	84	96	0	1	.994	5.53	4	20
C Barmes	2B	65.3	19	27	1	0	.979	6.34	3	3
D Hocking	2B	48.0	13	16	0	0	1.000	5.44	2	1
R Clayton	SS	1241.0	213	416	5	4	.986	4.56	44	39
C Barmes	SS	76.0	17	36	1	0	.981	6.28	3	3
L Gonzalez	SS	61.0	9	18	0	0	1.000	3.98	2	2
D Hocking	SS	57.3	13	25	2	1	.927	5.97	2	2
V Castilla	3B	1286.0	125	315	2	4	.987	3.08	25	0
L Gonzalez	3B	99.0	13	21	0	1	.971	3.09	1	0
G Atkins	3B	27.0	2	4	0	0	1.000	2.00	1	0
K Pellow	3B	13.3	2	1	0	0	1.000	2.03	0	0
A Tracy	3B	6.0	0	1	0	0	1.000	1.50	0	0
D Hocking	3B	3.3	1	0	0	0	1.000	2.70	0	0
M Holliday	LF	917.0	177	4	3	3	.963	1.78	2	0
J Burnitz	LF	151.7	36	0	1	0	.973	2.14	0	0
L Gonzalez	LF	110.3	20	0	0	0	1.000	1.63	0	0
J Piedra	LF	79.3	12	0	0	0	1.000	1.36	0	0
M Sweeney	LF	53.3	13	1	0	0	1.000	2.36	0	0
D Hocking	LF	52.3	19	0	0	1	.950	3.27	0	0
K Pellow	LF	47.0	8	0	0	0	1.000	1.53	0	0
G Atkins	LF	14.0	5	0	0	0	1.000	3.21	0	0
B Hawpe	LF	9.3	2	0	0	0	1.000	1.93	0	0
R Reyes	LF	1.0	1	0	0	0	1.000	9.00	0	0
J Burnitz	CF	517.0	114	3	1	2	.975	2.04	0	0
P Wilson	CF	436.0	118	3	0	6	.953	2.50	1	0
C Freeman	CF	245.0	69	1	0	1	.986	2.57	0	0
J Piedra	CF	103.7	32	1	0	0	1.000	2.86	2	0
R Reyes	CF	96.3	25	0	0	0	1.000	2.34	0	0
D Hocking	CF	37.3	16	0	0	0	1.000	3.86	0	0
J Burnitz	RF	528.3	105	6	0	3	.974	1.89	2	0
L Walker	RF	265.7	63	4	0	0	1.000	2.27	1	0
B Hawpe	RF	233.0	52	1	0	1	.981	2.05	2	0
K Pellow	RF	145.0	20	2	0	0	1.000	1.37	1	0
M Sweeney	RF	118.3	29	2	0	0	1.000	2.36	1	0
L Gonzalez	RF	75.7	13	0	0	0	1.000	1.55	0	0
R Reyes	RF	35.0	5	1	0	0	1.000	1.54	1	0
J Piedra	RF	23.7	5	0	0	0	1.000	1.90	0	0
D Hocking	RF	10.7	4	0	0	0	1.000	3.38	0	0

Florida Marlins

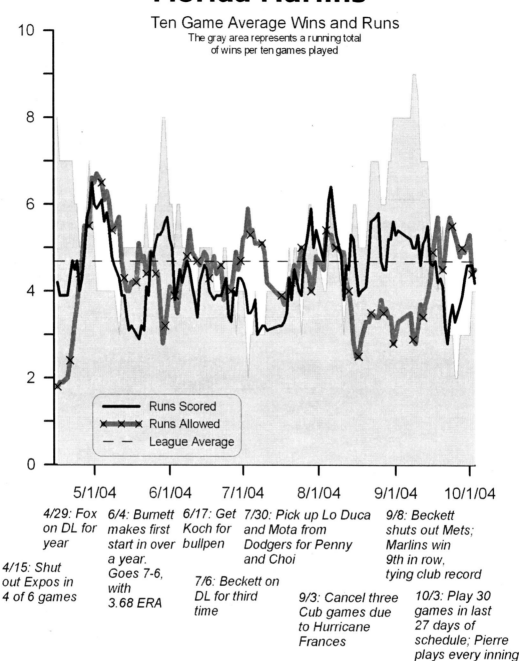

Ten Game Average Wins and Runs
The gray area represents a running total
of wins per ten games played

4/29: Fox on DL for year

4/15: Shut out Expos in 4 of 6 games

6/4: Burnett makes first start in over a year. Goes 7-6, with 3.68 ERA

6/17: Get Koch for bullpen

7/30: Pick up Lo Duca and Mota from Dodgers for Penny and Choi

7/6: Beckett on DL for third time

9/3: Cancel three Cub games due to Hurricane Frances

9/8: Beckett shuts out Mets; Marlins win 9th in row, tying club record

10/3: Play 30 games in last 27 days of schedule; Pierre plays every inning of season in CF

Team Batting and Pitching/Fielding Stats by Month						
	April	May	June	July	Aug	Sept
Wins	15	15	11	11	16	15
Losses	9	13	16	14	10	17
OBP	.328	.335	.316	.343	.338	.320
SLG	.443	.411	.386	.407	.401	.396
FIP	4.14	4.62	3.98	3.87	4.01	4.55
DER	.725	.724	.693	.689	.738	.706

Batting Stats

Player	RC	Runs	RBI	PA	Outs	H	BB	HR	TB	BA	OBP	SLG	GPA	ISO	SB	CS	GDP
Lowell M.	103	87	85	671	439	175	64	27	302	.293	.365	.505	.291	.212	5	1	15
Pierre J.	102	100	49	748	488	221	45	3	276	.326	.374	.407	.270	.081	45	24	7
Cabrera M.	97	101	112	685	448	177	68	33	309	.294	.366	.512	.293	.219	5	2	20
Castillo L.	84	91	47	649	418	164	75	2	196	.291	.373	.348	.255	.057	21	4	14
Conine J.	82	55	83	579	394	146	48	14	225	.280	.340	.432	.261	.152	5	5	14
Gonzalez A.	63	67	79	599	447	130	27	23	235	.232	.270	.419	.226	.187	3	1	15
Choi H.	58	48	40	340	207	76	52	15	139	.270	.388	.495	.298	.224	1	0	2
Easley D.	37	26	43	257	177	53	24	9	102	.238	.331	.457	.263	.220	4	1	6
Lo Duca P.	28	27	31	213	145	48	14	3	70	.258	.314	.376	.235	.118	2	1	6
Redmond M.	28	19	25	273	193	63	14	2	84	.256	.315	.341	.227	.085	1	0	10
Encarnacion	24	21	19	182	124	38	17	3	61	.238	.320	.381	.240	.144	2	1	1
Mordecai M.	9	7	5	90	67	19	6	1	25	.226	.278	.298	.199	.071	0	1	1
Castro R.	5	9	8	108	84	13	11	3	25	.135	.231	.260	.169	.125	0	0	1
Treanor M.	4	7	1	61	44	13	4	0	15	.236	.311	.273	.208	.036	0	0	2
Harris L.	4	7	17	99	76	20	3	1	28	.211	.232	.295	.178	.084	0	0	1
Aguila C.	4	10	5	48	35	10	2	3	23	.222	.255	.511	.243	.289	0	0	0
Willis D.	4	5	3	84	61	15	4	1	22	.203	.244	.297	.184	.095	0	0	2
Cordero W.	4	6	6	72	55	13	3	1	19	.197	.250	.288	.184	.091	1	0	2
Pavano C.	3	4	6	79	56	13	1	2	22	.191	.214	.324	.177	.132	0	0	1
Nunez A.	3	9	5	75	58	11	9	1	17	.172	.274	.266	.190	.094	1	2	3
Mota G.	2	1	1	6	4	2	0	0	3	.333	.333	.500	.275	.167	0	0	0
Willingham J	1	2	1	29	21	5	4	1	8	.200	.310	.320	.220	.120	0	0	1
Beckett J.	1	2	2	55	37	7	2	0	8	.159	.196	.182	.133	.023	0	0	0
Sutton L.	1	0	1	6	4	1	1	0	1	.200	.333	.200	.200	.000	0	0	0
Valdez I.	1	2	0	18	13	4	1	0	5	.235	.278	.294	.199	.059	0	0	0
Burnett A.	0	4	1	37	26	4	0	0	4	.138	.138	.138	.097	.000	0	0	1
Oliver D.	0	0	1	21	18	3	0	0	3	.158	.158	.158	.111	.000	0	0	2
Benitez A.	0	0	0	1	1	0	0	0	0	.000	.000	.000	.000	.000	0	0	0
Manzanillo J	0	0	0	1	1	0	0	0	0	.000	.000	.000	.000	.000	0	0	0
Kensing L.	0	0	0	3	2	0	0	0	0	.000	.000	.000	.000	.000	0	0	0
Small A.	0	0	0	2	2	0	0	0	0	.000	.000	.000	.000	.000	0	0	0
Wayne J.	0	0	0	4	3	0	0	0	0	.000	.000	.000	.000	.000	0	0	0
Howard B.	0	0	0	3	3	0	0	0	0	.000	.000	.000	.000	.000	0	0	0
Weathers D.	0	0	0	3	3	0	0	0	0	.000	.000	.000	.000	.000	0	0	0
Bump N.	-1	0	0	5	5	0	0	0	0	.000	.000	.000	.000	.000	0	0	0
Phelps T.	-1	0	0	6	6	0	0	0	0	.000	.000	.000	.000	.000	0	0	0
Penny B.	-3	1	1	48	45	3	0	0	3	.064	.064	.064	.045	.000	0	0	1

Pitching Stats

Player	IP	BFP	G	GS	P/PA	H	K	BB	HR	W	L	Sv	Op	Hld	RA	ERA	FIP	DER
Pavano C.	222.3	909	31	31	3.47	212	139	49	16	18	8	0	0	0	3.24	3.00	3.57	.718
Willis D.	197.0	848	32	32	3.68	210	139	61	20	10	11	0	0	0	4.52	4.02	4.04	.694
Beckett J.	156.7	654	26	26	3.75	137	152	54	16	9	9	0	0	0	4.14	3.79	3.61	.716
Penny B.	131.3	545	21	21	3.85	124	105	39	10	8	8	0	0	0	3.43	3.15	3.43	.706
Burnett A.	120.0	490	20	19	3.71	102	113	38	9	7	6	0	0	0	3.75	3.68	3.22	.715
Bump N.	73.7	329	50	2	3.67	86	44	32	7	2	4	1	4	5	5.62	5.01	4.54	.675
Benitez A.	69.7	262	64	0	3.92	36	62	21	6	2	2	47	51	0	1.42	1.29	3.32	.827
Oliver D.	58.7	260	18	8	3.48	74	33	17	13	2	3	0	0	0	6.75	6.44	5.75	.689
Valdez I.	56.0	242	11	11	3.67	61	30	18	12	5	3	0	0	0	4.82	4.50	5.76	.731
Perisho M.	47.0	212	66	0	3.86	45	42	26	6	5	3	0	2	10	4.40	4.40	4.74	.713
Howard B.	37.7	167	31	0	3.76	37	33	21	6	1	1	0	0	3	5.50	5.50	5.15	.708
Phelps T.	34.0	144	19	4	3.77	34	28	12	6	1	1	0	0	4	5.29	4.76	4.78	.714
Mota G.	33.7	134	26	0	4.02	24	33	10	4	1	4	3	7	13	4.81	4.81	3.73	.765
Wayne J.	32.7	148	19	1	3.91	35	20	18	6	3	3	0	2	1	6.61	5.79	6.08	.716
Manzanillo	32.3	151	26	0	3.87	38	27	15	6	3	3	1	4	2	6.68	6.12	5.49	.680
Koch B.	25.7	115	23	0	3.94	21	25	20	3	1	2	0	0	3	3.51	3.51	4.99	.731
Seanez R.	23.0	93	23	0	4.10	18	25	8	3	3	1	0	1	3	2.74	2.74	3.64	.737
Borland T.	18.3	86	18	0	3.90	18	18	12	2	1	1	0	1	3	5.40	5.40	5.20	.717
Weathers	16.7	64	8	2	3.70	13	10	7	2	1	0	0	0	1	2.70	2.70	4.70	.756
Small A.	16.3	78	7	0	3.36	24	8	7	5	0	0	0	0	1	8.27	8.27	7.36	.672
Kensing L.	13.7	66	5	3	3.85	19	7	9	5	0	3	0	0	0	9.88	9.88	9.00	.682
Fox C.	10.7	49	12	0	4.47	9	17	8	1	0	1	0	2	5	6.75	6.75	3.64	.636
Tejera M.	4.0	23	2	2	4.26	6	3	6	0	0	1	0	0	0	18.00	18.00	6.83	.538
Neu M.	4.0	18	1	0	3.22	5	2	2	1	0	0	0	0	0	4.50	4.50	6.83	.692
Gracesqui	4.0	23	7	0	3.52	6	1	3	0	0	1	1	1	0	11.25	11.25	6.33	.647

Fielding Stats

Catchers

Name	Innings	SBA/G	CS%	ERA	WP+PB/G
Redmond	604.3	0.92	18%	4.59	0.283
Lo Duca	413.0	1.13	25%	3.64	0.305
Castro	243.0	0.52	36%	3.56	0.259
Treanor	147.7	0.85	21%	4.39	0.244
Willingham	23.0	1.57	0%	3.13	0.783
Mordecai	8.0	4.50	0%	4.50	0.000

Infielders and Outfielders

Name	POS	Inn	PO	A	TE	FE	FPct	RF	DPS	DPT
H Choi	1B	712.7	719	41	0	5	.990	9.60	9	1
J Conine	1B	489.3	475	48	3	1	.992	9.62	5	1

Florida Marlins

Name	POS	Inn	PO	A	TE	FE	FPct	RF	DPS	DPT
D Easley	1B	138.0	121	8	1	1	.985	8.41	3	0
W Cordero	1B	97.0	105	4	0	1	.991	10.11	0	0
L Sutton	1B	2.0	1	0	0	0	1.000	4.50	0	0
L Castillo	2B	1274.0	273	404	2	4	.991	4.78	39	53
D Easley	2B	158.3	28	53	1	2	.964	4.60	5	5
M Mordecai	2B	6.3	2	2	1	0	.800	5.68	0	0
A Gonzalez	SS	1351.0	225	425	8	8	.976	4.33	47	48
D Easley	SS	65.3	6	24	1	0	.968	4.13	2	2
M Mordecai	SS	22.0	5	8	0	0	1.000	5.32	2	2
M Lowell	3B	1326.0	117	272	2	5	.982	2.64	25	2
M Mordecai	3B	67.0	10	16	0	2	.929	3.49	2	0
D Easley	3B	42.0	4	11	0	0	1.000	3.21	0	0
L Harris	3B	4.0	0	0	0	0	.000	0.00	0	0
J Conine	LF	709.7	174	5	0	1	.994	2.27	4	0
M Cabrera	LF	504.0	92	6	1	1	.980	1.75	0	0
A Nunez	LF	123.3	28	0	0	0	1.000	2.04	0	0
L Harris	LF	43.0	9	0	0	0	1.000	1.88	0	0
J Willingham	LF	21.0	6	0	0	0	1.000	2.57	0	0
W Cordero	LF	19.0	5	0	0	0	1.000	2.37	0	0
C Aguila	LF	19.0	3	0	0	0	1.000	1.42	0	0
J Pierre	CF	1439.0	365	3	0	2	.995	2.30	2	0
M Cabrera	RF	856.0	170	6	0	7	.962	1.85	2	0
J Encarnacio	RF	398.7	96	2	2	0	.980	2.21	0	0
C Aguila	RF	70.0	16	1	1	1	.895	2.19	0	0
A Nunez	RF	61.0	15	0	0	0	1.000	2.21	0	0
D Easley	RF	32.0	10	0	0	1	.909	2.81	0	0
L Harris	RF	21.3	3	0	0	0	1.000	1.27	0	0

Houston Astros

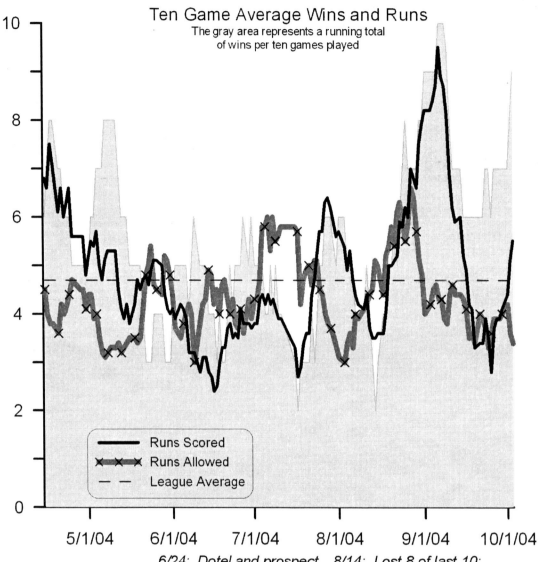

Ten Game Average Wins and Runs
The gray area represents a running total
of wins per ten games played

- Runs Scored
- Runs Allowed
- — League Average

6/24: Dotel and prospect
traded for Carlos Beltran

6/26: Miller on
DL; out for year

7/14: Garner replaces
Williams as manager

8/14: Lost 8 of last 10;
will go 36-10 the rest of
the way

8/18: Pettitte out for
season; pitched only
83 innings

Team Batting and Pitching/Fielding Stats by Month						
	April	**May**	**June**	**July**	**Aug**	**Sept**
Wins	14	14	12	12	17	23
Losses	9	14	15	14	11	7
OBP	.365	.343	.324	.329	.358	.334
SLG	.465	.425	.378	.429	.462	.458
FIP	4.07	4.01	3.83	4.50	4.53	3.59
DER	.723	.713	.683	.715	.689	.689

Batting Stats

Player	RC	Runs	RBI	PA	Outs	H	BB	HR	TB	BA	OBP	SLG	GPA	ISO	SB	CS	GDP
Berkman L.	110	92	92	602	341	147	118	27	269	.312	.455	.571	.348	.259	6	7	10
Bagwell J.	94	93	75	588	369	134	85	24	235	.272	.386	.477	.293	.205	4	4	6
Biggio C.	78	90	55	614	405	160	36	21	265	.288	.347	.477	.275	.189	7	2	7
Kent J.	74	83	90	530	354	135	43	21	242	.285	.343	.512	.282	.226	6	1	15
Beltran C.	55	59	50	307	188	68	44	23	157	.269	.384	.621	.328	.352	22	0	3
Ensberg M.	50	45	57	410	281	101	33	8	150	.274	.331	.408	.251	.133	6	3	11
Everett A.	49	65	31	435	285	105	17	8	148	.273	.317	.385	.239	.112	13	2	4
Lamb M.	48	34	56	261	165	72	25	12	127	.309	.372	.545	.304	.236	1	1	3
Vizcaino J.	32	31	30	317	215	83	18	3	116	.284	.324	.397	.245	.113	0	1	5
Ausmus B.	30	34	31	402	284	92	30	5	123	.255	.313	.341	.226	.086	2	2	13
Hidalgo R.	22	21	30	220	156	51	17	4	82	.256	.309	.412	.242	.156	1	2	6
Lane J.	17	18	15	144	97	29	15	3	49	.232	.315	.392	.240	.160	1	0	1
Palmeiro O.	17	19	12	146	96	30	17	3	44	.242	.347	.355	.245	.113	1	1	1
Chavez R.	8	7	16	150	115	28	10	0	35	.204	.259	.255	.180	.051	0	1	5
Bruntlett E.	7	9	7	52	34	10	6	3	20	.227	.308	.455	.252	.227	2	0	0
Backe B.	4	2	4	12	6	3	1	1	6	.333	.400	.667	.347	.333	0	0	0
Oswalt R.	3	0	6	77	52	9	3	0	10	.150	.200	.167	.132	.017	0	0	1
Clemens R.	3	1	7	67	51	11	3	0	11	.180	.219	.180	.144	.000	0	0	1
Pettitte A.	2	0	2	29	19	4	3	0	5	.174	.269	.217	.176	.043	0	0	0
Miller W.	2	2	3	35	20	7	0	0	7	.259	.259	.259	.181	.000	0	0	0
Hernandez C.	1	0	1	12	7	1	0	0	1	.125	.125	.125	.088	.000	0	0	0
Miceli D.	0	0	0	2	1	1	0	0	1	.500	.500	.500	.350	.000	0	0	0
Alfaro J.	0	1	0	2	1	1	0	0	1	.500	.500	.500	.350	.000	0	0	0
Griffiths J.	0	0	0	2	1	0	1	0	0	.000	.500	.000	.225	.000	0	0	0
Burke C.	0	2	0	12	9	0	3	0	0	.000	.250	.000	.113	.000	0	0	0
Duckworth B.	0	1	1	10	7	2	1	0	2	.222	.300	.222	.191	.000	0	0	0
Bullinger K.	0	0	0	4	3	0	1	0	0	.000	.250	.000	.113	.000	0	0	0
Lidge B.	0	0	0	1	1	0	0	0	0	.000	.000	.000	.000	.000	0	0	0
Gallo M.	0	0	0	1	1	0	0	0	0	.000	.000	.000	.000	.000	0	0	0
Harville C.	0	0	0	1	1	0	0	0	0	.000	.000	.000	.000	.000	0	0	0
Taveras W.	0	0	0	1	1	0	0	0	0	.000	.000	.000	.000	.000	0	0	0
Oliver D.	-1	0	0	4	4	0	0	0	0	.000	.000	.000	.000	.000	0	0	1
Munro P.	-1	3	1	31	24	2	2	0	2	.077	.138	.077	.081	.000	0	0	0
Redding T.	-2	1	0	30	25	4	0	0	4	.138	.138	.138	.097	.000	0	0	0

Pitching Stats

Player	IP	BFP	G	GS	P/PA	H	K	BB	HR	W	L	Sv	Op	Hld	RA	ERA	FIP	DER
Oswalt R.	237.0	983	36	35	3.65	233	206	62	17	20	10	0	0	0	3.80	3.49	3.19	.686
Clemens	214.3	878	33	33	3.91	169	218	79	15	18	4	0	0	0	3.19	2.98	3.14	.725
Redding T.	100.7	465	27	17	3.83	125	56	43	15	5	7	0	0	0	6.53	5.72	5.33	.682
Munro P.	99.7	446	21	19	3.75	120	63	26	12	4	7	0	0	0	5.33	5.15	4.46	.678
Lidge B.	94.7	369	80	0	4.00	57	157	30	8	6	5	29	33	17	2.00	1.90	2.00	.708
Miller W.	88.7	383	15	15	4.07	76	74	44	11	7	7	0	0	0	3.55	3.35	4.51	.744
Pettitte A.	83.0	346	15	15	3.90	71	79	31	8	6	4	0	0	0	4.01	3.90	3.55	.724
Miceli D.	77.7	336	74	0	3.96	74	83	27	10	6	6	2	8	24	3.94	3.59	3.73	.701
Backe B.	67.0	293	33	9	3.76	75	54	27	10	5	3	0	0	3	4.43	4.30	4.66	.677
Harville C.	53.0	238	56	0	3.82	54	46	26	8	3	2	0	4	3	5.94	4.75	4.89	.705
Gallo M.	49.3	223	69	0	3.59	55	34	20	12	2	0	0	1	4	4.93	4.74	6.44	.715
Hernandez	42.0	200	9	9	3.87	50	26	23	11	1	3	0	0	0	6.64	6.43	7.24	.711
Duckworth	39.3	180	19	6	3.96	55	23	13	11	1	2	0	0	0	6.86	6.86	6.53	.669
Dotel O.	34.7	146	32	0	4.25	27	50	15	4	0	4	14	17	0	3.89	3.12	3.08	.697
Qualls C.	33.0	141	25	0	3.66	34	24	8	3	4	0	1	2	9	3.55	3.55	3.89	.696
Weathers	32.0	137	26	0	3.78	31	26	13	5	1	4	0	3	5	5.63	4.78	4.98	.711
Bullinger K	30.7	140	27	0	3.56	36	11	10	5	1	0	1	2	1	6.46	6.16	5.55	.726
Stone R.	19.0	92	16	0	3.47	26	16	7	5	1	1	0	0	1	5.68	5.68	6.39	.656
Wheeler D	14.3	55	14	0	3.25	11	9	3	1	0	0	0	0	2	2.51	2.51	3.57	.756
Oliver D.	14.0	54	9	2	3.91	12	13	4	1	1	0	0	0	0	3.86	3.86	3.01	.694
Springer R	13.7	62	16	0	4.24	15	9	6	1	0	1	0	0	5	2.63	2.63	4.25	.689
Griffiths J.	4.3	20	1	1	3.90	4	5	3	1	0	0	0	0	0	10.38	10.38	5.85	.727
Fernandez	1.0	14	2	1	3.71	6	0	5	0	0	0	0	0	0	54.00	54.00	18.08	.333

Fielding Stats

Catchers

Name	Innings	SBA/G	CS%	ERA	WP+PB/G
Ausmus	1018.3	0.89	23%	4.08	0.274
Chavez	423.7	0.70	30%	3.97	0.382
Tremie	1.0	0.00	0%	9.00	0.000

Infielders and Outfielders

Name	POS	Inn	PO	A	TE	FE	FPct	RF	DPS	DPT
J Bagwell	1B	1328.0	1195	93	3	3	.995	8.73	8	0
M Lamb	1B	65.0	76	4	0	0	1.000	11.08	0	0
J Vizcaino	1B	32.3	42	3	0	0	1.000	12.53	0	0
J Lane	1B	13.0	13	1	0	1	.933	9.69	0	0
L Berkman	1B	4.0	5	1	0	0	1.000	13.50	0	0
J Kent	2B	1189.0	272	376	3	4	.989	4.90	23	50
J Vizcaino	2B	173.7	45	51	0	0	1.000	4.98	1	14

Houston Astros

Name	POS	Inn	PO	A	TE	FE	FPct	RF	DPS	DPT
M Lamb	2B	40.3	9	12	0	1	.955	4.69	0	0
C Burke	2B	25.7	7	14	0	0	1.000	7.36	1	2
E Bruntlett	2B	14.0	3	5	0	0	1.000	5.14	0	0
A Everett	SS	842.0	138	277	3	7	.976	4.44	30	23
J Vizcaino	SS	455.3	66	153	3	4	.969	4.33	15	9
E Bruntlett	SS	127.0	17	28	0	3	.938	3.19	5	4
J Alfaro	SS	16.7	2	3	0	0	1.000	2.70	1	0
M Ensberg	SS	2.0	0	0	0	0	.000	0.00	0	0
M Ensberg	3B	920.7	80	163	6	7	.949	2.38	26	0
M Lamb	3B	453.7	41	106	6	· 7	.919	2.92	9	1
J Vizcaino	3B	68.7	10	11	1	3	.840	2.75	0	0
C Biggio	LF	654.3	116	2	0	9	.929	1.62	0	0
L Berkman	LF	608.7	93	2	0	2	.979	1.40	0	0
J Lane	LF	101.7	24	2	1	0	.963	2.30	0	0
O Palmeiro	LF	73.3	17	0	0	0	1.000	2.09	0	0
W Taveras	LF	4.0	0	0	0	0	.000	0.00	0	0
E Bruntlett	LF	1.0	0	0	0	0	.000	0.00	0	0
C Beltran	CF	772.3	200	8	1	4	.977	2.42	3	0
C Biggio	CF	570.7	134	1	0	0	1.000	2.13	0	0
J Lane	CF	49.0	8	0	0	0	1.000	1.47	0	0
O Palmeiro	CF	27.0	8	0	0	0	1.000	2.67	0	0
L Berkman	CF	9.0	2	0	0	0	1.000	2.00	0	0
E Bruntlett	CF	9.0	1	0	0	0	1.000	1.00	0	0
W Taveras	CF	6.0	1	0	0	0	1.000	1.50	0	0
L Berkman	RF	780.3	148	9	0	0	1.000	1.81	2	0
R Hidalgo	RF	452.3	107	4	0	2	.982	2.21	0	0
J Lane	RF	140.7	28	0	0	0	1.000	1.79	0	0
O Palmeiro	RF	68.7	12	0	0	0	1.000	1.57	0	0
W Taveras	RF	1.0	0	0	0	0	.000	0.00	0	0

Los Angeles Dodgers

Ten Game Average Wins and Runs
The gray area represents a running total
of wins per ten games played

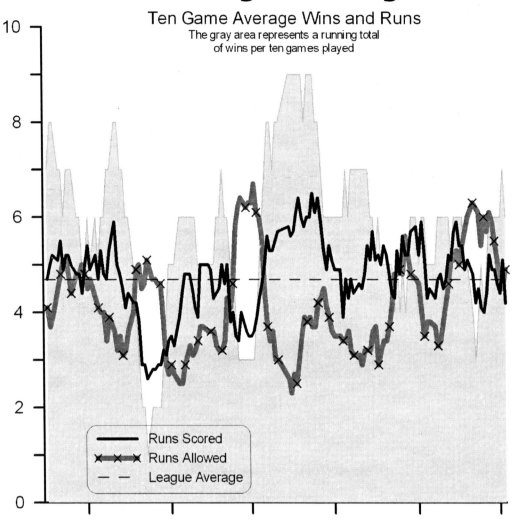

Runs Scored
Runs Allowed
League Average

5/1/04   6/1/04   7/1/04   8/1/04   9/1/04   10/1/04

*5/12: Cora sees 18
pitches before HR
in one at bat*

*7/3: Beltre hits two
homers; beat Angels
8-5; win 24 of next
30 games*

*8/9: Penny
strains biceps,
only makes
one more start*

*10/2: Huge comeback
against Giants to win
division, 7-3, capped
by Finley's grand slam*

*7/30: Trade Lo Duca, Mota;
pick up Penny, Finley, Choi*

*9/28: Beltre's 48th HR
ties MLB 3B record*

Team Batting and Pitching/Fielding Stats by Month						
	April	**May**	**June**	**July**	**Aug**	**Sept**
Wins	15	12	13	20	17	16
Losses	8	15	13	7	11	15
OBP	.342	.316	.337	.353	.334	.312
SLG	.447	.387	.424	.471	.427	.393
FIP	4.79	3.98	4.43	4.23	4.01	4.97
DER	.719	.726	.708	.744	.727	.706

Batting Stats

Player	RC	Runs	RBI	PA	Outs	H	BB	HR	TB	BA	OBP	SLG	GPA	ISO	SB	CS	GDP
Beltre A.	128	104	121	657	415	200	53	48	376	.334	.388	.629	.332	.294	7	2	15
Izturis C.	98	90	62	728	491	193	43	4	255	.288	.330	.381	.243	.093	25	9	5
Green S.	83	92	86	671	449	157	71	28	271	.266	.352	.459	.273	.193	5	2	14
Bradley M.	75	72	67	597	398	138	71	19	219	.267	.362	.424	.269	.157	15	11	9
Cora A.	64	47	47	484	311	107	47	10	154	.264	.364	.380	.259	.116	3	4	9
Lo Duca P.	54	41	49	381	261	105	22	10	155	.301	.351	.444	.269	.143	2	4	13
Werth J.	50	56	47	326	215	76	30	16	141	.262	.338	.486	.274	.224	4	1	0
Roberts D.	43	45	21	270	177	59	28	2	83	.253	.340	.356	.242	.103	33	1	2
Encarnacion	41	42	43	350	258	76	21	13	135	.235	.289	.417	.234	.182	3	3	7
Finley S.	37	31	46	250	172	59	21	13	110	.263	.324	.491	.269	.228	1	3	4
Hernandez J.	36	32	29	238	154	61	26	13	114	.289	.370	.540	.301	.251	3	1	3
Ventura R.	26	19	28	175	118	37	22	5	55	.243	.337	.362	.242	.118	0	0	3
Grabowski J.	22	18	20	192	139	38	19	7	66	.220	.297	.382	.229	.162	0	0	4
Saenz O.	19	17	22	128	84	31	12	8	56	.279	.352	.505	.284	.225	0	0	4
Ross D.	12	13	15	190	139	28	15	5	48	.170	.253	.291	.186	.121	0	0	2
Choi H.	5	5	6	76	54	10	11	0	15	.161	.289	.242	.191	.081	0	0	2
Weaver J.	3	3	2	78	55	15	1	0	19	.214	.225	.271	.169	.057	0	0	0
Mayne B.	3	5	5	113	80	18	14	0	18	.188	.286	.188	.175	.000	0	0	2
Sanchez D.	1	1	2	5	3	1	0	0	2	.250	.250	.500	.238	.250	0	0	0
Ishii K.	1	7	6	62	48	7	1	1	10	.127	.143	.182	.110	.055	0	0	0
Perez A.	1	5	0	14	10	3	0	0	4	.231	.286	.308	.205	.077	1	0	0
Jackson E.	1	0	1	6	3	1	0	0	1	.250	.250	.250	.175	.000	0	0	0
Thurston J.	1	1	1	18	14	3	0	0	6	.176	.167	.353	.163	.176	0	0	0
Lima J.	1	1	2	57	41	9	1	0	9	.188	.204	.188	.139	.000	0	0	2
Flores J.	0	0	0	5	3	1	1	0	1	.250	.400	.250	.243	.000	0	0	0
Dessens E.	0	0	0	4	3	1	0	0	1	.250	.250	.250	.175	.000	0	0	0
Falkenborg B	0	1	0	3	2	0	1	0	0	.000	.333	.000	.150	.000	0	0	0
Dreifort D.	0	0	0	1	1	0	0	0	0	.000	.000	.000	.000	.000	0	0	0
Brazoban Y.	0	0	0	1	1	0	0	0	0	.000	.000	.000	.000	.000	0	0	0
Carrara G.	0	0	0	2	2	0	0	0	0	.000	.000	.000	.000	.000	0	0	0
Wilson T.	0	1	0	8	7	1	0	0	1	.125	.125	.125	.088	.000	0	0	0
Gagne E.	0	0	0	3	3	0	0	0	0	.000	.000	.000	.000	.000	0	0	0
Penny B.	0	0	0	4	4	0	0	0	0	.000	.000	.000	.000	.000	0	0	0
Chen C.	-1	1	0	10	9	0	2	0	0	.000	.200	.000	.090	.000	0	0	1
Mota G.	-1	0	0	6	6	0	0	0	0	.000	.000	.000	.000	.000	0	0	0
Nomo H.	-1	2	1	27	23	3	0	1	6	.115	.115	.231	.110	.115	0	0	0
Alvarez W.	-1	4	0	34	28	5	1	0	5	.161	.188	.161	.125	.000	0	0	2
Perez O.	-1	5	2	70	58	7	2	0	9	.113	.141	.145	.100	.032	0	0	3

Pitching Stats

Player	IP	BFP	G	GS	P/PA	H	K	BB	HR	W	L	Sv	Op	Hld	RA	ERA	FIP	DER
Weaver J.	220.0	935	34	34	3.67	219	153	67	19	13	13	0	0	0	4.21	4.01	3.91	.707
Perez O.	196.3	787	31	31	3.58	180	128	44	26	7	6	0	0	0	3.48	3.25	4.21	.737
Ishii K.	172.0	749	31	31	3.74	155	99	98	21	13	8	0	0	0	5.08	4.71	5.29	.746
Lima J.	170.3	702	36	24	3.43	178	93	34	33	13	5	0	0	1	4.28	4.07	5.12	.732
Alvarez W.	120.7	499	40	15	3.80	109	102	31	12	7	6	1	2	2	4.18	4.03	3.57	.722
Nomo H.	84.0	393	18	18	3.88	105	54	42	19	4	11	0	0	0	8.25	8.25	6.37	.686
Gagne E.	82.3	326	70	0	3.89	53	114	22	5	7	3	45	47	0	2.62	2.19	2.08	.733
Sanchez D.	80.0	343	67	0	3.64	81	44	27	9	3	1	0	1	4	3.83	3.38	4.68	.720
Mota G.	63.0	259	52	0	4.11	51	52	27	4	8	4	1	1	17	2.14	2.14	3.63	.730
Carrara G.	53.7	227	42	0	3.65	46	48	20	1	5	2	2	3	6	2.52	2.18	2.70	.713
Dreifort D.	50.7	227	60	0	4.10	43	63	36	5	1	4	1	4	15	4.44	4.44	4.00	.691
Brazoban Y.	32.7	133	31	0	4.25	25	27	15	2	6	2	0	0	5	2.48	2.48	3.60	.742
Martin T.	28.3	132	47	0	4.14	32	18	14	3	0	1	1	1	5	4.13	4.13	4.98	.691
Jackson E.	24.7	112	8	5	3.89	31	16	11	7	2	1	0	0	0	7.30	7.30	6.81	.692
Dessens E.	19.7	82	12	1	4.27	16	18	8	4	1	0	0	1	0	3.20	3.20	5.11	.769
Falkenborg B	14.3	73	6	0	3.84	19	11	9	2	1	0	0	0	0	8.79	7.53	5.87	.646
Stewart S.	12.3	60	11	0	3.38	20	8	6	3	1	0	0	0	0	5.84	5.84	6.40	.605
Penny B.	11.7	45	3	3	4.20	6	6	6	2	1	2	0	0	0	3.86	3.09	5.82	.871
Venafro M.	9.0	42	17	0	3.57	11	6	3	1	0	0	0	0	2	5.00	4.00	4.85	.667
Kida M.	4.7	19	3	0	4.26	4	5	1	0	0	0	0	0	0	0.00	0.00	2.22	.667
Myers R.	2.0	6	1	0	3.17	1	1	0	0	0	0	0	0	0	0.00	0.00	2.08	.800
Ventura R.	1.0	4	1	0	3.00	1	0	0	0	0	0	0	0	0	0.00	0.00	3.08	.750

Fielding Stats

Catchers

Name	Innings	SBA/G	CS%	ERA	WP+PB/G
Lo Duca	691.7	0.91	23%	3.94	0.442
Ross	451.7	0.76	29%	4.24	0.379
Mayne	293.0	0.58	21%	3.78	0.123
Wilson	17.0	0.00	0%	4.24	0.529

Infielders and Outfielders

Name	POS	Inn	PO	A	TE	FE	FPct	RF	DPS	DPT
S Green	1B	926.7	879	53	1	4	.995	9.05	5	0
R Ventura	1B	210.0	214	14	0	0	1.000	9.77	1	0
H Choi	1B	155.0	161	10	0	1	.994	9.93	1	0
O Saenz	1B	126.0	124	12	0	2	.986	9.71	1	2
P Lo Duca	1B	19.0	11	1	0	0	1.000	5.68	0	0
J Hernandez	1B	12.7	15	2	0	0	1.000	12.08	0	0
J Grabowski	1B	4.0	2	1	0	0	1.000	6.75	0	0

Los Angeles Dodgers

Name	POS	Inn	PO	A	TE	FE	FPct	RF	DPS	DPT
A Cora	2B	1091.0	260	345	5	3	.987	4.99	25	62
J Hernandez	2B	341.7	80	113	4	0	.980	5.08	6	16
J Thurston	2B	11.3	2	3	0	0	1.000	3.97	0	1
A Perez	2B	8.0	2	1	0	1	.750	3.38	0	1
J Flores	2B	1.0	0	0	0	0	.000	0.00	0	0
C Izturis	SS	1386.0	233	430	8	2	.985	4.31	54	37
J Hernandez	SS	62.3	8	26	1	0	.971	4.91	1	4
A Perez	SS	4.0	1	2	0	0	1.000	6.75	0	1
A Beltre	SS	1.0	0	1	0	0	1.000	9.00	0	0
A Beltre	3B	1340.0	121	322	7	2	.978	2.98	30	1
R Ventura	3B	62.0	13	11	0	0	1.000	3.48	5	0
J Hernandez	3B	38.0	4	7	0	0	1.000	2.61	1	0
J Flores	3B	8.0	0	1	0	0	1.000	1.13	0	0
O Saenz	3B	5.0	0	2	0	0	1.000	3.60	0	0
J Werth	LF	526.0	116	6	2	2	.968	2.09	4	0
D Roberts	LF	378.7	77	0	1	1	.975	1.83	0	0
J Grabowski	LF	216.7	36	0	0	1	.973	1.50	0	0
M Bradley	LF	128.0	34	1	0	0	1.000	2.46	0	0
J Encarnacio	LF	79.0	10	0	0	0	1.000	1.14	0	0
P Lo Duca	LF	69.0	13	0	0	0	1.000	1.70	0	0
J Hernandez	LF	40.0	6	0	0	0	1.000	1.35	0	0
C Chen	LF	16.0	8	0	0	0	1.000	4.50	0	0
M Bradley	CF	792.7	231	2	1	3	.983	2.65	1	0
S Finley	CF	484.7	145	0	0	1	.993	2.69	0	0
D Roberts	CF	132.0	41	2	0	1	.977	2.93	2	0
J Werth	CF	44.0	11	0	0	0	1.000	2.25	0	0
J Encarnacio	RF	673.3	151	3	1	3	.975	2.06	0	0
S Green	RF	427.3	81	2	0	2	.976	1.75	1	0
M Bradley	RF	267.7	66	5	0	4	.947	2.39	0	0
J Werth	RF	74.0	19	0	0	0	1.000	2.31	0	0
J Grabowski	RF	11.0	6	0	0	0	1.000	4.91	0	0

Milwaukee Brewers

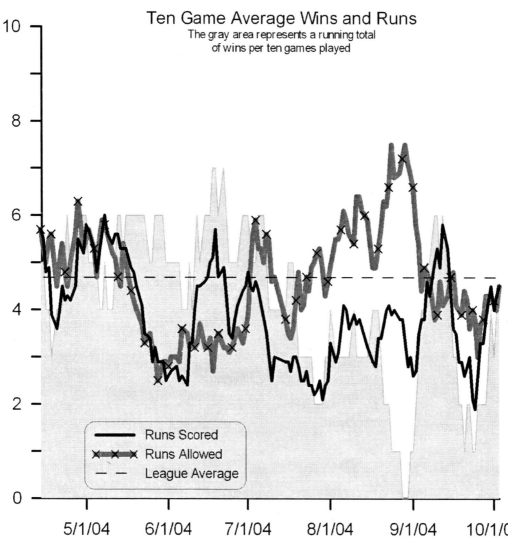

Ten Game Average Wins and Runs
The gray area represents a running total
of wins per ten games played

Legend:
— Runs Scored
—X—X— Runs Allowed
— — League Average

5/16: Sheets strikes out 18 Atlanta batters

7/15: Overbay starts 2nd half with a .344/.407/.555 batting line; hits just .245/.357/.379 after.

7/3: Spivey on DL and out for the year.

9/9: Podsednik swipes 55th base, breaking the team record; finishes with 70 steals and only 13 CS.

9/27: Selig family announces they will sell the Brewers

Team Batting and Pitching/Fielding Stats by Month						
	April	**May**	**June**	**July**	**Aug**	**Sept**
Wins	12	14	15	9	6	11
Losses	12	12	10	19	21	20
OBP	.336	.316	.347	.301	.306	.321
SLG	.428	.374	.402	.349	.372	.404
FIP	4.65	3.59	3.77	4.08	4.61	4.19
DER	.708	.725	.723	.719	.685	.714

Batting Stats

Player	RC	Runs	RBI	PA	Outs	H	BB	HR	TB	BA	OBP	SLG	GPA	ISO	SB	CS	GDP
Overbay L.	99	83	87	668	417	174	81	16	277	.301	.385	.478	.293	.178	2	1	11
Jenkins G.	80	88	93	681	474	163	46	27	292	.264	.325	.473	.264	.209	3	1	19
Podsednik S.	80	85	39	713	504	156	58	12	233	.244	.313	.364	.232	.120	70	13	7
Ginter K.	60	47	60	437	295	101	37	19	185	.262	.333	.479	.269	.218	8	1	9
Clark B.	57	41	46	420	271	99	53	7	140	.280	.385	.397	.272	.116	15	8	9
Counsell C.	48	59	23	551	368	114	59	2	149	.241	.330	.315	.227	.074	17	4	5
Hall B.	45	43	53	415	307	93	20	9	146	.238	.276	.374	.218	.136	12	6	4
Grieve B.	38	28	29	275	177	61	39	7	97	.261	.364	.415	.267	.154	0	0	4
Spivey J.	29	33	28	263	176	62	25	7	96	.272	.359	.421	.267	.149	5	3	7
Helms W.	29	24	28	306	213	72	24	4	99	.263	.331	.361	.239	.099	0	1	10
Branyan R.	25	21	27	182	122	37	20	11	83	.234	.324	.525	.277	.291	1	0	1
Bennett G.	16	18	20	246	179	49	22	3	72	.224	.297	.329	.216	.105	1	0	9
Moeller C.	15	25	27	349	264	66	21	5	96	.208	.265	.303	.195	.095	0	1	12
Obermueller	8	2	5	42	25	15	1	0	18	.385	.400	.462	.295	.077	0	0	1
Durrington T	8	13	4	87	64	19	4	2	33	.232	.267	.402	.221	.171	4	0	1
Magruder C.	8	11	10	101	72	21	8	2	35	.236	.310	.393	.238	.157	0	1	3
Kieschnick B	7	2	7	68	49	17	5	1	23	.270	.324	.365	.237	.095	0	0	3
Krynzel D.	4	6	3	47	32	9	3	0	10	.220	.319	.244	.205	.024	0	0	0
Liefer J.	3	2	5	31	24	6	2	1	11	.214	.258	.393	.214	.179	0	0	2
Capuano C.	3	0	2	32	24	6	1	0	8	.200	.250	.267	.179	.067	0	0	0
Johnson M.	1	1	2	15	10	1	3	0	1	.091	.267	.091	.143	.000	0	0	0
Kinney M.	0	0	1	10	7	2	0	0	2	.222	.222	.222	.156	.000	0	0	0
Erickson M.	0	0	0	6	5	1	0	0	1	.167	.167	.167	.117	.000	0	0	0
Liriano P.	0	0	0	1	1	0	0	0	0	.000	.000	.000	.000	.000	0	0	0
Phelps T.	0	0	0	1	1	0	0	0	0	.000	.000	.000	.000	.000	0	0	0
Hart C.	0	0	0	1	1	0	0	0	0	.000	.000	.000	.000	.000	0	0	0
Saenz C.	0	0	0	2	2	0	0	0	0	.000	.000	.000	.000	.000	0	0	0
Bennett J.	0	0	0	2	2	0	0	0	0	.000	.000	.000	.000	.000	0	0	0
Burba D.	0	0	0	3	3	0	0	0	0	.000	.000	.000	.000	.000	0	0	0
Wise M.	0	0	0	5	4	0	0	0	0	.000	.000	.000	.000	.000	0	0	0
Hernandez A.	0	0	0	5	4	0	0	0	0	.000	.000	.000	.000	.000	0	0	0
de la Rosa J	-1	0	0	7	6	0	0	0	0	.000	.000	.000	.000	.000	0	0	0
Hendrickson	-1	0	0	17	14	2	0	0	2	.125	.125	.125	.088	.000	0	0	0
Glover G.	-1	0	0	7	7	0	0	0	0	.000	.000	.000	.000	.000	0	0	0
Sheets B.	-1	2	1	81	60	9	5	0	9	.134	.194	.134	.121	.000	0	0	2
Santos V.	-2	0	1	47	37	2	2	0	3	.051	.098	.077	.063	.026	0	0	0
Davis D.	-6	0	0	71	64	1	1	0	1	.016	.031	.016	.018	.000	0	0	1

Pitching Stats

Player	IP	BFP	G	GS	P/PA	H	K	BB	HR	W	L	Sv	Op	Hld	RA	ERA	FIP	DER
Sheets B.	237.0	937	34	34	3.82	201	264	32	25	12	14	0	0	0	3.23	2.70	2.67	.712
Davis D.	207.3	880	34	34	3.87	192	166	79	14	12	12	0	0	0	3.65	3.39	3.59	.710
Santos V.	154.0	684	31	28	3.80	169	115	57	18	11	12	0	0	0	5.55	4.97	4.34	.690
Obermueller	118.0	529	25	20	3.63	138	59	42	15	6	8	0	0	0	6.10	5.80	4.86	.700
Capuano C.	88.3	385	17	17	3.84	91	80	37	18	6	8	0	0	0	5.60	4.99	5.33	.702
Vizcaino L.	72.0	298	73	0	4.10	61	63	24	12	4	4	1	5	21	4.38	3.75	4.53	.753
Bennett J.	71.3	316	60	0	3.63	78	45	26	12	1	5	0	1	8	5.43	4.79	5.17	.714
Burba D.	70.7	299	45	0	3.78	63	47	24	6	3	1	2	4	3	4.58	4.08	3.94	.741
Kinney M.	62.3	286	32	6	3.94	77	52	23	8	3	4	0	0	3	5.92	5.78	4.27	.657
Kolb D.	57.3	236	64	0	3.64	50	21	15	3	0	4	39	44	1	3.45	2.98	3.96	.758
Adams M.	53.0	225	46	0	3.82	50	39	14	5	2	3	0	5	12	3.57	3.40	3.73	.727
Wise M.	52.7	222	30	3	3.76	51	30	15	3	1	2	0	0	3	4.61	4.44	3.64	.721
Hendrickson	46.3	215	10	9	3.77	58	29	20	6	1	8	0	0	0	6.41	6.22	5.05	.667
Kieschnick	43.0	183	32	0	4.03	44	28	13	6	1	1	0	1	5	3.98	3.77	4.49	.721
Ford B.	24.0	107	19	0	3.56	25	13	10	4	1	1	0	3	2	6.38	6.38	5.65	.731
de la Rosa J	22.7	113	5	5	3.61	29	5	14	1	0	3	0	0	0	7.94	6.35	5.18	.696
Glover G.	18.0	82	4	3	3.74	18	8	8	2	2	1	0	0	0	4.50	3.50	5.29	.742
Hernandez	16.0	84	6	1	3.73	20	14	14	1	0	2	0	1	0	10.13	8.44	4.75	.655
Liriano P.	15.7	67	11	0	4.15	15	10	3	3	0	0	0	0	1	5.74	4.02	5.05	.760
Phelps T.	6.0	31	4	0	4.52	8	3	3	2	0	1	0	0	0	10.50	10.50	7.90	.739
Saenz C.	6.0	24	1	1	3.88	2	7	3	0	1	0	0	0	0	0.00	0.00	2.73	.846
Durrington T	0.3	1	1	0	1.00	0	0	0	0	0	0	0	0	0	0.00	0.00	3.07	1.000

Fielding Stats

Catchers

Name	Innings	SBA/G	CS%	ERA	WP+PB/G
Moeller	827.0	0.71	20%	3.67	0.457
Bennett	584.0	0.65	21%	5.12	0.354
Johnson	31.0	1.45	20%	4.06	0.290

Infielders and Outfielders

Name	POS	Inn	PO	A	TE	FE	FPct	RF	DPS	DPT
L Overbay	1B	1360.0	1311	113	1	10	.992	9.42	8	2
W Helms	1B	71.0	68	3	1	1	.973	9.00	0	0
R Branyan	1B	10.7	7	0	0	0	1.000	5.91	0	0
J Spivey	2B	517.7	111	177	3	7	.963	5.01	12	25
K Ginter	2B	459.3	91	126	3	2	.973	4.25	9	10
B Hall	2B	418.3	95	113	4	5	.959	4.47	10	18
T Durrington	2B	38.7	12	12	0	0	1.000	5.59	0	1
M Erickson	2B	8.0	1	3	0	0	1.000	4.50	1	0

Milwaukee Brewers

Name	POS	Inn	PO	A	TE	FE	FPct	RF	DPS	DPT
C Counsell	SS	1130.0	165	357	3	6	.983	4.16	38	33
B Hall	SS	303.7	59	116	2	6	.956	5.19	17	9
M Erickson	SS	4.0	0	4	0	0	1.000	9.00	0	0
J Spivey	SS	3.7	1	1	0	0	1.000	4.91	0	0
W Helms	3B	546.0	45	105	5	11	.904	2.47	10	0
K Ginter	3B	396.3	28	80	1	2	.973	2.45	8	0
R Branyan	3B	361.0	35	91	1	4	.962	3.14	7	1
B Hall	3B	72.0	6	22	1	1	.933	3.50	4	0
T Durrington	3B	66.3	3	12	0	3	.789	2.04	1	0
C Counsell	3B	0.3	0	0	0	0	.000	0.00	0	0
G Jenkins	LF	1362.0	261	10	0	1	.996	1.79	5	0
C Magruder	LF	59.0	9	1	0	0	1.000	1.53	0	0
B Clark	LF	21.0	7	0	0	0	1.000	3.00	0	0
S Podsednik	CF	1361.0	392	5	1	3	.990	2.63	3	0
B Clark	CF	63.0	22	1	0	0	1.000	3.29	2	0
D Krynzel	CF	18.0	8	0	0	0	1.000	4.00	0	0
B Clark	RF	784.7	219	4	2	2	.982	2.56	2	2
B Grieve	RF	470.3	106	0	0	4	.964	2.03	0	0
C Magruder	RF	87.0	23	0	0	0	1.000	2.38	0	0
D Krynzel	RF	60.0	21	1	0	1	.957	3.30	2	0
J Liefer	RF	25.0	4	0	0	0	1.000	1.44	0	0
K Ginter	RF	15.0	5	0	0	0	1.000	3.00	0	0

Montreal Expos

Ten Game Average Wins and Runs
The gray area represents a running total
of wins per ten games played

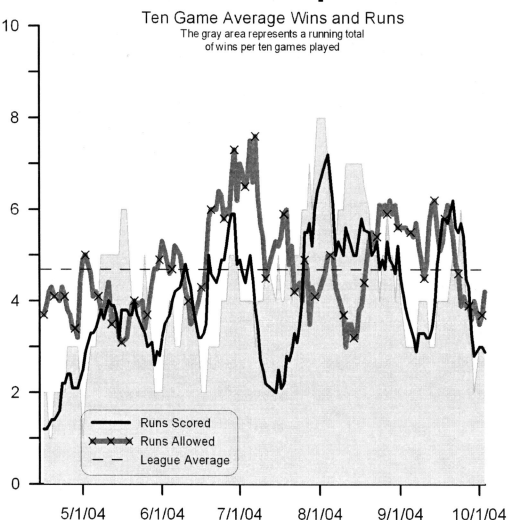

Runs Scored
Runs Allowed
League Average

4/15: Lose 3-0 at home to Florida; scored only three runs in a six-game homestand

4/30: Lose 13-4 to LA, team is 5-19 in April; lowest-scoring month in team history.

5/30: Pitcher Ohka bats 8th as Robinson shakes up lineup

6/16: Draw just 3,763 fans against the Twins

7/18: Everett traded to the White Sox for Majewski and Rauch.

8/7: Rauch beats the Astros 8-3 in first Expo start

9/29 - MLB announces that the Expos will move to Washington in 2005, and the Expos lose their final home game, 9-1 to Florida

Team Batting and Pitching/Fielding Stats by Month						
	April	May	June	July	Aug	Sept
Wins	5	11	10	15	15	11
Losses	20	15	16	12	13	19
OBP	.261	.302	.328	.328	.343	.305
SLG	.293	.391	.437	.383	.449	.379
FIP	4.92	4.25	5.37	4.44	4.74	4.50
DER	.721	.719	.698	.703	.711	.702

Batting Stats

Player	RC	Runs	RBI	PA	Outs	H	BB	HR	TB	BA	OBP	SLG	GPA	ISO	SB	CS	GDP
Wilkerson B.	103	112	67	688	438	146	106	32	285	.255	.374	.498	.293	.243	13	6	6
Batista T.	75	76	110	650	480	146	26	32	276	.241	.272	.455	.236	.215	14	6	14
Sledge T.	70	45	62	446	296	107	40	15	184	.269	.336	.462	.267	.193	3	3	2
Rivera J.	64	48	49	426	284	120	34	12	182	.307	.364	.465	.280	.159	6	2	11
Vidro J.	62	51	60	467	306	121	49	14	187	.294	.367	.454	.279	.160	3	1	14
Chavez E.	59	65	34	547	376	139	30	5	186	.277	.318	.371	.236	.094	32	7	6
Schneider B.	55	40	49	488	334	112	42	12	174	.257	.325	.399	.246	.142	0	1	9
Cabrera O.	39	41	31	425	310	96	28	4	131	.246	.298	.336	.218	.090	12	3	13
Johnson N.	38	35	33	295	196	63	40	7	100	.251	.359	.398	.261	.147	6	3	5
Carroll J.	29	36	16	256	159	63	32	0	81	.289	.378	.372	.263	.083	5	1	3
Gonzalez A.	15	19	16	144	103	32	8	4	51	.241	.289	.383	.226	.143	1	1	1
Everett C.	14	8	14	141	103	32	8	2	48	.252	.319	.378	.238	.126	0	0	8
Diaz E.	9	9	11	159	114	31	11	1	42	.223	.293	.302	.207	.079	2	0	6
Hernandez L.	9	2	10	97	62	20	1	1	30	.247	.256	.370	.208	.123	0	0	1
Izturis M.	8	10	4	121	86	22	10	1	34	.206	.286	.318	.208	.112	4	0	1
Pascucci V.	5	6	6	74	54	11	10	2	18	.177	.297	.290	.206	.113	1	0	3
Kim S.	4	1	5	32	22	6	0	0	8	.214	.214	.286	.168	.071	1	0	0
Calloway R.	3	4	10	91	73	14	5	1	19	.167	.211	.226	.152	.060	2	0	3
Cepicky M.	2	4	3	61	48	13	1	1	20	.217	.230	.333	.187	.117	1	0	1
Rauch J.	2	1	2	6	5	1	0	1	4	.167	.167	.667	.242	.500	0	0	0
Church R.	2	6	6	71	55	11	7	1	15	.175	.257	.238	.175	.063	0	0	3
Bergeron P.	2	2	1	45	34	9	2	0	9	.214	.250	.214	.166	.000	0	1	0
Harris B.	1	4	2	53	42	8	2	1	13	.160	.208	.260	.158	.100	0	0	0
Mateo H.	1	3	0	46	36	12	1	0	14	.273	.289	.318	.210	.045	2	3	1
Eischen J.	1	2	0	4	1	2	0	0	2	.667	.667	.667	.467	.000	0	0	0
Horgan J.	1	0	1	4	3	1	0	0	1	.250	.250	.250	.175	.000	0	0	0
Beltran F.	0	0	0	2	1	1	0	0	1	.500	.500	.500	.350	.000	0	0	0
Bentz C.	0	0	0	2	1	1	0	0	1	.500	.500	.500	.350	.000	0	0	0
Downs S.	0	1	0	22	14	1	1	0	1	.067	.125	.067	.073	.000	0	0	0
Ayala L.	0	0	0	10	6	3	0	0	4	.333	.333	.444	.261	.111	0	0	0
Cordero C.	0	0	0	3	2	0	0	0	0	.000	.000	.000	.000	.000	0	0	0
Hill S.	0	0	0	3	2	0	0	0	0	.000	.000	.000	.000	.000	0	0	0
Majewski G.	0	0	0	2	2	0	0	0	0	.000	.000	.000	.000	.000	0	0	0
Patterson J.	0	0	1	39	31	4	1	0	4	.121	.147	.121	.096	.000	0	0	2
Tucker T.	-1	1	0	12	11	1	0	0	1	.083	.083	.083	.058	.000	0	0	0
Biddle R.	-1	0	0	14	11	0	0	0	0	.000	.000	.000	.000	.000	0	0	0
Lopez L.	-1	0	0	27	23	4	0	0	4	.154	.185	.154	.122	.000	0	0	1
Armas Jr. T.	-1	0	0	21	16	0	0	0	0	.000	.000	.000	.000	.000	0	0	0
Ohka T.	-2	0	0	26	23	2	1	0	2	.080	.115	.080	.072	.000	1	0	0
Labandeira J	-2	0	0	14	15	0	0	0	0	.000	.000	.000	.000	.000	0	0	1
Day Z.	-2	1	1	32	28	1	0	1	4	.034	.034	.138	.050	.103	0	0	0
Vargas C.	-2	0	0	29	22	1	0	0	1	.045	.045	.045	.032	.000	0	0	1
Fox A.	-3	2	1	43	40	4	0	1	7	.093	.093	.163	.083	.070	0	0	1

Pitching Stats

Player	IP	BFP	G	GS	P/PA	H	K	BB	HR	W	L	Sv	Op	Hld	RA	ERA	FIP	DER
Hernandez	255.0	1053	35	35	3.73	234	186	83	26	11	15	0	0	0	3.71	3.60	4.03	.722
Kim S.	135.7	603	43	17	3.50	145	87	55	17	4	6	0	0	2	5.31	4.58	4.92	.703
Vargas C.	118.3	530	45	14	4.03	120	89	64	26	5	5	0	0	3	5.70	5.25	6.22	.727
Day Z.	116.7	496	19	19	3.68	117	61	45	13	5	10	0	0	0	4.09	3.93	4.73	.721
Patterson	98.3	445	19	19	4.07	100	99	46	18	4	7	0	0	0	5.31	5.03	5.08	.701
Ayala L.	90.3	367	81	0	3.60	92	63	15	6	6	12	2	7	21	2.99	2.69	3.20	.691
Ohka T.	84.7	367	15	15	3.40	98	38	20	11	3	7	0	0	0	4.25	3.40	4.60	.707
Cordero C.	82.7	357	69	0	4.24	68	83	43	8	7	3	14	18	8	3.05	2.94	3.91	.730
Biddle R.	78.0	364	47	9	3.73	98	51	31	15	4	8	11	15	1	7.96	6.92	5.76	.680
Armas Jr.	72.0	320	16	16	4.15	66	54	45	13	2	4	0	0	0	5.13	4.88	5.96	.740
Tucker T.	67.7	291	54	1	3.64	73	44	17	5	4	2	0	2	3	3.72	3.72	3.66	.692
Downs S.	63.0	284	12	12	3.69	79	38	23	9	3	6	0	0	0	6.71	5.14	4.96	.668
Horgan J.	40.0	178	47	0	3.70	35	30	22	5	4	1	2	3	12	4.05	3.15	5.07	.746
Bentz C.	27.7	126	36	0	3.97	23	18	23	5	0	3	0	0	5	6.18	5.86	6.83	.769
Fikac J.	25.0	112	19	0	3.87	26	22	13	5	1	2	0	0	2	5.76	5.40	5.47	.708
Rauch J.	23.3	88	9	2	4.10	14	18	7	1	3	0	0	0	0	1.54	1.54	2.98	.790
Majewski	21.0	95	16	0	3.89	28	12	5	2	0	1	1	2	0	6.43	3.86	4.16	.649
Eischen J.	18.3	80	21	0	3.81	16	17	8	2	0	1	0	1	2	4.91	3.93	4.10	.731
Beltran F.	14.3	69	11	0	3.80	20	8	5	3	0	0	1	1	0	7.53	7.53	6.14	.667
Hill S.	9.0	51	3	3	3.94	17	10	7	1	1	2	0	0	0	16.00	16.00	4.96	.500
Corcoran	5.3	28	5	0	3.64	7	4	5	0	0	0	0	0	0	6.75	6.75	4.38	.632
Beltran R.	0.7	3	2	0	4.00	1	0	0	0	0	0	0	0	0	13.50	13.50	3.07	.667

Fielding Stats

Catchers

Name	Innings	SBA/G	CS%	ERA	WP+PB/G
Schneider	1114.0	0.56	48%	3.86	0.259
Diaz	333.0	0.73	19%	5.89	0.486

Infielders and Outfielders

Name	POS	Inn	PO	A	TE	FE	FPct	RF	DPS	DPT
B Wilkerson	1B	701.7	694	66	3	0	.995	9.75	4	12
N Johnson	1B	610.0	618	43	0	4	.994	9.75	4	1
T Sledge	1B	61.3	63	6	0	0	1.000	10.13	0	0
L Lopez	1B	55.0	53	2	0	0	1.000	9.00	0	0
V Pascucci	1B	18.0	14	0	0	1	.933	7.00	0	0
A Fox	1B	1.0	2	0	0	0	1.000	18.00	0	0
J Vidro	2B	879.3	175	269	1	5	.987	4.54	23	42
J Carroll	2B	344.7	84	97	0	1	.995	4.73	11	21
M Izturis	2B	88.0	18	25	0	1	.977	4.40	4	2
B Harris	2B	82.0	15	20	1	0	.972	3.84	0	6

Montreal Expos

Name	POS	Inn	PO	A	TE	FE	FPct	RF	DPS	DPT
H Mateo	2B	37.0	12	17	4	0	.879	7.05	1	4
A Fox	2B	10.0	0	5	0	0	1.000	4.50	0	0
J Labandeira	2B	6.0	0	0	0	0	.000	0.00	0	0
O Cabrera	SS	867.7	148	290	4	3	.984	4.54	32	34
A Gonzalez	SS	293.3	57	88	1	5	.960	4.45	5	16
M Izturis	SS	187.0	32	71	3	4	.936	4.96	9	10
J Carroll	SS	59.0	11	16	0	0	1.000	4.12	1	3
A Fox	SS	21.0	0	5	0	0	1.000	2.14	0	0
J Labandeira	SS	19.0	2	3	1	0	.833	2.37	0	0
T Batista	3B	1326.0	83	308	5	14	.954	2.65	34	4
J Carroll	3B	78.0	8	26	1	1	.944	3.92	1	0
B Harris	3B	25.0	2	3	1	0	.833	1.80	0	0
A Fox	3B	17.0	1	6	0	0	1.000	3.71	0	0
E Diaz	3B	1.0	0	0	0	0	.000	0.00	0	0
T Sledge	LF	579.7	133	4	0	3	.979	2.13	2	0
B Wilkerson	LF	439.3	94	4	1	1	.980	2.01	4	0
C Everett	LF	149.7	24	1	0	2	.926	1.50	0	0
R Church	LF	72.0	16	2	0	0	1.000	2.25	0	0
J Rivera	LF	71.0	17	1	0	0	1.000	2.28	0	0
M Cepicky	LF	59.7	15	0	0	0	1.000	2.26	0	0
R Calloway	LF	39.7	2	0	0	0	1.000	0.45	0	0
V Pascucci	LF	26.0	4	0	0	0	1.000	1.38	0	0
J Carroll	LF	6.0	2	0	0	0	1.000	3.00	0	0
H Mateo	LF	4.0	1	0	0	0	1.000	2.25	0	0
E Chavez	CF	1081.0	301	9	2	3	.984	2.58	10	0
B Wilkerson	CF	140.0	46	3	0	1	.980	3.15	0	0
J Rivera	CF	97.3	24	0	0	0	1.000	2.22	0	0
P Bergeron	CF	97.0	21	0	0	2	.913	1.95	0	0
R Church	CF	16.0	7	0	0	0	1.000	3.94	0	0
T Sledge	CF	15.0	7	0	0	0	1.000	4.20	0	0
J Rivera	RF	721.7	151	13	2	1	.982	2.05	5	0
T Sledge	RF	293.3	76	1	0	0	1.000	2.36	0	0
C Everett	RF	112.0	37	1	0	1	.974	3.05	0	0
R Calloway	RF	96.7	25	0	0	0	1.000	2.33	0	0
V Pascucci	RF	93.3	25	0	0	0	1.000	2.41	0	0
B Wilkerson	RF	76.0	19	1	0	0	1.000	2.37	1	0
R Church	RF	38.0	12	1	0	0	1.000	3.08	0	0
M Cepicky	RF	16.0	9	0	0	0	1.000	5.06	0	0

New York Mets

Ten Game Average Wins and Runs

The gray area represents a running total
of wins per ten games played

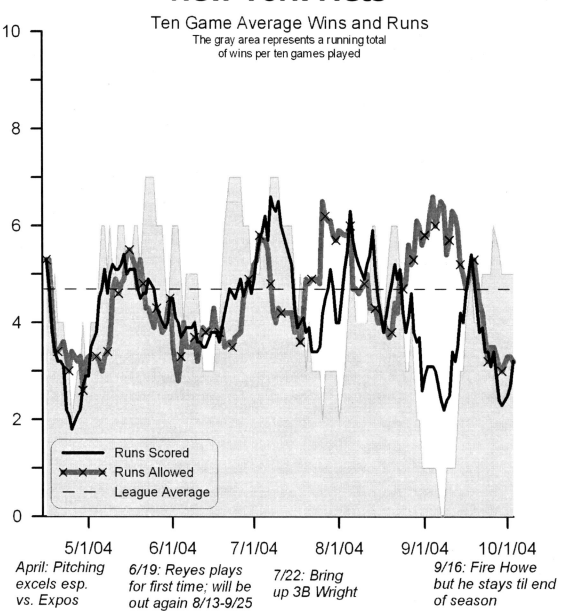

April: Pitching excels esp. vs. Expos

6/19: Reyes plays for first time; will be out again 8/13-9/25

7/2-7/4: Sweep Yankees

7/22: Bring up 3B Wright

7/31: "Black Friday": Trade top prospects for Zambrano and Benson.

9/16: Fire Howe but he stays til end of season

Team Batting and Pitching/Fielding Stats by Month						
	April	**May**	**June**	**July**	**Aug**	**Sept**
Wins	9	16	13	11	11	11
Losses	15	11	13	15	17	20
OBP	.319	.329	.309	.342	.309	.299
SLG	.377	.428	.406	.449	.414	.378
FIP	4.33	4.44	4.14	4.77	4.25	4.88
DER	.717	.737	.722	.695	.682	.741

Batting Stats

Player	RC	Runs	RBI	PA	Outs	H	BB	HR	TB	BA	OBP	SLG	GPA	ISO	SB	CS	GDP
Cameron M.	77	76	76	562	390	114	57	30	236	.231	.319	.479	.263	.247	22	6	5
Floyd C.	69	55	63	457	303	103	47	18	183	.260	.352	.462	.274	.202	11	4	6
Piazza M.	67	47	54	528	347	121	68	20	202	.266	.362	.444	.274	.178	0	0	13
Matsui K.	67	65	44	509	340	125	40	7	182	.272	.331	.396	.248	.124	14	3	2
Wright D.	45	41	40	283	193	77	14	14	138	.293	.332	.525	.281	.232	6	0	7
Wigginton T.	42	46	42	339	234	89	23	12	152	.285	.334	.487	.272	.202	6	1	10
Hidalgo R.	40	46	52	359	263	74	27	21	150	.228	.296	.463	.249	.235	3	2	11
Valent E.	38	39	34	300	208	72	28	13	130	.267	.337	.481	.272	.215	0	1	9
Zeile T.	38	30	35	396	279	81	44	9	124	.233	.319	.356	.233	.124	0	0	12
Spencer S.	31	21	26	204	134	52	13	4	76	.281	.332	.411	.252	.130	6	0	1
Phillips J.	31	34	34	412	295	79	35	7	118	.218	.298	.326	.215	.108	0	1	11
Reyes J.	27	33	14	229	167	56	5	2	82	.255	.271	.373	.215	.118	19	2	1
Wilson V.	25	18	21	177	117	43	11	4	67	.274	.335	.427	.258	.153	1	0	3
Garcia D.	23	23	17	174	107	32	22	3	50	.232	.371	.362	.257	.130	3	0	1
Delgado W.	20	11	13	147	93	38	15	2	50	.292	.366	.385	.261	.092	1	0	1
Garcia K.	19	24	22	202	153	45	10	7	77	.234	.272	.401	.223	.167	3	0	6
McEwing J.	18	17	16	154	104	35	9	1	43	.254	.297	.312	.212	.058	4	1	0
Williams G.	14	17	11	138	102	30	8	4	54	.233	.277	.419	.229	.186	2	1	2
Keppinger J.	11	9	9	123	90	33	6	3	44	.284	.317	.379	.238	.095	2	1	6
Glavine T.	7	5	8	72	45	11	10	0	13	.204	.328	.241	.208	.037	0	0	2
Diaz V.	6	8	8	53	39	15	1	3	27	.294	.321	.529	.277	.235	0	0	3
Gutierrez R.	3	2	5	70	54	11	6	0	13	.175	.257	.206	.167	.032	0	0	2
Brazell C.	2	3	3	35	26	9	1	1	14	.265	.286	.412	.232	.147	0	0	1
Ginter M.	1	1	1	19	11	3	2	0	4	.214	.313	.286	.212	.071	0	0	0
Trachsel S.	1	6	5	71	49	11	1	0	12	.186	.200	.203	.141	.017	0	0	1
Stanton M.	1	0	1	2	1	1	0	0	1	.500	.500	.500	.350	.000	0	0	0
Seo J.	1	2	1	38	28	5	2	0	6	.156	.229	.188	.150	.031	1	0	1
Duncan J.	1	2	1	17	14	1	1	0	1	.067	.125	.067	.073	.000	3	0	0
Wilson T.	0	0	0	5	3	1	1	0	1	.250	.400	.250	.243	.000	0	0	0
Wheeler D.	0	1	0	6	4	1	0	0	1	.200	.200	.200	.140	.000	0	0	0
Buchanan B.	0	0	0	4	3	0	1	0	0	.000	.250	.000	.113	.000	0	0	0
Moreno O.	0	0	0	1	1	0	0	0	0	.000	.000	.000	.000	.000	0	0	0
Bell H.	0	0	0	1	1	0	0	0	0	.000	.000	.000	.000	.000	0	0	0
Benson K.	0	1	2	25	18	1	1	0	1	.053	.100	.053	.058	.000	0	0	0
Bottalico R.	0	0	0	2	2	0	0	0	0	.000	.000	.000	.000	.000	0	0	0
Looper B.	0	0	0	2	2	0	0	0	0	.000	.000	.000	.000	.000	0	0	0
Baldwin J.	0	0	0	2	2	0	0	0	0	.000	.000	.000	.000	.000	0	0	0
Zambrano V.	0	0	0	7	5	1	0	0	1	.167	.167	.167	.117	.000	0	0	0
Erickson S.	0	0	0	3	3	0	0	0	0	.000	.000	.000	.000	.000	0	0	0
Heilman A.	-1	0	0	10	7	0	0	0	0	.000	.000	.000	.000	.000	0	0	0
Yates T.	-1	0	0	12	10	1	0	0	1	.091	.091	.091	.064	.000	0	0	0
Leiter A.	-2	0	0	59	50	5	3	0	6	.093	.140	.111	.091	.019	0	0	1

Pitching Stats

Player	IP	BFP	G	GS	P/PA	H	K	BB	HR	W	L	Sv	Op	Hld	RA	ERA	FIP	DER
Glavine T.	212.3	904	33	33	3.76	204	109	70	20	11	14	0	0	0	3.98	3.60	4.26	.739
Trachsel S.	202.7	881	33	33	3.80	203	117	83	25	12	13	0	0	0	4.62	4.00	4.83	.727
Leiter A.	173.7	750	30	30	4.33	138	117	97	16	10	8	0	0	0	3.37	3.21	4.79	.760
Seo J.	117.7	512	24	21	3.56	133	54	50	17	5	10	0	0	0	5.12	4.90	5.36	.702
Looper B.	83.3	346	71	0	3.68	86	60	16	5	2	5	29	34	0	3.02	2.70	3.10	.691
Stanton M.	77.0	337	83	0	3.74	70	58	33	6	2	6	0	6	25	3.74	3.16	3.95	.731
Ginter M.	69.3	313	15	14	3.70	82	38	20	8	1	3	0	0	0	5.32	4.54	4.56	.694
Bottalico R.	69.3	296	60	0	3.91	54	61	34	3	3	2	0	4	12	3.89	3.38	3.52	.737
Benson K.	68.0	290	11	11	3.70	65	51	17	8	4	4	0	0	0	4.90	4.50	4.03	.729
Wheeler D.	50.7	232	32	1	3.82	65	46	17	9	3	1	0	0	3	5.15	4.80	4.58	.650
Yates T.	46.7	228	21	7	3.94	61	35	25	6	2	4	0	0	2	6.94	6.36	5.05	.654
Franco J.	46.0	207	52	0	4.17	46	36	24	6	2	7	0	1	11	5.48	5.28	4.84	.714
Moreno O.	34.7	146	33	0	3.69	29	29	11	0	3	1	1	3	3	4.41	3.38	2.62	.718
Weathers D.	33.7	156	32	0	3.81	41	25	15	5	5	3	0	1	6	5.08	4.28	5.04	.670
Heilman A.	28.0	119	5	5	3.73	27	22	13	4	1	3	0	0	0	5.46	5.46	4.76	.713
Bell H.	24.3	94	17	0	4.05	22	27	6	5	0	2	0	1	1	3.33	3.33	4.27	.696
DeJean M.	21.3	91	17	0	3.52	21	24	5	0	0	0	0	0	2	2.11	1.69	1.81	.650
Fortunato B.	18.7	82	15	0	4.09	14	20	13	2	1	0	1	2	2	3.86	3.86	4.42	.745
Feliciano P.	18.3	82	22	0	4.11	14	14	12	2	1	1	0	0	2	5.89	5.40	5.09	.774
Parra J.	14.0	61	13	0	3.80	14	14	6	2	1	0	0	0	1	3.86	3.21	4.22	.692
Zambrano V.	14.0	62	3	3	3.90	12	14	6	0	2	0	0	0	0	5.79	3.86	2.36	.714
Erickson S.	8.0	42	2	2	3.40	15	3	4	1	0	1	0	0	0	10.13	7.88	5.45	.588
Baldwin J.	6.0	36	2	2	3.61	13	1	5	3	0	2	0	0	0	15.00	15.00	12.24	.615
Darensbourg	5.7	28	5	0	3.68	10	1	2	1	0	1	0	0	0	7.94	7.94	6.08	.625
Roberts G.	4.7	29	4	0	3.24	9	1	6	2	0	0	0	0	0	17.36	17.36	12.08	.650
Zeile T.	1.0	9	1	0	3.44	4	0	2	0	0	0	0	0	0	45.00	45.00	9.08	.429

Fielding Stats

Catchers

Name	Innings	SBA/G	CS%	ERA	WP+PB/G
Phillips	650.3	0.75	22%	3.87	0.180
Piazza	388.3	0.95	17%	3.99	0.278
Wilson	383.7	0.73	32%	4.46	0.399
Zeile	14.0	0.00	0%	4.50	0.000
Wilson	11.7	2.31	0%	8.49	0.000
Hietpas	1.0	0.00	0%	0.00	0.000

Infielders and Outfielders

Name	POS	Inn	PO	A	TE	FE	FPct	RF	DPS	DPT
M Piazza	1B	517.7	498	35	1	7	.985	9.27	4	0
T Zeile	1B	365.3	386	22	1	0	.995	10.05	4	2

New York Mets

Name	POS	Inn	PO	A	TE	FE	FPct	RF	DPS	DPT
J Phillips	1B	258.3	260	15	0	0	1.000	9.58	2	0
E Valent	1B	190.0	202	21	0	1	.996	10.56	2	0
T Wigginton	1B	41.0	48	7	1	0	.982	12.07	0	0
C Brazell	1B	35.0	34	4	0	1	.974	9.77	0	0
J McEwing	1B	21.7	20	1	0	0	1.000	8.72	1	0
S Spencer	1B	11.0	13	0	0	0	1.000	10.64	0	0
B Buchanan	1B	9.0	8	1	0	0	1.000	9.00	0	0
J Reyes	2B	352.0	75	117	3	1	.980	4.91	10	15
D Garcia	2B	344.0	99	92	3	3	.970	5.00	7	10
J Keppinger	2B	257.7	61	86	0	2	.987	5.13	6	15
T Wigginton	2B	183.7	30	68	2	1	.970	4.80	7	5
J McEwing	2B	159.7	47	52	0	2	.980	5.58	3	5
R Gutierrez	2B	128.0	31	44	0	0	1.000	5.27	6	6
K Matsui	2B	24.0	4	8	0	1	.923	4.50	2	1
K Matsui	SS	941.7	174	323	13	9	.956	4.75	29	36
W Delgado	SS	340.0	49	128	2	6	.957	4.69	20	8
J McEwing	SS	94.7	19	36	1	0	.982	5.23	2	3
J Reyes	SS	72.7	18	26	2	0	.957	5.45	1	3
D Wright	3B	603.7	39	139	5	6	.942	2.65	9	1
T Wigginton	3B	488.7	29	116	5	6	.924	2.67	7	2
T Zeile	3B	345.7	38	73	4	4	.933	2.89	7	0
R Gutierrez	3B	10.0	1	0	0	1	.500	0.90	0	0
J McEwing	3B	1.0	0	0	0	0	.000	0.00	0	0
C Floyd	LF	863.7	164	5	1	1	.988	1.76	2	0
S Spencer	LF	231.0	58	0	1	1	.967	2.26	0	0
E Valent	LF	213.3	39	1	0	0	1.000	1.69	0	0
G Williams	LF	72.0	9	2	0	1	.917	1.38	0	0
R Hidalgo	LF	42.3	7	0	0	0	1.000	1.49	0	0
J McEwing	LF	20.7	5	0	0	0	1.000	2.18	0	0
J Duncan	LF	5.0	1	0	0	0	1.000	1.80	0	0
E Snead	LF	1.0	0	0	0	0	.000	0.00	0	0
M Cameron	CF	1184.0	354	7	1	7	.978	2.74	4	0
G Williams	CF	160.0	38	1	0	0	1.000	2.19	0	0
S Spencer	CF	50.0	16	2	0	1	.947	3.24	0	0
J McEwing	CF	38.0	14	0	0	0	1.000	3.32	0	0
J Duncan	CF	17.0	6	0	0	0	1.000	3.18	0	0
R Hidalgo	RF	708.3	152	10	1	2	.976	2.06	5	0
K Garcia	RF	386.3	91	0	1	2	.968	2.12	0	0
S Spencer	RF	109.0	37	0	0	0	1.000	3.06	0	0
V Diaz	RF	108.0	29	0	0	2	.935	2.42	0	0
E Valent	RF	91.3	20	0	0	0	1.000	1.97	0	0
G Williams	RF	39.0	4	0	0	0	1.000	0.92	0	0
J McEwing	RF	7.0	4	0	0	0	1.000	5.14	0	0

Philadelphia Phillies

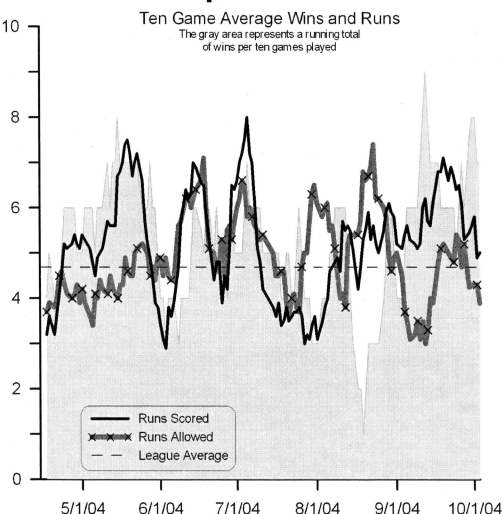

Ten Game Average Wins and Runs
The gray area represents a running total
of wins per ten games played

Runs Scored
Runs Allowed
League Average

4/12: Open new stadium,
Citizens Bank Park, with a
4-1 loss to Cincinnati

5/14: Wagner on DL;
first of two trips

7/4: Milton becomes
first 11-game winner
in NL. Will win just 3
of last 17 starts.

8/5: Millwood leaves
game with swelling
in elbow; will pitch
only four more innings

8/19: Bullpen gives up 7-3
lead versus Astros. Phils
went 1-9 in homestand,
blowing leads in seven games.

9/3: Floyd makes
MLB debut with 8-1
win vs. Mets

10/2: Bowa fired

Team Batting and Pitching/Fielding Stats by Month						
	April	**May**	**June**	**July**	**Aug**	**Sept**
Wins	10	17	14	12	12	21
Losses	12	11	13	15	16	9
OBP	.329	.347	.366	.332	.332	.360
SLG	.409	.443	.486	.377	.450	.479
FIP	4.01	4.62	5.66	4.85	4.75	4.11
DER	.705	.715	.702	.704	.708	.745

Batting Stats

Player	RC	Runs	RBI	PA	Outs	H	BB	HR	TB	BA	OBP	SLG	GPA	ISO	SB	CS	GDP
Abreu B.	142	118	105	713	409	173	127	30	312	.301	.428	.544	.328	.242	40	5	3
Rollins J.	108	119	73	725	480	190	57	14	299	.289	.348	.455	.270	.166	30	9	4
Thome J.	100	97	105	618	379	139	104	42	295	.274	.396	.581	.324	.307	0	2	8
Bell D.	87	67	77	603	391	155	57	18	244	.291	.363	.458	.278	.167	1	1	12
Burrell P.	72	67	84	534	341	115	78	24	204	.257	.365	.455	.278	.199	2	0	8
Polanco P.	70	74	55	555	368	150	27	17	222	.298	.345	.441	.266	.143	7	4	11
Lieberthal M	50	58	61	529	366	129	37	17	213	.271	.335	.447	.263	.176	1	1	18
Michaels J.	46	44	40	346	222	82	42	10	124	.274	.364	.415	.268	.140	2	2	3
Utley C.	37	36	57	287	202	71	15	13	125	.266	.308	.468	.256	.202	4	1	5
Byrd M.	35	48	33	378	276	79	22	5	111	.228	.287	.321	.209	.092	2	2	7
Ledee R.	24	19	26	145	90	35	22	7	63	.285	.393	.512	.305	.228	2	0	2
Perez T.	21	22	21	190	140	38	9	6	73	.216	.257	.415	.219	.199	0	0	2
Pratt T.	18	16	16	149	98	33	18	3	47	.258	.351	.367	.250	.109	0	0	3
Glanville D.	11	20	14	175	133	34	8	2	43	.210	.244	.265	.176	.056	8	0	5
Howard R.	7	5	5	42	30	11	2	2	22	.282	.333	.564	.291	.282	0	0	2
Wolf R.	6	6	8	55	33	12	1	3	23	.267	.277	.511	.252	.244	0	0	0
Collier L.	5	7	4	42	28	10	5	1	14	.278	.381	.389	.269	.111	1	0	2
Milton E.	3	4	5	75	55	10	4	0	11	.154	.200	.169	.132	.015	0	0	0
Lidle C.	1	1	4	24	17	3	0	1	8	.150	.150	.400	.168	.250	0	0	0
Abbott P.	1	1	2	14	9	2	0	0	2	.182	.182	.182	.127	.000	0	0	0
Millwood K.	1	0	1	53	39	8	2	0	10	.174	.208	.217	.148	.043	0	0	1
Myers B.	1	6	1	61	43	10	2	0	14	.196	.226	.275	.171	.078	0	0	2
Wooten S.	1	2	2	57	46	9	2	0	12	.170	.228	.226	.159	.057	0	0	2
Hinch A.	0	1	0	11	9	2	0	0	3	.182	.182	.273	.150	.091	0	0	0
Jones T.	0	0	0	1	0	0	1	0	0	.000	1.000	.000	.450	.000	0	0	0
Ramirez E.	0	0	0	1	0	0	1	0	0	.000	1.000	.000	.450	.000	0	0	0
Padilla V.	0	2	3	40	31	4	2	0	4	.114	.162	.114	.102	.000	0	0	0
Geary G.	0	0	0	1	1	0	0	0	0	.000	.000	.000	.000	.000	0	0	0
Cormier R.	0	0	0	1	1	0	0	0	0	.000	.000	.000	.000	.000	0	0	0
Hancock J.	0	0	0	2	2	0	0	0	0	.000	.000	.000	.000	.000	0	0	0
Wagner B.	0	0	0	2	2	0	0	0	0	.000	.000	.000	.000	.000	0	0	0
Madson R.	0	0	0	4	3	0	0	0	0	.000	.000	.000	.000	.000	0	0	0
Telemaco A.	0	0	0	4	4	0	0	0	0	.000	.000	.000	.000	.000	0	0	0
Powell B.	0	0	0	9	7	1	0	0	1	.125	.125	.125	.088	.000	0	0	0
Floyd G.	-1	0	0	10	10	0	0	0	0	.000	.000	.000	.000	.000	0	0	0

Pitching Stats

Player	IP	BFP	G	GS	P/PA	H	K	BB	HR	W	L	Sv	Op	Hld	RA	ERA	FIP	DER
Milton E.	201.0	862	34	34	3.99	196	161	75	43	14	6	0	0	0	4.93	4.75	5.39	.737
Myers B.	176.0	778	32	31	3.63	196	116	62	31	11	11	0	0	0	5.78	5.52	5.21	.707
Millwood K.	141.0	628	25	25	3.73	155	125	51	14	9	6	0	0	0	5.17	4.85	3.83	.673
Wolf R.	136.7	585	23	23	3.63	145	89	36	20	5	8	0	0	0	4.81	4.28	4.58	.713
Padilla V.	115.3	503	20	20	3.54	119	82	36	16	7	7	0	0	0	4.92	4.53	4.65	.713
Cormier R.	81.0	330	84	0	3.56	70	46	26	7	4	5	0	7	28	3.56	3.56	4.21	.744
Worrell T.	78.3	327	77	0	3.70	75	64	21	10	5	6	19	27	20	4.14	3.68	3.98	.717
Madson R.	77.0	312	52	1	3.87	68	55	19	6	9	3	1	2	7	2.69	2.34	3.60	.727
Lidle C.	62.3	255	10	10	3.43	54	33	17	3	5	2	0	0	0	4.04	3.90	3.70	.741
Hernandez R	56.7	260	63	0	3.83	66	44	29	9	3	5	0	4	9	6.19	4.76	5.18	.678
Telemaco A.	54.3	225	42	0	3.63	51	32	19	12	0	2	0	0	5	4.47	4.31	5.82	.759
Abbott P.	49.0	229	10	10	3.53	57	21	31	14	1	6	0	0	0	6.80	6.24	7.89	.735
Wagner B.	48.3	182	45	0	4.08	31	59	6	5	4	0	21	25	1	2.98	2.42	2.48	.764
Geary G.	44.7	200	33	0	3.77	52	30	16	8	1	0	0	0	0	5.84	5.44	5.34	.692
Powell B.	39.3	166	17	2	3.58	39	24	16	5	1	2	0	0	0	5.26	5.03	4.81	.717
Floyd G.	28.3	126	6	4	3.74	25	24	16	1	2	0	0	0	0	3.49	3.49	4.06	.700
Jones T.	25.3	123	27	0	3.76	35	22	8	3	3	3	1	2	5	4.97	4.97	4.42	.624
Rodriguez F.	21.0	90	23	0	4.28	18	28	10	1	2	3	1	1	7	3.00	3.00	2.60	.660
Ramirez E.	15.0	67	7	0	3.58	17	9	5	3	0	0	0	0	0	4.80	4.80	5.68	.714
Hancock J.	9.0	42	4	2	3.52	13	5	3	3	0	1	0	0	0	9.00	9.00	7.30	.677
Crowell J.	3.0	18	4	0	3.33	6	1	0	0	0	0	0	0	0	6.00	3.00	2.41	.647

Fielding Stats

Catchers

Name	Innings	SBA/G	CS%	ERA	WP+PB/G
Lieberthal	1104.0	0.76	20%	4.66	0.326
Pratt	333.0	0.86	13%	3.95	0.189
Hinch	25.7	1.05	67%	2.81	0.000

Infielders and Outfielders

Name	POS	Inn	PO	A	TE	FE	FPct	RF	DPS	DPT
J Thome	1B	1179.0	1089	84	2	3	.994	8.95	6	0
C Utley	1B	104.3	94	11	0	0	1.000	9.06	0	0
S Wooten	1B	62.0	70	3	0	0	1.000	10.60	0	0
R Howard	1B	60.7	59	6	0	0	1.000	9.64	4	0
T Perez	1B	56.0	49	4	1	1	.964	8.52	0	0
P Polanco	2B	944.0	265	303	2	1	.995	5.42	20	53
C Utley	2B	410.3	100	123	1	3	.982	4.89	12	16
T Perez	2B	108.3	27	32	0	0	1.000	4.90	4	2
J Rollins	SS	1376.0	213	398	3	6	.985	4.00	51	37

Philadelphia Phillies

Name	POS	Inn	PO	A	TE	FE	FPct	RF	DPS	DPT
T Perez	SS	86.0	14	26	1	1	.952	4.19	3	1
D Bell	3B	1239.0	89	307	10	13	.943	2.88	24	0
T Perez	3B	97.7	12	22	1	1	.944	3.13	1	0
P Polanco	3B	96.0	15	26	0	0	1.000	3.84	3	0
S Wooten	3B	26.3	2	4	0	0	1.000	2.05	0	0
L Collier	3B	3.0	0	1	0	0	1.000	3.00	1	0
P Burrell	LF	1060.0	217	9	0	4	.983	1.92	2	0
J Michaels	LF	227.3	49	3	0	0	1.000	2.06	4	0
R Ledee	LF	74.0	8	0	0	0	1.000	0.97	0	0
D Glanville	LF	65.3	22	0	0	0	1.000	3.03	0	0
L Collier	LF	36.0	3	0	0	0	1.000	0.75	0	0
M Byrd	CF	753.3	195	4	0	2	.990	2.38	0	1
J Michaels	CF	323.0	95	1	1	2	.970	2.67	0	0
D Glanville	CF	286.0	90	0	0	0	1.000	2.83	0	0
R Ledee	CF	100.3	38	3	0	0	1.000	3.68	2	0
B Abreu	RF	1394.0	311	13	2	3	.982	2.09	6	0
J Michaels	RF	67.0	22	1	0	0	1.000	3.09	0	0
R Ledee	RF	1.0	1	0	0	0	1.000	9.00	0	0

Pittsburgh Pirates

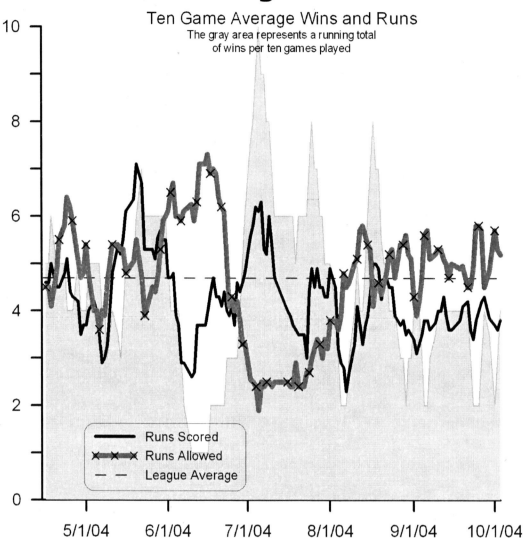

Ten Game Average Wins and Runs
The gray area represents a running total
of wins per ten games played

- Runs Scored
- ✕✕✕ Runs Allowed
- – – League Average

5/7: Bay comes
off DL

5/19: Release
Mondesi, citing
breach of
contract.

5/28: Mackowiak
hits game-winning
grand slam and
has first baby son

July: Perez is 3-1
2.16 ERA; staff
ERA is 2.64

7/30: Benson traded
to Mets for Wigginton
and MinL's

8/3: Kendall appears in
1,156th game behind
the plate for franchise
record

9/9: Perez K's 200th
batter; second Pirate
in history to do so

Team Batting and Pitching/Fielding Stats by Month						
	April	**May**	**June**	**July**	**Aug**	**Sept**
Wins	11	12	9	17	12	11
Losses	11	14	18	10	17	19
OBP	.337	.344	.293	.324	.322	.308
SLG	.414	.454	.372	.392	.403	.373
FIP	4.08	4.61	4.30	3.48	4.83	4.18
DER	.705	.682	.703	.705	.696	.706

Batting Stats

Player	RC	Runs	RBI	PA	Outs	H	BB	HR	TB	BA	OBP	SLG	GPA	ISO	SB	CS	GDP
Kendall J.	96	86	51	658	409	183	60	3	224	.319	.399	.390	.277	.071	11	8	10
Wilson C.	89	97	82	644	424	148	50	29	280	.264	.354	.499	.284	.235	2	2	9
Wilson J.	89	82	59	693	466	201	26	11	299	.308	.335	.459	.266	.150	8	4	11
Bay J.	79	61	82	472	310	116	41	26	226	.282	.358	.550	.298	.268	4	6	9
Mackowiak	76	65	75	555	377	121	50	17	206	.246	.319	.420	.249	.173	13	4	3
Redman T.	62	65	51	581	403	153	23	8	204	.280	.310	.374	.233	.093	18	6	4
Ward D.	43	39	57	321	228	73	22	15	139	.249	.305	.474	.256	.225	0	0	8
Castillo J.	40	44	39	415	301	98	23	8	141	.255	.298	.367	.226	.112	3	2	13
Hill B.	26	28	27	267	184	62	20	2	79	.266	.353	.339	.244	.073	0	3	10
Wigginton	22	17	24	206	145	40	22	5	62	.220	.306	.341	.223	.121	1	0	3
Mondesi R	16	8	14	110	74	28	11	2	42	.283	.355	.424	.266	.141	0	2	1
Nunez A.	13	17	13	194	147	43	10	2	58	.238	.276	.320	.204	.083	1	3	6
Simon R.	12	14	14	193	146	34	15	3	49	.194	.264	.280	.189	.086	0	0	5
Stynes C.	11	16	16	174	130	35	9	1	48	.216	.266	.296	.194	.080	0	0	3
Cota H.	7	10	8	70	52	15	3	5	33	.227	.271	.500	.247	.273	0	0	1
Mateo R.	7	4	7	39	26	8	5	3	17	.242	.359	.515	.290	.273	0	0	1
Alvarez T.	6	5	8	45	31	8	4	1	13	.211	.289	.342	.216	.132	0	0	1
Davis J.	2	4	3	40	30	5	4	0	6	.143	.225	.171	.144	.029	2	0	0
VanBnshot	2	2	2	11	7	1	1	1	4	.125	.222	.500	.225	.375	0	0	0
Vogelsong	2	2	3	44	25	7	2	0	9	.226	.265	.290	.192	.065	0	0	1
Sanchez F	2	2	2	20	16	3	0	0	3	.158	.158	.158	.111	.000	0	0	0
Wells K.	1	4	0	50	35	8	3	0	13	.186	.239	.302	.183	.116	0	0	0
Gonzalez	1	0	2	1	0	1	0	0	2	1.000	1.000	2.000	.950	1.000	0	0	0
Rivera C.	1	1	1	17	12	3	1	0	3	.200	.250	.200	.163	.000	0	0	0
Benson K.	1	2	3	50	32	7	1	0	7	.179	.200	.179	.135	.000	0	0	0
Torres S.	1	0	0	2	1	1	0	0	2	.500	.500	1.000	.475	.500	0	0	0
Bautista J.	1	1	0	43	33	8	2	0	10	.200	.238	.250	.170	.050	0	0	1
Perez O.	0	2	0	72	47	11	4	0	11	.190	.242	.190	.156	.000	0	0	0
Meadows	0	0	1	4	3	0	1	0	0	.000	.250	.000	.113	.000	0	0	0
Grabow J.	0	0	0	1	1	0	0	0	0	.000	.000	.000	.000	.000	0	0	0
Brooks F.	0	0	0	1	1	0	0	0	0	.000	.000	.000	.000	.000	0	0	0
Roberts W	0	0	0	1	1	0	0	0	0	.000	.000	.000	.000	.000	0	0	0
Corey M.	0	0	0	1	1	0	0	0	0	.000	.000	.000	.000	.000	0	0	0
Boehringer	0	0	0	1	1	0	0	0	0	.000	.000	.000	.000	.000	0	0	0
Snell I.	0	0	0	3	2	0	0	0	0	.000	.000	.000	.000	.000	0	0	0
Williams D	0	0	0	9	8	1	0	0	1	.111	.111	.111	.078	.000	0	0	0
Figueroa N	-1	0	1	7	6	1	0	0	1	.143	.143	.143	.100	.000	0	0	0
House J.	-1	1	0	9	9	1	0	0	2	.111	.111	.222	.106	.111	0	0	1
Fogg J.	-2	1	3	64	49	4	0	0	5	.075	.075	.094	.058	.019	0	0	0
Burnett S.	-2	0	0	27	23	0	2	0	0	.000	.080	.000	.036	.000	0	0	0

Pitching Stats

Player	IP	BFP	G	GS	P/PA	H	K	BB	HR	W	L	Sv	Op	Hld	RA	ERA	FIP	DER
Perez O.	196.0	805	30	30	3.89	145	239	81	22	12	10	0	0	0	3.26	2.98	3.47	.729
Fogg J.	178.3	770	32	32	3.62	193	82	66	17	11	10	0	0	0	4.95	4.64	4.64	.705
Wells K.	138.3	621	24	24	3.90	145	116	66	14	5	7	0	0	0	4.62	4.55	4.28	.687
Vogelsong R	133.0	610	31	26	3.77	148	92	67	22	6	13	0	0	0	6.56	6.50	5.58	.699
Benson K.	132.3	564	20	20	3.70	137	83	44	7	8	8	0	0	0	4.69	4.22	3.64	.693
Torres S.	92.0	380	84	0	3.63	87	62	22	6	7	7	0	4	30	3.23	2.64	3.49	.715
Meadows B.	78.0	323	68	0	3.43	76	46	19	7	2	4	1	2	13	4.62	3.58	3.79	.725
Burnett S.	71.7	318	13	13	3.55	86	30	28	9	5	5	0	0	0	5.15	5.02	5.09	.692
Mesa J.	69.3	295	70	0	3.61	78	37	20	6	5	2	43	48	0	3.38	3.25	4.04	.688
Grabow J.	61.7	285	68	0	3.72	81	64	28	8	2	5	1	7	11	5.69	5.11	4.05	.605
Gonzalez M.	43.3	169	47	0	3.92	32	55	6	2	3	1	1	4	13	1.45	1.25	1.62	.714
Williams D.	38.7	162	10	6	3.86	31	33	13	4	2	3	0	0	0	4.89	4.42	3.96	.752
Corey M.	35.7	164	31	0	3.71	39	28	19	3	1	2	0	1	2	5.05	4.54	4.37	.679
Van Bnschot	28.7	135	6	5	3.66	33	18	19	3	1	3	0	0	0	8.48	6.91	5.38	.677
Figueroa N.	28.3	121	10	3	3.51	32	10	11	4	0	3	0	0	0	5.72	5.72	5.37	.708
Boehringer	25.3	115	21	0	4.20	27	20	17	2	1	1	0	2	1	4.97	4.62	4.66	667
Johnston M.	22.7	110	24	0	4.06	29	18	15	2	0	3	0	1	4	6.35	4.37	4.89	.630
Brooks F.	17.3	73	11	1	3.99	13	18	9	5	0	1	0	0	0	5.19	4.67	6.31	.805
Boyd J.	13.0	64	12	0	3.63	13	12	8	4	1	0	0	0	0	6.23	5.54	7.77	.757
Roberts W.	12.0	56	9	0	3.55	12	7	9	0	0	0	0	0	2	5.25	5.25	4.66	.684
Snell I.	12.0	56	3	1	3.52	14	9	9	2	0	1	0	0	0	7.50	7.50	5.99	.667
Nunez A.	0.3	1	1	0	3.00	0	0	0	0	0	0	0	0	0	0.00	0.00	3.08	1.000

Fielding Stats

Catchers

Name	Innings	SBA/G	CS%	ERA	WP+PB/G
Kendall	1259.0	0.69	32%	4.48	0.300
Cota	133.0	0.34	20%	3.59	0.338
House	19.0	0.00	0%	0.95	0.000
Wilson	17.0	1.59	0%	1.06	0.000

Infielders and Outfielders

Name	POS	Inn	PO	A	TE	FE	FPct	RF	DPS	DPT
D Ward	1B	559.0	548	34	1	3	.991	9.37	4	0
C Wilson	1B	494.3	459	34	1	2	.994	8.98	8	0
R Simon	1B	335.3	347	24	1	1	.992	9.96	3	0
C Rivera	1B	39.0	35	2	0	0	1.000	8.54	1	0
R Mackowiak	1B	0.3	0	0	0	0	.000	0.00	0	0
J Castillo	2B	951.0	230	300	6	5	.980	5.02	21	54
B Hill	2B	255.0	70	89	0	1	.994	5.61	9	12
A Nunez	2B	197.0	59	70	2	0	.985	5.89	8	16

Pittsburgh Pirates

Name	POS	Inn	PO	A	TE	FE	FPct	RF	DPS	DPT
F Sanchez	2B	25.0	3	4	0	0	1.000	2.52	0	1
J Wilson	SS	1357.0	235	493	7	9	.977	4.83	75	51
A Nunez	SS	58.3	10	15	0	0	1.000	3.86	3	1
F Sanchez	SS	10.0	1	2	1	0	.750	2.70	0	0
J Castillo	SS	2.0	0	0	0	0	.000	0.00	0	0
T Wigginton	3B	442.7	34	92	1	5	.955	2.56	7	0
R Mackowiak	3B	411.3	37	90	0	5	.962	2.78	15	0
C Stynes	3B	391.0	28	87	1	0	.991	2.65	9	0
B Hill	3B	159.7	10	24	1	0	.971	1.92	2	0
A Nunez	3B	21.3	0	5	0	1	.833	2.11	0	0
F Sanchez	3B	2.0	0	0	0	0	.000	0.00	0	0
J Bay	LF	963.0	208	3	0	2	.991	1.97	0	0
R Mackowiak	LF	153.0	33	2	0	0	1.000	2.06	0	0
C Wilson	LF	136.0	22	0	0	1	.957	1.46	0	0
R Mondesi	LF	117.0	21	0	0	2	.913	1.62	1	0
T Alvarez	LF	25.0	4	0	0	0	1.000	1.44	0	0
J Davis	LF	20.0	2	0	0	1	.667	0.90	0	0
R Mateo	LF	14.0	1	0	1	0	.500	0.64	0	0
T Redman	CF	1207.0	338	2	0	5	.986	2.54	2	0
R Mackowiak	CF	123.0	27	1	0	1	.966	2.05	0	0
R Mateo	CF	37.3	8	1	0	0	1.000	2.17	1	0
T Alvarez	CF	25.0	6	0	0	0	1.000	2.16	0	0
J Bay	CF	21.0	3	0	0	0	1.000	1.29	0	0
J Bautista	CF	14.0	6	0	1	1	.750	3.86	0	0
C Wilson	RF	627.7	145	2	0	3	.980	2.11	0	0
R Mackowiak	RF	438.7	78	6	1	2	.966	1.72	7	0
R Mondesi	RF	105.0	23	2	0	1	.962	2.14	0	0
D Ward	RF	78.3	10	0	0	0	1.000	1.15	0	0
J Davis	RF	61.0	14	1	0	1	.938	2.21	0	0
J Bautista	RF	61.0	13	0	1	0	.929	1.92	0	0
T Alvarez	RF	36.0	7	0	0	0	1.000	1.75	0	0
R Mateo	RF	20.3	4	0	0	0	1.000	1.77	0	0

St. Louis Cardinals

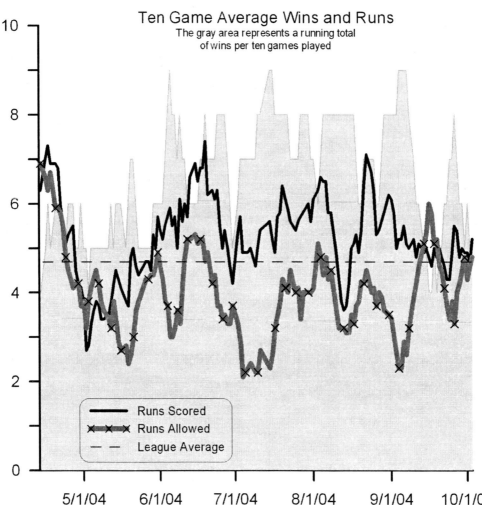

Ten Game Average Wins and Runs
The gray area represents a running total
of wins per ten games played

6/11: Move into first
place; go 70-31 on
out

8/6: Trade for
Larry Walker

9/11: Rolen out
for 16 games with
strained calf

6/8: After first loss 4/14,
Carpenter goes 6-0
with 2.73 ERA in 9 starts

8/29: 100 RBI for
Pujols for fourth time
in each of his first four
seasons

9/24: 100th
win

9/20: Carpenter strains
biceps; misses postseason

Team Batting and Pitching/Fielding Stats by Month						
	April	**May**	**June**	**July**	**Aug**	**Sept**
Wins	12	16	18	20	21	18
Losses	12	11	9	5	7	13
OBP	.342	.321	.350	.354	.358	.340
SLG	.504	.410	.427	.519	.469	.439
FIP	5.01	4.53	3.61	4.51	4.00	3.63
DER	.728	.737	.704	.726	.748	.705

Batting Stats

Player	RC	Runs	RBI	PA	Outs	H	BB	HR	TB	BA	OBP	SLG	GPA	ISO	SB	CS	GDP
Pujols A.	148	133	123	692	419	196	84	46	389	.331	.415	.657	.351	.326	5	5	18
Rolen S.	126	109	124	593	353	157	72	34	299	.314	.409	.598	.333	.284	4	3	7
Edmonds J.	118	102	111	612	355	150	101	42	320	.301	.418	.643	.349	.341	8	3	4
Womack T.	75	91	38	606	394	170	36	5	213	.307	.349	.385	.254	.078	26	5	6
Renteria E.	75	84	72	642	441	168	39	10	235	.287	.327	.401	.247	.114	17	11	12
Sanders R.	67	64	67	487	340	116	33	22	215	.260	.315	.482	.262	.222	21	5	5
Mabry J.	38	32	40	275	174	71	26	13	121	.296	.363	.504	.289	.208	0	1	4
Matheny M.	32	28	50	419	302	95	23	5	134	.247	.292	.348	.219	.101	0	2	10
Walker L.	30	29	27	178	113	42	24	11	84	.280	.393	.560	.317	.280	4	0	5
Cedeno R.	29	22	23	223	151	53	19	3	75	.265	.327	.375	.241	.110	5	1	3
Taguchi S.	27	26	25	206	135	52	12	3	75	.291	.337	.419	.256	.128	6	3	5
Lankford R.	25	36	22	235	154	51	29	6	85	.255	.349	.425	.263	.170	2	2	3
Anderson M.	24	31	28	271	200	60	12	8	96	.237	.269	.379	.216	.142	6	2	5
Luna H.	20	25	22	192	135	43	13	3	63	.249	.304	.364	.228	.116	6	3	2
Molina Y.	15	12	15	151	104	36	13	2	48	.267	.329	.356	.237	.089	0	1	4
Marquis J.	8	6	9	76	54	21	1	0	27	.292	.297	.375	.228	.083	1	0	3
McKay C.	5	7	6	79	58	17	2	0	19	.230	.269	.257	.185	.027	0	0	1
Morris M.	4	4	6	75	52	10	4	0	11	.161	.209	.177	.138	.016	0	0	0
Porter C.	3	3	2	35	26	11	0	1	15	.314	.314	.429	.249	.114	0	0	2
Reyes A.	1	0	0	1	0	1	0	0	1	1.000	1.000	1.000	.700	.000	0	0	0
Simontacchi	0	1	0	2	1	1	0	0	1	.500	.500	.500	.350	.000	0	0	0
Isringhausen	0	1	2	3	2	1	0	0	1	.333	.333	.333	.233	.000	0	0	0
Hart B.	0	0	2	14	11	2	1	0	2	.154	.214	.154	.135	.000	0	0	0
Ankiel R.	0	0	0	2	1	0	1	0	0	.000	.500	.000	.225	.000	0	0	0
Williams W.	0	3	2	70	50	11	1	0	15	.180	.200	.246	.151	.066	0	0	0
Kline S.	0	1	0	1	0	0	0	0	0	.000	.000	.000	.000!	.000	0	0	0
Calero K.	0	0	0	1	1	0	0	0	0	.000	.000	.000	.000	.000	0	0	0
King R.	0	0	0	2	2	0	0	0	0	.000	.000	.000	.000	.000	0	0	0
Flores R.	0	0	0	2	2	0	0	0	0	.000	.000	.000	.000	.000	0	0	0
Eldred C.	-1	0	0	6	6	0	0	0	0	.000	.000	.000	.000	.000	0	0	1
Haren D.	-2	1	0	14	13	0	0	0	0	.000	.000	.000	.000	.000	0	0	1
Carpenter C.	-2	1	1	67	57	5	1	0	5	.081	.095	.081	.063	.000	0	0	0
Suppan J.	-4	3	0	65	54	4	1	0	4	.070	.086	.070	.056	.000	0	0	1

Pitching Stats

Player	IP	BFP	G	GS	P/PA	H	K	BB	HR	W	L	Sv	Op	Hld	RA	ERA	FIP	DER
Morris M.	202.0	850	32	32	3.62	205	131	56	35	15	10	0	0	0	5.17	4.72	4.95	.727
Marquis J.	201.3	874	32	32	3.80	215	138	70	26	15	7	0	0	0	4.02	3.71	4.58	.700
Williams W.	189.7	817	31	31	3.83	193	131	58	20	11	8	0	0	0	4.41	4.18	4.13	.711
Suppan J.	188.0	811	31	31	3.76	192	110	65	25	16	9	0	0	0	4.60	4.07	4.80	.723
Carpenter C.	182.0	747	28	28	3.61	169	152	38	24	15	5	0	0	0	3.71	3.46	3.88	.724
Isringhausen	75.3	308	74	0	3.82	55	71	23	5	4	2	47	54	0	3.23	2.87	3.05	.758
Eldred C.	67.0	282	52	0	4.06	71	54	17	11	4	2	1	3	9	4.16	3.76	4.41	.698
Tavarez J.	64.3	268	77	0	3.73	57	48	19	1	7	4	4	6	19	2.94	2.38	2.95	.711
King R.	62.0	248	86	0	3.82	43	40	24	1	5	2	0	1	31	2.76	2.61	3.30	.767
Kline S.	50.3	202	67	0	3.68	37	35	17	3	2	2	3	4	15	2.15	1.79	3.71	.762
Haren D.	46.0	194	14	5	3.89	45	32	17	4	3	3	0	0	0	4.50	4.50	4.05	.705
Calero K.	45.3	168	41	0	4.13	27	47	10	5	3	1	2	3	13	2.78	2.78	3.16	.790
Lincoln M.	17.3	71	13	0	3.76	10	14	6	1	3	2	0	2	1	6.23	5.19	3.42	.816
Simontacchi	15.3	67	13	0	3.66	17	3	7	5	0	0	0	0	0	5.87	5.28	8.49	.765
Flores R.	14.0	57	9	1	3.19	13	7	3	0	1	0	0	0	0	1.93	1.93	3.36	.705
Reyes A.	12.0	41	12	2	4.17	3	11	2	0	0	0	0	0	0	0.75	0.75	1.74	.893
Ankiel R.	10.0	43	5	0	4.00	10	9	1	2	1	0	0	0	2	5.40	5.40	4.78	.724
Cali C.	7.3	40	10	0	3.55	13	8	6	1	0	0	0	0	0	8.59	8.59	5.12	.520
Pearce J.	2.3	9	3	0	2.44	3	0	0	0	0	0	0	0	0	3.86	3.86	3.08	.667
McKay C.	2.0	7	1	0	2.57	0	0	1	0	0	0	0	0	0	0.00	0.00	4.58	1.000

Fielding Stats

Catchers

Name	Innings	SBA/G	CS%	ERA	WP+PB/G
Matheny	977.7	0.49	28%	3.88	0.267
Molina	344.0	0.44	47%	3.64	0.392
McKay	132.0	0.75	45%	3.00	0.477

Infielders and Outfielders

Name	POS	Inn	PO	A	TE	FE	FPct	RF	DPS	DPT
A Pujols	1B	1338.0	1456	114	4	6	.994	10.56	13	1
J Mabry	1B	98.0	92	14	0	2	.981	9.73	0	0
J Edmonds	1B	9.0	9	1	0	0	1.000	10.00	0	0
M Anderson	1B	4.0	3	0	0	0	1.000	6.75	0	0
C McKay	1B	3.0	2	0	0	0	1.000	6.00	0	0
M Matheny	1B	1.0	1	0	0	0	1.000	9.00	0	0
T Womack	2B	1113.0	225	389	5	10	.976	4.96	44	37
M Anderson	2B	224.0	55	70	4	0	.969	5.02	10	11
H Luna	2B	92.7	24	33	0	0	1.000	5.54	1	5
B Hart	2B	24.0	6	9	0	0	1.000	5.63	1	3

St. Louis Cardinals

Name	POS	Inn	PO	A	TE	FE	FPct	RF	DPS	DPT
E Renteria	SS	1307.0	222	418	2	9	.983	4.41	44	47
H Luna	SS	144.3	33	56	5	0	.947	5.55	4	7
B Hart	SS	2.0	0	0	0	0	.000	0.00	0	0
S Rolen	3B	1228.0	93	324	1	8	.977	3.06	23	1
J Mabry	3B	122.3	10	27	1	2	.925	2.72	3	0
H Luna	3B	87.7	5	19	1	1	.923	2.46	2	2
C McKay	3B	15.7	1	2	0	1	.750	1.72	0	0
R Lankford	LF	392.0	82	1	0	4	.954	1.91	0	0
R Sanders	LF	297.3	65	2	0	1	.985	2.03	1	0
J Mabry	LF	225.0	48	0	0	1	.980	1.92	0	0
S Taguchi	LF	192.0	40	0	0	2	.952	1.88	0	0
M Anderson	LF	165.0	35	2	0	1	.974	2.02	1	0
R Cedeno	LF	133.7	18	2	0	0	1.000	1.35	0	0
H Luna	LF	32.3	7	0	0	0	1.000	1.95	0	0
C Porter	LF	15.3	5	0	0	0	1.000	2.93	0	0
J Simontacch	LF	1.0	0	0	0	0	.000	0.00	0	0
J Edmonds	CF	1241.0	314	11	1	3	.988	2.36	4	0
S Taguchi	CF	176.7	43	0	0	0	1.000	2.19	0	0
R Lankford	CF	21.0	3	0	0	0	1.000	1.29	0	0
H Luna	CF	10.0	2	0	0	0	1.000	1.80	0	0
C Porter	CF	2.7	0	0	0	0	.000	0.00	0	0
L Walker	CF	1.0	0	0	0	0	.000	0.00	0	0
J Mabry	CF	0.7	0	0	0	0	.000	0.00	0	0
R Sanders	RF	652.0	132	4	0	3	.978	1.88	0	0
L Walker	RF	337.3	58	1	0	1	.983	1.57	0	0
R Cedeno	RF	202.0	29	0	0	0	1.000	1.29	0	0
J Mabry	RF	114.3	21	0	0	0	1.000	1.65	0	0
S Taguchi	RF	76.3	16	1	0	0	1.000	2.00	0	0
C Porter	RF	39.0	7	0	0	0	1.000	1.62	0	0
M Anderson	RF	32.7	8	0	1	1	.800	2.20	0	0

San Diego Padres

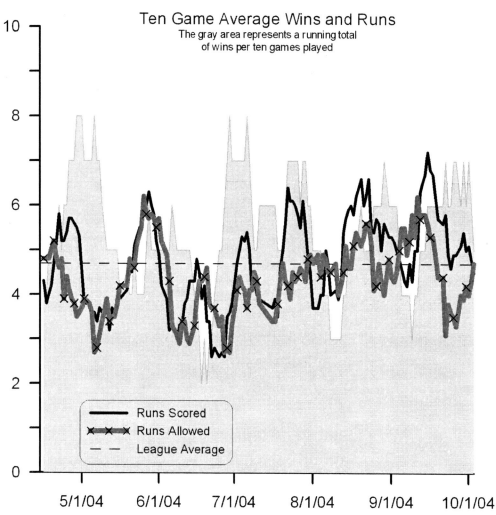

Ten Game Average Wins and Runs
The gray area represents a running total
of wins per ten games played

Legend:
— Runs Scored
✗✗✗ Runs Allowed
– – League Average

4/8: Petco Park opens with a thrilling 4-3 ten-inning Padre victory

6/13: Lose to Yankees 6-5 as bullpen blows two leads; starts six-game loss streak

7/5: Nevin has knee surgery; misses only two weeks; Pads fall out of first place two days later

9/13: Greene breaks finger, essentially ending his season

9/26: Peavy goes 6 strong innings in 7-1 victory over Arizona, essentially clinching ERA title

Team Batting and Pitching/Fielding Stats by Month						
	April	May	June	July	Aug	Sept
Wins	16	12	13	16	13	16
Losses	9	15	13	9	14	15
OBP	.350	.330	.322	.344	.358	.347
SLG	.396	.385	.369	.435	.450	.440
FIP	4.01	4.48	4.07	4.74	4.51	3.69
DER	.710	.702	.724	.741	.701	.687

Batting Stats

Player	RC	Runs	RBI	PA	Outs	H	BB	HR	TB	BA	OBP	SLG	GPA	ISO	SB	CS	GDP
Loretta M.	118	108	76	707	423	208	58	16	307	.335	.391	.495	.300	.160	5	3	8
Giles B.	107	97	94	711	451	173	89	23	289	.284	.374	.475	.287	.190	10	3	12
Nevin P.	102	78	105	623	404	158	66	26	269	.289	.368	.492	.288	.203	0	0	15
Klesko R.	80	58	66	480	294	117	73	9	180	.291	.399	.448	.291	.157	3	2	7
Greene K.	78	67	65	554	363	132	53	15	216	.273	.349	.446	.269	.174	4	2	9
Burroughs S.	71	76	47	564	377	156	31	2	191	.298	.348	.365	.248	.067	5	4	6
Payton J.	63	57	55	511	351	119	43	8	168	.260	.326	.367	.238	.107	2	0	12
Hernandez R.	54	45	63	432	294	106	35	18	183	.276	.341	.477	.273	.201	1	0	16
Long T.	32	31	28	313	217	85	19	3	121	.295	.335	.420	.256	.125	3	2	12
Ojeda M.	24	23	26	174	117	39	15	8	66	.252	.316	.426	.249	.174	0	0	1
Aurilia R.	14	22	16	158	105	35	15	2	53	.254	.331	.384	.245	.130	0	0	2
Robinson K.	10	20	5	101	69	27	5	0	31	.293	.330	.337	.233	.043	11	4	0
Vazquez R.	9	12	13	132	91	27	11	1	37	.235	.297	.322	.214	.087	1	1	2
Nady X.	8	7	9	84	62	19	5	3	32	.247	.301	.416	.239	.169	0	0	4
Cirillo J.	7	12	7	81	59	16	5	1	22	.213	.259	.293	.190	.080	0	0	0
Eaton A.	6	9	8	76	53	13	6	0	20	.203	.282	.313	.205	.109	2	0	2
Quintero H.	6	7	10	78	60	18	5	2	27	.250	.295	.375	.226	.125	0	2	4
Guzman F.	4	8	5	80	62	16	3	0	19	.211	.250	.250	.175	.039	5	2	0
Gonzalez A.	3	2	3	25	19	4	2	0	7	.174	.240	.304	.184	.130	0	0	0
Peavy J.	3	5	3	68	50	10	4	0	11	.169	.222	.186	.147	.017	0	0	1
Buchanan B.	2	7	6	68	50	12	6	2	20	.200	.279	.333	.209	.133	0	0	2
Bragg D.	1	2	0	9	6	1	2	0	1	.143	.333	.143	.186	.000	0	0	0
Knott J.	1	1	1	15	11	3	1	0	5	.214	.267	.357	.209	.143	0	0	0
Valdez I.	1	4	5	41	30	6	2	0	9	.171	.211	.257	.159	.086	0	0	1
Fick R.	0	2	0	15	10	2	2	0	2	.167	.333	.167	.192	.000	0	0	0
Tankersley D	0	0	1	10	6	2	1	0	2	.250	.333	.250	.213	.000	0	0	0
Stone R.	0	0	0	1	1	0	0	0	0	.000	.000	.000	.000	.000	0	0	0
Otsuka A.	0	0	0	1	1	0	0	0	0	.000	.000	.000	.000	.000	0	0	0
Szuminski J.	0	0	0	1	1	0	0	0	0	.000	.000	.000	.000	.000	0	0	0
Linebrink S.	0	0	0	3	2	0	0	0	0	.000	.000	.000	.000	.000	0	0	0
Hansen D.	0	1	0	31	27	4	3	0	4	.143	.226	.143	.137	.000	0	0	3
Sweeney B.	0	0	0	4	4	0	0	0	0	.000	.000	.000	.000	.000	0	0	0
Germano J.	-1	0	0	8	7	0	0	0	0	.000	.000	.000	.000	.000	0	0	0
Witasick J.	-1	0	0	5	6	0	0	0	0	.000	.000	.000	.000	.000	0	0	1
Wells D.	-1	2	3	69	52	6	3	0	6	.105	.164	.105	.100	.000	0	0	1
Hitchcock S.	-1	0	0	7	8	0	0	0	0	.000	.000	.000	.000	.000	0	0	1
Lawrence B.	-3	5	2	73	57	6	3	0	7	.097	.138	.113	.091	.016	0	0	1

Pitching Stats

Player	IP	BFP	G	GS	P/PA	H	K	BB	HR	W	L	Sv	Op	Hld	RA	ERA	FIP	DER
Lawrence	203.0	870	34	34	3.47	226	121	55	26	15	14	0	0	0	4.48	4.12	4.47	.697
Eaton A.	199.3	848	33	33	3.84	204	153	52	28	10	14	0	0	0	5.10	4.61	4.30	.709
Wells D.	195.7	804	31	31	3.49	203	101	20	23	12	8	0	0	0	3.91	3.73	3.91	.726
Peavy J.	166.3	694	27	27	3.86	146	173	53	13	15	6	0	0	0	2.65	2.27	3.17	.700
Valdez I.	114.0	509	23	20	3.53	141	37	31	21	9	6	0	0	0	5.92	5.53	5.69	.713
Linebrink	84.0	326	73	0	3.87	61	83	26	8	7	3	0	5	28	2.36	2.14	3.37	.743
Otsuka A.	77.3	312	73	0	4.03	56	87	26	6	7	2	2	7	34	1.86	1.75	2.84	.741
Witasick J.	61.7	266	44	0	3.82	57	57	26	8	0	1	1	3	2	4.09	3.21	4.23	.718
Hoffman T	54.7	209	55	0	3.70	42	53	8	5	3	3	40	44	0	2.30	2.30	2.77	.741
Neal B.	42.0	183	40	0	3.79	49	36	11	6	1	1	0	2	3	4.07	4.07	4.15	.664
Osuna A.	36.7	151	31	0	4.21	32	36	11	3	2	1	0	2	2	2.70	2.45	3.16	.710
Tankersley	35.0	157	9	6	4.00	35	29	17	3	0	5	0	0	1	6.43	5.14	4.08	.701
Stone R.	32.7	146	27	0	3.31	40	22	9	6	1	1	0	0	0	7.44	6.89	5.22	.679
Beck R.	24.0	108	26	0	3.68	27	15	9	8	0	2	0	0	5	6.75	6.38	7.29	.750
Hitchcock	21.3	91	4	4	3.66	22	14	8	5	0	3	0	0	0	6.33	6.33	5.94	.734
Germano	21.3	109	7	5	3.77	31	16	14	2	1	2	0	0	0	10.13	8.86	4.76	.623
Puffer B.	18.0	89	14	0	3.85	24	12	11	3	0	1	0	0	0	6.50	5.50	5.91	.661
Sweeney	14.3	63	7	2	3.52	20	10	2	1	1	0	0	0	0	5.65	5.65	3.01	.620
Watkins S.	14.3	65	11	0	3.66	17	7	4	3	0	0	0	0	0	6.28	6.28	6.08	.714
Szuminski	10.0	57	7	0	3.91	12	5	11	3	0	0	0	0	0	8.10	7.20	9.88	.750
Oropesa E	9.0	45	16	0	4.49	6	6	13	1	2	1	0	0	1	12.00	11.00	7.52	.800
McLeary	3.7	20	3	0	4.40	7	4	2	2	0	0	0	0	0	14.73	14.73	9.62	.583
Ashby A.	2.0	7	2	0	3.57	1	2	0	0	0	0	0	0	0	0.00	0.00	1.08	.800
Bynum M.	0.7	6	2	0	4.17	1	0	3	0	0	1	0	0	0	54.00	54.00	16.58	.667

Fielding Stats

Catchers

Name	Innings	SBA/G	CS%	ERA	WP+PB/G
Hernandez	925.3	0.69	25%	4.02	0.243
Ojeda	340.0	0.29	27%	4.31	0.185
Quintero	171.7	0.47	11%	3.67	0.210
Nevin	4.0	0.00	0%	0.00	0.000

Infielders and Outfielders

Name	POS	Inn	PO	A	TE	FE	FPct	RF	DPS	DPT
P Nevin	1B	1207.0	1140	85	3	8	.989	9.13	8	0
R Klesko	1B	139.0	138	16	0	2	.987	9.97	2	0
J Cirillo	1B	53.7	61	1	0	0	1.000	10.40	0	0
D Hansen	1B	17.0	15	1	0	0	1.000	8.47	0	0
R Fick	1B	8.0	9	0	0	0	1.000	10.13	0	0

San Diego Padres

Name	POS	Inn	PO	A	TE	FE	FPct	RF	DPS	DPT
B Buchanan	1B	7.0	9	0	0	0	1.000	11.57	0	0
R Vazquez	1B	6.0	8	0	0	0	1.000	12.00	0	0
R Aurilia	1B	3.0	7	0	0	0	1.000	21.00	0	0
M Loretta	2B	1339.0	288	451	5	5	.987	4.97	47	54
R Vazquez	2B	55.0	12	17	0	0	1.000	4.75	2	3
R Aurilia	2B	25.0	6	9	0	1	.938	5.40	0	3
J Cirillo	2B	22.0	4	9	0	2	.867	5.32	1	1
K Greene	SS	1189.0	176	380	9	11	.965	4.21	47	33
R Vazquez	SS	136.0	22	35	0	1	.983	3.77	2	3
A Gonzalez	SS	68.0	10	18	0	0	1.000	3.71	0	4
R Aurilia	SS	47.3	8	17	0	1	.962	4.75	0	2
S Burroughs	3B	1060.0	99	208	6	8	.956	2.61	21	2
R Aurilia	3B	231.7	16	42	3	2	.921	2.25	2	1
J Cirillo	3B	78.3	8	10	0	0	1.000	2.07	1	0
R Vazquez	3B	54.0	8	6	0	0	1.000	2.33	2	0
D Hansen	3B	17.0	0	1	0	0	1.000	0.53	0	0
R Klesko	LF	723.7	135	2	0	1	.986	1.70	1	0
T Long	LF	330.7	85	1	0	2	.977	2.34	0	0
K Robinson	LF	121.0	34	0	0	0	1.000	2.53	0	0
X Nady	LF	105.0	16	1	1	1	.895	1.46	0	0
B Buchanan	LF	86.7	10	0	0	0	1.000	1.04	0	0
J Payton	LF	48.0	8	0	0	0	1.000	1.50	0	0
J Knott	LF	24.0	4	0	0	0	1.000	1.50	0	0
J Cirillo	LF	2.0	0	0	0	0	.000	0.00	0	0
J Payton	CF	1027.0	333	11	1	3	.989	3.01	2	0
T Long	CF	198.3	49	1	0	0	1.000	2.27	0	0
F Guzman	CF	139.0	46	2	0	2	.960	3.11	0	0
K Robinson	CF	48.0	14	0	0	0	1.000	2.63	0	0
X Nady	CF	28.7	5	0	0	0	1.000	1.57	0	0
B Giles	RF	1383.0	323	8	2	5	.979	2.15	5	0
T Long	RF	29.3	6	0	0	0	1.000	1.84	0	0
X Nady	RF	14.0	2	0	0	0	1.000	1.29	0	0
B Buchanan	RF	11.7	2	0	0	0	1.000	1.54	0	0
K Robinson	RF	3.0	0	0	0	0	.000	0.00	0	0

San Francisco Giants

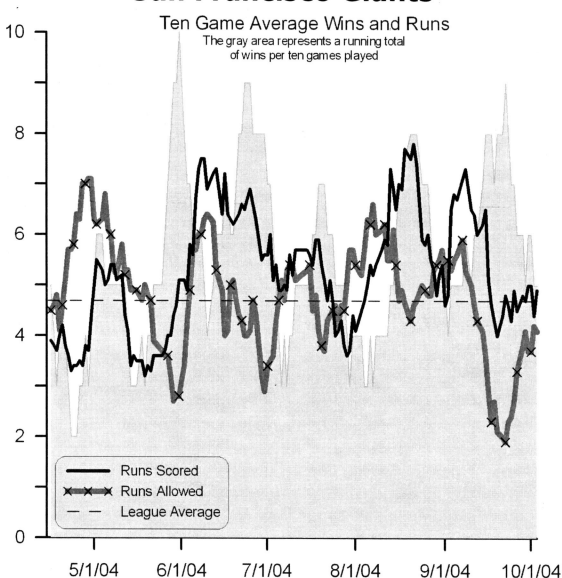

Ten Game Average Wins and Runs
The gray area represents a running total
of wins per ten games played

Runs Scored
Runs Allowed
League Average

5/1/04   6/1/04   7/1/04   8/1/04   9/1/04   10/1/04

4/16: Schmidt comes off DL

4/27: Durham on DL; back 6/15

6/22: Cruz goes 5-5 and replaces Perez

7/4: JT Snow hits PH HR, beginning second half surge

8/4: Hermanson becomes closer

8/26: Tomko blanks Marlins, staff ace in September

Team Batting and Pitching/Fielding Stats by Month						
	April	**May**	**June**	**July**	**Aug**	**Sept**
Wins	11	15	18	13	16	18
Losses	14	11	10	14	12	10
OBP	.347	.333	.380	.347	.372	.361
SLG	.392	.395	.466	.427	.495	.443
FIP	4.76	4.34	4.53	4.78	3.81	4.04
DER	.694	.726	.703	.701	.685	.752

Batting Stats

Player	RC	Runs	RBI	PA	Outs	H	BB	HR	TB	BA	OBP	SLG	GPA	ISO	SB	CS	GDP
Bonds B.	177	129	101	617	244	135	232	45	303	.362	.609	.812	.477	.450	6	1	5
Durham R.	85	95	65	542	347	133	57	17	228	.282	.364	.484	.285	.202	10	4	5
Snow J.	82	62	60	417	236	113	58	12	183	.327	.429	.529	.325	.202	4	0	3
Grissom M.	75	78	90	606	425	157	37	22	253	.279	.323	.450	.258	.171	3	1	19
Alfonzo E.	75	66	77	576	386	150	46	11	211	.289	.350	.407	.259	.118	1	1	16
Tucker M.	69	77	62	547	352	119	70	13	191	.256	.353	.412	.262	.155	5	2	5
Feliz P.	60	72	84	531	381	139	23	22	244	.276	.305	.485	.259	.209	5	2	15
Pierzynski A	60	45	77	510	370	128	19	11	193	.272	.319	.410	.246	.138	0	1	26
Cruz D.	55	46	55	431	296	116	17	7	171	.292	.322	.431	.252	.139	1	3	12
Mohr D.	44	52	28	324	198	72	46	7	115	.274	.394	.437	.287	.163	0	3	4
Perez N.	26	28	33	353	252	74	21	2	94	.232	.276	.295	.198	.063	0	1	6
Torrealba Y.	19	19	23	196	140	39	17	6	70	.227	.302	.407	.238	.180	2	0	7
Ransom C.	10	13	11	78	55	17	6	1	26	.250	.320	.382	.240	.132	2	2	2
Hammonds	9	14	6	113	77	20	15	3	34	.211	.336	.358	.241	.147	1	0	2
Minor D.	9	8	6	74	46	14	12	0	16	.241	.405	.276	.251	.034	0	0	2
Dallimore B.	6	8	7	49	32	12	4	1	17	.279	.347	.395	.255	.116	0	1	0
Ellison J.	3	4	3	4	2	2	0	1	5	.500	.500	1.250	.538	.750	2	0	0
Torcato T.	3	1	2	12	4	5	1	0	5	.556	.583	.556	.401	.000	0	0	0
Hennessey	1	1	2	15	10	3	1	0	3	.231	.267	.231	.178	.000	0	0	0
Schmidt J.	1	4	3	84	56	9	4	2	15	.138	.200	.231	.148	.092	0	0	0
Rueter K.	1	4	2	67	53	8	3	0	10	.131	.172	.164	.118	.033	0	0	0
Correia K.	1	1	0	4	2	1	1	0	2	.333	.500	.667	.392	.333	0	0	0
Ledee R.	1	6	4	60	48	6	5	0	8	.113	.200	.151	.128	.038	1	0	1
Linden T.	1	6	1	40	27	5	5	0	6	.156	.289	.188	.177	.031	0	0	0
Franklin W.	1	2	2	5	2	1	1	0	1	.333	.400	.333	.263	.000	0	0	0
Brower J.	0	1	0	3	1	1	1	0	1	.500	.667	.500	.425	.000	0	0	0
Lowry N.	0	2	0	36	27	6	0	0	8	.182	.182	.242	.142	.061	0	0	0
Burba D.	0	0	0	1	1	0	0	0	0	.000	.000	.000	.000	.000	0	0	0
Knoedler J.	0	0	0	1	1	0	0	0	0	.000	.000	.000	.000	.000	0	0	0
Rodriguez F	0	0	0	1	1	0	0	0	0	.000	.000	.000	.000	.000	0	0	0
Eyre S.	0	0	0	2	2	0	0	0	0	.000	.000	.000	.000	.000	0	0	0
Cooper B.	0	0	0	3	3	0	0	0	0	.000	.000	.000	.000	.000	0	0	0
Walker T.	-1	0	0	7	7	0	0	0	0	.000	.000	.000	.000	.000	0	0	0
Hermanson	-1	2	1	37	27	3	0	0	3	.100	.129	.100	.083	.000	0	0	0
Williams J.	-2	1	0	43	32	5	1	0	5	.139	.162	.139	.108	.000	0	1	0
Tomko B.	-3	3	0	77	56	7	2	0	8	.113	.141	.129	.096	.016	0	0	1

Pitching Stats

Player	IP	BFP	G	GS	P/PA	H	K	BB	HR	W	L	Sv	Op	Hld	RA	ERA	FIP	DER
Schmidt J.	225.0	907	32	32	3.97	165	251	77	18	18	7	0	0	0	3.36	3.20	2.95	.737
Tomko B.	194.0	825	32	31	3.84	196	108	64	19	11	7	0	0	0	4.55	4.04	4.23	.721
Rueter K.	190.3	840	33	33	3.91	225	56	66	21	9	12	0	0	0	5.11	4.73	4.98	.707
Hermanson	131.0	565	47	18	3.72	132	102	46	15	6	9	17	20	1	4.88	4.53	4.13	.707
Williams J.	129.3	559	22	22	3.59	123	80	44	14	10	7	0	0	0	4.80	4.24	4.66	.730
Brower J.	93.0	401	89	0	3.63	90	63	36	6	7	7	1	5	24	4.06	3.29	3.85	.712
Lowry N.	92.0	383	16	14	3.65	91	72	28	10	6	0	0	0	0	4.01	3.82	3.84	.703
Herges M.	65.3	301	70	0	3.70	90	39	21	8	4	5	23	31	5	6.06	5.23	4.58	.643
Walker T.	63.7	275	52	0	3.86	69	48	24	8	5	1	1	1	5	4.38	4.24	4.38	.686
Eyre S.	52.7	229	83	0	4.14	43	49	27	8	2	2	1	5	23	4.44	4.10	4.73	.759
Franklin W.	50.7	227	43	2	3.97	55	40	22	11	2	1	0	1	5	6.57	6.39	5.80	.709
Rodriguez F	44.7	199	53	0	4.29	43	31	19	7	3	5	0	3	13	3.63	3.43	5.27	.739
Christiansen	36.0	167	60	0	3.87	34	22	26	3	4	3	3	6	8	5.00	4.50	5.35	.726
Hennessey	34.3	163	7	7	3.85	42	25	15	2	2	2	0	0	0	6.29	4.98	3.69	.669
Correia K.	19.0	92	12	1	3.74	25	14	10	3	0	1	0	0	0	9.47	8.05	5.39	.656
Cooper B.	13.3	61	5	2	3.38	15	7	5	4	0	2	0	0	0	8.78	8.78	7.28	.750
Aardsma D.	10.7	61	11	0	3.87	20	5	10	1	1	0	0	1	1	6.75	6.75	6.73	.558
Burba D.	6.3	27	6	0	2.93	7	3	2	1	1	0	0	1	1	5.68	5.68	5.13	.714
Walker K.	1.7	10	5	0	5.30	3	1	2	1	0	0	0	0	1	16.20	16.20	15.08	.600
Valdez M.	1.7	12	2	0	4.75	4	2	3	1	0	0	0	0	0	27.00	27.00	13.88	.500
Estrella L.	1.3	13	2	0	2.62	8	0	1	0	0	0	0	0	0	27.00	27.00	5.33	.333
Foppert J.	1.0	4	1	0	4.50	1	2	0	0	0	0	0	0	0	0.00	0.00	-0.92	.500

Fielding Stats

Catchers

Name	Innings	SBA/G	CS%	ERA	WP+PB/G
Pierzynski	1022.0	0.55	18%	4.30	0.396
Torrealba	433.0	0.56	22%	4.47	0.374
Knoedler	2.0	0.00	0%	0.00	0.000

Infielders and Outfielders

Name	POS	Inn	PO	A	TE	FE	FPct	RF	DPS	DPT
J Snow	1B	793.0	799	55	0	4	.995	9.69	9	1
P Feliz	1B	535.7	524	41	1	4	.991	9.49	7	0
D Minor	1B	128.3	131	9	0	0	1.000	9.82	1	0
R Durham	2B	990.3	243	314	4	12	.972	5.06	25	40
N Perez	2B	291.7	80	115	1	0	.995	6.02	6	15
C Ransom	2B	80.3	28	21	1	0	.980	5.49	2	3
B Dallimore	2B	49.7	8	18	0	1	.963	4.71	1	2
E Alfonzo	2B	42.0	5	10	1	1	.882	3.21	1	1

San Francisco Giants

Name	POS	Inn	PO	A	TE	FE	FPct	RF	DPS	DPT
D Cruz	2B	3.0	0	0	0	0	.000	0.00	0	0
D Cruz	SS	800.7	127	266	0	8	.980	4.42	35	26
N Perez	SS	440.0	67	157	3	1	.978	4.58	15	14
P Feliz	SS	119.7	17	48	2	3	.929	4.89	6	3
C Ransom	SS	96.7	20	35	1	2	.948	5.12	5	6
E Alfonzo	3B	1081.0	87	246	8	4	.965	2.77	17	2
P Feliz	3B	339.3	32	85	2	1	.975	3.10	6	1
B Dallimore	3B	29.0	4	8	1	0	.923	3.72	0	0
N Perez	3B	5.3	1	0	0	0	1.000	1.69	0	0
D Cruz	3B	1.0	0	0	0	0	.000	0.00	0	0
C Ransom	3B	1.0	0	0	1	0	.000	0.00	0	0
B Bonds	LF	1130.0	214	11	0	4	.983	1.79	0	0
D Mohr	LF	219.3	55	2	0	0	1.000	2.34	2	0
T Linden	LF	51.7	6	0	0	0	1.000	1.05	0	0
J Hammonds	LF	45.3	8	1	0	0	1.000	1.79	0	0
R Ledee	LF	7.0	1	0	0	0	1.000	1.29	0	0
P Feliz	LF	2.0	1	0	0	0	1.000	4.50	0	0
C Ransom	LF	1.0	0	0	0	0	.000	0.00	0	0
M Grissom	CF	1219.0	341	3	0	1	.997	2.54	3	0
M Tucker	CF	168.0	52	1	0	2	.964	2.84	1	0
D Mohr	CF	32.0	9	0	0	0	1.000	2.53	0	0
R Ledee	CF	19.0	6	0	0	0	1.000	2.84	0	0
J Ellison	CF	10.0	5	0	0	0	1.000	4.50	0	0
J Hammonds	CF	9.0	2	0	0	0	1.000	2.00	0	0
M Tucker	RF	838.0	209	1	0	4	.981	2.26	3	0
D Mohr	RF	377.3	89	4	0	3	.969	2.22	1	0
J Hammonds	RF	149.3	39	2	0	0	1.000	2.47	0	0
R Ledee	RF	72.0	17	0	0	1	.944	2.13	0	0
T Linden	RF	16.3	3	0	0	0	1.000	1.65	0	0
P Feliz	RF	4.0	0	0	0	0	.000	0.00	0	0

Lee Sinins' RCAA and RSAA

Runs Created Above Average (RCAA) and Runs Saved Above Average (RSAA) are the two mainstay statistics maintained and reported by Lee Sinins. Lee is the creator of the Sabermetric Baseball Encyclopedia (a must-have for the serious baseball fan) and he is also a daily contributor to the Hardball Times. You can subscribe to his daily e-mail on the Hardball Times site, and to order the Encyclopedia, visit www.baseball-encyclopedia.com.

National League RCAA by Team

DIAMONDBACKS	
Gonzalez	11
Alomar	3
Hillenbrand	3
Sexson	3
Finley	2
Snyder	0
Hill	-2
Zinter	-2
McCracken	-3
Sadler	-3
Colbrunn	-5
DeVore	-6
Kata	-6
Mayne	-6
Baerga	-7
Tracy	-7
Olson	-8
Kroeger	-9
Terrero	-9
Hairston	-11
Gil	-12
Green	-12
Hammock	-13
Bautista	-15
Brito	-18
Cintron	-29

BRAVES	
Drew	66
Marrero	14
Giles	13
Jones	11
Estrada	9
Franco	6
Thomas	5
LaRoche	2
Furcal	1
Hollins	1
Jones	0
Wise	-5
Betemit	-6

Green	-8
Garcia	-9
Hessman	-9
Perez	-11
DeRosa	-20

CUBS	
Alou	30
Ramirez	24
Lee	13
Hollandsworth	10
Sosa	5
Walker	5
Perez	4
Garciaparra	0
Grieve	0
DiFelice	-1
Dubois	-1
Barrett	-2
Grudzielanek	-2
Jackson	-2
Kelton	-2
Patterson	-8
Macias	-9
Ordonez	-9
Goodwin	-10
Bako	-13
Gonzalez	-14
Martinez	-15

REDS	
Dunn	52
Casey	40
Griffey Jr.	12
Freel	8
Mo Pena	6
Jimenez	3
LaRue	1
Machado	1
Larkin	0
Lopez	-2
Romano	-2

Clark	-4
Kearns	-4
Larson	-4
Bragg	-5
Vander Wal	-5
Cruz	-6
Valentin	-7
Hummel	-8
Miller	-8
Castro	-15

ROCKIES	
Helton	78
Walker	16
Burnitz	12
Sweeney	4
Atkins	3
Piedra	-2
Tracy	-2
Closser	-3
Barmes	-4
Holliday	-4
Greene	-7
Hawpe	-8
Castilla	-9
Pellow	-9
Johnson	-10
Reyes	-10
Gonzalez	-11
Freeman	-12
Hocking	-15
Wilson	-16
Clayton	-31
Miles	-32

MARLINS	
Cabrera	26
Lowell	26
Choi	18
Pierre	10
Easley	1

Aguila	-1
Castillo	-1
Conine	-2
Willingham	-2
Encarnacion	-4
Treanor	-4
Cordero	-5
Mordecai	-5
Nunez	-7
Harris	-8
Lo Duca	-8
Castro	-10
Redmond	-12
Gonzalez	-26

ASTROS	
Berkman	69
Beltran	28
Bagwell	17
Kent	12
Lamb	11
Biggio	8
Lane	3
Bruntlett	2
Tremie	0
Alfaro	-2
Burke	-3
Palmeiro	-4
Hidalgo	-9
Everett	-11
Ensberg	-12
Vizcaino	-14
Chavez	-19
Ausmus	-26

DODGERS	
Beltre	64
Hernandez	13
Green	9
Werth	9
Bradley	3

Lee Sinins' RCAA and RSAA

Lee Sinins' RCAA and RSAA

Roberts	3
Saenz	3
Finley	1
Flores	-1
Lo Duca	-1
Perez	-1
Chen	-2
Thurston	-2
Ventura	-3
Cora	-4
Choi	-5
Grabowski	-7
Izturis	-8
Mayne	-9
Encarnacion	-13
Ross	-14

BREWERS	
Overbay	24
Branyan	3
Ginter	2
Clark	1
Grieve	0
Erickson	-1
Johnson	-1
Krynzel	-2
Spivey	-2
Liefer	-3
Durrington	-4
Magruder	-5
Jenkins	-6
Helms	-12
Bennett	-16
Podsednik	-20
Counsell	-21
Hall	-23
Moeller	-31

EXPOS	
Wilkerson	30
Rivera	12
Vidro	9
Sledge	7
Carroll	4
Johnson	1
Labandeira	-3
Lopez	-3
Bergeron	-4
Gonzalez	-4
Mateo	-4

Cepicky	-5
Harris	-5
Izturis	-5
Pascucci	-5
Everett	-6
Church	-7
Fox	-7
Schneider	-7
Chavez	-9
Calloway	-10
Diaz	-10
Batista	-20
Cabrera	-20

METS	
Wright	7
Floyd	6
Piazza	4
Cameron	2
Wigginton	2
Delgado	1
Spencer	0
Valent	0
Buchanan	-1
Diaz	-1
Garcia	-1
Wilson	-1
Wilson	-2
Duncan	-3
Matsui	-4
Keppinger	-6
Williams	-6
McEwing	-7
Gutierrez	-8
Reyes	-9
Garcia	-10
Hidalgo	-11
Zeile	-17
Phillips	-23

PHILLIES	
Abreu	69
Thome	43
Rollins	14
Bell	10
Burrell	9
Ledee	6
Michaels	3
Collier	0
Howard	0
Polanco	0
Hinch	-1

Utley	-3
Pratt	-4
Lieberthal	-6
Wooten	-7
Perez	-10
Glanville	-16
Byrd	-25

PIRATES	
Wilson	19
Bay	18
Kendall	15
Wilson	6
Mateo	1
Mondesi	0
Cota	-1
Rivera	-1
Alvarez	-2
House	-2
Mackowiak	-2
Sanchez	-2
Ward	-3
Bautista	-4
Davis	-4
Wigginton	-8
Hill	-10
Stynes	-11
Redman	-13
Nunez	-15
Simon	-16
Castillo	-18

PADRES	
Loretta	44
Giles	30
Nevin	23
Klesko	21
Greene	9
Hernandez	5
Ojeda	1
Aurilia	-1
Bragg	-1
Burroughs	-1
Fick	-1
Gonzalez	-1
Knott	-1
Robinson	-1
Long	-3
Nady	-3
Buchanan	-4
Hansen	-4
Cirillo	-5

Quintero	-5
Guzman	-6
Vazquez	-6
Payton	-9

GIANTS	
Bonds	152
Snow	35
Durham	15
Mohr	6
Ellison	3
Torcato	2
Dallimore	-1
Tucker	-1
Minor	-2
Hammonds	-3
Linden	-4
Ransom	-4
Alfonzo	-7
Ledee	-8
Torrealba	-9
Cruz	-11
Feliz	-11
Grissom	-12
Pierzynski	-23
Perez	-27

CARDINALS	
Pujols	75
Edmonds	73
Rolen	57
Walker	12
Mabry	7
Sanders	4
Womack	3
Lankford	-1
Porter	-1
Hart	-2
Taguchi	-4
Cedeno	-5
Molina	-5
Luna	-6
McKay	-6
Renteria	-12
Anderson	-14
Matheny	-23

National League RSAA by Team

DIAMONDBACKS	
Johnson	50
Webb	20
Aquino	5
Koplove	4
Valverde	1
Villafuerte	1
Bruney	0
Gosling	0
Reynolds	0
Choate	-1
Nance	-2
Dessens	-3
Durbin	-4
Good	-4
Villarreal	-5
Service	-6
Fetters	-9
Mantei	-9
Randolph	-10
Daigle	-15
Cormier	-19
Sparks	-21
Gonzalez	-25
Fossum	-35

BRAVES	
Wright	21
Alfonseca	14
Smoltz	14
Ramirez	13
Thomson	13
Cruz	12
Gryboski	8
Byrd	5
Ortiz	4
Colon	2
Reitsma	2
Martin	1
Drew	0
Hampton	0
McConnell	0
Nitkowski	0
Almanza	-2
Cunnane	-4
Capellan	-6
Smith	-9

CUBS	
Zambrano	42

Clement	18
Hawkins	18
Rusch	16
Maddux	13
Wood	13
Mercker	12
Prior	7
Remlinger	5
Leicester	3
Dempster	1
Wuertz	1
Beltran	0
Farnsworth	-1
Pratt	-3
Wellemeyer	-4
Borowski	-8
Mitre	-12

REDS	
Hudson	8
Jones	1
Graves	0
Bong	-1
Myette	-2
Hancock	-3
Valentine	-4
Wagner	-4
Sanchez	-6
Wilson	-7
Matthews	-8
Norton	-8
Haynes	-9
Reith	-9
Riedling	-10
White	-10
Padilla	-11
Harang	-15
Claussen	-16
Lidle	-22
Van Poppel	-27
Acevedo	-34

ROCKIES	
Kennedy	27
Reed	11
Cook	10
Wright	9
Dohmann	5
Harikkala	3
Tsao	1

Francis	0
Simpson	0
Bernero	-1
Driskill	-1
Fuentes	-2
Wendell	-3
Fassero	-4
Jarvis	-5
Nunez	-5
Jennings	-7
Young	-7
Gissell	-9
Lopez	-11
Chacon	-14
Estes	-15
Stark	-18
Elarton	-21

MARLINS	
Pavano	27
Benitez	22
Penny	14
Burnett	6
Beckett	5
Seanez	3
Weathers	3
Koch	2
Willis	2
Perisho	-2
Valdez	-2
Borland	-3
Fox	-3
Gracesqui	-3
Mota	-3
Phelps	-3
Howard	-6
Tejera	-6
Wayne	-6
Bump	-7
Manzanillo	-7
Small	-8
Kensing	-9
Oliver	-15

ASTROS	
Clemens	32
Lidge	26
Oswalt	22
Miller	10
Miceli	6

Dotel	5
Pettitte	4
Qualls	3
Springer	3
Wheeler	3
Oliver	1
Backe	0
Gallo	-2
Harville	-2
Weathers	-2
Griffiths	-3
Stone	-3
Bullinger	-6
Munro	-9
Hernandez	-10
Duckworth	-11
Redding	-15

DODGERS	
Perez	19
Gagne	18
Mota	14
Carrara	12
Sanchez	7
Brazoban	6
Weaver	3
Dessens	2
Kida	2
Alvarez	1
Lima	1
Myers	1
Penny	1
Martin	0
Venafro	0
Ventura	0
Dreifort	-2
Stewart	-2
Falkenborg	-5
Jackson	-9
Ishii	-11
Nomo	-38

BREWERS	
Sheets	45
Davis	24
Kolb	9
Adams	6
Vizcaino	5
Burba	3
Kieschnick	3

Lee Sinins' RCAA and RSAA

Saenz	3
Glover	2
Liriano	1
Durrington	0
Wise	0
Bennett	-3
Phelps	-4
de la Rosa	-5
Ford	-5
Capuano	-6
Hernandez	-7
Hendrickson	-9
Kinney	-9
Santos	-9
Obermueller	-18

EXPOS

Ayala	14
Hernandez	14
Cordero	11
Rauch	7
Ohka	6
Horgan	4
Tucker	3
Day	2
Majewski	1
Eischen	0
Beltran	-1
Corcoran	-2
Fikac	-4
Beltran	-5
Bentz	-5
Armas	-6
Downs	-7
Kim	-7
Patterson	-10
Hill	-12
Vargas	-15
Biddle	-25

METS

Leiter	20
Glavine	16
Looper	15
Stanton	10
Bottalico	7
DeJean	6

Trachsel	6
Bell	3
Moreno	3
Parra	2
Fortunato	1
Zambrano	1
Weathers	0
Benson	-2
Darensbourg	-2
Feliciano	-2
Ginter	-2
Erickson	-3
Wheeler	-3
Heilman	-4
Franco	-5
Zeile	-5
Baldwin	-7
Roberts	-7
Seo	-8
Yates	-11

PHILLIES

Madson	17
Wagner	10
Cormier	7
Worrell	6
Floyd	3
Lidle	3
Rodriguez	3
Wolf	1
Telemaco	0
Ramirez	-1
Jones	-2
Hernandez	-3
Padilla	-3
Powell	-3
Hancock	-5
Geary	-6
Millwood	-8
Milton	-9
Abbott	-10
Myers	-23

PIRATES

Perez	25
Torres	15
Gonzalez	14

Mesa	7
Meadows	5
Nunez	0
Benson	-1
Boehringer	-1
Brooks	-1
Johnston	-1
Roberts	-1
Williams	-1
Boyd	-2
Corey	-2
Snell	-4
Figueroa	-5
Burnett	-7
Grabow	-7
Wells	-7
Van Benschoten	-9
Fogg	-10
Vogelsong	-35

PADRES

Peavy	31
Otsuka	19
Linebrink	17
Hoffman	10
Osuna	6
Wells	5
Witasick	5
Ashby	1
Neal	0
Lawrence	-3
Puffer	-3
Sweeney	-3
Bynum	-4
McLeary	-4
Szuminski	-4
Watkins	-4
Tankersley	-5
Beck	-6
Hitchcock	-6
Oropesa	-7
Stone	-11
Germano	-12
Eaton	-14
Valdez	-20

GIANTS

Schmidt	31
Brower	12
Tomko	9
Lowry	6
Rodriguez	5
Williams	3
Eyre	2
Walker	1
Christiansen	0
Foppert	0
Burba	-1
Hermanson	-1
Hennessey	-2
Walker	-2
Aardsma	-3
Estrella	-3
Valdez	-4
Cooper	-6
Herges	-6
Rueter	-6
Correia	-8
Franklin	-11

CARDINALS

Carpenter	14
Kline	13
Tavarez	13
Isringhausen	11
King	11
Marquis	10
Calero	7
Reyes	5
Eldred	3
Flores	3
McKay	1
Pearce	0
Suppan	0
Williams	0
Ankiel	-1
Haren	-2
Lincoln	-2
Simontacchi	-2
Cali	-4
Morris	-12

American League RCAA by Team

ANGELS	
Guerrero	56
Guillen	15
Quinlan	15
DaVanon	10
Glaus	9
Anderson	8
Figgins	5
Erstad	2
Galarraga	0
McPherson	0
Kennedy	-1
Paul	-3
Pride	-3
Riggs	-4
Mondesi	-5
Kotchman	-8
Halter	-9
Salmon	-9
Molina	-10
Amezaga	-12
Molina	-14
Eckstein	-17

ORIOLES	
Mora	54
Tejada	23
Lopez	21
Newhan	10
Hairston Jr.	2
Palmeiro	2
Surhoff	2
Segui	0
Bautista	-1
Gil	-1
Bigbie	-2
Huckaby	-2
Majewski	-2
Mottola	-2
McDonald	-4
Garcia	-5
Osik	-5
Raines Jr.	-6
Leon	-10
Lopez	-10
Machado	-10
Roberts	-10
Gibbons	-17
Matos	-24

REDSOX	
Ramirez	49
Ortiz	46
Damon	25
Varitek	19
Millar	15
Bellhorn	10
Nixon	7
Mirabelli	6
Garciaparra	5
Mueller	5
Hyzdu	2
Youkilis	2
Cabrera	-1
Martinez	-1
Daubach	-2
Dominique	-2
Roberts	-2
Burks	-3
Gutierrez	-3
McCarty	-5
Mientkiewicz	-9
Crespo	-11
Kapler	-11
Reese	-21

WHITESOX	
Lee	26
Thomas	26
Rowand	25
Konerko	14
Burke	2
Gload	2
Ordonez	2
Dransfeldt	-1
Olivo	-2
Everett	-3
Uribe	-4
Valdez	-5
Alomar	-8
Davis	-9
Alomar Jr.	-12
Harris	-16
Valentin	-16
Borchard	-18
Perez	-22
Crede	-23

INDIANS	
Hafner	51

Broussard	18
Martinez	15
Blake	9
Bard	5
Lawton	5
Crisp	2
Phelps	2
Sizemore	1
Belliard	0
Martinez	0
Gonzalez	-2
Little	-2
Ludwick	-2
Peralta	-2
Phillips	-3
Vizquel	-3
Merloni	-4
Gerut	-5
Escobar	-7
McDonald	-8
Laker	-11

TIGERS	
Guillen	36
Rodriguez	29
Monroe	10
Pena	7
Young	7
Inge	6
Thames	3
White	2
Infante	0
Torres	0
Granderson	-1
Higginson	-1
Logan	-2
DiFelice	-3
Shelton	-3
Raburn	-4
Smith	-4
Munson	-5
Sanchez	-7
Norton	-8
Vina	-9

ROYALS	
Beltran	18
Sweeney	15
Stairs	4

Stinnett	3
Blanco	1
Pickering	1
Randa	1
Brown	0
Thompson	0
Castillo	-1
DeJesus	-1
Gomez	-1
Gonzalez	-1
Harvey	-1
Jackson	-1
Phillips	-1
Gettis	-2
Bautista	-3
Guerrero	-3
Murphy	-3
Berger	-5
Gotay	-5
Lopez	-6
Santiago	-6
Graffanino	-7
Brown	-8
Mateo	-8
Buck	-9
Nunez	-10
Guiel	-11
Berroa	-15
Relaford	-24

TWINS	
Ford	19
Stewart	12
Morneau	10
Mauer	9
Koskie	8
Ojeda	5
Kubel	1
Offerman	0
Restovich	0
Tiffee	0
Borders	-1
Bartlett	-2
Prieto	-2
Cuddyer	-3
Punto	-3
Bowen	-4
Hunter	-5
LeCroy	-6
Ryan	-6

Mientkiewicz	-10
Rivas	-11
Jones	-15
Guzman	-24
Blanco	-26

YANKEES

Matsui	44
Sheffield	40
Rodriguez	35
Posada	18
Jeter	14
Williams	4
Cairo	1
Lofton	1
Olerud	1
Navarro	0
Phillips	0
Bush	-1
Escalona	-1
Lee	-3
Giambi	-4
Sierra	-4
Clark	-5
Crosby	-5
Flaherty	-5
Wilson	-18

A'S

Durazo	38
Chavez	21
Kotsay	21
Byrnes	13
Hatteberg	8
Rose	0
Swisher	0
Dye	-2
Castro	-3

Melhuse	-3
German	-4
Menechino	-6
McLemore	-7
Kielty	-8
McMillon	-8
Karros	-9
Miller	-11
Crosby	-15
Scutaro	-17

MARINERS

Suzuki	56
Ibanez	16
Winn	7
Reed	6
Jacobsen	5
Hansen	3
Leone	0
Olerud	-1
Rivera	-1
Bocachica	-2
Dobbs	-3
McCracken	-3
Martinez	-4
Santiago	-4
Borders	-6
Davis	-6
Bloomquist	-7
Boone	-7
Olivo	-8
Cabrera	-9
Lopez	-9
Aurilia	-13
Spiezio	-15
Wilson	-16

DEVIL RAYS

Huff	28
Crawford	14
Martinez	13
Cantu	3
Cummings	3
Cruz Jr.	2
Baldelli	0
Diaz	0
Gipson	0
Lugo	0
Upton	0
Bautista	-1
Romano	-1
Gomes	-2
Perez	-2
Simon	-2
Gathright	-3
McGriff	-5
Fick	-12
Fordyce	-12
Rolls	-15
Sanchez	-16
Blum	-20
Hall	-21

RANGERS

Teixeira	30
Young	13
Blalock	10
Mench	10
Matthews Jr.	4
Ardoin	0
Soriano	0
Alexander	-1
Fox	-2
Dellucci	-3
Gonzalez	-3

Nivar	-3
Allen	-5
Huckaby	-5
Young	-6
Conti	-7
Perry	-8
Fullmer	-10
Laird	-15
Nix	-15
Barajas	-16
Jordan	-18

BLUEJAYS

Delgado	19
Menechino	13
Adams	2
Estalella	-1
Hermansen	-1
Myers	-1
Wells	-1
Crozier	-2
Zaun	-3
Catalanotto	-5
Hudson	-5
Quiroz	-5
Pond	-6
Clark	-8
Gross	-8
Gomez	-11
Berg	-12
Rios	-13
Phelps	-14
Woodward	-15
Cash	-17
Johnson	-24
Hinske	-28

American League RSAA by Team

ANGELS	
Rodriguez	26
Escobar	15
Shields	15
Percival	9
Donnelly	7
Gregg	4
Turnbow	3
Ortiz	2
Dunn	-1
Hensley	-1
Washburn	-1
Bergman	-2
Lackey	-2
Sele	-7
Weber	-9
Colon	-10

ORIOLES	
Ryan	25
Lopez	23
Parrish	12
Chen	10
Williams	7
Bedard	3
Grimsley	2
Julio	2
Bauer	1
Groom	0
Rakers	0
Rodriguez	0
Cubillan	-1
Borkowski	-2
Maine	-2
Cabrera	-3
DeJean	-6
Riley	-6
Bautista	-7
Ponson	-12
DuBose	-13
Ainsworth	-17

REDSOX	
Schilling	42
Foulke	25
Martinez	24
Arroyo	18
Williamson	12
Timlin	7
Embree	5

Mendoza	5
Leskanic	4
DiNardo	2
Seibel	2
Castillo	1
Malaska	1
McCarty	1
Myers	1
Wakefield	1
Jones	0
Anderson	-1
Brown	-1
Alvarez	-2
Adams	-3
Kim	-3
Martinez	-4
Nelson	-4
Astacio	-5
Lowe	-10

WHITESOX	
Buehrle	29
Takatsu	18
Marte	13
Garcia	6
Politte	3
Adkins	2
Darensbourg	1
Garland	1
Loaiza	1
Wunsch	1
Jackson	0
Koch	-1
Rauch	-1
Contreras	-3
Bajenaru	-5
Cotts	-5
Wright	-6
Munoz	-8
Schoeneweis	-8
Stewart	-9
Diaz	-10
Grilli	-12

INDIANS	
Westbrook	28
Howry	9
Miller	9
Sabathia	9
Riske	7

Betancourt	5
Stanford	5
Cabrera	1
Laker	1
Wickman	1
Bartosh	0
Elarton	0
Guthrie	0
Robbins	0
Dawley	-1
Pote	-1
Tadano	-1
Cressend	-3
Lee	-3
Anderson	-4
Cruceta	-4
Stewart	-4
White	-6
Denney	-9
D'Amico	-11
Davis	-12
Durbin	-12
Robertson	-12
Jimenez	-16
Lee	-18

TIGERS	
Walker	9
Yan	6
Maroth	3
Ledezma	0
Urbina	0
Levine	-1
Patterson	-1
Novoa	-3
German	-5
Urdaneta	-6
Colyer	-7
Dingman	-7
Ennis	-7
Bonderman	-9
Robertson	-10
Cornejo	-11
Knotts	-12
Johnson	-15

ROYALS	
Greinke	7
Cerda	6
Camp	4

Grimsley	3
Bukvich	1
Field	1
Seanez	1
MacDougal	-1
Serrano	-1
Carrasco	-2
Sullivan	-2
Villacis	-3
Affeldt	-4
Appier	-4
Reyes	-4
Kinney	-5
Bautista	-6
Leskanic	-6
Huisman	-7
George	-13
Gobble	-15
Wood	-17
Anderson	-22
May	-25

TWINS	
Santana	54
Radke	31
Nathan	25
Rincon	19
Silva	12
Romero	10
Crain	8
Balfour	2
Roa	2
Durbin	-2
Fultz	-2
Guerrier	-2
Thomas	-4
Pulido	-5
Mulholland	-6
Beimel	-7
Greisinger	-8
Lohse	-13

YANKEES	
Gordon	22
Rivera	22
Hernandez	11
Brown	5
Lieber	2
Karsay	1
Padilla	1

Lee Sinins' RCAA and RSAA

DePaula	-1
Prinz	-2
Mussina	-3
Proctor	-3
Quantrill	-3
Nitkowski	-5
Osborne	-5
Halsey	-7
Heredia	-8
Graman	-9
Sturtze	-9
White	-9
Vazquez	-10
Contreras	-13
Loaiza	-19

A'S

Hudson	24
Duchscherer	15
Harden	14
Hammond	12
Mecir	6
Mulder	6
Rincon	5
Zito	4
Dotel	3
Bradford	2
Saarloos	1
Harville	0
Blanton	-1
Redman	-1
Lehr	-2
Rhodes	-2
Garcia	-5

MARINERS

Garcia	13
Madritsch	10
Guardado	7
Atchison	2
Villone	2
Sherrill	1
Thornton	0
Williams	-1
Myers	-2
Taylor	-2
Mateo	-3
Putz	-3
Soriano	-3
Baek	-4
Kida	-4
Jarvis	-6
Hasegawa	-7
Pineiro	-7
Meche	-11
Nageotte	-13
Franklin	-14
Blackley	-17
Moyer	-22

DEVIL RAYS

Carter	9
Miller	7
Baez	6
Colome	5
Harper	5
Seay	5
Fortunato	1
Bell	0
Zambrano	0
Gonzalez	-1
Gaudin	-2

Nunez	-2
Webb	-3
Halama	-4
Ritchie	-4
Brazelton	-5
Kazmir	-5
Standridge	-5
Hendrickson	-8
Moss	-11
Abbott	-12
Sosa	-12
Waechter	-12
Gonzalez	-14

RANGERS

Cordero	24
Drese	21
Mahay	19
Shouse	14
Almanzar	11
Francisco	10
Rodriguez	9
Rogers	8
Brocail	6
Powell	5
Dominguez	3
Ramirez	3
Lewis	2
Young	2
Bacsik	1
Garcia	0
Loe	0
Bierbrodt	-1
Hughes	-1
Nelson	-1
Erickson	-2
Narron	-2
Regilio	-2

Snare	-2
Tejera	-3
Callaway	-4
Park	-4
Dickey	-6
Benoit	-7
Wasdin	-12

BLUEJAYS

Lilly	19
Bush	14
Halladay	11
Speier	8
Frasor	6
Adams	5
Chacin	4
Batista	3
League	3
Chulk	2
Glynn	2
File	0
Menechino	0
de los Santos	-2
Lopez	-2
Towers	-2
Kershner	-3
Peterson	-4
Frederick	-5
Douglass	-6
Maurer	-7
Nakamura	-7
Ligtenberg	-9
Miller	-10
Hentgen	-18

Win Shares and Net Win Shares Value

Net Win Shares Value is the total contractual value a player brought to his team, compared to the average baseball player's contract in 2004. It is based on the status of the player (free agent, arbitration-eligible or not arbitration eligible), the contract he signed and his total Win Shares Above Replacement (WSR). The full documentation of this methodology can be found at *http://www.hardballtimes.com/main/article/net-win-shares-value/*.

For this table, we researched the status of each player individually, but there are no official MLB sources for a player's status. These represent our best educated guesses. The table lists each player's THT Win Shares, WSR, and salary in order of most to least Net Win Shares Value. Salary is listed in thousands. If a player played for more than one team during the year, we show his statistics in total.

Name	POS	FA?	WS	WSR	Salary	Net WS Value
Bonds B	OF	FA	53	41	$18,000.0	$23,442.8
Rolen S	3B	FA	38	26	$7,781.0	$16,991.5
Beltre A	3B	A	37	23	$5,000.0	$14,731.6
Dunn A	OF	NA	31	17	$445.0	$14,599.5
Pujols A	1B	A	40	26	$7,000.0	$14,581.3
Loretta M	2B	FA	33	19	$2,500.0	$14,390.6
Edmonds J	OF	FA	36	23	$9,333.3	$14,039.3
Drew J	OF	A	34	21	$4,200.0	$13,520.0
Santana J	P	A	27	17	$1,600.0	$13,332.4
Abreu B	OF	FA	37	23	$10,600.0	$12,763.2
Tejada M	SS	FA	30	16	$4,789.0	$11,057.1
Hafner T	1B	NA	21	13	$316.3	$10,963.4
Blalock H	3B	A	26	13	$550.0	$10,290.7
Ortiz D	1B	FA	25	15	$4,587.5	$9,949.4
Zambrano C	P	NA	19	12	$450.0	$9,650.4
Young M	SS	NA	25	11	$450.0	$9,246.9
Snow J	1B	FA	20	12	$1,500.0	$9,153.0
Matsui H	OF	FA	29	16	$7,000.0	$9,114.2
Lidge B	P	NA	17	11	$360.0	$9,097.8
Mora M	3B	A	25	13	$2,333.3	$8,929.4
Rowand A	OF	NA	21	11	$340.0	$8,870.3
Teixeira M	1B	NA	25	13	$2,625.0	$8,681.1
Izturis C	SS	NA	25	10	$358.5	$8,612.3
Nathan J	P	A	16	10	$440.0	$8,545.0
Peavy J	P	NA	16	10	$350.0	$8,474.6
Guillen C	SS	A	24	13	$2,500.0	$8,472.4
Berkman L	OF	A	32	18	$6,500.0	$8,437.5
Perez O	P	NA	17	10	$321.0	$8,374.4
Rodriguez F	P	NA	15	10	$375.0	$8,187.9
Durazo E	1B	A	20	12	$2,100.0	$8,129.8
Sheffield G	OF	FA	31	18	$12,029.1	$8,110.9
Helton T	1B	FA	31	18	$11,600.0	$7,914.7
Giles M	2B	NA	18	9	$430.0	$7,789.4
Casey S	1B	A	30	18	$6,800.0	$7,774.7
Kennedy J	P	NA	15	9	$320.0	$7,669.2

Name	POS	FA?	WS	WSR	Salary	Net WS Value
Martinez V	C	NA	20	9	$304.5	$7,637.9
Clemens R	P	FA	20	12	$4,751.7	$7,605.0
Bellhorn M	2B	A	21	9	$490.0	$7,524.4
Sheets B	P	A	20	11	$2,425.0	$7,290.0
Jimenez D	2B	A	23	10	$1,615.0	$7,156.9
Estrada J	C	NA	19	8	$312.5	$7,138.3
Greene K	SS	NA	20	8	$300.5	$7,104.9
Crawford C	OF	NA	21	8	$320.0	$7,073.0
Benitez A	P	FA	16	11	$3,500.0	$7,006.5
Guerrero V	OF	FA	29	16	$11,000.0	$7,000.8
Suzuki I	OF	FA	27	13	$6,528.0	$6,957.4
Wilkerson B	1B	NA	22	8	$375.0	$6,896.6
Cabrera M	OF	NA	22	8	$320.0	$6,666.5
Rollins J	SS	A	25	11	$2,425.0	$6,662.1
Rincon J	P	NA	12	8	$330.0	$6,631.3
Pena W	OF	NA	15	8	$345.0	$6,560.9
Guillen J	OF	FA	21	9	$2,200.0	$6,560.0
Lopez R	P	NA	15	8	$365.0	$6,518.6
Figgins C	3B	NA	20	8	$320.0	$6,453.8
Lowell M	3B	FA	26	12	$6,500.0	$6,445.9
Pavano C	P	A	20	12	$3,800.0	$6,440.1
Gordon T	P	FA	15	10	$3,500.0	$6,369.0
Bay J	OF	NA	17	7	$305.0	$6,176.9
Uribe J	2B	NA	18	7	$350.0	$6,124.9
Westbrook J	P	A	17	8	$925.0	$6,103.0
Cordero F	P	A	15	9	$2,000.0	$6,071.4
Damon J	OF	FA	26	13	$8,000.0	$5,963.1
Wilson J	SS	A	23	9	$1,850.0	$5,939.1
Byrnes E	OF	NA	19	7	$328.0	$5,848.9
Schneider B	C	NA	17	7	$350.0	$5,751.1
Foulke K	P	FA	15	9	$3,500.0	$5,724.3
Takatsu S	P	FA	11	7	$750.0	$5,711.1
Broussard B	1B	NA	16	7	$324.1	$5,654.6
Marquis J	P	A	14	7	$525.0	$5,649.6
Rodriguez I	C	FA	22	11	$6,521.6	$5,593.9

Win Shares and Net Win Shares Value

Name	POS	FA?	WS	WSR	Salary	Net WS Value		Name	POS	FA?	WS	WSR	Salary	Net WS Value
Lugo J	SS	A	21	8	$1,750.0	$5,564.7		Franco J	1B	FA	12	5	$750.0	$3,852.9
Otsuka A	P	FA	11	7	$700.0	$5,473.3		Burnitz J	OF	FA	18	6	$2,500.0	$3,821.3
Freel R	3B	NA	18	6	$320.0	$5,461.4		Marte D	P	A	9	5	$500.0	$3,815.4
Overbay L	1B	NA	20	6	$326.0	$5,357.5		Castillo L	2B	FA	21	8	$4,666.7	$3,771.7
Pierre J	OF	A	24	9	$2,400.0	$5,112.8		Giles B	OF	FA	25	11	$8,563.0	$3,707.0
Mench K	OF	NA	15	6	$345.0	$5,051.2		Cairo M	2B	FA	13	5	$900.0	$3,690.0
Beltran C	OF	A	31	17	$9,000.0	$5,017.1		Webb B	P	NA	12	4	$335.0	$3,687.8
Davis D	P	A	14	6	$450.0	$4,998.7		Baldelli R	OF	NA	15	4	$320.0	$3,683.2
Torres S	P	A	11	6	$775.0	$4,959.3		Clark B	OF	A	13	4	$376.0	$3,673.9
Sledge T	OF	NA	15	6	$300.0	$4,931.2		Almanzar C	P	FA	8	4	$420.0	$3,653.3
Duchscherer	P	NA	10	6	$302.5	$4,866.9		Carpenter C	P	FA	11	4	$500.0	$3,611.5
Shields S	P	NA	11	6	$375.0	$4,859.3		Blake C	3B	NA	17	4	$352.4	$3,607.1
Lamb M	3B	NA	12	6	$352.0	$4,855.0		Durham R	2B	FA	20	9	$7,200.0	$3,591.6
Linebrink S	P	NA	10	6	$326.0	$4,848.9		Nevin P	1B	FA	23	10	$8,500.0	$3,574.0
Lilly T	P	A	16	8	$1,900.0	$4,843.9		Michaels J	OF	NA	11	4	$335.0	$3,540.5
Oswalt R	P	A	18	9	$3,250.0	$4,820.6		Johnson R	P	FA	25	16	$16,500.0	$3,494.2
Kendall J	C	FA	25	12	$8,571.4	$4,796.1		Furcal R	SS	A	21	8	$3,700.0	$3,489.1
Madson R	P	NA	9	6	$300.0	$4,788.9		Cruz J	P	NA	7	4	$370.0	$3,416.1
Alou M	OF	FA	26	12	$9,500.0	$4,707.5		Lo Duca P	C	A	21	9	$4,066.7	$3,357.2
Wright J	P	A	13	6	$850.0	$4,700.3		Alfonseca A	P	FA	8	5	$1,350.0	$3,324.5
Silva C	P	NA	14	6	$340.0	$4,659.3		Wilson C	OF	A	18	5	$1,150.0	$3,280.3
Cora A	2B	A	17	7	$1,300.0	$4,634.5		Schilling C	P	FA	22	13	$12,000.0	$3,270.6
Cordero C	P	NA	10	5	$300.0	$4,597.0		Marrero E	OF	A	13	7	$3,000.0	$3,261.8
Hudson O	2B	NA	16	5	$320.0	$4,539.8		Gagne E	P	A	16	10	$5,000.0	$3,247.8
Werth J	OF	NA	12	5	$303.0	$4,508.1		DaVanon J	OF	NA	10	4	$375.0	$3,195.9
Choi H	1B	NA	14	5	$310.0	$4,506.5		Roberts D	OF	A	12	5	$975.0	$3,136.8
Schmidt J	P	FA	19	11	$7,937.5	$4,472.9		Tavarez J	P	FA	8	5	$1,600.0	$3,119.5
Rivera J	OF	NA	14	5	$312.0	$4,467.9		Millar K	1B	FA	17	6	$3,300.0	$3,115.6
Ryan B	P	A	11	7	$1,275.0	$4,462.0		Barrett M	C	FA	15	5	$1,550.0	$3,096.4
Klesko R	OF	FA	19	9	$6,000.0	$4,372.1		Mackowiak R	OF	NA	15	4	$335.0	$3,091.2
Conine J	OF	FA	19	7	$3,000.0	$4,199.2		Mauer J	C	NA	6	4	$300.0	$3,053.2
Huff A	3B	A	20	8	$2,666.7	$4,159.7		Cameron M	OF	FA	18	7	$4,333.3	$3,034.2
Belliard R	2B	FA	18	6	$1,100.0	$4,159.0		Jones T	P	FA	8	4	$425.0	$3,002.6
Kent J	2B	FA	24	12	$9,517.6	$4,146.9		Burroughs S	3B	NA	15	4	$340.0	$2,998.2
Patterson C	OF	A	19	5	$480.0	$4,136.5		Thomson J	P	FA	12	5	$2,250.0	$2,980.1
Hawkins L	P	FA	12	7	$2,666.7	$4,053.3		Mohr D	OF	NA	10	4	$342.5	$2,950.3
Sanders R	OF	FA	16	6	$2,000.0	$4,027.2		Payton J	OF	FA	15	4	$1,500.0	$2,943.0
Crisp C	OF	NA	15	5	$319.4	$4,027.1		Carter L	P	NA	7	3	$320.0	$2,911.0
Kotsay M	OF	FA	22	9	$6,500.0	$4,025.1		Romero J	P	A	8	4	$820.0	$2,899.0
Bell D	3B	FA	20	8	$4,400.0	$4,015.5		Lee C	OF	A	24	11	$6,500.0	$2,856.6
Buehrle M	P	A	19	9	$3,500.0	$3,959.7		Dellucci D	OF	FA	11	4	$750.0	$2,841.9
Mota G	P	A	11	6	$1,475.0	$3,940.3		Looper B	P	FA	10	5	$2,000.0	$2,823.1
Mahay R	P	FA	8	5	$500.0	$3,928.8		Mesa J	P	FA	9	4	$800.0	$2,798.9
Ayala L	P	NA	9	5	$317.5	$3,915.6		Thomas F	1B	FA	12	8	$6,000.0	$2,784.5
Walker T	2B	FA	14	6	$1,750.0	$3,863.1		Larkin B	SS	FA	11	4	$700.0	$2,783.5

Win Shares and Net Win Shares Value

Name	POS	FA?	WS	WSR	Salary	Net WS Value
Sierra R	OF	FA	9	4	$1,000.0	$2,754.5
Menechino F	2B	A	9	3	$400.0	$2,748.7
Lopez J	C	FA	19	7	$6,000.0	$2,747.3
Hoffman T	P	FA	9	5	$2,500.0	$2,685.5
Everett A	SS	NA	12	3	$370.0	$2,643.6
Gload R	1B	NA	8	3	$302.0	$2,630.9
Zambrano V	P	NA	9	3	$325.0	$2,626.5
Willis D	P	NA	10	3	$353.5	$2,611.8
Ginter K	2B	NA	12	3	$383.3	$2,611.5
King R	P	A	7	4	$900.0	$2,587.9
Kolb D	P	A	9	5	$1,500.0	$2,568.7
Brower J	P	A	8	3	$662.5	$2,557.5
Posada J	C	FA	20	9	$9,000.0	$2,515.8
LaRue J	C	A	15	6	$2,750.0	$2,494.0
Kieschnick B	P	NA	4	3	$380.0	$2,480.8
Jennings J	P	NA	10	3	$340.0	$2,470.9
Maroth M	P	NA	12	3	$332.5	$2,468.0
Easley D	2B	FA	8	3	$300.0	$2,456.8
Surhoff B	OF	FA	10	3	$800.0	$2,423.1
Miller D	C	A	15	6	$3,000.0	$2,422.9
Lane J	OF	NA	6	3	$307.5	$2,391.9
Mirabelli D	C	A	7	3	$825.0	$2,356.0
Calero K	P	NA	5	3	$305.0	$2,306.0
Mercker K	P	FA	6	3	$1,200.0	$2,289.9
Miceli D	P	FA	7	3	$600.0	$2,286.8
Sanchez D	P	NA	6	3	$305.0	$2,280.1
Lackey J	P	NA	11	3	$375.0	$2,267.5
Castilla V	3B	FA	16	3	$1,195.2	$2,256.0
Griffey Jr. K	OF	FA	16	9	$9,142.6	$2,250.6
Parrish J	P	NA	6	3	$320.0	$2,224.3
Koplove M	P	NA	7	3	$330.0	$2,212.6
Reed S	P	FA	6	3	$600.0	$2,197.3
Cuddyer M	3B	NA	10	3	$307.5	$2,184.3
Monroe C	OF	NA	12	3	$335.0	$2,175.5
Rogers K	P	FA	13	4	$2,406.6	$2,157.4
Roberts B	2B	NA	16	3	$345.0	$2,120.9
Arroyo B	P	NA	10	3	$332.5	$2,093.1
Grissom M	OF	FA	16	4	$2,125.0	$2,082.7
Ojeda M	C	NA	6	2	$305.0	$2,060.5
Winn R	OF	FA	18	5	$3,500.0	$2,041.1
Kline S	P	FA	6	3	$1,700.0	$2,025.2
Ramirez A	3B	A	22	10	$6,000.0	$1,996.7
Tucker M	OF	FA	14	3	$1,500.0	$1,991.6
Miller T	P	FA	5	3	$650.0	$1,977.9
Escobar K	P	FA	15	6	$5,750.0	$1,965.5

Name	POS	FA?	WS	WSR	Salary	Net WS Value
Infante O	2B	NA	13	2	$305.0	$1,952.4
Betancourt R	P	NA	6	2	$305.2	$1,948.4
Gryboski K	P	NA	5	2	$377.5	$1,940.8
Hollandsworth	OF	FA	6	3	$1,000.0	$1,890.0
Hatteberg S	1B	A	17	5	$2,300.0	$1,870.4
Biggio C	OF	FA	18	4	$3,000.0	$1,858.1
Sweeney M	OF	FA	6	2	$400.0	$1,854.3
Gregg K	P	NA	6	2	$301.5	$1,847.5
Wells D	P	FA	10	3	$1,250.0	$1,843.5
Radke B	P	FA	19	10	$10,750.0	$1,811.2
Hudson T	P	A	16	8	$5,000.0	$1,807.8
Wells V	OF	A	14	3	$870.0	$1,776.5
Clark T	1B	FA	8	2	$750.0	$1,731.5
Vizcaino L	P	A	6	2	$550.0	$1,729.9
Rivera M	P	FA	16	10	$10,890.0	$1,675.5
Punto N	2B	NA	4	2	$307.5	$1,672.6
Hammond C	P	FA	6	4	$2,400.0	$1,670.7
Grieve B	OF	FA	8	2	$700.0	$1,654.4
Riske D	P	A	7	3	$1,025.0	$1,642.0
Walker J	P	A	6	3	$775.0	$1,614.6
Ventura R	1B	FA	6	3	$1,200.0	$1,613.5
Anderson G	OF	FA	15	6	$6,200.0	$1,594.3
Lieber J	P	FA	11	4	$2,700.0	$1,587.4
Beckett J	P	A	9	3	$1,509.4	$1,512.8
Ramirez H	P	NA	4	2	$330.0	$1,511.1
Mueller B	3B	FA	12	3	$2,100.0	$1,466.0
Estes S	P	FA	9	2	$600.0	$1,455.0
Grudzielanek	2B	FA	9	2	$2,500.0	$1,453.0
Bigbie L	OF	NA	12	2	$340.0	$1,436.9
Molina B	C	A	11	4	$2,025.0	$1,429.2
Day Z	P	NA	6	2	$315.0	$1,406.3
Speier J	P	A	7	3	$1,600.0	$1,386.6
Chavez E	3B	A	19	8	$5,325.0	$1,329.0
Ledee R	OF	FA	6	2	$1,225.0	$1,307.3
Dotel O	P	A	11	5	$2,800.0	$1,301.4
Stairs M	OF	FA	11	4	$1,000.0	$1,284.1
Stewart S	OF	FA	13	5	$5,500.0	$1,233.9
Burba D	P	FA	5	2	$440.0	$1,224.5
Villone R	P	FA	7	2	$1,000.0	$1,215.5
Young E	OF	FA	9	2	$1,000.0	$1,209.4
Tomko B	P	FA	9	2	$1,200.0	$1,188.2
Melhuse A	C	FA	6	1	$357.5	$1,181.7
Moreno O	P	NA	3	1	$317.5	$1,139.1
Polanco P	2B	A	17	6	$3,950.0	$1,138.8
Ramirez E	P	NA	3	1	$303.8	$1,127.0

Win Shares and Net Win Shares Value

Name	POS	FA?	WS	WSR	Salary	Net WS Value
Williams J	P	NA	6	1	$308.0	$1,082.7
Baez D	P	A	8	3	$1,750.0	$1,068.9
Meadows B	P	FA	5	2	$625.0	$1,065.8
Pena C	1B	NA	12	1	$330.0	$935.2
Towers J	P	NA	6	1	$340.0	$931.4
Sabathia C	P	A	12	4	$2,700.0	$930.9
Cruz J	OF	FA	15	3	$2,500.0	$911.4
Stanton M	P	FA	7	3	$3,000.0	$895.9
Osuna A	P	FA	3	1	$750.0	$866.4
Taguchi S	OF	FA	6	2	$1,200.0	$847.9
Roa J	P	NA	4	1	$320.0	$827.2
Grimsley J	P	FA	5	1	$1,000.0	$818.0
Camp S	P	NA	4	1	$300.0	$806.5
Harris W	2B	NA	10	1	$318.5	$799.8
Thome J	1B	FA	22	10	$12,166.7	$794.7
Barajas R	C	A	9	1	$500.0	$790.6
Carroll J	2B	NA	6	1	$310.0	$769.4
Ramirez M	OF	FA	28	16	$20,409.5	$749.5
Yan E	P	FA	6	1	$650.0	$729.8
Wilson V	C	A	5	1	$715.0	$716.8
Myers M	P	FA	3	1	$550.0	$713.2
Palmeiro O	OF	FA	4	1	$750.0	$713.0
Halama J	P	FA	6	1	$600.0	$702.6
Guardado E	P	FA	7	4	$4,000.0	$696.1
Torcato T		NA	1	1	$302.0	$690.8
Field N	P	NA	3	1	$306.5	$682.7
Crosby B	SS	NA	13	1	$300.0	$662.7
Reitsma C	P	A	6	2	$950.0	$662.5
Perisho M	P	NA	3	1	$300.0	$659.7
Wuertz M	P	NA	2	1	$300.0	$641.8
Cormier R	P	FA	7	3	$3,000.0	$639.4
Isringhausen	P	FA	12	6	$7,750.0	$638.7
Rodriguez A	3B	FA	30	17	$21,726.9	$631.2
La Roche A	1B	NA	8	1	$300.0	$629.7
German E	3B	NA	2	1	$301.0	$598.9
Valentin J	SS	FA	14	4	$5,000.0	$582.3
Bauer R	P	NA	3	1	$335.0	$572.8
Bruntlett E	SS	NA	2	1	$307.5	$568.9
Munson E	3B	NA	9	2	$1,487.5	$568.0
White R	OF	FA	11	2	$2,750.0	$543.3
Adams T	P	FA	5	2	$1,700.0	$537.8
Hansen D	1B	FA	3	1	$750.0	$531.3
Choate R	P	NA	3	1	$325.8	$518.4
Ensberg M	3B	NA	10	1	$380.0	$514.0
Merloni L	1B	A	5	1	$560.0	$512.7

Name	POS	FA?	WS	WSR	Salary	Net WS Value
Hernandez R	C	A	13	4	$2,937.5	$505.9
Podsednik S	OF	NA	15	1	$400.0	$493.0
McEwing J	2B	A	4	1	$500.0	$479.1
Timlin M	P	FA	6	2	$2,500.0	$469.4
Eldred C	P	FA	4	1	$900.0	$469.0
Stanford J	P	NA	1	1	$302.5	$457.7
Scutaro M	2B	NA	10	1	$301.5	$445.3
Fogg J	P	NA	7	1	$342.0	$426.0
Molina J	C	NA	5	1	$335.0	$425.6
Wise D	OF	NA	4	1	$325.0	$421.2
Alvarez W	P	FA	6	1	$1,500.0	$418.0
Pratt T	C	FA	4	1	$875.0	$412.6
Rincon R	P	FA	4	2	$1,750.0	$412.4
Vizquel O	SS	FA	17	5	$6,250.0	$403.7
Grabowski J	OF	NA	4	0	$300.0	$390.4
Matsui K	SS	FA	14	4	$5,066.7	$342.3
Julio J	P	NA	5	0	$385.0	$333.4
Olivo M	C	NA	7	0	$320.0	$332.6
Ibanez R	OF	FA	13	3	$3,916.7	$326.2
Floyd C	OF	FA	14	5	$6,500.0	$322.2
Hairston Jr. J	OF	A	8	2	$1,650.0	$314.7
Ransom C	SS	NA	2	0	$303.0	$313.5
Paul J	C	NA	2	0	$335.0	$291.9
Wheeler D	P	NA	3	0	$311.5	$286.8
Adkins J	P	NA	3	0	$301.0	$281.4
Hendrickson	P	NA	8	0	$315.0	$272.7
Lewis C	P	NA	1	0	$337.5	$271.6
Gomez C	SS	FA	8	1	$750.0	$266.8
Levine A	P	FA	4	1	$825.0	$252.1
Gonzalez L	2B	NA	7	0	$300.0	$244.1
Mulder M	P	A	15	6	$4,450.0	$233.3
Bonderman J	P	NA	8	0	$330.0	$222.6
Fultz A	P	A	3	1	$550.0	$221.4
Daubach B	1B	FA	2	0	$500.0	$210.0
Carrasco D	P	NA	2	0	$320.5	$208.4
Eyre S	P	A	4	1	$1,000.0	$198.2
Rivas L	2B	A	9	2	$1,500.0	$164.5
Mateo J	P	NA	3	0	$345.0	$161.9
Miles A	2B	NA	11	0	$300.0	$153.9
Hall T	C	NA	9	0	$320.0	$153.7
Bradford C	P	A	4	1	$965.0	$146.0
Reyes D	P	FA	5	0	$550.0	$87.6
Nix L	OF	NA	8	0	$300.0	$87.2
Luna H	SS	NA	4	0	$300.0	$74.8
Cotts N	P	NA	3	0	$301.0	$66.1

Win Shares and Net Win Shares Value

Name	POS	FA?	WS	WSR	Salary	Net WS Value
Valverde J	P	NA	2	0	$320.0	$62.6
Politte C	P	FA	3	0	$800.0	$45.7
Phelps J	1B	NA	6	0	$342.0	$9.4
Wellemeyer T	P	NA	1	0	$310.0	$5.8
Prior M	P	NA	7	3	$2,600.0	($2.6)
Worrell T	P	FA	7	2	$2,750.0	($7.5)
Cust J		NA	0	(0)	$305.0	($16.4)
Thompson R	OF	NA	0	(0)	$300.0	($22.8)
Kearns A	OF	NA	5	0	$400.0	($23.3)
Batista M	P	FA	11	2	$3,600.0	($26.1)
Lincoln M	P	A	1	0	$450.0	($27.2)
Pratt A	P	NA	0	(0)	$300.0	($56.7)
Estrella L	P	NA	0	(0)	$316.0	($61.4)
Olmedo R	SS	NA	0	(0)	$322.0	($66.3)
Torrealba Y	C	NA	4	(0)	$334.0	($67.5)
Perez E	1B	FA	1	0	$750.0	($73.5)
Miller W	P	A	7	4	$3,400.0	($77.4)
Thomas B	P	NA	0	(0)	$300.0	($93.0)
Flaherty J	C	FA	3	0	$775.0	($94.0)
Offerman J	1B	FA	3	0	$500.0	($110.0)
Obermueller	P	NA	4	(0)	$314.0	($115.6)
Jackson M	P	FA	2	0	$500.0	($116.8)
Dinardo L	P	NA	1	(0)	$300.0	($120.9)
Randolph S	P	NA	3	(0)	$322.5	($121.6)
Capuano C	P	NA	3	(0)	$305.0	($123.4)
Fuentes B	P	NA	2	(0)	$320.0	($124.6)
Gobble J	P	NA	6	(0)	$304.0	($125.0)
Fikac J	P	NA	1	(0)	$350.0	($125.0)
Appier K	P	FA	0	(0)	$300.0	($139.5)
Robinson K	OF	A	2	0	$450.0	($158.1)
Crosby B	OF	NA	1	(0)	$301.4	($169.8)
Feliz P	1B	A	11	1	$850.0	($171.7)
Kim S	P	NA	5	(0)	$303.0	($191.7)
Weaver J	P	FA	12	4	$6,250.0	($200.2)
Affeldt J	P	NA	4	(0)	$350.0	($225.5)
Walker K	P	A	0	(0)	$450.0	($235.8)
Robertson N	P	NA	8	(0)	$345.0	($239.4)
Greene T	C	FA	4	(0)	$550.0	($240.9)
Hart B	2B	NA	0	(0)	$307.0	($246.0)
Thurston J	2B	NA	0	(0)	$301.0	($258.2)
Perez T	2B	A	4	0	$750.0	($264.0)
Zito B	P	A	12	3	$3,000.0	($265.9)
Martinez T	1B	FA	15	5	$7,500.0	($282.0)
Rivera C	1B	NA	0	(0)	$312.0	($301.0)
Suppan J	P	FA	7	0	$1,000.0	($307.2)

Name	POS	FA?	WS	WSR	Salary	Net WS Value
Hall B	2B	NA	8	(0)	$310.0	($314.7)
Nitkowski C	P	FA	1	(0)	$350.0	($321.3)
Szuminski J	P	NA	0	(0)	$300.0	($331.1)
Vizcaino J	SS	FA	8	0	$1,200.0	($338.3)
Randa J	3B	FA	12	2	$3,250.0	($341.0)
Cota H	C	NA	1	(0)	$303.0	($341.5)
Cabrera J	3B	A	8	0	$1,000.0	($342.1)
Fassero J	P	FA	4	(0)	$500.0	($348.4)
Telemaco A	P	FA	2	(0)	$525.0	($350.3)
Dickey R	P	NA	4	(0)	$337.5	($352.4)
Nivar R	OF	NA	0	(0)	$300.0	($353.9)
Gerut J	OF	NA	10	(0)	$325.6	($355.2)
Wagner R	P	NA	2	(0)	$302.5	($362.3)
Lee C	P	NA	7	(0)	$303.2	($372.2)
Escobar A	OF	NA	3	(0)	$302.2	($373.6)
Macias J	3B	A	4	0	$750.0	($376.6)
Hermanson D	P	FA	6	(0)	$800.0	($379.9)
Garcia J	SS	NA	2	(0)	$312.5	($391.4)
Callaway M	P	NA	0	(0)	$320.0	($415.1)
Valentin J	C	NA	4	(0)	$385.0	($419.0)
Glavine T	P	FA	15	7	$10,765.6	($419.7)
Aardsma D	P	NA	0	(1)	$300.0	($431.0)
Stinnett K	C	FA	1	(0)	$500.0	($432.4)
Kata M	2B	NA	3	(0)	$315.0	($433.0)
Kennedy A	2B	A	13	2	$2,500.0	($437.4)
Encarnacion J	OF	FA	13	2	$3,565.0	($466.6)
Penny B	P	A	9	4	$3,725.0	($471.2)
Falkenborg B	P	NA	0	(1)	$302.5	($471.9)
Lee D	1B	A	21	7	$6,166.7	($475.5)
Harville C	P	NA	2	(1)	$307.0	($479.4)
Mondesi R	OF	FA	3	0	$1,150.0	($481.1)
Lopez L	1B	FA	0	(1)	$350.0	($489.4)
Boyd J	P	NA	0	(1)	$350.0	($492.3)
Durrington T	3B	NA	1	(1)	$305.0	($502.9)
Garland J	P	A	11	2	$2,300.0	($505.5)
Sadler D	SS	A	0	(0)	$400.0	($507.0)
Harvey K	1B	NA	8	(1)	$317.5	($507.6)
Graffanino T	2B	FA	6	(0)	$1,100.0	($509.0)
Halter S	3B	FA	2	(0)	$575.0	($509.2)
Wilson E	2B	FA	5	(0)	$700.0	($520.1)
Simontacchi J	P	NA	0	(1)	$350.0	($546.5)
Embree A	P	FA	4	1	$3,000.0	($571.5)
McCarty D	1B	FA	3	(1)	$500.0	($574.4)
Riley M	P	NA	2	(1)	$310.0	($576.7)
Larson B	3B	NA	2	(1)	$318.0	($587.5)

Win Shares and Net Win Shares Value

Name	POS	FA?	WS	WSR	Salary	Net WS Value
MacDougal M	P	NA	0	(1)	$346.5	($598.5)
Cressend J	P	NA	0	(1)	$322.4	($603.5)
Almanza A	P	A	0	(0)	$500.0	($604.0)
Quantrill P	P	FA	6	1	$3,000.0	($604.3)
Witasick J	P	FA	3	0	$1,750.0	($614.1)
Castillo J	2B	NA	8	(1)	$300.0	($617.4)
Mordecai M	3B	FA	1	(1)	$425.0	($630.4)
Trachsel S	P	FA	10	3	$5,000.0	($645.1)
Estalella B	C	FA	0	(1)	$550.0	($650.6)
Mendoza R	P	FA	3	2	$3,600.0	($651.0)
Burrell P	OF	A	15	4	$4,250.0	($651.7)
Berroa A	SS	NA	10	(1)	$372.5	($652.4)
Wright D	P	NA	0	(1)	$340.0	($655.9)
Villarreal O	P	NA	0	(1)	$325.0	($671.5)
Rodriguez F	P	A	6	3	$3,050.0	($679.0)
Myers G	C	FA	0	(0)	$900.0	($679.6)
Davis J	OF	NA	0	(1)	$300.0	($686.4)
Koskie C	3B	A	14	5	$4,500.0	($709.4)
Varitek J	C	A	18	8	$6,900.0	($709.5)
Osborne D	P	FA	0	(1)	$450.0	($709.6)
Knotts G	P	NA	5	(1)	$316.0	($713.8)
Cunnane W	P	A	0	(1)	$525.0	($713.8)
Burks E		FA	0	(1)	$750.0	($717.2)
Pettitte A	P	FA	6	3	$5,500.0	($726.0)
Perez T	OF	A	6	(0)	$850.0	($730.7)
Shelton C	1B	NA	0	(1)	$300.0	($752.3)
Lopez M	2B	NA	0	(1)	$330.0	($760.8)
LeCroy M	1B	NA	4	(1)	$340.0	($770.5)
Bergeron P	OF	NA	0	(1)	$300.0	($775.2)
Redman T	OF	NA	11	(1)	$321.0	($776.9)
Gonzalez A	SS	A	15	2	$2,800.0	($782.6)
Erstad D	1B	FA	15	5	$7,750.0	($786.3)
Lofton K	OF	FA	7	1	$2,985.6	($791.0)
Maddux G	P	FA	12	4	$7,500.0	($795.1)
Lopez A	P	NA	0	(1)	$318.0	($802.5)
de los Santos	P	FA	0	(1)	$850.0	($802.5)
Wilson P	P	FA	8	1	$3,500.0	($804.1)
Norton P	P	NA	2	(1)	$303.5	($805.6)
Gaudin C	P	NA	1	(1)	$302.5	($809.2)
Martinez R	SS	A	6	(0)	$900.0	($809.3)
Pond S	OF	NA	0	(1)	$300.0	($825.6)
Kershner J	P	NA	0	(1)	$315.0	($828.5)
Baerga C	1B	FA	1	(0)	$1,000.0	($835.4)
Johnson R	OF	NA	10	(1)	$318.0	($849.1)
Wendell T	P	FA	0	(1)	$700.0	($849.7)
Sullivan S	P	FA	3	0	$2,100.0	($853.2)
McDonald J	SS	NA	1	(1)	$324.4	($858.4)
Hillenbrand S	1B	A	14	2	$2,600.0	($869.4)
Alomar R	2B	FA	3	(1)	$924.2	($874.7)
Batista T	3B	FA	13	(0)	$1,500.0	($882.6)
Finley S	OF	FA	18	4	$7,000.0	($882.8)
Williamson S	P	A	4	3	$3,175.0	($888.2)
Johnston M	P	NA	0	(1)	$300.0	($890.3)
Fernandez J	P	NA	(1)	(1)	$325.0	($902.8)
Alfonzo E	3B	FA	15	4	$6,500.0	($906.6)
Bennett J	P	NA	2	(1)	$300.0	($908.6)
Catalanotto F	OF	FA	5	0	$2,300.0	($920.2)
Bloomquist W	3B	NA	3	(1)	$325.0	($925.0)
Perez O	P	A	12	5	$5,000.0	($931.7)
Leskanic C	P	fa	2	(0)	$1,250.0	($939.6)
Hill B	2B	NA	4	(1)	$315.0	($947.5)
Martin T	P	FA	2	(0)	$1,400.0	($950.3)
Redman M	P	A	9	1	$2,000.0	($961.1)
Garcia F	P	A	16	7	$6,875.0	($973.3)
Lawrence B	P	A	7	(0)	$925.0	($973.7)
Wagner B	P	FA	8	5	$8,000.0	($977.9)
Wigginton T	3B	NA	10	(1)	$316.0	($979.0)
Kielty B	OF	NA	4	(1)	$347.5	($983.6)
Bentz C	P	NA	0	(1)	$300.0	($999.1)
Jeter D	SS	FA	26	12	$18,600.0	($1,007.4)
Roberts G	P	NA	(1)	(1)	$319.5	($1,022.0)
Ford B	P	NA	0	(1)	$300.0	($1,026.4)
Reith B	P	NA	0	(1)	$327.3	($1,031.0)
Baldwin J	P	FA	(1)	(1)	$320.0	($1,042.1)
Soriano R	P	NA	(1)	(1)	$335.0	($1,047.2)
Ryan M	OF	NA	0	(1)	$305.0	($1,068.5)
Reyes R	OF	NA	0	(1)	$300.0	($1,091.2)
Sosa J	P	NA	3	(1)	$312.5	($1,101.4)
Matthews M	P	FA	0	(1)	$300.0	($1,105.8)
Fox C	P	FA	0	(1)	$1,200.0	($1,112.1)
Nelson J	P	FA	1	(0)	$1,789.8	($1,120.9)
Pierzynski A	C	A	13	3	$3,500.0	($1,130.3)
Smith J	2B	NA	2	(1)	$310.0	($1,147.6)
Benoit J	P	NA	3	(1)	$335.0	($1,164.2)
Phelps T	P	NA	0	(1)	$307.5	($1,177.7)
Colyer S	P	NA	0	(1)	$302.0	($1,187.4)
Boehringer B	P	FA	1	(0)	$2,000.0	($1,189.8)
Wayne J	P	NA	0	(1)	$301.0	($1,195.1)
Sweeney M	1B	FA	14	6	$11,000.0	($1,197.8)
Renteria E	SS	FA	17	4	$7,250.0	($1,205.4)

Win Shares and Net Win Shares Value

Name	POS	FA?	WS	WSR	Salary	Net WS Value
Wooten S	1B	A	0	(1)	$575.0	($1,208.0)
Powell J	P	FA	2	1	$3,500.0	($1,217.3)
Weathers D	P	FA	5	1	$3,933.3	($1,232.6)
Redmond M	C	A	5	(1)	$840.0	($1,233.5)
DeJean M	P	FA	2	(1)	$1,500.0	($1,233.6)
Groom B	P	FA	3	1	$3,000.0	($1,235.1)
Martinez E		FA	8	0	$3,000.0	($1,278.1)
Patterson J	P	NA	2	(2)	$310.0	($1,285.0)
Guzman C	SS	A	15	3	$3,725.0	($1,298.0)
Pellow K	OF	NA	1	(2)	$310.0	($1,307.8)
Christiansen J	P	FA	2	0	$2,433.3	($1,312.0)
Palmeiro R	1B	FA	13	1	$4,000.0	($1,315.0)
Nunez V	P	FA	0	(1)	$700.0	($1,327.3)
Duckworth B	P	NA	0	(1)	$390.0	($1,327.9)
D'Amico J	P	FA	0	(1)	$750.0	($1,350.2)
Douglass S	P	NA	0	(2)	$305.0	($1,353.1)
Alomar Jr. S	C	FA	2	(1)	$700.0	($1,358.3)
Cordero W	1B	FA	0	(1)	$600.0	($1,376.8)
Rhodes A	P	FA	2	(1)	$1,800.0	($1,381.8)
Kapler G	OF	FA	5	(1)	$750.0	($1,386.1)
Osik K	C	FA	(1)	(1)	$500.0	($1,386.5)
Lee T	1B	FA	0	(0)	$2,000.0	($1,391.7)
Byrd M	OF	NA	6	(2)	$355.0	($1,397.7)
Laker T	C	FA	1	(2)	$450.0	($1,415.1)
Farnsworth K	P	A	3	(0)	$1,400.0	($1,427.2)
Vazquez R	SS	NA	1	(2)	$342.5	($1,456.1)
Hammonds J	OF	FA	1	(1)	$1,000.0	($1,458.3)
Franco J	P	FA	1	(1)	$1,100.0	($1,459.2)
Leiter A	P	FA	12	6	$10,295.6	($1,460.3)
Ohka T	P	A	4	1	$2,337.5	($1,461.3)
Calloway R	OF	NA	0	(2)	$312.5	($1,462.4)
Matheny M	C	FA	10	1	$4,000.0	($1,462.4)
Sanchez A	OF	NA	5	(2)	$385.0	($1,466.0)
Hernandez A	P	FA	(1)	(2)	$425.0	($1,471.6)
Lopez L	3B	FA	0	(2)	$350.0	($1,473.2)
Harris L	OF	FA	0	(2)	$400.0	($1,499.4)
Ishii K	P	FA	6	(0)	$2,497.3	($1,514.1)
McCracken Q	OF	FA	3	(1)	$1,750.0	($1,546.8)
Wells K	P	A	6	1	$2,575.0	($1,555.3)
Buchanan B	1B	A	0	(1)	$650.0	($1,558.7)
Harang A	P	NA	4	(2)	$360.0	($1,560.8)
Clayton R	SS	FA	11	(2)	$650.0	($1,572.8)
Mitre S	P	NA	0	(2)	$305.0	($1,580.4)
McMillon B	OF	FA	0	(2)	$450.0	($1,582.6)
Waechter D	P	NA	1	(2)	$300.0	($1,608.4)

Name	POS	FA?	WS	WSR	Salary	Net WS Value
Lopez J	P	NA	0	(2)	$317.5	($1,629.0)
Stewart S	P	A	0	(1)	$850.0	($1,664.8)
Crede J	3B	NA	9	(2)	$340.0	($1,674.5)
Miller C	C	NA	(1)	(2)	$317.0	($1,691.1)
Hernandez R	P	FA	1	(2)	$750.0	($1,722.7)
Konerko P	1B	A	20	8	$8,000.0	($1,737.5)
Cedeno R	OF	FA	6	2	$5,375.0	($1,742.4)
Santiago B	C	FA	3	(1)	$2,150.0	($1,758.4)
Cornejo N	P	NA	(1)	(2)	$335.0	($1,773.6)
Karros E	1B	FA	0	(2)	$550.0	($1,782.2)
DuBose E	P	NA	1	(2)	$305.0	($1,787.4)
Fox A	2B	FA	(1)	(2)	$450.0	($1,788.8)
Grabow J	P	NA	1	(2)	$300.0	($1,789.8)
Ortiz R	P	A	7	2	$3,266.7	($1,797.9)
Perez E	C	FA	2	(2)	$625.0	($1,826.1)
Everett C	OF	FA	5	(0)	$3,000.0	($1,835.3)
Woodward C	SS	A	3	(2)	$775.0	($1,838.5)
Hasegawa S	P	FA	3	(0)	$2,750.0	($1,840.2)
Lohse K	P	NA	6	(2)	$395.0	($1,843.5)
Stone R	P	NA	0	(2)	$395.0	($1,860.9)
Franklin W	P	NA	0	(2)	$360.0	($1,874.4)
Kinney M	P	NA	1	(2)	$400.0	($1,888.2)
Colbrunn G	1B	FA	0	(0)	$2,750.0	($1,896.4)
Riedling J	P	A	2	(2)	$650.0	($1,901.5)
Bump N	P	NA	1	(2)	$305.0	($1,911.4)
Gonzalez J	OF	FA	3	0	$4,000.0	($1,919.1)
Hammock R	C	NA	2	(2)	$315.0	($1,925.8)
Goodwin T	OF	FA	0	(2)	$650.0	($1,949.0)
Laird G	C	NA	1	(2)	$300.0	($1,980.6)
Bautista D	OF	FA	12	0	$4,000.0	($1,991.7)
Hocking D	SS	FA	0	(2)	$700.0	($1,994.6)
Bagwell J	1B	FA	23	9	$16,000.0	($1,996.4)
Meche G	P	A	5	(0)	$1,950.0	($2,015.5)
Lidle C	P	FA	7	(1)	$2,750.0	($2,029.6)
Castro R	3B	A	0	(2)	$400.0	($2,042.7)
Hessman M	1B	NA	(1)	(2)	$300.0	($2,048.5)
Berg D	OF	FA	1	(2)	$800.0	($2,066.1)
Valdez I	P	FA	4	(2)	$800.0	($2,082.7)
Wilson D	C	FA	7	(0)	$3,500.0	($2,083.3)
Percival T	P	FA	7	3	$7,833.3	($2,088.3)
Schoeneweis	P	A	4	(1)	$1,725.0	($2,116.9)
Fick R	OF	FA	2	(2)	$800.0	($2,121.8)
Vargas C	P	NA	2	(3)	$307.5	($2,123.6)
Durbin C	P	NA	0	(3)	$315.0	($2,130.2)
Fullmer B	1B	FA	2	(2)	$1,000.0	($2,183.1)

Win Shares and Net Win Shares Value

Name	POS	FA?	WS	WSR	Salary	Net WS Value
Lawton M	OF	FA	15	3	$7,250.0	($2,223.6)
Smoltz J	P	FA	12	6	$11,666.7	($2,234.8)
Nunez A	2B	NA	1	(3)	$300.0	($2,243.7)
Anderson M	2B	A	3	(2)	$600.0	($2,249.8)
Crespo C	SS	NA	(1)	(3)	$309.5	($2,251.1)
Mecir J	P	A	4	1	$3,300.0	($2,261.0)
Sanchez R	2B	FA	4	(2)	$1,000.0	($2,268.0)
Glanville D	OF	FA	1	(3)	$550.0	($2,283.3)
Daigle C	P	NA	(1)	(3)	$300.0	($2,310.2)
Nunez A	OF	A	4	(2)	$625.0	($2,324.4)
Garcia K	OF	FA	3	(2)	$800.0	($2,334.3)
Yates T	P	NA	(1)	(3)	$300.0	($2,347.0)
Chavez R	C	NA	1	(3)	$315.0	($2,350.6)
Weber B	P	A	(1)	(2)	$900.0	($2,357.9)
Wakefield T	P	FA	8	0	$4,350.0	($2,386.4)
Gonzalez L	OF	FA	12	3	$8,250.0	($2,387.6)
Davis J	P	NA	2	(3)	$326.8	($2,400.2)
Clement M	P	A	11	4	$6,000.0	($2,407.4)
Heredia F	P	FA	0	(2)	$1,800.0	($2,424.2)
Halladay R	P	A	10	4	$6,000.0	($2,429.4)
Patterson D	P	FA	1	(1)	$2,800.0	($2,431.6)
Wolf R	P	A	7	2	$4,375.0	($2,444.8)
Soriano A	2B	A	16	4	$5,400.0	($2,465.1)
Ligtenberg K	P	FA	1	(2)	$2,000.0	($2,466.6)
Spivey J	2B	A	5	(0)	$2,367.5	($2,481.3)
Cash K	C	NA	1	(3)	$302.0	($2,484.8)
Oliver D	P	FA	0	(3)	$750.0	($2,497.9)
Jones J	OF	A	14	2	$4,350.0	($2,499.5)
Guiel A	OF	NA	0	(3)	$320.0	($2,540.7)
Kim B	P	FA	0	(1)	$3,425.0	($2,555.8)
Moss D	P	A	(2)	(2)	$850.0	($2,560.7)
Helms W	3B	A	5	(1)	$1,687.5	($2,569.6)
Bako P	C	A	1	(2)	$865.0	($2,582.8)
Norton G	3B	FA	(1)	(3)	$600.0	($2,583.9)
Ross D	C	NA	1	(3)	$310.0	($2,604.3)
Reese P	SS	FA	3	(3)	$1,000.0	($2,614.4)
Young D	1B	FA	9	2	$7,750.0	($2,644.3)
Padilla V	P	A	4	(0)	$2,600.0	($2,651.4)
Eaton A	P	A	6	(1)	$1,925.0	($2,654.6)
Haynes J	P	FA	(1)	(2)	$2,500.0	($2,691.4)
Rolls D	3B	A	0	(3)	$800.0	($2,707.8)
Castro J	3B	A	4	(2)	$1,000.0	($2,723.0)
Perry H	1B	A	1	(1)	$1,700.0	($2,747.5)
Ainsworth K	P	NA	(2)	(3)	$315.0	($2,771.6)
Higginson B	OF	FA	13	3	$8,850.0	($2,778.1)

Name	POS	FA?	WS	WSR	Salary	Net WS Value
Jones A	OF	FA	19	6	$12,500.0	($2,781.4)
Perez N	SS	FA	7	(2)	$2,750.0	($2,805.8)
Pineiro J	P	A	6	0	$3,000.0	($2,817.4)
Williams W	P	FA	8	1	$6,562.2	($2,847.5)
Myers B	P	NA	3	(3)	$362.5	($2,853.5)
Jones C	3B	FA	19	8	$15,333.3	($2,871.8)
Vina F	2B	FA	1	(1)	$3,000.0	($2,931.5)
Van Poppel T	P	FA	1	(3)	$300.0	($2,937.4)
Phillips J	C	NA	5	(3)	$318.0	($2,950.8)
Elarton S	P	FA	3	(3)	$480.0	($2,975.8)
Jarvis K	P	FA	0	(1)	$4,250.0	($2,987.9)
Fordyce B	C	FA	0	(3)	$650.0	($3,021.2)
Sparks S	P	FA	1	(3)	$500.0	($3,058.3)
Davis B	C	A	2	(2)	$1,400.0	($3,068.9)
Hunter T	OF	A	15	4	$6,500.0	($3,194.5)
Redding T	P	NA	0	(4)	$395.0	($3,209.9)
Blanco H	C	A	4	(3)	$750.0	($3,211.5)
Counsell C	SS	A	11	(0)	$3,166.7	($3,250.1)
Jordan B	OF	FA	1	(3)	$1,250.0	($3,267.0)
Ausmus B	C	FA	6	(3)	$1,000.0	($3,336.0)
Ortiz R	P	A	11	4	$6,200.0	($3,346.6)
Abbott P	P	FA	0	(4)	$600.0	($3,347.2)
Stynes C	3B	FA	0	(4)	$750.0	($3,351.2)
Ponson S	P	FA	7	(2)	$3,000.0	($3,356.2)
Dessens E	P	A	5	1	$4,000.0	($3,383.5)
Mayne B	C	FA	1	(4)	$800.0	($3,460.5)
White G	P	FA	0	(3)	$1,925.0	($3,525.4)
Johnson J	P	FA	6	(2)	$3,000.0	($3,527.3)
Williams B	OF	FA	16	5	$12,357.1	($3,580.1)
Cintron A	SS	NA	8	(4)	$335.0	($3,595.0)
Franklin R	P	A	6	(2)	$1,800.0	($3,600.9)
Zeile T	1B	FA	4	(4)	$1,000.0	($3,646.7)
Bennett G	C	FA	1	(4)	$600.0	($3,730.6)
Long T	OF	A	6	(0)	$3,575.0	($3,748.9)
Simon R	1B	FA	0	(4)	$800.0	($3,751.6)
May D	P	A	5	(3)	$1,750.0	($3,879.8)
Herges M	P	A	1	(4)	$1,100.0	($3,911.1)
Borowski J	P	A	(1)	(3)	$2,000.0	($3,968.1)
Hentgen P	P	FA	0	(3)	$2,200.0	($3,998.9)
Jimenez J	P	FA	(2)	(4)	$1,025.0	($3,999.6)
Segui D	1B	FA	1	0	$6,815.4	($4,007.7)
Relaford D	3B	FA	4	(4)	$900.0	($4,038.4)
Matos L	OF	A	3	(4)	$975.0	($4,041.9)
Vogelsong R	P	NA	0	(5)	$311.5	($4,071.4)
Gibbons J	OF	A	5	(2)	$2,600.0	($4,097.8)

Win Shares and Net Win Shares Value

Name	POS	FA?	WS	WSR	Salary	Net WS Value
Washburn J	P	A	8	2	$5,450.0	($4,104.6)
Gonzalez J	P	A	(1)	(3)	$1,700.0	($4,111.5)
Stark D	P	NA	(4)	(5)	$321.0	($4,207.5)
Gutierrez R	2B	FA	0	(2)	$4,166.7	($4,320.8)
Olerud J	1B	FA	10	0	$7,700.0	($4,341.4)
Rueter K	P	FA	6	(1)	$6,133.3	($4,381.1)
Diaz E	C	A	1	(2)	$2,587.5	($4,415.9)
Gonzalez A	SS	FA	5	(1)	$5,750.0	($4,462.0)
Loaiza E	P	FA	5	(3)	$4,000.0	($4,531.7)
Eckstein D	SS	A	9	(3)	$2,150.0	($4,587.2)
DeRosa M	3B	A	2	(5)	$725.0	($4,610.4)
Moeller C	C	NA	2	(5)	$370.0	($4,673.3)
Spiezio S	3B	FA	4	(4)	$2,566.7	($4,766.2)
Benson K	P	A	9	2	$6,150.0	($4,805.2)
Martinez P	P	FA	16	7	$17,500.0	($4,830.3)
Blum G	3B	A	3	(4)	$1,500.0	($4,909.5)
Aurilia R	SS	FA	5	(4)	$3,150.0	($5,063.5)
Hinske E	3B	A	7	(5)	$900.0	($5,065.9)
Biddle R	P	A	0	(4)	$1,950.0	($5,091.8)
Anderson B	P	FA	3	(4)	$3,250.0	($5,156.7)
Fossum C	P	NA	(1)	(6)	$345.0	($5,273.1)
Hampton M	P	FA	9	3	$12,975.3	($5,382.1)
Giambi J	1B	FA	8	2	$12,428.6	($5,468.3)
Colon B	P	FA	10	1	$11,000.0	($5,543.4)
Johnson C	C	FA	7	(0)	$9,000.0	($5,556.4)
Sele A	P	FA	5	(0)	$8,666.7	($5,620.0)
Dye J	OF	FA	13	2	$11,666.7	($5,652.8)
Chacon S	P	A	0	(5)	$1,850.0	($5,769.4)
Wood K	P	A	8	3	$8,000.0	($5,789.1)
Acevedo J	P	NA	(1)	(7)	$340.0	($5,816.9)
Mientkiewicz	1B	A	5	(4)	$2,800.0	($5,859.4)
Lieberthal M	C	FA	9	(2)	$7,500.0	($5,974.6)
Lowe D	P	A	6	(2)	$4,500.0	($6,147.9)
Moyer J	P	FA	6	(2)	$7,000.0	($6,187.3)
Graves D	P	A	5	(0)	$6,000.0	($6,358.6)
Koch B	P	A	3	0	$6,375.0	($6,364.2)
Delgado C	1B	FA	17	7	$19,700.0	($6,519.3)
Glaus T	3B	A	9	5	$10,450.0	($6,602.1)
Brown K	P	FA	9	4	$15,714.3	($6,634.2)
Salmon T	OF	FA	2	(1)	$9,900.0	($6,859.6)
Contreras J	P	FA	5	(2)	$8,500.0	($6,935.2)
Vidro J	2B	A	12	3	$9,000.0	($7,112.0)
Mussina M	P	FA	10	3	$16,000.0	($7,119.6)
Wilson P	OF	FA	2	(2)	$9,000.0	($7,395.8)
Dreifort D	P	FA	2	(1)	$11,400.0	($7,418.3)
Green S	1B	FA	17	3	$16,666.7	($7,493.4)
Millwood K	P	FA	4	(1)	$11,000.0	($7,547.6)
Boone B	2B	FA	9	(3)	$8,000.0	($7,731.3)
Sosa S	OF	FA	14	3	$16,875.0	($7,770.9)
Vazquez J	P	A	10	2	$9,000.0	($7,926.5)
Cabrera O	SS	A	11	(2)	$6,000.0	($8,180.0)
Sexson R	1B	A	3	1	$8,725.0	($8,306.5)
Piazza M	1B	FA	12	2	$16,071.4	($8,330.0)
Park C	P	FA	4	0	$13,879.2	($8,440.1)
Milton E	P	A	8	1	$9,000.0	($8,742.3)
Jenkins G	OF	A	14	0	$8,737.5	($8,965.5)
Mantei M	P	A	(2)	(3)	$7,000.0	($9,617.2)
Ordonez M	OF	A	8	4	$14,000.0	($11,513.4)
Nomo H	P	FA	(6)	(9)	$9,000.0	($13,052.1)
Morris M	P	A	7	(0)	$12,500.0	($13,402.2)
Hidalgo R	OF	A	11	(1)	$12,500.0	($13,837.9)

Fielding Win Shares by Position

Fielding Win Shares were developed by Bill James to calculate the number of Wins that could be attributed to a player as a result of his contributions while fielding his position. They include the impact of a number of fielding statistics, such as range, assists, error rates, double plays and catchers' caught stealing. The following table lists the Fielding Win Shares of each player who played at leat 300 innings at a specific position in 2004. Players are ranked in order of Fielding Win Shares per 1000 innings played.

Catchers

Player	Team	Innings	FWS	WS/1000
American League				
D Miller	OAK	963.7	7.90	8.20
A Melhuse	OAK	504.7	3.82	7.58
J Molina	ANA	524.3	3.84	7.32
D Wilson	SEA	827.3	5.90	7.13
M Olivo	SEA	394.0	2.68	6.80
J Mauer	MIN	257.0	1.66	6.46
B Molina	ANA	762.0	4.87	6.40
H Blanco	MIN	872.3	4.74	5.43
T Hall	TBD	1011.0	5.30	5.25
A Castillo	KC	242.3	1.27	5.23
G Laird	TEX	397.0	2.06	5.18
J Burke	CHW	292.0	1.49	5.12
K Cash	TOR	460.3	2.35	5.10
J Lopez	BAL	1092.0	5.23	4.79
R Barajas	TEX	916.7	4.32	4.72
G Zaun	TOR	789.0	3.55	4.50
B Fordyce	TBD	400.7	1.77	4.43
B Davis	CHW	397.0	1.74	4.38
J Varitek	BOS	1071.0	4.60	4.29
S Alomar Jr.	CHW	377.0	1.58	4.19
I Rodriguez	DET	1051.0	4.21	4.01
J Posada	NYY	1102.0	4.19	3.80
B Santiago	KC	416.0	1.56	3.76
M Olivo	CHW	366.3	1.35	3.68
T Laker	CLE	298.7	1.08	3.61
B Inge	DET	312.7	1.12	3.59
J Buck	KC	575.0	1.95	3.39
V Martinez	CLE	1108.0	3.70	3.33
J Flaherty	NYY	328.3	1.05	3.19
D Mirabelli	BOS	375.7	0.85	2.25
National League				
B Schneider	MON	1114.0	10.60	9.52
M Matheny	STL	977.7	8.15	8.34
Y Molina	STL	344.0	2.54	7.39
P Lo Duca	LAD	691.7	5.09	7.36
R Hammock	ARI	376.7	2.40	6.37
C Snyder	ARI	247.3	1.53	6.20
J Phillips	NYM	650.3	4.00	6.16
C Moeller	MIL	836.0	5.13	6.14

Player	Team	Innings	FWS	WS/1000
R Chavez	HOU	423.7	2.43	5.74
J Kendall	PIT	1259.0	6.85	5.44
B Ausmus	HOU	1018.0	5.46	5.36
Y Torrealba	SFG	433.0	2.29	5.30
R Castro	FLO	243.0	1.20	4.92
J Brito	ARI	461.7	2.21	4.78
A Pierzynski	SFG	1022.0	4.88	4.77
B Mayne	LAD	293.0	1.38	4.71
R Hernandez	SDP	924.7	4.33	4.68
P Lo Duca	FLO	413.0	1.91	4.63
P Bako	CHC	377.7	1.73	4.58
V Wilson	NYM	381.7	1.75	4.57
B Mayne	ARI	236.7	1.05	4.44
E Diaz	MON	341.0	1.51	4.43
M Barrett	CHC	1081.0	4.71	4.35
M Ojeda	SDP	340.7	1.44	4.23
T Pratt	PHI	333.0	1.33	3.99
J LaRue	CIN	930.0	3.58	3.85
M Piazza	NYM	390.3	1.48	3.78
J Valentin	CIN	409.7	1.54	3.75
M Redmond	FLO	604.3	2.15	3.56
D Ross	LAD	451.7	1.56	3.45
E Perez	ATL	408.0	1.34	3.29
M Lieberthal	PHI	1104.0	3.63	3.29
J Estrada	ATL	1042.0	3.06	2.94
G Bennett	MIL	584.0	1.57	2.69
J Closser	COL	259.0	0.68	2.61
C Johnson	COL	746.3	1.45	1.94
T Greene	COL	421.0	0.60	1.42
All Catchers				**4.93**

First Basemen

Player	Team	Innings	FWS	WS/1000
American League				
M Teixeira	TEX	1231.0	2.66	2.16
D Erstad	ANA	1065.0	2.29	2.15
C Kotchman	ANA	270.3	0.51	1.90
C Delgado	TOR	1038.0	1.94	1.87
T Clark	NYY	623.7	1.13	1.81
J Morneau	MIN	538.3	0.95	1.77
J Olerud	NYY	400.0	0.69	1.72

Player	Team	Innings	FWS	WS/1000
D Mientkiewi	MIN	668.7	1.15	1.72
A Huff	TBD	274.3	0.47	1.70
B Broussard	CLE	1019.0	1.72	1.69
J Giambi	NYY	375.0	0.63	1.68
R Gload	CHW	218.3	0.35	1.62
L Merloni	CLE	297.7	0.47	1.59
P Konerko	CHW	1177.0	1.87	1.59
T Martinez	TBD	959.7	1.50	1.56
R Palmeiro	BAL	1137.0	1.65	1.45
S Hatteberg	OAK	1280.0	1.70	1.33
S Spiezio	SEA	279.0	0.35	1.26
J Olerud	SEA	645.3	0.81	1.26
D McCarty	BOS	297.0	0.36	1.21
K Harvey	KC	630.0	0.75	1.19
D Mientkiewi	BOS	272.0	0.32	1.18
M Sweeney	KC	471.0	0.55	1.18
D Young	DET	211.3	0.24	1.15
K Millar	BOS	512.0	0.58	1.13
C Pena	DET	1159.0	1.29	1.11
D Ortiz	BOS	260.3	0.29	1.11
M Stairs	KC	229.0	0.23	1.01
National League				
T Helton	COL	1320.0	4.04	3.06
D Lee	CHC	1432.0	3.61	2.52
J Conine	FLO	489.3	0.89	1.81
R Ventura	LAD	210.0	0.38	1.80
H Choi	FLO	712.7	1.22	1.72
S Green	LAD	926.7	1.50	1.62
J Bagwell	HOU	1328.0	2.14	1.61
A Pujols	STL	1338.0	2.13	1.59
J Snow	SFG	793.0	1.15	1.45
T Zeile	NYM	365.3	0.53	1.45
L Overbay	MIL	1369.0	1.97	1.44
J Phillips	NYM	258.3	0.36	1.41
P Feliz	SFG	535.7	0.75	1.41
B Wilkerson	MON	701.7	0.98	1.40
N Johnson	MON	610.0	0.85	1.39
S Hillenbran	ARI	1113.0	1.51	1.36
M Piazza	NYM	517.7	0.66	1.28
J Thome	PHI	1179.0	1.42	1.20
R Simon	PIT	335.3	0.38	1.14
S Casey	CIN	1245.0	1.40	1.13
D Ward	PIT	559.0	0.59	1.06
C Wilson	PIT	494.3	0.51	1.04
P Nevin	SDP	1207.0	1.23	1.02
J Franco	ATL	631.3	0.60	0.96
A La Roche	ATL	720.0	0.67	0.93
All First Basemen				**1.55**

Second Basemen

Player	Team	Innings	FWS	WS/1000
American League				
L Rivas	MIN	860.3	6.47	7.52
M Cuddyer	MIN	327.3	2.02	6.18
M McLemore	OAK	373.3	2.21	5.92
O Hudson	TOR	1124.0	6.63	5.90
M Cairo	NYY	856.0	4.75	5.55
W Harris	CHW	673.7	3.49	5.18
M Scutaro	OAK	968.7	4.98	5.14
E Wilson	NYY	564.7	2.86	5.06
J Uribe	CHW	616.7	3.10	5.03
F Menechino	TOR	237.3	1.10	4.62
T Graffanino	KC	630.3	2.75	4.36
A Kennedy	ANA	1225.0	5.03	4.11
M Bellhorn	BOS	1053.0	4.16	3.95
A Soriano	TEX	1256.0	4.85	3.86
R Belliard	CLE	1320.0	4.81	3.65
D Relaford	KC	278.3	0.97	3.50
F Vina	DET	248.3	0.86	3.47
R Sanchez	TBD	696.0	2.31	3.32
J Smith	DET	258.0	0.83	3.23
B Roberts	BAL	1322.0	4.27	3.23
R Gotay	KC	368.3	1.05	2.84
O Infante	DET	868.7	2.38	2.74
G Blum	TBD	364.7	0.98	2.70
J Cantu	TBD	274.0	0.69	2.50
B Boone	SEA	1308.0	2.13	1.63
National League				
M Grudzielan	CHC	568.0	3.64	6.41
J Kent	HOU	1189.0	7.45	6.26
B Hill	PIT	255.0	1.47	5.76
P Polanco	PHI	944.0	5.22	5.53
M Giles	ATL	789.0	4.33	5.49
N Green	ATL	572.0	3.03	5.30
M Loretta	SDP	1339.0	6.77	5.06
L Castillo	FLO	1274.0	6.36	4.99
T Walker	CHC	749.3	3.69	4.92
J Hernandez	LAD	341.7	1.64	4.79
A Cora	LAD	1091.0	5.23	4.79
N Perez	SFG	291.7	1.39	4.76
C Utley	PHI	410.3	1.91	4.65
J Castillo	PIT	951.0	4.38	4.61
L Gonzalez	COL	293.0	1.34	4.58
A Miles	COL	1029.0	4.53	4.40
T Womack	STL	1113.0	4.51	4.05
M Anderson	STL	224.0	0.87	3.89
J Keppinger	NYM	257.7	0.84	3.25
R Durham	SFG	990.3	3.15	3.18
J Reyes	NYM	352.0	1.07	3.03
M Kata	ARI	320.7	0.87	2.72

Player	Team	Innings	FWS	WS/1000
D Garcia	NYM	344.0	0.92	2.67
D Jimenez	CIN	1263.0	3.35	2.65
J Carroll	MON	344.7	0.82	2.38
J Vidro	MON	887.3	2.00	2.26
S Hairston	ARI	704.0	1.50	2.13
J Spivey	MIL	517.7	1.02	1.96
K Ginter	MIL	459.3	0.68	1.47
B Hall	MIL	427.3	0.61	1.43
All Second Basemen				**4.18**

Player	Team	Innings	FWS	WS/1000
E Renteria	STL	1307.0	4.92	3.76
A Gonzalez	MON	293.3	1.06	3.63
J Rollins	PHI	1376.0	4.77	3.47
R Clayton	COL	1241.0	4.04	3.26
F Lopez	CIN	391.0	1.26	3.23
J Gil	ARI	212.3	0.64	3.02
B Larkin	CIN	684.3	2.05	3.00
A Cintron	ARI	1099.0	3.13	2.85
All Shortstops				**4.60**

Shortstops

Player	Team	Innings	FWS	WS/1000
American League				
J Uribe	CHW	287.3	2.14	7.44
C Guzman	MIN	1304.0	9.61	7.37
J Valentin	CHW	1025.0	6.06	5.91
B Crosby	OAK	1356.0	7.49	5.53
D Jeter	NYY	1341.0	7.21	5.38
J Lugo	TBD	1238.0	6.56	5.30
M Tejada	BAL	1421.0	7.17	5.05
P Reese	BOS	516.7	2.43	4.71
C Guillen	DET	1151.0	5.19	4.51
M Young	TEX	1394.0	5.82	4.18
A Berroa	KC	1143.0	4.16	3.64
O Vizquel	CLE	1245.0	4.49	3.60
D Eckstein	ANA	1191.0	4.29	3.60
C Woodward	TOR	514.7	1.71	3.33
O Cabrera	BOS	491.0	1.61	3.29
R Aurilia	SEA	634.0	2.07	3.26
C Gomez	TOR	638.0	1.95	3.05
N Garciaparr	BOS	311.3	0.91	2.94
J Lopez	SEA	490.0	1.21	2.47
National League				
J Wilson	PIT	1357.0	9.31	6.86
B Hall	MIL	303.7	2.05	6.70
R Furcal	ATL	1134.0	6.93	6.12
A Everett	HOU	842.0	4.84	5.75
A Gonzalez	FLO	1351.0	7.46	5.52
J Vizcaino	HOU	455.3	2.45	5.39
R Martinez	CHC	529.7	2.81	5.31
C Izturis	LAD	1386.0	7.08	5.11
C Counsell	MIL	1139.0	5.78	5.07
A Gonzalez	CHC	297.3	1.48	4.98
K Greene	SDP	1189.0	5.62	4.73
N Perez	SFG	440.0	2.02	4.60
N Garciaparr	CHC	364.7	1.67	4.57
D Cruz	SFG	800.7	3.54	4.43
O Cabrera	MON	875.7	3.62	4.13
W Delgado	NYM	340.0	1.38	4.05
K Matsui	NYM	941.7	3.63	3.86

Third Basemen

Player	Team	Innings	FWS	WS/1000
American League				
J Cabrera	SEA	277.7	1.41	5.09
K Youkilis	BOS	515.0	2.41	4.67
S Spiezio	SEA	587.7	2.52	4.30
A Rodriguez	NYY	1364.0	5.80	4.25
H Blalock	TEX	1385.0	5.55	4.00
B Mueller	BOS	827.7	3.19	3.86
S Halter	ANA	213.3	0.81	3.79
R Quinlan	ANA	218.0	0.80	3.68
E Chavez	OAK	1129.0	3.63	3.22
J Randa	KC	1021.0	3.26	3.19
C Figgins	ANA	707.3	2.19	3.10
M McLemore	OAK	202.0	0.60	2.98
J Leone	SEA	242.0	0.70	2.89
D Relaford	KC	315.7	0.88	2.78
W Bloomquist	SEA	221.3	0.61	2.77
B Inge	DET	524.7	1.45	2.76
E Hinske	TOR	1310.0	3.55	2.71
C Koskie	MIN	1004.0	2.65	2.64
C Blake	CLE	1352.0	3.53	2.61
J Crede	CHW	1235.0	3.06	2.48
G Blum	TBD	382.0	0.94	2.45
E Munson	DET	740.7	1.77	2.39
A Huff	TBD	705.0	1.65	2.33
M Mora	BAL	1210.0	2.41	1.99
M Cuddyer	MIN	338.0	0.58	1.73
National League				
S Rolen	STL	1228.0	5.57	4.53
A Beltre	LAD	1340.0	6.04	4.51
R Branyan	MIL	361.0	1.42	3.94
M Lowell	FLO	1326.0	4.90	3.70
D Bell	PHI	1239.0	4.44	3.59
T Batista	MON	1334.0	4.51	3.38
R Freel	CIN	392.3	1.29	3.30
P Feliz	SFG	339.3	1.11	3.27
V Castilla	COL	1286.0	4.10	3.18
M Lamb	HOU	453.7	1.42	3.13
C Stynes	PIT	391.0	1.17	3.00

Player	Team	Innings	FWS	WS/1000
R Mackowiak	PIT	411.3	1.22	2.96
C Jones	ATL	802.0	2.34	2.92
F Lopez	CIN	207.7	0.61	2.91
K Ginter	MIL	396.3	1.07	2.70
S Burroughs	SDP	1060.0	2.80	2.64
E Alfonzo	SFG	1081.0	2.81	2.60
C Tracy	ARI	1062.0	2.63	2.48
T Wigginton	PIT	442.7	1.08	2.44
M DeRosa	ATL	556.0	1.36	2.44
J Castro	CIN	378.7	0.89	2.35
M Ensberg	HOU	920.7	2.16	2.35
A Ramirez	CHC	1245.0	2.67	2.14
B Larson	CIN	272.3	0.54	1.99
W Helms	MIL	555.0	1.09	1.96
R Aurilia	SDP	231.7	0.44	1.92
T Zeile	NYM	345.7	0.61	1.76
D Wright	NYM	603.7	1.00	1.66
T Wigginton	NYM	488.7	0.77	1.58
All Third Basemen				**3.06**

Left Fielders

Player	Team	Innings	FWS	WS/1000
American League				
C Crisp	CLE	293.3	1.27	4.33
G Gross	TOR	289.7	1.21	4.18
K Mench	TEX	372.3	1.35	3.62
D Dellucci	TEX	647.0	2.31	3.57
L Ford	MIN	680.7	2.19	3.21
C Crawford	TBD	1010.0	3.21	3.18
E Young	TEX	326.3	1.01	3.10
J Guillen	ANA	1165.0	3.19	2.74
C Lee	CHW	1277.0	3.48	2.73
R Johnson	TOR	461.3	1.26	2.72
M Lawton	CLE	1070.0	2.90	2.71
E Byrnes	OAK	871.3	2.32	2.66
M Thames	DET	298.7	0.78	2.62
M Ramirez	BOS	1096.0	2.72	2.48
B Surhoff	BAL	268.3	0.65	2.42
R Ibanez	SEA	949.3	2.23	2.34
B Kielty	OAK	366.7	0.85	2.33
R Winn	SEA	288.0	0.67	2.32
F Catalanott	TOR	309.7	0.70	2.28
L Bigbie	BAL	915.0	2.06	2.25
A Guiel	KC	307.3	0.66	2.14
S Stewart	MIN	639.3	1.28	2.00
H Matsui	NYY	1388.0	2.62	1.89
D Berg	TOR	226.7	0.41	1.81
D Brown	KC	433.0	0.78	1.80
R White	DET	614.7	0.95	1.54
C Monroe	DET	446.0	0.52	1.17

Player	Team	Innings	FWS	WS/1000
National League				
C Thomas	ATL	560.7	2.08	3.71
J Conine	FLO	709.7	2.62	3.70
R Sanders	STL	297.3	1.05	3.53
D Mohr	SFG	219.3	0.77	3.51
E Marrero	ATL	375.0	1.25	3.34
J Michaels	PHI	227.3	0.69	3.02
J Mabry	STL	225.0	0.63	2.80
T Sledge	MON	579.7	1.55	2.67
S Spencer	NYM	231.0	0.61	2.66
B Wilkerson	MON	439.3	1.15	2.63
M Cabrera	FLO	504.0	1.30	2.59
M Alou	CHC	1338.0	3.43	2.57
E Valent	NYM	213.3	0.53	2.49
C Floyd	NYM	863.7	2.15	2.49
C Jones	ATL	238.0	0.59	2.49
P Burrell	PHI	1060.0	2.62	2.48
R Lankford	STL	392.0	0.97	2.47
T Long	SDP	330.7	0.81	2.46
J Werth	LAD	526.0	1.27	2.42
B Bonds	SFG	1130.0	2.68	2.37
G Jenkins	MIL	1371.0	3.15	2.29
M Holliday	COL	917.0	1.86	2.03
J Bay	PIT	963.0	1.91	1.99
L Berkman	HOU	608.7	1.20	1.97
D Roberts	LAD	378.7	0.71	1.88
R Klesko	SDP	723.7	1.30	1.80
L Gonzalez	ARI	900.3	1.52	1.69
C Biggio	HOU	654.3	1.04	1.59
Q McCracken	ARI	223.7	0.35	1.56
A Dunn	CIN	1327.0	1.36	1.03
All Left Fielders				**2.50**

Center Fielders

Player	Team	Innings	FWS	WS/1000
American League				
G Matthews J	TEX	221.7	1.91	8.61
J Damon	BOS	1265.0	7.09	5.60
E Byrnes	OAK	215.3	1.19	5.53
R Johnson	TOR	265.0	1.39	5.25
L Ford	MIN	341.0	1.68	4.92
R Baldelli	TBD	1047.0	5.10	4.87
L Nix	TEX	883.7	4.29	4.86
T Hunter	MIN	1100.0	5.34	4.86
J DaVanon	ANA	247.7	1.18	4.75
C Crawford	TBD	225.0	1.07	4.75
M Kotsay	OAK	1255.0	5.93	4.72
G Sizemore	CLE	348.3	1.60	4.58
V Wells	TOR	1135.0	5.06	4.46
L Bigbie	BAL	242.7	1.03	4.23

Fielding Win Shares by Position

Player	Team	Innings	FWS	WS/1000
A Rowland	CHW	1018.0	4.06	3.99
N Logan	DET	359.7	1.38	3.83
C Beltran	KC	597.0	2.28	3.82
K Lofton	NYY	539.3	2.02	3.74
R Winn	SEA	1070.0	3.89	3.63
G Anderson	ANA	791.7	2.80	3.54
L Matos	BAL	781.3	2.69	3.44
C Figgins	ANA	336.0	1.10	3.28
D DeJesus	KC	732.3	2.36	3.23
C Crisp	CLE	807.3	2.44	3.02
W Harris	CHW	222.7	0.59	2.64
B Williams	NYY	830.3	2.07	2.49
A Sanchez	DET	661.0	1.24	1.87
National League				
A Jones	ATL	1347.0	7.39	5.49
J Edmonds	STL	1241.0	6.50	5.24
D Glanville	PHI	286.0	1.45	5.06
J Payton	SDP	1027.0	5.13	5.00
M Cameron	NYM	1184.0	5.91	4.99
C Beltran	HOU	772.3	3.85	4.98
C Patterson	CHC	1367.0	6.26	4.58
C Freeman	COL	245.0	1.12	4.57
S Finley	LAD	484.7	2.03	4.20
J Michaels	PHI	323.0	1.31	4.05
M Grissom	SFG	1219.0	4.87	4.00
E Chavez	MON	1089.0	4.35	3.99
M Bradley	LAD	792.7	3.13	3.95
S Podsednik	MIL	1370.0	5.25	3.83
P Wilson	COL	436.0	1.66	3.81
C Biggio	HOU	570.7	2.15	3.78
J Pierre	FLO	1439.0	5.25	3.65
W Pena	CIN	378.3	1.34	3.54
M Byrd	PHI	753.3	2.55	3.38
T Redman	PIT	1207.0	4.02	3.33
S Finley	ARI	896.3	2.85	3.18
L Terrero	ARI	488.7	1.25	2.56
J Burnitz	COL	517.0	1.31	2.53
R Freel	CIN	271.3	0.60	2.19
K Griffey Jr	CIN	656.3	1.12	1.70
All Center Fielders				**4.14**

Right Fielders

Player	Team	Innings	FWS	WS/1000
American League				
K Mench	TEX	491.0	2.71	5.51
B Jordan	TEX	368.3	1.69	4.59
G Matthews J	TEX	482.7	2.20	4.57
J Jones	MIN	1237.0	4.70	3.80
G Kapler	BOS	592.7	2.21	3.73
A Rios	TOR	943.7	2.94	3.11

Player	Team	Innings	FWS	WS/1000
T Nixon	BOS	306.0	0.94	3.06
K Millar	BOS	432.7	1.30	3.00
V Guerrero	ANA	1234.0	3.67	2.98
J Gerut	CLE	1009.0	2.97	2.95
M Ordonez	CHW	364.0	1.05	2.89
T Perez	CHW	383.7	1.09	2.84
R Johnson	TOR	382.7	1.07	2.79
C Monroe	DET	386.0	1.07	2.77
J Dye	OAK	1178.0	3.16	2.68
I Suzuki	SEA	1405.0	3.65	2.60
J Cruz	TBD	1301.0	3.35	2.58
A Nunez	KC	459.3	1.10	2.40
J Borchard	CHW	460.7	1.07	2.32
B Surhoff	BAL	302.0	0.70	2.31
J Gibbons	BAL	555.3	1.26	2.26
G Sheffield	NYY	1178.0	2.52	2.14
M Stairs	KC	450.3	0.96	2.12
B Higginson	DET	979.3	1.92	1.96
National League				
T Hollandswo	CHC	232.3	1.09	4.68
R Hidalgo	HOU	452.3	1.86	4.11
L Walker	COL	265.7	1.07	4.02
B Clark	MIL	785.7	2.77	3.53
J Drew	ATL	1193.0	4.16	3.49
S Sosa	CHC	1097.0	3.66	3.34
T Sledge	MON	293.3	0.97	3.29
J Encarnacio	FLO	398.7	1.26	3.16
L Berkman	HOU	780.3	2.42	3.11
M Bradley	LAD	267.7	0.81	3.03
J Rivera	MON	721.7	2.17	3.01
R Hidalgo	NYM	708.3	2.13	3.00
R Sanders	STL	652.0	1.95	2.99
D Bautista	ARI	1178.0	3.23	2.74
B Abreu	PHI	1394.0	3.75	2.69
D Mohr	SFG	377.3	1.01	2.69
M Tucker	SFG	838.0	2.23	2.66
J Burnitz	COL	528.3	1.34	2.54
L Walker	STL	337.3	0.84	2.48
K Garcia	NYM	386.3	0.94	2.43
M Cabrera	FLO	856.0	1.96	2.29
R Freel	CIN	265.0	0.60	2.27
B Giles	SDP	1383.0	3.14	2.27
J Encarnacio	LAD	673.3	1.52	2.25
R Cedeno	STL	202.0	0.43	2.11
C Wilson	PIT	627.7	1.29	2.05
B Grieve	MIL	478.3	0.95	1.99
S Green	LAD	427.3	0.84	1.96
R Mackowiak	PIT	438.7	0.79	1.81
A Kearns	CIN	508.3	0.58	1.15
W Pena	CIN	339.7	0.29	0.85
All Right Fielders				**2.88**

Plate Appearance Outcomes by Pitcher

Following is a list of the types of outcome of each plate appearance in the major leagues last year, for pitchers with at least 100 batters faced, sorted by the pitcher's name. If the pitcher played for more than one team, his totals for each team are listed separately. The columns show the total number of batters faced by the pitcher (BFP), along with the percent of plate appearances that resulted in a strikeout (K), Walk (BB), Groundball (GB), Outfield fly (OF), Infield fly (IF) and line drive (LD). For many pitchers, the percentages do not quite add up to 100% due to other types of batted balls such as bunts.

Background information about this data can be found at http://www.hardballtimes.com/main/article/who-gave-up-what/. For comparison, here are the Major League averages:

K	BB	GB	OF	IF	LD
17%	10%	32%	22%	4%	13%

Player	Team	BFP	K	BB	GB	OF	IF	LD
Average	MLB		17%	10%	32%	22%	4%	13%
Abbott P.	TBD	222	11%	14%	29%	28%	5%	12%
Abbott P.	PHI	229	9%	14%	30%	28%	4%	13%
Acevedo J.	CIN	704	17%	7%	28%	27%	5%	14%
Adams M.	MIL	225	17%	7%	28%	27%	3%	13%
Adams T.	BOS	119	18%	6%	39%	21%	3%	12%
Adams T.	TOR	197	18%	12%	41%	12%	4%	13%
Adkins J.	CHW	271	16%	8%	34%	22%	2%	16%
Affeldt J.	KC	344	14%	10%	33%	23%	1%	16%
Ainsworth K.	BAL	151	13%	17%	29%	23%	4%	12%
Alfonseca A.	ATL	313	14%	9%	45%	14%	1%	13%
Almanzar C.	TEX	298	15%	8%	37%	24%	4%	11%
Alvarez W.	LAD	499	20%	7%	23%	28%	4%	13%
Anderson B.	KC	745	9%	7%	28%	30%	4%	19%
Aquino G.	ARI	147	18%	13%	35%	19%	2%	12%
Armas Jr. T.	MON	320	17%	15%	23%	24%	4%	15%
Arroyo B.	BOS	764	19%	9%	30%	24%	3%	14%
Atchison S.	SEA	133	27%	11%	32%	17%	2%	11%
Ayala L.	MON	367	17%	5%	41%	17%	3%	15%
Backe B.	HOU	293	18%	10%	28%	23%	4%	15%
Baez D.	TBD	295	18%	12%	28%	24%	5%	12%
Balfour G.	MIN	172	24%	13%	21%	23%	3%	13%
Batista M.	TOR	867	12%	11%	39%	20%	2%	14%
Bauer R.	BAL	230	16%	10%	41%	19%	2%	12%
Bautista D.	KC	127	14%	10%	35%	24%	2%	14%
Beck R.	SDP	108	14%	8%	26%	35%	3%	14%
Beckett J.	FLO	654	23%	9%	30%	20%	4%	11%
Bedard E.	BAL	633	19%	12%	26%	24%	5%	13%
Bell R.	TBD	529	11%	9%	36%	24%	4%	15%
Beltran F.	CHC	152	26%	14%	26%	20%	3%	8%
Benitez A.	FLO	262	24%	8%	20%	29%	7%	11%
Bennett J.	MIL	316	14%	9%	33%	27%	2%	14%
Benoit J.	TEX	456	21%	9%	23%	27%	5%	14%
Benson K.	NYM	290	18%	7%	30%	26%	4%	14%
Benson K.	PIT	564	15%	9%	32%	23%	4%	15%
Bentz C.	MON	126	14%	20%	37%	18%	2%	9%
Bernero A.	COL	147	14%	12%	20%	39%	5%	10%
Betancourt R	CLE	286	27%	6%	25%	23%	6%	12%
Biddle R.	MON	364	14%	11%	35%	25%	1%	12%
Blackley T.	SEA	134	12%	17%	22%	33%	4%	11%
Boehringer B	PIT	115	17%	16%	26%	23%	3%	14%
Bonderman J	DET	793	21%	10%	32%	21%	2%	12%
Borkowski D.	BAL	247	18%	7%	32%	23%	2%	16%
Borowski J.	CHC	106	16%	14%	23%	26%	5%	14%
Bottalico R.	NYM	296	21%	13%	25%	25%	2%	13%

Player	Team	BFP	K	BB	GB	OF	IF	LD
Average	MLB		17%	10%	32%	22%	4%	13%
Bradford C.	OAK	251	14%	12%	44%	15%	2%	12%
Brazelton D.	TBD	535	12%	12%	27%	29%	7%	12%
Brazoban Y.	LAD	133	20%	11%	20%	26%	6%	13%
Brocail D.	TEX	232	19%	11%	38%	15%	3%	13%
Brower J.	SFG	401	16%	10%	39%	17%	2%	12%
Brown K.	NYY	551	15%	7%	35%	24%	4%	15%
Bruney B.	ARI	135	25%	21%	17%	19%	3%	13%
Buehrle M.	CHW	1016	16%	6%	37%	21%	3%	14%
Bullinger K.	HOU	140	8%	8%	43%	21%	1%	18%
Bump N.	FLO	329	13%	11%	41%	16%	2%	15%
Burba D.	MIL	299	16%	9%	29%	27%	4%	13%
Burnett A.	FLO	490	23%	9%	33%	19%	3%	11%
Burnett S.	PIT	318	9%	9%	44%	22%	1%	11%
Bush D.	TOR	412	16%	8%	32%	27%	5%	12%
Byrd P.	ATL	482	16%	4%	28%	30%	5%	14%
Cabrera D.	BAL	662	11%	14%	31%	25%	4%	12%
Calero K.	STL	168	28%	7%	28%	24%	2%	10%
Camp S.	KC	286	18%	7%	42%	20%	1%	12%
Capuano C.	MIL	385	21%	11%	25%	24%	5%	13%
Carpenter C.	STL	746	20%	6%	38%	19%	2%	13%
Carrara G.	LAD	227	21%	9%	22%	25%	4%	13%
Carrasco D.	KC	163	13%	11%	42%	18%	3%	10%
Carter L.	TBD	336	11%	7%	26%	37%	4%	14%
Cerda J.	KC	206	16%	16%	21%	28%	4%	13%
Chacon S.	COL	316	16%	18%	21%	25%	5%	12%
Chen B.	BAL	196	16%	8%	28%	26%	7%	14%
Choate R.	ARI	232	21%	14%	37%	15%	1%	12%
Christiansen	SFG	167	13%	17%	36%	20%	1%	13%
Chulk V.	TOR	248	18%	11%	28%	25%	2%	14%
Claussen B.	CIN	313	14%	12%	26%	24%	7%	14%
Clemens R.	HOU	878	25%	10%	31%	19%	2%	11%
Clement M.	CHC	775	25%	11%	31%	17%	3%	10%
Colome J.	TBD	169	24%	11%	20%	25%	4%	12%
Colon B.	ANA	897	18%	8%	28%	29%	3%	12%
Colyer S.	DET	147	21%	17%	22%	24%	3%	12%
Contreras J.	CHW	333	20%	13%	32%	17%	4%	13%
Contreras J.	NYY	425	19%	11%	28%	28%	4%	9%
Cook A.	COL	433	9%	11%	46%	18%	2%	12%
Cordero C.	MON	357	23%	12%	18%	28%	3%	13%
Cordero F.	TEX	304	26%	11%	25%	22%	3%	12%
Corey M.	PIT	164	17%	13%	32%	20%	3%	15%
Cormier L.	ARI	218	11%	12%	35%	21%	2%	17%
Cormier R.	PHI	330	14%	9%	39%	21%	1%	12%
Cornejo N.	DET	125	10%	10%	41%	23%	2%	10%

Plate Appearance Outcomes by Pitcher

Player Average	Team MLB	BFP	K 17%	BB 10%	GB 32%	OF 22%	IF 4%	LD 13%
Cotts N.	CHW	281	21%	12%	30%	21%	3%	14%
Crain J.	MIN	109	13%	12%	32%	28%	6%	8%
Cruz J.	ATL	300	23%	11%	29%	20%	2%	13%
Daigle C.	ARI	230	7%	13%	36%	27%	4%	11%
D'Amico J.	CLE	144	11%	5%	29%	37%	4%	13%
Davis D.	MIL	880	19%	10%	32%	21%	3%	13%
Davis J.	CLE	540	13%	10%	38%	20%	2%	14%
Day Z.	MON	496	12%	10%	41%	18%	3%	15%
de la Rosa J	MIL	113	4%	13%	38%	24%	2%	17%
DeJean M.	BAL	197	18%	17%	29%	16%	4%	14%
Dessens E.	ARI	386	14%	6%	38%	20%	3%	17%
Diaz F.	CHW	226	15%	8%	25%	26%	7%	17%
Dickey R.	TEX	480	12%	8%	34%	25%	4%	14%
Dinardo L.	BOS	130	16%	11%	42%	10%	2%	18%
Dingman C.	DET	141	11%	18%	28%	24%	4%	13%
Dohmann S.	COL	198	25%	10%	22%	27%	5%	11%
Donnelly B.	ANA	172	33%	9%	18%	24%	4%	10%
Dotel O.	HOU	146	34%	11%	14%	26%	3%	9%
Dotel O.	OAK	210	34%	10%	15%	24%	4%	10%
Douglass S.	TOR	179	20%	17%	25%	18%	3%	15%
Downs S.	MON	284	13%	9%	38%	20%	1%	14%
Dreifort D.	LAD	227	28%	16%	31%	10%	2%	10%
Drese R.	TEX	897	11%	8%	43%	18%	2%	17%
DuBose E.	BAL	338	14%	14%	30%	21%	4%	15%
Duchscherer	OAK	398	15%	9%	31%	26%	4%	13%
Duckworth B.	HOU	180	13%	7%	31%	26%	4%	17%
Durbin C.	CLE	239	16%	12%	27%	22%	5%	19%
Eaton A.	SDP	848	18%	7%	27%	28%	4%	13%
Elarton S.	COL	199	12%	10%	28%	29%	6%	14%
Elarton S.	CLE	498	16%	9%	24%	32%	5%	13%
Eldred C.	STL	282	19%	6%	28%	24%	5%	15%
Embree A.	BOS	217	17%	6%	29%	25%	4%	18%
Escobar K.	ANA	878	22%	9%	29%	23%	4%	12%
Estes S.	COL	904	13%	13%	37%	21%	2%	13%
Eyre S.	SFG	229	21%	12%	25%	28%	3%	9%
Farnsworth K	CHC	298	26%	12%	24%	22%	3%	11%
Fassero J.	COL	505	12%	10%	38%	22%	3%	14%
Field N.	KC	191	16%	11%	25%	32%	5%	10%
Figueroa N.	PIT	121	8%	9%	39%	26%	1%	12%
Fikac J.	MON	112	20%	12%	29%	18%	2%	17%
File B.	TOR	154	10%	9%	40%	20%	2%	19%
Floyd G.	PHI	126	19%	17%	30%	17%	3%	13%
Fogg J.	PIT	770	11%	10%	36%	24%	2%	15%
Ford B.	MIL	107	12%	11%	33%	30%	2%	11%
Fossum C.	ARI	652	18%	11%	28%	22%	4%	14%
Foulke K.	BOS	333	24%	6%	24%	31%	3%	11%
Francis J.	COL	164	20%	9%	31%	27%	4%	9%
Francisco F.	TEX	216	28%	14%	16%	24%	6%	12%
Franco J.	NYM	207	17%	12%	35%	15%	3%	14%
Franklin R.	SEA	870	12%	8%	27%	29%	6%	16%
Franklin W.	SFG	227	18%	11%	28%	23%	5%	12%
Frasor J.	TOR	299	18%	13%	31%	20%	4%	13%
Frederick K.	TOR	133	17%	13%	35%	23%	2%	11%
Fuentes B.	COL	201	24%	11%	20%	23%	4%	14%
Fultz A.	MIN	216	17%	11%	30%	26%	2%	13%
Gagne E.	LAD	326	35%	8%	23%	17%	4%	10%
Gallo M.	HOU	223	15%	12%	34%	21%	4%	13%
Garcia F.	CHW	432	24%	9%	30%	22%	2%	12%
Garcia F.	SEA	446	18%	8%	29%	26%	4%	11%
Garland J.	CHW	923	12%	9%	35%	26%	3%	13%
Gaudin C.	TBD	201	15%	10%	25%	29%	2%	18%

Player Average	Team MLB	BFP	K 17%	BB 10%	GB 32%	OF 22%	IF 4%	LD 13%
Geary G.	PHI	200	15%	10%	29%	29%	4%	13%
George C.	KC	207	7%	12%	27%	29%	3%	20%
Germano J.	SDP	109	15%	13%	38%	17%	0%	16%
Ginter M.	NYM	313	12%	8%	34%	26%	4%	14%
Glavine T.	NYM	904	12%	8%	39%	21%	2%	15%
Gobble J.	KC	638	8%	7%	31%	32%	6%	15%
Gonzalez E.	ARI	228	14%	10%	30%	23%	4%	18%
Gonzalez J.	TBD	235	9%	10%	29%	24%	7%	20%
Gonzalez M.	PIT	169	33%	4%	30%	17%	2%	11%
Good A.	ARI	177	15%	9%	24%	30%	5%	16%
Gordon T.	NYY	342	28%	7%	30%	22%	2%	10%
Gosling M.	ARI	112	13%	13%	34%	26%	1%	12%
Grabow J.	PIT	285	22%	10%	31%	18%	1%	15%
Graves D.	CIN	290	14%	5%	42%	23%	2%	13%
Gregg K.	ANA	377	22%	8%	29%	22%	4%	12%
Greinke Z.	KC	599	17%	6%	26%	29%	5%	16%
Greisinger S	MIN	233	15%	7%	31%	26%	5%	13%
Grilli J.	CHW	203	13%	11%	30%	29%	3%	13%
Grimsley J.	KC	118	15%	14%	50%	8%	1%	11%
Grimsley J.	BAL	167	13%	13%	49%	12%	1%	10%
Groom B.	BAL	236	14%	7%	36%	25%	4%	14%
Gryboski K.	ATL	217	11%	11%	47%	13%	2%	15%
Guardado E.	SEA	176	26%	9%	18%	32%	4%	11%
Halama J.	TBD	513	12%	7%	40%	26%	2%	13%
Halladay R.	TOR	561	17%	7%	44%	17%	2%	11%
Halsey B.	NYY	153	16%	10%	31%	25%	3%	12%
Hammond C.	OAK	224	15%	7%	32%	22%	4%	18%
Hampton M.	ATL	760	11%	9%	41%	20%	1%	16%
Hancock J.	CIN	251	12%	10%	35%	24%	3%	12%
Harang A.	CIN	711	18%	8%	30%	24%	3%	14%
Harden R.	OAK	803	21%	10%	30%	21%	4%	12%
Haren D.	STL	195	16%	10%	32%	24%	4%	11%
Harikkala T.	COL	262	11%	9%	34%	32%	3%	9%
Harper T.	TBD	330	18%	9%	31%	21%	4%	16%
Harville C.	HOU	238	19%	12%	37%	16%	2%	12%
Hasegawa S.	SEA	300	15%	11%	28%	24%	3%	16%
Hawkins L.	CHC	333	21%	5%	28%	25%	4%	15%
Heilman A.	NYM	119	18%	11%	34%	18%	1%	13%
Hendrickson	MIL	215	13%	11%	38%	19%	2%	14%
Hendrickson	TBD	803	11%	7%	37%	26%	3%	16%
Hennessey B	SFG	163	15%	9%	36%	21%	1%	15%
Hensley M.	ANA	120	25%	8%	23%	21%	8%	13%
Hentgen P.	TOR	373	9%	12%	29%	27%	5%	18%
Heredia F.	NYY	182	14%	12%	31%	24%	4%	14%
Herges M.	SFG	301	13%	8%	33%	26%	4%	14%
Hermanson	SFG	565	18%	9%	30%	25%	3%	12%
Hernandez C	HOU	200	13%	14%	26%	27%	4%	14%
Hernandez L.	MON	1053	18%	9%	33%	23%	2%	14%
Hernandez O	NYY	359	23%	11%	23%	24%	5%	13%
Hernandez R	PHI	260	17%	12%	37%	18%	3%	9%
Hoffman T.	SDP	209	25%	4%	21%	26%	7%	15%
Horgan J.	MON	178	17%	14%	35%	22%	2%	10%
Howard B.	FLO	167	20%	13%	21%	29%	2%	12%
Howry B.	CLE	178	22%	8%	22%	24%	3%	19%
Hudson L.	CIN	204	19%	13%	21%	30%	2%	11%
Hudson T.	OAK	793	13%	7%	47%	16%	2%	14%
Huisman J.	KC	116	11%	8%	49%	16%	3%	14%
Ishii K.	LAD	749	13%	14%	22%	30%	5%	13%
Isringhausen	STL	308	23%	8%	30%	21%	4%	13%
Jackson E.	LAD	113	14%	10%	32%	24%	5%	13%
Jackson M.	CHW	210	12%	9%	31%	27%	3%	17%

285

Plate Appearance Outcomes by Pitcher

Player Average	Team MLB	BFP	K 17%	BB 10%	GB 32%	OF 22%	IF 4%	LD 13%
Jennings J.	COL	925	14%	12%	34%	19%	2%	16%
Jimenez J.	CLE	170	12%	11%	48%	16%	1%	12%
Johnson J.	DET	859	15%	8%	37%	22%	2%	15%
Johnston M.	PIT	110	16%	15%	34%	24%	3%	6%
Jones T.	PHI	123	18%	11%	33%	22%	2%	12%
Jones T.	CIN	235	16%	11%	27%	23%	5%	16%
Julio J.	BAL	306	23%	14%	25%	24%	4%	9%
Kazmir S.	TBD	152	27%	15%	23%	21%	5%	9%
Kennedy J.	COL	705	17%	11%	34%	20%	5%	12%
Kershner J.	TOR	103	15%	8%	38%	19%	3%	17%
Kieschnick B	MIL	183	15%	7%	34%	24%	6%	11%
Kim S.	MON	603	14%	11%	37%	20%	2%	14%
King R.	STL	248	16%	11%	36%	20%	2%	13%
Kinney M.	MIL	286	18%	9%	22%	25%	4%	20%
Kline S.	STL	202	17%	10%	40%	16%	3%	10%
Knotts G.	DET	599	14%	10%	32%	25%	4%	14%
Koch B.	CHW	114	22%	16%	27%	19%	2%	14%
Koch B.	FLO	115	22%	17%	23%	22%	3%	11%
Kolb D.	MIL	236	9%	8%	52%	13%	3%	14%
Koplove M.	ARI	371	15%	11%	39%	17%	2%	12%
Lackey J.	ANA	855	17%	8%	32%	26%	3%	12%
Lawrence B.	SDP	870	14%	7%	40%	21%	2%	14%
Ledezma W.	DET	225	13%	9%	35%	26%	4%	13%
Lee C.	CLE	802	20%	11%	23%	27%	3%	14%
Lehr J.	OAK	144	11%	11%	33%	24%	2%	17%
Leicester J.	CHC	175	20%	9%	34%	22%	2%	13%
Leiter A.	NYM	750	16%	14%	28%	23%	4%	12%
Leskanic C.	BOS	119	18%	14%	34%	19%	0%	12%
Levine A.	DET	310	10%	8%	34%	30%	3%	13%
Lidge B.	HOU	369	43%	10%	15%	19%	3%	10%
Lidle C.	PHI	255	13%	9%	38%	23%	2%	14%
Lidle C.	CIN	656	14%	7%	38%	19%	3%	16%
Lieber J.	NYY	749	14%	3%	40%	26%	2%	15%
Ligtenberg K	TOR	263	19%	10%	26%	28%	5%	11%
Lilly T.	TOR	845	20%	11%	24%	25%	6%	13%
Lima J.	LAD	702	13%	5%	35%	25%	4%	15%
Linebrink S.	SDP	326	25%	9%	21%	25%	4%	14%
Loaiza E.	NYY	214	16%	13%	26%	27%	2%	16%
Loaiza E.	CHW	604	14%	8%	32%	27%	4%	14%
Lohse K.	MIN	883	13%	9%	34%	25%	3%	14%
Looper B.	NYM	346	17%	5%	47%	14%	3%	12%
Lopez J.	COL	187	11%	16%	40%	13%	3%	17%
Lopez R.	BAL	714	17%	8%	34%	24%	3%	13%
Lowe D.	BOS	839	13%	9%	48%	14%	1%	13%
Lowry N.	SFG	383	19%	7%	29%	26%	3%	14%
Maddux G.	CHC	872	17%	5%	38%	20%	2%	15%
Madritsch B.	SEA	359	17%	10%	29%	21%	6%	17%
Madson R.	PHI	312	18%	8%	39%	17%	3%	14%
Mahay R.	TEX	290	19%	11%	30%	24%	5%	10%
Manzanillo J	FLO	151	18%	12%	29%	24%	6%	10%
Maroth M.	DET	928	12%	7%	36%	26%	3%	14%
Marquis J.	STL	874	16%	9%	41%	17%	2%	14%
Marte D.	CHW	303	22%	12%	23%	26%	3%	11%
Martin T.	LAD	132	14%	13%	33%	20%	4%	14%
Martinez P.	BOS	903	25%	9%	25%	24%	4%	12%
Mateo J.	SEA	248	17%	8%	23%	34%	4%	13%
Matthews M.	CIN	137	11%	13%	28%	24%	5%	16%
May D.	KC	832	14%	7%	27%	32%	4%	14%
Meadows B.	PIT	323	14%	6%	40%	19%	4%	15%
Meche G.	SEA	565	18%	9%	27%	28%	4%	14%
Mecir J.	OAK	212	23%	11%	35%	16%	3%	10%

Player Average	Team MLB	BFP	K 17%	BB 10%	GB 32%	OF 22%	IF 4%	LD 13%
Mendoza R.	BOS	119	11%	7%	38%	24%	4%	15%
Mercker K.	CHC	223	23%	13%	22%	21%	5%	15%
Mesa J.	PIT	295	13%	7%	35%	26%	3%	14%
Miceli D.	HOU	336	25%	9%	28%	22%	5%	10%
Miller J.	TOR	375	13%	13%	33%	23%	2%	15%
Miller M.	CLE	226	24%	13%	33%	14%	3%	12%
Miller T.	TBD	208	21%	9%	37%	17%	3%	12%
Miller W.	HOU	383	19%	11%	25%	26%	5%	11%
Millwood K.	PHI	628	20%	9%	28%	22%	3%	14%
Milton E.	PHI	862	19%	9%	21%	30%	7%	12%
Mitre S.	CHC	244	15%	10%	44%	16%	2%	11%
Moreno O.	NYM	146	20%	10%	37%	13%	7%	12%
Morris M.	STL	850	15%	7%	39%	22%	2%	12%
Mota G.	FLO	134	25%	9%	29%	21%	4%	10%
Mota G.	LAD	259	20%	11%	32%	18%	4%	12%
Moyer J.	SEA	888	14%	8%	30%	28%	5%	13%
Mulder M.	OAK	952	15%	10%	41%	19%	1%	13%
Mulholland T	MIN	549	11%	7%	39%	23%	3%	16%
Munro P.	HOU	446	14%	8%	38%	20%	2%	15%
Mussina M.	NYY	697	19%	6%	32%	23%	3%	15%
Myers B.	PHI	778	15%	9%	35%	22%	3%	14%
Myers M.	SEA	126	18%	15%	31%	19%	3%	11%
Nageotte C.	SEA	185	13%	17%	39%	14%	3%	13%
Nakamura M.	TOR	114	21%	8%	26%	29%	4%	11%
Nathan J.	MIN	284	31%	9%	21%	23%	6%	10%
Neal B.	SDP	183	20%	7%	32%	23%	3%	13%
Nelson J.	TEX	103	21%	18%	30%	24%	2%	3%
Nomo H.	LAD	393	14%	12%	19%	28%	6%	20%
Norton P.	CIN	296	16%	14%	39%	16%	2%	11%
Nunez V.	COL	114	19%	13%	23%	31%	4%	9%
Obermueller	MIL	529	11%	9%	39%	23%	2%	15%
Ohka T.	MON	367	10%	6%	35%	29%	4%	14%
Oliver D.	FLO	260	13%	7%	31%	27%	4%	14%
Ortiz R.	ANA	543	15%	8%	29%	29%	3%	14%
Ortiz R.	ATL	896	16%	13%	29%	23%	3%	15%
Osuna A.	SDP	151	24%	8%	25%	25%	5%	13%
Oswalt R.	HOU	983	21%	7%	30%	20%	4%	16%
Otsuka A.	SDP	312	28%	8%	30%	17%	4%	11%
Padilla V.	PHI	503	16%	9%	32%	25%	3%	13%
Park C.	TEX	428	15%	11%	33%	26%	3%	11%
Parrish J.	BAL	353	20%	16%	33%	17%	1%	12%
Patterson D.	DET	179	13%	12%	37%	24%	3%	9%
Patterson J.	MON	445	22%	12%	20%	26%	4%	13%
Pavano C.	FLO	909	15%	7%	37%	22%	2%	15%
Peavy J.	SDP	694	25%	9%	27%	20%	4%	13%
Penny B.	FLO	545	19%	8%	30%	23%	4%	14%
Percival T.	ANA	211	16%	10%	24%	31%	7%	12%
Perez O.	LAD	787	16%	6%	39%	20%	3%	12%
Perez O.	PIT	805	30%	11%	20%	24%	4%	9%
Perisho M.	FLO	212	20%	13%	24%	22%	5%	14%
Pettitte A.	HOU	346	23%	9%	36%	14%	3%	14%
Phelps T.	FLO	144	19%	8%	31%	26%	2%	10%
Pineiro J.	SEA	596	19%	8%	32%	24%	4%	13%
Politte C.	CHW	225	21%	11%	27%	23%	3%	15%
Powell B.	PHI	166	14%	10%	29%	25%	7%	13%
Powell J.	TEX	103	17%	11%	31%	20%	3%	17%
Prinz B.	NYY	124	18%	12%	31%	29%	4%	6%
Prior M.	CHC	510	27%	10%	22%	22%	5%	12%
Proctor S.	NYY	118	18%	12%	26%	31%	3%	10%
Putz J.	SEA	275	17%	11%	37%	20%	3%	11%
Qualls C.	HOU	141	17%	9%	43%	18%	1%	13%

286

Plate Appearance Outcomes by Pitcher

Player Average	Team MLB	BFP	K 17%	BB 10%	GB 32%	OF 22%	IF 4%	LD 13%
Quantrill P.	NYY	424	9%	6%	40%	27%	2%	14%
Radke B.	MIN	901	16%	4%	34%	26%	5%	15%
Ramirez E.	TEX	148	14%	7%	38%	24%	3%	13%
Ramirez H.	ATL	259	12%	12%	40%	16%	3%	15%
Randolph S.	ARI	393	16%	20%	19%	30%	3%	12%
Redding T.	HOU	465	12%	10%	30%	25%	2%	17%
Redman M.	OAK	832	12%	9%	31%	27%	4%	15%
Reed S.	COL	285	13%	8%	32%	24%	7%	14%
Reith B.	CIN	128	19%	17%	23%	17%	4%	17%
Reitsma C.	ATL	344	17%	7%	40%	23%	1%	12%
Remlinger M.	CHC	156	22%	11%	23%	26%	4%	12%
Reyes D.	KC	483	19%	11%	34%	20%	1%	11%
Rhodes A.	OAK	182	19%	12%	27%	26%	3%	12%
Riedling J.	CIN	365	13%	12%	38%	18%	1%	15%
Riley M.	BAL	292	21%	15%	23%	23%	3%	13%
Rincon J.	MIN	327	32%	10%	25%	19%	3%	9%
Rincon R.	OAK	201	20%	11%	29%	21%	7%	11%
Riske D.	CLE	336	23%	13%	23%	25%	4%	12%
Rivera M.	NYY	316	21%	8%	42%	14%	6%	8%
Roa J.	MIN	318	15%	9%	31%	25%	4%	13%
Robertson N.	DET	852	18%	8%	36%	21%	2%	13%
Rodriguez E.	BAL	193	19%	18%	16%	36%	1%	9%
Rodriguez F.	SFG	199	16%	12%	24%	26%	8%	14%
Rodriguez F.	ANA	335	37%	10%	23%	17%	2%	10%
Rodriguez R.	TEX	119	13%	10%	36%	24%	4%	13%
Rogers K.	TEX	935	13%	8%	33%	24%	4%	17%
Romero J.	MIN	319	22%	13%	35%	15%	3%	10%
Rueter K.	SFG	840	7%	8%	41%	24%	2%	16%
Rusch G.	CHC	545	17%	7%	30%	24%	3%	17%
Ryan B.	BAL	361	34%	10%	22%	17%	3%	12%
Saarloos K.	OAK	112	9%	13%	40%	17%	3%	16%
Sabathia C.	CLE	787	18%	10%	28%	25%	4%	14%
Sanchez D.	LAD	342	13%	10%	39%	22%	3%	12%
Santana J.	MIN	881	30%	7%	25%	22%	4%	10%
Santos V.	MIL	684	17%	9%	29%	26%	5%	13%
Schilling C.	BOS	910	22%	4%	30%	24%	4%	14%
Schmidt J.	SFG	907	28%	9%	28%	21%	3%	10%
Schoeneweis	CHW	500	14%	10%	33%	25%	2%	14%
Seanez R.	KC	100	21%	11%	33%	20%	4%	9%
Sele A.	ANA	593	9%	9%	35%	31%	3%	13%
Seo J.	NYM	512	11%	10%	29%	27%	4%	16%
Serrano J.	KC	141	18%	9%	26%	28%	6%	13%
Sheets B.	MIL	937	28%	4%	29%	24%	3%	11%
Sherrill G.	SEA	104	15%	10%	30%	26%	9%	11%
Shields S.	ANA	454	24%	9%	37%	17%	3%	9%
Shouse B.	TEX	184	18%	10%	40%	12%	3%	14%
Silva C.	MIN	869	9%	5%	43%	23%	3%	15%
Simpson A.	COL	183	25%	13%	19%	23%	4%	14%
Smith T.	ATL	180	14%	7%	36%	26%	2%	13%
Smoltz J.	ATL	323	26%	4%	33%	22%	1%	12%
Sosa J.	TBD	447	21%	12%	23%	27%	4%	11%
Sparks S.	ARI	545	10%	9%	32%	27%	4%	16%
Speier J.	TOR	294	18%	10%	23%	31%	3%	13%
Stanton M.	NYM	337	17%	10%	31%	23%	3%	12%
Stark D.	COL	150	7%	12%	26%	27%	2%	23%
Stone R.	SDP	146	15%	8%	34%	27%	1%	14%
Sturtze T.	NYY	337	17%	12%	28%	25%	5%	12%
Sullivan S.	KC	273	16%	11%	23%	27%	5%	16%
Suppan J.	STL	811	14%	9%	36%	22%	3%	14%
Tadano K.	CLE	225	17%	9%	24%	27%	5%	16%
Takatsu S.	CHW	245	20%	9%	26%	26%	6%	10%

Player Average	Team MLB	BFP	K 17%	BB 10%	GB 32%	OF 22%	IF 4%	LD 13%
Tankersley D	SDP	157	18%	11%	31%	17%	4%	15%
Tavarez J.	STL	268	18%	9%	35%	19%	2%	15%
Telemaco A.	PHI	225	14%	8%	31%	28%	7%	11%
Thomson J.	ATL	834	16%	7%	35%	23%	2%	14%
Thornton M.	SEA	148	20%	17%	24%	17%	7%	12%
Timlin M.	BOS	320	18%	8%	36%	18%	3%	16%
Tomko B.	SFG	825	13%	8%	33%	24%	5%	16%
Torres S.	PIT	380	16%	7%	43%	17%	2%	11%
Towers J.	TOR	518	10%	7%	39%	25%	3%	15%
Trachsel S.	NYM	881	13%	10%	32%	25%	4%	13%
Tucker T.	MON	291	15%	7%	36%	22%	4%	14%
Urbina U.	DET	234	24%	15%	18%	29%	5%	8%
Valdez I.	FLO	242	12%	7%	27%	30%	6%	16%
Valdez I.	SDP	509	7%	6%	33%	33%	3%	16%
Valentine J.	CIN	136	21%	20%	20%	19%	6%	13%
Valverde J.	ARI	131	29%	14%	20%	16%	5%	14%
VanBenschot	PIT	135	13%	16%	29%	21%	3%	14%
Van Poppel	CIN	502	14%	7%	27%	28%	6%	16%
Vargas C.	MON	530	17%	13%	23%	28%	4%	15%
Vazquez J.	NYY	849	18%	8%	28%	27%	4%	14%
Villone R.	SEA	523	16%	15%	25%	26%	3%	13%
Vizcaino L.	MIL	298	21%	8%	24%	27%	7%	12%
Vogelsong R.	PIT	610	15%	13%	24%	25%	6%	16%
Waechter D.	TBD	309	12%	12%	22%	38%	5%	11%
Wagner B.	PHI	182	32%	4%	27%	21%	4%	9%
Wagner R.	CIN	242	15%	12%	36%	18%	1%	17%
Wakefield T.	BOS	831	14%	10%	35%	23%	7%	10%
Walker J.	DET	277	19%	5%	26%	29%	5%	15%
Walker T.	SFG	275	17%	9%	30%	24%	3%	15%
Wasdin J.	TEX	301	12%	9%	26%	34%	5%	13%
Washburn J.	ANA	640	13%	7%	30%	28%	4%	16%
Wayne J.	FLO	148	14%	14%	35%	22%	3%	14%
Weathers D.	HOU	137	19%	12%	34%	20%	3%	10%
Weathers D.	NYM	156	16%	11%	35%	19%	3%	14%
Weaver J.	LAD	935	16%	9%	29%	24%	5%	15%
Webb B.	ARI	933	18%	14%	43%	11%	1%	11%
Weber B.	ANA	117	9%	13%	43%	18%	0%	17%
Wellemeyer	CHC	119	25%	17%	14%	24%	3%	15%
Wells D.	SDP	804	13%	3%	39%	25%	3%	14%
Wells K.	PIT	621	19%	12%	31%	19%	3%	15%
Westbrook J.	CLE	895	13%	7%	49%	17%	2%	11%
Wheeler D.	NYM	232	20%	7%	27%	22%	6%	17%
White G.	NYY	104	8%	9%	21%	38%	7%	14%
White G.	CIN	161	20%	3%	17%	36%	7%	14%
White R.	CLE	340	13%	9%	37%	23%	2%	14%
Wickman B.	CLE	129	20%	9%	40%	16%	3%	11%
Williams D.	PIT	162	20%	10%	36%	20%	1%	10%
Williams J.	SFG	559	14%	11%	38%	21%	3%	12%
Williams T.	BAL	126	10%	11%	54%	13%	1%	10%
Williams W.	STL	817	16%	8%	28%	27%	4%	15%
Williamson S	BOS	120	23%	18%	25%	24%	3%	7%
Willis D.	FLO	848	16%	8%	33%	23%	3%	14%
Wilson P.	CIN	798	15%	9%	32%	25%	4%	13%
Wise M.	MIL	222	14%	8%	37%	27%	1%	13%
Witasick J.	SDP	266	21%	10%	30%	23%	2%	13%
Wolf R.	PHI	585	15%	7%	26%	29%	3%	16%
Wood K.	CHC	595	24%	10%	29%	17%	5%	12%
Wood M.	KC	432	13%	8%	41%	22%	2%	13%
Worrell T.	PHI	327	20%	7%	32%	22%	5%	13%
Wright J.	COL	361	11%	14%	37%	17%	4%	16%
Wright J.	ATL	781	20%	9%	31%	22%	2%	13%

287

Player Average	Team MLB	BFP	K 17%	BB 10%	GB 32%	OF 22%	IF 4%	LD 13%
Wuertz M.	CHC	124	24%	14%	17%	29%	3%	10%
Yan E.	DET	379	18%	9%	36%	20%	2%	13%
Yates T.	NYM	228	15%	12%	39%	14%	4%	15%
Young C.	TEX	158	17%	8%	23%	26%	9%	13%

Player Average	Team MLB	BFP	K 17%	BB 10%	GB 32%	OF 22%	IF 4%	LD 13%
Zambrano C.	CHC	887	21%	11%	33%	18%	3%	12%
Zambrano V.	TBD	588	19%	19%	28%	21%	3%	11%
Zito B.	OAK	926	18%	10%	26%	26%	5%	13%

Plate Appearance Outcomes by Batter

Following is a list of the types of outcome of each plate appearance in the major leagues last year, for batters with at least 100 plate appearances, sorted by the player's name. If the batter played for more than one team, his totals for each team are listed separately. The columns show the total number of plate appearances (PA), along with the percent of plate appearances that resulted in a strikeout (K), Walk (BB), Groundball (GB), Flyball (FB), line drive (LD) and Other (Oth), which is most often a bunt.

Background information about this data can be found at http://www.hardballtimes.com/main/article/who-hit-what/. For comparison, here are the Major League averages:

K	BB	GB	FB	LD	Oth
17%	10%	32%	27%	13%	2%

Player Average	Team MLB	PA	K 17%	BB 10%	GB 32%	FB 27%	LD 13%	Oth 2%
Abreu B.	PHI	713	16%	19%	27%	24%	14%	0%
Alfonzo E.	SFG	576	7%	9%	31%	33%	19%	1%
Alomar Jr. S	CHW	164	8%	8%	43%	25%	13%	2%
Alomar R.	ARI	125	14%	10%	38%	18%	11%	8%
Alou M.	CHC	675	12%	10%	30%	33%	15%	0%
Amezaga A.	ANA	105	23%	6%	36%	15%	5%	15%
Anderson G.	ANA	475	16%	6%	33%	27%	18%	0%
Anderson M.	STL	271	14%	5%	38%	26%	15%	1%
Aurilia R.	SDP	158	18%	11%	30%	27%	14%	1%
Aurilia R.	SEA	292	15%	8%	28%	33%	14%	2%
Ausmus B.	HOU	448	13%	8%	40%	23%	14%	2%
Bagwell J.	HOU	679	19%	15%	26%	26%	13%	0%
Bako P.	CHC	157	18%	11%	33%	22%	13%	3%
Baldelli R.	TBD	565	16%	7%	39%	26%	10%	2%
Barajas R.	TEX	389	16%	4%	22%	44%	11%	2%
Barrett M.	CHC	506	13%	8%	38%	25%	16%	1%
Batista T.	MON	650	12%	5%	30%	40%	13%	1%
Bautista D.	ARI	582	11%	7%	43%	22%	16%	1%
Bay J.	PIT	472	27%	11%	24%	26%	11%	1%
Bell D.	PHI	603	12%	10%	31%	28%	17%	0%
Bellhorn M.	BOS	620	29%	15%	24%	21%	11%	0%
Belliard R.	CLE	663	15%	9%	33%	28%	15%	0%
Beltran C.	KC	309	14%	13%	27%	33%	12%	2%
Beltran C.	HOU	399	14%	15%	27%	32%	10%	1%
Beltre A.	LAD	657	13%	8%	32%	32%	14%	0%
Bennett G.	MIL	246	13%	10%	38%	27%	11%	1%
Berg D.	TOR	162	17%	4%	32%	30%	18%	0%
Berkman L.	HOU	687	15%	20%	26%	25%	14%	0%
Berroa A.	KC	554	16%	6%	39%	24%	12%	2%
Bigbie L.	BAL	531	21%	9%	37%	18%	14%	1%
Biggio C.	HOU	700	13%	8%	29%	29%	17%	3%
Blake C.	CLE	668	21%	12%	29%	27%	12%	0%
Blalock H.	TEX	713	21%	11%	23%	32%	12%	0%
Blanco H.	MIN	353	16%	7%	26%	37%	11%	4%
Bloomquist	SEA	201	24%	5%	29%	26%	14%	2%
Blum G.	TBD	369	16%	7%	35%	31%	11%	2%
Bocachica H.	SEA	107	25%	12%	24%	24%	10%	4%
Bonds B.	SFG	617	7%	39%	19%	25%	10%	0%
Boone B.	SEA	658	21%	9%	34%	26%	10%	1%
Borchard J.	CHW	222	26%	9%	28%	24%	13%	0%
Bradley M.	LAD	597	21%	13%	30%	22%	12%	2%
Bragg D.	CIN	103	28%	8%	25%	23%	14%	2%
Branyan R.	MIL	182	37%	12%	14%	26%	9%	1%
Brito J.	ARI	184	22%	5%	44%	16%	11%	1%
Broussard B.	CLE	485	20%	13%	26%	28%	13%	0%
Brown D.	KC	209	24%	6%	32%	25%	12%	0%
Buck J.	KC	258	31%	6%	28%	24%	10%	2%
Burke J.	CHW	133	10%	8%	41%	19%	19%	4%
Burnitz J.	COL	606	20%	10%	27%	30%	13%	0%
Burrell P.	PHI	534	24%	15%	21%	28%	12%	0%

Plate Appearance Outcomes by Batter

Player Average	Team MLB	PA	K 17%	BB 10%	GB 32%	FB 27%	LD 13%	Oth 2%
Burroughs S.	SDP	564	9%	7%	44%	21%	18%	0%
Byrd M.	PHI	378	18%	8%	42%	20%	11%	1%
Byrnes E.	OAK	632	18%	9%	25%	35%	13%	0%
Cabrera J.	SEA	391	18%	6%	30%	28%	15%	3%
Cabrera M.	FLO	685	22%	11%	31%	24%	13%	0%
Cabrera O.	BOS	248	9%	5%	37%	33%	16%	1%
Cabrera O.	MON	425	7%	7%	38%	32%	15%	1%
Cairo M.	NYY	408	12%	8%	33%	27%	15%	4%
Cameron M.	NYM	562	25%	12%	19%	33%	10%	1%
Cantu J.	TBD	185	24%	6%	30%	24%	16%	0%
Carroll J.	MON	256	8%	13%	38%	22%	18%	1%
Casey S.	CIN	633	6%	9%	37%	29%	20%	0%
Cash K.	TOR	197	30%	7%	28%	21%	14%	0%
Castilla V.	COL	648	17%	9%	30%	31%	13%	0%
Castillo A.	KC	105	10%	13%	37%	22%	15%	3%
Castillo J.	PIT	414	22%	6%	42%	17%	12%	1%
Castillo L.	FLO	649	10%	12%	49%	14%	13%	2%
Castro J.	CIN	316	16%	4%	35%	31%	12%	1%
Castro R.	FLO	108	28%	11%	19%	35%	6%	0%
Catalanotto	TOR	274	12%	8%	36%	23%	21%	0%
Cedeno R.	STL	223	18%	9%	35%	20%	17%	1%
Chavez E.	MON	547	7%	6%	46%	23%	13%	6%
Chavez E.	OAK	577	17%	17%	27%	28%	12%	0%
Chavez R.	HOU	176	22%	6%	36%	20%	13%	3%
Choi H.	FLO	340	23%	16%	22%	28%	11%	1%
Cintron A.	ARI	613	10%	5%	37%	30%	15%	3%
Clark B.	MIL	420	11%	15%	30%	28%	14%	2%
Clark H.	TOR	133	11%	10%	35%	29%	13%	2%
Clark T.	NYY	283	33%	10%	30%	20%	7%	0%
Clayton R.	COL	652	19%	8%	37%	17%	11%	8%
Closser J.	COL	124	18%	6%	38%	21%	15%	2%
Conine J.	FLO	579	13%	9%	27%	34%	16%	0%
Cora A.	LAD	484	8%	13%	35%	28%	13%	2%
Counsell C.	MIL	551	16%	12%	32%	21%	16%	4%
Crawford C.	TBD	672	12%	5%	38%	26%	16%	2%
Crede J.	CHW	543	15%	8%	26%	37%	12%	1%
Crisp C.	CLE	538	13%	7%	38%	24%	15%	4%
Crosby B.	OAK	623	23%	11%	29%	25%	11%	2%
Cruz D.	SFG	431	7%	5%	43%	29%	14%	2%
Cruz J.	CIN	167	26%	12%	31%	18%	13%	0%
Cruz J.	TBD	636	18%	12%	25%	32%	11%	1%
Cuddyer M.	MIN	382	19%	10%	27%	29%	13%	1%
Damon J.	BOS	702	10%	11%	39%	26%	14%	0%
DaVanon J.	ANA	337	16%	14%	25%	31%	9%	5%
Davis B.	CHW	171	23%	6%	28%	29%	13%	1%
DeJesus D.	KC	413	13%	10%	35%	24%	13%	5%
Delgado C.	TOR	551	21%	15%	23%	28%	14%	0%
Delgado W.	NYM	147	20%	10%	29%	25%	14%	2%
Dellucci D.	TEX	387	23%	13%	26%	27%	11%	0%
DeRosa M.	ATL	345	15%	8%	36%	24%	15%	1%
Devore D.	ARI	114	27%	6%	32%	20%	14%	0%
Diaz E.	MON	159	6%	9%	38%	23%	21%	2%
Drew J.	ATL	645	18%	19%	27%	24%	12%	0%

Player Average	Team MLB	PA	K 17%	BB 10%	GB 32%	FB 27%	LD 13%	Oth 2%
Dunn A.	CIN	681	29%	17%	18%	26%	11%	0%
Durazo E.	OAK	578	18%	11%	28%	29%	15%	0%
Durham R.	SFG	542	11%	12%	32%	30%	13%	2%
Dye J.	OAK	590	22%	9%	27%	29%	13%	0%
Easley D.	FLO	257	14%	12%	30%	30%	14%	0%
Eckstein D.	ANA	637	8%	9%	39%	24%	17%	4%
Edmonds J.	STL	612	25%	17%	19%	26%	12%	0%
Encarnacion	FLO	182	18%	11%	27%	30%	13%	1%
Encarnacion	LAD	350	15%	7%	35%	32%	11%	0%
Ensberg M.	HOU	456	10%	8%	36%	28%	16%	1%
Erstad D.	ANA	543	14%	8%	44%	21%	13%	1%
Escobar A.	CLE	179	23%	13%	28%	22%	9%	3%
Estrada J.	ATL	517	13%	10%	33%	27%	17%	0%
Everett A.	HOU	435	13%	6%	29%	32%	11%	9%
Everett C.	MON	141	13%	9%	35%	28%	14%	0%
Everett C.	CHW	169	15%	8%	37%	27%	13%	0%
Feliz P.	SFG	531	16%	4%	37%	30%	12%	0%
Fick R.	TBD	238	13%	9%	26%	37%	14%	0%
Figgins C.	ANA	638	15%	8%	26%	28%	18%	5%
Finley S.	LAD	250	12%	8%	28%	34%	16%	1%
Finley S.	ARI	456	11%	9%	32%	30%	15%	3%
Flaherty J.	NYY	135	19%	4%	27%	32%	16%	3%
Floyd C.	NYM	457	23%	13%	28%	26%	11%	0%
Ford L.	MIN	658	11%	12%	39%	24%	13%	1%
Fordyce B.	TBD	163	21%	7%	31%	28%	13%	1%
Franco J.	ATL	361	19%	10%	38%	16%	17%	1%
Freel R.	CIN	592	15%	13%	34%	20%	14%	4%
Freeman C.	COL	105	20%	13%	37%	17%	11%	1%
Fullmer B.	TEX	290	10%	10%	38%	31%	10%	0%
Furcal R.	ATL	632	11%	9%	37%	25%	12%	5%
Garcia D.	NYM	174	20%	18%	26%	24%	11%	2%
Garcia J.	ATL	118	14%	2%	36%	31%	12%	6%
Garcia K.	NYM	202	17%	5%	35%	31%	11%	1%
Garciaparra	BOS	169	9%	7%	22%	40%	21%	0%
Garciaparra	CHC	185	8%	10%	34%	30%	19%	1%
Gerut J.	CLE	548	11%	11%	36%	29%	12%	1%
Giambi J	NYY	322	19%	17%	25%	32%	6%	0%
Gibbons J.	BAL	380	17%	8%	34%	31%	10%	0%
Giles B.	SDP	711	11%	13%	27%	33%	15%	0%
Giles M.	ATL	434	16%	10%	31%	26%	16%	1%
Ginter K.	MIL	437	23%	10%	25%	28%	13%	1%
Glanville D.	PHI	175	12%	5%	36%	30%	14%	4%
Glaus T.	ANA	242	21%	14%	25%	29%	10%	0%
Gload R.	CHW	260	14%	8%	30%	27%	19%	1%
Gomez C.	TOR	377	11%	8%	36%	25%	20%	1%
Gonzalez A.	CHC	135	19%	3%	34%	29%	13%	2%
Gonzalez A.	MON	144	22%	6%	35%	24%	11%	1%
Gonzalez A.	FLO	599	21%	5%	24%	37%	11%	2%
Gonzalez J.	KC	138	14%	7%	33%	33%	13%	0%
Gonzalez L.	COL	351	19%	5%	31%	25%	17%	3%
Gonzalez L.	ARI	451	13%	16%	25%	34%	12%	0%
Goodwin T.	CHC	114	19%	7%	32%	21%	19%	1%
Gotay R.	KC	166	22%	7%	28%	27%	14%	3%

Plate Appearance Outcomes by Batter

Player Average	Team MLB	PA	K 17%	BB 10%	GB 32%	FB 27%	LD 13%	Oth 2%
Grabowski J.	LAD	192	26%	10%	23%	31%	10%	0%
Graffanino T	KC	314	12%	10%	34%	26%	15%	3%
Green A.	ARI	119	14%	5%	32%	32%	12%	5%
Green N.	ATL	290	22%	6%	29%	26%	14%	4%
Green S.	LAD	671	17%	12%	39%	22%	11%	0%
Greene K.	SDP	554	17%	11%	26%	33%	13%	0%
Greene T.	COL	209	18%	6%	26%	39%	11%	0%
Grieve B.	MIL	275	24%	14%	31%	20%	11%	0%
Griffey Jr.	CIN	348	19%	13%	25%	31%	11%	1%
Grissom M.	SFG	606	14%	6%	38%	29%	13%	0%
Gross G.	TOR	149	21%	13%	31%	23%	11%	1%
Grudzielanek	CHC	278	12%	6%	33%	28%	20%	2%
Guerrero V.	ANA	680	11%	9%	34%	30%	17%	0%
Guiel A.	KC	157	27%	13%	29%	22%	10%	1%
Guillen C.	DET	583	15%	9%	31%	28%	17%	1%
Guillen J.	ANA	621	15%	8%	36%	26%	14%	0%
Guzman C.	MIN	624	10%	5%	46%	22%	13%	4%
Hafner T.	CLE	576	19%	15%	25%	28%	12%	1%
Hairston Jr.	BAL	334	9%	11%	28%	31%	18%	2%
Hairston S.	ARI	364	24%	6%	26%	30%	14%	1%
Hall B.	MIL	415	29%	5%	27%	24%	13%	2%
Hall T.	TBD	441	9%	7%	34%	37%	13%	0%
Halter S.	ANA	121	25%	6%	30%	26%	12%	2%
Hammock R.	ARI	210	19%	6%	30%	32%	12%	1%
Hammonds J	SFG	113	19%	16%	24%	29%	12%	0%
Harris W.	CHW	472	17%	11%	34%	19%	13%	6%
Harvey K.	KC	494	18%	7%	41%	20%	13%	0%
Hatteberg S.	OAK	638	8%	12%	33%	32%	14%	0%
Hawpe B.	COL	118	29%	10%	32%	16%	13%	0%
Helms W.	MIL	306	20%	9%	30%	27%	13%	0%
Helton T.	COL	683	11%	19%	24%	31%	15%	0%
Hernandez J.	LAD	238	26%	11%	28%	25%	9%	0%
Hernandez R	SDP	432	10%	9%	36%	28%	15%	1%
Hidalgo R.	HOU	220	24%	8%	22%	30%	15%	0%
Hidalgo R.	NYM	359	21%	9%	25%	32%	13%	0%
Higginson B.	DET	531	16%	15%	26%	32%	11%	1%
Hill B.	PIT	267	15%	12%	35%	22%	16%	0%
Hillenbrand	ARI	604	8%	6%	39%	28%	18%	0%
Hinske E.	TOR	634	17%	9%	32%	29%	14%	0%
Hocking D.	COL	106	19%	7%	33%	20%	13%	8%
Hollandswort	CHC	167	16%	11%	37%	20%	16%	1%
Holliday M.	COL	439	20%	8%	35%	23%	13%	0%
Hudson O.	TOR	551	18%	10%	34%	23%	14%	1%
Huff A.	TBD	667	11%	9%	36%	29%	15%	0%
Hummel T.	CIN	125	14%	8%	38%	25%	11%	5%
Hunter T.	MIN	569	18%	8%	35%	28%	11%	0%
Ibanez R.	SEA	524	14%	7%	34%	28%	17%	0%
Infante O.	DET	556	20%	7%	24%	32%	14%	2%
Inge B.	DET	458	16%	8%	32%	29%	14%	2%
Izturis C.	LAD	728	10%	6%	40%	25%	17%	3%
Izturis M.	MON	121	17%	10%	28%	26%	16%	4%
Jacobsen B.	SEA	176	27%	9%	32%	25%	7%	0%
Jenkins G.	MIL	681	22%	9%	30%	26%	13%	0%

Player Average	Team MLB	PA	K 17%	BB 10%	GB 32%	FB 27%	LD 13%	Oth 2%
Jeter D.	NYY	721	14%	8%	36%	24%	15%	3%
Jimenez D.	CIN	652	15%	13%	30%	26%	15%	0%
Johnson C.	COL	362	25%	15%	26%	23%	10%	1%
Johnson N.	MON	295	20%	15%	31%	22%	13%	0%
Johnson R.	TOR	582	17%	7%	40%	19%	14%	4%
Jones A.	ATL	646	23%	11%	31%	24%	11%	0%
Jones C.	ATL	567	17%	16%	31%	26%	10%	0%
Jones J.	MIN	608	19%	8%	40%	22%	10%	2%
Jordan B.	TEX	233	15%	7%	33%	30%	15%	0%
Kapler G.	BOS	310	16%	5%	38%	26%	13%	2%
Karros E.	OAK	111	14%	6%	37%	32%	11%	0%
Kata M.	ARI	178	16%	7%	33%	28%	13%	3%
Kearns A.	CIN	246	29%	12%	29%	23%	7%	0%
Kendall J.	PIT	658	6%	12%	41%	24%	17%	0%
Kennedy A.	ANA	533	17%	10%	28%	28%	14%	3%
Kent J.	HOU	606	16%	9%	27%	33%	15%	0%
Keppinger J.	NYM	123	6%	5%	45%	28%	16%	0%
Kielty B.	OAK	278	17%	14%	29%	28%	12%	0%
Klesko R.	SDP	480	14%	15%	30%	25%	16%	0%
Konerko P.	CHW	643	17%	12%	30%	30%	12%	0%
Koskie C.	MIN	488	21%	13%	24%	33%	10%	0%
Kotchman C.	ANA	128	9%	9%	45%	23%	15%	0%
Kotsay M.	OAK	673	10%	8%	30%	32%	17%	2%
La Roche A.	ATL	356	22%	8%	31%	24%	13%	1%
Laird G.	TEX	168	21%	8%	30%	24%	13%	4%
Laker T.	CLE	128	22%	6%	31%	23%	16%	2%
Lamb M.	HOU	312	20%	10%	31%	24%	15%	0%
Lane J.	HOU	156	21%	11%	23%	31%	13%	1%
Lankford R.	STL	235	23%	13%	24%	28%	11%	0%
Larkin B.	CIN	386	10%	9%	42%	23%	15%	1%
Larson B.	CIN	135	26%	12%	40%	14%	8%	0%
LaRue J.	CIN	445	24%	11%	27%	24%	13%	1%
Lawton M.	CLE	680	12%	13%	36%	25%	13%	0%
LeCroy M.	MIN	287	21%	7%	37%	22%	13%	0%
Ledee R.	PHI	145	19%	15%	34%	21%	10%	2%
Lee C.	CHW	658	13%	9%	26%	37%	15%	0%
Lee D.	CHC	688	19%	11%	29%	28%	13%	0%
Leone J.	SEA	115	28%	10%	28%	26%	7%	1%
Lieberthal M	PHI	529	13%	9%	26%	36%	17%	0%
Lo Duca P.	FLO	213	10%	8%	34%	30%	14%	4%
Lo Duca P.	LAD	381	7%	7%	37%	29%	18%	1%
Lofton K.	NYY	313	9%	10%	40%	27%	13%	2%
Logan N.	DET	152	16%	9%	34%	21%	11%	9%
Long T.	SDP	313	16%	6%	37%	26%	15%	0%
Lopez F.	CIN	295	27%	9%	27%	23%	11%	2%
Lopez J.	SEA	218	14%	4%	33%	30%	17%	1%
Lopez J.	BAL	638	15%	8%	35%	27%	14%	0%
Loretta M.	SDP	707	6%	9%	32%	32%	19%	1%
Lowell M.	FLO	671	11%	10%	25%	38%	15%	0%
Lugo J.	TBD	655	16%	9%	35%	24%	13%	3%
Luna H.	STL	192	19%	8%	30%	24%	17%	2%
Mabry J.	STL	275	23%	10%	27%	26%	12%	2%
Macias J.	CHC	204	19%	3%	37%	22%	17%	2%

Plate Appearance Outcomes by Batter

Player Average	Team MLB	PA	K 17%	BB 10%	GB 32%	FB 27%	LD 13%	Oth 2%
Mackowiak R	PIT	555	21%	10%	32%	23%	14%	1%
Magruder C.	MIL	101	21%	10%	31%	27%	10%	2%
Marrero E.	ATL	280	18%	9%	33%	29%	12%	0%
Martinez E.	SEA	549	19%	11%	31%	24%	14%	0%
Martinez R.	CHC	298	13%	9%	29%	31%	14%	3%
Martinez T.	TBD	538	13%	14%	30%	31%	12%	0%
Martinez V.	CLE	591	12%	11%	31%	34%	13%	0%
Matheny M.	STL	419	20%	6%	36%	24%	12%	1%
Matos L.	BAL	359	17%	7%	34%	27%	13%	3%
Matsui H.	NYY	680	15%	13%	29%	28%	14%	0%
Matsui K.	NYM	509	19%	8%	34%	20%	16%	2%
Matthews Jr.	TEX	317	20%	11%	31%	21%	16%	0%
Mauer J.	MIN	122	11%	10%	35%	29%	15%	0%
Mayne B.	ARI	111	15%	12%	31%	19%	21%	3%
Mayne B.	LAD	113	21%	12%	29%	24%	12%	1%
McCarty D.	BOS	168	24%	10%	32%	24%	11%	0%
McCracken	ARI	172	13%	8%	35%	27%	14%	2%
McDonald J.	CLE	100	11%	4%	34%	36%	12%	3%
McEwing J.	NYM	154	21%	6%	27%	28%	12%	6%
McLemore M	OAK	295	11%	14%	38%	21%	13%	2%
McMillon B.	OAK	102	22%	9%	31%	29%	9%	0%
Melhuse A.	OAK	231	20%	7%	33%	24%	14%	1%
Mench K.	TEX	481	13%	8%	28%	37%	14%	0%
Menechino F	TOR	276	16%	14%	29%	26%	13%	1%
Merloni L.	CLE	214	19%	8%	29%	27%	14%	3%
Michaels J.	PHI	346	23%	13%	25%	25%	13%	1%
Mientkiewicz	BOS	119	15%	9%	29%	31%	16%	0%
Mientkiewicz	MIN	328	12%	13%	33%	29%	13%	2%
Miles A.	COL	566	9%	5%	44%	23%	15%	3%
Millar K.	BOS	588	15%	13%	26%	34%	12%	0%
Miller D.	OAK	442	20%	9%	31%	23%	17%	0%
Mirabelli D.	BOS	182	25%	12%	24%	27%	12%	0%
Moeller C.	MIL	349	21%	7%	34%	27%	9%	2%
Mohr D.	SFG	324	20%	17%	25%	26%	11%	2%
Molina B.	ANA	363	10%	6%	41%	30%	13%	1%
Molina J.	ANA	218	24%	5%	33%	25%	10%	4%
Molina Y.	STL	151	13%	9%	35%	26%	15%	1%
Mondesi R.	PIT	110	25%	10%	19%	34%	13%	0%
Monroe C.	DET	481	16%	6%	35%	29%	14%	0%
Mora M.	BAL	636	15%	12%	28%	28%	15%	3%
Morneau J.	MIN	312	17%	10%	28%	34%	12%	0%
Mueller B.	BOS	460	12%	12%	33%	27%	16%	0%
Munson E.	DET	357	25%	10%	24%	30%	11%	1%
Nevin P.	SDP	623	19%	11%	30%	26%	13%	0%
Newhan D.	BAL	412	17%	8%	34%	24%	14%	3%
Nix L.	TEX	400	28%	6%	29%	24%	12%	1%
Nixon T.	BOS	167	14%	10%	28%	35%	13%	0%
Nunez A.	PIT	195	18%	5%	46%	18%	9%	3%
Nunez A.	KC	247	19%	10%	31%	27%	12%	1%
Offerman J.	MIN	202	15%	14%	24%	31%	15%	0%
Ojeda M.	SDP	174	20%	9%	27%	30%	13%	1%
Olerud J.	NYY	188	11%	12%	34%	26%	17%	0%
Olerud J.	SEA	312	13%	15%	33%	26%	13%	0%

Player Average	Team MLB	PA	K 17%	BB 10%	GB 32%	FB 27%	LD 13%	Oth 2%
Olivo M.	CHW	156	19%	6%	30%	31%	10%	4%
Olivo M.	SEA	173	32%	8%	32%	20%	8%	1%
Olson T.	ARI	114	16%	14%	29%	30%	7%	4%
Ordonez M.	CHW	222	10%	9%	40%	30%	12%	0%
Ortiz D.	BOS	669	20%	12%	24%	31%	13%	0%
Overbay L.	MIL	668	19%	12%	31%	22%	16%	0%
Palmeiro O.	HOU	156	12%	13%	28%	30%	14%	2%
Palmeiro R.	BAL	651	9%	14%	25%	35%	16%	0%
Patterson C.	CHC	687	24%	7%	25%	26%	12%	5%
Payton J.	SDP	511	11%	9%	32%	33%	14%	1%
Pellow K.	COL	133	32%	9%	25%	23%	11%	0%
Pena C.	DET	562	26%	13%	24%	27%	10%	1%
Pena W.	CIN	364	30%	8%	32%	21%	10%	0%
Perez E.	ATL	188	15%	7%	31%	28%	17%	2%
Perez N.	SFG	353	10%	6%	37%	26%	15%	6%
Perez T.	PHI	190	23%	5%	22%	32%	13%	5%
Perez T.	CHW	321	9%	5%	36%	31%	12%	6%
Perry H.	TEX	153	12%	11%	42%	25%	10%	0%
Phelps J.	TOR	321	23%	8%	38%	18%	14%	0%
Phillips J.	NYM	412	10%	10%	35%	30%	14%	1%
Piazza M.	NYM	528	15%	13%	29%	28%	15%	0%
Pickering C.	KC	142	30%	13%	30%	15%	12%	0%
Pierre J.	FLO	748	5%	7%	45%	19%	17%	8%
Pierzynski A	SFG	510	5%	7%	40%	30%	17%	0%
Podsednik S.	MIL	713	15%	9%	34%	25%	12%	5%
Polanco P.	PHI	555	7%	7%	40%	25%	19%	2%
Posada J.	NYY	547	17%	18%	34%	20%	11%	0%
Pratt T.	PHI	149	26%	13%	26%	21%	14%	1%
Pujols A.	STL	692	8%	13%	33%	33%	14%	0%
Punto N.	MIN	103	18%	12%	20%	26%	20%	3%
Quinlan R.	ANA	177	15%	9%	36%	24%	16%	1%
Raines Jr T.	BAL	101	16%	5%	36%	21%	15%	8%
Ramirez A.	CHC	606	10%	9%	27%	35%	19%	0%
Ramirez M.	BOS	663	19%	13%	28%	29%	10%	0%
Randa J.	KC	539	14%	9%	30%	32%	15%	0%
Redman T.	PIT	581	9%	4%	45%	23%	15%	3%
Redmond M.	FLO	273	10%	8%	37%	26%	17%	1%
Reese P.	BOS	268	22%	6%	28%	26%	14%	3%
Relaford D.	KC	430	13%	10%	34%	29%	13%	1%
Renteria E.	STL	642	12%	6%	37%	25%	18%	2%
Reyes J.	NYM	229	14%	2%	34%	30%	15%	6%
Rios A.	TOR	460	18%	7%	42%	17%	15%	0%
Rivas L.	MIN	358	15%	4%	36%	31%	12%	3%
Rivera J.	MON	426	11%	8%	40%	25%	17%	0%
Roberts B.	BAL	736	13%	10%	29%	29%	16%	4%
Roberts D.	BOS	101	17%	11%	36%	26%	3%	8%
Roberts D.	LAD	270	11%	12%	31%	22%	13%	11%
Robinson K.	SDP	101	8%	6%	44%	19%	15%	9%
Rodriguez A.	NYY	698	19%	13%	31%	27%	11%	0%
Rodriguez I.	DET	575	16%	8%	34%	25%	17%	0%
Rolen S.	STL	593	16%	14%	21%	34%	15%	0%
Rollins J.	PHI	725	10%	8%	34%	28%	16%	3%
Rolls D.	TBD	132	27%	8%	30%	23%	10%	2%

Plate Appearance Outcomes by Batter

Player Average	Team MLB	PA	K 17%	BB 10%	GB 32%	FB 27%	LD 13%	Oth 2%
Ross D.	LAD	190	33%	11%	18%	28%	8%	3%
Rowand A.	CHW	534	17%	7%	33%	26%	14%	2%
Saenz O.	LAD	128	26%	11%	21%	30%	12%	0%
Salmon T.	ANA	206	20%	8%	23%	32%	17%	0%
Sanchez A.	DET	352	14%	2%	35%	15%	15%	19%
Sanchez R.	TBD	307	9%	5%	44%	22%	18%	2%
Sanders R.	STL	487	24%	8%	25%	28%	15%	0%
Santiago B.	KC	189	17%	5%	34%	31%	11%	2%
Schneider B.	MON	488	13%	9%	37%	25%	15%	1%
Scutaro M.	OAK	477	12%	3%	36%	30%	17%	2%
Sexson R.	ARI	104	20%	13%	32%	25%	10%	0%
Sheffield G.	NYY	684	12%	15%	30%	30%	13%	0%
Sierra R.	NYY	338	16%	7%	32%	30%	14%	0%
Simon R.	PIT	193	9%	9%	45%	27%	10%	1%
Sizemore G.	CLE	159	21%	12%	29%	24%	13%	1%
Sledge T.	MON	446	15%	9%	31%	29%	13%	3%
Smith J.	DET	169	22%	5%	28%	26%	13%	5%
Snow J.	SFG	417	15%	16%	26%	27%	16%	0%
Snyder C.	ARI	110	23%	12%	24%	27%	15%	0%
Soriano A.	TEX	658	18%	7%	25%	36%	14%	0%
Sosa S.	CHC	539	25%	11%	27%	24%	12%	0%
Spencer S.	NYM	204	18%	7%	33%	27%	13%	1%
Spiezio S.	SEA	415	14%	10%	25%	37%	13%	1%
Spivey J.	MIL	263	18%	12%	29%	24%	17%	0%
Stairs M.	KC	496	19%	11%	35%	26%	9%	0%
Stewart S.	MIN	430	10%	11%	33%	29%	17%	0%
Stynes C.	PIT	174	13%	6%	39%	30%	10%	1%
Surhoff B.	BAL	378	12%	8%	33%	29%	16%	1%
Suzuki I.	SEA	762	8%	7%	53%	15%	15%	1%
Sweeney M.	COL	215	24%	16%	23%	28%	10%	0%
Sweeney M.	KC	452	10%	9%	30%	39%	13%	0%
Taguchi S.	STL	206	11%	7%	36%	24%	15%	6%
Teixeira M.	TEX	625	19%	12%	27%	27%	14%	0%
Tejada M.	BAL	725	10%	8%	38%	28%	16%	0%
Terrero L.	ARI	255	31%	10%	24%	19%	11%	5%
Thames M.	DET	184	23%	10%	22%	32%	13%	0%
Thomas C.	ATL	267	17%	11%	36%	20%	14%	2%
Thomas F.	CHW	311	18%	23%	17%	32%	11%	0%
Thome J.	PHI	618	23%	17%	22%	27%	11%	0%
Torrealba Y.	SFG	196	16%	10%	42%	22%	7%	3%
Tracy C.	ARI	532	11%	8%	28%	35%	17%	0%
Tucker M.	SFG	547	19%	13%	27%	26%	12%	3%
Upton B.	TBD	177	26%	9%	36%	19%	9%	1%

Player Average	Team MLB	PA	K 17%	BB 10%	GB 32%	FB 27%	LD 13%	Oth 2%
Uribe J.	CHW	553	17%	6%	28%	33%	13%	2%
Utley C.	PHI	287	14%	6%	34%	27%	17%	1%
Valent E.	NYM	300	20%	10%	29%	27%	14%	0%
Valentin J.	CIN	222	16%	8%	27%	32%	17%	0%
Valentin J.	CHW	504	28%	9%	18%	35%	9%	2%
Varitek J.	BOS	536	24%	13%	26%	24%	13%	0%
Vazquez R.	SDP	132	18%	8%	34%	19%	17%	4%
Ventura R.	LAD	175	18%	13%	27%	33%	10%	0%
Vidro J.	MON	467	9%	10%	40%	24%	15%	1%
Vina F.	DET	131	7%	11%	41%	20%	17%	5%
Vizcaino J.	HOU	385	10%	5%	43%	23%	18%	2%
Vizquel O.	CLE	651	10%	9%	33%	28%	17%	4%
Walker L.	COL	138	17%	21%	27%	20%	15%	1%
Walker L.	STL	178	19%	16%	33%	25%	7%	0%
Walker T.	CHC	424	12%	11%	29%	29%	18%	0%
Ward D.	PIT	321	14%	8%	29%	37%	12%	0%
Wells V.	TOR	590	14%	9%	34%	29%	14%	0%
Werth J.	LAD	326	26%	10%	20%	27%	16%	1%
White R.	DET	498	15%	9%	37%	28%	10%	0%
Wigginton T.	PIT	206	17%	11%	33%	27%	13%	0%
Wigginton T.	NYM	339	14%	7%	35%	27%	16%	1%
Wilkerson B.	MON	688	22%	16%	19%	29%	13%	1%
Williams B.	NYY	651	15%	13%	32%	27%	13%	0%
Williams G.	NYM	138	19%	6%	25%	33%	14%	4%
Wilson C.	PIT	644	26%	12%	27%	22%	12%	0%
Wilson D.	SEA	359	16%	8%	31%	25%	18%	2%
Wilson E.	NYY	262	8%	6%	41%	32%	12%	2%
Wilson J.	PIT	693	10%	4%	37%	29%	17%	2%
Wilson P.	COL	222	22%	9%	30%	24%	15%	0%
Wilson V.	NYM	177	14%	9%	32%	33%	12%	1%
Winn R.	SEA	703	14%	9%	39%	22%	14%	2%
Wise D.	ATL	175	16%	6%	35%	23%	16%	4%
Womack T.	STL	606	10%	6%	39%	23%	18%	4%
Woodward C	TOR	232	20%	6%	28%	29%	16%	1%
Wright D.	NYM	283	14%	6%	27%	36%	17%	0%
Youkilis K.	BOS	248	18%	15%	25%	28%	14%	0%
Young D.	DET	432	16%	9%	33%	25%	16%	0%
Young E.	TEX	402	7%	13%	32%	30%	16%	3%
Young M.	TEX	739	12%	6%	31%	31%	20%	0%
Zaun G.	TOR	392	16%	14%	31%	22%	17%	1%
Zeile T.	NYM	396	21%	11%	31%	23%	12%	2%

Who's Who at the Hardball Times

Alex Belth has been writing about baseball since the fall of 2002 on his site, *Bronx Banter* (www.all-baseball.com/bronxbanter/). Belth spent close to a decade working his way up to assistant film editor in New York's film industry. He was fortunate enough to work for Ken Burns, Woody Allen and the Coen brothers. However his resume is dominated by movies like "Swimfan," "Belly," and "The Blair Witch Project II." After Belth turned 30, he realized the movie business was not for him. He currently holds down a 9-5 job. In addition to following the Yankees for All Baseball.com, Belth is writing a biography of Curt Flood for a young adult audience, which due out in the fall of 2005.

Craig Burley writes for *Batter's Box* (www.battersbox.ca), a website presenting baseball news and analysis from a Canadian perspective. He works in Toronto and lives in Hamilton, Ontario. Craig is a longtime Blue Jays and Expos fan and considers the Expos' loss on "Blue Monday" to be one of the most important events in his life. A devotee of baseball history and statistics, Craig is a SABR member and has founded what he believes is the very first fantasy baseball league for NPB, Japan's professional baseball league. Craig would like to thank his wife Sonya and son Jay for their support, and Kent Williams and Jordan Furlong for sharing their passion.

Joe Dimino is a Yankees/Expos fan who has said that everyone, even Red Sox fans, should get to experience their team winning a championship at least once, but now he's having second thoughts about that one. Joe conceived of the *Hall of Merit* (though Robert Dudek contributed the name) and runs the project at www.baseballthink-factory.org He'd like to thank his girlfriend Crissy, his parents and the rest of his family and friends for making his life an absolute blast. He'd also like to thank John Murphy and everyone who has participated in the Hall of Merit, for making the project better than he ever could have imagined.

Robert Dudek is an author at the *Batter's Box*, home of baseball news and analysis from a Canadian perspective.

Aaron Gleeman is a journalism student at the University of Minnesota. His writing has appeared at Baseball Primer, Rotoworld, InsiderBaseball.com, FOXSports.com, and at AaronGleeman.com, home of *Aaron's Baseball Blog*.

Brian Gunn runs *Redbird Nation*, "A St. Louis Cardinals Obsession Site." (redbirdnation.blog-spot.com/). During the day, he works as a screenwriter in Los Angeles.

Ben Jacobs graduated from the University of Rochester (N.Y.) with a degree in Philosophy and currently works as a sports reporter at the Ithaca (N.Y.) Journal. Ben sends his thanks to Stacy for putting up with his sports fanaticism and his parents for reading almost everything he writes.

Vinay Kumar is a baseball fanatic and fledgling writer. A software developer by day, Vinay is a die-hard Padre fan. Vinay would like to thank his family for their love and support through the years.

Larry Mahnken is a freelance baseball writer living in Fairport, New York. In addition to writing for The Hardball Times, he publishes the *Replacement Level Yankees Weblog* (yankeefan.blogspot.com), which was named the Best Baseball Blog by Forbes.com in 2003. Larry is a passionate Yankees fan and just as big a Civil War buff. Larry would like to thank his parents Donald and Joanne, his sister Beth Anne, and his best friend Stefanie Yawman for their unconditional and unwavering love and support, and would also like to thank Mike Barker, Ken Burns and Doug Pappas for inspiring him to always learn more.

Matthew Namee is the former research assistant to baseball author Bill James, and lives in Lawrence, Kansas.

Lee Sinins is the man behind both the Around the Majors daily e-mail report and the *Sabermetric Baseball Encyclopedia* (www.baseball-encyclopedia.com/), two essentials for any serious baseball fan. He is also a huge history and political buff, as well as a TV addict.

Bryan Smith writes at *Wait 'Til Next Year*, part of the All-Baseball.com network. He is a college student at the University of Iowa, where he is currently studying journalism. In the summers, he calls suburban Chicago home, where he attempts to make it to Wrigley as much as possible. Bryan considers the Kerry Wood, 20-strikeout game to be the most influential baseball happening of his lifetime. Without the love and support from his parents Chuck and Laurie, as well as his girlfriend Molly, this baseball writing hobby would have ended long ago.

Dave Studenmund is the creator of the *Baseball Graphs* website (www.baseballgraphs.com), which features historic and historical baseball graphs and Win Shares research. Dave lives in the greater Chicagoland area with his wonderful family: Joan, Daniel, Emily and James. To thank his family for their Bondsian patience over the past two months, Dave has promised them free hot dogs during their next trip to Wrigley Field.

Steve Treder is Vice President for Strategic Development for Western Management Group, a compensation consulting firm headquartered in California. Several of his articles have been published in *Nine: A Journal of Baseball History and Culture*. A lifelong San Francisco Giants fan, he has never really gotten over the Orlando Cepeda-for-Ray Sadecki trade.

Be sure to visit us all year long at:

www.hardballtimes.com